Culture Evolves

Culture Evolves

Edited by

Andrew Whiten

Professor of Evolutionary and Developmental Psychology,
and Wardlaw Professor,
University of St Andrews
Scotland, UK

Robert A. Hinde

Fellow, St. John's College,
University of Cambridge,
Cambridge, UK

Christopher B. Stringer

Research Leader in Human Origins,
The Natural History Museum,
London, UK

Kevin N. Laland

Professor of Behavioural and Evolutionary Biology,
University of St Andrews
Scotland, UK

PHILOSOPHICAL
TRANSACTIONS
— OF —
THE ROYAL
SOCIETY B

OXFORD
UNIVERSITY PRESS

OXFORD

UNIVERSITY PRESS

Great Clarendon Street, Oxford ox2 6DP

Oxford University Press is a department of the University of Oxford.
It furthers the University's objective of excellence in research, scholarship,
and education by publishing worldwide in

Oxford New York

Auckland Cape Town Dar es Salaam Hong Kong Karachi
Kuala Lumpur Madrid Melbourne Mexico City Nairobi
New Delhi Shanghai Taipei Toronto

With offices in

Argentina Austria Brazil Chile Czech Republic France Greece
Guatemala Hungary Italy Japan Poland Portugal Singapore
South Korea Switzerland Thailand Turkey Ukraine Vietnam

Oxford is a registered trade mark of Oxford University Press
in the UK and in certain other countries

Published in the United States
by Oxford University Press Inc., New York

British Library Cataloguing in Publication Data
Data available

Library of Congress Cataloging in Publication Data
Library of Congress Control Number: 2011943636

Typeset in Minion by Cenveo, Bangalore, India
Printed and bound by
CPI Group (UK) Ltd, Croydon, CR0 4YY

ISBN 978–0–19–960896–6

10 9 8 7 6 5 4 3 2 1

Whilst every effort has been made to ensure that the contents of this book are as complete,
accurate and up-to-date as possible at the date of writing, Oxford University Press is not
able to give any guarantee or assurance that such is the case. Readers are urged to take
appropriately qualified medical advice in all cases. The information in this book is intended
to be useful to the general reader, but should not be used as a means of self-diagnosis or
for the prescription of medication.

Preface

Leaving aside its subject matter, which we survey in the introductory chapter, this volume of *Philosophical Transactions* is unusual in two ways we wish to highlight here. First, the issue is based on one of the relatively small but growing number of Discussion Meetings organized and supported jointly by the Royal Society and the British Academy. This partly explains the large size of the volume, which includes chapters authored by all 24 of those who presented talks over the 3-day meeting.

Second, as part of its celebrations of its 350th anniversary, the Royal Society opted to locate this Discussion Meeting in the Queen Elizabeth Hall of the Southbank complex, as part of its 10-day-long 'Festival of Science and Arts'. This allowed an unusually large audience to participate and we are grateful to the Society for facilitating this unique event.

In addition, we thank the Society for supporting a complementary 2-day satellite meeting, 'Social Learning in Humans and Non-human Animals: Theoretical and Empirical Dissections' at the Kavli Royal Society International Centre for the Advancement of Science.

At the Royal Society, we are particularly indebted to Madalina Black, for her organization of the Discussion Meeting, to Kirstie Eaton for organization of the satellite meeting, to Stephen Cox, Aosaf Afzal, Katherine Jarrett, Madeleine Bell and Rachel Francis for their support at the Southbank event and to Claire Rawlinson and Joanna Bolesworth for their assistance at *Philosophical Transactions*. At the British Academy, we especially thank Robin Jackson and Angela Pusey for their support.

Finally, we wish to express our gratitude to those who so expertly chaired the six sessions of the Discussion Meeting: Pat Bateson, Bill McGrew, Paul Mellars, Colin Renfrew, Gary Runciman and Uta Frith.

Andrew Whiten, Robert A. Hinde,
Christopher B. Stringer and Kevin N. Laland
September 2010

Contents

Contributors

Quentin D. Atkinson
Department of Psychology,
University of Auckland,
Auckland, New Zealand

Nicola Atton
Centre for Social Learning and
Cognitive Evolution,
School of Biology,
University of St Andrews,
St Andrews, UK

Robert Boyd
Department of Anthropology,
University of California,
Los Angeles, CA, USA

Adam H. Boyette
Department of Anthropology,
Washington State University,
Vancouver, WA, USA

James Broesch
Robert Wood Johnson Health
and Society Scholar,
Department of Population Health Sciences,
University of Wisconsin-Madison,
Madison, WI, USA

Briggs Buchanan
Laboratory of Human
Evolutionary Studies,
Department of Archaeology,
Simon Fraser University,
Burnaby, BC, Canada;
Department of Anthropology,
University of Missouri,
Columbia, MO, USA

Judith M. Burkart
Anthropologisches Institut and Museum,
Universität Zürich,
Zürich, Switzerland

Andreea S. Calude
School of Biological Sciences,
University of Reading,
Reading, UK

Tim Clutton-Brock
Department of Zoology,
University of Cambridge,
Cambridge, UK

Mark Collard
Laboratory of Human
Evolutionary Studies,
Department of Archaeology,
Simon Fraser University,
Burnaby, BC, Canada;
Department of Anthropology,
University of Missouri,
Columbia, MO, USA

Kathleen H. Corriveau
Graduate School of Education,
Harvard University,
Cambridge, MA, USA

Andre Costopoulos
Department of Anthropology,
McGill University,
Montreal, QC, Canada

Gergely Csibra
Cognitive Development Center,
Central European University,
Budapest, Hungary

Thomas E. Currie
Evolutionary Cognitive Science
Research Centre,
Graduate School of Arts and Sciences,
University of Tokyo, Tokyo, Japan;
Human Evolutionary Ecology Group,
Department of Anthropology,
University College London,
London, UK

Diana H. Damrosch
Department of Psychology,
Yale University,
New Haven, CT, USA

Magnus Enquist
Department of Zoology,
and Centre for the Study of
Cultural Evolution,
Stockholm University,
Stockholm, Sweden;
Department of Biological Sciences,
Stanford University,
Stanford, CA, USA

Francesco d'Errico
CNRS UMR 5199 PACEA,
University of Bordeaux,
Talence, France;
Institute of Archaeology, History,
Cultural Studies and Religion,
University of Bergen
Bergen, Norway

Marcus W. Feldman
Centre for Social Learning and
Cognitive Evolution,
School of Biology,
University of St Andrews,
St Andrews, Fife, UK

Laurel Fogarty
Centre for Social Learning and
Cognitive Evolution,
School of Biology,
University of St Andrews,
St Andrews, Fife, UK

R. A. Foley
Leverhulme Centre for Human
Evolutionary Studies,
University of Cambridge,
The Henry Wellcome Building,
Cambridge, UK

Hillary N. Fouts
Department of Child and
Family Studies,
University of Tennessee, TN, USA

György Gergely
Cognitive Development Center,
Central European University,
Budapest, Hungary

Luc-Alain Giraldeau
Département des Sciences Biologiques,
Université du Québec à Montréal,
Montréal, Québec, Canada

Naama Goren-Inbar
Institute of Archaeology,
The Hebrew University of Jerusalem,
Mt. Scopus,
Jerusalem, Israel

Russell D. Gray
Department of Psychology,
University of Auckland,
Auckland, New Zealand

Simon J. Greenhill
Department of Psychology,
University of Auckland,
Auckland, New Zealand

Yfke Hager
Department of Zoology,
University of Cambridge,
Cambridge, UK

Paul L. Harris
Graduate School of Education,
Harvard University,
Cambridge, MA, USA

Joseph Henrich
Department of Psychology and
Department of Economics,
University of British Columbia,
Vancouver, BC, Canada

Barry S. Hewlett
Department of Anthropology,
Washington State University,
Vancouver, WA, USA;
Program in Anthropology,
Hawassa University,
Hawassa, Ethiopia

Bonnie L. Hewlett
Department of Anthropology,
Washington State University,
Vancouver, WA, USA;
Program in Anthropology,
Hawassa University,
Hawassa, Ethiopia

Robert A. Hinde
St John's College,
Cambridge, UK

Frank C. Keil
Department of Psychology,
Yale University,
New Haven, CT, USA

M. Mirazón Lahr
Leverhulme Centre for Human
Evolutionary Studies,
University of Cambridge,
The Henry Wellcome Building,
Cambridge, UK

Kevin N. Laland
Centre for Social Learning and
Cognitive Evolution,
School of Biology,
University of St Andrews,
St Andrews, Fife, UK

Jennifer K. Lin
Department of Psychology,
Yale University,
New Haven, CT, USA

Derek E. Lyons
Department of Psychology,
Yale University,
New Haven, CT, USA;
Department of Informatics,
University of California,
Irvine, CA, USA

Ruth Mace
Human Evolutionary Ecology Group,
Department of Anthropology,
University College London,
London, UK

Deanna M. Macris
Department of Psychology,
Yale University,
New Haven, CT, USA;
Department of Cognitive, Linguistic
and Psychological Sciences,
Brown University,
Providence, RI, USA

Jesse Morin
Department of Anthropology,
University of British Columbia,
Vancouver, BC, Canada

Mark Pagel
School of Biological Sciences,
University of Reading,
Reading, UK

Susan Perry
Department of Anthropology,
UCLA;
Behavior, Evolution and Culture Program,
UCLA, University of California-Los Angeles,
Los Angeles, CA, USA

Simon M. Reader
Department of Biology and
Helmholtz Institute,
Utrecht University,
Utrecht, The Netherlands;
Department of Biology,
McGill University,
Montreal, QC, Canada

Luke Rendell
Centre for Social Learning and
Cognitive Evolution,
School of Biology,
University of St Andrews,
St Andrews, Fife, UK

Guillaume Rieucau
Laboratoire Évolution et Diversité
Biologique CNRS UMR 5174,
Université Paul Sabatier,
Toulouse, France

Stephen Shennan
UCL Institute of Archaeology and
AHRC Centre for the Evolution
of Cultural Diversity,
London, UK

Tore Slagsvold
Department of Biology,
Centre for Ecological and Evolutionary
Synthesis (CEES),
University of Oslo,
Blindern, Oslo, Norway

Dietrich Stout
Department of Anthropology,
Emory University,
Atlanta, GA, USA

Christopher B. Stringer
Department of Palaeontology,
The Natural History Museum,
London, UK

Alex Thornton
Department of Zoology,
and Department of Experimental
Psychology,
University of Cambridge,
Cambridge, UK

Ignacio de la Torre
Institute of Archaeology,
University College London,
London, UK

Carel P. van Schaik
Anthropologisches Institut
and Museum,
Universität Zürich,
Zürich, Switzerland

Michael M. Webster
Centre for Social Learning and
Cognitive Evolution,
School of Biology,
University of St Andrews,
St Andrews, UK

Andrew Whiten
Centre for Social Learning and
Cognitive Evolution,
and Scottish Primate Research Group,
School of Psychology,
University of St Andrews,
St Andrews, UK

Karen L. Wiebe
Department of Biology,
University of Saskatchewan,
Saskatoon, SK, Canada

A Note to the Reader and Early Bibliography Concerning Anthropology and Cultural Evolution

This prefatory note offers interested readers a bibliography and accompanying explanatory note on the history of the topic of cultural evolution in relation to anthropology, which is beyond the scope of the Introduction which follows, but important to acknowledge. It originally appeared in the supplementary electronic information accompanying the Introduction in *Philosophical Transactions*. This bibliography is selective and not intended in any way to be exhaustive ([1] can be consulted for perhaps the most comprehensive recent historical review), but is designed to facilitate sufficient entry points to the earlier literature that will allow interested readers to readily achieve a substantial degree of scholarly depth. It is usefully complemented by Currie and Mace [2], extending to the more comprehensive bibliography they supplied in the electronic supplementary information accompanying their article.

We describe this as a 'note' only, to emphasize that we are not offering any substantial historical analysis. Our more modest intention is simply to properly acknowledge that efforts to address the evolution of culture has deep origins going back to Darwin (and in some respects, to yet earlier times) and to the foundations of anthropology, with writings on the topic to be found through the whole period since, contributed from cultural and other branches of anthropology as well as other disciplines. Here we take the listing only as far as the 1980s, when we consider the 'modern era' of studies to have been launched by the works of Cavalli-Sforza, Feldman, Boyd and Richerson.

The bibliography is listed below by ascending date. It includes some of the most oft-cited works by cultural anthropologists as well as selected key publications concerning the evolution of culture that are listed in order to help appreciation of the history of different perspectives in the field and potential cross-references between them (a potential by no means always fulfilled: Pitt-Rivers (1906), for example, is rarely cited in the works that followed).

The listing starts with the *Origin*, in which Darwin already drew attention to the principles shared by biological evolution and language evolution, using the latter to introduce his radical new ideas about the former. Several linguists of the time were already primed to think the same way and indeed had already written about language evolution, including August Schleicher, who went on to publish *Die Darwinische Theorie und die Sprachwissenschaft* by 1863. Soon, authors like Ernst Haeckel were illustrating language trees alongside the Darwinian 'tree of life'.

Influential works by Spencer and Tylor soon followed, setting out scenarios of cultural evolution, and Darwin then referred back to these himself in the *Descent*, with cross-references between these and other authors continuing through later editions of these works and others. In the *Descent*, Darwin accordingly referred not only to cultural evolution within languages, but to other cultural topics including marriage, morality and religion. He also referred to the early evolution of paleolithic and neolithic technologies, to tool use in primates, and to social learning, particularly in the form of imitation, thus anticipating multiple topics addressed in the present volume.

The approaches of Spencer, Tylor and their followers in the late nineteenth and early twentieth century focused heavily on one particular aspect of evolution, its tendency to progressively generate more complex and sophisticated forms, in culture as in biology. Unfortunately, this was largely treated as exemplifying a linear sequence rising from phases of 'savagery' and 'barbarism' up to 'civilisation', with evolution erroneously seen as inherently and directionally driven towards greater complexity. Analyses were often heavily based upon comparisons of contemporary peoples allocated to such supposed stages, and some came to be laced with implicit (and explicit) political and racial interpretations.

For these reasons and others, much of this early literature came under heavy criticism as the twentieth century dawned, so much so that, with an onslaught generally acknowledged to have been particularly driven by Franz Boas, cultural evolution came to be disparaged and largely ignored in American anthropology for over the first quarter of the new century. Ripples from this apparently spread internationally. In Europe, anti-evolutionist stances were associated with such celebrated anthropologists as Malinowski and Radcliffe-Brown. Fascinating and pithy accounts of this period are offered by White (1959) in his preface to *The Evolution of Culture* and in his foreword to the volume edited the following year by Sahlins and Service. Hallpike (1986) surveys and analyses several aspects of the debates of the time and more recent overviews and critiques are offered by Laland and Brown [3] and, from a contemporary anthropologist's perspective, by Kuper [4].

It was only in the second half of the twentieth century that a new generation of anthropologists recognised that in all this turmoil 'the baby had been thrown out with the bathwater'. Figures including White, Steward, Sahlins and Service accordingly resurrected the topic of the evolution of culture within cultural anthropology. However, these contributions display a noticeably different character from those presented in the present volume, particularly in being highly theoretical and discursive, with rather little empirical content. Quantification, tables, figures and graphs are noticeably rare. In Kroeber's (1952) compilation of his works, for example, there is just one (quite intriguing) quantitative analysis of cultural evolution, based on extensive measurements of changes in women's wear ('Three centuries of dress fashions: A quantitative analysis', 1940). The scope of cultural evolution is also often highly restricted, typically limited to humans and moreover to 'symbolic culture', so that although White (1959), at least, made reference to primates, this was essentially to emphasise that culture in his terms was uniquely human (although at that time, little was known of the behaviour of wild primates, so that inferences were limited to sources such as Kohler's experiments with captive chimpanzees and Zuckerman's observations of captive baboons).

The next notable developments were due to Cavalli-Sforza, Feldman, Boyd and Richerson, whose efforts many authors in the present volume would see as more directly scientifically 'ancestral' to their current work, and it is there we end our historical bibliography. Carneiro [1] provides perhaps the closest contemporary cultural anthropologists' account of cultural evolution in the intellectual tradition of White and his followers. It must also be finally noted, however, that the bulk of contemporary cultural anthropologists today appear to remain uninterested or even negatively disposed towards evolutionary perspectives, with post-modern, even anti-scientific attitudes being common. For an anthropologist's lament on this, see d'Andrade [5].

Chronological selected bibliography

1859 Darwin, C. *The origin of species*. London: Murray.

1861 Maine, H. M. *Ancient law*. Oxford: Oxford University Press.

1862 Spencer, H. *First principles*. London: Williams and Norgate.

1863 Schleicher A. *Die Darwinische Theorie und die Sprachwissenschaft*.

1871 Tylor, E. B. *Primitive culture*. London: Murray.

1871 Darwin, C. *The descent of man and selection in relation to sex*. London: Murray

1873 Spencer, H. *The study of sociology*. London: Williams and Norgate.

1877 Morgan, L. H. *Ancient society*. Chicago, IL: Kerr & Co.

1881 Tylor, E. B. *Anthropology*. London.

1906 Pitt-Rivers, A. H. L.-F. *The evolution of culture and other essays*. Oxford: Clarendon Press.

1932 Murdock, G. P. The science of culture. *American Anthropologist* **3b4**, 200–215.

1949 White, L. A. *The science of culture*. New York: Grove Press.

1959 White, L. A. *The evolution of culture*. New York: McGraw-Hill.

1952 Kroeber, A. L. *The nature of culture*. Chicago, IL: Chicago University Press.

1955 Steward, J. *Theory of culture change*. Urbana, IL: University of Illinois Press.

1955 Huxley. J. S. Evolution, cultural and biological. In *Yearbook of Anthropology*, pp. 3–25. New York: Wenner-Gren Foundation.

1960 Dole, G. E. & Carneiro, R. L. (eds.) *Essays in the science of culture. In honor of Leslie A. White*. New York: Thomas Y. Crowell.

1960 Sahlins, M. D. & Service, E. R. (eds.) *Evolution and culture*. Ann Arbor, MI: University of Michigan Press.

1965 Campbell, D. T. Variation and selective retention in socio-cultural evolution. In H. R. Barringer *et al.* (eds) *Social change in developing areas*, pp 19–49. Cambridge, MA: Schenkman.

1971 Service, E. R. *Cultural evolutionism: Theory in practice*. New York: Holt, Rinehart and Winston.

1977 May, R. M. Population genetics and cultural inheritance. *Nature* **268**, 11–13.

1979 Cavalli-Sforza, L. L. & Feldman, M. W. Towards a theory of cultural evolution. *Interdisciplinary Science Review* **3**, 99–107.

1980 Bonner, J. T. *The evolution of culture in animals*. Princeton, NJ: Princeton University Press.

1981 Cavalli-Sforza, L. L. & Feldman, M. W.. *Cultural transmission and evolution*: A quantitative approach. Princeton, NJ: Princeton University Press.

1985 Boyd, R. and Richerson, P. J. *Culture and the evolutionary process*. Chicago, IL: Chicago University Press.

1986 Hallpike, C. R. *The principles of social evolution*. Oxford: Clarendon Press.

References

1 Carneiro, R. L. 2003 *Evolutionism and cultural anthropology*. Boulder, CO: Westview Press.

2 Currie, T. E. & Mace, R. 2011 Mode and tempo in the evolution of socio-political organization: Reconciling 'Darwinian' and 'Spencerian' evolutionary approaches in anthropology. *Phil. Trans. R. Soc. B* **366**, 1108–1117.

3 Laland, K. N. & Brown, G. R. 2011 *Sense and nonsense: Evolutionary perspectives on human behaviour (2nd Edition)*. Oxford: Oxford University Press.

4 Kuper, A. 2005 *Invention of primitive society: transformations of a myth*. London: Routledge.

5 D'Andrade, R. 2000 The sad story of anthropology 1950–1999. *Cross Cultural Research* **34**, 219–232.

Chapter 1

Introduction: Culture Evolves[*]

Andrew Whiten, Robert A. Hinde, Kevin N. Laland
and Christopher B. Stringer

Culture pervades human lives and has allowed our species to create niches
all around the world and its oceans, in ways quite unlike any other primate.
Indeed, our cultural nature appears so distinctive that it is often thought to
separate humanity from the rest of nature and the Darwinian forces that
shape it. A contrary view arises through the recent discoveries of a diverse
range of disciplines, here brought together to illustrate the scope of a
burgeoning field of cultural evolution and to facilitate cross-disciplinary
fertilization. Each approach emphasizes important linkages between culture
and evolutionary biology rather than quarantining one from the other.
Recent studies reveal that processes important in cultural transmission are
more widespread and significant across the animal kingdom than earlier
recognized, with important implications for evolutionary theory. Recent
archaeological discoveries have pushed back the origins of human culture
to much more ancient times than traditionally thought. These developments
suggest previously unidentified continuities between animal and human
culture. A third new array of discoveries concerns the later diversification of
human cultures, where the operations of Darwinian-like processes are
identified, in part, through scientific methods borrowed from biology.
Finally, surprising discoveries have been made about the imprint of cultural
evolution in the predispositions of human minds for cultural transmission.

Keywords: culture; cultural evolution; traditions; social learning; human evolution;
cognition

1.1 Introduction and overview

Culture, broadly conceived as all that individuals learn from others that endures to generate customs and traditions, shapes vast swathes of human lives. Cumulative cultural
achievements, from technology to social institutions, have allowed our species to invade

---

[*] Electronic supplementary material is available at http://dx.doi.org/10.1098/rstb.2010.0372 or via
  http://rstb.royalsocietypublishing.org.

and exploit virtually every region of the planet. Accordingly, this special capacity for culture is often thought to represent a qualitative distinction between our species and the rest of nature, and our relative independence from the Darwinian forces that shape the natural world.

A different perspective has grown in a diverse range of disciplines that instead focus on the evolution of culture,[1] and thus address continuities as well as discontinuities. Here, we bring these different endeavours together to facilitate cross-fertilization among them and encourage the building of a more coherent science embracing the different strands of the evolution of culture. We have sought to include a breadth of studies that illustrate the importance, excitement and extensive scope of this rapidly expanding field. In introducing the chapters, we allocate them to four main themes (parts 1–4), each of which has seen substantial and radical progress in recent years.

The first theme concerns the evolution of social learning, traditions and other culturally related phenomena, which have proved to be far more widespread across the animal kingdom than imagined a half-century ago, and more complex in their manifestations [1–8] (here, Chapters 2–9). The pace of discovery in this area has accelerated markedly in this century [9–11]. A rich variety of underlying social learning processes, strategies and behavioural consequences has also been identified [12–17]. These discoveries are of considerable scientific importance from several perspectives. One is that the identification and understanding of this 'second inheritance system' [18–20], operating in addition to and in interaction with genetic inheritance, has far-reaching consequences for our broader understanding of evolutionary biology. A second is that the nature of human culture becomes less mysterious as allied manifestations are charted among non-human animals and early hominins, and inferences drawn about the evolutionary foundations of humanity's distinctive cultural faculties.

The sense of 'culture evolves' in this first part of the volume thus refers to the *emergence* and nature of cultural processes and capabilities in the animal kingdom. In the next two parts, which focus specifically on the hominin case, the sense of 'culture evolves' widens to embrace the evolution of culture and its products *per se*, because a distinctive hominin development is that culture has become cumulative, with progressive changes building on previous generations' achievements. Today, such accumulation is evident within our lifetimes, as exemplified by digital technology and genetic engineering. By contrast, evidence for cumulative achievements is both minimal and controversial among all the diverse manifestations of animal culture analysed in part 1.

Part 2 turns to the beginnings of hominin culture traced in the early records of stone tool manufacture, which now extend back to approximately 2.6 Ma [21], with recent evidence suggesting stone tool use for butchery as long as 3.4 Ma [22]. Given that metal blades generally replaced stones a mere few thousand years ago, lithic cultures must have pervaded millions of years of recent hominin evolution. Of course other, non-preserved elements of both material and non-material culture were likely coevolving in these times and before: but we are immensely fortunate that the ancient and rich lithic record is available. Hundreds of millennia of reliance on the cultural information required is likely to have profoundly shaped the evolving human mind. The four chapters of part 2 [23–26] (here, Chapters 10–13) together assess the most important recent discoveries about how culture evolves through these Stone Ages.

Here, we highlight two significant sets of discoveries. The first concerns the understanding achieved by a combination of remarkable re-fitting ('retro-manufacture') of flakes knapped from cores 2 Ma, coupled with skilled reconstruction of knapping techniques [27] and the archaeological recovery of ancient artefacts. Such advances have revealed more sophisticated early technological skills than previously imagined as well as subtle markers of cumulative culture. The second set of discoveries, something of a scientific revolution, concerns the emergence of symbolic culture, classically identified with the era of European cave paintings, approximately 12–30 Ka. The latter, together with evidence such as burials, led to a long-standing hypothesis that this period represented an 'Upper Palaeolithic revolution' in culture [28]. However, over the last decade or so, an extensive body of much more ancient discoveries has revealed surprisingly rich cultural achievements, including such apparently aesthetic items as shell beads, dating back at least 100 Ka [26, 29].

The surprising cultural achievements suggested by these latter developments provide a bridge to the third part of the volume [30–37] (here, Chapters 14–21), where chapters address the later accelerating, tree-like growth of regional cultural diversity. Two major aspects of what has recently been achieved in such work deserve emphasis here. The first is the extent to which various well-established methodologies in the natural sciences have been applied to the subject of culture, traditionally tackled in disciplines such as cultural anthropology through more qualitative approaches. Scientific approaches to culture exemplified by systematic methodologies, quantification, hypothesis-testing, mathematical modelling, rigorous statistical evaluation, objectivity, inter-observer reliability and experimentation have become more prominent in recent years. The methodological aspirations embodied in this new work integrate it more closely with natural sciences approaches evident in parts 1 and 2, and raise optimism about the prospects for a more unified and broad-based 'science of culture' [19, 38–40].[2]

A second development we highlight is engagement with the parallels between biological and cultural evolution. Such parallels concerning language were recognized long ago by Darwin himself, initially in the *Origin* [41], and later in the *Descent* [42] where he remarked that 'We find in distinct languages striking homologies due to community of descent, and analogies due to a similar process of formation. The manner in which certain letters or sounds change when others change is very like correlated growth. We have in both cases the reduplication of parts, the effects of long-continued use, and so forth. The frequent presence of rudiments, both in languages and in species, is still more remarkable'. A more generalized recognition of such similarities was made famous in Dawkins' [43] concept of the 'meme', proposed as a cultural unit analogous to the gene. The application of the meme concept in serious research on culture has remained relatively minimal and much debated [44]. Here, however, Shennan [31] (Chapter 14) argues that the 'meme's eye view' offers a significant theoretical perspective that the field ought to embrace. Shennan also builds on the now extensive body of cultural evolution theory built in the last 30 years, largely stimulated through the foundational work of Cavalli-Sforza & Feldman [18] and Boyd & Richerson [19, 45]. These authors have pioneered a rigorous science of culture that spans biology, psychology and anthropology, using methods adapted from evolutionary biology. Cultural evolution theory recognizes and exploits parallels between biological and cultural change, but tailors its mathematical models and methods to the specific and unique processes of culture. Further impetus has come from the application of phylogenetic methods to interpret aspects of human cultural variation, and reconstruct cultural histories [30, 33, 46].

Mesoudi *et al.* [47] pointed out that since Darwin set out his theory without the knowledge of genes, many questions about the extent to which cultural evolution exhibits Darwinian features can be addressed while skirting the 'meme debate'. Instead, Mesoudi *et al.* worked directly from the core concepts in the Origin [41] to explore the extent and manner in which cultural evolution, like biological evolution, encompasses (or if not, in what ways it differs interestingly from) Darwinian processes that include variation, competition, selection, inheritance, accumulation of modifications, adaptation, geographical distribution, convergent evolution and changes of function. Further below, we return to how chapters in part 3 address such matters.

A different perspective is provided in the four chapters of part 4, which do not so much address cultural evolution itself, as how it has shaped minds to acquire complex cultural repertoires [48–51] (here, Chapters 22–25). In principle, this is an issue relevant for the subjects of part 1, insofar as the young of any species that displays some degree of culture is expected to be subject to selection pressures shaping ontogenetic processes to facilitate cultural learning. However, we judged that the unique scale of cultural acquisitions in the human case justifies focusing part 4 on the cultural and socio-cognitive worlds of humans, with a particular focus on children.

Of course social learning, especially imitation, has long been studied in developmental psychology and continues to be so [17]. Two particularly relevant contemporary developments are addressed here. One concerns the capacity for selecting *what* to imitate; the other concerns the capacity for selecting *whom* to learn from.

With regard to the first capacity, recent ingenious studies have shown that already in infancy, novel actions of others are selectively copied in ways that show a sophisticated grasp of the logic of human action: infants were more likely to copy the rather bizarre action of switching on a light by touching it with one's head if the hands were free, than if they were bound up in a blanket (so the head had to be used), a phenomenon called 'rational imitation' [52]. Here, Csibra & Gergely [48] (Chapter 22) offer additional evidence that infants are sensitive to other's signals that certain actions are pedagically directed at them, and 'for' them. However, equally surprising have been demonstrations that young children can be prone to what has recently been called 'over-imitation', being apparently involuntarily motivated to copy certain intentional adult actions that are visibly ineffectual in gaining a desirable outcome [49] (here, Chapter 23). On the face of it, these findings appear to be in direct opposition to those dubbed 'rational imitation', an intriguing contrast discussed further in part 4.

With regard to the second capacity, theoretical models of cultural learning have long suggested that the young might be biased to learn from some informants or models rather than others [18, 19]. Two chapters in part 4 provide convergent evidence for such selectivity (see also [37], (here, Chapter 21)). Hewlett *et al.* [50] (here, Chapter 24) provide the first detailed observational evidence for such learning biases among children growing up in hunter–gatherer communities, while Harris and Corriveau [51] (here, Chapter 25) use experimental procedures to demonstrate the early emergence and developmental time-course of such biases.

Such developmental studies remind us of the complexity of the processes that lie between biological propensities and culture, but this is true across all four themes. Hinde [53] emphasized the need to understand the diachronic and dialectical relations between a species' cultural propensities, behaviour, dyadic interactions, interpersonal relationships, environment and socio-cultural structures. This is perhaps most challenging in relation to the foci of parts 3 and 4.

We return to each of the four main themes further below and highlight contributions made to them in the constituent chapters. First, however, we briefly address some important core definitions.

1.2 **Definitions of core concepts**

The field covered by this volume has often been bedeviled by confusing variations in the definitions of several technical terms, from 'imitation' to 'culture' itself. Famously, Kroeber & Kluckhohn [54] listed 168 definitions of 'culture' in the literature extant at the time; more have arisen since. Here, we address three concepts we judge central to the present volume.

We begin with 'traditions', since this has been important in the work reviewed in part 1, and the basic concept appears less contentious than 'culture' itself. Fragaszy & Perry [55, p. xiii] offered an oft-cited but minimal definition of a tradition as 'a distinctive behaviour pattern shared by two or more individuals in a social unit, which persists over time and that new practitioners acquire in part through socially aided learning'. The minimum of two individuals required makes sense insofar as we might say 'my friend and I have developed a tradition of dining out on Mondays'. However, the concept of tradition becomes of more interest when an idea or behaviour pattern spreads by social learning across multiple individuals, to become a population-level phenomenon (with different populations potentially developing different traditions, although this is not necessary to define tradition *per se*). Thus, traditions may vary in number of practitioners, from two to many (elsewhere Fragaszy [56, p. 61]) refers to a tradition as 'a behavioural practice that is shared among members of a group'. 'Persists over time' in Fragaszy & Perry [55] may also seem regrettably elastic, yet this makes sense insofar as a continuum is possible, from mere fads and fashions (perhaps lasting only weeks or even much less) to those that pass down very many generations (well illustrated in the chapters of part 2). No neat cut-off on this continuum will circumscribe traditions; rather, particularly robust evidence of traditions comes from those that are of long duration, or rely on multiple transmission events, whether between generations or within them.

The crucial component of 'social learning' embedded within the concept of tradition refers to learning from others, more formally defined by Heyes [57] as 'learning that is influenced by observation of, or interaction with, another animal (typically a conspecific) or its products'. The last part of this definition acknowledges that social learning may extend to learning from such things as objects made or used by others, or more generally the results of other's actions, such as the availability of part-processed foods (e.g. cracked shells or nuts). This overarching concept of social learning can be dissected into numerous alternative or constituent underlying processes, from the very elementary, such as stimulus enhancement, in which the learner's attention is simply drawn to some locus by the model's actions, to more sophisticated ones such as the imitative learning of complex skills. These are classified and defined elsewhere in comprehensive recent taxonomies [14, 15] and as they arise in chapters in this volume. Such social learning is a necessary ingredient of, although not a sufficient criterion for, the existence of traditions as described above.

The term 'culture' itself is more contentious. Some authors essentially equate 'culture' with 'tradition' as described above, a long-standing practice such that we regularly find in the literature such titles as 'the cultural transmission of bird song' [58] and 'cultural transmission of feeding behaviour in the black rat' [59], the latter referring to specific techniques for stripping pine cones, that pups were shown to 'inherit' from their mothers through social learning. Other authors, noting the gulf between such cases as birdsong dialects and pine-cone-stripping traditions on the one hand, and the richness of human cultures on the other hand, have required additional criteria for use of the term 'culture' in relation to animal traditions. For example, Galef [60] and Tomasello [61] were concerned that animal cases such as these might be too readily assumed to be homologous (sharing evolutionary ancestry) with human culture, when they might really be merely analogous (dependent on different forms of social learning, for example). These authors argued that the term 'culture' should be reserved for cases dependent on processes of social transmission known to be influential in the human case, such as imitation and teaching. Other authors suggest further criteria that pick out closer links to human culture, such as multiple traditions spanning different modes of behaviour, like technology and social customs [62] or accumulation over generations [63]. Clearly, nobody can legislate for a 'correct' definition (there can be no such thing) and variant usages are by now well-embedded in existing literatures. In these circumstances our policy is, first, to urge all authors writing in this volume to define their terms to clearly facilitate good scientific communication; and second to counsel readers to be alert to the variations in the wider literature noted above. In any case the interesting questions in relation to human culture are not so much about whether certain animals can or cannot be said to 'have culture' (evidently, non-human species described as cultural will not display all the components of *human* culture), but rather whether such animals display significant elements of culture that suggest a deeper understanding of the roles of such phenomena in the biological world, as well as the potential foundations they provided for the emergence of uniquely human culture. Social learning and traditions are widely seen as two such elements.

1.3 **Culture evolves in the animal kingdom**

Studies of social learning, traditions and culture in non-human animals (henceforth 'animals') have blossomed in recent times, becoming one of the six major areas to populate the latest, gargantuan *Encyclopedia of Animal Behaviour* [64]. This would not have been the case a decade or two ago. The coming of age for this area of research means that a now vast literature cannot comprehensively be addressed by the eight chapters that make up our part 1. We have instead invited contributions that emphasize what we see as two major classes of discovery in this area of research: first, that social learning and traditions exist widely across the animal kingdom, and second, that their significance pervades many—indeed arguably most—dimensions of some animals' lives. The first of these points is illustrated by chapters reviewing recent findings spanning fish, birds, primates and other mammals [2–7] (here, Chapters 3–8), and the second by reference to the extensive range of phenomena incorporated into traditions described here, including foraging techniques, tool use, food types and sites, travel routes, predator recognition, social customs and mate choice.

The rise to prominence of this work has multiple sources. One appears to be that at least for long-lived species like primates and cetaceans, the discovery of major roles for cultural processes represents the fruition of decades of patient field studies at multiple different sites, allowing the documentation of putative regional cultural variations as well as the rise, spread and loss of traditions over time. Other factors include advances in methodologies that include long-term, systematic observational studies that minutely trace the ontogeny, rise, spread and in some cases demise of traditional behaviour patterns; cross-fostering and translocation experiments (recently elegantly achieved in birds by careful transfers of eggs and in fishes through the transfer of individuals and populations); diffusion experiments of varied kinds in which new behaviour patterns are seeded in one or two individuals, allowing quantification of subsequent spread across a community; and the development of formal theory (for instance, on social learning strategies), which has stimulated empirical research and led to testable predictions.

The importance and significance of this body of work can be appreciated from more than one perspective. For some authors this is an anthropocentric one. What do the discoveries described in part 1 suggest were the pre-hominin evolutionary foundations on which humans' distinctive cultural nature has been built? A primary answer to this question should in principle be provided by a series of comparative analyses, beginning with inferences about our last common ancestor with chimpanzees and then the other great apes, based on shared features of cultural transmission. This procedure can be repeated to make inferences about such increasingly distant ancestors as those shared in turn with other primates, mammals, vertebrates and perhaps beyond. The evidence remains too patchy to underwrite any such comprehensive analyses to be pursued with confidence as yet—unlike, say, anatomy where it was feasible to establish phylogenies long ago. Here, Whiten [6] offers an initial attempt at the task for the most-recent great ape phylogeny, but even here, data for bonobos and gorillas remain minimal when compared with those available for common chimpanzees and orangutans.

Such analyses aspire to establish homologies between different taxa in the cultural phenomena they display, the critical inferences being about similarity through descent from common ancestors. But striking similarities can also arise through convergent evolution. This means that studies of species only distantly related to ourselves can nevertheless cast light on fundamental principles that illuminate aspects of human culture and are often of considerable interest in their own right. An example concerns 'teaching', defined in functional terms (rather than the intentional terms more familiar to us in the human case), as actions costly to a teacher yet beneficial to a pupil in such consequences as enhanced levels of skill, and here identified in meerkats by elegant field experiments [4], but observed in diverse avian and other taxa too. Another example concerns the functional rules that animals and human children deploy when they engage in social learning. Articles in several parts of this collection (e.g. [2, 5, 6, 25, 37, 50, 51] (Chapters 3, 6, 7, 12, 21, 24, 25, this volume)) describe experimental evidence that rules such as 'conform to the majority behaviour', 'copy the most successful individual' and 'learn from familiar individuals' are used by a range of distantly related animals, as well as humans, although differing underlying processes may be involved.

Illuminating the roots of human culture, however, is far from the only reason for current interest in animal culture. Understanding cultural transmission in animals carries much more general significance because it constitutes a second inheritance system [18–20] that has emerged on the back of the antecedent genetic inheritance, with which it may interact in turn. Coupled with a capacity for innovation, this provides a means for adjustment and accommodation to local conditions on a much more rapid timescale than its genetically based equivalents. Such changes may occur with respect to an animal's environment in ways paralleling biological adaptation, examples of which are provided in this collection in relation to such activities as foraging and predator avoidance [2–6] (here, Chapters 3–7). In addition, an existing culture may itself become part of the selective regime, an instance of niche construction [65]. Social conventions illustrate this point well, as in those described for capuchin monkeys by Perry [5] (here, Chapter 6). Once certain social conventions exist, whether they be the supposed bond-testing 'games' of capuchins, or local human languages, cultural transmission becomes the key to interacting successfully with others in such communities. In humans, cultural niche construction reaches its zenith, with recent genetic data suggesting that cultural practices extensively modified the biological selection acting on our species [66, 67]. The articles by van Schaik & Burkart [7] and Reader et al. [8] (here, Chapters 8 and 9) provide other, non-human examples, in which social learning is thought to have driven brain evolution and favoured a suite of other cognitive capabilities in the process.

Further parallels with biological evolution are provided by the potential of cultural processes to generate variations in behaviour over time and in space (regional traditions). As noted above, culture can provide faster adaptation than is possible through genetic change. Moreover, learning from others can allow the learner to reap the benefits of much prior filtering by others of what is locally adaptive [68]. Such benefits are highlighted in several chapters in part 1 (e.g. [2–7] here, Chapters 3–8) as well as elsewhere [36]. However, over-reliance on what others in one's community do carries the danger of maladaptive behaviour when environments change, a point powerfully made in the influential cultural modelling work of Boyd & Richerson [19, 69]. This and the animal social foraging literature [70] have emphasized the frequency-dependent quality of social learning. Social learning can be viewed as 'information parasitism' and accordingly, some balance of social learning (information 'scrounging') and asocial learning ('information producing') is expected in a population (but see Rendell *et al.* [35] (here, Chapter 19), for a counter perspective). This and other theoretical reasons for why social learning might not be expected to be as common in nature as some of the above considerations might predict are set out by Rieucau & Giraldeau [1] (here, Chapter 2) in the opening chapter of part 1.

1.4 Cumulative culture evolves in ancient hominins

A panoramic view across the 2.6 Myr record of hominin stone tool-making reveals the beginnings of a capacity for cumulative cultural progress, which was ultimately to transform *Homo sapiens* into the richly cultural species we are today. This became particularly clear as the Oldowan phase of relatively elementary stone flaking was surpassed after about 1.6 Myr by the Acheulian phase, characterized by artefacts with consistent shapes that were the clearly intended endpoints of a more sophisticated knapping process. Notable was a double bilateral symmetry appearing as a rough pear shape from one perspective, much thinned by skilled flaking, to 'flatten' it from the orthogonal perspective [23–25] (here, Chapters 10–12). However, the potential cultural accumulation inferred appears to span at least two hominin genera, so the cumulative cultural capability of each genus requires untangling. The evidence for cultural borrowing across hominin species, such as the Chatelperronian and other transitional technologies, implies that gain of cumulative knowledge could plausibly have occurred across different lineages.

Our understanding of the cumulative cultural achievements of the Stone Age has been transformed over the last dozen years or so by the integrated exploitation of a diverse range of evidential sources, often depending on extremely careful, painstaking and effortful work. These sources include (i) the primary one of archaeology, which in this period has established much earlier dates than known before, both for the emergence of lithic tool-making and for skilled knapping; (ii) inferences drawn by highly skilled re-creation by scientists of knapping techniques that produce the kinds of artefacts recovered; (iii) linked observations of knapping and other techniques used by peoples such as the Irian Jaya, who preserved a complex lithic tool culture; and (iv) the careful refitting of recovered sets of flakes to their cores, allowing the retro-construction of the knapping sequences used by their makers [23–25, 71] (here, Chapters 10–12). Here, Stout [25] (Chapter 12) builds on these combined sources to generate a systematic analysis of the complexity of manufacturing techniques, tentatively concluding from this that through the whole Stone Age (extending beyond the Acheulian to later, more sophisticated achievements such as the Levallois), there has been an approximately exponential increase in quantifiable complexity of techniques.

Intriguingly, such progress appears remarkably lacking in the Oldowan. The above-listed sources of evidence applied to the oldest known Oldowan artefacts show their manufacture to have relied on a good appreciation of fracture processes in stone-working, which exceeded that apparent in the efforts of great apes who have knapped sharp flakes in recent experimental contexts [21]. Over the next approximately 1 Myr, Oldowan arte-facts showed little if any progress beyond this—indeed, later ones often appear less sophisticated [23, 25] (Chapters 10 and 12).

However, Oldowan knapping itself may plausibly have represented a cumulative step built on the prior use of stone tools for butchery, which recent evidence dates back to about 3.4 Ma [22]. We note that this latter date takes our perspective back more clearly than does the 2.6 Myr figure, to pre-*Homo* times, when there was as yet no discernable rise in brain size beyond that of a great ape. Indeed, the Oldowan and pre-Oldowan record now stretches back half way to the time of our inferred common ancestor with chimpanzees. This, combined with our rich knowledge of varied chimpanzee percussive wooden-tool-use, and the use of unmodified stone tools to crack nuts on anvils, suggests a step-wise, cumulative transition from such a repertoire in our common ancestor to pre-Oldowan and then Oldowan achievements [72].

By contrast with the Oldowan, technological progress within the Acheulian is better documented [24, 25] (here, Chapters 11 and 12), but its pace was still inordinately slow when compared with recent rates of cumulative cultural change. For example, Goren-Inbar's [24] (here, Chapter 11) studies of a rich archaeological assemblage spanning 800–700 Ka reveals 'a cultural continuum over at least 50 000 years' marked by essentially similar artefact characteristics. Such an age of cultural stability is scarcely imaginable from the perspective of our recent and current rates of cultural turnover. Indeed, the whole million-year-long Acheulian period has frequently been seen as reflecting such stasis. Recent studies summarized in this collection [24, 25] (here, Chapters 11 and 12) take issue with this, demonstrating increasingly rich variations, and ever-earlier signatures of sophis-ticated manufacturing processes from some of the earliest Acheulian assemblages. Similarly, even the Oldowan, despite the lack of clear 'progress' within it, should not be regarded as monolithic; it incorporated geographical and temporal patterning in variants described in this section [23, 25] (here, Chapters 10 and 12).

Inferences about cultural transmission processes at these times are naturally limited. Cautious inferences are made here through a combination of direct observational evi-dence from the present-day stone knapping cultures and inferences drawn from scien-tists' own experiences in learning different grades of knapping techniques [23–25] (here, Chapters 10–12). Of course, present-day knappers have brains much larger than the hom-inins who knapped in the early Acheulian period. Nevertheless, Goren-Inbar [24] (here, Chapter 11) is led to conclude that given the intimate and far-reaching roles of linguistic interchange described in cultural transmission among the present-day knapping peoples, the complex techniques implicated in her 700–800 Ka artefacts also imply the necessity of significant linguistic pedagogical support. This may be an area where some of the experi-mental techniques developed to study cultural transmission in animals could usefully be brought to bear on the processes of social learning necessary for different grades of stone working. At the time of writing, more than one such exploratory effort is underway.

As we move beyond the Acheulian to survey the most recent quarter-million years or so, we again note dramatic reappraisals of our picture of cultural evolution, this time driven mainly by the sheer weight of increasingly early and diverse archaeological discoveries, including blade and microlithic technology, bone tools, various kinds of artwork and decorations, like beads and pigments, as well as refined tools like spear points and awls [26] (here, Chapter 13). This has transformed the picture from one of a cultural 'symbolic' revolution around 30 Ka to a longer, drawn-out history extending back long before 100 Ka and taking the form of a bush, with multiple growth points and extinctions, governed by factors including ecology and population structures, of the kind familiar in biological evolution [26, 73] (here, Chapter 13). The evidence again suggests cross-species cultural transmission.

1.5 Human culture evolves and diversifies: how Darwinian is cultural evolution?

The last chapter of part 2 provides a natural bridge to the eight chapters that make up part 3. These are largely organized around two related themes: first, the spread and diversification of human cultures, and second, the question of how the underlying processes reflect, extend or differ from the Darwinian principles already familiar in the case of biological evolution.

The first two of these chapters offer broad overviews. In their different ways these provide an overarching context for the chapters that follow, as well as linking to the earlier sections. Shennan [31] (here, Chapter 14) provides a concise overview of key principles in biologically inspired approaches to cultural evolution, summarizing fundamental theoretical foundations [18, 19] and going on to illustrate the recent growth in empirical work that engages with cultural evolutionary theory. As Shennan shows, the scope of this body of work now ranges from Acheulian artefacts to more recent examples that include such diverse cases as hunter–gatherer projectile points, pottery designs, iron-smelting and baby names. Shennan defends the 'memes-eye view' of such cases, which focuses on the principles governing the evolution of cultural attributes themselves, as theoretically important in the way it complements person-centred analyses, as well as being pragmatic given the raw data typically available in archaeology and often in other disciplines.

The Foley & Mirazón Lahr [32] (here, Chapter 15) review also takes a broad perspective but a different, complementary one. They offer an overview of cultural evolution in *Homo sapiens*, from approximately 200 000 years ago to the present, analysed in terms of five successive phases which thus overlap and link with the studies of part 2. Each of the last four phases, from around 120 Ka on, is marked by accelerating cultural achievements (echoing the analysis of Stout [25] (here, Chapter 12) referring to even earlier times) and greater diversity. Phase 3 is also intertwined with migration out of Africa and the later phases with the spread of populations, which diversified both biologically and culturally as they spread and settled around the world.

A recurrent theme in these two chapters, others in this volume [26, 36] (here, Chapters 13 and 20) and elsewhere [73] concerns the ways in which these processes have been shaped, sometimes very severely, by interactions between demographic and environmental factors. Some of the principles revealed here echo biology, such as the relationships between diversity (both biological and cultural) and such basic factors as latitude, temperature and rainfall [32]. Such analyses have offered compelling explanations for the apparently sporadic growth and fading of early cultural developments in Africa in the period up to about 50 Ka, after which more continuity is observed [26, 31, 32, 73].

An intimate linkage between demographic factors and culture, in the form of language evolution, is also demonstrated by Gray [33] (here, Chapter 16) in cases such as the spreading of peoples and languages eastwards across the island communities of the Pacific in more recent times. This work provides an excellent example of the application of numerical phylogenetic methods, borrowed and modified from biological contexts, to reconstruct cultural phylogenies. These methods have been much elaborated over the last decade and applied to increasingly wider cultural forms, from languages to artefacts [46, 74, 75]. In this collection, these methods are extended for the first time to sociopolitical evolution [30] (here, Chapter 18). A remarkable linkage between culture and biology is graphically illustrated by the convergence between the picture of the peopling of the Pacific islands based on language phylogenies [33] (here, Chapter 16), and that derived from the analysis of gut flora [76]. In the case of socio-political phylogenies, Currie & Mace [30] (here, Chapter 18) address long-standing evolutionary theories in anthropology that are numerically tested here for the first time and as a result, supported in a new and objective fashion.

A different, but equally weighty numerical analysis is offered for another aspect of language evolution by Calude & Pagel [34] (here, Chapter 17). In the evolution of lexicons, some classes of word meanings are replaced by new word-forms relatively rapidly, while others have lives up to a hundredfold longer. Calude & Pagel identify fundamental principles concerning the frequency of usage and parts of speech that explain much of this evolutionary variance across a broad world sample of languages. The parallels with biological, Darwinian evolution are, once again, striking [77].

As Shennan [31] (following [18]) notes, cultural change can occur through 'cultural selection' (for example, people select the most efficient axes) and/or 'natural selection' in the conventional sense (the reproductive success of the best axe makers promotes the evolution of those axes). In addition, the forms that culture evolves into provide an array of selection pressures on the biological sphere, instances of which are the subject of diverse chapters here including van Schaik & Burkart [7] (here, Chapter 8) and those of part 4. One of the most fundamental forms of selection is likely to be upon capacities and strategies for social learning themselves. Rendell *et al.* [68] have taken a novel approach to this by organizing a computer-based tournament involving Darwinian competition among over 100 different learning strategies submitted. Strategies that fared most successfully in mastering the exploitation of an initially unknown environment were found to rely strongly on social learning. Here, Rendell *et al.* [35] (Chapter 19), extend this work to examine the wider implications of different learning strategies for cultural evolution. Drawing a distinction between effects on individuals' knowledge versus the behaviour they express, Rendell *et al.* discover intriguing differences in the effects of a heavy reliance on cultural transmission on these two factors, which together confer adaptive plasticity in relation to environmental change.

The theme of the adaptive nature of culture continues in the work of Collard *et al.* [36] (here, Chapter 20), who focus on the relationship between the complexity of material culture and the degree of risk involved in the local foraging niche. Here again we see an application of quantification to complex material, in this case the sophistication of the local hunting and gathering implements employed, which in some ways parallels and complements Stout's [25] (here, Chapter 12) numerical analysis of the complexity of stone tools. In the case study presented, Collard *et al.*'s data do not support the hypothesis tested, but this illustrates an important consequence of the numerical and objective approaches encouraged in this volume: that clarity is achieved whether the hypothesis chosen for examination is supported or not. Negative but reliable findings are as important in constructing a robust science of culture as are positive ones. In this case, they lead to new hypotheses about the distinct roles that different causes of cultural diversity play at different spatial scales.

Henrich & Broesch [37] (here, Chapter 21) provide a complementary analysis of cultural adaptation, building on the extensive foundations provided by the modelling literature discussed by Shennan [31] (here, Chapter 14), to which Henrich has made extensive contributions (e.g. [78]). Here, hypotheses derived from the theoretical literature concerning biases such as selective learning from high-prestige models are empirically tested, and supported. The data suggest a two-phase model of cultural learning, in which young children first learn from their primary attachment figures, then later become more selective in learning from the best available models. This analysis links directly with the studies of Harris & Corriveau in part 4, which experimentally demonstrate an ontogenetic shift of this kind, in which children become progressively skilled at discriminating the most useful sources of adaptive information.

1.6 **The evolution of cultural minds**

The extent and rate of cultural acquisition that a child's brain must handle is vast, and natural selection, in the course of tripling brain size over the period discussed in part 2, can be expected to have moulded the developmental processes profoundly to facilitate this. A similar principle is suggested in the 'cultural intelligence hypothesis' applied to the great ape case by van Schaik & Burkart [7] (here, Chapter 8), but the nature of human culture predicts a yet more profound scale of ontogenetic adaptation.

Since humans turned to agriculture a mere 10–12 Kyr ago, the long hunter–gatherer way of life that preceded this is likely to have provided the context for major aspects of this developmental adaptation. With reference to a range of sources of evidence from butchery millions of years ago [22] to javelin-like spears 400 Kyr old [79], some level of hunting–gathering has been inferred to have characterized our genus from its inception. Study of the present-day hunter–gatherer peoples has thus been seen as a valuable route to insights into the behavioural details corresponding to hunting and gathering niches. However, the corpus of studies of hunter–gatherer childhood [80], and in particular the study of children's acquisition of hunter–gatherer culture, has remained minuscule within developmental psychology, despite the above rationale for its great theoretical importance. Writers on cultural evolution have in recent years commented on a (largely anecdotal) literature suggesting that, contrary to claims that teaching makes human culture distinctive, teaching plays only a minimal role in hunter–gatherer culture, by comparison with observational learning. Two chapters in this section offer conceptual and empirical analysis of this issue. Csibra & Gergely [48] (here, Chapter 22) provide evidence that infants are sensitive to often subtle cues ('natural pedagogy' in the authors' terminology) that an adult's actions are performed 'for them' to learn from. Hewlett *et al.* [50] (here, Chapter 24) directly address the role of teaching in hunter–gatherer childhood with some of the first objective and numerical studies of its occurrence. Consistent with the proposal that pedagogy is natural and universal in humans [48], they find that deliberate teaching does occur, especially in the context of caregiver-to-child transmission.

Lyons *et al.* [49] (here, Chapter 23) present new data on the recently discovered phenomenon of 'over-imitation', in which young children copy actions of others despite those actions being visibly ineffectual. The authors present evidence that children are remarkably inflexible in learning to act otherwise. However, consistent with the proposal that they are receptive to deliberate demonstration, children do not reproduce a model's accidental or unintended actions. Such receptivity to deliberate demonstration is likely to facilitate children's adoption of 'opaque' procedures whose causal workings may be difficult for them to fully discern. Nevertheless, the final paper in this collection by Harris & Corriveau [51] (here, Chapter 25) emphasizes that even if children are sometimes hyper-receptive with respect to what they learn, they are selective about whom they learn from. Their findings support other papers in the collection in proposing that children have several biases in their selection of models and informants [37, 50]. Such biases are likely to promote vertical learning from familiar and reliable caregivers as well as oblique and horizontal efficient learning from other members of the local culture.

1.7 **Omissions**

A major goal of this volume is to indicate the current breadth and scope of contemporary scientific approaches to the evolution of social learning, traditions and culture. However, the field has become very large and some regrettably substantial omissions are inevitable. Here we can do no more than acknowledge some of these and indicate some entry points to the larger literature. We note some complementary collected works and recent books on our topic [81–88].

In relation to part 1, we must recognize inevitable gaps in our coverage both taxonomically, for example concerning cetaceans [89] and invertebrates [90], and in relation to the range of behaviour patterns concerned, such as vocal traditions [91].

We have not included chapters in the cultural evolution modelling tradition of Cavalli-Sforza & Feldman [18] and Boyd & Richerson [19], although several papers in this collection (e.g. [2, 31, 35, 37, 51] (here, Chapters 3, 14, 19, 21, and 25)) draw on this tradition. Moreover, we have opted to focus here on culture *per se*, at the cost of neglecting the larger subject of gene–culture coevolution. Recent reviews of this work draw on progress in genomics [66, 67]. More generally, mathematical modelling has also not been given great prominence in this volume, in favour of a relentless focus on heavily empirical studies. The powerful and indeed foundational role of modelling and associated theory [18, 19] is nevertheless acknowledged, and it continues with vigour [92].

In relation to part 3, we must acknowledge that the cultures that have evolved around the world, even through just the most recent few millennia, are so rich as to defy any comprehensive treatment. They are the subjects of vast literatures in archaeology, anthropology, history and kindred disciplines. However, systematic and evolutionary approaches to the associated databases of the kinds explored in this volume remain relatively few. We have striven to illustrate some of the most interesting ways in which this state of affairs is changing.

The final, developmental part in the volume has its own omissions. Perhaps, the most obvious is the study of language acquisition, which represents a substantial instance of cultural transmission, and about which a deep understanding has been achieved through decades of study [93]. Other relevant literatures include those dealing with comparative studies of children and non-human species (typically apes) [94] and cross-cultural developmental psychology [95].

1.8 **Concluding remarks**

We shall not attempt to reprise again here the overview of this volume we have offered above. We believe the contents of the volume offer a uniquely broad 'map' of many of the leading edges of current research addressing different aspects of the evolution of culture, particularly from the overtly scientific approaches we have favoured. In relation to this latter aspect of our endeavours, the array of both novel and well-tested, reliable methodologies included here are no less important to report than the resulting discoveries, exciting as so many of these are, for we think these methodologies are here shown to hold much promise for further revealing how and why culture evolves.

Acknowledgements

The authors of this Introduction wish to thank all those authors of chapters in the volume who commented on our earlier drafts, particularly James Broesch, Gergely Csibra, Tom Currie, Paul Harris, Barry Hewlett, Tore Slagsvold and Dietrich Stout.

Endnotes

1 Although the study of the evolution of culture has seen remarkable recent progress of the kind that underwrites this issue, it is important to recognize that the topic has a long history, largely associated with post-Darwinian cultural anthropology (e.g. [96, 97]: but see also [98]). A brief overview and selected bibliography of this work is offered in the electronic supplementary material (here, see pp. xiii–xvi). A more extended, complementary bibliography spanning 114 articles is in the electronic supplementary material provided by Currie & Mace [30].

2 Likewise, the creation of a 'science of culture' was an aspiration of many cultural anthropologists in the early twentieth century, including those concerned with the evolution of culture [99, 100], although such writings were typically discursive and theoretical, incorporating little empirical material (see electronic supplementary material).

References

1 Rieucau, G. & Giraldeau, L.-A. 2011 Exploring the costs and benefits of social information use: an appraisal of current experimental evidence. *Phil. Trans. R. Soc. B* **366**, 949–957.

2 Laland, K. N., Atton, N. & Webster, M. M. 2011 From fish to fashion: experimental and theoretical insights into the evolution of culture. *Phil. Trans. R. Soc. B* **366**, 958–968.

3 Slagsvold, T. & Wiebe, K. L. 2011 Social learning in birds and its role in shaping a foraging niche. Phil. *Trans. R. Soc. B* **366**, 969–977.

4 Thornton, A. & Clutton-Brock, T. 2011 Social learning and the development of individual and group behaviour in mammal societies. *Phil. Trans. R. Soc. B* **366**, 978–987.

5 Perry, S. 2011 Social traditions and social learning in capuchin monkeys (*Cebus*). *Phil. Trans. R. Soc. B* **366**, 988–996.

6 Whiten, A. 2011 The scope of culture in chimpanzees, humans and ancestral apes. *Phil. Trans. R. Soc. B* **366**, 997–1007.

7 van Schaik, C. P. & Burkart, J. M. 2011 Social learning and evolution: the cultural intelligence hypothesis. *Phil. Trans. R. Soc. B* **366**, 1008–1016.

8 Reader, S. M., Hager, Y. & Laland, K. N. 2011 The evolution of primate general and cultural intelligence. *Phil. Trans. R. Soc. B* **366**, 1017–1027.

9 Laland, K. N. & Galef, B. G. (eds) 2009 *The question of animal culture*. Cambridge, MA: Harvard University Press.

10 Price, E. E., Caldwell, C. A. & Whiten, A. 2010 Comparative cultural cognition. *Wiley Interdiscip. Rev. Cogn. Sci.* **1**, 23–31.

11 Kendal, R. L., Galef, B. G. & van Schaik, C. P. (eds) 2010 Capturing social learning in natural contexts: methodological insights and implications for culture. *Learn. Behav.* (special issue) **38**, 187–336.

12 Galef Jr, B. G. & Heyes, C. M. (eds) 2004 Social learning and imitation. *Learn. Behav.* (special issue) **32**, 1–144.

13 Laland, K. N. 2004 Social learning strategies. *Learn. Behav.* **32**, 4–14.

14 Whiten, A., Horner, V., Litchfield, C. & Marshall-Pescini, S. 2004 How do apes ape? *Learn. Behav.* **32**, 36–52.

15 Hoppitt, W. & Laland, K. N. 2008 Social processes influencing learning in animals: a review of the evidence. *Adv. Study Behav.* **38**, 105–165.

16 Thornton, A. & Raihani, N. J. 2008 The evolution of teaching. *Anim. Behav.* **75**, 1823–1836.

17 Heyes, C. M., Huber, L., Gergley, G. & Brass, M. (eds) 2009 Evolution, development and intentional control of imitation (whole issue). *Phil. Trans. R. Soc. B* **364**, 2291–2443.

18 Cavalli-Sforza, L. L. & Feldman, M. W. 1981 *Cultural transmission and evolution*. Princeton, NJ: Princeton University Press.

19 Boyd, R. & Richerson, P. J. 1985 *Culture and the evolutionary process*. Chicago, IL: Chicago University Press.

20 Whiten, A. 2005 The second inheritance system of chimpanzees and humans. *Nature* **437**, 52–55.

21 Toth, N. & Schick, K. (eds) 2006 *The Oldowan: case studies into the earliest stone age*. Gosport, IN: Stone Age Institute Press.

22 McPherron, S. P., Alemseged, Z., Marean, C. W., Wynn, J. G., Reed, D., Geraads, D., Bobe, R. & Bearat, H. A. 2010 Evidence for stone-tool-assisted consumption of animal tissues before 3.39 million years ago at Dikika, Ethiopia. *Nature* **466**, 857–860.

23 de la Torre, I. 2011 The origins of stone tool technology in Africa: a historical perspective. *Phil. Trans. R. Soc. B* **366**, 1028–1037.

24 Goren-Inbar, N. 2011 Culture and cognition in the Acheulian industry: a case study from Gesher Benot Yaàqov. *Phil. Trans. R. Soc. B* **366**, 1038–1049.

25 Stout, D. 2011 Stone toolmaking and the evolution of human culture and cognition. *Phil. Trans. R. Soc. B* **366**, 1050–1059.

26 d'Errico, F. & Stringer, C. B. 2011 Evolution, revolution or saltation scenario for the emergence of modern cultures? *Phil. Trans. R. Soc. B* **366**, 1060–1069.

27 Roux, V. & Bril, B. (eds) 2005 *Stone knapping: the necessary conditions for a uniquely hominin behaviour*. Cambridge, UK: McDonald Institute Monographs.

28 Mellars, P. & Stringer, C. 1989 *The human revolution: behavioural and biological perspectives on the orgins of modern humans*. Edinburgh, UK: Edinburgh University Press.

29 McBrearty, S. & Brooks, A. 2000 The revolution that wasn't: a new interpretation of the origin of modern human behavior. *J. Hum. Evol.* **39**, 453–563.

30 Currie, T. E. & Mace, R. 2011 Mode and tempo in the evolution of socio-political organization: reconciling 'Darwinian' and 'Spencerian' evolutionary approaches in anthropology. *Phil. Trans. R. Soc. B* **366**, 1108–1117.

31 Shennan, S. 2011 Descent with modification and the archaeological record. *Phil. Trans. R. Soc. B* **366**, 1070–1079.

32 Foley, R. A. & Mirazón Lahr, M. 2011 The evolution of the diversity of cultures. *Phil. Trans. R. Soc. B* **366**, 1080–1089.

33 Gray, R. D., Atkinson, Q. D. & Greenhill, S. J. 2011 Language evolution and human history: what a difference a date makes. *Phil. Trans. R. Soc. B* **366**, 1090–1100.

34 Calude, A. S. & Pagel, M. 2011 How do we use language? Shared patterns in the frequency of word use across seventeen world languages. *Phil. Trans. R. Soc. B* **366**, 1101–1107.

35 Rendell, L., Boyd, R., Enquist, M., Feldman, M. W., Fogarty, L. & Laland, K. N. 2011 How copying affects the amount, evenness and persistence of cultural knowledge: insights from the social learning strategies tournament. *Phil. Trans. R. Soc. B* **366**, 1118–1128.

36 Collard, M., Buchanan, B., Morin, J. & Costopoulos, A. 2011 What drives the evolution of hunter–gatherer subsistence technology? A reanalysis of the risk hypothesis with data from the Pacific Northwest. *Phil. Trans. R. Soc. B* **366**, 1129–1138.

37 Henrich, J. & Broesch, J. 2011 On the nature of cultural transmission networks: evidence from Fijian villages for adaptive learning biases. *Phil. Trans. R. Soc. B* **366**, 1139–1148.

38 Durham, W. H. 1990 *Coevolution: genes, culture and human diversity*. Stanford, CA: Stanford University Press.

39 Cronk, L. 1999 *That complex whole: culture and the evolution of human behaviour*. Bolder, CO: Westview Press.

40 Mesoudi, A., Whiten, A. & Laland, K. N. 2006 Towards a unified science of cultural evolution. *Behav. Brain Sci.* **29**, 329–383.

41 Darwin, C. 1859 *The origin of species*. London, UK: Murray.

42 Darwin, C. 1871 *The descent of man and selection in relation to sex*. London, UK: Murray.

43 Dawkins, R. 1976 *The selfish gene*. Oxford, UK: Oxford University Press.

44 Aunger, R. (ed.) 2000 *Darwinizing culture: the status of memetics as a science*. Oxford, UK: Oxford University Press.

45 Richerson, P. & Boyd, R. 2005 *Not by genes alone: how culture transformed human evolution*. Chicago, IL: Chicago University Press.

46 Mace, R., Holden, C. J. & Shennan, S. (eds) 2005 *The evolution of cultural diversity: a phylogenetic approach*. London, UK: UCL Press.

47 Mesoudi, A., Whiten, A. & Laland, K. N. 2004 Is human cultural evolution Darwinian? *Evolution* **58**, 1–11.

48 Csibra, G. & Gergely, G. 2011 Natural pedagogy as evolutionary adaptation. *Phil. Trans. R. Soc. B* **366**, 1149–1157.

49 Lyons, D. E., Damrosch, D. H., Lin, J. K., Macris, D. M. & Keil, F. C. 2011 The scope and limits of overimitation in the transmission of artefact culture. *Phil. Trans. R. Soc. B* **366**, 1158–1167.

50 Hewlett, B. S., Fouts, H. N., Boyette, A. H. & Hewlett, B. L. 2011 Social learning among Congo Basin hunter–gatherers. *Phil. Trans. R. Soc. B* **366**, 1168–1178.

51 Harris, P. L. & Corriveau, K. H. 2011 Young children's selective trust in informants. *Phil. Trans. R. Soc. B* **366**, 1179–1187.

52 Gergely, G., Bekkering, H. & Király, I. 2002 Rational imitation in preverbal infants. *Nature* **415**, 755.

53 Hinde, R. A. 1987 *Individuals, relationships and culture: links between ethology and the social sciences.* Cambridge, UK: Cambridge University Press.

54 Kroeber, A. L. & Kluckhohn, C. 1952 Culture: a critical review of concepts and definitions. *Pap. Peabody Museum Am. Archaeol. Ethnol.* **47**, 41–72.

55 Fragaszy, D. M. & Perry, S. (eds) 2003 *The biology of traditions: models and evidence.* Cambridge, UK: Cambridge University Press.

56 Fragaszy, D. M. 2003 Making space for traditions. *Evol. Anthropol.* **12**, 61–70.

57 Heyes, C. M. 1994 Social learning in animals: categories and mechanisms. *Biol. Rev.* **69**, 207–231.

58 Slater, P. J. B. 1986 The cultural transmission of bird song. *Trends Ecol. Evol.* **1**, 94–97.

59 Terkel, J. 1995 Cultural transmission in the black rat: pine-cone feeding. *Adv. Study Behav.* **24**, 119–154.

60 Galef, B. G. 1992 The question of animal culture. *Hum. Nat.* **3**, 157–178.

61 Tomasello, M. 1994 The question of chimpanzee culture. In *Chimpanzee cultures* (eds R. W. Wrangham, W. C. McGrew, F. B. M. de Waal & P. Heltne), pp. 301–317. Cambridge, MA: Harvard University Press.

62 Whiten, A. & van Schaik, C. P. 2007 The evolution of animal 'cultures' and social intelligence. *Phil. Trans. R. Soc. B* **362**, 603–620.

63 Levinson, S. C. & Jaisson, P. (eds) 2006 *Evolution and culture.* Cambridge, MA: MIT Press.

64 Breed, M. D. & Moore, J. (eds) 2010 *Encyclopedia of animal behaviour.* Oxford, UK: Academic Press.

65 Laland, K. N., Odling-Smee, J. & Feldman, M. W. 2000 Niche construction, biological evolution and cultural change. *Behav. Brain Sci.* **23**, 131–175.

66 Laland, K. N., Odling-Smee, F. J. & Myles, S. 2010 How culture has shaped the human genome: bringing genetics and the human sciences together. *Nat. Rev. Genet.* **11**, 137–148.

67 Richerson, P., Boyd, R. & Henrich, J. 2010 Gene-culture coevolution in the age of genomics. *Proc. Natl Acad. Sci. USA* **107**, 8985–8992.

68 Rendell, L. *et al.* 2010 Why copy others? Insights from the social learning strategies tournament. *Science* **328**, 208–213.

69 Boyd, R. & Richerson, P. 1996 Why culture is common but cultural evolution is rare. *Proc. Brit. Acad.* **88**, 73–93.

70 Giraldeau, A. & Caraco, T. 2000 *Social foraging theory.* Princeton, NJ: Princeton University Press.

71 Stout, D. 2006 The social and cultural context of stone-knapping skill acquisition. In *Stone knapping: the necessary conditions for a uniquely hominin behaviour* (eds V. Roux & B. Bril). Cambridge, UK: McDonald Institute Monographs.

72 Whiten, A., Schick, K. & Toth, N. 2009 The evolution and cultural transmission of percussive technology: integrating evidence from paleoanthropology and primatology. *J. Hum. Evol.* **57**, 420–435.

73 Powell, A., Shennan, S. J. & Thomas, M. G. 2009 Late Pleistocene demography and the appearance of modern human behavior. *Science* **324**, 1298–1301.

74 Lipo, C. P., O'Brien, M. J., Collard, M. & Shennan, S. J. (eds) 2006 *Mapping our ancestors: phylogenetic approaches in anthropology and prehistory.* New Brunswick, NJ: Aldine Transaction.

75 Forster, P. & Renfrew, C. (eds) 2006 *Phylogenetic methods and the prehistory of languages.* Cambridge, UK: McDonald Institute.

76 Renfrew, G. 2009 Where bacteria and languages concur. *Science* **323**, 467–468.

77 Pagel, M. 2009 Human language as a culturally transmitted replicator. *Nature Rev. Gen.* **10**, 405–415.

78 Henrich, J. & McElreath, R. 2007 Dual inheritance theory: the evolution of human cultural capacities and cultural evolution. In *Oxford handbook of evolutionary psychology* (eds R. I. M. Dunbar & L. Barrett), pp. 555–570. Oxford, UK: Oxford University Press.

79 Thieme, H. 1997 Lower Palaeolithic hunting spears from Germany. *Nature* **385**, 807–810.

80 Hewlett, B. S. & Lamb, M. E.(eds) 2005 *Hunter–gatherer childhoods: evolutionary, developmental and cultural perspectives*. London, UK: Aldine Transaction.

81 Wheeler, M., Ziman, J. & Boden, M. A. (eds) 2002 *The evolution of cultural entities*. Oxford, UK: Oxford University Press.

82 Carneiro, R. L. 2003 *Evolutionism in cultural anthropology: a critical history*. Boulder, CO: Westview Press.

83 Smith, K., Kalish, M. L., Griffiths, T. L. & Lewandowsky, S. 2008 Cultural transmission and the evolution of human behaviour. *Phil. Trans. R Soc. B* **363**, 3469–3476.

84 Shennan, S. (ed.) 2009 *Pattern and process in cultural evolution*. London, UK: University of California Press.

85 Linquist, S. (ed.) 2010 *The evolution of culture*. Farnham, UK: Ashgate Publishing.

86 Blute, M. 2010 *Darwinian sociocultural evolution: solutions to dilemmas in cultural and social theory*. Cambridge, UK: Cambridge University Press.

87 Runciman, G. 2010 *The theory of cultural and social selection*. Cambridge, UK: Cambridge University Press.

88 Mesoudi, A. 2011 *Cultural evolution: how Darwinian evolutionary theory can explain human culture and synthesize the social sciences*. Chicago, IL: University of Chicago Press.

89 Rendell, L. & Whitehead, H. 2001 Cultures in whales and dolphins. *Behav. Brain Sci.* **24**, 309–324.

90 Leadbeater, E. & Chittka, L. 2007 Social learning in insects—from miniature brains to consensus building. *Curr. Biol.* **17**, R703–R713.

91 Janik, V. M. & Slater, P. J. B. 2003 Traditions in mammalian and avian vocal communication. In *The biology of traditions: models and evidence* (eds D. M. Fragaszy & S. Perry), pp. 213–235. Cambridge, UK: Cambridge University Press.

92 Enquist, M., Eriksson, K. & Ghirlanda, S. 2007 Critical social learning: a solution to Rogers's paradox of non-adaptive culture. *Am. Anthropol.* **109**, 727–734.

93 Tomasello, M. & Bates, E. (eds) 2001 *Language development: the essential readings*. Oxford, UK: Blackwell.

94 Tomasello, M., Carpenter, C., Behne, T. & Moll, H. 2005 Understanding and sharing intentions: the origins of cultural cognition. *Behav. Brain Sci.* **28**, 675–691.

95 Rogoff, B. 2003 *The cultural nature of human development*. Oxford, UK: Oxford University Press.

96 White, L. A. 1959 *The evolution of culture*. New York, NY: McGraw-Hill.

97 Sahlins, M. D. & Service, E. R. (eds) 1960 *Evolution and culture*. Ann Arbor, MI: University of Michigan Press.

98 Pitt-Rivers, A. L.-F. 1906 *The evolution of culture and other essays*. Oxford, UK: Clarendon Press.

99 Murdock, G. P. 1932 The science of culture. *Am. Anthropol.* **34**, 200–215.

100 White, L. A. 1949 *The science of culture*. New York, NY: Grove Press.

Chapter 2

Exploring the Costs and Benefits of Social Information Use: An Appraisal of Current Experimental Evidence

Guillaume Rieucau and Luc-Alain Giraldeau

Research on social learning has focused traditionally on whether animals possess the cognitive ability to learn novel motor patterns from tutors. More recently, social learning has included the use of others as sources of inadvertent social information. This type of social learning seems more taxonomically widespread and its use can more readily be approached as an economic decision. Social sampling information, however, can be tricky to use and calls for a more lucid appraisal of its costs. In this four-part review, we address these costs. Firstly, we address the possibility that only a fraction of group members are actually providing social information at any one time. Secondly, we review experimental research which shows that animals are circumspect about social information use. Thirdly, we consider the cases where social information can lead to incorrect decisions and finally, we review studies investigating the effect of social information quality. We address the possibility that using social information or not is not a binary decision and present results of a study showing that nutmeg mannikins combine both sources of information, a condition that can lead to the establishment of informational cascades. We discuss the importance of empirically investigating the economics of social information use.

Keywords: social information; public information; social information costs; social learning; informational cascade

2.1 Introduction

Using the behaviour of others as a means to acquire novel behavioural techniques by social learning has been the focus of a considerable number of empirical and theoretical studies [1] (see also [2] for an example of an empirical study). More recently, the focus of social learning research has diverged slightly from just the acquisition of novel motor patterns to the acquisition and updating of information about the value of alternative options, social sampling of a sort [3–7]. In this review, we address specifically cases of the latter: social information use or social sampling.

Social sampling information is important because it is argued to afford the first building block for the evolution of traditions on the one hand, and to provide an advantage to group living on the other. As a result, considerable theoretical and empirical research has been directed to the ecological and cognitive requirements for its evolution [8–11]. Empirical research on the subject has focused on exploring whether animals do indeed acquire and use social information generated by the behaviour of others [1]. A number of empirical findings suggest that social sampling is taxonomically widespread, observed in fish, birds and mammals and useful in various ecological settings such as group foraging, anti-predatory behaviour, agonistic interaction, migration, dispersal, mate choice and breeding habitat selection. Moreover, it has been reported in both intra- and interspecific social interactions [5, 12–18].

Evidence of social information use comes usually in the form of 'copying': adopting the same option others are observed to choose. Research on copying focuses on the circumstances under which an animal copies rather than selects an option on the basis of its own personal information. Theoretical studies have explored the different rules that animals may adopt when faced with the decision of whether to copy others or learn by themselves [19]. These rules can take forms such as 'copy the majority' or 'copy if others are more successful', and which is best depends on the costs and benefits of social learning in a given ecological setting. Such an economic approach to social learning has enjoyed some empirical success (e.g. see [20] (here, Chapter 3) in this collection for an extensive review of social learning in fish). Empirical evidence arising mostly from the field of human culture (i.e. see the chapter entitled 'Culture is maladaptive' in [21]) suggests that socially acquired information can sometimes be incorrect and still spread within groups. This raises the issue that animals that use social information should perhaps use it with some caution, paying attention to the specific circumstances and the pay-offs associated with social and asocial acquisition of information [19, 22].

Our objective in this four-part review is to summarize the research that has been dedicated to the study of the costs associated with the use of social information. In the first section, we deal with the cost linked to the possibility that animals are incapable of simultaneously gathering social and asocial information. When this happens, they must choose which type of sampling they will engage in and the economic value of each alternative depends on how many individuals choose to sample socially. The more social samplers there are in a population, the fewer the asocial samplers. As a consequence a combination of asocial and social learners is expected [19, 22, 23], a situation which is similar to the producer–scrounger scenario [24, 25]. In the second section, we argue that if social information can be risky, then there should be evidence of this in studies providing subjects with a choice between both social and personal information that differ in reliability. The third section reviews experimental studies that explore the circumstances under which animals could use incorrect social information and consequently decide wrongly to adopt maladaptive behaviour. The fourth section presents a recent experimental study that shows how the persuasiveness of social information can influence individuals to the point where they disregard highly reliable personal information to copy the erroneous behaviour of others. Finally, we use these results to discuss the informational cascade, a phenomenon that has been reported to be widespread in human societies.

2.2 Only a fraction of any group provides social information

Almost all evolutionary models of social information use assume that within a group of animals engaged in searching for some resource, food, water, mates and nesting material, all individuals are actively occupied by exploration and search. During this exploratory process, each searching individual would be generating inadvertent social information and the success of each could be summed to provide a more representative corporate sample of current resource levels in that habitat. This idyllic view of the advantage of social information, however, is questionable because it assumes that all individuals in a group are engaged in searching for the resource while concurrently monitoring the success of others. If individuals cannot obtain both types of information concurrently, then they will have to choose which of the two to use. When this happens, at any instant the population is composed of pure asocial and pure social learners, a situation that was originally modelled by Rogers [23]. The gains of social learning depend on how many asocial learners there are to copy. Social learners initially do very well but as they spread and replace asocial learners in the population, their benefits decline as they become increasingly likely to copy a social learning individual whose information may be outdated. The incompatibility predicts an evolutionarily stable mixture of social and asocial learners within a population, a situation akin to a producer–scrounger game [19, 24–26]. That means that at best, in any group, only a fraction of its members are actively generating useful inadvertent social information, Kendal *et al.* [19] going as far as predicting that the expected social learning rule is the one that forms an equilibrium with the fewest asocial learners as possible.

Although the claim for frequency-dependent pay-offs associated with the social learning strategy can be traced as far back as Rogers [23] and is found in a number of recent studies [19, 22], there is yet no convincing empirical evidence for it. No study for instance has ever experimentally demonstrated that groups with increasing numbers of social learning strategists do more poorly than others. To date, no study has addressed whether the collection of social and asocial information are incompatible activities. Such an incompatibility could be sensory or include higher neural processes. Such studies remain dearly needed.

2.3 When animals can choose between social and asocial learning

Giraldeau *et al.* [22] suggested that social information may not be universally reliable and predicted that animals should be more discerning of its value before using it (see also [19, 27]). A recent study based on the results of a social learning tournament [28, 29] suggests instead that social learning is widely beneficial, showing that individuals do increasingly better in a changing world the more they use social as opposed to asocial learning, so long as asocial learners are present in the population. This theoretical result, which appears insensitive to the accuracy of social learning, is partly at odds with a large number of studies showing that animals use social information primarily as plan B, or a backup when personal information is too costly to obtain, unreliable or outdated. Many of those studies are devoted to considering the ecological circumstances under which animals choose socially over asocially acquired information. Such studies have been conducted on social insects, fishes, birds and mammals and relied on the use of experimental designs that allow precise control of the source of information available, creating situations where social and personal information are incompatible or in conflict [30–36].

Templeton & Giraldeau [31], in an experimental study on European starlings (*Sturnus vulgaris*), reported that birds relied only on public information (i.e. a specific type of inadvertent social information based on performance that provides indication about the quality of a resource [4, 37]) when personal information about the quality of different food patches was either difficult or costly to obtain. These results combined with findings from a previous study of Templeton & Giraldeau [30] suggest that starlings mostly use information obtained from their own sampling of the environment rather than social information when both types of information are not available concurrently. Starlings, it seems, are unwilling to forgo collection of any personal information in order to obtain public information. Since then, several other studies have explored the situations under which animals may use preferentially one source of information over the other.

Many studies have been devoted to the question of fish's propensity to rely on social information [20]. For instance, van Bergen *et al.* [35] in a study where nine-spined sticklebacks (*Pungitius pungitius*) were provided with conflicting asocial and social information found a preferential use of personal information over social information when fish had access to highly reliable personal information. However, as personal information became out-of-date, fish relied mostly on social information. van Bergen *et al.* [35] argue that sticklebacks can assess the reliability of both sources of information and choose to exploit the most reliable such that reliance on either social or personal information may vary according to circumstances.

Fletcher & Miller [38] also reported an effect of social information reliability on its use during offspring production of female cactus bugs (*Chelinidea vittiger*). This hemipteran is known to form foraging and reproductive aggregations on the prickly pear cactus (*Opuntia* spp.) where the prior presence of conspecific nymphs or eggs may provide social cues about the quality of a patch. Female bugs exposed to different sources of social information about the quality of the resource (the presence of juveniles was assumed to be more informative than the sole presence of eggs) were found to rely mostly on a recent and accurate type of social information than on outdated prior information. This, therefore, provides experimental support for the theoretical assumption that current information (either socially or personally acquired) should be used preferentially over prior knowledge because reliability of prior information is expected to degrade over time [16, 39, 40].

The costs of acquiring personal information may be a key determinant in an animal's decision to use social information. Boyd & Richerson [41] proposed that social learning will be favoured whenever personal information becomes costly to acquire directly; individuals should take advantage in this case of the cheaper source of information. From this formulation of the 'costly information hypothesis' [41], Laland [42] suggested that individuals could possibly adopt a 'copy when asocial learning is costly' social learning strategy. The nature of these asocial learning costs is multiple. They can arise from energetic, time or opportunity losses induced by the direct sampling of the environment or from an increasing vulnerability to predation when, for instance, gathering personal information interferes with anti-predator vigilance. Moreover, such asocial learning costs may also depend on the ecological context that an individual is facing. For instance, Bouliner *et al.* [43] argued that if estimating the overall quality of a food patch could be done quasi-instantaneously by a forager, this is clearly not the case when animals have to assess the quality of a breeding site where acquiring personal information requires at least that the individual experiences a complete reproductive event. As a consequence, one may expect that in some contexts, where asocial information is highly costly to obtain, such as choosing a breeding habitat and perhaps even a mate, individuals will be expected to rely on social rather than asocial information.

Empirical support for the 'copy when asocial learning is costly' hypothesis is accumulating. Webster & Laland [44] tested the hypothesis directly in European minnows (*Phoxinus phoxinus*), by giving these social fish a foraging patch choice under different levels of simulated predation risk (presence or not in the experimental tank of a life-sized dummy perch, *Perca* sp.). The minnows' propensity to rely on social information was mediated by the level of predation risk; under simulated situations of high danger, both naive fish and those provided with social information that conflicted with their reliable personal information choose to rely more on social information. Minnows, it seems, adopt a copy when asocial learning is costly strategy. In another shoaling species, Kendal *et al.* [34] reported that guppies (*Poecilia reticulata*) were willing to gather personal information rather than copy group members' decisions until it required losing visual contact with the rest of the shoal; a situation that is expected to reduce the security benefits provided by swimming in a group.

2.4 Using incorrect social information

While evidence that animals can gather adaptive information about the outside world and learn from others is becoming common, social learning can, under some specific circumstances, also promote the diffusion of maladaptive decisions throughout a population [22, 32, 45]. Under a rapidly changing environment, information diffused socially can lag behind environmental changes and so result in the transmission of outdated and perhaps maladaptive information [45]. In such a situation, individuals that decide only on the basis of their own personal information should be favoured, and so using socially learned information may not be universally adaptive [45].

Laland & Williams [32] tested this prediction with the guppy using a transmission chain design experiment. In such an experiment, a founder group of demonstrators is initially trained to access a floating feeder using either a long circuitous route or a short direct route, a pilot study having previously confirmed that guppies spontaneously prefer the short, more direct route. Founders are gradually replaced one by one by naive fish in each group throughout the experiment, until no founder eventually remains within either group. Not surprisingly, when placed with founders that use the short direct route, the preference persists in the group even when no founder remains within the group. Similarly, preference for the long route persists even when no founder remains within the group. Maladaptive information, using a long instead of a short route, therefore, can be socially transmitted throughout a population and promote the establishment of suboptimal traditions [32].

Bates & Chappell [33] argued that an anti-predatory component could account for the persistent preference for the long route even when no founders remain within the group; when fishes are shoaling, the security benefits of remaining with swimming mates can outweigh any energetic benefit associated with choosing the shorter route. To control for this anti-predatory benefit, Bates & Chappell [33] conducted an experiment where fish that have acquired the founders' preference for the suboptimal long route via social learning were tested individually when given a choice between long and short routes to a feeder. Under such conditions, fish that previously swam with long-route founders prefer the long route when tested in a shoaling condition, but clearly prefer the short route when tested alone [33]. The preference switch between the group and solitary conditions suggests a trade-off between anti-predatory and energetic benefits.

Experimental evidence of maladaptive choice following exposure to social information remains sparse and begs the development of stronger experimental procedures that control the quality of the social information provided to subjects. In a field experiment investigating breeding habitat choice of first-time breeding natal dispersing birds of the solitary Nelson's sharp-tailed sparrow (*Ammodramus nelsoni*) and social bobolink (*Dolichonyx oryzivorus*), Nocera *et al.* [46] provide strong evidence that only young inexperienced bobolinks rely on social information (location cues) provided by visual models and audio playbacks of adult males to choose a breeding habitat. Interestingly, they report that erroneous social information (i.e. when audio playbacks and visual models were played and placed in suboptimal habitats) induces young bobolinks to settle in and even defend these suboptimal territories the following spring. Nocera *et al.*'s [46] work is compelling because of the experimental technique that was adopted: audio playback. In such a situation, the experimenter controls the quality of the social information and as a result provides a convincing demonstration of the potential effect of false social information use directly and in field conditions.

2.5 Changing the quality of social information

Animals can use the number of demonstrators performing a given task as a warrant of social cue quality. Such a conformity effect was highlighted in experiments using groups of fishes in a context of food patch choice [34, 47] or escape route preference [48]. An observer will be more willing to follow a demonstrator group's decision the greater the number of individuals within the group. However, if such a conformity effect is handy for naive individuals because they can thus obtain information rapidly and at low cost, more experienced individuals with reliable and accurate personal knowledge seem more insulated from its effects [34].

Giraldeau *et al.* [22] argue that social information based on the actual quantitative value of a reward, public information, would be more reliable than information obtained from simply observing an individual's decision, a social cue. Public information that is more directly related to the actual state of the world should therefore be preferred when available concurrently with less informative social cues [49, 50]. A clever series of experiments with nine-spined sticklebacks provides the first empirical support for this preference [51]. A social cue in this experiment consists in observing a large and a small group of conspecifics each visiting a feeding location that has no food and so provides no public information about food quality. With these cues, the observer fish prefers to go where more fish had been observed [51], showing that they relied on social cues to choose a feeding location. However, when provided concurrently with social cues and public information, naive fish relied preferentially on public information, always choosing the location where the demonstrators were feeding, independently of the demonstrator group's size. Coolen *et al.* [51] concluded that when available, public information is preferred over social cues, providing the first empirical support for Doliguez *et al.* [49] and Koops' [50] prediction. Following up on Coolen *et al.*'s [51] work on preference for public information, Kendal *et al.* [27] show that sticklebacks use public information adaptively, switching their prior preference for a feeder only when the observed outcomes of a demonstrator fish at another feeder exceeded their own outcomes.

Up to now, the decision to use social as opposed to asocial learning has been approached as a dichotomous choice. When asocial information is outdated, costly to obtain or otherwise doubtful, the animal is predicted to use social information. Economists Bikhchandani *et al.* [52] break with this view and assume that individuals should always combine both asocial and social information when having to come to a decision about options. They argue that the best way to choose what to do is to combine personal cues obtained from one's own sampling to the combined social cues provided by the sequence of earlier decisions of other group members. Social information may be of little consequence when it is redundant with accurate and unambiguous asocial information. However, as asocial information is increasingly ambiguous, the contribution of social information on decision increases. This Bayesian combination of asocial and social information can generate a phenomenon known as an 'informational cascade', characterized by the explosive spread of a decision, whether correct or not [52]. Once an informational cascade is engaged, the weight of social information is such that it completely outweighs the value of asocial information and individuals appear to totally disregard their own personal experience. Informational cascades have been proposed as a possible explanation for a number of large-scale explosive copying events in humans, such as market crashes in economics and panic rushes in crowds as well as flock alarm flights, night roost selection in colonial birds or mate-choice copying in animals [22]. Even though establishment of informational cascades has been found in laboratory experiments involving human participants [53, 54], clear experimental evidence of an informational cascade in non-humans is still lacking.

One intriguing aspect of informational cascades is that animals may be called to disregard their current, asocially acquired information to conform to contradictory social information provided by a sequence of group mates. This may appear unlikely given the quantity of research previously reviewed which shows that animals are circumspect about social information, using it only as a backup for inaccurate or outdated personal information. However, few studies have explored whether the apparent high quality of social information when combined with reliable but contradictory asocial information can induce individuals to disregard their asocial information as predicted by the theory of informational cascades.

One earlier study explored whether budgies (*Psittacus undulatus*) foraging in groups would combine both personally acquired and socially acquired information about the distribution of seed patch quality [55]. The results indicated that the birds relied exclusively on their asocially acquired information (personal patch-sample information combined with prior knowledge of food distribution) and were apparently incapable of or unwilling to integrate socially acquired information into their foraging decisions. More recently, Rieucau & Giraldeau [36] provide some experimental evidence to suggest that nutmeg mannikins (*Lonchura punctulata*), small social estrildid finches from Southeast Asia, could be induced to integrate social and asocial sources of information in their assessment of the best foraging patch. Twenty food-deprived birds were individually given a choice to feed from one of two feeders that differed in their quality. One dish was filled with a large quantity of their highly preferred millet seeds and provided rapid access to a palatable source of food. The other contained only a thin layer of seeds covered by a thick layer of a non-edible substrate, forcing them to search through the substrate in order to access the food. The birds never knew ahead of time which of the right or the left feeder was the better one.

Before testing, half of the birds were provided with asocial information about dish quality by training them to recognize that a dish with a coloured dot always had more food. The other half of the birds had no asocial information about which was the better dish because they were trained in such a way that the dot had no predictive value for them. Once trained, birds from both groups were placed singly in a choice apparatus and were provided with social information. The birds were first confined to an observation compartment that contained no food and shown a video playback of birds feeding from one of two dishes in the adjacent feeding compartment (Figure 2.1). For each trial, only one of the dishes bore a dot and the playback could show companion birds at the marked dish or at the other. Once the video playback ended and conspecifics could no longer be seen, the bird was allowed into the feeding compartment where it could choose to feed in one of the dishes.

The quality of social information was manipulated in two ways: behaviourally and numerically. Behavioural persuasiveness depended on whether the companions were seen feeding or not. We assumed feeding birds were more persuasive than non-feeding birds. Numerical persuasiveness was based on the number of companions, assuming the more birds were in the playback, the more persuasive the social information. As expected,

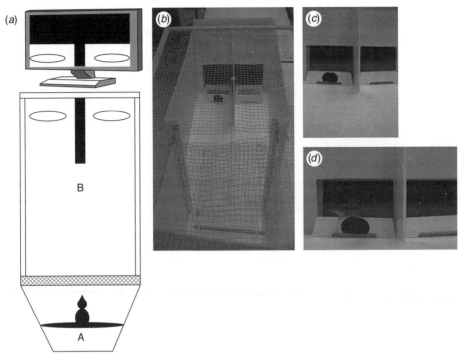

Figure 2.1 (*a, b*) Representations of the apparatus: each bird is individually introduced in the observation compartment A where it can observe the video sequences through the transparent partition. (*c*) Once in compartment A, the focal bird cannot see the content of the feeders in compartment B, and once let into compartment B by remote raising of the partition between compartments A and B, it can choose its feeder using the visual cue on one of the feeders with which it had previous experience or/and the social information that had been provided by a video playback of companions behind one of the feeders (*d*).

birds with no asocial information consistently chose the feeder according to the social information they had obtained irrespective of the number of companions or whether they were feeding or not (Figure 2.2). Companions did not so easily influence birds with asocial information. The birds continued to choose dishes according to their asocial information when companions did not feed, no matter how many there were. The result was quite different, however, when the playbacks showed feeding companions. In that case, the number of birds with asocial information that chose to copy the companions' choice of going to the poor-quality feeder increased as the number of companions increased (Figure 2.3). This result shows that the persuasive social information was probably combined with the bird's reliable asocial information, leading to a decision suggestive of individuals disregarding their reliable asocial information in a way that is entirely consistent with the establishment of informational cascades [22, 52]. This use of video playback provides a powerful and effective way of tackling questions of social information use. More laboratories should consider developing the technique further.

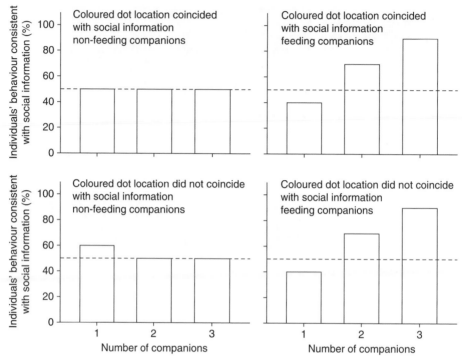

Figure 2.2 Proportion of focal birds (*n* = 10) for which prior training was such that the coloured dot failed to predict the location of the fast feeder that relied on social information to choose their feeder, expressed according to the number and the behaviour of virtual companions and whether the social information coincided or not with the location of the coloured dot. (Reproduced from *Behavioral Ecology*, **22**(3), Guillaume Rieucau, Luc-Alain Giraldeau, Persuasive companions can be wrong: the use of misleading social information in nutmeg mannikins, pp. 1217–1222, © 2009 with permission from Oxford University Press.)

Future research concerning cascades should consider situations where asocial information is more ambiguous than the experimental situation tested so far. If cascades can
occur, their duration, their rate of establishment and risk of being incorrect should all
depend crucially on the uncertainty associated with asocial information.

2.6 **Conclusion**

Social information use in a sampling context and social learning of new motor skills are
increasingly amalgamated under the topic of social learning. While both imply the use of
social information, they differ in important ways. Social sampling, for instance, appears
to be more common and taxonomically wide-spread, reported in species ranging
from invertebrates to primates, than social learning of new motor patterns. It may be
important in the future to pay more attention to the differences between the two. Our
review of studies devoted to social information in the context of sampling among foraging alternatives leads us to a number of conclusions. First of all, although the claims for

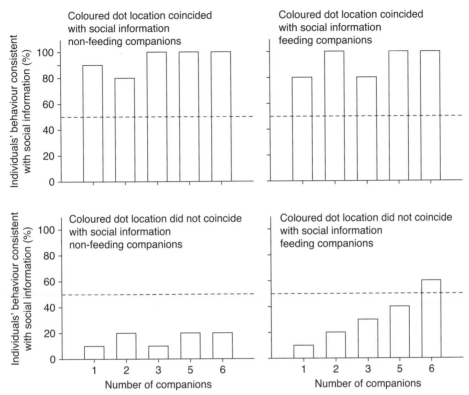

Figure 2.3 Proportion of focal birds (*n* = 10) for which prior training was such that the coloured dot provided a strong predictor of the location of the fast feeder that relied on social information to choose their feeder, expressed according to the number and the behaviour of virtual companions and whether the social information coincided or not with the location of the coloured dot. (Reproduced from *Behavioral Ecology*, **22**(3), Guillaume Rieucau, Luc-Alain Giraldeau, Persuasive companions can be wrong: the use of misleading social information in nutmeg mannikins, pp. 1217–1222, © 2009 with permission from Oxford University Press.)

the frequency-dependent nature of the value of social information are increasing, empirical evidence is suspiciously lacking. We cannot argue more forcefully for the pressing need to investigate the frequency dependence of social information empirically. More specifically, it would be important to establish the extent to which the collection of both asocial and social information is incompatible. Second, the results of a recent and already widely cited social learning tournament [29] indicate that, while some asocial learners still persist in the population, increasing the use of social learning, irrespective of the informative nature of social information on which it is based, provides the best strategy in a changing world. This result is somewhat surprising given the impressive number of empirical studies which show that when given a choice between asocial and social information, animals tend to rely primarily on asocial information and only use social information as a backup when asocial information is unsatisfactory. This discrepancy between the results of the social learning tournament and reported caution exercised by animals that use social information now needs to be addressed. One possibility is that the tournament simulates a situation of adopting novel motor patterns rather than a case of merely sampling alternatives. This issue deserves further investigation. Third, we have highlighted that up to now the use of social versus asocial learning has been presented as a more or less dichotomous decision. Animals are predicted to use social information or not. Some theoreticians have pointed out the superiority a Bayesian combination of both social and asocial information in the evaluation of the quality of alternative options. We showed the results of one study in which individuals provided with strong asocial information were increasingly led to choosing the incorrect option when increasingly convincing social information contradicted their asocial information. This combination of the two sources of information paves the way to the establishment of informational cascades. Researchers should now turn to investigating whether informational cascades, whether for correct or incorrect decisions, can actually be induced within animal groups. We encourage researchers to develop further the playback approaches, whether auditory, video or involving any other relevant modality, as a means to control experimentally the social information provided to subjects. In the end, we encourage all those engaged in social learning research to consider more seriously whether the economics of using social information in a sampling context differ from those presiding over the social learning of novel motor patterns and hence technical traditions such as food-handling techniques in orangutans [56] or over-imitation [57].

Acknowledgements

We wish to thank Andy Whiten for inviting us to contribute to this special volume and Kevin Laland who kindly commented on an earlier version. G.R. is financially supported by a Fyssen Foundation Postdoctoral Fellowship.

References

1 Galef Jr, B. G. & Giraldeau, A. 2001 Social influences on foraging in vertebrates: causal mechanisms and adaptive functions. *Anim. Behav.* **61**, 3–15.

2 Thornton, A. & Clutton-Brock, T. 2011 Social learning and the development of individual and group behaviour in mammal societies. *Phil. Trans. R. Soc. B* **366**, 978–987.

3 Brown, C. & Laland, K. N. 2003 Social learning in fishes: a review. *Fish Fish.* **4**, 280–288.

4 Danchin, E., Giraldeau, L.-A., Valone, T. J. & Wagner, R. H. 2004 Public information: from nosy neighbors to cultural evolution. *Science* **305**, 487–491.

5 Griffin, A. S. 2004 Social learning about predators: a review and prospectus. *Learn. Behav.* **32**, 131–140.

6 Bonnie, K. E. & Earley, R. L. 2007 Expanding the scope for social information use. *Anim. Behav.* **74**, 171–181.

7 Blanchet, S., Clobet, J. & Danchin, E. 2010 The role of public information in ecology and conservation: an emphasis on inadvertent social information. *Ann. N. Y. Acad. Sci.* **1195**, 149–168.

8 Henrich, J. 2001 Cultural transmission and the diffusion of innovations: adoption dynamics indicate that biased cultural transmission is the predominate force in behavioral change and much of sociocultural evolution. *Am. Anthropol.* **103**, 992–1013.

9 Henrich, J. & McElreath, R. 2003 The evolution of cultural evolution. *Evol. Anthropol.* **12**, 123–135.

10 Dunbar, R. I. M. & Shultz, S. 2007 Evolution in the social brain. *Science* **317**, 1344–1347.

11 Henrich, J., Boyd, R. & Richerson, P. J. 2008 Five misunderstandings about cultural evolution. *Hum. Nat.* **19**, 119–137.

12 Coolen, I., van Bergen, Y., Day, R. L. & Laland, K. N. 2003 Species difference in adaptive use of public information by sticklebacks. *Proc. R. Soc. Lond. B* **270**, 2413–2419.

13 Coolen, I., Dangles, O. & Casas, J. 2005 Social learning in noncolonial insects? *Curr. Biol.* **15**, 1931–1935.

14 Pajero, D., Danchin, E. & Aviles, J. M. 2005 The hetero-specific habitat copying hypothesis: can competitors indicate habitat quality? *Behav. Ecol.* **16**, 96–105.

15 Seppänen, J. T. & Forsman, J. T. 2007 Interspecific social learning: novel preference can be acquired from a competing species. *Curr. Biol.* **17**, 1248–1252.

16 Seppänen, J. T., Forsman, J. T., Monkkonen, M. & Thomson, R. L. 2007 Social information use is a process across time, space, and ecology, reaching heterospecifics. *Ecology* **88**, 1622–1633.

17 Cote, J. & Clobert, J. 2007 Social information and emigration: lessons from immigrants. *Ecol. Lett.* **10**, 411–417.

18 Mery, F., Varela, S. A. M., Danchin, E., Blanchet, S., Parejo, D., Coolen, I. & Wagner, R. H. 2009 Public versus personal information for mate copying in an invertebrate. *Curr. Biol.* **19**, 730–734.

19 Kendal, J., Giraldeau, L.-A. & Laland, K. 2009 The evolution of social learning rules: payoff-biased and frequency-dependent biased transmission. *J. Theor. Biol.* **260**, 210–219.

20 Laland, K. N., Atton, N. & Webster, M. M. 2011 From fish to fashion: experimental and theoretical insights into the evolution of culture. *Phil. Trans. R. Soc. B* **366**, 958–968.

21 Richerson, P. J. & Boyd, R. 2005 *Not by genes alone: how culture transformed human evolution.* Chicago, IL: University of Chicago Press.

22 Giraldeau, L.-A., Valone, T. J. & Templeton, J. J. 2002 Potential disadvantages of using socially acquired information. *Phil. Trans. R. Soc. Lond. B* **357**, 1559–1566.

23 Rogers, A. 1989 Does biology constrain culture? *Am. Anthropol.* **90**, 819–831.

24 Barnard, C. J. & Sibly, R. M. 1981 Producers and scroungers: a general model and its application to captive flocks of house sparrows. *Anim. Behav.* **29**, 543–555.

25 Giraldeau, L.-A. & Caraco, T. 2000 *Social foraging theory.* Princeton, NJ: Princeton University Press.

26 Giraldeau, L.-A. & Dubois, F. 2008 Social foraging and the study of exploitative behaviour. *Adv. Study Behav.* **38**, 59–104.

27 Kendal, J. R., Rendell, L., Pike, T. & Laland, K. N. 2009 Nine-spined sticklebacks deploy a hill-climbing social learning strategy. *Behav. Ecol.* **20**, 238–244.

28 Rendell, L., Boyd, R., Enquist, M., Feldman, M. W., Fogarty, L. & Laland, K. N. 2011 How copying affects the amount, evenness and persistence of cultural knowledge: insights from the social learning strategies tournament. *Phil. Trans. R. Soc. B* **366**, 1118–1128.

29 Rendell, L. *et al.* 2010 Why copy others? Insights from the social learning strategies tournament. *Science* **328**, 208–213.

30 Templeton, J. J. & Giraldeau, A. 1995 Patch assessment in foraging flocks of European starlings: evidence for the use of public information. *Behav. Ecol.* **6**, 65–72.

31 Templeton, J. J. & Giraldeau, L.-A. 1996 Vicarious sampling: the use of personal and public information by starlings foraging in a simple patchy environment. *Behav. Ecol. Sociobiol.* **38**, 105–114.

32 Laland, K. N. & Williams, K. 1998 Social transmission of maladaptive information in the guppy. *Behav. Ecol.* **9**, 493–499.

33 Bates, L. & Chappell, J. 2002 Inhibition of optimal behavior by social transmission in the guppy depends on shoaling. *Behav. Ecol.* **13**, 827–831.

34 Kendal, R. L., Coolen, I. & Laland, K. N. 2004 The role of conformity in foraging when personal and social information conflict. *Behav. Ecol.* **15**, 269–277.

35 van Bergen, Y., Coolen, I. & Laland, K. N. 2004 Nine-spined sticklebacks exploit the most reliable source when public and private information conflict. *Proc. R. Soc. Lond. B* **271**, 957–962.

36 Rieucau, G. & Giraldeau, L.-A. 2009 Persuasive companions can be wrong: the use of misleading social information in nutmeg mannikin. *Behav. Ecol.* **20**, 1217–1222.

37 Valone, T. J. & Templeton, J. J. 2002 Public information for the assessment of quality: a widespread social phenomenon. *Phil. Trans. R. Soc. Lond. B* **357**, 1549–1557.

38 Fletcher, R. J. & Miller, C. W. 2008 The type and timing of social information alters offspring production. *Biol. Lett.* **4**, 482–485.

39 Boyd, R. & Richerson, P. J. 1995 Why does culture increase human adaptability. *Ethol. Sociobiol.* **16**, 125–143.

40 Henrich, J. & Gil-White, F. J. 2001 The evolution of prestige: freely conferred deference as a mechanism for enhancing the benefits of cultural transmission. *Evol. Hum. Behav.* **22**, 165–196.

41 Boyd, R. & Richerson, P. J. 1985 *Culture and the evolutionary process.* Chicago, IL: University of Chicago Press.

42 Laland, K. N. 2004 Social learning strategies. *Learn. Behav.* **32**, 4–14.

43 Boulinier, T., Mariette, M., Doligez, B. & Danchin, É. 2008 Choosing where to reproduce— breeding habitat selection. In *Behavioural ecology* (eds É. Danchin, L.-A. Giraldeau & F. Cézilly), pp. 285–321. Oxford, UK: Oxford University Press.

44 Webster, M. M. & Laland, K. N. 2008 Social learning strategies and predation risk: minnows copy only when using private information would be costly. *Proc. R. Soc. B* **275**, 2869–2876.

45 Feldman, M., Aoki, K. & Kumm, J. 1996 Individual versus social learning: evolutionary analysis in a fluctuating environment. *Anthropol. Sci.* **104**, 209–232.

46 Nocera, J. J., Forbes, G. J. & Giraldeau, L.-A. 2006 Inadvertent social information in breeding site selection of natal dispersing birds. *Proc. R. Soc. B* **273**, 349–355.

47 Pike, T. W. & Laland, K. N. 2010 Conformist learning in nine-spined sticklebacks' foraging decisions. *Biol. Lett.* **6**, 466–468.

48 Brown, C. & Laland, K. N. 2002 Social learning of a novel avoidance task in the guppy, *P. reticulata*: conformity and social release. *Anim. Behav.* **64**, 41–147.

49 Doligez, B., Cadet, C., Danchin, E. & Boulinier, T. 2003 When to use public information for breeding habitat selection? The role of environmental predictability and density dependence. *Anim. Behav.* **66**, 973–988.

50 Koops, M. A. 2004 Reliability and the value of information. *Anim. Behav.* **67**, 103–111.

51 Coolen, I., Ward, A. J. W., Hart, P. J. B. & Laland, K. N. 2005 Foraging nine-spined sticklebacks prefer to rely on public information over simpler social cues. *Behav. Ecol.* **16**, 865–870.

52 Bikhchandani, S., Hirshleifer, D. & Welch, I. 1998 Learning from the behavior of others: conformity fads and informational cascades. *J. Econ. Perspect.* **12**, 151–170.

53 Anderson, L. R. & Holt, C. A. 1997 Information cascades in the laboratory. *Am. Econ. Rev.* **87**, 847–862.

54 Noth, M. & Weber, M. 2003 Information aggregation with random ordering: cascades and overconfidence. *Econ. J.* **113**, 166–189.

55 Valone, T. J. & Giraldeau, L.-A. 1993 Patch estimation in group foragers: what information is used? *Anim. Behav.* **45**, 721–728.

56 van Schaik, C. P. & Burkart, J. M. 2011 Social learning and evolution: the cultural intelligence hypothesis. *Phil. Trans. R. Soc. B* **366**, 1008–1016.

57 Lyons, D. E., Damrosch, D. H., Lin, J. K., Macris, D. M. & Keil, F. C. 2011 The scope and limits of overimitation in the transmission of artefact culture. *Phil. Trans. R. Soc. B* **366**, 1158–1167.

Chapter 3

From Fish to Fashion: Experimental and Theoretical Insights into the Evolution of Culture

Kevin N. Laland, Nicola Atton and Michael M. Webster

Recent years have witnessed a re-evaluation of the cognitive capabilities of fishes, including with respect to social learning. Indeed, some of the best experimental evidence for animal traditions can be found in fishes. Laboratory experimental studies reveal that many fishes acquire dietary, food site and mating preferences, predator recognition and avoidance behaviour, and learn pathways, through copying[1] other fishes. Concentrating on foraging behaviour, we will present the findings of laboratory experiments that reveal social learning, behavioural innovation, the diffusion of novel behaviour through populations and traditional use of food sites. Further studies reveal surprisingly complex social learning strategies deployed by sticklebacks. We will go on to place these observations of fish in a phylogenetic context, describing in which respects the learning and traditionality of fish are similar to, and differ from, that observed in other animals. We end by drawing on theoretical insights to suggest processes that may have played important roles in the evolution of the human cultural capability.

Keywords: culture; social learning; tradition; fishes; gene–culture coevolution; teaching

3.1 Introduction

Humans are a remarkably successful species, both demographically in terms of our burgeoning numbers, and ecologically in terms of the broad range of terrestrial environments in which we thrive. Our capacity for culture is the major factor underlying these accomplishments [1, 2]. By 'culture' we mean the ability to acquire valuable knowledge and skills from other individuals through social learning and teaching, and to build on this reservoir of shared knowledge, iteratively, generation after generation, building ever more efficient solutions to life's challenges [3]. Other animals, including fishes, are capable of social learning and traditionality in behaviour, and in many respects these resemble aspects of human culture and cognition. Nonetheless, the fact remains that humans alone have sequenced genomes, built satellites and Large Hadron Colliders, written plays and novels and composed moonlight sonatas, while the most culturally accomplished non-human animals sit naked in the jungle cracking nuts. It may be tempting to view culture as the faculty that sets humans apart from the rest of nature—and to some extent this is justifiable. However, the human cultural capability obviously must have evolved too.

Herein lies a major challenge facing the biological and social sciences: how could the extraordinary and unique human capacity for culture have evolved out of something resembling the simple behavioural traditions observed in other animals? While a comprehensive answer to this question may still be some way off, we will endeavour in this chapter to provide a sketch of some factors that we believe to be important. Our position is informed by both experimental studies of social learning, innovation, diffusion and tradition in animals, and by theoretical studies that use mathematical models to investigate aspects of human social evolution.

We will concentrate disproportionately on the insights into animal traditions that can be gained from experimental studies of fishes. Our 'fishy focus' is only partly because other contributors to this volume have been given the remit to cover alternative taxonomic groups. Fishes provide, we believe, highly informative and practical model systems for experimental investigation of the biological bases of culture. Naturally, we understand that to most social scientists, as well as to the layperson, fishes seem so distant—both intellectually and taxonomically—from humans, that it is extremely difficult to envisage how the study of their behaviour could shed light on human cognitive evolution. However, the cognitive capabilities of fishes have historically been underestimated, and in many respects their intellectual faculties are comparable to birds and mammals [4, 5]. Recent years have witnessed a shift away from the belief that animal intelligence mirrors the degree of relatedness to humans towards the notion of convergent evolution of intelligence in distinct taxonomic groups [6, 7]. This has the dual implication that, among the 28 000 species of fishes, there might well be some with interesting cognitive capabilities, and that the blanket dismissal of cognitive prowess of an entire taxon based on experimental studies of a small number of species would be scientifically unjustifiable.

As we describe in the following sections, there is now extensive experimental evidence that social learning and tradition play an important role in the behavioural development of many fishes, and frequently underlie differences in the behavioural repertoires of different populations. Most fishes are social animals and, like other vertebrates, their behaviour is far from rigidly controlled by a genetic programme, but constantly and flexibly adjusted to exploit information and resources in their social and asocial environment. The behaviour of others constitutes important sources of information to many fish species, providing them with valuable clues as to what to eat, where to find it, how to process it, what a predator looks like, how to escape, how to move safely through their environment, whom to mate with and many other challenges. Social learning is now known to play an important role in all of these domains in many fishes.

Given the knowledge that fishes are both competent at, and naturally widely reliant on, social learning and tradition, experimental studies of fish behaviour take on a new light. That is because fishes offer practical advantages over many other vertebrates for the study of social learning. After all, the diffusion of innovations and animal traditions are group-level phenomena, and if they are to be studied reliably researchers require not just replicate animals but replicate populations of animals. While it would be economically and practically challenging to set up large numbers of replicate populations of chimpanzees or Japanese macaques, it is extremely straightforward and cheap to set up large numbers of populations of small fishes in the laboratory, and subject them to experimentation. For instance, guppies are commercially available, thrive in simple aquaria, and cost virtually nothing to buy and keep, while sticklebacks are ubiquitous in the temperate Northern Hemisphere, can easily be fished out of local streams, and are equally effective laboratory subjects. Fish experimentalists enjoy the twin luxuries of the multiple conditions that good experimental design frequently demands and good statistical power, bringing experimental rigour to any social learning investigation.

Before we turn to a consideration of the social learning capabilities of fishes, we note in passing that biological interest in 'animal culture' goes beyond interest in reconstructing the evolution of human culture [8]. This is of relevance, because most of the experimental work that we will describe was not motivated by a wish to throw comparative light on human cognitive evolution. Biologists have their own agenda in studying animal traditions and culture. Perhaps, the most obvious determinant of biological interest is the observation that social learning is a source of adaptive behaviour; individuals can efficiently acquire solutions to problems such as 'what to eat?' and 'with whom to mate?' by copying others. But the recent fascination of biologists with culture also relates to its capability to propagate behaviour in a manner that is to some degree independent of the ecological environment, generate patterns of phenotypic variation in space, allow arbitrary and even maladaptive information to spread, and underpin niche construction. The social sciences may have been studying culture in humans prior to biologists, but they no longer have a monopoly of interest. The challenge that we laid out at the outset of this chapter, to understand the evolution of culture, is fundamentally a multi-disciplinary challenge, and a satisfactory solution will require a genuinely multi-disciplinary research effort.

3.2 Social learning in fishes

We begin this review with a brief account of how social learning is used by fishes under several different contexts, including moving through space, finding food, avoiding predators and choosing a mate (see [4, 5] for more extensive overviews).

3.2.1 Fish migrations

For most fish species, biologically important locations, such as profitable foraging sites, areas safe from predation, resting sites, suitable areas to find mates and reproduce, as well as safe routes between these locations, must be learned. Many fishes are now known to exhibit traditionality in their use of mating sites, preferred schooling sites, resting sites, feeding sites and pathways through their natural environments [4, 5]. A straightforward method for acquiring knowledge of the location of important resources is simply to follow others and in the process to learn the site or route for themselves.

Laland & Williams [9] trained 'demonstrator' guppies to take one of two alternative routes to a food source over repeated trials in laboratory aquaria. They then introduced naive subjects into the populations, who tended to shoal with their demonstrators, and thereby take the same route to food. After 5 days of trials, the subjects were tested alone, and showed a significant preference for taking the same route as had their demonstrators, despite there being an alternative route of equal distance and complexity (Figure 3.1a).

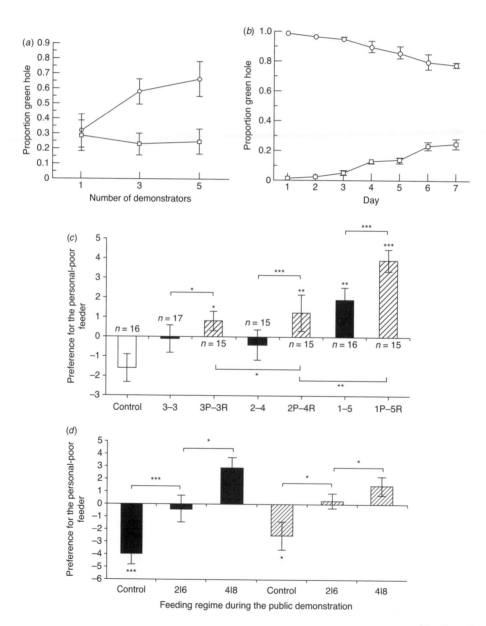

(Continued)

Thus simply by shoaling with knowledgeable conspecifics individuals can learn a route to food. Laland & Williams [9, 10] then went on to demonstrate how this simple process could underlie the natural migratory traditions that are observed in many fishes. They conducted experiments using a transmission chain design, where small shoals were trained to take one of two routes, and these trained founders were then gradually replaced by naive individuals to see if the route preferences were retained. Several days after the trained founders had been removed the route preferences were maintained in the groups (Figure 3.1b). Even when one route was substantially longer, and more energetically costly, than the alternative, the longer route was still being widely used by individuals whose founders had previously been trained to take it.

While many animals, notably chimpanzees [13], orangutans [14] and capuchin monkeys [15], exhibit behavioural traditions in nature (see [16–18]), the evidence that these are underpinned by social learning is, at best, circumstantial, leading to considerable controversy over the legitimacy of claims of animal culture [8, 19]. In contrast, for fish

---

Figure 3.1 (a) The proportion (mean ± s.e.) of trials in which observer guppies tested singly took the green hole to a food source, given that their demonstrators were trained to take the green (circle) or red (square) hole, and that they had one, three or five demonstrators. (b) The proportion of trials in which subjects took the green hole to a food source, in transmission chains where founder populations were trained to take the green (circle) or red (square) hole. Each point represents the mean of the pooled performances of the fish in each group. (c) Mean (± s.e.) preference for the personal-poor feeder (time spent near the personal-poor feeder minus time spent near the personal-rich feeder from instantaneous sampling every 6 s for 90 s) in the personal-information only condition ('control', white bar), the social-information only conditions (black bars, where 3–3 denotes three fish shoaling at one feeder and three fish at the other feeder) and the public-information conditions (hashed bars, where 3P–3R denotes three fish feeding at the public-poor feeder and three fish at the public-rich feeder, respectively). See text for full details. Asterisks above bars indicate a significant difference from the control group; horizontal lines indicate orthogonal pairwise comparisons between groups. $*p < 0.05$, $**p < 0.01$ and $***p < 0.001$. (d) Mean (± s.e.) standard error difference (personal-poor minus personal-rich) in the number of instances that the fish was present in the 'goal zone' around each feeder (from instantaneous sampling of the fish's location every 6 s for the first 90 s following the start of the choice test), in fish trained on a 6|2 (i.e. 6 and 2 deliveries to rich and poor feeders, respectively; black bars) or 8|4 (hashed bars) regime and subsequently exposed to either a 2|6 or a 4|8 public demonstration (denoted as '2|6' or '4|8', respectively). Controls received no public demonstration (see text for full details). Asterisks denote either a significant difference from zero (in controls) or a significant difference between groups: $***p < 0.001$, $*p < 0.05$. (Reprinted from *Animal Behaviour*, **53**(6), Kevin N. Laland and Kerry Williams, Shoaling generates social learning of foraging information in guppies, pp. 1161–1169, Copyright (1997), with permission from Elsevier (a,b); *Behavioral Ecology*, **6**(4), Jeremy R. Kendal, Luke Rendell, Thomas W. Pike, and Kevin N. Laland, Nine-spined sticklebacks deploy a hill-climbing social learning strategy, pp. 466–468, © 2009 with permission from Oxford University Press (c); and *Biology Letters*, **6**, Pike, T.W. and Laland, K.N., Conformist learning in nine-pined sticklebacks' foraging decision © 2010, pp. 466–468 with permission from the Royal Society (d).)

there exists highly compelling experimental evidence that natural traditions are maintained through social learning, stemming from transplant experiments (see also [20]). Helfman & Schultz [21] transplanted French grunts, *Haemulon flavolineatum*, between populations and found that the moved individuals subsequently learn the daily migration routes between the foraging and resting sites used by resident conspecifics. The transplanted individuals only needed to follow the informed residents twice before being able to navigate the route themselves in the absence of all previous residents. Migratory traditions have also been shown to be present in bluehead wrasse, *Thalassoma bifascatum*, which have mating-site locations that remain in place over many generations. When entire populations were removed and replaced with transplanted populations, the wrasses were observed to establish entirely new mating sites, which remained constant over the 12-year period of the study [22]. However, when Warner replaced newly established populations after one month, he found the introduced fish reused the same sites as their immediate predecessors [23]. Thus, these sites are not fully determined by habitat structure; rather, Warner's findings suggest that site use is initially based on resource assessment but then preserved through social learning.

3.2.2 Foraging

Social learning is also a means by which fishes increase their foraging efficiency [5]. For instance, when a fish discovers a food patch, the foraging behaviour of that individual will frequently attract others to the same area. Fish also often appear attuned to the feeding movements of others. For example, juvenile Atlantic salmon, *Salmo salar*, dart to the water's surface to catch prey items from their benthic foraging stations. This darting motion is used as a cue by conspecifics that indicate food is available [24]. Fishes do not just learn of the location of food socially, but have been found to learn novel food types [24, 25] as well as to acquire novel foraging behaviour. A striking example of the latter is provided by Schuster *et al.* [26], who demonstrate experimentally that archer fish (*Toxotes jaculatrix*) can learn to shoot down moving aerial prey through observation of the successful performance of conspecifics.

3.2.3 Anti-predator behaviour

Fishes also learn anti-predator behaviour from conspecifics. One mechanism by which this can be attained in fishes is via a chemical cue, known as Shreckstoff, released as a result of damage to the skin [27] or, in some species, voluntarily, as 'disturbance pheromones' [28]. When these cues are detected by conspecifics, or heterospecifics, the receivers typically exhibit an anti-predator response [29]. Extensive experimental evidence, in multiple species, has established that fish can learn the identity of predators through associating predator cues with the detection of Schreckstoff released by other fish. For instance, Hall & Suboski [30] found that control of the alarm reaction could be transferred to previously neutral stimuli via paired conditioning and could provide a mechanism whereby naive animals learn to recognize predators without ever coming into direct contact with them. Similarly, Chivers & Smith [31] demonstrated that minnows could associate these alarm substances with chemical cues emanating from predators.

Minnows also learn to exhibit anti-predator behaviour in response to olfactory cues from a novel predator when these cues are received at the same time as seeing a fright response from conspecifics [32]. They can associate spatial areas, and even chemical cues associated with the water, with predator risk through the same mechanism [33], allowing fishes to recognize habitats with high predation risk. Chivers & Smith [34] and Suboski *et al.* [32] recorded that naive minnows (*Pimphales promelas*) and zebra danios (*Danio rerio*), respectively, receiving visual cues of a fright response from demonstrators through a clear barrier, acquire anti-predator responses to predator cues, if experiencing them simultaneously. It is also known that the observed fright behaviour of one individual will induce a similar response in others despite them having not seen the predator themselves [35]. This phenomenon is known as the 'Trafalgar effect' [36]. Shoaling fish are therefore made aware of a potential predator earlier than they would if solitary and the shoal can respond to the threat more effectively with coordinated evasion behaviour [35]. Magurran & Higham [37] discovered that minnows, *Phoxinus phoxinus*, even though unable to see the predator, exhibited predator avoidance behaviour upon observing the fright reaction of conspecifics to a model pike, *Esox* sp.

3.2.4 Aggressive interactions

Social learning also allows fishes to learn about the fighting potential of rivals. Male Siamese fighting fish, *Betta splendens*, monitor aggressive interactions between neighbouring conspecifics and use the information to guide subsequent aggressive interactions with the males they have observed [38]. Similarly, green swordtails (*Xiphophorus helleri*, Poeciliidae) were less likely to initiate fights, escalate fights or win against the winners of the contests they had observed [39]. This exploitation of communicated signals in a network has become known as 'eavesdropping' [40]; it provides a means whereby individuals can gain information about the social status of others without having to expend energy or risk injury in social contests. Grosenick *et al.* [41] report that, following observation of conspecific fights, the cichlid (*Astatotilapia burtoni*) deploys an impressive capability for transitive inference to compute a linear hierarchy among its rivals, which then influences which fish it fights.

3.2.5 Mate choice

Social learning has also been shown to influence mate choice in several species of fish including species from at least four families [5]. Perhaps, the most widely known example of mate-choice copying is in the guppy. Dugatkin [42] conducted a series of experiments in which two males were secured at either end of an aquarium, with a model female residing near one of the males. A focal female was then placed into the middle of the tank and allowed to observe the males. After the model female was removed, the focal female was then allowed to swim freely within the aquarium during which time it was observed that focal females would spend a significantly larger amount of time with the male that had been near to the model female. This effect was upheld even when the male's locations were reversed after the observation period, strong enough to reverse prior preferences [43], and increases with the size, and hence age, of the model female [44]. It is also observed in mollies, where it has been demonstrated in a native river, establishing that it is no laboratory artefact [45]. Interestingly, male Atlantic mollies (*Poecilia mexicana*), which also exhibit mate-choice copying, have been found to court the lesser preferred of two females when watched by an observing male, an act of deception thought to function to alleviate sperm competition [46].

3.3 Laboratory studies of fish observational learning and tradition

We now switch to describing some experimental studies from our own laboratory, which illustrate some interesting and relevant features of fish social learning and tradition.

3.3.1 Laboratory 'traditions' and the role of conformity

Stanley *et al.* [47] demonstrated that foraging techniques can be maintained as traditions in laboratory populations of guppies, as well as in another poeciliid, the platy (*Xiphophorus maculates*). Demonstrator fish were trained to collect food from inside vertical tubes, requiring them to swim in a vertical position not normally observed. Demonstrators were initially trained to feed by swimming into horizontal tubes to collect food held at the far end. Over a period of several exposures these tubes were rotated to vertical. This was a foraging task that the fish could not solve by themselves without training; while trained fish reliably fed from these tubes, no naive fish presented with a vertical tube learned to feed from it on its own. When placed in groups with experienced demonstrators however, naive fish readily learned to feed from the vertical tubes, establishing the social transmission of a novel feeding behaviour. When the experienced demonstrators were gradually removed and replaced with further naive fish, other group members continued to exploit the feeding tubes. Larger groups of fish showed more stable transmission of this behaviour than smaller groups, although this was found to be related to their slower rate of turnover rather than a direct effect of group size.

The Stanley *et al.* [48] and Laland & Williams [9, 10] studies show that simple traditions can be established in the experimental laboratory. While these laboratory traditions are short-term, lasting days or weeks rather than years, such experiments suggest potential mechanisms for the cross-generational transmission of arbitrary behavioural preferences to be maintained within fish populations, as observed in the aforementioned field experiments of Helfman & Schultz [21] and Warner [22, 23]. Such traditions are stable because the natural shoaling tendencies of the fish bring about a simple form of conformity. Fish prefer to join and follow large shoals compared with small shoals [48], thereby lending them a tendency to adopt the majority behaviour that becomes stabilized through positive frequency dependence, generating the 'cultural inertia' that can characterize behavioural traditions [1]. This process is sufficiently powerful that it can maintain arbitrary and even maladaptive traditions [10], which helps explain why the mating and schooling sites of natural populations cannot always be predicted from features of the environment [23].

Lachlan *et al.* [48] showed that individual guppies preferred to follow larger groups of conspecifics over smaller ones, and that by following such a group on just three occasions they were able to learn the route to a food patch. Conformity effects are stronger in larger groups, where more individuals are available to act as demonstrators. For example, Day *et al.* [49] found that the latency of the first and focal fish to find food was lower in larger shoals compared with smaller shoals when foraging in open water. However, when fish were required to pass through a small hole in an opaque barrier to locate food the opposite was seen; the latency for the first and focal fish to reach the food patch was now significantly higher in the larger groups compared with smaller groups. They suggest that this is a consequence of conformity; individuals may be unwilling to break visual contact with the shoal, with the effect that, at least early on in the diffusion, the tendency to remain with the shoal discourages individuals from leaving to locate the prey patch, with large shoals exerting more pull than small shoals. This prediction was confirmed in a second experiment, where a transparent rather than opaque barrier was used. Here, fish no longer had to break visual contact with their shoal mates, and, as in the open water trial, the latency of the first and focal fish to find the food was once again lower in larger shoals compared with the smaller ones.

While the aforementioned studies are strongly suggestive of conformist learning, they do not provide unequivocal evidence for it. However, Pike & Laland [12] showed that ninespine sticklebacks (*Pungitius pungitius*) do indeed follow a 'copy-the-majority' or conformist social learning strategy. Fish were trained to expect greater prey yield from one food patch, then were given conflicting public information from foraging conspecifics that another food patch was richer, and finally tested for their patch choice. Pike & Laland found that as the number of demonstrators at the patch demonstrated to be richer increased, so did the likelihood that the observer would select this patch. Moreover, this likelihood increased disproportionately and not linearly with increasing demonstrator number (Figure 3.1c), a definitive feature of conformist social learning [1]. Control experiments in which the demonstrators received no food, ruled out the possibility that this was simply a shoaling response. Pike & Laland's finding provides clear support for the predictions of theoretical analyses, which suggest that animals should exhibit conformist behaviour when basing decisions upon social information [1, 50].

3.3.2 Public information use and efficient copying in ninespine sticklebacks

The aforementioned Pike & Laland study is the latest in a series of studies that we have carried out to investigate public information use in sticklebacks. 'Public information use' refers to the capability of an animal to assess the quality of a resource vicariously, through monitoring the success and failure of others interacting with it [51]. It allows individuals to collect information, for instance, about the richness of a foraging patch, without the costs associated with personal sampling, such as increased exposure to predators and travel time incurred between patches to make comparisons.

This capability was first demonstrated in a fish, the ninespine stickleback, *P. pungitius*, by Coolen *et al.* [52]. We placed observer fish in a central compartment from where, through transparent partitions, they could observe two groups of demonstrators being fed through artificial feeders at different rates. The observer could not see the food in the feeder, only the reactions of the demonstrators to the food. After a period of 10 min, all demonstrators and remaining food items were removed from the tank and the observer was released. It was observed that the observers spent a significantly larger proportion of time in the feeding zone that formerly housed the demonstrator group that was fed at the faster rate, and disproportionately chose to enter this goal zone first, implying that they were able to use the behaviour of the demonstrators to establish which of the two foraging patches was the more profitable. Coolen *et al.* [52] compared public information use in the ninespine stickleback and the closely related threespine stickleback (*Gasterosteus aculeatus*), finding that only the nine-spines were able to use public information about patch quality when tested later in the absence of demonstrators. This species difference seems robust, with public information use seen in ninespines in a number of subsequent studies, described below, while several recent investigations have found no evidence for public information use in threespines, in spite of the fact that threespines are capable of other forms of social learning [53, 54].

We believe that the explanation for this species difference may be related to the observation that three-spines possess greater armour, in the form of lateral plates and longer dorsal spines [55], than do ninespines. Indeed, this morphological difference is to such an extent that predatory fishes have been shown to display a preference for consuming ninespines over threespines [56]. The superior defences of threespines mean that they are more likely to withstand the higher predation risk associated with personal sampling and therefore benefit more from maximizing their opportunities to feed. In contrast, the ninespines are more vulnerable to predation and hide in refuge when predators are near. Seemingly, natural selection has fashioned the ninespines' ability to use public information as a means of acquiring valuable foraging information through observation, from the safety of refuge.

Coolen *et al.* [52] also demonstrated that ninespines are not only capable of using public information in a foraging context from conspecifics but from the heterospecific threespines as well. As these fish were collected from the same rivers and streams, and are sympatric throughout their range, this finding raises the possibility that the opportunity to acquire public information from heterospecifics may underlie a preference in the ninespines for mixed-species shoaling. We have collected ninespine and threespine sticklebacks from all round the world, assaying them for public information use, and also raised both species in the laboratory under a variety of rearing conditions. We have found no other aspect of the fishes' ecology, morphology, social system or rearing conditions that affect the incidence of public information use. Rather, we observe a robust species difference, with ninespines always, and threespines never, exhibiting this capability.

Building on our Coolen *et al.* [52] study, we have adopted the ninespine stickleback as a model organism for studying public information use and social learning strategies, using the aforementioned procedure and apparatus. The advantage of this paradigm is that it is extremely flexible, allowing us to vary, for example, the ratio of food delivered by each feeder in order to simulate rich and poor feeding patches, the number, phenotype or species of the demonstrators, or to provide the observer with various forms of prior experience (or 'private information') about one or both of the patches. This approach enables us to investigate the social learning strategies that govern the ways in which individuals weight different sources of information when they are in conflict.

Such studies reveal that ninespines are capable of adaptive tradeoffs in their reliance on social and asocial sources of information, mixing their own prior knowledge of patch quality with the information gleaned from observation of others, in a surprisingly sophisticated way. For instance, van Bergen et al. [57] first gave ninespine subjects the opportunity to learn through direct foraging that one of two prey patches either consistently or on average yielded a larger number of prey items, followed by conflicting public information which implied that the previously lower yielding patch was now richer. Subjects were then tested as before. We found that fish that had received reliable private information ignored public information and chose the patch they had previously experienced to be richer, while those which had unreliable (noisy) private information were more inclined to copy, and base their patch choice at test on the richer patch for the demonstrators. Moreover, the magnitude of copying increased with the degree of noisiness in their private information. A second experiment devalued the private information in a different way, by manipulating its age, but to similar effect. Fish would base their patch choice on private information in preference to conflicting public information if only 1 day had elapsed since they last sampled the patch, but as the private information got more and more out-of-date, they increasingly ignored their private information and copied the demonstrators. If 7 days had elapsed since they last updated their private information, subjects had switched completely to using public information, and copied at the same rate as individuals that had not previously sampled the patches. Thus, these fish are not always or mindlessly using public information, but rather switching between reliance on different sources of information according to their probable reliability.

Use of this paradigm reveals evidence for theoretically predicted optimal learning strategies in our fish. Kendal et al. [58] found that ninespines deploy a 'hill-climbing' social learning strategy when they exploit public information. Specifically, they saw that fish with previous experience of finding food at one prey patch switched patch preferences when the prey capture rate of demonstrators suggested that the yield of the alternative patch was greater than that at the rich patch according to their private experience. Conversely, they were far less likely to switch to the alternative patch if the prey capture rate of the demonstrators was lower than that of the 'rich' patch based on their private information. Such a strategy, if widely deployed, potentially allows individuals in a population to steadily increase their foraging efficiency by gradually homing in on the most profitable foraging locations, which lends it a 'hill climbing' quality. Pike et al. [11] showed that the probability of an observing fish selecting a demonstrated richer prey patch was proportionally dependent solely upon the returns to the foraging demonstrators (in terms of prey item yielded by the patch). The degree of copying by the observing fish increased with the absolute rate of feeding by the demonstrators (Figure 3.1d). What is particularly interesting about this finding is that the ninespines behaviour is precisely that predicted by an evolutionary game theory analysis conducted by economist Karl

Schlag [59]; theory of course developed to predict humans' behaviour. In other words, humans and a species of stickleback exhibit the same optimal learning rule when they copy, a rule that Schlag terms 'proportional observation'—they both follow a *payoff-based* copying strategy. Schlag's analysis demonstrated that 'proportional observation' is an optimal social learning strategy, which will take populations to the fitness maximizing behaviour. The use of a relatively simple rule by individuals (proportional copying) could lead to a surprisingly complex outcome in a population (cumulative knowledge gain). In this respect, these results may be of general significance, since they establish that the proportional observation rule, which possesses the hill-climbing properties necessary to allow optimal solutions to be reached over repeated iterations, is actually observed in nature. The deployment of a strategy with this potential ratcheting quality has, to our knowledge, never been demonstrated before in a non-human, and has hitherto been considered absent in animals. Utilization of such a strategy by ninespine sticklebacks may allow them to exhibit cumulative increases in the efficiency with which they exploit diverse prey in their natural environments, for instance, as they colonize new regions.

3.4 **The psychological processes underlying fish social learning**

Thus far, we have focused upon functional aspects of social learning, such as where to forage, and what route to follow. We now briefly consider the psychological mechanisms that underlie such behaviour, drawing on Hoppitt & Laland's [60] classification of social learning processes.

The above studies imply that route preference learning, described for both laboratory studies of guppy shoaling behaviour [48] and in the wild in several species of reef fishes [21–23], is underpinned by simple local enhancement mechanisms, whereby an observer is attracted to a location where it detects or has recently detected the presence of others. Conversely, mate choice copying, widely reported in poeciliid fishes, is probably brought about through stimulus enhancement, whereby the presence of receptive demonstrators interacting with potential mates cause the observer to become more likely to interact with mates with similar phenotypes to themselves. Public information use, described above for foraging ninespine sticklebacks, might operate through observational conditioning, in which observation of a demonstrator exposes the observer to a relationship between stimuli at t_1, and exposure to this relationship effects a change in the observer detected, in any behaviour, at t_2. A 'simple' case of local enhancement is ruled out because observers were not responding to the mere presence of demonstrators but to the rate of feeding itself. One plausible explanation is that observers formed S–S associations of different strengths between each food patch and food, as a result of a previously formed association between the sight of a feeding conspecific and food. Anti-predator learning (e.g. [61]) may also be supported by observational conditioning, or possibly observational R-S learning, in which observation of a demonstrator exposes the observer to a relationship between a response and a reinforcer at t_1, and exposure to this relationship effects a change in the observer detected, in any behaviour, at t_2. Finally, learning to exploit novel foods (e.g. [24]) may be brought about by response facilitation, where the presence of a demonstrator performing an act increases the probability of an animal that sees it doing the same.

We know of no convincing laboratory evidence that fish are capable of imitation, that is, learning to produce particular bodily movements through observation of others, although there is plenty of experimental evidence for observational learning in fishes [26, 41, 52], and several studies produce evidence consistent with imitation, although other mechanisms are perhaps more likely (e.g. [26, 47]). Suggestive circumstantial evidence of imitation is also provided by Mazeroll & Montgomery's [62] report that in the local migrations of brown surgeonfish (*Acanthurus nigrofuscus, Acanthuridae*), followers not only take the route of leaders but reproduce their postural changes (e.g. dips and rolls). However, it is a feature of animal social learning that simple processes are sufficient both to allow individuals to acquire adaptive information, and to mediate behavioural traditions in populations.

3.5 **From animal tradition to human cultures**

In this final section, we endeavour to place the social learning of fishes in a more general context, before going on briefly to address the issue of the evolution of human culture. While this account is inevitably speculative, we describe the theoretical findings that lead us to favour this argument.

The preceding sections establish a number of points about the social learning capabilities of fishes. First, social learning is widespread in fishes, as demonstrated by extensive and rigorous laboratory investigation. Second, while much social learning in fishes results from simple local enhancement or following mechanisms, as it does in other animals, many fishes are highly competent social learners, exhibiting forms of learning that are reliant on seemingly more complex forms of social learning. For instance, we have described cases of observational learning, conformist learning, proportional observation and acquisition of novel motor patterns through observation. Third, the social learning exhibited by individual fish species is frequently expressed across multiple domains. For instance, in guppies alone, experimental evidence reveals the social learning of routes to food sites, food patch preferences, natural and artificial predator evasion behaviour, female mating preferences, and predator inspection. This means that some fish species cannot accurately be characterized as 'one trick ponies' [63]. Fourth, not just social learning, but also the diffusion of innovations through populations [64, 65] and the maintenance of traditions, has been reproduced and investigated in the laboratory. Fifth, the social learning of fishes is not restricted to the experimental laboratory: field experiments demonstrate that social learning is used under natural conditions [45, 66] while relocation experiments provide clear evidence that fish traditions are underpinned by social learning [21–23]. Finally, fishes are excellent model systems for studying social learning, and there is much still to be done, for instance, concerning the biological basis, development and phylogenetic history of social learning capabilities where fishes could usefully be deployed. When we add to this the broader recent insights into fish Machiavellian intelligence [67], tracking third-part relations [38], computing transitive inference [41], tool and substrate use [68] and cooperation [69, 70], we witness a far richer conception of fish cognition than hitherto conceived.

Notwithstanding the above, the observation that fishes in general exhibit much richer social learning than might be predicted on the basis of examinations of relative brain size among the animalia need not, in and of itself, lead us to challenge our conceptions of fish intelligence. The most probable explanation for this pattern is that social learning and tradition do not inherently require complex cognition. A major finding of the social learning strategies tournament [71] is that copying is typically far more effective than trial-and-error learning, which explains why social learning is widespread in nature, not just in vertebrates but even in crickets, bumblebees and fruitflies [72]. However, another clear conclusion from Rendell *et al.*'s [71] analysis is that the strategic use of copying is far more effective than random copying, and that there are fitness benefits associated with copying efficiently. Such strategic copying is now widely reported in fishes [11, 12, 57, 73].

In many respects, the social learning of fishes is very much comparable to that of birds and mammals. Similar experiments in mammals and birds, such as transmission chains or diffusion studies, generate broadly similar patterns, and appear to be reliant on similar processes, as those described in fishes [74–77]. While individual species or genera of primates, such as chimpanzees, orangutans, macaques and capuchins, may arguably exhibit more sophisticated cultural capabilities, there is little reason to suppose that the social learning of fishes is any less impressive than that observed in, say, bushbabies, lemurs or gibbons. A broad sweep of the social learning capabilities of animals in general suggests convergent selection in distinct lineages for those cognitive capabilities that might be considered the rudimentary foundations of culture, a perspective that receives support from a recent meta-analysis of primate intelligence [78]. Certain lineages have apparently witnessed selection for more strategic forms of copying, such as payoff-based rules like proportional observation, or effective sampling rules like conformity, which gave individuals an edge over their competitors. There is now considerable evidence that strategic copying is a general feature of animal learning [79, 80].

The Great Apes are one such lineage, and it is here that we envisage certain feedback processes began to operate, or to operate at a greater pace, triggering the cascade of events that culminated in our own extraordinary culture (see [17] for a similar argument). One process that we believe to be important is a 'cultural' or 'behavioural drive' [81]. Reader & Laland [82] found that, across non-human primates, the incidence of behavioural innovation and social learning increases positively with brain size, controlling for research effort, phylogeny and a number of other factors. This led them to endorse the argument, originally conceived by Allan Wilson [81], that the ability to invent new behaviour, and to copy the inventions of others, would give an individual a selective advantage in the struggle to survive and reproduce. As these abilities must have some neural substrate, Wilson argued that innovation and social learning would generate selection for larger and larger brains among primates, culminating in humans—the most innovative and culturally reliant species with the largest relative brain size. (Whiten & van Schaik [83] make a similar argument.) However, while Reader & Laland's data are consistent with Wilson's hypothesis, we believe that the primate lineage leading to humans is not just characterized by more and more social learning, but rather better and better social learning. Indeed, these factors are probably related, since more efficient forms of social learning will allow for greater amounts of socially transmitted information. Moreover, big brains allow for a number of capabilities that enhance the efficiency of copying, including better perceptual systems (allowing copying from distance and supporting accurate imitation), more cross-modal mapping allowing integration across modalities and generalization across modular structures, better comprehension of the goals of the demonstrator, and the ability to monitor payoff or compute frequency-dependence.

The importance of improvements in the efficiency of social learning is another take-home message of the social learning strategies tournament [71], where strategies that copied highly strategically, timing their copying to be optimal so as to maximize their payoffs, thrived. The winning strategy engaged in a form of mental time travel, monitoring rates of change in the environment, and then evaluating information based on its age to devalue out-of-date knowledge, and judging how valuable its current behaviour will be in the future and whether further learning was likely to be profitable. We suspect that humans alone are capable of copying in this manner, although, as van Bergen *et al.*'s sticklebacks demonstrate, animals may well be capable of adjusting their reliance on information according to its age. However, efficiency in copying can be gained through other means, such as following conformity and payoff-based copying rules [1], as again illustrated by the sticklebacks [11, 12].

Our thinking is also highly influenced by a recent theoretical analysis by Enquist *et al.* [84], which, through stochastic simulation, reveals an accelerating relationship between the fidelity or accuracy of information transmission during copying and the length of time that a cultural trait stays in a population. In simple terms, the study reveals that a small increase in fidelity can make a big difference to how long a cultural trait persists, with the knock-on consequence that high-fidelity transmission mechanisms support much more culture than low-fidelity mechanisms. Moreover, more culture, and more long-lasting culture, means greater opportunities for cumulative culture, since the longer cultural variants last the more likely an improvement or refinement will be devised, and the greater the opportunities there are for cross-fertilization of ideas from different cultural traits, leading to further accumulation. Common chimpanzees are reported to have 37 cultural traits [13] while the number of cultural variants possessed by humans is far too numerous to count. The Enquist *et al.* study suggests that a large part of the difference in the extent of chimpanzee and human culture can be attributed to differences in the fidelity of copying. In particular, humans, but not chimpanzees, possess a capacity for teaching, supported by language, which greatly increases the accuracy with which complex knowledge can be transmitted between individuals. Tomasello [85] was probably correct to link fidelity to cumulative culture. Moreover, theoretical work conducted in our laboratory suggests that cumulative culture broadens the conditions that favour teaching, which completes the feedback loop [86].

In summary, we believe that teaching, language and cumulative culture reinforce each other, each enhancing the utility and potency of the others. Teaching is far more effective with language, language becomes critical in a rich and diverse cultural context, and cumulative culture promotes reliance on teaching. The hominins, a taxonomic group that like other Great Apes was already comparatively rich in its social learning capabilities, were probably one of several primate lineages experiencing selection favouring more and more efficient and accurate copying, which led in turn to a richer culture. At some juncture our ancestors crossed a threshold when the fidelity of their copying was sufficient to support cumulative knowledge gain, and the aforementioned feedback mechanism kicked in. We now know that much recent human evolution was probably dominated by gene–culture coevolution, as humans evolved in response to their agricultural and other cultural practices, such as the domestication of animals and plants, and the new densities, diseases and diets these practices afforded [87]. Humans and their ancestors constructed a cultural niche, and evolved to excel in it [88].

Acknowledgements

Research supported in part by an ERC Advanced grant (EVOCULTURE, 232823) and NERC grant (NE/D010365/1) to K.N.L.

Note

[1] By the term 'copying' we mean any form of social learning, and do not necessarily imply imitation.

References

1 Boyd, R. & Richerson, P. J. 1985 *Culture and the evolutionary process*. Chicago, IL: University of Chicago Press.

2 Richerson, P. J. & Boyd, R. 2005 *Not by genes alone*. Chicago, IL: University of Chicago Press.

3 Laland, K. N. & Hoppitt, W. J. E. 2003 Do animals have culture? *Evol. Anthropol.* **12**, 150–159.

4 Brown, C. & Laland, K. N. 2003 Social learning in fishes: a review. *Fish Fisheries* (Special Edn) **4**, 280–288.

5 Brown, C. & Laland, K. N. 2011 Social learning in fishes. In *Fish cognition and behaviour*, Second Edition (eds C. Brown, K. N. Laland & J. Krause), pp. 240–259. Oxford, UK: Blackwell Publishing.

6 Shettleworth, S. J. 2001 Animal cognition and animal behaviour. *Anim. Behav.* **61**, 277–286.

7 Emery, N. J. & Clayton, N. S. 2004 The mentality of crows: convergent evolution of intelligence in corvids and apes. *Science* **306**, 1903–1907.

8 Laland, K. N. & Galef, B. G. 2009 *The question of animal culture*. Cambridge, MA: Harvard University Press.

9 Laland, K. N. & Williams, K. 1997 Shoaling generates social learning of foraging information in guppies. *Anim. Behav.* **53**, 1161–1169.

10 Laland, K. N. & Williams, K. 1998 Social transmission of maladaptive information in the guppy. *Behav. Ecol.* **9**, 493–499.

11 Pike, T. W., Kendal, J. R., Rendell, L. & Laland, K. N. 2010 Learning by proportional observation in a species of fish. *Behav. Ecol.* **20**, 238–244.

12 Pike, T. W. & Laland, K. N. 2010 Conformist learning in nine-spined sticklebacks' foraging decisions. *Biol. Lett.* **6**, 466–468.

13 Whiten, A., Goodall, J., McGrew, W. C., Nishida, T., Reynolds, V., Sugiyama, Y., Tutin, C. E. G., Wrangham, R. W. & Boesch, C. 1999 Culture in chimpanzees. *Nature* **399**, 682–685.

14 van Schaik, C. P., Ancrenaz, M., Borgen, G., Galdikas, B., Knott, C. D., Singleton, I., Suzuki, A., Utami, S. S. & Merrill, M. 2003 Orangutan cultures and the evolution of material culture. *Science* **299**, 102–105.

15 Perry, S. *et al.* 2003 Social conventions in wild white-faced capuchins: evidence for traditions in a Neotropical primate. *Curr. Anthropol.* **44**, 241–268.

16 Whiten, A. 2011 The scope of culture in chimpanzees, humans and ancestral apes. *Phil. Trans. R. Soc. B* **366**, 997–1007.

17 van Schaik, C. P. & Burkart, J. M. 2011 Social learning and evolution: the cultural intelligence hypothesis. *Phil. Trans. R. Soc. B* **366**, 1008–1016.

18 Perry, S. 2011 Social traditions and social learning in capuchin monkeys (*Cebus*). *Phil. Trans. R. Soc. B* **366**, 988–996.

19 Laland, K. N. & Janik, V. 2006 The animal cultures debate. *Trends Ecol. Evol.* **21**, 542–547.

20 Slagsvold, T. & Wiebe, K. L. 2011 Social learning in birds and its role in shaping a foraging niche. *Phil. Trans. R. Soc. B* **366**, 969–977.

21 Helfman, G. S. & Schultz, E. T. 1984 Social transmission of behavioural traditions in a coral reef fish. *Anim. Behav.* **32**, 379–384.

22 Warner, R. R. 1988 Traditionality of mating-site preferences in a coral reef fish. *Nature* **335**, 719–721.

23 Warner, R. R. 1990 Male versus female influences on mating-site determination in a coral-reef fish. *Anim. Behav.* **39**, 540–548.

24 Brown, C. & Laland, K. N. 2002 Social enhancement and social inhibition of foraging behaviour in hatchery-reared Atlantic salmon. *J. Fish Biol.* **61**, 987–998.

25 Brown, C. & Laland, K. N. 2001 Suboski and Templeton revisited: social learning and life skills training for hatchery reared fish. *J. Fish Biol.* **59**, 471–493.

26 Schuster, S., Wohl, S., Griebsch, M. & Klostermeier, I. 2006 Animal cognition: how archer fish learn to down rapidly moving targets. *Curr. Biol.* **16**, 378–383.

27 von Frisch, K. 1938 Zur Psychologie des Fisch-Schwarmes. *Naturwissenschaften* **26**, 601–606.

28 Wisenden, B. D., Chivers, D. P., Brown, G. E. & Smith, R. J. F. 1995 The role of experience in risk assessment: avoidance of areas chemically labelled with fathead minnow alarm pheromone by conspecifics and heterospecifics. *Ecoscience* **2**, 115–122.

29 Brown, G. E. & Godin, G. J. 1997 Anti-predator responses to conspecific and heterospecific skin extracts by threespine sticklebacks: alarm pheromones revisited. *Behaviour* **134**, 1123–1134.

30 Hall, D. & Suboski, M. D. 1995 Visual and olfactory stimuli in learned release of alarm reactions by zebra danio fish (*Brachydanio rerio*). *Neurobiol. Learn. Mem.* **63**, 229–240.

31 Chivers, D. P. & Smith, R. J. F. 1995 Free-living fathead minnows rapidly learn to recognize pike as predators. *J. Fish Biol.* **46**, 949–954.

32 Suboski, M. D., Bain, S., Carty, A. E. & McQuoid, L. M. 1990 Alarm reaction in acquisition and social transmission of simulated-predator recognition by zebra danio (*Brachydanio rerio*). *J. Comp. Psychol.* **104**, 101–112.

33 Chivers, D. P. & Smith, R. J. F. 1995 Fathead minnows (*Pimephales promelas*) learn to recognize chemical stimuli from high-risk habitats by the presence of alarm substance. *Behav. Ecol.* **6**, 155–158.

34 Chivers, D. P.& Smith, R. J. F. 1994 Fathead minnows *Pimephales promelas*, acquire predator recognition when alarm substance is associated with the sight of unfamiliar fish. *Anim. Behav.* **48**, 597–605.

35 Krause, J. 1993 Transmission of fright reaction between different species of fish. *Behaviour* **127**, 37–48.

36 Treherne, J. E. & Foster, W. A. 1981 Group transmission of predator avoidance behaviour in a marine insect: the Trafalgar effect. *Anim. Behav.* **32**, 536–542.

37 Magurran, A. E. & Higham, A. 1988 Information transfer across fish shoals under predator threat. *Ethology* **78**, 153–158.

38 Oliveira, R. F., McGregor, P. K. & Latruffe, C. 1998 Know thine enemy: fighting fish gather information from observing conspecific interactions. *Proc. R. Soc. Lond. B* **265**, 1045–1049.

39 Early, R. L. & Dugatkin, L. A. 2002 Eavesdropping on visual cues in green swordtail (*Xiphophorus helleri*) fights: a case for networking. *Proc. R. Soc. Lond. B* **269**, 943–952.

40 McGregor, P. K. 1993 Signaling in territorial systems—a context for individual identification, ranging and eavesdropping. *Phil. Trans. R. Soc. Lond. B* **340**, 237–244.

41 Grosenick, L., Clement, T. S. & Fernald, R. D. 2007 Fish can infer social rank by observation alone. *Nature* **445**, 429–432.

42 Dugatkin, L. A. 1992 Sexual selection and imitation: females copy the mate choice of others. *Am. Nat.* **139**, 1384–1389.

43 Dugatkin, L. A. & Godin, J. 1992 Reversal of female mate choice by copying in the guppy (*Poecilia reticulata*). *Proc. R. Soc. Lond. B* **249**, 179–184.

44 Dugatkin, L. A. & Godin, J. 1993 Female mate copying in the guppy (*Poecilia reticulata*)—age-dependent effects. *Behav. Ecol.* **4**, 289–292.

45 Witte, K. & Ryan, M. J. 2002 Mate choice in the sailfin molly (*Poecilia latipinna*) in the wild. *Anim. Behav.* **63**, 943–949.

46 Plath, M., Blum, D., Tiedemann, R. & Schlupp, I. 2008 A visual audience effect in a cavefish. *Behaviour* **145**, 931–947.

47 Stanley, E. L., Kendal, R. L., Kendal, J. R., Grounds, S. & Laland, K. N. 2008 The effects of group size, rate of turnover and disruption to demonstration on the stability of foraging traditions in fish. *Anim. Behav.* **75**, 565–572.

48 Lachlan, R. F., Crooks, L. & Laland, K. N. 1998 Who follows whom? Shoaling preferences and social learning of foraging information in guppies. *Anim. Behav.* **56**, 181–190.

49 Day, R. L., MacDonald, T., Brown, C., Laland, K. N. & Reader, S. M. 2001 Interactions between shoal size and conformity in guppy social foraging. *Anim. Behav.* **62**, 917–925.

50 Henrich, J. & Boyd, R. 1998 The evolution of conformist transmission and between-group differences. *Evol. Hum. Behav.* **19**, 215–242.

51 Templeton, J. J. & Giraldeau, A. 1996 Vicarious sampling: the use of personal and public information by starlings in a simple patchy environment. *Behav. Ecol. Sociobiol.* **38**, 105–114.

52 Coolen, I., Van Bergen, Y., Day, R. L. & Laland, K. N. 2003 Species difference in adaptive use of public information in sticklebacks. *Proc. R. Soc. Lond. B* 270, 2413–2419.

53 Webster, M. M. & Hart, P. 2006 Subhabitat selection by foraging threespine stickleback (*Gasterosteus aculeatus*): previous experience and social conformity. *Behav. Ecol. Sociobiol.* **60**, 77–86.

54 Harcourt, J. L., Biau, S., Johnstone, R. & Manica, A. 2010 Boldness and information use in three-spined sticklebacks. *Ethology* **116**, 440–447.

55 FitzGerald, G. J. & Wooton, R. J. 1996 The behavioural ecology of sticklebacks. In *Behaviour of teleost fishes* (ed. T. J. Pitcher), pp. 537–572, 2nd edn. London, UK: Chapman & Hall.

56 Hoogland, R. D., Morris, D. & Tinbergen, N. 1957 The spines of sticklebacks (*Gasterosteus* and *Pygosteus*) as a means of defence against predators (*Perca* and *Esox*). *Behaviour* **10**, 205–237.

57 van Bergen, Y., Coolen, I. & Laland, K. N. 2004 Nine-spined sticklebacks exploit the most reliable source when public and private information conflict. *Proc. R. Soc. Lond. B* **271**, 957–962.

58 Kendal, J. R., Rendell, L., Pike, T. & Laland, K. N. 2009 Nine-spined sticklebacks deploy a hill-climbing social learning strategy. *Behav. Ecol.* **20**, 238–244.

59 Schlag, K. H. 1998 Why imitate and if so, how? A boundedly rational approach to multi-armed bandits. *J. Econ. Theory* **78**, 130–156.

60 Hoppitt, W. J. E. & Laland, K. N. 2008 Social processes influencing learning in animals: a review of the evidence. *Adv. Study Behav.* **38**, 105–165.

61 Brown, G. E. & Chivers, D. P. 2006 Learning about danger: chemical alarm cues and predation risk assessment by fishes. In *Fish cognition and behaviour* (eds C. Brown, K. N. Laland & J. Krause), pp. 49–69. Oxford, UK: Blackwell Publishing.

62 Mazeroll, A. I. & Montgomery, W. L. 1995 Structure and organization of local migrations in brown surgeon-fish (*Acanthurus nigrofuscus*). *Ethology* **99**, 89–106.

63 McGrew, W. 2004 *The cultured chimpanzee*. Cambridge, UK: Cambridge University Press.

64 Reader, S. M. & Laland, K. N. 2000 Diffusion of foraging innovation in the guppy. *Anim. Behav.* **60**, 175–180.

65 Swaney, W., Kendal, J. R., Capon, H., Brown, C. & Laland, K. N. 2001 Familiarity facilitates social learning of foraging behaviour in the guppy. *Anim. Behav.* **62**, 591–598.

66 Reader, S. M., Kendal, J. R. & Laland, K. N. 2003 Social learning of foraging sites and escape routes in wild Trinidadian guppies. *Anim. Behav.* **66**, 729–739.

67 Bshary, R. 2001 The cleaner fish market. In *Economics in nature* (eds R. Noë, J. van Hooff & P. Hammerstein), pp. 146–172. Cambridge, UK: Cambridge University Press.

68 Wirtz, P. 1996 Werkzeuggebrauch bei Lippfischen. *Aquar. Terr. Z.* **1**, 4–5.

69 Millinski, M. 1987 Tit for tat in sticklebacks and the evolution of cooperation. *Nature* **325**, 433–435.

70 Croft, D. P., James, R., Thomas, P. O. R., Hathaway, C., Mawdsley, D., Laland, K. N. & Krause, J. 2005 Social structure and co-operative interactions in a wild population of guppies (*Poecilia reticulata*). *Behav. Ecol. Sociobiol.* **59**, 644–650.

71 Rendell, L. *et al.* 2010 Why copy others? Insights from the social learning strategies tournament. *Science* **328**, 208–213.

72 Leadbeater, E. & Chittka, L. 2007 The dynamics of social learning in an insect model, the bumblebee (*Bombus terrestris*). *Behav. Ecol. Sociobiol.* **61**, 1789–1796.

73 Webster, M. M. & Laland, K. N. 2011 Reproductive state affects reliance on public information in sticklebacks. *Proc. R. Soc. B* **278**, 619–627.

74 Curio, E. 1988 Cultural transmission of enemy recognition by birds. In *Social learning: psychological and biological perspectives* (eds T. Zentall & B. G. Galef), pp. 75–97. Hillsdale, NJ: Lawrence Erlbaum.

75 Laland, K. N. & Plotkin, H. C. 1991 Excretory deposits surrounding food sites facilitate social learning of food preferences in Norway rats. *Anim. Behav.* **41**, 997–1005.

76 Laland, K. N. & Plotkin, H. C. 1993 Social transmission of food preferences amongst Norway rats by marking of food sites, and by gustatory contact. *Anim. Learn. Behav.* **21**, 35–41.

77 Lefebvre, L. & Palameta, B. 1988 Mechanisms, ecology, and population diffusion of socially-learned food-finding behaviour in feral pigeons. In *Social learning: psychological and biological perspectives* (eds T. Zentall & B. G. Galef), pp. 141–164. Hillsdale, NJ: Lawrence Erlbaum Associates.

78 Reader, S. M., Hager, Y. & Laland, K. N. 2011 The evolution of primate general and cultural intelligence. *Phil. Trans. R. Soc. B* **366**, 1017–1027.

79 Laland, K. N. 2004 Social learning strategies. *Learn. Behav.* **32**, 4–14.

80 Kendal, R. L., Coolen, I., van Bergen, Y. & Laland, K. N. 2005 Tradeoffs in the adaptive use of social and asocial learning. *Adv. Stud. Behav.* **35**, 333–379.

81 Wilson, A. C. 1985 The molecular basis of evolution. *Sci. Am.* **253**, 148–157.

82 Reader, S. M. & Laland, K. N. 2002 Social intelligence, innovation and enhanced brain size in primates. *Proc. Natl Acad. Sci. USA* **99**, 4436–4441.

83 Whiten, A. & van Schaik, C. P. 2007 The evolution of animal 'cultures' and social intelligence. *Phil. Trans. R. Soc. B* **362**, 603–620.

84 Enquist, M., Strimling, P., Eriksson, K., Laland, K. & Sjostrand, J. 2010 One cultural parent makes no culture. *Anim. Behav.* **79**, 1353–1362.

85 Tomasello, M. 1994 *Chimpanzee cultures* (ed. R. Wrangham *et al.*), pp. 301–317. Cambridge, MA: Harvard University Press.

86 Fogarty, L., Strimling, P. & Laland, K. N. 2011 The evolution of teaching. *Evolution* **65**, 2760–2770.

87 Laland, K. N., Odling-Smee, F. J. & Myles, S. 2010 How culture has shaped the human genome: bringing genetics and the human sciences together. *Nat. Rev. Genet.* **11**, 137–148.

88 Odling-Smee, F. J., Laland, K. N. & Feldman, M. W. 2003 *Niche construction: the neglected process in evolution*. Monographs in Population Biology, 37. Princeton, NJ: Princeton University Press.

Chapter 4

Social Learning in Birds and its Role in Shaping a Foraging Niche*

Tore Slagsvold and Karen L. Wiebe

We briefly review the literature on social learning in birds, concluding that strong evidence exists mainly for predator recognition, song, mate choice and foraging. The mechanism of local enhancement may be more important than imitation for birds learning to forage, but the former mechanism may be sufficient for faithful transmission depending on the ecological circumstances. To date, most insights have been gained from birds in captivity. We present a study of social learning of foraging in two passerine birds in the wild, where we cross-fostered eggs between nests of blue tits, *Cyanistes caeruleus* and great tits, *Parus major*. Early learning causes a shift in the foraging sites used by the tits in the direction of the foster species. The shift in foraging niches was consistent across seasons, as showed by an analysis of prey items, and the effect lasted for life. The fact that young birds learn from their foster parents, and use this experience later when subsequently feeding their own offspring, suggests that foraging behaviour can be culturally transmitted over generations in the wild. It may therefore have both ecological and evolutionary consequences, some of which are discussed.

Keywords: cultural transmission; ecological niche; foraging conservatism; habitat preferences; speciation

4.1 Introduction

Social learning is widely used among vertebrates to acquire information about a fluctuating environment [1–3]. In birds, there is ample opportunity for social learning because parents may provide care for their offspring for several weeks, and because birds may join conspecific or mixed species flocks, allowing both vertical and horizontal transmission of behaviour. Here, we briefly review the literature on social learning in birds. Most insights on social learning in animals come from studies in captivity, and the role of social

* Electronic supplementary material is available at http://dx.doi.org/10.1098/rstb.2010.0343 or via http://rstb.royalsocietypublishing.org

learning in nature remains rather poorly understood [4, 5]. We therefore conducted a study of social learning in the wild, where we cross-fostered eggs of blue tits, *Cyanistes caeruleus*, to nests of great tits, *Parus major*, and vice versa, enabling us to quantify the consequences of being reared in a different social context but in an environment otherwise natural to the birds. To our knowledge, the study is the most extensive of its kind of any animal group. Here we report on foraging behaviour and on the foraging niche.

4.1.1 Social learning in birds

Social learning may be involved in migration of some, but not all, avian species, where inexperienced birds may be guided by adults to find suitable migration routes and wintering areas. This knowledge has been successfully used to train naive, captive-reared endangered birds during migration using a microlight aircraft as 'foster parents' [6]. Social learning early in life may also be important in habitat selection [7, 8], and birds may use 'public information', viz. the breeding performance of other species, in choice of habitats and nest sites [9].

On the other hand, little social learning seems to be involved in nest building. Some species build quite complex nests, yet conditioning probably is a sufficient developmental mechanism, with only a limited repertoire of stereotyped movements needed [10]. In a few birds, males may build courtship display sites (bowers) and for these, there is some circumstantial evidence that social learning is involved in the choice of decoration objects [11].

Social learning has a role in the recognition of predators [12, 13] and brood parasites [14]; conservation strategies for endangered species attempt to teach inexperienced birds [13]. Alarm calls are considered to be quite stereotypic. Social learning may be involved in responding to such calls [13, 15], but not necessarily in producing them [16], although great tits seem to learn from foster parents of another species (blue tits) in the wild [17].

Convincing examples of social learning in birds come from studies of song. Some details about the ontogeny of song have been well studied such as the brain pathways for vocal learning, the sensitive period during which a juvenile must learn songs, and which individuals the juvenile learns from [18, 19]. Apparently, the strongest cases of 'production learning' come from vocal mimics copying calls of other species and environmental sounds [20]. Such mimicry is not confined to song birds [19]. Most experiments with song have been done in captivity but song copying also occurs in the wild, e.g. many birds have song dialects, and the dialects in a given local area may change over time. A few experimental studies on song copying in the wild suggest horizontal transmission, e.g. adult pied flycatchers, *Ficedula hypoleuca*, may pick up and sing novel playback songs [21].

Social learning is also important for mate choice in birds, primarily by vertical transmission through sexual imprinting early in life [22, 23]. Most data are from studies in captivity, but there is some support from experiments in the wild [24–26], where sexual imprinting as a juvenile lasts for life [27]. However, sexual imprinting does not seem to be equally important in all species: pied flycatchers did not imprint on blue tit or great tit foster parents in the wild [28]. Mate choice and species recognition seem to have a strong genetic basis in the flycatcher and may be linked to the sex chromosomes [29]. A challenge is to understand the variation in the degree of sexual imprinting among species [28]. Interestingly, male pied flycatchers raised by tits did include tit song elements in their song repertoire, suggesting that different mechanisms are involved in the development of mate choice preferences and song acquisition [30].

In addition to sexual imprinting early in life, using parents as role models when choosing a mate, birds may use social information gained later in life such as 'public information' and eavesdropping by observing the mating choices of other individuals [31]. Costs and benefits may differ between the sexes, and so also their use of information [32], e.g. females may modify their song preferences by attending to the vocal behaviour of other females [33]. There is some evidence for mate choice copying in polygynous birds but results are more mixed in monogamous birds [34–36].

Many bird species also depend on social learning to learn aspects of foraging such as feeding sites [8, 37], food items [38–40], hunting skills [41], handling and feeding techniques [42, 43], and tool use [44]. Social learning of foraging may take place early in life, using parents as role models [8, 40, 45], and later in life by observing others [20, 43, 46]. The efficiency of learning may depend on whether the demonstrator is rewarded and on which other birds are present [47], e.g. in the presence of familiar birds, males and females [48], and producers and scroungers [49].

Social learning in birds, such as that involved in foraging, may only be owing to social learning in the weakest sense, e.g. learning of foraging sites through stimulus and local enhancement, rather than any true imitation; see [20] for definitions of levels and mechanisms of learning. There is little evidence for true imitation in the wild [20, 50], although an increasing number of experimental studies suggests that birds are capable of motor imitation and production imitation [20, 51]. New Caledonian crows, *Corvus monedu-loides*, are the most sophisticated tool manufacturers other than humans. The behaviour is primarily based on trial-and-error learning but offspring also seem to learn from observing their parents [44, 52]. Apparently, the social learning is sufficient to cause consistent differences in tool designs between separate geographical sites in the wild without any obvious ecological correlates [53]. Note that even relatively simple ways of social learning might lead to faithful transmission of behaviours [20, 54, 55], and that even with imitation, ecological and physiological factors may be important for faithful transmission [5, 56].

Teaching was previously treated as a high-order intentionality attribute, largely restricted to humans. In recent years, it has been viewed as a functional category of behaviours serving to promote the learning of others [57]. The strongest evidence of teaching in wild birds may be the 'food' calls uttered by parents when arriving with food to the nestlings [58], and when foraging on preferable food items with the offspring after leaving the nest [40].

We conclude that although social learning is expected to be common in birds, strong evidence mainly exists for predator recognition, song, mate choice, and foraging. Although mainly lower level learning mechanisms may be involved in foraging, these may be sufficient both for vertical and horizontal transmission of behaviours.

4.1.2 **Experimental testing**

Strong evidence for social learning requires controlled experiments in the laboratory and in the field [57, 59–61]. The classical method has been to compare the behaviour of an animal allowed to observe a conspecific, with an animal not allowed to observe another, using a single transmission event [20, 50]. An improvement is to apply 'diffusion' experiments, in which founder behaviours are experimentally manipulated and their spread across multiple individuals tested [62]. This method has been applied with success in fish, birds and mammals [62], and has shown that birds use social learning when responding to predators [12], and when developing foraging behaviour [38, 42, 43, 63].

Cross-fostering in animals with parental care and translocation in species without parental care are powerful methods to study the influence of early learning, as shown by the famous studies of filial imprinting in geese by Lorenz [64]. More recently, these methods have been successfully applied to a range of taxa, from fish [65, 66] to mammals [67], although the focus has been on song learning and sexual imprinting in birds, as mentioned above. Perhaps, this is because it is relatively easy to cross-foster birds' eggs when compared with the more limited tools for studying vertical transmission in mammals.

4.2 **Cross-fostering experiments on tits**

We conducted a large-scale, long-term, heterospecific, cross-fostering experiment of blue tits and great tits in the wild, showing that many behaviours are affected, including sexual imprinting on the foster species [26, 27], alarm calls [17], song [68] and foraging [8]. Blue tits and great tits live in sympatry in large parts of their breeding ranges. The two species forage in mixed flocks except during breeding, with little overlap in feeding niches. Outside the breeding season, the blue tit feeds mainly high in trees on twigs and buds, whereas the great tit feeds mainly on the ground or on the trunks and thicker branches of trees [69]. We have shown previously that the foraging height and amount of foraging on twigs during autumn and early spring shifts in the direction of the foster species as a result of early learning [8]. Here, we ask whether such learning influences the type and size of prey delivered to offspring in the breeding season. The answer is not obvious because the two species may overlap in food choice during breeding, causing competition [70]. In addition, studies of foraging of hand-reared tits in captivity indicate a strong genetic predisposition to the foraging habitat [71]. In the present study, we filmed cross-fostered and control parents as they delivered prey to young.

4.2.1 **Fieldwork and video analyses**

Our study was conducted in a woodland area near Oslo over 4 years (2005–2008), and was approved by the Norwegian Animal Care Committee. Each year, about 500 nest boxes were available for breeding, of which about 110 were used annually by blue tits and 80 by great tits. Local recruits were given a unique colour combination of rings. Because of a possible difference in habitat of origin, immigrants (= not raised in our nest boxes) may have provided different prey items than the local recruits. Hence, the immigrants were excluded from all analyses except for an analysis within pairs presented in the electronic supplementary material. We compared prey items delivered by cross-fostered birds versus controls (= birds reared by parents of their own species). We also took several other variables into account: sex, age of parent, year, date of filming, brood size and geographical position of the nest site. The broods were filmed only once, for 1.5 h when about 10–12 days old. The tits are single prey loaders, and we estimated the length (l) and width (w) of each prey item in proportion to bill length of the focal parent (e.g. $l = 0.5$ means that prey length was half of parent bill length). Notice, therefore, that this is not an absolute measure. Prey volume was calculated using $s = \pi(0.5w)^2 l$ [72]. Type of prey was recorded as green, white or brown larvae, spider, adult Diptera ('fly'), adult Lepidoptera or 'others' (see electronic supplementary material for further details).

4.2.2 Statistical analyses

We used the mean prey volume for each individual as a single sample. The volumes of individual prey items were log-transformed for statistical analyses (and when calculating the mean values) but for easy interpretation in the figures, we back-transformed the log values. Statistical tests were two-tailed. The statistical analyses of prey volume, and the proportion of a given prey type, were done in two steps. Initially, we tested for random effects using general linear models (GLM) in R [73] because a few birds and nest boxes were filmed in more than 1 year. Hence, to account for repeated measures, bird identity and nest-box number were treated as random factors. Fixed effects tested were: species, sex, age (yearling or older), year, date, brood size, altitude, longitude and latitude (position of nest site on the study area). The analysis showed that including random effects did not result in model improvement (see electronic supplementary material). Hence, in the final analyses reported below, random effects were excluded and we used GLM-ANOVA (analysis of variance) in SPSS v. 17.0.

4.2.3 Results

The main factors of interest were species and treatment. Hence, to test for interaction, we started with a global ANOVA for prey volume including only these factors. The analysis showed a significant main effect of species ($F_{1,277} = 22.9, p < 0.0001$), but not of treatment ($F_{1,277} = 0.05, p = 0.83$). However, there was a highly significant interaction between the two variables ($F_{1,277} = 16.9, p = 0.0001$) because cross-fostered blue tits provided larger prey than controls, but it was the reverse in great tits, with cross-fostered birds providing smaller prey than controls, as predicted (Figure 4.1).

Because of the interaction, separate ANOVAs were conducted on each species and we included the following potentially confounding variables: treatment, year, date of filming, sex, age (first year or older), brood size, altitude, longitude and latitude of nest site. Forward stepwise selection was used, and variables, and interactions between these, were included only if significant at the 5 per cent level. In blue tits ($n = 137$), the final model included treatment ($F_{1,130} = 22.2, p < 0.0001$), year ($F_{3,130} = 11.4, p < 0.0001$), sex ($F_{1,130} = 7.88$, $p = 0.006$) and brood size ($F_{1,130} = 4.12, p = 0.045$). No second-order interactions were

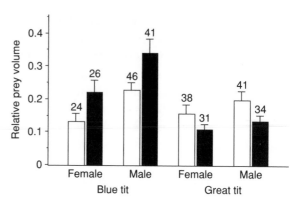

Figure 4.1 Mean (+s.e.) volume of prey items provided by female and male blue tit and great tit parents. Open bars, controls; filled bars, cross-fostered (reared by the other species). Prey volume was estimated from length and width of prey relative to bill length of parent. Sample size (number of parents) is shown above the bars.

significant. In great tits ($n = 144$), the final model included treatment ($F_{1,136} = 6.71$, $p = 0.011$), year ($F_{3,136} = 5.03$, $p = 0.002$), date of filming ($F_{1,136} = 5.57$, $p = 0.020$), age ($F_{1,136} = 4.24$, $p = 0.041$) and the interaction between treatment and age ($F_{1,136} = 6.36$, $p = 0.013$). See electronic supplementary material for the global ANOVA analysis for both species combined.

Prey volume was smaller for cross-fostered great tits than controls (Figure 4.1), except for yearlings (Figure 4.2). Apparently, this was because controls collected disproportionately smaller prey early in life compared with later, whereas cross-fostered birds provided small prey at all ages (Figure 4.2). To test this in more detail, we compared individual

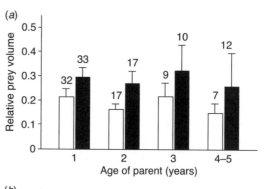

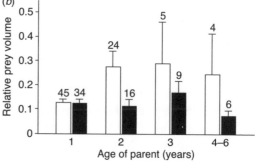

Figure 4.2 Mean (+s.e.) volume of prey items provided by (a) blue tit and (b) great tit parents in relation to the age of parent. Open bars, controls; filled bars, cross-fostered (reared by the other species). Prey volume was estimated from length and width of prey relative to bill length of parent. Sample size (number of parents) is shown above the bars.

birds filmed when they were 1 year old and when they were older (mean value in case of more than 1 year of filming as older). Prey volume did not change significantly in either cross-fostered or control blue tits, nor in cross-fostered great tits (paired t-tests, all $ps > 0.20$, $n = 8$–12), only in control great tits ($t_{17} = 3.90$, $p = 0.001$).

In our analyses, prey volume was estimated from length and width of the prey relative to bill length of the parent. To obtain a rough estimate of absolute prey volumes, we used mean (absolute) values of bill length recorded separately for each of the two species (for details see electronic supplementary material). The mean volumes of prey provided by the control birds were roughly 0.10 and 0.24 cm^3 for blue tit and great tit controls, respectively, and 0.16 cm^3 for the cross-fostered birds of both species. Thus, great tit controls provided larger prey than blue tits, but with cross-fostering, the difference disappeared and both groups provided prey intermediate in volume to the two control groups.

The main prey provided by the two tit species were green larvae, followed by brown larvae, flies and spiders (Figure 4.3). Blue tits provided more green larvae than did great tits (blue tits: mean values of 59%, s.d. = 18, $n = 137$; great tits: 51%, s.d. = 26, $n = 144$; $t_{277} = 3.17$, $p = 0.002$). Blue tits also provided more spiders (U-test, $z = -2.39$, $p = 0.017$), but fewer flies ($z = -2.62$, $p = 0.009$) than did great tits, whereas no difference existed between the species in the proportion of brown larvae ($z = -0.89$, $p = 0.38$). For the latter prey types, the Mann–Whitney U-test was used because of deviations from normality.

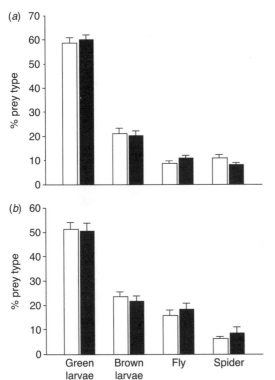

Figure 4.3 Mean proportion (+s.e.) of various prey types provided by (a) blue tit and (b) great tit parents. Open bars, controls (70 blue tits, 79 great tits); filled bars, cross-fostered (reared by the other species; 67 blue tits, 65 great tits).

A global ANOVA for the proportion of green larvae showed a significant main effect of tit species ($F_{1,277} = 10.1$, $p = 0.002$), but not of treatment ($F_{1,277} = 0.003$, $p = 0.96$), or the interaction between the two variables ($F_{1,277} = 0.19$, $p = 0.66$). We also analysed the proportion of green larvae for each species separately, including all potentially confounding variables as above, but there was no significant effect of cross-fostering even though there were a few other significant main effects (for blue tits: date of filming and longitude of nest site; for great tits: year of filming; tests not shown). See electronic supplementary material for a global ANOVA for both species combined.

Cross-fostered blue tits ($n = 67$) provided a higher proportion of flies than controls ($n = 70$; U-test, $z = -2.19$, $p = 0.029$), whereas no significant differences existed between the two groups in proportion of brown larvae ($z = -0.38$, $p = 0.70$), or spiders ($z = -1.13$, $p = 0.26$). However, cross-fostered females ($n = 26$) provided relatively fewer spiders than control females ($n = 24$; $z = 2.57$, $p = 0.010$; Figure 4.4). In great tits, no difference was found between cross-fostered birds ($n = 65$) and controls ($n = 79$) in the proportion of brown larvae ($z = -0.67$, $p = 0.50$), flies ($z = -0.56$, $p = 0.58$), or spiders ($z = -1.07$, $p = 0.29$).

Any difference in habitat quality surrounding the nest sites used by cross-fostered birds versus controls cannot account for our results. For instance, there was an effect of cross-fostering on prey volume even when comparing the prey provided by each member of a pair, where one parent was cross-fostered and the other parent was not (see electronic supplementary material). Furthermore, the differences in foraging between cross-fostered birds and controls cannot be explained by differences in body size. In blue tits, cross-fostered birds and controls had similar body size; in great tits, the cross-fostered

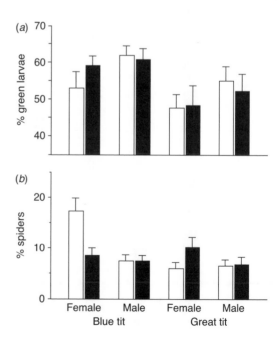

Figure 4.4 Mean (+s.e.) proportion of (a) green larvae, and (b) spiders, provided by female and male blue tit and great tit parents. Open bars, controls; filled bars, cross-fostered (reared by the other species). Sample sizes as in Figure 4.1.

birds tended to be slightly larger than the controls (T. Slagsvold 1997–2008, unpublished data). Larger birds may prefer larger prey, yet in our study, cross-fostered great tits provided smaller prey than controls.

4.3 Significance of the experiment

4.3.1 Social learning of foraging

The social learning hypothesis was supported. Great tits in the wild typically provide much larger prey to offspring than blue tits. Hence, we predicted that blue tits reared by great tit foster parents would bring larger prey items than control blue tits, and this was confirmed. The opposite prediction was confirmed for cross-fostered great tits; they provided smaller prey items than control great tits. Our study shows that not only does early social learning influence foraging during the non-breeding season [8], but also during the breeding season. The effect of social learning seemed to be equally strong in both species, although earlier work [7, 8] indicated that the response was stronger in the species with the more generalist diet (the great tit) than the one with the more specialized food niche (the blue tit).

Cross-fostering had a greater impact on the size of prey chosen than on the type of prey. However, our classification of prey types was quite coarse, and if we had been able to identify species of green larvae or other insects more precisely, more differences between the treatment groups might have been apparent. Nevertheless, cross-fostered blue tits provided more flies than the conspecific controls as would be predicted with social learning because, control great tits provided more flies than blue tits.

Another explanation for the lack of a pronounced difference in prey types between cross-fostered birds and conspecific controls may be an effect of genetic predispositions. This explanation is supported by the fact that cross-fostered birds of both species provided food items intermediate in (absolute) size to those provided by the controls of the two species. However, such intermediate patterns would also be expected if strong innovative and trial-and-error learning are involved, behaviours that are commonly seen in tits [74–76]. Trial-and-error learning may lead individuals to prefer food they can deal with more easily, and learning of such skills would presumably be rapid and early. Hence, the changes in food preferences reported here may only be due to social learning in the weakest sense, e.g. learning of foraging sites through stimulus and local enhancement [77] rather than imitation. Further studies are needed to see whether the young tits pick up foraging techniques from their parents, and whether they are influenced by the specific prey items provided by the parents.

Individual-based learning would probably shift the foraging technique and the choice of food items by the cross-fostered birds in the direction of the conspecific controls, i.e. to fill the feeding niche to which the species is morphologically and physiologically adapted. However, if innovation and trial-and-error learning were important in the tits, it must have been restricted primarily to a short time-window early in life because we neither found a significant effect of age in the present study, nor in a previous study where an effect of cross-fostering on foraging location was detectable already in the autumn soon after the young had left the parents [8].

Our results suggest that early social learning lasts for life. Recent studies indicate that animals in general are reluctant to include new prey items in their diets [78, 79], and avoid new nutritional stimuli [80]. Such dietary conservatism may be adaptive because the food items chosen by parents have already proven to be successful. Thus, early social learning in life may help the offspring to identify favourable food items, avoid other items, and develop search images more efficiently [81–83].

4.3.2 Ecological and evolutionary consequences

The fact that young birds learned from their foster parents, and used this experience later in life when subsequently feeding their own offspring, suggests that foraging behaviour can be culturally transmitted over generations in the wild, and may therefore have both ecological and evolutionary consequences. Recently, it has been recognized that non-genetic factors, such as phenotypic plasticity and epigenetics ('inclusive heritability' [84]), must be included in order to more fully understand phenotypic evolution [5, 84, 85]. According to theory, phenotypic plasticity may accelerate evolutionary change, depending on whether the genotypes that are already fitter have a proportionally higher gain in fitness owing to plasticity than those of the genetically less-fit individuals [4, 86]. Social learning may be favoured in fluctuating environments and when prey capture is difficult [1, 2]. Throughout the year, blue tits and great tits forage on a wide variety of food items that have evolved counter-measures to predation, like mimicry and camouflage [82, 87]. However, we do not know to what extent the individual tits gained in fitness from the social learning; it is not always obvious that social information is more valuable than personal information [4].

A cornerstone of ecological theory is that each species has a unique niche, which encompasses its habitat and use of resources in the presence of competing species and other biotic interactions [88]. A primary characteristic of the ecological niche involves exploitation of food. Much is known about animal foraging [89], and feeding niches are well documented in many species, yet little is known about how individuals come to adopt the niches [90, 91]. According to the present study, social learning may be important, even in two species that appear to have quite distinct foraging niches [69]. Our findings indicate strong phenotypic plasticity and hence suggest an ability of the focal populations to adapt rather quickly to environmental changes, such as those involving climate and anthropogenic factors [2, 92]. Knowledge of the ontogeny of foraging preferences may also help to understand patterns of competition among species, viz. juveniles may learn from their parents early in life to avoid excessive overlap with the foraging niches of competing species.

Early social learning, combined with dietary conservatism later in life, may influence natal dispersal and the use of micro- and macro-habitats, and explain a preference for the natal habitat [7, 93]. In turn, this may influence reproductive isolation, potentially causing hybridization and speciation [91, 94]. A social learning mechanism for foraging, rather than a strong genetic control, may reduce problems that hybrids face when the two parental species feed on different types of food [95].

Other consequences of the foraging niche may include plumage colour caused by variation in levels of carotenoids in the diet [96, 97], breeding time, growth rate and risk of predation. Foraging behaviour may thus have a strong influence on life history and fitness traits such as reproductive success and survival [89, 98]. We are currently addressing some of these questions in our long-term cross-fostering project.

Acknowledgements

We thank numerous assistants and graduate students for help in the field, P. McLoughlin for help with the statistics, and K. Laland, A. Thornton, A. Whiten, J. Whittington and an anonymous referee for comments on the manuscript.

References

1 Borenstein, E., Feldman, M. W. & Aoki, K. 2008 Evolution of learning in fluctuating environments: when selection favors both social and exploratory individual learning. *Evolution* **62**, 586–602.

2 van der Post, D. J. & Hogeweg, P. 2009 Cultural inheritance and diversification of diet in variable environments. *Anim. Behav.* **78**, 155–166.

3 Whiten, A., Hinde, R. A., Laland, K. N. & Stringer, C. B. 2011 Culture evolves. *Phil. Trans. R. Soc. B* **366**, 938–948.

4 Rieucau, G. & Giraldeau, L.-A. 2011 Exploring the costs and benefits of social information use: an appraisal of current experimental evidence. *Phil. Trans. R. Soc. B* **366**, 949–957.

5 Thornton, A. & Clutton-Brock, T. 2011 Social learning and the development of individual and group behaviour in mammal societies. *Phil. Trans. R. Soc. B* **366**, 978–987.

6 Boere, G. C., Galbraith, C. A. & Stroud, D. A. (eds) 2006 *Waterbirds around the world*. Edinburgh, UK: The Stationery Office.

7 Davis, J. M. 2008 Patterns of variation in the influence of natal experience on habitat choice. *Quart. Rev. Biol.* **83**, 363–380.

8 Slagsvold, T. & Wiebe, K. L. 2007 Learning the ecological niche. *Proc. R. Soc. B* **274**, 19–23.

9 Doligez, B., Danchin, E. & Clobert, J. 2002 Public information and breeding habitat selection in a wild bird population. *Science* **297**, 1168–1170.

10 Gould, J. L. & Gould, C. G. 2007 *Animal architects. Building and the evolution of intelligence.* New York, NY: Basic Books.

11 Madden, J. R., Lowe, T. J., Fuller, H.V., Dasmahapatra, K. K. & Coe, R. L. 2004 Local traditions of bower decoration by spotted bowerbirds in a single population. *Anim. Behav.* **68**, 759–765.

12 Curio, E., Ernst, U. & Vieth, W. 1978 Cultural transmission of enemy recognition: one function of mobbing. *Science* **202**, 899–901.

13 Griffin, A. S. 2004 Social learning about predators: a review and prospectus. *Learn. Behav.* **32**, 131–140.

14 Davies, N. B. & Welbergen, J. A. 2009 Social transmission of a host defence against cuckoo parasitism. *Science* **324**, 1318–1320.

15 Davies, N. B., Madden, J. R., Butchart, S. H. M. & Rutila, J. 2006 A host-race of the cuckoo *Cuculus canorus* with nestlings attuned to the parental alarm calls of the host species. *Proc. R. Soc. B* **273**, 693–699.

16 Hollén, L. I. & Radford, A. N. 2009 The development of alarm call behaviour in mammals and birds. *Anim. Behav.* **78**, 791–800.

17 Slagsvold, T. & Hansen, B. T. 2001 Sexual imprinting and the origin of obligate brood parasitism in birds. *Am. Nat.* **158**, 354–367.

18 Jarvis, E. D. 2006 Selection for and against vocal learning in birds and mammals. *Ornithol. Sci.*
    5, 5–14.

19 Catchpole, C. K. & Slater, P. J. B. 2008 *Bird song. Biological themes and variations.* Cambridge, UK:
    Cambridge University Press.

20 Hoppitt, W. & Laland, K. N. 2008 Social processes influencing learning in animals: a review of the
    evidence. *Adv. Stud. Behav.* **38**, 105–165.

21 Eriksen, A., Slagsvold, T. & Lampe, H. M. 2011 Vocal plasticity—are pied flycatchers (*Ficedula
    hypoleuca*) open-ended learners? *Ethology* **117**, 188–198.

22 ten Cate, C. & Vos, D. R. 1999 Sexual imprinting and evolutionary processes in birds: a
    reassessment. *Adv. Stud. Behav.* **28**, 1–31.

23 Freeberg, T. M. 2004 Social transmission of courtship behavior and mating preferences in
    brown-headed cowbirds, *Molothrus ater. Learn. Behav.* **32**, 122–130.

24 Harris, M. P. 1970 Abnormal migration and hybridization of *Larus argentatus* and *L. fuscus* after
    interspecies fostering experiments. *Ibis* **112**, 488–498.

25 Grant, P. R. & Grant, B. R. 1997 Hybridization, sexual imprinting, and mate choice. *Am. Nat.*
    149, 1–18.

26 Slagsvold, T., Hansen, B. T., Johannessen, L. E. & Lifjeld, L. T. 2002 Mate choice and imprinting in
    birds studied by cross-fostering in the wild. *Proc. R. Soc. Lond. B* **269**, 1449–1455.

27 Hansen, B. T., Johannessen, L. E. & Slagsvold, T. 2008 Imprinted species recognition lasts for life in
    free-living great tits and blue tits. *Anim. Behav.* **75**, 921–927.

28 Slagsvold, T. 2004 Cross-fostering of pied flycatchers (*Ficedula hypoleuca*) to heterospecific hosts in
    the wild: a study of sexual imprinting. *Behaviour* **14**, 1079–1102.

29 Sæther, S. A. *et al.* 2007 Sex chromosome-linked species recognition and evolution of reproductive
    isolation in flycatchers. *Science* **318**, 95–97.

30 Eriksen, A., Lampe, H. M. & Slagsvold, T. 2009 Inter-specific cross-fostering affects song acquisition
    but not mate choice in pied flycatchers, *Ficedula hypoleuca. Anim. Behav.* **78**, 857–863.

31 Swaddle, J. P., Cathey, M. G., Correll, M. & Hodkinson, B. P. 2005 Socially transmitted mate
    preferences in a monogamous bird: a non-genetic mechanism of sexual selection. *Proc. R. Soc. B*
    272, 1053–1058.

32 White, D. J. 2004 Influence of social learning on mate-choice decisions. *Learn. Behav.* **32**,
    105–113.

33 Freed-Brown, G. & White, D. J. 2009 Acoustic mate copying: female cowbirds attend to other
    females' vocalizations to modify their song preferences. *Proc. R. Soc. B* **276**, 3319–3325.

34 Galef, B. G. & White, D. J. 1998 Mate choice copying in Japanese quail, *Coturnix coturnix japonica.
    Anim. Behav.* **55**, 545–552.

35 Drullion, D. & Dubois, F. 2008 Mate choice copying by female zebra finches *Taeniopygia guttata*:
    what happens when model females provide inconsistent information? *Behav. Ecol. Sociobiol.*
    63, 269–276.

36 Slagsvold, T. & Viljugrein, H. 1999 Mate choice copying versus preference for actively displaying
    males by female pied flycatchers. *Anim. Behav.* **57**, 679–686.

37 Midford, P. E., Hailman, J. P. & Woolfenden, G. E. 2000 Social learning of a novel foraging patch in
    families of free-living Florida scrub-jays. *Anim. Behav.* **59**, 1199–1207.

38 Cloutier, S., Newberry, R. C., Honda, K. & Alldredge, R. 2002 Cannibalistic behaviour spread by
    social learning. *Anim. Behav.* **63**, 1153–1162.

39 Nicol, C. J. 2004 Development, direction, and damage limitation: social learning in domestic fowl.
    Learn. Behav. **32**, 72–81.

40 Clark, J. A. 2010 White-tailed ptarmigan food calls enhance chick diet choice: learning nutritional
    wisdom? *Anim. Behav.* **79**, 25–30.

41 Kitowski, I. 2009 Social learning of hunting skills in juvenile marsh harriers *Circus aeruginosus*. *J. Ethol.* **27**, 327–332.

42 Lefebvre, L. 1986 Cultural diffusion of a novel food-finding behaviour in urban pigeons: an experimental field test. *Ethology* **71**, 295–304.

43 Boogert, N. J., Reader, S. M., Hoppitt, W. & Laland, K. N. 2008 The origin and spread of innovations in starlings. *Anim. Behav.* **75**, 1509–1518.

44 Holzhaider, J. C., Hunt, G. R. & Gray, R. D. 2010 Social learning in New Caledonian crows. *Learn. Behav.* **38**, 206–219.

45 Norton-Griffiths, M. 1967 Some ecological aspects of the feeding behaviour of the oystercatcher *Haematopus ostralegus* on the edible mussel *Mytilus edulis*. *Ibis* **109**, 412–424.

46 Bouchard, J., Goodyer, W. & Lefebvre, L. 2007 Social learning and innovation are positively correlated in pigeons (*Columba livia*). *Anim. Cogn.* **10**, 259–266.

47 Laland, K. N. 2004 Social learning strategies. *Learn. Behav.* **32**, 4–14.

48 Cadieu, N., Fruchard, S. & Cadieu, J.-C. 2010 Innovative individuals are not always the best demonstrators: feeding innovation and social transmission in *Serinus canaria*. *PLoS ONE* **5**, e8841.

49 Giraldeau, L.-A. & Dubois, F. 2008 Social foraging and the study of exploitative behavior. *Adv. Stud. Behav.* **38**, 59–104.

50 Zentall, T. R. 2004 Action imitations in birds. *Learn. Behav.* **32**, 15–23.

51 Heyes, C. & Saggerson, A. 2002 Testing for imitative and nonimitative social learning in the budgerigar using a two-object/two-action test. *Anim. Behav.* **64**, 851–859.

52 Kenward, B., Rutz, C., Weir, A. A. S. & Kacelnik, A. 2006 Development of tool use in New Caledonian crows: inherited action patterns and social influences. *Anim. Behav.* **72**, 1329–1343.

53 Holzhaider, J. C., Gunt, G. R. & Gray, R. D. 2010 The development of pandanus tool manufacture in wild New Caledonian crows. *Behaviour* **147**, 553–586.

54 Heyes, C. M. 1993 Imitation, culture and cognition. *Anim. Behav.* **46**, 999–1010.

55 van der Post, D. J. & Hogeweg, P. 2008 Diet traditions and cumulative cultural processes as side-effects of grouping. *Anim. Behav.* **75**, 133–144.

56 Claidière, N. & Sperber, D. 2010 Imitation explains the propagation, not the stability of animal culture. *Proc. R. Soc. B* **277**, 651–659.

57 Thornton, A. & Raihani, N. J. 2010 Identifying teaching in wild animals. *Learn. Behav.* **38**, 297–309.

58 Raihani, N. J. & Ridley, A. R. 2008 Experimental evidence for teaching in wild pied babblers. *Anim. Behav.* **75**, 1–11.

59 Galef, B. G. J. 2004 Approaches to the study of traditional behaviors of free-living animals. *Learn. Behav.* **32**, 53–61.

60 Kendal, R. L., Galef, B. G. & van Schaik, C. P. 2010 Social learning research outside the laboratory: how and why? *Learn. Behav.* **38**, 187–194.

61 Reader, S. M. & Biro, D. 2010 Experimental identification of social learning in wild animals. *Learn. Behav.* **38**, 265–283.

62 Whiten, A. & Mesoudi, A. 2008 Establishing an experimental science of culture: animal social diffusion experiments. *Phil. Trans. R. Soc. B* **363**, 3477–3488.

63 Langen, T. A. 1996 Social learning of a novel foraging skill by white-throated magpie jays (*Calocitta formosa*, Corvidae): a field experiment. *Ethology* **102**, 157–166.

64 Lorenz, K. 1935 Der Kumpan in der Umwelt des Vogels. *J. Ornithol.* **83**, 137–214 (289–413).

65 Verzijden, M. N. & ten Cate, C. 2007 Early learning influences species assortative mating preferences in Lake Victoria cichlid fish. *Biol. Lett.* **3**, 134–136.

66 Laland, K. N., Atton, N. & Webster, M. M. 2011 From fish to fashion: experimental and theoretical insights into the evolution of culture. *Phil. Trans. R. Soc. B* **366**, 958–968.

67 Kendrick, K. M., Hinton, M. R. & Atkins, K. 1998 Mothers determine sexual preferences. *Nature* **395**, 229–230.

68 Johannessen, L. E., Slagsvold, T. & Hansen, B. T. 2006 Song structure and repertoire size affected by social rearing conditions: experimental evidence from the field. *Anim. Behav.* **72**, 83–95.

69 Lack, D. 1971 *Ecological isolation in birds*. London, UK: Blackwell Scientific Publications.

70 Dhondt, A. A. 2010 Effects of competition on great and blue tit reproduction: intensity and importance in relation to habitat quality. *J. Anim. Ecol.* **79**, 257–265.

71 Partridge, L. 1979 Differences in behaviour between blue and coal tits reared under identical conditions. *Anim. Behav.* **27**, 120–125.

72 Slagsvold, T. & Wiebe, K. L. 2007 Hatching asynchrony and early nestling mortality: the feeding constraint hypothesis. *Anim. Behav.* **73**, 691–700.

73 Pinheiro, J. C. & Bates, D. M. 2000 *Statistics and computing. Mixed-effects models in S and S-PLUS*. New York, NY: Springer.

74 Fisher, J. & Hinde, R. A. 1949 The opening of milk bottles by birds. *Br. Birds* **42**, 347–357.

75 Rowe, C., Linström, L. & Lyytinen, A. 2004 The importance of pattern similarity between Müllerian mimics in predator avoidance learning. *Proc. R. Soc. Lond. B* **271**, 407–413.

76 Estók, P., Zsebok, S. & Siemers, B. 2010 Great tits search for, capture, kill and eat hibernating bats. *Biol. Lett.* **6**, 59–62.

77 Krebs, J. R., MacRoberts, M. H. & Cullen, J. M. 1972 Flocking and feeding in the great tit *Parus major*: an experimental study. *Ibis* **114**, 507–530.

78 Marples, N. M., Roper, T. J. & Harper, D. G. C. 1998 Responses of wild birds to novel prey: evidence of dietary conservatism. *Oikos* **83**, 161–165.

79 Thomas, R.J., Bartlett, L.A., Marples, N.M., Kelly, D.J.& Cuthill, I. C. 2004 Prey selection by wild birds can allow novel prey and conspicuous colour morphs to spread in prey populations. *Oikos* **106**, 285–294.

80 Schaefer, H. M., Spitzer, K. & Bairlein, F. 2008 Long-term effects of previous experience determine nutrient discrimination abilities in birds. *Front. Zool.* **5**, 4.

81 Dall, S. R. X. & Cuthill, I. C. 1997 The information costs of generalism. *Oikos* **80**, 197–202.

82 Marples, N. M., Kelly, D. J. & Thomas, R. J. 2005 The evolution of warning coloration is not paradoxical. *Evolution* **59**, 933–940.

83 Salva, O. R., Daisley, J. N., Regolin, L. & Vallortigara, G. 2010 Time-dependent lateralization of social learning in the domestic chick (*Gallus gallus domesticus*): effects of retention delays in the observed lateralization pattern. *Behav. Brain Res.* **212**, 152–158.

84 Danchin, E. & Wagner, R. H. 2010 Inclusive heritability: combining genetic and non-genetic information to study animal behavior and culture. *Oikos* **119**, 210–218.

85 Pfenning, D. W., Wund, M. A., Snell-Rood, E. C., Cruickshank, T., Schlichting, C. D. & Moczek, A. P. 2010 Phenotypic plasticity's impact on diversification and speciation. *Trends Ecol. Evol.* **25**, 459–467.

86 Paenke, I., Sendhoff, B. & Kawecki, T. J. 2007 Influence of plasticity and learning on evolution under directional selection. *Am. Nat.* **170**, E47–E58.

87 Stevens, M. & Merilaita, S. 2009 Animal camouflage: current issues and new perspectives. *Phil. Trans. R. Soc. B* **364**, 423–427.

88 Begon, M., Townsend, C. R. & Harper, J. L. 2005 *Ecology. From individual to ecosystem*, 4th edn. Oxford, UK: Blackwell Publishing.

89 Stephens, D. W., Brown, J. S. & Ydenberg, R. C. 2007 *Foraging, behavior and ecology*. Chicago, IL: University of Chicago Press.

90 Davis, J. M. & Stamps, J. A. 2004 The effect of natal experience on habitat preferences. *Trends Ecol. Evol.* **19**, 411–416.

91 Tonnis, B., Grant, P. R., Grant, B. R. & Petren, K. 2005 Habitat selection and ecological speciation in Galápagos warbler finches (*Certhidea olivacea* and *Certhidea fusca*). *Proc. R. Soc. B* **272**, 819–826.

92 Chevin, L.-M., Lande, R. & Mace, G. M. 2010 Adaptation, plasticity, and extinction in a changing environment: towards a predictive theory. *PLoS Biol.* **8**, 1–8.

93 Stamps, J. A., Krishnan, V. V. & Willits, N. H. 2009 How different types of natal experience affect habitat preferences. *Am. Nat.* **174**, 623–630.

94 Beltman, J. B., Haccou, P. & ten Cate, C. 2004 Learning and colonization of new niches: a first step toward speciation. *Evolution* **58**, 35–46.

95 Grosch, K. 2003 Hybridization between two insectivorous bird species and the effect on prey-handling efficiency. *Evol. Ecol.* **17**, 1–17.

96 Slagsvold, T. & Lifjeld, J. T. 1985 Variation in plumage colour of the great tit *Parus major* in relation to habitat, season and food. *J. Zool.* **206**, 321–328.

97 Hill, G. E., Inouye, C. Y. & Montgomerie, R. 2002 Dietary carotenoids predict plumage coloration in wild house finches. *Proc. R. Soc. Lond. B* **269**, 1119–1124.

98 McLoughlin, P. D., Coulson, T. & Clutton-Brock, T. 2008 Cross-generational effects of habitat and density on life history in red deer. *Ecology* **89**, 3317–3326.

Chapter 5

Social Learning and the Development of Individual and Group Behaviour in Mammal Societies

Alex Thornton and Tim Clutton-Brock

As in human societies, social learning may play an important role in shaping individual and group characteristics in other mammals. Here, we review research on non-primate mammals, concentrating on work at our long-term meerkat study site, where longitudinal data and field experiments have generated important insights into the role of social learning under natural conditions. Meerkats live under high predation pressure and occupy a difficult foraging niche. Accordingly, pups make extensive use of social information in learning to avoid predation and obtain food. Where individual learning is costly or opportunities are lacking, as in the acquisition of prey-handling skills, adults play an active role in promoting learning through teaching. Social learning can also cause information to spread through groups, but our data suggest that this does not necessarily result in homogeneous, group-wide traditions. Moreover, traditions are commonly eroded by individual learning. We suggest that traditions will only persist where there are high costs of deviating from the group norm or where skill development requires extensive time and effort. Persistent traditions could, theoretically, modify selection pressures and influence genetic evolution. Further empirical studies of social learning in natural populations are now urgently needed to substantiate theoretical claims.

Keywords: culture; development; evolution; mammals; social learning; traditions

5.1 Introduction

In human societies, the ability to learn from others ('social learning') promotes the development of individual skills and shapes the behaviour of groups, giving rise to varied local cultures [1]. Understanding the extent to which social learning has similar effects in other species is one of the most fundamental questions in the life sciences. Theoretical models suggest that social learning may have major ecological and evolutionary implications, promoting the spread of adaptive information within groups and between generations, dissociating behavioural traits from ecological conditions and modifying selection pressures [2–4]. Furthermore, comparative studies of social learning are critical for understanding the biological basis of human culture [5–7].

In recognition of these implications, social learning has become a major research topic in recent years. Studies in captivity have revealed mechanisms of social learning across a range of taxa and shown that information can spread across chains of individuals and diffuse through groups, forming group-level behavioural characteristics or traditions [8]. However, patterns of social learning in artificial groups of animals in close proximity to one another, with freely available food and no predation pressure may not adequately reflect those found in nature. Descriptive, observational studies of animals in their natural environment provide greater ecological validity, but cannot generate unequivocal evidence that social learning shapes individual or group behaviour [9]. Consequently, the role of social learning in nature remains rather poorly understood.

In this review, we synthesize existing knowledge of the importance of social learning in wild animal societies, with a focus on non-primate mammals (primates [10, 11], birds [12] and fish [13] are topics of other contributions in this volume, and we discuss research on these and other taxa where relevant). We concentrate particularly on research at our long-term field site of cooperatively breeding meerkats (*Suricata suricatta*), where access to multiple groups of individually recognizable, habituated animals has allowed us to obtain detailed records of individual development and enabled experimental tests of social learning. We then turn our attention to two key questions: can socially transmitted traditions influence evolution; and can traditions themselves evolve?

5.2 Social learning and individual development

Young animals whose own skills are poorly developed may often benefit from the knowledge of more experienced individuals. Theory predicts a reliance on vertical or oblique transmission (from parents or other adults to offspring) when different generations experience similar environmental challenges, whereas horizontal transmission is favoured when environmental change is faster than generation time [14]. Consequently, horizontal transmission may allow the rapid spread of innovations and improve the efficiency of individuals foraging at ephemeral food patches, while vertical transmission may promote the development of fundamental skills. Indeed, there is now evidence that many key behavioural determinants of fitness, including the ability to avoid predators, obtain food and select mates are determined in part by social learning in early life.

5.2.1 Predator avoidance

A plethora of experiments have shown that naive animals can acquire a fear of novel predators as a result of exposure to the fearful responses of conspecifics (see [15] for a review). However, these experiments seldom consider social learning as a developmental process contributing to skill acquisition by the young, and no study has yet demonstrated that social learning affects anti-predator behaviour in wild mammals (though see [16, 17] for experiments on learned enemy avoidance in wild birds and fish).

Despite a lack of unequivocal evidence, social learning is likely to play a role in the development of anti-predator responses in many mammals. Inflexible anti-predator responses under tight genetic control are unlikely to be adaptive if predation risk varies in time and space, and learning about predators through direct experience is extremely dangerous. The high costs of individual learning should therefore favour a reliance on social information [2]. Young animals, whose small size, poor motor skills and lack of experience make them especially vulnerable to predators, may be particularly likely to benefit from attending to the anti-predator behaviour of older individuals.

In meerkats, social influences play a clear role in responses to humans. Wild meerkats normally flee upon sighting a human, so initial attempts to habituate groups at our study site to human observers took well over a year. However, once the first groups were habituated, all the pups born into them were unafraid of people (T. Clutton-Brock 1994, unpublished data). Social learning may also aid the development of mobbing behaviour, used by meerkats when encountering threats such as snakes. Pups are less likely than adults to mob snakes, but more likely to mob non-threatening Cape ground squirrels (*Xerus inauris*), suggesting that mobbing may be shaped by experience. Adults show heightened responses to snakes when pups are present. Although this probably reflects the greater need to drive away snakes when vulnerable pups are present, mobbing may additionally provide pups with relatively safe opportunities to learn about the characteristics of the threat [18].

Circumstantial evidence suggests that social learning also facilitates the development of meerkats' responses to alarm calls. Meerkats live in open habitats under high predation pressure and, like many primates, use functionally referential alarm calls, with predator-specific calls eliciting distinct responses [19]. While adults respond rapidly and appropriately to alarms (e.g. running to bolt-holes in response to aerial predator alarms), pups react more slowly and generally run to the nearest adult [20]. Pups may therefore gain opportunities to learn appropriate responses by following their elders. Interestingly, female pups, who spend more time near adults, are faster to react than males and are more likely to show adult-like responses [20]. Whether this results from greater opportunities for social learning is unclear, but a similar pattern is found in chimpanzees (*Pan troglodytes*), where sex differences in the development of termite fishing have been attributed to differences in offspring's attentiveness to mothers [21].

Meerkats' use of alarm calls is also likely to be influenced by social learning. In common with other young mammals (e.g. vervet monkeys, *Chlorocebus aethiops* [22]), meerkat pups often alarm inappropriately, for example producing terrestrial alarm calls in response to aerial predators or alarming in response to non-threatening birds. Differences in pup and adult call use are not adaptive responses to age-related differences in vulnerability, as predators that are more threatening to pups than adults do not elicit more alarm calling from pups. Rather, pups begin responding appropriately to common predators at an earlier age than to rarer predators, suggesting that alarm call usage improves with experience [23]. Given that adults' responses provide the only means for pups to learn associations between predators and call types, social learning is likely to be important.

Together, these findings suggest that meerkats' predator-avoidance skills are strongly linked to social information acquired in early life. Similar effects are likely to be common in small mammals with substantial periods of parental care. For instance, in Belding's ground squirrels (*Spermophilus beldingi*), the presence of mothers is strongly related to the development of pups' ability to discriminate between alarm and non-alarm calls [24]. Nevertheless, a role for social learning does not negate the importance of genetic effects and individual experience. Rather, it is likely that selection tailors animals with certain predispositions for responding to predators, which are then refined by social and asocial learning processes. In support of this view, experiments suggest that naive monkeys can learn to fear snakes more easily than flowers [25]. Similarly, passerines cross-fostered between species develop relatively weak responses to the alarm calls of their own species, suggesting that genetically controlled templates are refined through learning [26].

5.2.2 Foraging

Species with complex foraging techniques or generalist diets commonly have long periods of parental care [27], and an offspring's transition to nutritional independence is likely to rely heavily on information acquired from adults. In meerkats, social interactions help pups to learn where to look for food, what to eat and how to handle difficult prey (Figure 5.1).

Animals in heterogeneous environments typically target their foraging attempts towards particular microhabitats. Such preferences are major determinants of the foraging niche, and may thereby influence species coexistence and speciation (see [12]). Where habitats vary temporally or spatially, individual preferences must be moulded by experience. Meerkats' development of microhabitat preferences involves the integration of information acquired through personal experience and social cues obtained from adults [28]. Adult meerkats preferentially forage at the base of sparsely distributed vegetation. Pups initially show no such preference and their foraging attempts are highly unproductive, but become more productive and adult-like as they get older. This transition rests largely on learning through direct experience of the profitability of different micro-habitats (cf. [29]), but pups may also use cues obtained by foraging near adults and digging in holes already created by adults (Figure 5.1a). Digging in the existing holes offers few nutritional rewards, but may allow pups to obtain olfactory cues from prey removed by the original hole-digger, thereby raising the probability that a pup would dig in similar locations in future [28].

In many species, including rodents, dogs and fowl, social interactions can also facilitate learning of suitable items to incorporate into the diet [30]. This is particularly important in generalist species where the costs of learning by sampling novel items may be high owing to the presence of potentially toxic items. The varied diets of rats (*Rattus* spp.) are especially well-studied in this context [31]. Here, laboratory studies show that social influences on food preferences begin in the womb, as traces of mothers' food are transported across the placenta into the foetal blood system, influencing pups' food choices after birth [32]. Similarly, food preferences may be transmitted from mothers to nursing offspring through milk [33]. Social learning processes continue into adulthood, as naive

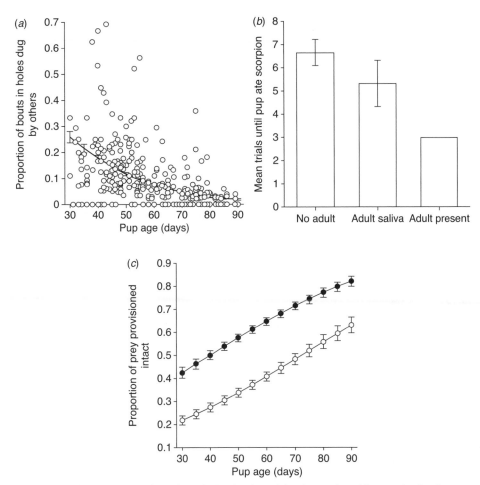

Figure 5.1 (a) Young pups often dig in holes dug by adults. (Reproduced from *Behavioral Ecology*, **20**(1), Alex Thornton and Sarah J. Hodge, The development of foraging microhabitat preferences in meerkats, pp. 103–110. © 2009 with permission from Oxford University Press.) (b) Young pups learn to eat dead scorpions more rapidly if they see helpers eating scorpions than if exposed to dead scorpions (unadulterated or covered in adult saliva) when alone. (Reprinted from *Animal Behaviour*, **76**(4), Alex Thornton, Social learning about novel foods in young meerkats, pp. 1411–1421, Copyright (2008), with permission from Elsevier.) (c) Adults increasingly provision pups with live, intact prey items as they grow older (open circles, scorpions; filled circles, other mobile prey). (Reprinted from *Science*, **313**(5784), Alex Thornton and Katherine McAuliffe, Teaching in wild meerkats, pp. 227–229, Copyright (2006), with permission from the American Association for the Advancement of Science.)

individuals show preferences for food associated with odours detected on the conspecifics' breath [34]. Similar effects have been found in other mammals, e.g. mice, *Mus musculus* [35], and dogs, *Canis familiaris* [36].

Numerous studies suggest that social information helps young mammals to learn what to eat in the wild [30, 37], although most evidence is inconclusive. The most direct evidence comes from meerkats, where pups are neophobic towards unfamiliar foods, but will incorporate them into their diet after interacting with older group members. In field experiments, young pups refused to eat hard-boiled egg (used at the study site to entice meerkats onto balances for the collection of weight data), but rapidly learned to eat it after exposure to adults eating egg [38]. Most pups were similarly reticent to eat dead scorpions (a common prey type in the meerkat diet), but were attracted to the sight of adults eating scorpions, causing them to sample the prey and subsequently incorporate it into their diet [38] (Figure 5.1*b*).

The most complex element of foraging behaviour is typically the ability to handle and process food types such as items encased in hard coverings or live, mobile prey. The difficulty in perfecting these skills through individual learning alone may favour a reliance on social learning from more experienced individuals. Developmental studies suggest that social learning may be important in the development of extractive foraging, hunting and tool use in primates, carnivores, rodents and cetaceans [37, 39]. For instance, bottlenose dolphin (*Tursiops* sp.) calves spend many years in close proximity to their mothers, and longitudinal data reveal strong correlations between certain maternal foraging tactics, including the use of sponges as foraging tools, and the acquisition of same skills by calves [40]. These data strongly suggest that social learning is involved in the development of foraging skills, but definitive experimental support is still lacking. Stronger evidence is provided by Terkel and colleagues, who found that black rats (*Rattus rattus*) in recently planted forests of Jerusalem pine in Israel had learned to extract seeds from pine cones. Subsequent laboratory experiments showed that experience of completing the stripping of cones started by others facilitated learning in naive individuals and that only young rats raised by dams that could strip cones learned to do so efficiently themselves [41]. Here, a simple mechanism of social learning allowed the rats to enter a previously unoccupied niche.

Although social influences on skill development are common, until recently it was generally thought that non-human animals never actively facilitate learning in others through teaching. This view stemmed from the anthropocentric assumption that teaching requires the capacity to understand the knowledge states of others and intentionally endeavour to correct their ignorance [42–44]. In contrast, the evolutionary approach promoted by Caro & Hauser [45] treats teaching as a functional category of behaviour whereby knowledgeable individuals incur short-term costs to promote learning in others. From this point of view, teaching is not contingent on particular cognitive mechanisms and may be favoured by selection if opportunities for individual learning are low or involve severe costs and passive social learning is ineffective [39]. For instance, meerkat pups seldom find mobile prey items and so lack opportunities to refine their prey-handling skills. Moreover, incompetent attempts to handle certain prey types, such as scorpions, may be dangerous and, as the development of the motor skills involved in prey-capture requires repeated practice [46], simply watching others is ineffective. Consequently, adults teach pups by providing them with otherwise unavailable opportunities to handle live prey. Young pups are primarily given dead or disabled prey items and are gradually introduced to live, intact prey as they grow older (Figure 5.1*c*). Provisioning pups with live prey that might escape is costly to adults, but experiments show that pups' skills improve as a result of handling practice [47]. Other clear examples of teaching occur in pied babblers (*Turdoides bicolor*), cooperatively breeding birds where helpers teach nestlings to associate particular calls with food [48], and in the ant *Temnothorax albipennis* where knowledgeable individuals teach colony members routes to food [49]. In the context of foraging skills, there is strong evidence that many solitary-hunting mammalian carnivores, particularly felids, teach their young to hunt in a similar manner to meerkats, by providing them with live prey [45]. Weaker evidence is also found in raptorial birds, cetaceans and primates (reviewed in [39]).

5.2.3 Mate selection

Where selecting a mate involves substantial costs, individuals may benefit from copying others. Female lek-breeding mammals, for instance, may reduce the risks of predation and harassment by following other females between territories [50]. In some fish and birds, females avoid the costs of mate assessment by preferentially affiliating with males chosen by other females. If such socially induced preferences generalize to other, phenotypically similar males [51, 52], they can generate long-term effects on mate choice. As well as influencing mate choice, social learning may affect the development of secondary sexual characteristics. In song-birds, for example, young males commonly learn to match their song to that of adults in the vicinity and females learn to prefer song types they hear in early life [53]. This may cause lifelong mating preferences, assortative mating and perhaps even speciation [54, 55]. Such downstream effects of social learning may be less common in mammals, where mate choice relies heavily on olfactory and morphological signals which are unaffected by learning, and where male coercion often masks the effects of female choice [56]. Nevertheless, developmental effects of social learning on mate choice may occur in certain species, particularly in bats and cetaceans that, like passerines, are capable of vocal learning and use vocalizations to attract mates [57, 58].

5.3 Social learning and group behaviour

Can social learning cause information to spread through groups of non-human animals, forming traditions akin to those of human societies? Much of the debate surrounding this question has centred on semantic issues concerning what precisely constitutes a tradition. The broad definition proposed by Fragaszy & Perry [59]—'a distinctive behaviour pattern shared by two or more individuals in a social unit, which persists over time and that new practitioners acquire in part through socially aided learning'—is widely accepted, but its requirement for persistence is ambiguous and could arguably exclude the short-term trends and fads that are so prevalent in human societies. Some authors would further stipulate a requirement that socially learned traits must become the norm within a group and endure across generations [60]. Conflicting views on the distinction between traditions and culture further complicate the issue. Some authors equate the terms [61], others treat culture as a collection of traditions (leaving open the question of how many traditions make a culture) [62] and yet others reserve the term 'culture' for traditions that signal group membership [63], or which increase in complexity over time [64].

An excessive focus on semantic issues may risk creating artificial dichotomies and obscuring central ecological and evolutionary issues. First, classifying traits as cultural (i.e. socially learned) or non-cultural is problematic because phenotypes are often shaped by combinations of genetic predispositions, epigenetic effects on gene regulation, and information acquired through individual exploration and social learning. Moreover, although social learning is commonly assumed to homogenize group behaviour [65], recent studies suggest that social learning may sometimes maintain behavioural heterogeneity [66–68]. Rather than fixating on terminology, we must determine the extent to which social learning shapes behavioural phenotypes and their stability at individual and group levels. Current attempts to address these issues have been limited by a heavy reliance on laboratory studies. In the wild, the popular ethnographic method (or method of exclusion) for identifying traditions by comparing the behaviour of geographically separated groups is generally unable to exclude genetic or ecological explanations for group differences [9]. Field experiments are therefore critical to bridge the divide between captive and observational studies.

To date, only a handful of field experiments have examined the spread of information through natural groups (reviewed in [8]). One powerful approach is to examine whether individuals translocated between groups subsequently adopt the behaviour of their new groups. Such experiments have generated strong evidence for socially learned mating sites and foraging routes in reef fish [69, 70], but are unlikely to be feasible with other vertebrates. With meerkats, we have used an alternative approach: training individual 'demonstrators' out of sight of the rest of the group (while foraging or babysitting) to perform a task, and then examining the adoption of demonstrators' behaviour by others. These experiments have generated a number of important insights. For instance, they show that the social transmission of information need not result in the adoption of uniform, group-wide traditions. In one experiment, we seeded six groups with demonstrators trained to obtain food from an experimental apparatus using one of two techniques, while a further three groups with no demonstrators served as controls for individual learning. Individuals in control groups were unlikely to obtain food, but in experimental groups, demonstrators' techniques preferentially spread to other group members. However, not all individuals learned. In particular, pups were more attentive than adults to demonstrators' behaviour, were more likely to follow demonstrators and scrounge scraps of food and consequently were more likely to learn (note that scrounging has variable effects on social learning depending on levels of social tolerance and task complexity [68]). This suggests that individuals' attentiveness, rather than their learning abilities, governs the spread of information (a similar effect is found in wild vervet monkeys, where selective attention to female demonstrators governs patterns of transmission of novel skills [71]). Moreover, a number of meerkats learned to use the technique on which their demonstrator was not trained, and this technique also spread to others, leading to the coexistence of alternative techniques within groups (Figure 5.2a). A lack of

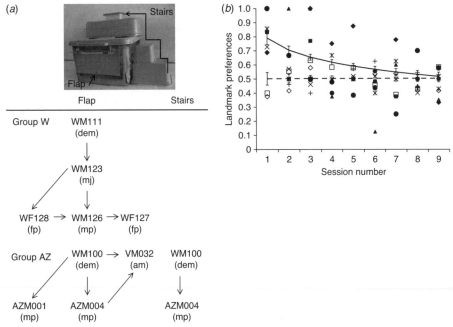

Figure 5.2 (a) Meerkats could obtain food from the experimental apparatus either by going through the flap or by climbing up the stairs and breaking a paper lid. In group W, the flap technique was transmitted from the trained demonstrator to other individuals. The flap technique also spread in group AZ, but here the demonstrator also discovered the stairs technique and was observed by a pup, who subsequently adopted the technique. dem, demonstrator; m, male; f, female; a, adult; j, juvenile; p, pup. (Reprinted from *Animal Behaviour*, **78**(2), Alex Thornton and Aurore Malapert, Experimental evidence for social transmission of food acquisition techniques in wild meerkats, pp. 225–264, Copyright (2009), with permission from Elsevier.) (b) Meerkats in control groups with no demonstrators showed no preference for either of the two equally rewarding landmarks; meerkats in experimental groups showed an initial preference for landmarks used by demonstrators, but this collapsed over time. Symbols are mean preferences for each group per session (open, control groups; filled, experimental groups); solid and dotted lines show combined means ± s.e. for experimental and control groups, respectively. (Reproduced from Thornton and Malapert, *Proceedings of the Royal Society B: Biological Sciences*, **276**(1660), pp.1269–1276, (c) 2009, The Royal Society with permission.)

stable behavioural homogeneity in groups need not, therefore, imply a lack of social transmission [68].

Our experiments suggest that the uniformity and stability of non-human animal traditions depend principally on the balance between social and individual learning. Where low-cost opportunities for individual learning are readily available, socially learned traditions are unlikely to persist (see also [72–75]). This is illustrated by a second experiment, which examined whether naive meerkats would adopt the preferences of demonstrators trained to obtain rewards from one of two adjacent and equally rewarding landmarks of distinctive shape and colour [76]. Here, social learning promoted an initial bias towards the landmark used by demonstrators, generating arbitrary traditions within groups. However, having learned that one landmark was profitable, individuals began exploring the other and learned that it provided equal rewards, so the tradition collapsed over time. This contrasts with human societies, where conformity to group norms and punishment of transgressors can maintain arbitrary traditions, regardless of the profitability of alternative options [1, 77].

In non-human animals, traditions may only persist when the net benefits of switching to alternative patterns of behaviour are low. Traditional foraging routes or food preferences, for example, may persist because the severe costs of leaving the safety of the group or sampling unknown foods outweigh any benefits. This may explain the persistence of group differences in emergence times in our meerkat population. Here, extensive gene flow precludes genetic differentiation between groups. Nevertheless, some groups consistently emerged from their sleeping burrows later in the morning than others for more than a decade, despite complete turnovers in group membership and the influx of immigrants. These differences do not appear to be driven by environmental factors, as group territories overlap, the same burrows are often used by different groups, and emergence times are unrelated to territory quality. Moreover, strong group effects remained even after accounting for ecological and meteorological factors in multi-factorial analyses. Group differences may therefore constitute local traditions maintained because individuals face large risks if they emerge from the burrow at a different time to the rest of the group [78].

Traditions may also persist if skills take extensive time and effort to perfect. If skill development is difficult and protracted, individuals may benefit from sticking with the first technique they learned, even if alternative techniques could be equally productive. This may explain the maintenance of complex food extraction skills, such as tool-use techniques in chimpanzee populations, negating the need to invoke human-like conformity to social norms (cf. [77]). For instance, in banded mongooses (*Mungos mungo*), communally breeding relatives of meerkats where pups form exclusive associations with one adult escort, pups take several months to learn to open encased food items by biting them or smashing them against anvils. Müller & Cant [66] experimentally presented escorts with food-filled plastic eggs and found that many escorts showed stable preferences for either biting or smashing. Pups tended to adopt their escorts' preferences and maintain them into adulthood, suggesting that the difficulty in perfecting techniques favours the maintenance of learned skills. However, both techniques coexisted within groups, providing further evidence that social learning can maintain within-group heterogeneity (see also [67]).

5.4 Broader implications

5.4.1 Can social learning affect evolution?

Theoretical models suggest that by allowing organisms to alter their environments and enter new niches, socially transmitted traits can modify selection pressures and thereby influence genetic evolution [2–4]. Empirical evidence is rapidly accumulating for human populations, with a recent survey identifying over 100 candidate genes, involved in a range of physiological, morphological and behavioural traits, which may have been influenced by culturally modified selective pressures [79]. However, data from other species are lacking. Among the most likely cases are those where social learning may affect sexual selection by influencing the development of secondary sexual traits and mate choice. For instance, in passerines and cetaceans where songs are learned, they must, by definition, be learned from others. As male song is commonly involved in female mate choice, female preferences for song dialects from their local area could theoretically cause pre-zygotic isolation between populations, ultimately leading to speciation [54, 55]. Explicit empirical tests of this prediction have yet to be conducted.

Social learning may also modify selection pressures through its long-term effects on foraging behaviour and habitat use. In humans, the invention of dairy farming resulted in the spread of alleles for lactose tolerance in pastoralist populations [80]. At our meerkat study site, social learning has resulted in a simple tradition of hard-boiled egg eating [38] which could, in theory, generate similar selective pressures for effective hard-boiled egg digestion over many generations. Social learning could also play an important role in the expansion of populations into new habitats. For example, the social transmission of innovative methods of food acquisition and mating site preferences may have played an important role in the expansion of many animals into urban areas. Subsequent exposure to new dangers, new food types and light regimes distorted by street lamps over many generations could well result in urban populations diverging genetically from their rural counterparts. Unfortunately, information on the role of social learning in urbanization is lacking. Indeed, excluding humans, the only well-documented case of niche invasion facilitated by social learning is in black rats, where social transmission of pine-cone stripping allowed invasion of pine forests [41]. Genetic comparisons of current forest populations with their counterparts outside the forest would provide an excellent test of gene–culture coevolution. Empirical analyses such as these are critical if we are to move beyond pure speculation as to the evolutionary implications of social learning.

5.4.2 Do non-human animal traditions evolve?

Human traditions are thought to evolve according to principles that are much in common with Darwinian evolution, with each generation building upon the innovations of the last [64, 81]. Apart from bird and cetacean song, however, the traditions of other species do not seem to show such incremental changes (though see [82] and [83] for tentative suggestions in the tool use of chimpanzees and New Caledonian crows, *Corvus moneduloides*). Kendal *et al.* [84] have suggested that social learning strategies such as copying others whose behaviour yields higher rewards than one's own may allow individuals to converge on fitness-maximizing behaviour over repeated iterations, thus promoting cumulative cultural evolution (see also [13]). However, although such strategies may allow sticklebacks in laboratory experiments to choose the best foraging patches [84], there is little direct evidence that they can allow the elaboration of technical innovations as seen in humans.

One common argument for the lack of cumulative culture in non-humans is that human culture is underpinned by higher fidelity mechanisms of social learning than those prevalent in other species. One such mechanism is imitation, which was commonly thought to be rare or absent in non-human animals [64, 85]. However, laboratory experiments have now generated evidence for imitation in a number of species [86]. Moreover, the fidelity of information transmission by imitation may not be as great as previously supposed [72], and in experiments on humans cumulative cultural evolution was observed in the absence of opportunities for imitation [87].

The ability to facilitate learning in others by teaching has also been suggested to be a uniquely human trait allowing high-fidelity information transmission and promoting cumulative cultural change [64, 85]. However, we now know that teaching is found across a range of taxa [39]. It now seems likely that neither imitation nor teaching *per se* provide the basis for cultural evolution. Rather, certain cognitive mechanisms that humans incorporate into some of their imitative and pedagogical activities may be important [88, 89]. For instance, non-human teaching is restricted to particular adaptive contexts (e.g. facilitating acquisition of hunting skills) and is not involved in the transmission of innovations [39, 90]. In contrast, humans' capacity for mental state attribution, joint attention and foresight may allow teachers to recognize and correct their pupils' ignorance, demonstrate novel actions, and thereby facilitate the transmission and improvement of cultural inventions across a range of contexts [91, 92] (see also [88, 93]).

5.5 **Conclusions**

Information transmitted between individuals is likely to have important effects in many mammal societies. In African elephant (*Loxodonta africana*) herds, for example, matriarchs are thought to act as repositories of social knowledge, and their removal may lead to decreases in the *per capita* reproductive success of remaining group members [94]. It is likely that many of the traits that behavioural ecologists model as genetically controlled adaptations, including anti-predator behaviour, foraging skills and social strategies, are to some extent shaped by social learning. However, the role of social learning remains poorly understood in wild mammal groups, and many common assumptions remain to be verified. For instance, great apes are often assumed to rely more heavily than other animals on socially transmitted information [60, 95], but the strongest experimental evidence that social learning influences individual and group behaviour in wild mammals is found in social carnivores [38, 47, 66, 68, 76]. This may simply reflect the greater tractability of small carnivores for field experiments, but claims of ape cultural supremacy nevertheless remain premature. Similarly, claims of cumulative traditions and evolutionary impacts of social learning currently amount to little more than tentative suggestions lacking in empirical support. Long-term field studies, incorporating field experiments and novel statistical techniques [6] provide the means to revealing the true importance of social learning in nature.

Acknowledgements

We thank Marta Manser for discussion and support, Katherine McAuliffe and Nichola Raihani for comments on the manuscript and Pembroke College, Cambridge for funding.

References

1 Richerson, P. J. & Boyd, R. 2005 *Not by genes alone: how culture transformed human evolution.* Chicago, IL: University of Chicago Press.

2 Boyd, R. & Richerson, P. 1985 *Culture and the evolutionary process.* Chicago, IL: University of Chicago Press.

3 Danchin, E., Giraldeau, L. A., Valone, T. J. & Wagner, R. H. 2004 Public information: from nosy neighbors to cultural evolution. *Science* **305**, 487–491.

4 Laland, K. N., Odling-Smee, J. & Feldman, M. W. 2000 Niche construction, biological evolution, and cultural change. *Behav. Brain Sci.* **23**, 131–175.

5 Heyes, C. M. & Galef Jr, B. G. 1996 *Social learning in animals: the roots of culture.* San Diego, CA: Academic Press.

6 Laland, K. N., Kendal, J. R. & Kendal, R. L. 2009 Animal culture: problems and solutions. In *The question of animal culture* (eds K. N. Laland & B. G. Galef), pp. 174–197. Cambridge, MA: Harvard University Press.

7 Whiten, A., Hinde, R. A., Laland, K. N. & Stringer, C. B. 2011 Culture evolves. *Phil. Trans. R. Soc. B* **366**, 938–948.

8 Whiten, A. & Mesoudi, A. 2008 Establishing an experimental science of culture: animal social diffusion experiments. *Phil. Trans. R. Soc. B* **363**, 3477–3488.

9 Laland, K. N. & Janik, V. M. 2006 The animal cultures debate. *Trends Ecol. Evol.* **21**, 542–547.

10 Perry, S. 2011 Social traditions and social learning in capuchin monkeys (*Cebus*). *Phil. Trans. R. Soc. B* **366**, 988–996.

11 Whiten, A. 2011 The scope of culture in chimpanzees, humans and ancestral apes. *Phil. Trans. R. Soc. B* **366**, 997–1007.

12 Slagsvold, T. & Wiebe, K. L. 2011 Social learning in birds and its role in shaping a foraging niche. *Phil. Trans. R. Soc. B.* **366**, 969–977.

13 Laland, K. N., Atton, N. & Webster, M. M. 2011 From fish to fashion: experimental and theoretical insights into the evolution of culture. *Phil. Trans. R. Soc. B* **366**, 958–968.

14 Laland, K. N. & Kendal, J. R. 2003 What the models say about social learning. In *The biology of traditions: models and evidence* (eds D. M. Fragaszy & S. Perry), pp. 33–55. Cambridge, UK: Cambridge University Press.

15 Griffin, A. S. 2004 Social learning about predators: a review and prospectus. *Learn. Behav.* **32**, 131–140.

16 Davies, N. B. & Welbergen, J. A. 2009 Social transmission of a host defense against cuckoo parasitism. *Science* **324**, 1318–1320.

17 Reader, S. M., Kendal, J. R. & Laland, K. N. 2003 Social learning of foraging sites and escape routes in wild Trinidadian guppies. *Anim. Behav.* **66**, 729–739.

18 Graw, B. & Manser, M. B. 2007 The function of mobbing in cooperative meerkats. *Anim. Behav.* **74**, 507–517.

19 Manser, M. B., Seyfarth, R. M. & Cheney, D. L. 2002 Suricate alarm calls signal predator class and urgency. *Trends Cogn. Sci.* **6**, 55–57.

20 Hollén, L. I. & Manser, M. B. 2006 Ontogeny of alarm call responses in meerkats, *Suricata suricatta*: the roles of age, sex and nearby conspecifics. *Anim. Behav.* **72**, 1345–1353.

21 Lonsdorf, E. V., Eberly, L. E. & Pusey, A. E. 2004 Sex differences in learning in chimpanzees. *Nature* **428**, 715–716.

22 Cheney, D. & Seyfarth, R. 1990 *How monkeys see the world: inside the mind of another species.* Chicago, IL: University of Chicago Press.

23 Hollén, L. I., Clutton-Brock, T. & Manser, M. B. 2008 Ontogenetic changes in alarm-call production and usage in meerkats (*Suricata suricatta*): adaptations or constraints? *Behav. Ecol. Sociobiol.* **62**, 821–829.

24 Mateo, J. M. & Holmes, W. G. 1997 Development of alarm-call responses in Belding's ground squirrels: the role of dams. *Anim. Behav.* **54**, 509–524.

25 Mineka, S. & Cook, M. 1988 Social learning and the acquisition of snake fear in monkeys. In *Social learning: psychological and biological perspectives* (eds T. R. Zentall & B. G. Galef), pp. 51–73. Hillsdale, NJ: Erlbaum.

26 Davies, N. B., Madden, J. R. & Butchart, S. H. M. 2004 Learning fine-tunes a specific response of nestlings to the parental alarm calls of their own species. *Proc. R. Soc. Lond. B* **271**, 2297–2304.

27 Heinsohn, R. G. 1991 Slow learning of foraging skills and extended parental care in cooperatively breeding white-winged choughs. *Am. Nat.* **137**, 864–881.

28 Thornton, A. & Hodge, S. J. 2009 The development of foraging microhabitat preferences in meerkats. *Behav. Ecol.* **20**, 103–110.

29 Giraldeau, L. A. 1984 Group foraging: the skill pool effect and frequency-dependent learning. *Am. Nat.* **124**, 72–79.

30 Galef, B. G. & Giraldeau, L. A. 2001 Social influences on foraging in vertebrates: causal mechanisms and adaptive functions. *Anim. Behav.* **61**, 3–15.

31 Galef, B. G. 2003 'Traditional' foraging behaviors of brown and black rats (*Rattus norvegicus and Rattus rattus*). In *The biology of traditions: models and evidence* (eds D. M. Fragaszy & S. Perry), pp. 159–186. Cambridge, UK: Cambridge University Press.

32 Hepper, P. G. 1988 Adaptive fetal learning: prenatal exposure to garlic affects postnatal preferences. *Anim. Behav.* **36**, 935–936.

33 Galef, B. G. & Sherry, D. F. 1973 Mothers milk: a medium for transmission of cues reflecting flavor of mother's diet. *J. Comp. Physiol. Psychol.* **83**, 374–378.

34 Galef, B. G. & Stein, M. 1985 Demonstrator influence on observer diet preference: analyses of critical social interactions and olfactory signals. *Anim. Learn. Behav.* **13**, 31–38.

35 Valsecchi, P. & Galef, B. G. 1989 Social influences on the food preferences of house mice (*Mus musculus*). *Int. J. Comp. Psychol.* **2**, 245–256.

36 Lupfer-Johnson, G. & Ross, J. 2007 Dogs acquire food preferences from interacting with recently fed con-specifics. *Behav. Processes* **74**, 104–106.

37 Box, H. O. & Gibson, K. R. (eds) 1999 *Mammalian social learning: comparative and ecological perspectives.* Cambridge, UK: Cambridge University Press.

38 Thornton, A. 2008 Social learning about novel foods by young meerkats. *Anim. Behav.* **76**, 1411–1421.

39 Thornton, A. & Raihani, N. J. 2008 The evolution of teaching. *Anim. Behav.* **75**, 1823–1836.

40 Sargeant, B. L. & Mann, J. 2009 Developmental evidence for foraging traditions in wild bottlenose dolphins. *Anim. Behav.* **78**, 715–721.

41 Terkel, J. 1996 Cultural transmission of feeding behavior in the black rat (*Rattus rattus*). In *Social learning in animals: the roots of culture* (eds C. M. Heyes & B. G. Galef Jr), pp. 17–47. San Diego, CA: Academic Press.

42 Premack, D. & Premack, A. J. 1996 Why animals lack pedagogy and some cultures have more of it than others. In *Handbook of education and human development: new models of learning, teaching and schooling* (eds D. R. Olson & N. Torrance), pp. 302–323. Oxford, UK: Blackwell.

43 Strauss, S., Ziv, M. & Stein, A. 2002 Teaching as a natural cognition and its relations to preschoolers' developing theory of mind. *Cogn. Dev.* **17**, 1473–1487.

44 Tomasello, M., Kruger, A. C. & Ratner, H. H. 1993 Cultural learning. *Behav. Brain Sci.* **16**, 495–552.

45 Caro, T. M. & Hauser, M. D. 1992 Is there teaching in nonhuman animals? *Q. Rev. Biol.* **67**, 151–174.

46 Caro, T. M. 1980 The effects of experience on the predatory patterns of cats. *Behav. Neural Biol.* **29**, 1–28.

47 Thornton, A. & McAuliffe, K. 2006 Teaching in wild meerkats. *Science* **313**, 227–229.

48 Raihani, N. J. & Ridley, A. R. 2008 Experimental evidence for teaching in wild pied babblers. *Anim. Behav.* **75**, 3–11.

49 Franks, N. R. & Richardson, T. 2006 Teaching in tandem-running ants. *Nature* **439**, 153.

50 McComb, K. & Clutton-Brock, T. 1994 Is mate choice copying or aggregation responsible for skewed distributions of females on leks? *Proc. R. Soc. Lond. B* **255**, 13–19.

51 Godin, J. G. J., Herdman, E. J. E. & Dugatkin, L. A. 2005 Social influences on female mate choice in the guppy, *Poecilia reticulata*: generalized and repeatable trait-copying behaviour. *Anim. Behav.* **69**, 999–1005.

52 White, D. J. & Galef, B. G. 2000 'Culture' in quail: social influences on mate choices of female *Coturnix japonica. Anim. Behav.* **59**, 975–979.

53 Janik, V. M. & Slater, P. J. B. 2000 The different roles of social learning in vocal communication. *Anim. Behav.* **60**, 1–11.

54 Beltman, J. B., Haccou, P. & Ten Cate, C. 2004 Learning and colonization of new niches: a first step toward speciation. *Evolution* **58**, 35–46.

55 Laland, K. N. 1994 On the evolutionary consequences of sexual imprinting. *Evolution* **48**, 477–489.

56 Clutton-Brock, T. & McAuliffe, K. 2009 Female mate choice in mammals. *Q. Rev. Biol.* **84**, 3–27.

57 Davidson, S. M. & Wilkinson, G. S. 2004 Function of male song in the greater white-lined bat, *Saccopteryx bilineata. Anim. Behav.* **67**, 883–891.

58 Rendell, L. & Whitehead, H. 2001 Culture in whales and dolphins. *Behav. Brain Sci.* **24**, 309–324.

59 Fragaszy, D. M. & Perry, S. 2003 Towards a biology of traditions. In *The biology of traditions: models and evidence* (eds D. M. Fragaszy & S. Perry), pp. 1–32. Cambridge, UK: Cambridge University Press.

60 McGrew, W. C. 2009 Ten dispatches from the chimpanzee culture wars, plus postcript (revisiting the battlefronts). In *The question of animal culture* (eds K. N. Laland & B. G. Galef). Cambridge, MA: Harvard University Press.

61 Laland, K. N. & Hoppitt, W. 2003 Do animals have culture? *Evol. Anthropol.* **12**, 150–159.

62 Whiten, A. & van Schaik, C. P. 2007 The evolution of animal 'cultures' and social intelligence. *Phil. Trans. R. Soc. B* **362**, 603–620.

63 Perry, S. 2009 Are nonhuman primates likely to exhibit cultural capacities like those of humans? In *The question of animal culture* (eds K. N. Laland & B. G. Galef). Cambridge, MA: Harvard University Press.

64 Tomasello, M. 1994 The question of chimpanzee culture. In *Chimpanzee cultures* (eds R. Wrangham, W. McGrew, F. de Waal & P. Heltne), pp. 301–317. Cambridge, MA: Harvard University Press.

65 Kendal, R. L., Kendal, J. R., Hoppitt, W. & Laland, K. N. 2009 Identifying social learning in animal populations: a new 'option-bias' method. *PLoS ONE* **4**, e6541.

66 Müller, C. A. & Cant, M. A. 2010 Imitation and traditions in wild banded mongooses. *Curr. Biol.* **20**, 1171–1175.

67 Sargeant, B. L. & Mann, J. 2009 From social learning to culture: intrapopulation variation in bottlenose dolphins. In *The question of animal culture* (eds K. N. Laland & B. G. Galef). Cambridge, MA: Harvard University Press.

68 Thornton, A. & Malapert, A. 2009 Experimental evidence for social transmission of food acquisition techniques in wild meerkats. *Anim. Behav.* **78**, 255–264.

69 Helfman,G.S.& Schultz,E.T.1984 Social transmission of behavioral traditions in a coral reef fish. *Anim. Behav.* **32**, 379–384.

70 Warner, R. R. 1988 Traditionality of mating site preferences in a coral reef fish. *Nature* **335**, 719–721.

71 van de Waal, E., Renevey, N., Favre, C. M. & Bshary, R. 2010 Selective attention to philopatric models causes directed social learning in wild vervet monkeys. *Proc. R. Soc. B* **277**, 2105–2111.

72 Claidière, N. & Sperber, D. 2010 Imitation explains the propagation, not the stability of animal culture. *Proc. R. Soc. B* **277**, 651–659.

73 Galef, B. G. & Allen, C. 1995 A new model system for studying behavioral traditions in animals. *Anim. Behav.* **50**, 705–717.

74 Giraldeau, L. A. & Lefebvre, L. 1987 Scrounging prevents cultural transmission of food-finding behavior in pigeons. *Anim. Behav.* **35**, 387–394.

75 Rieucau, G. & Giraldeau, L.-A. 2011 Exploring the costs and benefits of social information use: an appraisal of current experimental evidence. *Phil. Trans. R. Soc. B* **366**, 949–957.

76 Thornton, A. & Malapert, A. 2009 The rise and fall of an arbitrary tradition: an experiment with wild meerkats. *Proc. R. Soc. B* **276**, 1269–1276.

77 Henrich, J. *et al.* 2010 Markets, religion, community size, and the evolution of fairness and punishment. *Science* **327**, 1480–1484.

78 Thornton, A., Samson, J. & Clutton-Brock, T. 2010 Multi-generational persistence of traditions in neighbouring meerkat groups. *Proc. R. Soc. B* **277**, 3623–3629.

79 Laland, K. N., Odling-Smee, J. & Myles, S. 2010 How culture shaped the human genome: bringing genetics and the human sciences together. *Nat. Rev. Genet.* **11**, 137–148.

80 Durham, W. H. 1991 *Coevolution: genes, culture, and human diversity.* Stanford, CA: Stanford University Press.

81 Mesoudi, A., Whiten, A. & Laland, K. N. 2006 Towards a unified science of cultural evolution. *Behav. Brain Sci.* **29**, 329–383.

82 Boesch, C. 1993 Towards a new image of culture in wild chimpanzees. *Behav. Brain Sci.* **16**, 514–515.

83 Hunt, G. R. & Gray, R. D. 2003 Diversification and cumulative evolution in New Caledonian crow tool manufacture. *Proc. R. Soc. Lond. B* **270**, 867–874.

84 Kendal, J. R., Rendell, L., Pike, T. W. & Laland, K. N. 2009 Nine-spined sticklebacks deploy a hill-climbing social learning strategy. *Behav. Ecol.* **20**, 238–244.

85 Galef, B. G. 1992 The question of animal culture. *Hum. Nat.* **3**, 157–178.

86 Huber, L., Range, F., Voelkl, B., Szucsich, A., Viranyi, Z. & Miklosi, A. 2009 The evolution of imitation: what do the capacities of non-human animals tell us about the mechanisms of imitation? *Phil. Trans. R. Soc. B* **364**, 2299–2309.

87 Caldwell, C. A. & Millen, A. E. 2009 Social learning mechanisms and cumulative cultural evolution: is imitation necessary? *Psychol. Sci.* **20**, 1478–1483.

88 Csibra, G. & Gergely, G. 2011 Natural pedagogy as evolutionary adaptation. *Phil. Trans. R. Soc. B* **366**, 1149–1157.

89 Lyons, D. E., Damrosch, D. H., Lin, J. K., Macris, D. M. & Keil, F. C. 2011 The scope and limits of over-imitation in the transmission of artefact culture. *Phil. Trans. R. Soc. B* **366**, 1158–1167.

90 Thornton, A. & Raihani, N. J. 2010 Identifying teaching in wild animals. *Learn. Behav.* **38**, 297–309.

91 Hrdy, S. B. 2009 *Mothers and others: the evolutionary origins of mutual understanding.* Cambridge, MA: Harvard University Press.

92 Tomasello, M., Carpenter, M., Call, J., Behne, T. & Moll, H. 2005 Understanding and sharing intentions: the origins of shared cognition. *Behav. Brain Sci.* **28**, 675–735.

93 Hewlett, B. S., Fouts, H. N., Boyette, A. H. & Hewlett, B. L. 2011 Social learning among Congo Basin hunter–gatherers. *Phil. Trans. R. Soc. B* **366**, 1168–1178.

94 McComb, K., Moss, C., Durant, S. M., Baker, L. & Sayialel, S. 2001 Matriarchs as repositories of social knowledge in African elephants. *Science* **292**, 491–494.

95 Whiten, A. 2005 The second inheritance system of chimpanzees and humans. *Nature* **437**, 52–55.

Chapter 6

Social Traditions and Social Learning in Capuchin Monkeys (*Cebus*)*

Susan Perry

Capuchin monkeys (genus *Cebus*) have evolutionarily converged with humans and chimpanzees in a number of ways, including large brain size, omnivory and extractive foraging, extensive cooperation and coalitionary behaviour and a reliance on social learning. Recent research has documented a richer repertoire of group-specific social conventions in the coalition-prone *Cebus capucinus* than in any other non-human primate species; these social rituals appear designed to test the strength of social bonds. Such diverse social conventions have not yet been noted in *Cebus apella*, despite extensive observation at multiple sites. The more robust and widely distributed *C. apella* is notable for the diversity of its tool-use repertoire, particularly in marginal habitats. Although *C. capucinus* does not often use tools, white-faced capuchins do specialize in foods requiring multi-step processing, and there are often multiple techniques used by different individuals within the same social group. Immatures preferentially observe foragers who are eating rare foods and hard-to-process foods. Young foragers, especially females, tend to adopt the same foraging techniques as their close associates.

Keywords: capuchins; social traditions; social conventions; *Cebus*; social learning

6.1 Introduction

The quest to explain the evolutionary roots of human culture requires detailed comparative data on behavioural variation in populations of wild non-human species, along with data on the mechanisms that could potentially give rise to this variation. The best comparative datasets on behavioural diversity in wild populations within the order Primates currently come from two ape genera: (chimpanzees, *Pan troglodytes* [1, 2], and *Pongo*, orangutans [3, 4]), one Old World monkey species (Japanese macaques, *Macaca fuscata* [5, 6]), and one New World monkey genus (*Cebus*, capuchin monkeys: *Cebus capucinus* [7], and *Cebus apella* [8, 9]). This article will focus on capuchin researchers' discoveries from the past two decades.

---

* Electronic supplementary material is available at http://dx.doi.org/10.1098/rstb.2010.0317 or via http://rstb.royalsocietypublishing.org.

Capuchins are interesting for social-learning research because they exhibit many of the characteristics suggested as crucial for the emergence of material culture [10]: they are highly gregarious [9], and exhibit remarkable degrees of social tolerance while feeding [9, 11], thereby enabling regular exposure of naive individuals to models. Capuchins are long-lived (up to 55 years in captivity [12]) and develop slowly, reaching maturity at 5.5–8 years in females and 6–10 years in males [9] (S. Perry 1990–2010, unpublished data); thus, they have much time to acquire and use socially acquired information. *Cebus* has one of the largest brain sizes relative to body size of any primate [13] and generally excels at cognitive tasks [9]. Therefore, this genus is expected to be good at problem-solving, though opinions regarding the genus' capacity for imitation are mixed [9, 14–16]. Capuchins are omnivores specializing in extractive foraging [9, 17], so the foraging tasks they routinely need to solve are complex; therefore, it might be expected that they would benefit by having social cues to guide the acquisition of their foraging skills [18].

In this chapter, I review and synthesize findings about two broad categories of traditions: (i) socially transmitted group- or dyad-specific forms of social interaction, and (ii) foraging (food choice and food processing) behaviours. Although the theoretical predictions regarding which species should exhibit material culture are fairly clear [10], it is less clear what factors should predict the emergence of social communicative rituals, and this is also a topic of great interest for researchers interested in explaining the emergence of human culture. It might be argued that group-specific communicative rituals would be expected in those species that rely extensively on coalitionary aid, and therefore need to communicate more about their position in a complex society of shifting alliances. In this case, *C. capucinus* (though possibly not *C. apella*) is a prime candidate to have social conventions, because these monkeys form coalitions in a wide variety of contexts and are highly dependent on allies in order to successfully migrate, acquire high rank and defend their offspring from infanticidal males [9, 11].

Whereas there are some questions regarding the mechanisms of social learning and the cognitive potential to learn in various ways that can only be investigated in a captive experimental setting, there are other issues regarding cultural evolution that can be addressed only by observing wild animal populations. For example, even if we know that animals are capable of acquiring traits socially, we still need to know to what extent this really happens in nature, and what factors in a species' natural range of circumstances promote a reliance on social learning and affect the choice of the demonstrator to attend to. In order to understand the population dynamics of culture change, it is also important to have empirical data on the speed and fidelity with which traits are transmitted within and between groups living in natural conditions, and how this varies according to ecology, demographics, social dynamics and the utility of the trait in question.

6.2 Social conventions

6.2.1 Social conventions in *C. capucinus*

Most research on non-human animal traditions has focused on foraging skills rather than on group-specific communicative rituals [3, 6, 19]. However, human cultures are rich in social conventions, i.e. in social rituals that are unique to particular groups or cliques, and it is arguably the case that, relative to other species, humans devote a far greater portion of their cultural repertoire to these group-specific ways of conducting social interactions than to group-specific subsistence behaviours. Despite this, far less research has been devoted to social conventions than to foraging-related traditions in the animal literature, perhaps because the former are rarer in most species' repertoires.

White-faced capuchins are noteworthy for their innovative gestural repertoires. A comparative study was conducted of four populations of *C. capucinus* dwelling in tropical dry forest sites in Costa Rica, using the 'group contrasts' method [20]. In this study, social rituals were deemed to qualify as traditions if (i) they were common in some groups or sites (i.e. seen at a rate of at least once per 100 h) and never seen in other groups that had been studied for at least 250 h, (ii) the behaviour was observed to spread to additional group members over time, and (iii) it was durable, remaining in the behavioural repertoire for at least six months. According to these criteria, five behaviour patterns qualified as true traditions: (i) hand-sniffing (inserting one's fingers in or on the nostrils of the partner, often mutually, for prolonged periods of time), (ii) prolonged sucking of body parts, and (iii) three 'games', in which one partner bites firmly on something belonging to the other partner (a finger, a tuft of hair that has been bitten out of the face or shoulder or an inanimate non-edible object or 'toy') and the other partner works to retrieve the object, with the two partners frequently switching in the biting and retrieving roles. Since the publication of these results [20], another apparent bond-testing ritual, 'eye-poking' (the insertion of a partner's finger into one's own eye socket up to the first knuckle), has entered one group's repertoire and spread throughout the group, persisting after the death of its innovator though at low frequencies.

Table 6.1 documents the occurrence of particular social conventions across groups. Table 6.1 makes two important points: (i) all of these odd behaviours have been invented in multiple groups, and (ii) none of these behaviours is seen in all groups: they are present and are common in 2–8 of the 18 study groups, and completely absent in 4–10 of the well-studied groups. Table 6.2 provides more detail on temporal variation in the frequency (occurrence/unit time) and popularity (number of performing individuals and dyads) of one illustrative tradition: hand-sniffing. For example, in the FF group in 2004, hand-sniffing was observed between five and six times per 100 h of observation, and was practised by 40 dyads that included a total of 18 individuals. Note that even in groups exhibiting hand-sniffing, it goes in and out of fashion. Further details on the methods, the dataset and the interpretation of the results are presented in the electronic supplementary material.

6.2.2 Hypothesized function of *C. capucinus* social conventions

Whereas it is easy to understand how tool use and food choices impact fitness, it is less easy to understand exactly what is being accomplished by engaging in odd social rituals. Because non-participants seem uninterested in observing these rituals, and they typically occur on the periphery of the group, it seems unlikely that they function to display the

Table 6.1 Distribution of *C. capucinus* social conventions across study sites and social groups in Costa Rica. C, the behaviour is common (i.e. seen at a rate of > 1/100 h) during at least 1 year the group was studied; R, the behaviour was seen anecdotally; X, the behaviour was never seen in > 250 h of observation (see the table in the electronic supplementary material for number of hours each group was observed); ?, the behaviour was never seen, but the group was studied for < 250 h. Site names: SR, Santa Rosa; LB, Lomas Barbudal; PV, Palo Verde; CU, Curú

site name-group name	hand-sniffing	eye-poking	sucking	finger game	hair game	toy game
SR-SE	C	?	?	?	?	?
SR-CP	C	X	X	X	X	X
SR-LV	R	X	R	X	X	X
SR-NA	X	X	X	X	X	X
SR-CA	?	?	C	?	?	?
SR-CU	C	?	C	?	?	?
SR-BH	X	X	R	X	X	X
LB-AA	C	R	C	C	C	C
LB-FL	C	R	R	C	C	C
LB-RR	R	X	C	R	R	R
LB-MK	X	X	R	X	X	X
LB-CU	X	X	X	X	X	X
LB-FF	C	R	R	R[a]	X	X
LB-RF	C	R	X	X	X	X
LB-NM	?	?	?	?	?	?
PV-LT	?	?	?	?	?	?
PV-ST	C	X	R	X	X	X
CU-BE	X	X	R	X	X	C

[a]Rare variant using tail rather than finger.

quality of the performers' social relationship to third parties. Thus far, the available evidence best fits the hypothesis that these rituals function to test the quality of social bonds. Zahavi [21] has suggested that behaviours involving discomfort or risk can serve this function. In his verbal model, an actor imposes a small cost on a bond partner (the recipient). A tolerant or enthusiastic response from the recipient reliably signals the actor that s/he is in good standing with the recipient, whereas an aversive response reliably signals that the actor is in poor standing with the recipient. Thus, the same behaviour can elicit pleasurable or aversive responses, depending on the quality of their past interactions. The bond-testing hypothesis has been advanced to explain male–male greetings, including risky genital manipulation, in savannah baboons [22]. Sociologists have developed parallel arguments applicable to humans. For example, Collins [23] has argued that an important purpose of human conversations is for the interaction partners to convey to

Table 6.2 Temporal distribution of hand-sniffing in eight groups of monkeys at Lomas Barbudal. Cell values indicate (separated by commas) rate of hand-sniffing in ad libitum observation hours, number of individuals practising hand-sniffing and number of dyads practising hand-sniffing. 'Dash' indicates that no observations were conducted on that group in that year. For rate of hand-sniffing, 0, not observed, R, observed at a rate of < 1 time/100 h and C means 'common', with the number after the C indicating the approximate rate. C1, seen at a rate of 1–2 × /100 h; C2, seen at a rate of 2–3 × /100 h, etc.

year	AA	FL	RR	MK	CU	FF	RF	NM
1990	0,0,0	—	—	—	—	—	—	—
1991	C1,4,3	—	—	—	—	—	—	—
1992	C5,10,13	—	—	—	—	—	—	—
1993	C4,12,12	—	—	—	—	—	—	—
1994	C1,1,1(?)	—	—	—	—	—	—	—
1995	C1,4,3	—	—	—	—	—	—	—
1996	?	—	—	—	—	—	—	—
1997	C1,7,6	—	0,0,0	—	—	—	—	—
1998	0,0,0	—	0,0,0	—	—	—	—	—
1999	0,0,0	—	0,0,0	—	—	—	—	—
2000	0,0,0	—	0,0,0	—	—	—	—	—
2001	0,0,0	—	0,0,0	—	—	—	—	—
2002	R,16,16	—	R,4,2	—	—	—	—	—
2003	R,14,15	0,0,0	R,2,1	—	—	C2,15,20	—	—
2004	R,7,6	C2,5,4	R,2,1	0,0,0	—	C5,18,40	—	—
2005	R,2,1	C1,5,4	R,2,1	0,0,0	—	C3,12,18	—	—
2006	R,2,1	C1,3,3	0,0,0	0,0,0	—	C3,13,21	—	—
2007	R,8,5	R,6,4	0,0,0	0,0,0	0,0,0	C3,11,17	R,2,1	—
2008	0,0,0	C1,8,6	R,2,1	0,0,0	0,0,0	C3,13,13	C2,4,3	0,0,0

one another, via tone of voice, posture, eye contact and degree of enthusiasm, how committed they are to their relationship relative to relationships of other dyads in the coalitionary structure of the community. So, the precise verbal content of the conversation is not necessarily as meaningful as the non-verbal components that convey affect, except in the way in which the text of the conversation meaningfully references aspects of their social relationship (e.g. by referring to knowledge that is specific to their friendship, or things they have done together). Some human rituals, such as Yanomamö greetings at the start of feasts, and Newfoundland 'mumming' rituals, in which one group feigns an attack on the other party, who remains deliberately vulnerable, have been explained as 'rituals of trust' [24] according to the logic of Zahavi's bond-testing theory.

Why construct dyad-specific bond-testing behaviours? Other putative bond-testing behaviours do not involve innovative (and therefore easily misunderstood) behaviours— e.g. grooming, and non-conceptive sexual interactions, both of which are common throughout the order Primates. Like *C. capucinus* social conventions, these stereotyped signals (i) entail risk of injury as one party exposes vulnerable body parts to another individual whose actions s/he cannot necessarily visually monitor, and (ii) force individuals to signal partner preferences by allocating scarce social time [25]: if A is grooming B, s/he cannot simultaneously be grooming individual C. I speculate that dyad-specific rituals entail a 'start-up' time cost in addition to a risk cost and the time cost of each ritual performance, and are therefore more reliable signals than species-typical social behaviours such as grooming. The time costs (months, in some cases—S. Perry 1990–2010, unpublished data) required for partners to co-develop the particular elements of a social ritual are non-transferable to another dyadic relationship, and therefore strongly indicate degree of commitment to a particular relationship. Analogously, human romantic couples, friend dyads and parent–offspring dyads often devise dyadic-specific rituals (e.g. particular bedtime or mealtime rituals). If a couple breaks up and the two individuals go on to form new partnerships, they do not generally transfer these rituals to the new relationships, but rather, they form new rituals with the new partner. Further discussion of the probable function and design features of capuchin bond-testing signals can be found in Perry *et al.* [20].

Assuming that the apparent lack or at least rarity of social conventions for the purpose of bond-testing in most species is not an artefact of methods, but a true feature of their behavioural biology, why is it that white-faced capuchins have such a rich repertoire of such behaviours? It may be the case that coalitions are far more common, and also more important for maximizing fitness, in *C. capucinus* than in most species. Certainly, *C. capucinus* has one of the highest rates of coalitionary lethal aggression of conspecifics found in a mammal [11, 26] and coalitions are employed in a wide range of contexts [11, 27, 28]. The greater importance of alliances may necessitate a richer source of information about whom to trust.

6.3 Social learning of food choice: experimental and field studies

Capuchin foragers are unusually tolerant of frequent, close-range observations of other group members while they are eating, even permitting frequent scrounging. Perhaps because of this, *C. apella* is one of the best-studied primate species with regard to the issue of social learning about food (see [9] for a review). Experimental studies of captive animals indicate that the presence of foraging conspecifics facilitates sampling of novel foods, but that observers' behaviour is not affected by the specific properties of the food eaten by the observed foragers [29, 30]. Thus, it has been argued that capuchins do not pay close attention to the specific properties of foods eaten by others, but instead learn what to eat by coordinating their foraging in space and time (which, in the wild, would generally result in their eating the same items as group-mates). No analogous research has been done on *C. capucinus*, but the evidence from observational studies in the wild suggests a different view. For example, wild white-faced capuchins are more likely to target a forager for close-range observation ('peering' at a range of less than 10 cm) if the forager is consuming an item that is rare in the diet, suggesting that they are more interested in watching the consumption of foods they do not already know about [17]. Captive *C. apella* infants were more prone to show close-range interest in a forager's food if the food were novel rather than familiar, though they were just as likely to peer at others eating the novel food after trying it as they were before tasting it [31]. Thus, the function of close-range 'food interest' remains controversial (but see below).

6.4 Social learning of food-processing techniques: experimental and field studies

6.4.1 What do capuchins learn from close-range observation of food processing?

Another hypothesis about food interest/peering is that the monkeys need to observe at close range in order to learn details of food-processing techniques. Wild *C. capucinus* preferentially target foragers for close-range observation when they are feeding on foods that require two or more steps to process [17], and this result is not accounted for by differences in handling time (and hence observation opportunity) between the types of foods. Free-ranging *C. apella* preferentially observe the most skilled nut-cracking individuals [32][1], which could either indicate that they know who is best at nut-cracking and want to learn these skills, or that they have figured out that certain individuals obtain food more quickly and hence provide better scrounging opportunities. While these studies show that individuals are structuring their learning opportunities in a way that could enhance their knowledge, they do not show what is actually learned.

Early studies of the effects of observation opportunities on skill acquisition (reviewed in [9]) failed to produce much evidence that captive capuchins attend to the relevant details of observed food procurement tasks, even when allowed up to 75 observation opportunities of skilled demonstrators [33]. Later studies employed a two-action method in which an artificial fruit could be opened in one of two ways, and two groups of experimental subjects were exposed to a demonstrator who opened it in only one way. Custance *et al.*'s [14] study of human-reared capuchins and human demonstrators produced mixed results, whereas a more recent set of two-action studies, using a transmission chain design in which capuchins observed other capuchins, found much firmer evidence for faithful transmission [15, 16]. These researchers drew on the idea that the quality of social relationship between the demonstrator and the observer will affect the fidelity of transmission, such that dyads with close affiliative relationships will have an inherent desire to behave similarly (i.e. the bonding- and identification-based observational learning model [34, 35]). To facilitate tranquil, close-range observations of the demonstrations, demonstrator–observer pairs were restricted to those that had high rates of proximity and grooming and low tendencies to displace one another while co-feeding, and the demonstrator was slightly higher ranking, so that the observer would not disrupt demonstrations. The alpha male and alpha female were trained by humans in one of the two possible techniques for opening the fruit (lifting or sliding). Then they were allowed to demonstrate to another group member until satiated, at which point the observer had the opportunity to operate the apparatus. Monkeys were tested, pairwise, in this fashion, until there were five links in the transmission chain for lifting and four links for sliding. At the end of the study, the sixth monkey in the 'lifting' transmission chain was using lifting 95 per cent of the time, and the fifth monkey in the 'sliding' chain was using sliding 90 per cent of the time, whereas there was 100 per cent fidelity in transmission up until the last link in both chains [15]. Another study [16] trained two alpha males in two different techniques for opening a fruit and then reintroduced these males to their groups as demonstrators. In both groups, the group members preferentially adopted the technique used by the alpha male, even though 81 per cent also discovered the alternative technique. The degree of conformity obtained in these studies is much higher than that seen in wild groups of *C. capucinus* (§6.4.4), and this is most probably due to the care taken by Dindo *et al.* in choosing the demonstrator according to rank and tolerance of other group members in the two studies.

In a study conducted by de Waal & Bonnie [35] on *C. apella*, subjects first observed a model open one of three boxes, and then were given a chance to choose a box to open themselves. Dyads that had above-average 'relationship quality indices' (RQIs: relative hourly rates of exchanged grooming and resting in contact, divided by the relative hourly rate of dyadic agonism and aggression) were more prone to copy one another's choice of box to open than were dyads with below-average RQIs, at least in trials where the model's choice (but not the subject's) was rewarded [35].

It is likely that quality of social relationship also plays a factor in the desire of wild monkeys to copy one another, but in observational studies of wild animals, there is no way to control who has observational access to whom, or who demonstrates what techniques. So for most wild populations, the subset of practitioners of technique A will include both tolerant and intolerant dyads, as will the group consisting of practitioners of technique B.

6.4.2 Interpopulation variation in food-processing techniques in the wild

Capuchin monkeys exhibit between-population variation in food-processing techniques. *Cebus apella* create tool kits, some quite elaborate, which vary between sites in their size and composition (§6.5). But even *C. capucinus*, which rarely employs tools, displays between-group differences in the specific techniques used to process those foods that are part of the diet at multiple sites not connected by forest corridors [36]. In our comparison of four white-faced capuchin sites, all in tropical dry forest, we found that 20 of the 61 foods that were common to the diet at multiple sites were processed differently at different sites. In 17 of the 20 cases, the difference simply involved the use of a species-typical action (pounding, scrubbing, tapping and, in rare cases, a fulcrum action) to a food type at one site but not at another. All these actions were seen at all four sites, but they were not employed in the same contexts everywhere. A few more elaborate foraging practices (e.g. following army ants to catch the prey they flush up) were seen at some sites but not others.

It is difficult to attribute between-group differences in food processing to social learning, because even small ecological differences between sites could lead to differences in foraging behaviour (e.g. chimpanzees create longer ant-dipping sticks to forage on species of ants that are more aggressive or have more painful bites [37]). When there is homogeneity within groups and heterogeneity between groups, it is impossible to know whether members of the same group have converged owing to social-learning processes, or whether all group members are independently using trial-and-error learning to adapt to the same ecological constraints. It is easier to infer a role of social learning if there is within-group variation in a trait, and the patterning of variation can be compared with the association patterns within the group, to see whether closer associates are more likely to share techniques.

6.4.3 Cross-sectional studies of association patterns and shared food-processing techniques in the wild

Several researchers have investigated whether those individuals who more frequently associate with one another are also more prone to share the same foraging techniques (see the electronic supplementary material for a table summarizing these results). At Palo Verde National Park, performers of rare techniques (e.g. rubbing mangoes, or pounding *Annona* or *Randia* fruits) had mean dyadic proximity scores that were significantly higher than the mean proximity scores for dyads that did not share the same food-processing technique [36]. The capuchins of Santa Rosa National Park who shared the trait of pounding *Luehea candida* fruits had significantly higher mean dyadic proximity indices than dyads that did not exhibit that technique [38]. At Lomas Barbudal, monkeys who spent more time associating were significantly more likely to share the same technique for processing *Sloanea terniflora* fruits [17]. A study of wild *Cebus albifrons* [39] yielded mixed evidence for a positive effect of association time on sharing of techniques, depending on the analytical technique used and the types of food-processing tasks included in the analysis. Indeed, several studies have found non-significant or marginally significant trends towards associations between capuchin proximity patterns and shared food-processing techniques [36, 38, 39] (S. Perry 2001–2010, unpublished data). These mixed results may be attributable to the studies' cross-sectional designs: the subjects may have acquired their food-processing techniques while young, before acquiring their current social networks. This is almost certainly true of adult males, who have emigrated from their natal groups. Thus, it would be surprising to find strong effects of adult proximity patterns on techniques employed. A longitudinal design, focusing on the early years of development, is better suited to capturing meaningful relationships between proximity (and hence social-learning opportunity) and techniques acquired.

6.4.4 Longitudinal study of association patterns and shared food-processing techniques in the wild

Thus far, only one longitudinal study has examined the acquisition of foraging strategies in wild *Cebus* [40]. In this study, 48 immature individuals (21 females, 27 males) from three social groups were studied for a period of 7 years, covering the first 5 years of their development. The trait documented was the manner in which *L. candida* fruits were processed in order to extract the tiny seeds from the woody capsule in which they were embedded. *Luehea* is a food that is consumed at all three sites in Costa Rica where *C. capucinus* has been studied, and at all sites, the monkeys employ multiple techniques to obtain the seeds [17, 38, 41]. In their first year of life, infants simply pluck loose seeds from the end of the capsule. In their second year of life, they experiment with a variety of techniques, some efficient and some non-efficient. Gradually over the next few years, they narrow their range of techniques used until they settle on a single predominant technique, usually by age 5 years. There are two common techniques used by adults, pounding and scrubbing, which do not differ significantly in their efficiency. The proportions of pounding and scrubbing used vary according to social group. The main goal of this study was to examine the correspondence between the techniques observed by foraging individuals with the techniques they actually practised in any given *Luehea* season. Data on the techniques practised were collected on all group members, regardless of whether they were part of the developmental study, and information on gaze direction and proximity to other *Luehea* foragers was also noted.

The mother was presumed to be an important demonstrator for her young, and so observations of maternal technique were analysed both separately from, and jointly with, observations of other group members. The independent variable in the regression model was the proportion of *Luehea*-processing events observed that were pounding, as opposed to scrubbing. The outcome variable, 'practised technique', was the proportion of the focal animal's processing events that were pounding (i.e. the number of pounded fruits, divided by the sum total of fruits pounded plus fruits scrubbed). Regardless of whether the independent variable in the regression model was observations of maternal technique, non-maternal technique or both combined, females exhibited a highly significant impact of observed technique on practised technique for each of the first 5 years, showing the greatest impact (3.85% change in the proportion of pounding practised resulting from a 1% change in the observed technique, for maternal and non-maternal influence combined) during the second year of development. Males exhibited the same pattern, but to a far lesser extent, rarely attaining significance. With respect to maternal influence, males showed a significant impact ($p \leq 0.05$) of maternal technique observed upon male technique practised only in years 2 and 5. Overall, averaged across the 5 years of development, females exhibited a 2.79 per cent change in proportion of pounding practised resulting from a 1 per cent change in observed maternal and non-maternal techniques combined (s.d. = 0.49, $p < 0.0001$), whereas males exhibited only a 1.45 per cent change (s.d. = 0.34, $p < 0.0001$) [40].

Examining only the data on the most recent year available for *Luehea* processing, for all 106 individuals in the population for which maternity data were available, it was found that the 48 females were significantly likely to use the maternal technique, whereas the 58 males were not (Fisher's exact, $p = 0.002$ for females, $p = 0.18$ for males) [40].

It was not clear what factors caused the sex difference in tendency to conform. Males and females spent equal amounts of time in proximity to their mothers, and equal amounts of time alone, which suggests that their overall exposure to models did not differ [40]. The one available developmental study of chimpanzee termiting [42] found that sex differences in conformity to maternal tool style were probably due to differences in visual attention to the mother, rather than to the amount of time in proximity to her. But male and female capuchins devoted equal amounts of time to actively observing the techniques of foraging neighbours, both when neighbours were foraging on *Luehea* and when they were foraging on other foods [40]. According to de Waal's BIOL model [34], individuals will have an intrinsic desire to copy the behaviour of individuals with whom they have strong social bonds.[2] It may be that females, being the philopatric sex in this species, are more motivated to copy group-mates than males are, since males migrate multiple times and hence do not form lifelong alliances with group-mates. Female–female dyads groom and affiliate at higher rates than do male–male dyads, with male–female dyads typically showing intermediate values [11, 43]; these data, as well as data on the patterning of aggression in this species, indicate that females typically have more affiliative relationships and fewer conflictual relationships in their social groups than males do. Studies of captive brown capuchins have found that observing a model collect a reward does not influence the tendency to copy, nor is it necessary for the subject to obtain a reward in order to copy a model [44]. In the *Luehea*-processing study, subjects seemed capable of learning both techniques via trial-and-error learning, and there was no advantage to learning one technique over another, yet they still conformed to the technique they saw most [40].

6.5 Explaining the differences between *C. capucinus* and *C. apella* in social conventions and tool-use traditions

In the past few years, there has been an explosion of research on the behavioural diversity of *C. apella* at numerous sites throughout South America (see [8] for a recent review of tool use at 29 sites, and [9] for a review of tool use in both captive and field settings for all capuchin species). Although there is currently no evidence for traditional bond-testing rituals at any of these *C. apella* sites (P. Izar 2010, personal communication), there are numerous reports of traditions involving tool use [8]. Monkeys at 10 of these sites exhibit no tool use, though they do engage in complex object manipulations while foraging. At 12 sites, tool use is reported anecdotally; at six, stone tool use for nut-cracking is customary, and the monkeys at one site (Serra de Capivara) use an elaborate tool kit including many types of stone tools as well as stick tools [8, 45, 46]. *Cebus capucinus* has a far more impoverished tool-use repertoire, with no customary tool use reported for any site, and only scattered anecdotes from individual monkeys (e.g. use of a club to kill a snake [47]; wrapping of hairy fruits and caterpillars in leaves [36]). It is not yet entirely clear whether there is a species difference with regard to propensity to create tools and test social bonds, or whether the apparent differences between species in the frequency and types of traditions formed are due to differences in ecology. Tool use in *C. apella* is far more frequent in the arid savannah sites, where monkeys are often on the ground foraging on hard foods such as palm nuts and have ready access to stones. Although all of the well-studied sites for *C. capucinus* are in dry forest, most have ready access to water, and there are plenty of foods available that do not require tools to open. On the other hand, experiments done on captive *C. apella* and *C. capucinus* in equivalent housing conditions suggest that *C. apella* spontaneously engages in more complex object manipulations (combining an object with a substrate, or combining two objects together) and is less neophobic about handling new objects, relative to *C. capucinus* [48]. It may be the case that there are both ecological factors and evolved psychological dispositions contributing to the observed differences between species and populations of capuchins. Most studies of *C. apella* report that coalitionary aggression is less common than in *C. capucinus* [9, 49], which could explain why there is a greater need to test the quality of social bonds in *C. capucinus*.

6.6 Explaining the population dynamics of social transmission of bond-testing rituals and foraging traditions

Useful foraging traditions (e.g. nut-cracking in chimpanzees [50] and brown capuchins [51]) persist in a fairly stable form for many generations, even long enough to leave an archaeological record. In contrast, capuchin social conventions are not transmitted with high fidelity and are fairly transient in group repertoires (table 2). They typically last no longer than 10 years and are rarely, if ever, transmitted beyond three links in a social transmission chain before going extinct [20]. In this way, they are similar to human fads, though the reason for the transience is somewhat different in the two cases. In both dyadic bond-testing rituals and human fads (in which multiple individuals conform to the same behaviour), the specific content (e.g. what specific motor patterns are used to inflict discomfort in capuchin bond-testing rituals, or what dances or clothing styles are currently fashionable) is to some extent arbitrary. It does not matter whether it is a finger or a toy that is extracted from the partner's mouth, any more than it matters whether people wear lace or ruffles on their dress hems. What matters is that some sort of cost (in time or money) is being expended in order to assert a particular role in the social structure. In the case of the dyadic bond-testing signals, part of what is being tracked is the mutual devotion to developing the dyad-specific ritual, and so it is important that each dyad exhibits somewhat different twists on these general themes, and that it takes much time to construct a ritual that is mutually satisfying to both members of the dyad. This argument builds on Dunbar's [25] hypothesis that the preferential allocation of limited social (grooming) time reliably signals commitment to allies. So, whereas multiple dyads in the same group may be hand-sniffers, each dyad differs somewhat with regard to (i) where they insert their fingers (into the eye, mouth or nose), (ii) whether they grip one another's hands while they do it, and (iii) what postures they assume (with some partners clutching a particular body part with a free hand). In the case of human fashions, the purpose of adopting a fashion is not to test a dyadic relationship, but rather to advertise identification and/or membership in a group: it is important to be current in tracking what the high-prestige set of people is doing. High-status signals would lose their value if they remained static, because everyone would have time to conform; whereas if they shift constantly, only the wealthy and well-connected can rapidly conform [52, 53]. In contrast, greater stability is expected for foraging traditions, because certain techniques or tool forms are more useful at obtaining high foraging returns than others, and so there will be selection for keeping useful variants in the repertoire.

The capuchin bond-testing rituals were practised chiefly by adults. Young animals typically became regular practitioners of hand-sniffing or eyeball-poking only when they reached adolescence at Lomas Barbudal. Game-playing started somewhat earlier, as early as age 1, but most often included one adult practitioner. New bond-testing rituals could be acquired in adults of any age, as individuals remained creative and flexible regarding their gestural repertoires for their entire lives. In contrast, foraging techniques in the Lomas Barbudal population were acquired at a young age, and the greatest social influence upon the acquisition of these techniques occurred during the first 3 years. For *Luehea* processing in *C. capucinus*, the technique that predominated at age 5 remained the dominant technique (i.e. the technique used more than 95% of the time) for the rest of the animal's life.

6.7 Conclusions

Research on social learning in capuchins has yielded ample evidence for traditions in wild populations as well as evidence for various social-learning mechanisms in captive *Cebus*. There appear to be species differences in the propensities to create different types of traditions, with *C. apella* showing a greater propensity for material culture (especially in marginal habitats) and the more coalition-oriented *C. capucinus* developing more social conventions, apparently for the purpose of testing social bonds. Capuchins selectively observe models best capable of conveying knowledge they lack. They converge behaviourally with those whom they observe, particularly if they have high-quality relationships with the models. Thus far, there is no evidence that capuchins exhibit complex cumulative culture, social norms or ethnic markers.

Acknowledgements

I would like to thank the following people for contributing data to the Lomas Barbudal monkey project's long-term database from 2002 to 2008: B. Barrett, L. Beaudrot, M. Bergstrom, A. Bjorkman, L. Blankenship, J. Broesch, J. Butler, F. Campos, C. Carlson, N. Donati, G. Dower, R. Dower, K. Feilen, A. Fuentes J., M. Fuentes, C. Gault, H. Gilkenson, I. Godoy, S. Herbert, S. Hyde, E. Johnson, L. Johnson, M. Kay, E. Kennedy, D. Kerhoas-Essens, S. Kessler, T. Lord, W. Lammers, S. Leinwand, M. Mayer, W. Meno, M. Milstein, C. Mitchell, C. O'Connell, J. C. Ordoñez J., N. Parker, B. Pav, K. Potter, K. Ratliff, J. Rottman, H. Ruffler, I. Schamberg, C. Schmitt, S. Schulze, J. Vandermeer, J. Verge, A. Walker Bolton, E. Williams and J. Williams. I am particularly grateful to H. Gilkenson and W. Lammers for managing the field site. The Lomas Barbudal field site was supported by the Max Planck Institute for Evolutionary Anthropology, and by grants to S.P. from the National Science Foundation (grant nos 0613226 and 6812640), the National Geographic Society and the L.S.B. Leakey Foundation. Any opinions, findings and conclusions or recommendations expressed in this material are those of the author and do not necessarily reflect the views of the National Science Foundation or other funding agencies. The Costa Rican park service (SINAC), the Area de Conservacion Tempisque-Arenal (MINAET), Hacienda Pelon de la Bajura, Hacienda Brin D'Amor and the residents of San Ramon de Bagaces granted permission to work on their land. J. Manson, R. Lesure and K. Kajokaite provided useful comments and discussion.

Endnotes

1   There is a correlation between observation and proficiency of target, but not between nut-cracking frequency and proficiency.

2   The reverse is also true: capuchins are more affiliative to humans who copy them [54].

References

1   Whiten, A., Goodall, J., McGrew, W. C., Nishida, T., Reynolds, V., Sugiyama, Y., Tutin, C. E. G., Wrangham, R. W. & Boesch, C. 1999 Cultures in chimpanzees. *Nature* **399**, 682–685.

2   Whiten, A. 2011 The scope of culture in chimpanzees, humans and ancestral apes. *Phil. Trans. R. Soc. B* **366**, 997–1007.

3   van Schaik, C. P., Ancrenaz, M., Borgen, W., Galdikas, B., Knott, C. D., Singleton, I., Suzuki, A., Utami, S. S. & Merrill, M. 2003 Orangutan cultures and the evolution of material culture. *Science* **299**, 102–105.

4   Wich, S., Atmoko, S. S. U., Setia, T. M. & van Schaik, C. P. 2009 *Orangutans: geographic variation in behavioral ecology and conservation.* Oxford, UK: Oxford University Press.

5   Itani, J. & Nishimura, A. 1973 The study of infrahuman culture in Japan: a review. In *Symp. of the IVth Int. Congress of Primatology. Vol. 1: Precultural primate behavior*, pp. 26–50. Basel, Switzerland: Karger.

6   Perry, S. & Manson, J. H. 2003 Traditions in monkeys. *Evol. Anthropol* **12**, 71–81.

7   Perry, S. *et al.* 2003 Traditions in wild white-faced capuchin monkeys. In *The biology of traditions: models and evidence* (eds D. Fragaszy & S. Perry), pp. 391–425. Cambridge, UK: Cambridge University Press.

8   Ottoni, E. & Izar, P. 2008 Capuchin monkey tool use: overview and implications. *Evol. Anthropol.* **17**, 171–178.

9   Fragaszy, D., Visalberghi, E. & Fedigan, L. M. 2004 *The complete capuchin: the biology of the genus Cebus.* Cambridge, UK: Cambridge University Press.

10   van Schaik, C. P., Deaner, R. O. & Merrill, M. Y. 1999 The condition for tool use in primates: implications for the evolution of material culture. *J. Hum. Evol* **36**, 719–741.

11   Perry, S. & Manson, J. H. 2008 *Manipulative monkeys: the capuchins of Lomas Barbudal.* Cambridge, MA: Harvard University Press.

12   Hakeem, A., Sandoval, R. G., Jones, M. & Allman, J. 1996 Brain and life span in primates. In *Handbook of the psychology of aging* (eds J. E. Birren & K. W. Schaie), pp. 78–104, 4th edn. San Diego, CA: Academic Press.

13   Stephan, H., Barbon, G. & Frahm, H. D. 1988 Comparative size of brains and brain components. In *Comparative primate biology* (eds H. D. Steklis & J. Erwin), pp. 1–39. New York, NY: Wiley-Liss.

14   Custance, D., Whiten, A. & Fredman, T. 1999 Social learning of an artificial fruit task in capuchin monkeys (*Cebus apella*). *J. Comp. Psych.* **113**, 13–23.

15   Dindo, M., Thierry, B. & Whiten, A. 2008 Social diffusion of novel foraging methods in capuchin monkeys (*Cebus apella*). *Proc. R. Soc. B* **275**, 187–193.

16   Dindo, M., Whiten, A. & de Waal, F. B. M. 2009 In-group conformity sustains different foraging traditions in capuchin monkeys (*Cebus apella*). *PLoS ONE* **4**, e7858.

17 Perry, S. & Ordoñez Jiménez, J. C. 2006 The effects of food size, rarity, and processing complexity on white-faced capuchins' visual attention to foraging con-specifics. In *Feeding ecology in apes and other primates* (eds G. Hohmann, M. Robbins & C. Boesch), pp. 203–234. Cambridge, UK: Cambridge University Press.

18 Byrne, R. W. 2007 Culture in great apes: using intricate complexity in feeding skills to trace the evolutionary origin of human technical prowess. *Phil. Trans. R. Soc. B* **362**, 577–585.

19 McGrew, W. C. 1992 *Chimpanzee material culture*. Cambridge, UK: Cambridge University Press.

20 Perry, S. *et al.* 2003 Social conventions in wild white-faced capuchin monkeys: evidence for traditions in a neotropical primate. *Curr. Anthropol.* **44**, 241–268.

21 Zahavi, A. 1977 The testing of a bond. *Anim. Behav.* **25**, 246–247.

22 Smuts, B. B. & Watanabe, J. M. 1990 Social relationships and ritualized greetings in adult male baboons (*Papio cynocephalus anubis*). *Int. J. Primatol.* **11**, 147–172.

23 Collins, R. 1983 Emotional energy as the common denominator of rational action. *Ration. Soc.* **5**, 203–230.

24 Palmer, C. T. & Pomianek, C. N. 2007 Applying signaling theory to traditional cultural rituals. *Hum. Nat.* **18**, 295–312.

25 Dunbar, R. 1993 Coevolution of neocortex size, group size and language in humans. *Behav. Brain Sci.* **16**, 681–735.

26 Gros-Louis, J. G., Perry, S. & Manson, J. H. 2003 Violent coalitionary attacks and intraspecific killing in wild capuchin monkeys (*Cebus capucinus*). *Primates* **44**, 341–346.

27 Perry, S. 2003 Coalitionary aggression in white-faced capuchins, *Cebus capucinus*. In *Animal social complexity: intelligence, culture and individualized societies* (eds F. B. M. de Waal & P. Tyack), pp. 111–114. Cambridge, MA: Harvard University Press.

28 Perry, S., Barrett, H. C. & Manson, J. H. 2004 White-faced capuchin monkeys exhibit triadic awareness in their choice of allies. *Anim. Behav.* **67**, 165–170.

29 Visalberghi, E. & Addessi, E. 2000 Seeing group members eating a familiar food enhances the acceptance of novel foods in capuchin monkeys. *Anim. Behav.* **60**, 69–76.

30 Visalberghi, E. & Addessi, E. 2001 Acceptance of novel foods in *Cebus apella*: do specific social facilitation and visual stimulus enhancement play a role? *Anim. Behav.* **62**, 567–576.

31 Fragaszy, D., Visalberghi, E. & Galloway, A. 1997 Infant tufted capuchin monkeys' behaviour with novel foods: opportunism, not selectivity. *Anim. Behav.* **53**, 1337–1343.

32 Ottoni, E. B., de Resende, B. D. & Izar, P. 2005 Watching the best nutcrackers: what capuchin monkeys (*Cebus apella*) know about others' tool-using skills. *Anim. Cogn.* **24**, 215–219.

33 Visalberghi, E. 1993 Tool use in a South American monkey species: an overview of the characteristics and limits of tool use in *Cebus apella*. In *The use of tools by human and non-human primates* (eds A. Berthelet & J. Chavaillon), pp. 118–131. Oxford, UK: Clarendon Press.

34 de Waal, F. B. M. 2001 *The ape and the sushi-master: cultural reflections of a primatologist*. Cambridge, MA: Harvard University Press.

35 de Waal, F. B. M. & Bonnie, K. E. 2009 In tune with others: the social side of culture. In *The question of animal culture* (eds K. Laland & B. G. Galef), pp. 19–40. Cambridge, MA: Harvard University Press.

36 Panger, M., Perry, S., Rose, L., Gros-Louis, J., Vogel, E., MacKinnon, K. & Baker, M. 2002 Cross-site differences in the foraging behavior of white-faced capuchin monkeys (*Cebus capucinus*). *Am. J. Phys. Anthropol.* **119**, 52–66.

37 Humle, T. & Matsuzawa, T. 2002 Ant-dipping among the chimpanzees of Bossou, Guinea, and some comparisons with other sites. *Am. J. Primatol.* **58**, 133–148.

38 O'Malley, R. C. & Fedigan, L. M. 2005 Evaluating social influences on food processing behavior in white-faced capuchins (*Cebus capucinus*). *Am. J. Phys. Anthropol.* **127**, 481–491.

39 Matthews, L. 2009 Intragroup behavioral variation in white-fronted capuchin monkeys (*Cebus albifrons*): mixed evidence for social learning inferred from new and established analytical methods. *Behaviour* **146**, 295–324.

40 Perry, S. 2009 Conformism in the food processing techniques of white-faced capuchin monkeys (*Cebus capucinus*). *Anim. Cogn.* **12**, 705–717.

41 Panger, M. A. 1998 Object-use in free-ranging white-faced capuchins (*Cebus capucinus*) in Costa Rica. *Am. J. Phys. Anthropol.* **106**, 311–321.

42 Lonsdorf, E., Eberly, L. E. & Pusey, A. E. 2004 Sex differences in learning in chimpanzees. *Nature* **428**, 715–716.

43 Perry, S. 1996 Female–female social relationships in wild white-faced capuchin monkeys, *Cebus capucinus. Am. J. Primatol* **40**, 167–182.

44 Bonnie, K. E. & de Waal, F. B. M. 2007 Copying without rewards: socially influenced foraging decisions among brown capuchin monkeys. *Anim. Cogn.* **10**, 283–292.

45 Mannu, M. & Ottoni, E. B. 2009 The enhanced tool-kit of two groups of wild bearded capuchin monkeys in the caatinga: tool making, associative use, and secondary tools. *Am. J. Primatol.* **71**, 242–251.

46 Moura, A. C. A. & Lee, P. 2004 Capuchin stone tool use in caatinga dry forest. *Science* **306**, 1909.

47 Boinski, S. 1988 Use of a club by a wild white-faced capuchin (*Cebus capucinus*) to attack a venomous snake (*Bothrops asper*). *Am. J. Primatol.* **14**, 177–179.

48 Herrenschmidt, M. 2007 Object manipulation in captive white-faced capuchins (*Cebus capucinus*) and tufted capuchins (*Cebus apella*). Masters thesis, Roehampton University, London, UK.

49 Ferreira, R. G., Izar, P. & Lee, P. C. 2006 Exchange, affiliation, and protective interventions in semifree-ranging brown capuchin monkeys (*Cebus apella*). *Am. J. Primatol.* **68**, 765–776.

50 Mercader, J., Panger, M. & Boesch, C. 2002 Excavation of a chimpanzee stone tool site in the African rainforest. *Science* **296**, 1452–1455.

51 Visalberghi, E., Fragaszy, D., Ottoni, E., Izar, P., de Oliveira, M. G. & Andrade, F. R. D. 2007 Characteristics of hammer stones and anvils used by wild bearded capuchin monkeys (*Cebus libidinosus*) to crack open palm nuts. *Am. J. Phys. Anthropol.* **132**, 426–444.

52 Veblen, T. 1899/1994 *The theory of the leisure class*. New York, NY: Penguin.

53 Bell, Q. 1992 *On human finery*. London, UK: Allison & Busby.

54 Paukner, A., Suomi, S. J., Visalberghi, E. & Perrari, P. F. 2009 Capuchin monkeys display affiliation toward humans who imitate them. *Science* **325**, 880–883.

Chapter 7

The Scope of Culture in Chimpanzees, Humans and Ancestral Apes*

Andrew Whiten

More studies have focused on aspects of chimpanzee behaviour and cognition relevant to the evolution of culture than on any other species except our own. Accordingly, analysis of the features shared by chimpanzees and humans is here used to infer the scope of cultural phenomena in our last common ancestor, at the same time clarifying the nature of the special characteristics that advanced further in the hominin line. To do this, culture is broken down into three major aspects: the large scale, population-level patterning of traditions; social learning mechanisms; and the behavioural and cognitive contents of culture. Each of these is further dissected into subcomponents. Shared features, as well as differences, are identified in as many as a dozen of these, offering a case study for the comparative analysis of culture across animal taxa and a deeper understanding of the roots of our own cultural capacities.

Keywords: culture; traditions; cultural evolution; social learning; apes; chimpanzees

7.1 Introduction

From the perspective of our now-voluminous data [1] it is extraordinary that half a century ago, virtually nothing was known about wild chimpanzees, the animals with whom we share the most recent common ancestry. Today, we have a fund of evidence about the cultural nature of our sister genus that appears unrivalled in animal behaviour and exceeded only by our knowledge of human cultures. Applying the comparative method to reconstruct the scope of culture in the common ancestors of humans and chimpanzees may thus offer a more comprehensive analysis than is yet feasible for other animal groups. This is a prime aim of the current chapter. However, no less important are the conceptual and empirical tools developed in doing this, which should be applicable to similar exercises across the animal kingdom, as the necessary data accumulate.

* Electronic supplementary material is available at http://dx.doi.org/10.1098/rstb.2010.0334 or via http://rstb.royalsocietypublishing.org.

Both the popular and scientific press often ask whether a particular species 'has culture'. Rather than assume the unitary conception of culture this implies, I dissect cultural phenomena into several major and subsidiary subcomponents organized within a hierarchically structured taxonomy, so as to compare species on each component. This leaves open for empirical investigation whether certain subcomponents vary together in systematic ways across species, or instead evolve in mosaic-like fashion, shaped perhaps by different phylogenetic and ecological factors.

Explorations of this approach in recent years have themselves evolved [2–4] and continue to do so here. However, distinguishing three main classes of variation among cultural phenomena has emerged as a resilient taxonomic approach. The first of these three classes concerns the patterned distribution of traditions in space and time. For this I adopt Fragaszy & Perry's [5, p. xiii] definition of a tradition, namely 'A distinctive behaviour pattern shared by two or more individuals in a social unit, which persists over time and that new practitioners acquire in part through socially aided learning'. As noted in this collection's introduction [6] (here, Chapter 1), this definition can and should accommodate at least two continua, whereby traditions become more *substantial* as they spread from a minimum of two individuals, across potentially large communities or populations, and more *enduring* as they last longer, potentially persisting across generations. Such variance is inherent in this first class of analyses. In the present chapter, my emphasis is on traditions that have spread to become common in a community and are relatively enduring.

The second category in my taxonomy concerns the varied processes by which social learning can occur, such as imitation or teaching. The third class focuses on the content of cultural phenomena, such as action-types (e.g. 'tool use'), ideas and beliefs.

If we imagine comparing the scope of culture in two or more species, we can appreciate that a high degree of independent variation in each of these three classes may, in principle, be found. Thus, the two species might exhibit similar patterns in the distribution of their traditions (for example, displaying minimal cultural overlap between communities), whatever the transmission mechanisms and particular cultural contents involved. Likewise, they might or might not share certain processes like teaching, irrespective of the distribution of traditions and their content. Finally, specific cultural contents, such as tool use, might vary independently of the other two classes.

Although it would be relevant for more wide-ranging comparisons across the animal kingdom to assess evidence for the very existence of traditions in each taxon, for economy I here take the existence of tradition *per se* (and thence some kind of social learning) for the species of interest (i.e. humans and chimpanzees) as a well-established given [4, 7]. This means that each subcomponent of the three major classes dissected here (Figure 7.1) is selected to address some way in which human culture clearly goes beyond the mere existence of a tradition, and about which recent empirical discoveries about similar cultural phenomena in chimpanzees and human children allow comparisons with real interest to be made. A central goal of doing this is to establish both the shared features parsimoniously attributed to our common ancestry, and those which differ, reflecting changes since the ancestral divergence about 6–7 Myr ago.

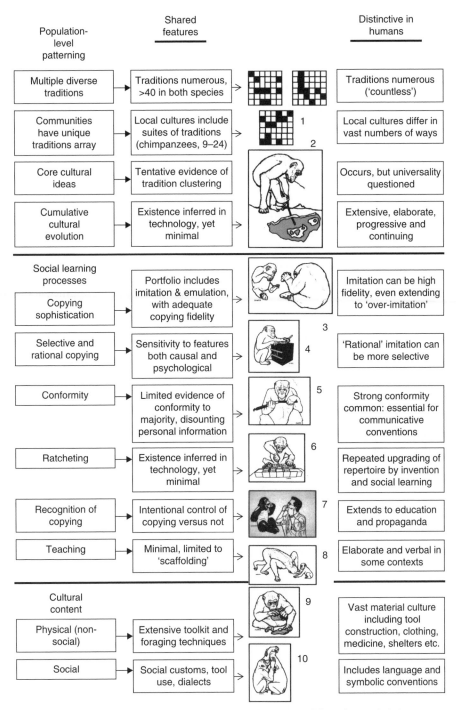

Figure 7.1 Features of culture shared by chimpanzees, humans and (by inference) their common ancestor, and features of culture distinctive in humans. Features (rows) are nested under three main headings (see text for extended discussion). Images represent examples discussed in the text: further explanation for each numbered image is given in the electronic supplementary material.

Note that in this procedure, it is not being assumed that the common ancestor was particularly chimpanzee-like [8]; the crucial inferences about ancestry instead rely upon cultural features that are shared by the descendant taxa. Of course, species may share features because of convergent evolution rather than common descent, but when the features are shared by a closely related group of species, the parsimonious inference is that this is due to shared ancestry—the underlying logic of the comparative method in biology. Such inferences can be argued to be stronger the larger the related clade of taxa becomes; feathers and wings are confidently attributed to the common avian ancestor. From this perspective, inferences about the common ancestor of just two sister species (human and chimpanzee) must be viewed as more tentative. In some of what follows, it is possible to go beyond this to stronger inferences about the common cultural ancestry of the whole great ape clade (henceforth 'apes'), but at present a greater range of data is available to explore human–chimpanzee commonalities specifically.

7.2 Comparing chimpanzee and human cultures

In the following, I address the three major classes of cultural variation outlined above in turn, and within each, a series of nested subcomponents.

7.2.1 Variation among traditions in time and space

Culture is by its very nature a community-level phenomenon, minimally defined above by traditions shared by at least two individuals, but typically many more. When we talk of different human cultures we refer to attributes of communities, typically contrasted either regionally (e.g. Scottish versus Chinese) or across historical time (e.g. Scottish culture in the twentieth century versus the tenth century). Within the first of these contrasts, note that different (sub)cultures may coexist within a larger local population [9]. Four aspects of variation in the patterning of traditions in time and space are distinguished.

7.2.1.1 Existence of multiple and diverse traditions

Many of the published examples of traditions in fishes, birds and mammals concern only a single pattern of behaviour, such as birdsong dialect [10] or pine-cone stripping in black rats [11]. Human culture differs from this in encompassing countless variations, spanning a huge diversity of behaviour, technology, ideas and much else. No other species comes close to this. However, multiple traditions have been identified in some species, and chimpanzees have provided evidence for the greatest number, which also span a diversity of behavioural domains including foraging techniques, tool use, social behaviour and sexual courtship. Systematically identifying these by pooling data across field sites and excluding environmental and genetic explanations for the differences led to an initial count of 39 traditions [12], since significantly expanded by supplementary studies [3, 7, 13–15], although a formal synthesis of these accumulating cases remains in progress.

So far, it has not proved possible to contrive field experiments to test the social learning inferred to underlie these putative traditions. Indeed, only recently was the first such field experiment achieved for any wild primate, with alternative techniques for opening 'artificial fruits' introduced into different vervet monkey groups. The subsequent spread of these techniques in their respective groups clearly implicated social learning [16]. However, it was with captive chimpanzees that an extensive battery of these primate 'diffusion experiments' was first developed [17–20][1]. These experiments confirmed that chimpanzees can sustain multiple traditions transmitted from group to group, each spreading across over 20 individuals ([20]; Figure 7.2), a finding consistent with the inferences drawn about the cultural nature of wild chimpanzees.

The number and diversity of behavioural traditions described for chimpanzees are of course more than matched among humans. Among non-human species, it has only been significantly approached by another great ape, the orangutan, for whom over 30 different traditions have been described, again spanning behavioural diversity that ranges from tool use to social communication [21]. Among other species, it is other primates, notably capuchin monkeys [22], that have revealed multiple and diverse traditions, but enumeration of these suggests less-rich cultures than in orangutans and chimpanzees [23]. Accordingly, on the basis of the comparisons described above, the scope of culture in the

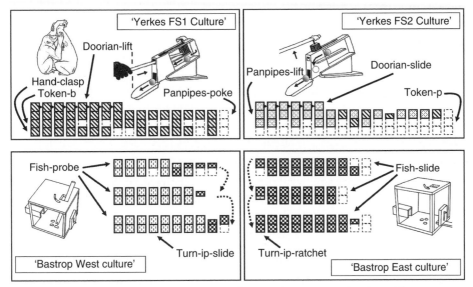

Figure 7.2 Spread of experimentally seeded, multiple traditions generating four chimpanzee 'cultures'. At each pair of locations, alternative techniques were experimentally seeded in a single individual and spread locally. Each column represents a single chimpanzee, with hatching corresponding to the alternative techniques seeded in the leftmost individual in each case. At Yerkes, row 1 = *lift* versus *slide* methods to open door in 'doorian fruit', run as a diffusion chain [18]; row 2 = *poke* versus *lift* panpipes techniques spread in an open (unconstrained) diffusion [17]; row 3 = *bucket* versus *pipe* posting option for tokens in an open diffusion [19]; row 4 = hand-clasp grooming, which arose and spread spontaneously in only Yerkes FS1 community. At Bastrop, row 1 = *fish-probe* versus *fish-slide* techniques; row 2 = *turn-ip-slide* versus *turn-ip-ratchet* techniques, used to extract food from two different devices; each technique spread to a second group (middle) and then a third (bottom) [20].

chimpanzee–human common ancestor is inferred as incorporating numerous and diverse traditions.[2] The orangutan data additionally suggest the principal evolutionary step towards this complexity existed already in the common ancestor of all the great apes, approximately 14 Ma (equivalent studies for gorillas have yet to be published, and remain limited for bonobos [24]).

7.2.1.2 Local cultures incorporating, and differentiated by, multiple traditions

Not only do chimpanzees as a species evidence numerous traditions, but also each community displays its own unique cultural profile, defined by a subset of traditions. Accordingly, as for humans, if enough of a chimpanzee's behaviour is observed, that individual can be assigned to its community on the basis of its cultural profile. Importantly, this has been replicated in the experimental studies noted above, where four different chimpanzee 'cultures' emerged, each defined by multiple, experimentally initiated traditions shown to spread by social learning (Figure 7.2). Local cultures incorporating and differentiated by multiple traditions are thus also inferred in the chimpanzee–human common ancestor.

Although the adaptive significance of many such patterns in living chimpanzees remains to be formally established, the majority that involve food processing manifestly yield access to sources not otherwise available, in many cases through tool use. For some of the latter, there is evidence this carries the community through seasonal nutritional bottlenecks [25]. A potentially important implication of the cultural richness outlined above is thus that there should be a significant selection pressure on the underlying cultural abilities. These have clearly been massively selected for in the cultural learning capacities of our own species [26–29], but Whiten & van Schaik [23] suggested that selection for cultural knowledge acquisition and storage may also help explain great apes' distinctively high degree of encephalization among primates (the 'cultural intelligence' hypothesis [23, 30]).

A further implication of chimpanzees' cultural niche is that more often than in other species, immigrating adolescents or adults (most typically females, in apes) from other communities may be the bearers of cultural variants not yet known locally, from which residents may learn. Conversely, immigrants may observe cultural variants new to them, and learn them. For example, when T. Matsuzawa and co-workers introduced novel nuts into a community in West Africa that uses hammer stones and anvils to crack nuts, just one female was quick to crack these new nuts, inferred to be a known habit in the community from which she had emigrated. Over several years, the new nuts came to be routinely cracked by most of the population [31]. Studies of subtly different grooming techniques in adjacent communities have also shown immigrant females adopting the local approach of their new community, with one female adapting her existing technique and in turn eliciting some corresponding adaptation in the residents who groomed with her [32].

7.2.1.3 Linkage of traditions through core cultural ideas

The above analyses view cultures in terms of multiple independent traditions that can be enumerated to facilitate species comparisons. Although this basic approach was also used in the earliest twentieth-century analyses of human cultures by anthropologists, this was later challenged by the view that a set of core ideas links together suites of local cultural phenomena, such that a culture is 'an organization of ideas rather than aggregate of independent traits' [33]. Examples include an individualistic and analytic world view in the west, contrasted with more holistic and collective orientations in eastern cultures that pervade many different aspects of cognition and behaviour [34]. This view, although challenged by others in turn [35], is sufficiently central to many cultural anthropologists' conception of culture (see 'core principles' in [36]) that it begs to be addressed from the comparative perspective.

Doing so is clearly a challenge, since much of the evidence for 'cultural cores' in the human case appears fundamentally verbal, even if sometimes constrained by sanctions that can include non-verbal actions [36]. Whiten et al. [2] suggested that the central hypothesis can perhaps be best addressed for non-verbal animals like chimpanzees by testing whether particular local communities have underlying cognitive representations that steer them towards particular cultural options. It was suggested that differences between some West African chimpanzee communities that display extensive and varied tool use, and others in East Africa that display a poverty of tool use, might reflect an underlying cognitive orientation in the former to see new problems as calling for a variant on their tool repertoire. The alternative that the East/West difference is primarily genetic [37] is countered by a recent experiment showing that East African, non-nutcracking chimpanzees can become proficient in cracking nuts by observing existing experts [38]. Lycett et al. [39] have also completed a series of numerical phylogenetic analyses of the distribution of behavioural variation among chimpanzee communities that they conclude is incompatible with genetic explanations.

A recent experiment that may address the hypothesis of cultural 'cores' more directly presented a novel experimental situation—honey in a vertically drilled hole in a fallen log—to two different chimpanzee communities in Uganda [40]. One community habitually uses sticks and stems for gaining water from tree holes, and they applied a similar technique to the new honey source. A second community that does not use sticks as tools, but does make masticated leaf-sponges to gain water from tree-holes, instead applied this method (with less success) to the new problem. The interpretation of Gruber et al. [40], summarized in their title, is that 'Wild chimpanzees rely on [their] cultural knowledge to solve an experimental honey acquisition task'. More evidence is required to test this interpretation, but it is consistent with the essence of the 'core cultural ideas' principle, in which certain behavioural variants are proposed to be cognitively linked, rather than mere cultural 'beans in a bag'.

7.2.1.4 Cumulative cultural evolution

Human cultural achievements have progressively and repeatedly built upon earlier ones to create the vast complexity and variety in our cultures of today, including technologies, languages and social institutions [41, 42]. In the view of some, such cumulative cultural evolution is essentially absent in other species [43]. Others argue for the existence of cumulative culture in animals [7], but the cases discussed appear rudimentary compared with the achievements of humans [41, 42, 44].

A good example that implies accumulation but at the same time illustrates the 'rudimentary' epithet comes from recent studies of tool use by chimpanzees in the Goualougo locality of central Africa. Sanz *et al.* [45] described how these chimpanzees first drive a stout stick deep into the earth (often aided by combined foot and hand pressure), puncturing a channel into a subterranean termite nest. They then modify one of several stems they have brought to the site, fraying the end by drawing it through their teeth to create a brush tip, then carefully inserting this down the channel to fish for termites. The brush tip makes fishing more efficient. This multi-stage procedure is unknown in other communities, where termite-fishing chimpanzees often bite off the ends of used probes, rather than fraying them. Sanz *et al.* therefore conclude that the Goualougo technique must have been elaborated by cumulative modification of the more basic technique observed elsewhere. This conclusion seems compelling. Indeed, the first evidence of hominins exceeding such cumulative achievements did not become apparent until the manufacture of bifaced Acheulian stone tools around 1.6 Ma [46].

Why cumulative culture is so minimal in non-human species remains poorly understood. It is possible that no particular kinds of accumulation could significantly enhance their technologies and their reproductive success in the ecological niches they successfully exploit. Recent experimental work that focuses instead on the possible role of biases in social learning of chimpanzees versus humans is discussed in §7.2.2.4, below.

7.2.2 Social learning processes

Galef [47] urged that unless processes as sophisticated as those assumed to transmit human culture (notably imitation and teaching) could be shown to underlie a species' traditions, the term 'culture' should be eschewed in favour of talk of 'traditions' only. Over the last century, a considerable range of social learning processes has been identified and those available to any one species are likely to shape the scope of culture in that species. For example, if a species is limited only to stimulus enhancement, where an observer simply has its attention drawn to certain objects or locations by another, it may be able to sustain traditions favouring such foci, but it will not be able to acquire novel behavioural techniques that require imitative copying. In the following, I compare chimpanzee social learning to some of the more sophisticated forms such learning can take in the human case.

7.2.2.1 Copying sophistication and fidelity

Over the last two decades a debate has unfolded, fuelled by numerous ingenious and revealing studies, about whether social learning in chimpanzees can accurately be described as imitation or emulation, and how this may constrain their cultures. Imitation and emulation have been defined, respectively, as the copying of others' actions, versus copying of only the results of those actions, with chimpanzees characterized as dependent on emulation, in contrast with the high imitative competence of children [44, 48]. Such a difference could have important implications for the nature of culture in the two species. If chimpanzees rely only on emulation, there should be little scope for the transmission of behavioural techniques or gestural communication. Indeed, the fidelity of copying that distinguishes imitation has been argued to be crucial to facilitate cumulative cultural evolution, which first requires accurate copying across generations, on which progressive elaborations can be built. Accordingly, humanity's unique capacity for cumulative culture has been linked to imitative prowess, suggested to be lacking in chimpanzees [25].

Accumulating studies have converged towards a consensus across research groups that the imitative ability and motivation of children are indeed typically superior to that of chimpanzees [43, 49]. However, several lines of evidence have led our research group to question whether this represents the stark species dichotomy outlined above. First, the chimpanzee diffusion experiments (Figure 7.2) have demonstrated a capacity to sustain different traditional techniques applied to the same foraging task, in different groups. For example, Whiten *et al.* [20] found that for each of two different tasks, one dependent on tool use, the other on a sequence of two separate sets of manipulations, alternative techniques seeded in different groups were maintained not only in the original groups but also were transmitted by observational learning across two further groups. To be sure, the copying fidelity involved (Figure 7.2) does not match the perfect transmission of 'panpipes' techniques along a chain of 20 individuals that we recorded in children [50]. Nevertheless, the differential spread of techniques across two sets of three groups [20] shows that chimpanzees have sufficient copying fidelity for the inter-community spread of complex behavioural techniques, consistent with the picture for African chimpanzees inferred from field observations. Moreover, our first replications of 'open' diffusion experiments with groups of young children revealed patterns more similar to those seen in chimpanzees: initial differentiation of traditional techniques was followed by a degree of corruption as some children discovered the technique seeded in the other group [51].

These experimental results for chimpanzees can aptly be described in terms of 'copying', because quite elaborate techniques are being replicated as they spread across communities. However, that might still rely on high-fidelity *emulation*, with learning focusing on the way the foraging devices operate to deliver food rewards. One approach to testing this hypothesis has been through 'ghost' experiments, which remove the model from the scene and display only the object movements the model would normally cause, which is what an emulation hypothesis suggests the apes are actually learning from. When this was done with the panpipes (Figure 7.2), using fishing line to create the normal effects of tool use in delivering food rewards, chimpanzees showed a stark absence of learning [52]. This contrasts markedly with the learning evidenced in the earlier open diffusion study, where chimpanzees could observe existing tool users in action [17]. This implies copying actions is important. With a much simpler task that involved only a small door being slid to one side or the other to reveal a food reward, Hopper *et al.* [53] elicited the first evidence for emulation in such a ghost experiment with primates, but the effect was fleeting (trial-1 only) and subjects then explored either way to slide the door. This contrasted strikingly with a condition in which a chimpanzee acted as the model, when the direction in which the model slid the door was copied in 99 per cent of trials. Hopper *et al.* [53] concluded that emulation evidenced in this ghost context may operate with respect to the simpler tasks, but for those more challenging to chimpanzee intelligence, observing individuals need to gain information on how another individual actually performs the crucial actions, together with its desirable outcome.

7.2.2.2 Selective and 'rational' copying

One way in which human imitation evidences sophistication is in selectivity, which has been identified in a number of different guises. These include what has been called 'rational imitation'. In one example, even infants tended to copy a model's novel and bizarre action of using their head to butt a noise-making device so long as the model's hands were free, but not if the hands were occupied, such as in holding a blanket round one's shoulders [54]. Buttelmann *et al.* [55] have subsequently demonstrated a similar phenomenon in what they call 'enculturated' chimpanzees (having extensive interaction with human caretakers), although the effect was weaker than in child studies, consistent with child/chimpanzee contrasts in social learning outlined above. The same authors failed to find such selective copying in non-enculturated (mother-reared) chimpanzees, although they did record it in non-enculturated orangutans [56].

Selectivity has also been identified in relation to evidence for physical causality in what children witness. For example, Lyons *et al.* [28] have shown that children would not copy an adult's actions on an object physically separate from another where the adult then achieved a desirable goal. Similarly, Horner & Whiten [57] showed that young chimpanzees were significantly less likely to copy aspects of tool use that could be seen to be physically separate from desirable outcomes compared with those displaying contact with such outcomes (gaining food). When an apparatus was used that was identical except that it was opaque, masking the lack of physical connection between tool and outcome, chimpanzees instead tended to incorporate such actions into a more complete imitation of the elaborate sequence they witnessed. This demonstrated a flexible capacity to switch between imitative and emulative modes of social learning, according to context.

Laland [58] has described selective social learning in terms of different learning 'strategies' concerning when and from whom to learn. Such flexibility appears increasingly to be widespread in the animal kingdom [59]. The child and chimpanzee studies described above illustrate selectivity resting on relatively complex cognitive distinctions in relation to rationality of actions in others, and plausibility of physical causation. These illustrate selectivity in what Laland distinguishes as 'when' to copy, in relation to structural aspects of what the observer witnesses. We have recently completed an experiment ([60], see also [29, 61] that focuses instead on 'whom' to copy [58]). In an earlier diffusion experiment we noted that one low-ranking individual generated an action different from the rest of her group—yet she was not copied by others [19]. To further explore this apparent selectivity in copying, we tested the preference of chimpanzees to copy the behaviour of a model that was either high ranking, with a strong track record of being a useful model to copy, or low ranking with no such record [60]. In each of two groups, chimpanzees showed a significant preference to copy the first of these two options. In humans, similar effects are described as a bias to copy individuals with high prestige [62]. The preference displayed by the chimpanzees does not imply that exactly the same cognitive processes are involved,[3] but it does demonstrate a basic bias shared between the two species. Its function in chimpanzees is not known, but Horner *et al.* [60] note that the preference demonstrated is likely to involve learning from a model who often achieves particularly beneficial outcomes.

7.2.2.3 Conformity

In humans, the motivation to be like others can lead to extreme degrees of conformity, long studied by social psychologists [63]. Such conformity can take various forms, such as following the majority, or copying others despite personal experience favouring an alternative course of action.

Whiten *et al.* [17] first attached the term 'conformity' to chimpanzee social learning on finding that, after some individuals discovered the non-seeded behavioural option in a diffusion experiment, they showed a significant tendency to 'return to the fold' and match the behaviour of the majority of their group (the experimentally seeded technique) at a later time. An allied effect was obtained in a recent study in which we tested chimpanzees' ability to learn from conspecific models how to combine two sticks into a long tool that could be used to rake in distant food [64]. Most subjects could learn this only from others, but a few achieved the combination by their own individual efforts. The surprising later finding was that when flexibility of action was tested by arranging problems in which the tool was not needed (target within manual reach), chimpanzees who had learned individually did not make a long tool, whereas those who had learned socially tended to persist in making and using the now-redundant long tool. Price *et al.* [64] described this as a particularly 'potent' effect of social learning.

Whether such potency, as suggested by these studies, is special among chimpanzees, as well as humans, remains to be established. Galef & Whiskin [65], responding to the chimpanzee conformity study [17], showed that in rats, such potency appears sufficiently strong that individual experience, even the consequences of eating highly noxious foods, will be rejected in favour of others' observed preferences for the food. What we are seeing in the above chimpanzee and human results may not be a special potency of social learning *per se* (perhaps widespread among animals in certain ecological conditions), but rather its interaction with the more elaborate forms of social learning, notably copying complex forms of action such as tool use.

7.2.2.4 Ratcheting versus conservatism

In §7.2.1, it was noted that a major contrast between human and non-human cultures lies in the inflated role of progressive accumulation in humans. Tomasello *et al.* [48] suggested that the contrast is explained by chimpanzees' tendency to emulate rather than imitate.

However, the diffusion experiments outlined above cast doubt on whether copying fidelity constrains cumulative culture in chimpanzees. A recent experiment [66] accordingly attempted to directly test chimpanzees' capacity for cumulative social learning. Young chimpanzees first learned, by observation, to open a cover in a honey dispenser and extract honey using a probe. They then observed a more complex approach in which the probe was first used to free a lid, so the probe could be inserted into the usual hole to lever open the lid and gain access to both nuts and honey. Despite this greater payoff, the second, cumulative step was not learned, although control conditions showed it was within chimpanzees' capability. Young children, by contrast, were later shown to acquire the second step [49]. It may be, then, that a cognitive capacity for progressive social learning of the kind needed in this study arose only much later in the hominin line, and was limited in our common ancestors. Other experimental studies have identified a similar conservatism in chimpanzee social learning, convergent with that described above [67].

7.2.2.5 Recognition of copying

Older children become increasingly able to play copying games ('Simon says') that rely on knowing what imitation is. Evidence that chimpanzees have an appreciation of the same kind comes from their ability to learn, and be tested in a 'Do-as-I-do' paradigm in which having grasped the rule to copy on a command like 'Do this!', they evidence copying of novel actions. Apes (both chimpanzees and orangutans) have shown a proficiency in mastering this, where extensive parallel efforts with monkeys failed [2, 68]. This apparently meta-cognitive grasp of the nature of copying may accordingly represent a significant achievement that appeared only in the common ancestor of the great ape clade.

7.2.2.6 Teaching

Galef [48] expressed a common view that teaching may be a distinctive characteristic of social learning in humans. To the extent that much human teaching is verbal, that is probably correct, although it has been suggested that a lack of teaching in hunter–gatherer societies may mean that teaching has not figured as much in the evolution of human cultures as those of us living in societies with formal schooling might assume ([2], but see [27, 69]).

We tend to think of teaching in humans in intentional terms—as based upon an intent to inform or educate a person in the role of pupil. However, if this intentional element is replaced as a criterion by its functional equivalent—actions that serve to support the development of competencies in a pupil, at some cost to the teacher—then we find that recent studies offer evidence of teaching in a wide variety of species [9, 70]. Such behaviour is little in evidence in chimpanzees and other apes. At most it seems to extend to tolerant support of difficult skills like nutcracking, where mothers donate tools and nuts to their offspring [71]. Arguably better evidence for such functional teaching in primates comes from callitrichid monkeys, which like meerkats [9] may draw the attention of youngsters to prey and make it available to them [72]. The contrast may appear strange from the socio-cognitive perspective, since recent evidence suggests chimpanzees have a sufficiently sophisticated 'theory of mind' to recognize ignorance in others [73], supporting intentional teaching. However, from a functional and ecological perspective the contrast may make more sense. Functional-level teaching appears often to be found in species for whom such challenges as hunting live prey is obligatory, and may help young make the leap from incompetence to the highly skilled abilities required for success. By contrast, a more gradual transition to adult competence is feasible for an animal with the dietary profile of a chimpanzee, including all the forms of tool use employed in this quest. Hoppitt *et al.* [70] suggest that particularly well-developed observational learning capacities in chimpanzees may counter pressures for teaching that are more significant in some other taxa.

7.2.3 Cultural content

From the perspective of biocultural anthropology, Hill [44] suggests two major differences between human culture and its closest matches in non-humans. The first is cumulative culture, discussed in §7.2.1.4 above. The second concerns what I shall refer to as the specific *contents* of culture, where Hill picks out human 'symbolic reinforcement of particular systems of rules and institutions that regulate behaviour' (p. 285) as distinctive. But one can list a considerable range of other cultural contents that are special even to those human cultures in which the total material contents can be carried on nomadic hunter–gatherers' backs. These include such aspects of material culture as hafted and other, multi-component weapons and other tools, clothing, fire and medicines; and social components ranging from language itself to ceremonial behaviour, dance, music and religion. Murdock *et al.* [74] distinguished 569 subcategories of cultural contents used to compile the data of the human relations area files (HRAFs), including such examples (under a heading 'leather, textiles and fabrics') as work in skins, knots and lashings, mats and basketry and woven fabrics. Most of these 569 will not apply to chimpanzees, a measure of the species-gulf in cultural content. However, some chimpanzee cultural content may be absent in humans, such as certain grooming customs and forms of sexual courtship-like oral 'leaf-clipping' and other kinds of noisy vegetation-manipulation used to attract a potential partner's attention.[4]

Nevertheless, it is possible to start to identify features of cultural content that chimpanzees and humans share. These are probably most aptly described at some intermediate level of abstraction. For example, we shall not expect to see an act as specific as chimpanzee 'pestle pounding' of the growing points of palm trees in humans; what is shared is rather a tool culture that includes a range of such pounding tools as well as puncturing, probing and wiping tools, used for a diversity of functions that include aiding foraging (e.g. nut-cracking), comfort (e.g. leaf seats on wet ground) and hygiene (e.g. leaf wipes for blood, faeces or semen on the body). Shared contents of social behaviour appear less easy to identify, but include vocal differences between communities [75].

However, one might question whether such questions about content really address the core of cultural phenomena. Content differences in culture appear rather more to do with the range of behaviours that humans and chimpanzees, respectively (the first with brains three times larger than the latter's) can generate, and which are assimilated into those category (a) and (b) type cultural phenomena analysed earlier. Nevertheless, such content differences suggest some of the most striking differences when we compare the scope of cultures in the two species. They merit more systematic studies and comparisons in future.

7.3 Discussion

This chapter began by noting how little we knew of our closest relatives just a half century ago. Now we know so much that the scope of the three categories of findings summarized in Figure 7.1 is extensive indeed and based upon many scores of publications. I have aimed to illustrate some of the most significant of these discoveries, but it is important to stress that the depth and detail of our knowledge goes far beyond what can be summarized here, as perusal of the more extensive literature reviewed in the publications cited will demonstrate.

A central objective of this chapter is to identify significant similarities and differences between chimpanzee and human cultures in the categories indicated, using the similarities to make inferences about our common ancestor, and the differences to identify what has evolved after the split occurred. From this perspective we can distinguish two levels at which to assess the scientific robustness of the conclusions drawn. The first level concerns the facts of the matter in respect of present day humans, chimpanzees and the other reference species compared with them. The next level concerns second-order inferences to ancestral states, and these inferences must logically be viewed as inherently more tentative than the first-order ones upon which they are based. This makes it important to recognize that, although we now possess a vast archive of relevant chimpanzee (and human) observation and experiments, the conclusions about cultural ancestry that should properly be drawn from these remain contentious [76].

Acknowledging this, Figure 7.1 offers a summary of the conclusions I currently draw. At the level of population-level patterning, the shared features are principally the first two of the four listed, which reflect two aspects of cultural richness in terms of multiplicity of traditions. Insofar as this state of affairs is shared with orangutans but not, according to present data, so much with old world monkeys, inferences about its occurrence in our ancestry appears to be most probably attributable to the common ancestor of the great ape clade of about 14 Ma, rather than the earlier ancestor of these old world primates. Evidence for the second two features is minimal, but not non-existent, which suggests corresponding foundations on which later evolving cumulative culture and cognitive inter-linking could have built.

Two potential anomalies in this picture should be noted, however. One is that evidence to date has outlined only a much smaller set of multiple-tradition cultures in chimpanzees' sister species, the bonobo, especially concerning tool use [24]. Similarly there remains a dearth of information about potential gorilla culture. Both cases may, however, reflect relatively limited field studies, and/or lack of focused attention to the topic by the field workers concerned.

Turning to social learning processes, most of the features listed in Figure 7.1 necessarily remain focused upon human characteristics shared with chimpanzees, rather than apes as a group, because so many more studies have focused upon chimpanzees [68]. One apparently qualitatively distinct feature that has been documented in children, chimpanzees and orangutans but not in monkeys is the recognition of copying (§7.2.2.4). Perhaps, the more quantitatively distinct features, notably sophistication in copying, may be related to this. In such copying, it is not so much bodily imitation that is distinctive—that has been shown in birds [77]—but rather the complexity of manipulative techniques, both in the wild and that have been shown to be transmissible in the diffusion experiments summarized above. Indeed, the tool use copying shown in these has not been found in experiments with other taxa, including capuchin monkeys, despite the tool use this genus shows in the wild [72].

This may be of particular significance in relation to the cultural innovations documented in the chapters that follow this one, concerning early hominin stone tool making. Although the present chapter was at pains to distinguish several quasi-independent aspects of culture (Figure 7.1), their significance for our own cultural ancestry may have lain in specific links between them. In particular, we may infer a shared ancestor that used varied forms of 'power' tool (e.g. clubbing and pounding [78]), possibly extending to the unique style of percussive nut-cracking we still see socially learned in local chimpanzee cultures, or at least a special propensity to develop such a culture that evolving hominins took to such world-changing heights [41, 42, 46].

Acknowledgements

I thank the BBSRC, ESRC, Leverhulme Trust and The Royal Society for funding the studies by my research group summarized within this chapter. I am particularly grateful to Robert Hinde, Lydia Hopper, Victoria Horner, Sarah Marshall-Pescini and Bess Price for comments and discussions on the subject matter of this chapter.

Endnotes

[1] Later field experiments of this kind with other mammals are described in Thornton & Clutton-Brock [9].

[2] Langergraber *et al.* [37] have shown a correlation between variation in chimpanzees' behaviour patterns across Africa, and genetic variation, that they suggest weakens the inference that the variations are traditions. However, such a correlation would be expected for even as cultural a species as humans, at least before recent levels of migration and mixing (e.g. before 100 Ka) A fuller analysis of Langergraber *et al.* [37] is in the electronic supplementary material.

[3] Henrich & Gil-White [62] note that prestige in humans is not to be simply equated with dominance rank. Consistent with this, the demonstration that chimpanzees preferentially copied higher-ranked, experienced models [62], as well as treating these individuals with the respect in agonistic conflicts that defines high rank, suggests the kind of convergence in deference across contexts that signify prestige. Of course, this does not imply identical underlying cognitive mechanisms.

[4] An anthropologist reader of this chapter noted that the hunter–gatherer peoples he works with also 'sit in rows and groom each other and use vegetation noises to attract a potential partner'. Much remains to be systematically compared between the species, concerning the behavioural contents of cultures.

References

1 Lonsdorf, E. V., Ross, S. R. & Matsuzawa, T. (eds) 2010 *The mind of the chimpanzee: ecological and experimental perspectives*. Chicago, IL: Chicago University Press.

2 Whiten, A., Horner, V. & Marshall-Pescini, S. R. J. 2003 Cultural panthropology. *Evol. Anthropol.* **12**, 92–105.

3 Whiten, A. 2005 The second inheritance system of chimpanzees and humans. *Nature* **437**, 52–55.

4 Whiten, A. 2009 The identification of culture in chimpanzees and other animals: from natural history to diffusion experiments. In *The question of animal culture* (eds K. N. Laland & B. G. Galef), pp. 99–124. Cambridge, MA: Harvard University Press.

5 Fragaszy, D. M. & Perry, S. (eds) 2003 *The biology of traditions: models and evidence*. Cambridge, UK: Cambridge University Press.

6 Whiten, A., Hinde, R. A., Laland, K. N. & Stringer, C. B. 2011 Culture evolves. *Phil. Trans. R. Soc. B* **366**, 938–948.

7 McGrew, W. C. 2004 *The cultured chimpanzee: reflections on cultural primatology*. Cambridge, UK: Cambridge University Press.

8 Whiten, A. *et al.* 2010 Using extant species to model our past. *Science* **327**, 410.

9 Thornton, A. & Clutton-Brock, T. 2011 Social learning and the development of individual and group behaviour in mammal societies. *Phil. Trans. R. Soc. B* **366**, 978–987.

10 Catchpole, C. K. & Slater, P. J. B. 1995 *Bird song: biological themes and variations*. Cambridge, UK: Cambridge University Press.

11 Terkel, J. 1995 Cultural transmission in the black rat: pine-cone feeding. *Adv. Study Behav.* **24**, 119–154.

12 Whiten, A. *et al.* 1999 Cultures in chimpanzees. *Nature* **399**, 682–685.

13 Möbius, Y., Boesch, C., Koops, K., Matsuzawa, T. & Humle, T. 2008 Cultural differences in army ant predation by West African chimpanzees? A comparative study of microecological variables. *Anim. Behav.* **76**, 37–45.

14 Shöning, C., Humle, T., Möbius, Y. & McGrew, W. C. 2008 The nature of culture: technological variation in chimpanzee predation on army ants revisited. *J. Hum. Evol.* **55**, 48–59.

15 Whiten, A. 2010 Coming of age for cultural panthropology. In *The mind of the chimpanzee* (eds E. Lonsdorf, S. Ross & T. Matsuzawa). Chicago, IL: Chicago University Press.

16 van de Waal, E., Renevy, N., Favre, C. M. & Bshary, R. 2010 Selective attention to philopatric models causes directed social learning in wild vervet monkeys. *Proc. R. Soc. B* **277**, 2105–2111.

17 Whiten, A., Horner, V. & de Waal, F. B. M. 2005 Conformity to cultural norms of tool use in chimpanzees. *Nature* **437**, 737–740.

18 Horner, V., Whiten, A., Flynn, E. & de Waal, F. B. M. 2006 Faithful replication of foraging techniques along cultural transmission chains by chimpanzees and children. *Proc. Natl Acad. Sci. USA* **103**, 13878–13883.

19 Bonnie, K. E., Horner, V., Whiten, A. & de Waal, F. B. M. 2007 Spread of arbitrary customs among chimpanzees: a controlled experiment. *Proc. R. Soc. B* **274**, 367–372.

20 Whiten, A., Spiteri, A., Horner, V., Bonnie, K. E., Lambeth, S. P., Schapiro, S. J. & de Waal, F. B. M. 2007 Transmission of multiple traditions within and between chimpanzee groups. *Curr. Biol.* **17**, 1038–1043.

21 van Schaik, C. P., Ancrenaz, M., Borgen, G., Galdikas, B., Knott, C. D., Singleton, I., Suzuki, A., Utami, S. S. & Merrill, M. 2003 Orangutan cultures and the evolution of material culture. *Science* **299**, 102–105.

22 Perry, S. *et al.* 2003 Social conventions in white-face capuchin monkeys: evidence for behavioral traditions in a neotropical primate. *Curr. Anthropol.* **44**, 241–268.

23 Whiten, A. & van Schaik, C. P. 2007 The evolution of animal 'cultures' and social intelligence. *Phil. Trans. R. Soc. B* **362**, 603–620.

24 Hohmann, G. & Fruth, B. 2003 Culture in bonobos? Betweens-species and within-species variation in behaviour. *Curr. Anthropol.* **44**, 563–571.

25 Whiten, A. 2006 The significance of socially transmitted information for nutrition and health in the great ape clade. In *Social information transmission and human biology* (eds J. C. K. Wells, K. N. Laland & S. S. Strickland), pp. 118–134. London, UK: CRC Press.

26 Tomasello, M. 1999 *The cultural origins of human cognition*. Cambridge, MA: Harvard University Press.

27 Csibra, G. & Gergely, G. 2011 Natural pedagogy as evolutionary adaptation. *Phil. Trans. R. Soc. B* **366**, 1149–1157.

28 Lyons, D. E., Damrosch, D. H., Lin, J. K., Macris, D. M. & Keil, F. C. 2011 The scope and limits of overimitation in the transmission of artefact culture. *Phil. Trans. R. Soc. B* **366**, 1158–1167.

29 Harris, P. L. & Corriveau, K. H. 2011 Young children's selective trust in informants. *Phil. Trans. R. Soc. B* **366**, 1179–1187.

30 van Schaik, C. P. & Burkart, J. M. 2011 Social learning and evolution: the cultural intelligence hypothesis. *Phil. Trans. R. Soc. B* **366**, 1008–1016.

31 Biro, D., Inoue-Nakamura, N., Tonooka, R., Yamakoshi, G., Sousa, C. & Matasuzawa, T. 2003 Cultural innovation and transmission of tool use in wild chimpanzees: evidence from field experiments. *Anim. Cogn.* **6**, 213–223.

32 Nakamura, M. & Uehara, S. 2004 Proximate factors of different types of grooming hand-clasp in Mahale chimpanzees: implications for chimpanzee social customs. *Curr. Anthropol.* **45**, 108–114.

33 Levine, R. A. 1984 Properties of culture: an ethnographic view. In *Culture theory: essays on mind, self and emotion* (eds R. A. Schweder & R. A. Levine), pp. 67–87. Cambridge, UK: Cambridge University Press.

34 Nisbett, R., Peng, K., Choi, I. & Norenzayan, A. 2001 Culture and systems of thought: holistic vs analytic cognition. *Psych. Rev.* **108**, 291–310.

35 Boyd, R., Borgerhoff-Mulder, M., Durham, W. H. & Richerson, P. J. 1997 Are cultural phylogenies possible? In *Human by nature: between biology and the human sciences* (eds P. Weingart, P. J. Mitchell, P. J. Richerson & S. Maasen), pp. 355–386. Mahwah, NJ: Lawrence Erlbaum Associates.

36 Hallpike, C. R. 1986 *The principles of social evolution*. Oxford, UK: Clarendon Press.

37 Langergraber, K. E. *et al.* 2010 Genetic and 'cultural' similarity in chimpanzees. *Proc. R. Soc. B.* **277**, 408–416.

38 Marshall-Pescini, S. & Whiten, A. 2008 Social learning of nut-cracking behaviour in East African sanctuary-living chimpanzees (*Pan troglodytes schweinfurthii*). *J. Comp. Psychol.* **122**, 186–194.

39 Lycett, S. J., Collard, M. & McGrew, W. C. 2010 Are behavioral differences among wild chimpanzee communities genetic or cultural? An assessment using tool-use data and phylogenetic methods. *Am. J. Phys. Anthropol.* **142**, 461–467.

40 Gruber, T., Muller, M. N., Strimling, P., Wrangham, R. & Zuberbuhler, K. 2009 Wild chimpanzees rely on cultural knowledge to solve an experimental honey acquisition task. *Curr. Biol.* **19**, 1846–1852.

41 Gray, R. D., Atkinson, Q. D. & Greenhill, S. J. 2011 Language evolution and human history: what a difference a date makes. *Phil. Trans. R. Soc. B* **366**, 1090–1100.

42 Currie, T. E. & Mace, R. 2011 Mode and tempo in the evolution of socio-political organization: reconciling 'Darwinian' and 'Spencerian' evolutionary approaches in anthropology. *Phil. Trans. R. Soc. B* **366**, 1108–1117.

43 Tennie, C., Call, J. & Tomasello, M. 2009 Ratcheting up the ratchet: on the evolution of cumulative culture. *Phil Trans. R. Soc. B* **364**, 2405–2415.

44 Hill, K. 2009 Animal 'culture'? In *The question of animal culture* (eds K. N. Laland & B. G. Galef), pp. 269–287. Cambridge, MA: Harvard University Press.

45 Sanz, C., Call, J. & Morgan, D. 2009 Design complexity in termite-fishing tools of chimpanzees (*Pan troglodytes*). *Biol. Lett.* **5**, 293–296.

46 Goren-Inbar, N. 2011 Culture and cognition in the Acheulian industry: a case study from Gesher Benot Ya'aqov. *Phil. Trans. R. Soc. B* **366**, 1038–1049.

47 Galef, B. G. 1992 The question of animal culture. *Hum. Nat.* **3**, 157–178.

48 Tomasello, M., Kruger, A. E. & Ratner, H. 1993 Cultural learning. *Behav. Brain Sci.* **16**, 595–652.

49 Whiten, A., McGuigan, H., Hopper, L. M. & Marshall-Pescini, S. 2009 Imitation, over-imitation, emulation and the scope of culture for child and chimpanzee. *Phil. Trans. R. Soc. B* **364**, 2417–2428.

50 Hopper, L.M., Flynn, E. G., Wood, L. A. N. & Whiten, A. 2010 Observational learning of tool use in children: investigating cultural spread through diffusion chains and learning mechanisms through ghost displays. *J. Exp. Child Psychol.* **106**, 82–97.

51 Whiten, A. & Flynn, E. G. 2010 The transmission and evolution of experimental 'microcultures' in groups of young children. *Dev. Psychol.* **46**, 1694–1709.

52 Hopper, L. M., Spiteri, A., Lambeth, S. P., Schapiro, S. J., Horner, V. & Whiten, A. 2007 Experimental studies of traditions and underlying transmission processes in chimpanzees. *Anim. Behav.* **73**, 1021–1032.

53 Hopper, L. M., Lambeth, S. P., Schapiro, S. J. & Whiten, A. 2008 Observational learning in chimpanzees and children studied through 'ghost' conditions. *Proc. R. Soc. B* **275**, 835–840.

54 Gergely, G., Bekkering, H. & Kiraly, I. 2002 Rational imitation in preverbal infants. *Nature* **415**, 755.

55 Buttelmann, D., Carpenter, M., Call, J. & Tomasello, M. 2007 Enculturated chimpanzees imitate rationally. *Dev. Sci.* **10**, 31–38.

56 Buttelmann, D., Carpenter, M., Call, J. & Tomasello, M. 2008 Rational tool use and tool choice in human infants and great apes. *Child Dev.* **79**, 609–626.

57 Horner, V. K. & Whiten, A. 2005 Causal knowledge and imitation/emulation switching in chimpanzees (*Pan troglodytes*) and children. *Anim. Cogn.* **8**, 164–181.

58 Laland, K. N. 2004 Social learning strategies. *Learn. Behav.* **32**, 4–14.

59 Laland, K. N., Atton, N. & Webster, M. M. 2011 From fish to fashion: experimental and theoretical insights into the evolution of culture. *Phil. Trans. R. Soc. B* **366**, 958–968.

60 Horner, V. K., Proctor, D., Bonnie, K. E., Whiten, A. & de Waal, F. B. M. 2010 Prestige affects cultural learning in chimpanzees. *PLoS ONE* **5**, e10625.

61 Henrich, J. & Broesch, J. 2011 On the nature of cultural transmission networks: evidence from Fijian villages for adaptive learning biases. *Phil. Trans. R. Soc. B* **366**, 1139–1148.

62 Henrich, J. & Gil-White, F. J. 2001 The evolution of prestige: freely conferred deference as a mechanism for enhancing the benefits of cultural transmission. *Evol. Hum. Behav.* **22**, 165–196.

63 Asch, S.E. 1956 Studies of independence and conformity: I. A minority of one against a unanimous majority. *Psychol. Monogr.* **70**, 1–70.

64 Price, E. E., Lambeth, S. P., Schapiro, S. J. & Whiten, A. 2009 A potent effect of observational learning on chimpanzee tool construction. *Proc. R. Soc. B* **276**, 3377–3383.

65 Galef, B. G. & Whiskin, E. E. 2008 'Conformity' in Norway rats? *Anim. Behav.* **75**, 2035–2039.

66 Marshall-Pescini, S. & Whiten, A. 2008 Chimpanzees (*Pan troglodytes*) and the question of cumulative culture: an experimental approach. *Anim. Cogn.* **11**, 449–456.

67 Hrubesch, C., Preuschoft, S. & van Schaik, C. 2008 Skill mastery inhibits adoption of observed alternative solutions among chimpanzees (*Pan troglodytes*). *Anim. Cogn.* **12**, 209–216.

68 Whiten, A., Horner, V., Litchfield, C. A. & Marshall-Pescini, S. 2004 How do apes ape? *Learn. Behav.* **32**, 36–52.

69 Hewlett, B. S., Fouts, H. N., Boyette, A. H. & Hewlett, B. L. 2011 Social learning among Congo Basin hunter–gatherers. *Phil. Trans. R. Soc. B* **366**, 1168–1178.

70 Hoppitt, W. J. E., Brown, G. E., Kendal, R., Rendell, L., Thornton, A., Webster, M. M. & Laland, K. N. 2008 Lessons from animal teaching. *Trends Ecol. Evol.* **23**, 486–493.

71 Boesch, C. & Boesch-Achermann, H. 2000 *The chimpanzees of the Tai Forest: behavioural ecology and evolution*. Oxford, UK: Oxford University Press.

72 Whiten, A. In press. Primate social learning, traditions and culture. In *The evolution of primate societies* (eds J. Mitani, J. Call, P. Kappeler, R. Palombit & J. Silk), Chicago, IL: Chicago University Press.

73 Call, J. & Tomasello, M. 2008 Does the chimpanzee have a theory of mind? 30 years later. *Trends Cogn. Sci.* **12**, 187–192.

74 Murdock, G. P., Ford, C. S., Hudson, A. E., Kennedy, R., Simmons, L. W. & Whiting, J. M. 1987 *Outline of cultural materials*, 5th revised edn. New Haven, CT: Connecticut: Human Relations Area Files.

75 Crockford, C., Herbinger, I., Vigilant, L. & Boesch, C. 2004 Wild chimpanzees produce group-specific calls: a case for vocal learning? *Ethology* **10**, 221–243.

76 Laland, K. N. & Galef, B. G. (eds) 2009 *The question of animal culture*. Cambridge, MA: Harvard University Press.

77 Zentall, T. R. 2004 Action imitation in birds. *Learn. Behav.* **32**, 15–23.

78 Whiten, A., Schick, K. & Toth, N. 2009 The evolution and cultural transmission of percussive technology: integrating evidence from paleoanthropology and primatology. *J. Hum. Evol.* **57**, 420–435.

Chapter 8

Social Learning and Evolution: The Cultural Intelligence Hypothesis*

Carel P. van Schaik and Judith M. Burkart

If social learning is more efficient than independent individual exploration, animals should learn vital cultural skills exclusively, and routine skills faster, through social learning, provided they actually use social learning preferentially. Animals with opportunities for social learning indeed do so. Moreover, more frequent opportunities for social learning should boost an individual's repertoire of learned skills. This prediction is confirmed by comparisons among wild great ape populations and by social deprivation and enculturation experiments. These findings shaped the cultural intelligence hypothesis, which complements the traditional benefit hypotheses for the evolution of intelligence by specifying the conditions in which these benefits can be reaped. The evolutionary version of the hypothesis argues that species with frequent opportunities for social learning should more readily respond to selection for a greater number of learned skills. Because improved social learning also improves asocial learning, the hypothesis predicts a positive interspecific correlation between social-learning performance and individual learning ability. Variation among primates supports this prediction. The hypothesis also predicts that more heavily cultural species should be more intelligent. Preliminary tests involving birds and mammals support this prediction too. The cultural intelligence hypothesis can also account for the unusual cognitive abilities of humans, as well as our unique mechanisms of skill transfer.

Keywords: social learning; intelligence; brain size; enculturation; cross-fostering; social deprivation

8.1 **Introduction**

Intelligence is the ability to respond flexibly to new or complex situations, to learn and to innovate [1]. This ability is anchored in genetic predispositions towards faster reaction times, greater working memory, inhibitory control and greater response to novelty [2].

---

* Electronic supplementary material is available at http://dx.doi.org/10.1098/rstb.2010.0304 or via http://rstb.royalsocietypublishing.org.

However, intelligence poses an evolutionary puzzle. What is heritable, and therefore mal-leable by natural selection, is the ability to invent effective solutions. But what contributes to fitness is not the ability to learn *per se* but rather these innovative solutions: the learned skills. Rare, serendipitous inventions may make major contributions to fitness, yet they are not heritable because their acquisition depends on many additional factors, such as the constellation of environmental conditions and sheer serendipity. Thus, selection to favour increased cognitive abilities beyond mere conditioning, towards innovative solutions to problems, i.e. true intelligence, must face a high threshold.

Nonetheless, many species are intelligent. Here, we argue this is largely because socially mediated learning (henceforth: social learning, for short) by offspring or other relatives makes inventions heritable, thus lowering the threshold for selection on intelligence. Opportunities for social learning allow an individual to acquire many learned skills during development that it could not acquire on its own. If the social system is such that such opportunities are frequent over many generations, selection may favour increased individual learning ability, i.e. intelligence, but it should certainly favour improved social-learning ability, which, as an inevitable by-product, will improve intelligence.

The 'Vygotskian intelligence hypothesis' [3] considers cultural effects on cognitive development, and assumes them to be unique to humans [4, 5]. However, several schol-ars have highlighted the presence of similar developmental effects in apes (e.g. [6–8]). Allan Wilson [9] went further and suggested that these cultural effects could also have affected the evolution of intelligence in our lineage and others (see also [10, 11]), an idea called the cultural intelligence hypothesis by Whiten & van Schaik [12]. This hypothesis builds on a long tradition suggesting that social learning, and thus culture, may affect evolution (e.g. [13]), and can also be linked to Reader & Laland's [14] hypothesis that general behavioural flexibility, which includes social learning, may have favoured the evolution of intelligence. Here we examine both the developmental and evolutionary aspects of the cultural intelligence hypothesis.

This hypothesis was motivated by observations on great ape cultures. Maturing chim-panzees and orangutans would not have acquired these cultural variants, which are com-plex learned skills, on their own, if it were not for social learning [15–18]. This is evident for tool-assisted nut cracking in chimpanzees [19] or seed extraction from *Neesia* fruits in orangutans, which improves fitness by bringing unusual energetic benefits but which is rarely invented and hence patchily distributed [20]. However, numerous less spectacular examples [21, 22] may also contribute to fitness and may also be difficult to invent, as suggested by their patchy geographical distribution [23]. Their acquisition should, there-fore, also be dependent on social learning. Comparisons across populations indicated that the set of learned (cultural) skills, in particular difficult tool-using skills, is larger where opportunities for social learning are more abundant [11, 24]. But the importance of social learning may extend beyond the acquisition of cultural skills and also include non-culturally varying (i.e. universal), learned skills [18, 25]. Indeed, there is little explo-ration and learning by maturing apes in nature that is not socially guided, suggesting they prefer social learning when possible [18]. All this suggests that they acquire their reper-toire of learned skills less through individual exploration and invention (arrow labelled 1

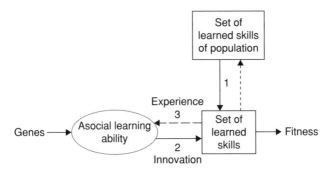

Figure 8.1 The sources of an individual's set of learned skills as acquired during development: (1) the skills learned through social learning from the population's pool of learned skills, and (2) the skills acquired through innovation from its own asocial (individual)-learning ability. The dashed arrow 3 reflects the effect of experience on asocial-learning ability.

in Figure 8.1) than through social learning (arrow 2; see also [26]). Similar processes may occur in capuchin monkeys [27, 28], and possibly to some extent in other non-primate lineages (cf. [29]). After having reviewed this developmental evidence in more detail, we will examine the evolutionary consequences of this reliance on social inputs for skill acquisition.

8.2 The cultural intelligence hypothesis

Social learning can be defined as learning influenced by observation of, or interaction with, another animal [30]. It thus encompasses two rather different processes. Learning through social interaction, including social play and agonistic interactions, generally involves the acquisition of social skills. Learning via social information is essential for the acquisition of non-social skills, although it may also be used in the acquisition of social skills (e.g. through eavesdropping: [31]). This second kind of social learning can take different forms of varying complexity, ranging from mechanisms as simple as local or stimulus enhancement to complex forms of imitation (e.g. summarized in [32]). It must be pointed out, however, that most social learning in animals is not direct copying. Indeed, along with a variable involvement of dedicated cognitive mechanisms [33–35], social learning almost invariably includes an important element of individual evaluation [36], and may indeed largely rely on existing asocial-learning mechanisms [37].

Social learning is not necessarily adaptive [38]. However, whereas horizontal social learning (i.e. from peers) to acquire perishable information about the state of the biotic or social environment can sometimes be maladaptive, vertical and oblique social learning (i.e. from parents or others in that generation) of cognitively demanding skills by naive immatures is most likely to be adaptive (cf. [39]). Throughout, we will focus on these adaptive forms.

The cultural intelligence hypothesis assumes that social learning is more efficient than individual, or asocial, exploration and learning, and that individuals in practice tend to rely on social learning to acquire skills, i.e. prefer it to asocial learning. We expect higher efficiency for social learning because asocial learners face the fundamental problem of identifying which environmental stimuli they should attend to, forcing them to explore in a less directed fashion. Thus, the signal-to-noise (relevant versus irrelevant) ratio of stimuli encountered by immatures is higher for those relying on social learning, making it more likely that they acquire a skill through either socially directed trial-and-error learning (enhancement effects) or observational forms of social learning (i.e. copying of actions, goals or results). Asocial learners, on the other hand, have a far lower signal-to-noise ratio since social inputs do not help them to filter out irrelevant stimuli (cf. [40]). Thus, at constant cognitive abilities, they will on average be less likely or take longer to find a solution to a problem than social learners.

A test of the assumption that social learning is more efficient requires that social learning be operationalized. A commonly used definition is that subjects acquire particular behaviours or skills faster when exposed to skilled role models than they do in a control situation, in which they can independently explore and eventually learn the skill individually. This assumption has been validated in many taxa, and especially in primates [34], although success rates vary across lineages [41], as do known mechanisms [35]. It is also supported by experiments in humans [39]. Thus, social learning acts to speed up the acquisition of behaviour patterns that are universal in the species concerned and thus probably have an innate component [42–44], such as nest building in great apes. It also improves their adult deployment, as shown for nest building in chimpanzees [45, 46]. However, social learning also allows acquisition of novel behaviours (innovations) that the animals would not learn at all otherwise. In many experiments, the control animals fail to find the solution (e.g. [47, 48]), a finding supported by the patchy geographical incidence of learned skills in wild populations [21, 22].

A second critical assumption is that animals able to learn socially do so preferentially rather than rely on individual exploration to acquire skills (as humans should do: [39]). Field observations show that infants in several primate species show relatively little independent exploration, but strongly increase selective exploration of potential food items after mothers fed on them [25], to the point that among orangutans their diets have become identical with those of their mothers by weaning [18], which cannot be attributed to genetic predispositions, because mothers from the same population differ with regard to their feeding repertoires from each other. Vertical inheritance of foraging specializations in dolphins suggests the same process [49]. Experiments similarly show that infants of some species avoid novel foods until their mothers or others have tried them (e.g. *Daubentonia*: [44]). Rats likewise avoid foods not eaten by others, focusing instead on those eaten by others [50].

Interspecific cross-fostering experiments are the most powerful tool to demonstrate a preference for social learning, if they produce a bias towards the behaviour of the adopting species. Although most examples in rodents and birds refer to sexual imprinting [51], a few experiments have examined the effects of more long-term exposure to heterospecific parents. They found powerful effects on diet, foraging, movement and even styles of social behaviour in birds [52–54] and mammals [55, 56], suggesting that social learning (through social information and social interaction) prevails over asocial learning in these domains. Enculturation studies, reviewed below, show equally powerful effects. Overall, these findings support the assumption that especially the young and naive of various species actually show a preference for social learning over individual exploration, although the exceptions (e.g. [57]) might provide a useful testing ground for the cultural intelligence hypothesis.

8.3 Testing the developmental prediction

The main prediction of the developmental version of the cultural intelligence hypothesis is that the number of learned skills acquired by a maturing individual depends on its opportunities for social learning during this period. While we already noted that observational data from wild apes support this prediction, we now discuss experiments that artificially reduce access to role models for social learning (deprivation) or provide better role models with larger skill repertoires (enculturation).

8.3.1 Deprivation effects

For several decades following World War II, many deprivation experiments were conducted in which infant monkeys or apes were reared without access to their mothers or other adult conspecifics. Monkeys and apes reared in partial social deprivation (i.e. with peers only) tend to have near-normal sexual and social competence, which can largely be learned through social interaction, but clearly reduced maternal competence [58–61]. For physical skills, learned through social information, the effects are stronger. Infant chimpanzees reared without adult role models show much reduced competence in many physical skills, such as nest building [45, 46] and tool use [62], or fail to develop them altogether, despite showing otherwise normal behaviour. Thus, primates, especially apes, deprived of adult role models acquire a smaller set of learned skills (see electronic supplementary material for more details).

8.3.2 Enculturation studies

Enculturation is interspecific cross-fostering, in which an animal is reared by humans and treated more or less like a human child, thus exposed to human artefacts and rules through joint attention and active teaching. Enculturation thus provides increased opportunities for socially guided learning, including in domains not present in normal conspecific individuals (e.g. complex artefacts, language). Usually, the cross-fostered individuals were apes, but where monkeys were studied, the results were in the same direction (e.g. [63]). Enculturation brings about more rapid behavioural and motor development [8] and an increased number of learned skills (reviewed in e.g. [64–66]), including more interest in objects and more sophisticated object manipulation [66, 67] and more skilful tool use [63, 68]. Perhaps most strikingly, some great apes developed unusually elaborate comprehension and some use of human language systems despite the complete absence of such symbolic signalling in the wild [6]. Further details are provided in the electronic supplementary material. Thus, enculturation studies not only show the strong preference for socially guided learning and interest in role models' actions of infant primates, but also the remarkable potential for apes to acquire learned skills well outside the range of acquisition during normal development if appropriate role models are available.

8.3.3 A stronger version of cultural intelligence

A stronger version of the cultural intelligence hypothesis is that social learning not merely increases the set of learned skills, as examined so far, but also affects the asocial-learning ability (intelligence) itself. Where an individual has a greater set of learned skills, it may become a better asocial learner through the experience it has gathered in learning the other skills, either because affordance learning has increased its scope of possible innovations or because learning has produced transfer of experience and abilities to new situations. This experience effect is ubiquitous in humans [69] and has long been known for captive primates [70], but also explains why wild primates generally show poor performance on cognitive tasks requiring familiarity with human artefacts or tasks [16, 71, 72]. Thus, where the population has a large pool of skills and social learning is possible, this should allow the individual not only to increase its set of learned skills, but also, through experience, to improve its asocial-learning ability (arrow labelled 3 in Figure 8.1).

The critical prediction of this stronger version is that the frequency of opportunities for social learning during development affects asocial-learning ability, i.e. intelligence. Indeed, social deprivation reduces learning ability in rodents [73] and probably primates [74, 75]. On the other hand, enculturation effects improve it [67, 76, 77]. For instance, only enculturated individuals master delayed imitation. However, because the exact nature of enculturation effects remains unclear (see detailed discussion in the electronic supplementary material) and systematic cognitive tests of primates deprived only of adult role models have not yet been conducted, this conclusion is preliminary. If further, systematic tests support this prediction, the evolutionary effects envisaged by the cultural intelligence hypotheses, reviewed below, are even stronger.

8.4 The evolutionary version of the cultural intelligence hypothesis

The observations and experiments reviewed above show that individuals with more opportunities for social learning systematically acquire a larger set of learned skills and also become better asocial learners. This effect of social learning may have two opposing evolutionary consequences. If individuals in lineages with systematically increased opportunities for social learning can more efficiently acquire the minimum number of skills to survive and reproduce, but derive no fitness benefit from enlarging the set of learned skills, then selection would favour smaller brains in these lineages than in less sociable ones. However, given that relative brain size has consistently increased over evolutionary time [78], the opposite outcome is more likely. Thus, if the number and complexity of skills acquired through social learning positively impact survival and/or reproduction, lineages with more opportunities for social learning can more readily respond to selection for an increased set of learned skills than lineages with limited contact between the generations or tolerant independent animals.

The increased set of learned skills is actually achieved through selection on improved social-learning ability. However, this can lead to improved asocial-learning ability, i.e. intelligence, in two distinct ways (Figure 8.2). First, better social-learning performance automatically improves asocial-learning processes [26], owing to the high overlap of the cognitive processes involved in social and asocial learning [37]. For instance, at the simplest level, selection on enhancement learning favours the causal understanding of agent–object relations. All forms of observational social learning benefit from increased inhibitory control, attention and memory—components of executive functions that enhance individual learning [2]. Emulation critically requires goal understanding; production imitation requires inhibitory control and working memory. In the extreme case, social-learning abilities may merely function as input channels for the asocial-learning mechanisms [37]. Thus, selection for more effective social learning indirectly or directly improves asocial-learning abilities. A second way in which improved social-learning ability can improve asocial-learning ability is direct. It arises whenever the experience effect operates and the increased set of learned skills leads to a direct improvement of the asocial-learning ability.

In lineages with opportunities for social learning, a positive coevolutionary process between social-learning ability and brain size may ensue, until increases in brain size no longer provide sufficient additional pay-off in survival or reproduction in the current environment. Different lineages are expected to go different distances in this eco-evolutionary process, with the position of the equilibrium depending on where the fitness costs of continued investment in neural structures begin to balance the benefits.

The cultural intelligence hypothesis therefore makes two evolutionary predictions, which can be tested comparatively. The first prediction is that social-learning abilities and asocial-learning abilities show correlated evolution. The second is that intelligence and frequency of opportunities for social learning show correlated evolution.

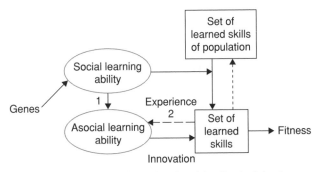

Figure 8.2 The evolution of intelligence through cultural feedback. Selection on an increased set of learned skills is achieved by improved social learning. Owing to the high cognitive overlap, social learning improves the asocial (individual)-learning ability (i.e. intelligence; shown by arrow 1). More learned skills also improve the latter through stronger experience effects (arrow 2).

8.4.1 Coevolution of social and asocial learning

The prediction of a positive interspecific relationship between the abilities for social and asocial learning is a strong one because under other hypotheses for the evolution of intelligence (see §8.5), greater individual intelligence is not necessarily accompanied by greater ability for social learning.

Reader & Laland [14] and Reader *et al.* [79] provided comparative support for this prediction by showing that among primates, reports of social learning, regardless of mechanism, show a significant positive correlation with reports of innovation, and both show significant positive correlations with the executive brain ratio, i.e. (neocortex + striatum/ brain-stem). Similarly, Lefebvre [80] reviewed evidence for a positive interspecific correlation between performance in social learning and individual learning experiments among birds.

A more detailed test compares the asocial-learning ability with the cognitive complexity of social learning across a set of taxa. We compared four primate grades: prosimians (lemurs, galagos and lorises, and in principle tarsiers), monkeys (i.e. both Old and New World monkeys), great apes (i.e. leaving out the gibbons and humans) and humans. While these grades do not correspond to actual clades, they are fairly homogeneous with respect to lifestyle and relative brain size (e.g. [81]). The summary of Table S1 in the electronic supplementary material shows that the performance in both social and asocial learning increases systematically from prosimians, to monkeys, to great apes and finally humans. It is generally assumed that observational forms of social learning, including all forms of emulation and imitation, involve more complex cognitive mechanisms than the non-observational forms, such as facilitation and enhancement. There is no evidence for observational learning in prosimians [34]. Almost all the observational forms of social learning documented so far among monkeys refer to contextual imitation [33] or imitation of species-typical actions [11], whereas among great apes, we see evidence for copying of novel actions, complex action sequences (also production imitation) or deferred imitation (see also electronic supplementary material). Subiaul [35] argues that this distinction is supported by neurobiological differences between these latter two lineages, with production imitation requiring neural adaptations that mediate the planning and coordination of gross and fine motor patterns. In support, human children can copy known motor acts before they can copy novel actions or action sequences [82].

8.4.2 Opportunities for social learning and brain size

The second prediction is that selection would be most likely to favour the evolution of improved domain-general cognitive abilities where opportunities for social learning are present, and should do so more when such opportunities are systematically more abundant. This is a *ceteris paribus* prediction. Thus, not all lineages satisfying the condition need to have evolved greater intelligence, but conversely all highly intelligent species should have excellent opportunities for social learning. In short, prediction 2 is that the most intelligent species should all be highly cultural species.

A proper test of the second prediction requires knowledge of the distribution and extent of culture among taxa in the wild. This information is woefully incomplete, forcing us to use indirect estimates of the amount of social learning in the wild as a first approach to testing this prediction. Opportunities for social learning correlate with a number of non-exclusive variables that can therefore be used as proxies for it: presence of stable social units containing overlapping generations, a long period of close association with one or more parents, the presence of cooperative breeding and extent of social tolerance in social units [24, 83]. Because the effect of social tolerance outweighs that of group size, in both theoretical [26] and empirical studies [14], group size is not a relevant variable, although group living *per se* probably is.

Intelligence must likewise be assayed indirectly, using neuro-anatomical measures, although theoretically there is no obvious best measure [84]. Results obtained with different measures are often the same (e.g. [85]) or similar (e.g. [14]), but not always [86].

As yet, no systematic analyses have been done for mammals, but among birds, several patterns are consistent with the cultural intelligence hypothesis. First, young of altricial species generally have far longer and more intensive contact with parents than precocial ones, and thus more opportunities for social learning. Accordingly, altricial birds have far larger average relative brain size than precocial ones [87]. Second, among altricial birds, the duration of post-fledging parental care, a period during which various skills improve [88], is positively correlated with relative brain size [89], as predicted. Third, among bower-birds, learning of bower building has been argued to be socially mediated [90], and the species that build bowers are larger brained than either non-bower-building relatives or ecologically similar but unrelated species [91]. Finally, among precocial birds, post-hatching care consists largely of protecting and less of provisioning, allowing a test of the effect of opportunities for social learning without being confounded by that of direct energy inputs to the young. This care is highly variable, but largely homogeneous within families (because most variation is at the higher taxonomic levels, we therefore consider patterns at the level of family). As predicted, the number of caretakers in a family strongly predicts relative brain size (K. Isler & C. van Schaik, 2010, unpublished data).

8.5 Discussion

8.5.1 The evolution of intelligence

The cultural intelligence hypothesis makes plausible assumptions that were empirically supported: (i) social learning is more efficient than individual learning, and (ii) animals appear to rely on it preferentially. The developmental effects on skill repertoires it predicts were found as well, whereas we also found preliminary support for the predicted evolutionary effects: interspecific correlation between individual and social-learning abilities and a relationship between opportunities for social learning and cognitive abilities across taxa. Future tests should focus on aspects not yet sufficiently evaluated. For instance, species with high social tolerance, as well as species with demonstrated traditions in natural conditions, should have a larger relative brain size than sister taxa lacking these features. If future tests remain favourable, then cultural intelligence should be part of the explanation for variation in intelligence and brain size across species.

Unlike the cultural intelligence hypothesis, currently popular hypotheses for the evolution of intelligence emphasize specific benefits. For the lineage that gave rise to humans, the primates, the most popular idea is that the challenges and opportunities of living in individualized, stable social groups have provided the strongest selective pressure towards increased cognitive abilities (social brain hypothesis), but ecological pressures, such as foraging demands, have probably contributed as well [92]. More specific benefits may have applied in particular lineages (e.g. acoustic foraging in aye-ayes: [93]). All of these hypotheses enjoy some support from comparative tests using brain size as a proxy for cognitive performance (e.g. [94]), although all hypotheses positing domain-specific benefits must explain how more generalized cognitive abilities, i.e. intelligence, subsequently arose from these specific cognitive adaptations. An alternative approach assumes domain-general benefits in the form of general problem-solving abilities, bringing fitness-enhancing behavioural flexibility [14, 79]. This idea is supported by the high correlations among performance measures on various and sundry cognitive tasks, suggesting the existence of general intelligence in animals, at least primates [95, 96]. There is also a good relationship between this general intelligence and aspects of brain size [79, 86].

Such benefits alone may not be sufficient to explain patterns in the evolution of brain size and intelligence. Brain tissue is metabolically more costly than many other tissues in the body, and consequently larger brains lead to developmental delays in precocial species [97] or require species to have higher metabolic turnover [98]. Therefore, benefits owing to increased brain size must be greater than those owing to equal changes in the size of most other tissues. Indeed, variation in the strength of these costs or ability to bear them explains much interspecific variation in brain size [97, 99]. By arguing that social learning leads to a more efficient use of brain tissue than individual exploration, the cultural intelligence hypothesis explicitly acknowledges these costs.

The efficiency argument holds regardless of the exact nature of the benefits or whether the benefits are domain-general or domain-specific, provided learning of skills is involved. Thus, the cultural intelligence hypothesis complements the benefit hypotheses mentioned above by specifying the conditions in which these benefits are likely to be cost-effective enough to be favoured by natural selection. The cultural intelligence hypothesis is therefore not meant to replace the benefit hypotheses because intelligence will not be favoured by natural selection merely because the costs are low, but only if it also provides clear improvements in survival or reproductive success. Rather, the cultural intelligence hypothesis specifies the conditions in which these potential benefits can be realized, namely whenever the social conditions allow sufficient social learning.

The complementarity with the benefits hypotheses makes it difficult to independently test the cultural intelligence hypothesis, at least until information on the taxonomic incidence of the expression of culture and oblique and vertical social learning is available. However, the cultural intelligence hypothesis correctly predicts the interspecific correlation between asocial and social learning, which is not predicted by the benefit hypotheses. It can also account for correlated evolution between opportunities for social learning and relative brain size, independent of living in stable groups.

8.5.2 Cultural intelligence and human evolution

Species vary dramatically in cognitive abilities. Much of this variation should be linked to the extent to which social learning is possible and improves survival and/or reproductive success. The equilibrium reached in a particular taxon will depend on (i) its social system and life history, i.e. its aggregate measure of opportunities for social learning, and (ii) the degree to which the possession of any skills or knowledge will improve survival or reproductive success. The latter need not be true for organisms in habitats with high unavoidable mortality. Some species will therefore end up relying more on social learning and on more sophisticated forms of it than others, even if opportunities for social learning are similar. Evidently, taxa with highly tolerant social systems, slow development and low rates of unavoidable mortality are expected to have evolved the most extensive forms of social learning. Great apes, capuchin monkeys, dolphins and toothed whales, elephants, corvids and parrots, all lineages with known social-learning abilities [100, 101], fit these conditions.

The evolution of uniquely human cognitive abilities is entirely consistent with the cultural intelligence hypothesis. Although the term cultural intelligence had been proposed earlier [11] to apply to animals generally, Herrmann *et al.* [5] soon thereafter used the term cultural intelligence to specifically refer to humans (i.e. the Vygotskian intelligence hypothesis [3]). Their comparison of adult chimpanzees and orangutans with human toddlers showed that human infants outperformed apes in the social, but not the physical domains of cognition, suggesting that socio-cognitive abilities (including social learning) and physical cognition have become dissociated in humans. This may seem inconsistent with the broader cultural intelligence hypothesis, but note that human *adults* clearly outperform all great apes in both social and physical cognition, indicating the social cognitive abilities simply mature earlier than the physical cognitive abilities. Herrmann *et al.* [5] version of the cultural intelligence hypothesis thus is that humans show specific adaptations fostering social learning that become apparent early in ontogeny and enable a further, socially constructed amplification of cognitive skills. This position is paralleled by the concept of pedagogy proposed as a specifically human adaptation by Gergely *et al.* [102], which encompasses specialized communicative acts on the part of the role model and specific sensitivity to these acts on the part of the infant. These human-specific adaptations are entirely consistent with the broad cultural intelligence hypothesis developed here (cf. [103]), and probably arose after humans adopted cooperative breeding [104, 105].

Acknowledgements

We thank Stephan Lehner for help in literature searches, and Christine Hrubesch, Adrian Jaeggi, Claudia Rudolf von Rohr, Andrea Strasser, Maria van Noordwijk and

Andrew Whiten for discussion, and several reviewers, as well as Kevin Laland and Andy Whiten for comments on the manuscript. Supported by SNF 3100A0-111915 and SNF 105312-114107.

References

1 Byrne, R. W. 1995 *The thinking ape: evolutionary origins of intelligence*. Oxford, UK: Oxford University Press.

2 Geary, D. C. 2005 *The origin of mind: evolution of brain, cognition, and general intelligence*. Washington, DC: American Psychological Association.

3 Moll, H. & Tomasello, M. 2007 Cooperation and human cognition: the Vygotskian intelligence hypothesis. *Phil. Trans. R. Soc. B* **362**, 639–648.

4 Tomasello, M. 1999 *The cultural origins of human cognition*. Cambridge, MA: Harvard University Press.

5 Herrmann, E., Call, J., Hernandez-Lloreda, M. V., Hare, B. & Tomasello, M. 2007 Humans have evolved specialized skills of social cognition: the cultural intelligence hypothesis. *Science* **317**, 1360–1366.

6 Savage-Rumbaugh, S., Fields, W. M., Segerdahl, P. & Rumbaugh, D. 2005 Culture prefigures cognition in *Pan/Homo* bonobos. *Theoria* **54**, 311–328.

7 Boesch, C. 2007 What makes us human (Homo sapiens)? The challenge of cognitive cross-species comparison. *J. Comp. Psychol.* **121**, 227–240.

8 Gardner, B. T. & Gardner, R. A. 1989 Prelinguistic development of children and chimpanzees. *Hum. Evol.* **4**, 433–460.

9 Wilson, A. C. 1991 From molecular evolution to body and brain evolution. In *Perspectives on cellular regulation: from bacteria to cancer* (eds J. Campisi & A. B. Pardee), pp. 331–340. New York, NY: J. Wiley & Sons.

10 van Schaik, C. P. 2004 *Among orangutans: red apes and the rise of human culture*. Cambridge, MA: Harvard University Press (Belknap).

11 van Schaik, C. P. 2006 Why are some animals so smart? *Sci. Am.* **294**, 64–71.

12 Whiten, A. & van Schaik, C. P. 2007 The evolution of animal 'cultures' and social intelligence. *Phil. Trans. R. Soc. B* **362**, 603–620.

13 Richerson, P. J., Boyd, R. & Henrich, J. 2010 Gene–culture coevolution in the age of genomics. *Proc. Natl Acad. Sci. USA* **107**, 8985–8992.

14 Reader, S. M. & Laland, K. N. 2002 Social intelligence, innovation and enhanced brain size in primates. *Proc. Natl Acad. Sci. USA* **99**, 4436–4441.

15 Nishida, T. & Turner, L. A. 1996 Food transfer between mother and infant chimpanzees of the Mahale Mountains National Park, Tanzania. *Intl J. Primatol.* **17**, 947–968.

16 van Schaik, C. P., Deaner, R. O. & Merrill, M. Y. 1999 The conditions for tool use in primates: implications for the evolution of material culture. *J. Hum. Evol.* **36**, 719–741.

17 Lonsdorf, E. V., Eberly, L. E. & Pusey, A. E. 2004 Sex differences in learning in chimpanzees. *Nature* **428**, 715–716.

18 Jaeggi, A., Dunkel, L., van Noordwijk, M. A., Wich, S. A., Sura, A. A. L. & van Schaik, C. P. 2010 Social learning of diet and foraging skills by wild immature Bornean orangutans: implications for culture. *Am. J. Primatol.* **72**, 62–71.

19 Boesch, C. & Boesch-Achermann, H. 2000 *The chimpanzees of the Taï forest: behavioral ecology and evolution*. Oxford, UK: Oxford University Press.

20 van Schaik, C. P. 2009 Geographic variation in the behavior of wild great apes: is it really cultural? In *The question of animal culture* (eds K. N. Laland & B. G. Galef), pp. 70–98. Cambridge, MA: Harvard University Press.

21 Whiten, A., Goodall, J., McGrew, W. C., Nishida, T., Reynolds, V., Sugiyama, Y., Tutin, C. E. G., Wrangham, R. W. & Boesch, C. 1999 Cultures in chimpanzees. *Nature* **399**, 682–685.

22 van Schaik, C. P., Ancrenaz, M., Borgen, G., Galdikas, B., Knott, C. D., Singleton, I., Suzuki, A., Utami, S. S. & Merrill, M. 2003 Orangutan cultures and the evolution of material culture. *Science* **299**, 102–105.

23 van Schaik, C. P., van Noordwijk, M. A. & Wich, S. A. 2006 Innovation in wild Bornean orangutans (*Pongo pygmaeus wurmbii*). *Behaviour* **143**, 839–876.

24 van Schaik, C. P. 2003 Local traditions in orangutans and chimpanzees: social learning and social tolerance. In *The biology of traditions: models and evidence* (eds D. M. Fragaszy & S. Perry), pp. 297–328. Cambridge, UK: Cambridge University Press.

25 Rapaport, L. G. & Brown, R. B. 2008 Social influences on foraging behavior in young nonhuman primates: learning what, where, and how to eat. *Evol. Anthropol.* **17**, 189–201.

26 van Schaik, C. P. & Pradhan, G. R. 2003 A model for tool-use traditions in primates: implications for the evolution of culture and cognition. *J. Hum. Evol.* **44**, 645–664.

27 Ottoni, E. & Izar, P. 2008 Watching the best nutcrackers: what capuchin monkeys (*Cebus apella*) know about others' tool-using skills. *Evol. Anthropol.* **17**, 171–178.

28 Perry, S. 2009 Are non-human primates likely to exhibit cultural capacities like those of humans? In *The question of animal culture* (eds K. N. Laland & B. G. Galef), pp. 247–268. Cambrdige, MA: Harvard University Press.

29 Terkel, J. 1996 Cultural transmission of feeding behavior in the black rat (*Rattus rattus*). In *Social learning in animals: the roots of cultures* (eds C. M. Heyes Jr & B. G. Galef Jr,), pp. 17–48. San Diego, CA: Academic Press.

30 Box, H. O. 1984 *Primate behavior and social ecology*. London, UK: Chapman and Hall.

31 Valone, T. J. 2007 From eavesdropping on performance to copying the behavior of others: a review of public information use. *Behav. Ecol. Sociobiol.* **62**, 1–14.

32 Whiten, A., Horner, V., Litchfield, C. A. & Marshall-Pescini, S. 2004 How do apes ape? *Learn. Behav.* **32**, 36–52.

33 Byrne, R. W. 2002 Imitation of novel complex action: what does the evidence from animals mean? *Adv. Study Behav.* **31**, 77–105.

34 Caldwell, C. & Whiten, A. 2007 Social learning in monkeys and apes: cultural animals? In *Primates in perspective* (eds C. J. Campbell, A. Fuentes, K. C. MacKinnon, M. Panger & S. Bearder), pp. 652–664. Oxford, UK: Oxford University Press.

35 Subiaul, F. 2007 The imitation faculty in monkeys: evaluating its features, distribution and evolution. *J. Anthropol. Sci.* **85**, 35–62.

36 Galef, B. G. 1995 Why behaviour patterns that animals learn socially are locally adaptive. *Anim. Behav.* **49**, 1325–1334.

37 Heyes, C. 1994 Social learning in animals: categories and mechanisms. *Biol. Rev.* **69**, 702–731.

38 Boyd, R. & Richerson, P. J. 1985 *Culture and the evolutionary process*. Chicago, IL: University of Chicago Press.

39 Rendell, L. *et al.* 2010 Why copy others? Insights from the social learning strategies tournament. *Science* **328**, 208–213.

40 Bandura, A. 1977 *Social learning theory*. Englewood Cliffs, NJ: Prentice Hall.

41 Custance, D. M., Whiten, A. & Fredman, T. 2002 Social learning and primate reintroduction. *Int. J. Primatol.* **23**, 479–499.

42 Byrne, R. W. 2007 Culture in great apes: using intricate complexity in feeding skills to trace the evolutionary origin of human technical prowess. *Phil. Trans. R. Soc. B* **362**, 577–585.

43 Kenward, B., Weir, A. A. S., Rutz, C. & Kacelnik, A. 2005 Tool manufacture by naive juvenile crows. *Nature* **433**, 121.

44 Krakauer, E. B. 2005 *Development of aye-aye (Daubentonia madagascariensis) foraging skills: independent exploration and social learning.* Durham, NC: Duke University.

45 Videan, E. N. 2006 Bed-building in capitve chimpanzees (*Pan traglodytes*): the importance of early rearing. *Am. J. Primatol.* **68**, 745–751.

46 Morimura, N. & Mori, Y. 2010 Effects of early rearing conditions on problem-solving skill in captive male chimpanzees (*Pan troglodytes*). *Am. J. Primatol.* **71**, 1–8.

47 Burkart, J. M., Foglia, M. & Strasser, A. 2009 Trade-offs between social learning and individual innovativeness in common marmosets, *Callithrix jacchus. Anim. Behav.* **77**, 1291–1301.

48 Whiten, A., Horner, V. & de Waal, F. B. M. 2005 Conformity to cultural norms of tool use in chimpanzees. *Nature* **437**, 737–740.

49 Sargent, B. & Mann, J. 2009 From social learning to culture: intrapopulation variation in bottlenose dolphins. In *The question of animal culture* (eds K. N. Laland & B. G. Galef), pp. 152–173. Cambridge, MA: Harvard University Press.

50 Galef, B. G. & Whiskin, E. E. 2001 Interaction of social and individual learning in food preferences of Norway rats. *Anim. Behav.* **62**, 41–46.

51 Slagsvold, T. 2004 Cross-fostering of pied flycatchers (*Ficedula hypoleuca*) to heterospecific hosts in the wild: a study of sexual imprinting. *Behaviour* **141**, 1079–1102.

52 Harris, M. P. 1970 Abnormal migration and hybridization of *Larus argentatus* and *L. fuscus* after interspecies fostering experiments. *IBIS* **112**, 488–498.

53 Rowley, I. & Chapman, G. 1986 Cross-fostering, imprinting and learning in two sympatric species of cockatoo. *Behaviour* **96**, 1–16.

54 Slagsvold, T. & Wiebe, K. L. 2007 Learning the ecological niche. *Proc. R. Soc. B* **274**, 19–23.

55 Hawkins, L. K. & Cranford, J. A. 1992 Long-term effects of intraspecific and interspecific cross-fostering on two species of *Peromyscus. J. Mammal.* **73**, 802–807.

56 De Waal, F. B. M. & Johanowicz, D. L. 1993 Modification of reconciliation behavior through social experience: an experiment with two macaque species. *Child Develop.* **64**, 897–908.

57 Taggart, D. A., Schultz, D., White, C., Whitehead, P., Underwood, G. & Phillips, K. 2005 Cross-fostering, growth and reproductive studies in the brush-tailed wallaby, *Petrogale penicillata* (Marsupialia: Macropodidae): efforts to accelerate breeding in a threatened marsupial species. *Aust. J. Zool.* **53**, 313–323.

58 Mason, W. A., Davenport, R. K. & Menzel, E. W. 1968 Early experience and the social development of rhesus monkeys and chimpanzees. In *Early experience and behavior: the psychological and physiological effects of early environmental variaton* (eds G. Newton & S. Levine), pp. 440–480. Springfield, IL: Charles C. Thomas.

59 Gilmer, W. S. & McKinney, W. T. 2003 Early experience and depressive disorders: human and non-human primate studies. *J. Affect. Disord.* **75**, 97–113.

60 Smith, H. J. 2005 *Parenting for primates.* Cambridge, MA: Harvard University Press.

61 Ruppenthal, G. C., Arling, G. L., Harlow, H. F., Sackett, G. P. & Suomi, S. J. 1976 A 10-year perspective of motherless-mother monkey behavior. *J. Abnorm. Psychol.* **85**, 341–349.

62 Menzel, E. W., Davenport, R. K. & Rogers, C. M. 1970 The development of tool using in wild-born and restriction-reared chimpanzees. *Folia Primatol.* **12**, 273–283.

63 Fredman, T. & Whiten, A. 2008 Observational learning from tool using models by human-reared and mother-reared capuchin monkeys (*Cebus apella*). *Anim. Cogn.* **11**, 295–309.

64 Bjorklund, D. F. 2006 Mother knows best: epigenetic inheritance, maternal effects, and the evolution of human intelligence. *Dev. Rev.* **26**, 213–242.

65 Tomasello, M. & Call, J. 2004 The role of humans in the cognitive development of apes revisited. *Anim. Cogn.* **7**, 213–215.

66 Bard, K. A. & Gardner, K. H. 1996 Influences on development in infant chimpanzees: enculturation, temperament, and cognition. In *Reaching into thought: the mind of great apes* (eds A. Russon, K. Bard & S. T. Parker), pp. 235–255. Cambridge, UK: Cambridge University Press.

67 Call, J. & Tomasello, M. 1996 The effects of humans on the cognitive development of apes. In *Reaching into thought: the mind of great apes* (eds A. Russon, K. Bard & S. T. Parker), pp. 371–403. Cambridge, UK: Cambridge University Press.

68 Furlong, E., Boose, K. & Boysen, S. 2007 Raking it in: the impact of enculturation on chimpanzee tool use. *Anim. Cogn.* **11**, 83–97.

69 Nisbett, R. E. 2009 *Intelligence and how to get it: why schools and cultures count.* New York, NY: W.W. Norton & Company.

70 Harlow, H. F. 1949 The formation of learning sets. *Psychol. Rev.* **56**, 51–65.

71 Halsey, L. G., Bezerra, B. M. & Souto, A. S. 2006 Can wild common marmosets (*Callithrix jacchus*) solve the parallel strings task? *Anim. Cogn.* **9**, 229–233.

72 Laidre, M. E. 2008 Spontaneous performance of wild baboons on three novel food-access puzzles. *Anim. Cogn.* **11**, 223–230.

73 Schrijver, N. C. A., Pallier, P. N., Brown, V. J. & Würbel, H. 2004 Double dissociation of social and environmental stimulation on spatial learning and reversal learning in rats. *Behav. Brain Res.* **152**, 307–314.

74 Brent, L., Bloomsmith, M. A. & Fisher, S. D. 1995 Factors determining tool-using ability in two captive chimpanzee (*Pan troglodytes*) colonies. *Primates* **36**, 265–274.

75 Clarke, A. S. & Snipes, M. 1998 Early behavioral development and temperamental traits in mother- versus peer-reared rhesus monkeys. *Primates* **39**, 433–448.

76 Miles, H. L., Mitchell, R. W. & Harper, S. E. 1996 Simon says: the development of imitation in an enculturated orangutan. In *Reaching into thought: the minds of the great apes* (eds A. E. Russon, K. A. Bard & S. T. Parker), pp. 278–299. Cambridge, UK: Cambridge University Press.

77 Premack, D. 1983 The codes of man and beasts. *Behav. Brain Sci.* **6**, 125–167.

78 Finarelli, J. A. 2008 Testing hypotheses of the evolution of brain-body size scaling in the Canidae (Carnivora, Mammalia). *Paleobiology* **34**, 35–45.

79 Reader, S. M., Hager, Y. & Laland, K. N. 2011 The evolution of primate general and cultural intelligence. *Phil. Trans. R. Soc. B* **366**, 1017–1027.

80 Lefebvre, L. 2000 Feeding innovations and their cultural transmission in bird populations. In *The evolution of cognition* (eds C. Heyes & L. Huber), pp. 311–328. Cambridge, MA: MIT Press.

81 Martin, R. D. 1990 *Primate origins and evolution; a phylogenetic reconstruction.* London, UK: Chapman & Hall.

82 Masur, E. F. 1988 Infants' imitation of novel and familiar behaviors. In *Social learning: psychological and biological perspectives* (eds T. R. Zentall Jr & B. G. Galef Jr), pp. 301–318. Hillsdale, NJ: Erlbaum.

83 Coussi-Korbel, S. & Fragaszy, D. M. 1995 On the relation between social dynamics and social learning. *Anim. Behav.* **50**, 1441–1453.

84 Deaner, R. O., Nunn, C. L. & van Schaik, C. P. 2000 Comparative tests of primate cognition: different scaling methods produce different results. *Brain Behav. Evol.* **55**, 44–52.

85 Dunbar, R. I. M. 1992 Neocortex size as a constraint on group size in primates. *J. Hum. Evol.* **20**, 469–493.

86 Deaner, R. O., Isler, K., Burkart, J. M. & van Schaik, C. P. 2007 Overall brain size, and not encephalization quotient, best predicts cognitive ability across non-human primates. *Brain Behav. Evol.* **70**, 115–124.

87 Bennett, P. M. & Owens, I. P. F. 2002 *Evolutionary ecology of birds: life histories, mating systems and extinction.* Oxford, UK: Oxford University Press.

88 Wunderle Jr, J. M. 1991 Age-specific foraging proficiency in birds. *Curr. Ornithol.* **8**, 273–324.

89 Iwaniuk, A. N. & Nelson, J. E. 2003 Developmental differences are correlated with relative brain size in birds: a comparative analysis. *Can. J. Zool.* **81**, 1913–1928.

90 Madden, J. 2008 Do bowerbirds exhibit culture? *Anim. Cogn.* **11**, 1–12.

91 Madden, J. 2001 Sex, bowers and brains. *Proc. R. Soc. Lond. B* **268**, 833–838.

92 Byrne, R. W. & Bates, L. A. 2007 Sociality, evolution and cognition. *Curr. Biol.* **17**, R714–R723.

93 Stephan, H., Baron, G. & Frahm, H. D. 1988 Comparative size of brains and brain components. In *Neurosciences: comparative primate biology*, vol. 4 (eds H. D. Steklis & J. D. Erwin), pp. 1–38. New York, NY: Liss.

94 Dunbar, R. I. M. & Shultz, S. 2007 Evolution in the social brain. *Science* **317**, 1344–1347.

95 Deaner, R. O., van Schaik, C. P. & Johnson, V. 2006 Do some taxa have better domain-general cognition than others? A meta-analysis of non-human primate studies. *Evol. Psychol.* **4**, 149–196.

96 Banerjee, K., Charbis, C. F., Johnson, V. E., Lee, J. J., Tsao, F. & Hauser, M. D. 2009 General intelligence in another primate: individual differences across cognitive task performance in a New World monkey (*Saguinus oedipus*). *PLoS ONE* 4, e5883.

97 Isler, K. & van Schaik, C. P. 2009 The expensive brain: a framework for explaining evolutionary changes in brain size. *J. Hum. Evol.* **57**, 392–400.

98 Isler, K. & van Schaik, C. P. 2006 Costs of encephalization: the energy trade-off hypothesis tested on birds. *J. Hum. Evol.* **51**, 228–243.

99 Aiello, L. C. & Wheeler, P. 1995 The expensive tissue hypothesis: the brain and digestive system in human and primate evolution. *Curr. Anthropol.* **36**, 199–221.

100 Emery, N. J. & Clayton, N. S. 2004 The mentality of crows: convergent evolution of intelligence in corvids and apes. *Science* **306**, 1903–1907.

101 Poole, J. H. & Moss, C. J. 2008 Elephant sociality and complexity: the scientific evidence. In *Never forgetting: elephants and ethics* (eds C. Wemmer & C. A. Christen). Baltimore, MD: Johns Hopkins University Press.

102 Gergely, G., Egyed, K. & Kiraly, I. 2007 On pedagogy. *Dev. Sci.* **10**, 139–146.

103 de Waal, F. B. M. & Ferrari, P. F. 2010 Towards a bottom–up perspective on animal and human cognition. *Trends Cogn. Sci.* **14**, 201–207.

104 Hrdy, S. 2009 *Mothers and others: the evolutionary origins of mutual understanding*. Cambridge, UK: Harvard University Press.

105 Burkart, J. M., Hrdy, S. B. & van Schaik, C. P. 2009 Cooperative breeding and human cognitive evolution. *Evol. Anthropol.* **18**, 175–186.

Chapter 9

The Evolution of Primate General and Cultural Intelligence*

Simon M. Reader, Yfke Hager and Kevin N. Laland

There are consistent individual differences in human intelligence, attributable to a single 'general intelligence' factor, g. The evolutionary basis of g and its links to social learning and culture remain controversial. Conflicting hypotheses regard primate cognition as divided into specialized, independently evolving modules versus a single general process. To assess how processes underlying culture relate to one another and other cognitive capacities, we compiled ecologically relevant cognitive measures from multiple domains, namely reported incidences of behavioural innovation, social learning, tool use, extractive foraging and tactical deception, in 62 primate species. All exhibited strong positive associations in principal component and factor analyses, after statistically controlling for multiple potential confounds. This highly correlated composite of cognitive traits suggests social, technical and ecological abilities have coevolved in primates, indicative of an across-species general intelligence that includes elements of cultural intelligence. Our composite species-level measure of general intelligence, 'primate g_S', covaried with both brain volume and captive learning performance measures. Our findings question the independence of cognitive traits and do not support 'massive modularity' in primate cognition, nor an exclusively social model of primate intelligence. High general intelligence has independently evolved at least four times, with convergent evolution in capuchins, baboons, macaques and great apes.

Keywords: social learning; behavioural innovation; tool use; cognitive evolution; brain evolution; culture

9.1 **Introduction**

Intelligence has been described as 'a very general mental ability that ... involves the ability to reason, plan, solve problems, think abstractly, comprehend complex ideas, learn quickly and learn from experience' [1]. It has been suggested that social learning

---

* Electronic supplementary material is available at http://dx.doi.org/10.1098/rstb.2010.0342 or via http://rstb.royalsocietypublishing.org.

and culture are a cause as well as a consequence of enhanced human and primate intelligence [2–7].

In humans, performance on diverse tests of cognitive ability typically show positive correlations, with substantial variation accounted for by a single factor, termed general intelligence or 'g'. g is composed of subfactors that represent more specific abilities, such as 'verbal comprehension' or 'working memory' [1, 8–10]. Considerable controversy surrounds the meaning of g, particularly whether it can be linked to underlying factors, such as brain size, neural plasticity or processing speed [9–11]. Unfortunately, IQ-test-based approaches are not appropriate for other animals, and understanding of the evolutionary origins of human intelligence and of the relationship between intelligence and culture remains limited.

In primates, numerous hypotheses address the evolution of intelligence, typically based on correlates of increased brain volume, assumed to covary with cognitive capacity (e.g. [12–16]). 'Ecological intelligence' hypotheses suggest that foraging challenges (e.g. 'extractive foraging' or 'cognitive mapping') drove cognitive evolution, while 'social intelligence' hypotheses postulate a connection between the complex social lives of primates and their large brains and advanced cognition [12–14]. Several researchers have envisaged a key role for social learning, one aspect of social intelligence, in driving the evolution of intelligence [3–7]. Wilson [4] suggested that through social learning, individuals expose themselves to novel environmental conditions and experiences, thereby increasing the rate of genetic change, and also driving brain expansion. Boyd & Richerson [5] view human cognition as having evolved to be specifically adapted to the acquisition of cultural knowledge, a view now termed the 'cultural intelligence' hypothesis and supported by comparative analysis [2]. Similar claims are made by several authors [3, 6, 7]. For example, a related cultural intelligence hypothesis argues that evolved changes in the reliance on social learning favoured the evolution of enhancements in other cognitive capacities such as individual learning [3, 7]. We use the term cultural intelligence to refer to the cognitive capacities underlying culture. Social intelligence hypotheses have attracted recent support but the debate is not settled, and several authors have pointed out that the domains are difficult to separate [6, 17–21]. This issue, together with controversies over whether social cognition and social learning are adaptive specializations [22, 23] and over modularity in primate cognition [24, 25], would be clarified by knowledge about the extent to which measures of social and ecological performance covary [20]. While factors ranging from social group size to diet [12, 16, 20, 26] correlate positively with primate brain volumes, the patterns of association between these factors [20], their relationship to a concept of primate intelligence and the consanguinity of non-human primate and human intelligence remain contentious and poorly understood.

Experimental studies of primates are a productive vehicle for exploring the psychological abilities of small numbers of species, and have been effective at delineating commonalities and differences in ape and human cognition [2, 27]. Primate genera differ in their performance in laboratory tests of cognition, with great apes typically outperforming other primates [27, 28]. Similarly, within two primate species, individual performance covaried across 11 laboratory tasks in cotton-top tamarins *Saguinus oedipus* and five laboratory tasks in common chimpanzees *Pan troglodytes* [29, 30]. These and related data from other mammals and birds [31–33] can be viewed as consistent with the hypothesis that a single general factor may underlie laboratory performance. This in turn raises the possibility that general intelligence may explain interspecific variation in the capacity to modify behaviour (i.e. behavioural flexibility; [34]) outside of the laboratory, including variation in social learning, innovation and tool use. However, comparative estimates of learning and cognition using experimental data are challenging, and laboratory tests have been criticized as being unfair to particular species, of questionable ecological validity and for failing to provide data on large numbers of species or on a broad range of cognitive capabilities [6, 17, 35].

An alternative approach, taken here, is to collate and analyse data from the published literature on the incidence of traits associated with behavioural flexibility in animal populations, on the assumption that the rate of incidence reflects the cognitive abilities of that species [34, 36–38]. Such an approach, which is feasible in groups such as primates and birds where there is a tradition of reporting such behaviour, circumvents the aforementioned problems with experimental studies and provides useful, quantitative, continuous measures of performance for large numbers of species across broad domains. While such data are subject to reporting and other biases, these can be addressed statistically. These behavioural flexibility measures thus provide a valuable complement to experimental data.

Here, the tendencies to (i) discover novel solutions to environmental or social problems (henceforth 'innovation' [6]), (ii) learn skills and acquire information from others ('social learning'), (iii) use tools, (iv) extract concealed or embedded food (extractive foraging [12, 39]), and (v) engage in tactical deception [40] were used as five ecologically relevant measures of behavioural flexibility. These are broad domains, each probably encompassing a range of underlying neurocognitive processes [41]. Further analyses incorporated (vi) diet breadth, (vii) percentage of fruit in the diet, and (viii) measures of social group size, thought to reflect the cognitive demands of exploiting/locating foods and tracking social relationships [12, 20]. We compiled measures of (i)–(iv) and (vi), while the remaining measures came from published compilations (§9.2).

We had two objectives. First, we investigated the relations between numerous measures of behavioural flexibility in primates, using statistical methods that control for potential confounds and simultaneously incorporating continuous variables relevant to social, cultural, ecological and technical intelligence. Plausibly, underlying general processes linking different aspects of cognitive performance would lead to cross-species associations in cognitive measures. If, on the other hand, primate intelligence is organized into domain-specific modules that reflect species-specific ecological and social demands, cognitive measures need not covary across species.

Second, we examined the pattern of phylogenetic variation to determine whether enhanced cognitive abilities have evolved independently on multiple occasions and, if so, in which lineages. If cognitive performance reflects evolutionarily conserved abilities homologous with human intelligence, then the high-scoring species might be those most closely related to humans. Conversely, if performance is dominated by past convergent selection favouring high intelligence, the data will not necessarily fit an 'apes outperform monkeys, who outperform prosimians' model. Our previous work has examined pairwise correlations between three measures of behavioural flexibility [6], and extensive past research has examined the relation between socio-ecological variables, cognitive measures and brain volume (see above). Here we examine, for the first time in a single set of analyses, multiple and ecologically relevant measures of behavioural flexibility from several behavioural domains together with socio-ecological variables, brain measures and laboratory-learning data.

9.2 Material and methods

The electronic supplementary material provides additional information on data, methods and analysis, and details supplemental analyses and validation of measures.

9.2.1 Data collection

Over 4000 articles published over a 75-year period, mainly drawn from four leading primate behaviour journals, were examined for examples of innovation, social learning, tool use and extractive foraging in all living primates, using keywords (e.g. 'novel' or 'traditional') to classify behaviour patterns (e.g. as innovation or social learning). Inter-observer reliabilities are high [6]. The observation frequencies for each of these four measures of behavioural flexibility were calculated as the total number of reported examples of each class. The innovation, social learning and tool-use compilations expanded on previously compiled datasets [6], while the extractive foraging compilation was new. Examples of innovation, social learning and tool use came from varied behavioural contexts, including foraging behaviour, locomotion, anti-predator behaviour and social displays. Social learning included learning from both family members and other individuals. We removed cases that simultaneously qualified as more than one of our measures of behavioural flexibility (e.g. innovative tool use), with the exception of reports of social learning and another measure, which we maintain are independent, since the innovator/original tool user/extractive forager is not the social learner. Tactical deception data were compiled from a published source [40]. This resulted in 62 species (electronic supplementary material) with non-zero scores in at least one of the five behavioural flexibility measures. Dietary breadth data were compiled by allocating foodstuffs to 13 categories (invertebrate prey, vertebrate prey, fruit, etc.) with species thus scored between 1 and 13. Extractive foraging and dietary breadth data were successfully validated against existing categorizations (electronic supplementary material). Data are archived online in the Dryad repository (http://datadryad.org). Group size, tactical deception and dietary data were compiled from published sources (electronic supplementary material). Where appropriate, these measures were (i) corrected for research effort by taking the perpendicular offset residuals from a linear regression of number of published articles on each species in the *Zoological Record* on observation frequency, and (ii) repeated after first partialing out the potential confounding effect of body mass, brain volume or research effort. We discuss and assess the reliability of the measures employed in the electronic supplementary material.

The most appropriate measure of brain size is controversial with no single preferred measure [17, 42], so we considered four measures: (i) neocortex ratio (neocortex/rest of brain), (ii) executive brain ratio (neocortex + striatum/brainstem), (iii) neocortex size, and (iv) residuals of neocortex on rest of brain (excluding cerebellum). Brain component volumes were taken from multiple sources, providing data for 56 species (electronic supplementary material).

9.2.2 Analysis

We used principal components and factor analysis (PCA/FA) to examine interrelations between variables. We conducted PCA and FA with and without diet and group-size measures because, depending on perspective, these measures can be viewed as measures of behavioural flexibility, correlates of cognitive performance or sources of selection for intelligence. The inclusion of diet and group-size measures with our five measures of behavioural flexibility allowed us to examine the pattern of covariation of the eight measures, and to investigate whether the behavioural flexibility measures clustered together more strongly with each other than with the socio-ecological variables. Where we addressed evolutionary questions, we corrected for phylogeny using independent contrasts [43], implemented with the computer program Comparative Analysis by Independent Contrasts [44]. Other potential confounding variables considered included brain volume, body size, group size, research effort and correlated error in research effort, and data were also reanalysed without the great apes, and at the genus level (see §9.3 and electronic supplementary material). Since data were not available for all species for all variables, analyses differ in sample size depending on data availability. All statistical tests were two-tailed with $\alpha = 0.05$.

9.3 Results

9.3.1 Across-species analyses

A PCA of cognitive measures alone, including research-effort-corrected measures of innovation, social learning, tool use, extractive foraging and tactical deception, in all 62 primate species for which full data were available, revealed a single dominant component, henceforth referred to as primate g_{S1}, which explained over 65 per cent of the variance in cognitive measures (Table 9.1). The 'S' subscript denotes that primate g is an across-species construct. Loadings for all measures were positive and ranged from 0.74 for tactical deception to 0.88 for tool use. A second eight-variable PCA that also incorporated the three socio-ecological variables (diet breadth, percentage fruit in diet and group size) generated a major component (henceforth g_{S2}) that explained 47 per cent of the variance (eigenvalue = 3.77, significantly higher than all other components), on which the five original measures and, to a lesser extent, diet breadth loaded significantly (Table 9.2), and which covaried strongly with g_{S1} ($r = 0.95$, $p = 0.0001$). The eight-variable PCA also extracted a second component, on which diet breadth, percentage fruit in diet

Table 9.1 Principal components analysis (PCA) on five primate cognitive measures extracts a single dominant component. PCA used a roots > 1 extraction criterion. $n = 62$, d.f. $= 14$, g_{S1} variance contribution $= 0.65$, Bartlett's $\chi^2 = 145.4$, $p < 0.0001$. See electronic supplementary material, Figure S1, for scree plot, and main text for details of measures

	component 1 (g_{S1})
extractive foraging	0.84
innovation	0.75
social learning	0.82
tactical deception	0.74
tool use	0.88

Table 9.2 PCA (orthogonal solution) across primate species of eight cognitive and socio-ecological measures. PCA used a roots > 1 extraction criterion. $n = 44$, d.f. $= 35$, g_{S2} variance contribution $= 0.47$, component 2 variance contribution $= 0.16$, Bartlett's $\chi^2 = 152.4$, $p < 0.0001$. See electronic supplementary material, Figure S1, for scree plot, and main text for details of measures

	component 1 (g_{S2})	component 2
diet breadth	0.32	0.71
extractive foraging	0.88	0.11
innovation	0.78	−0.002
percentage fruit	0.13	0.69
social group size	−0.046	0.69
social learning	0.80	0.29
tactical deception	0.68	0.35
tool use	0.88	0.045

and group size loaded (Table 9.2). The results of the eight-variable PCA thus support the interpretation of the primary component as a general cognitive measure. All 10 pair-wise correlations between the five cognitive measures were strongly significant ($p = 0.001$; Table 9.3). There was no significant correlation between diet breadth and innovation rate, suggesting that innovation rate is not simply an index of diet breadth (see also [41]). FAs gave equivalent results to the PCAs (electronic supplementary material, Table S1).

We took several approaches to address potential confounding variables. The observed associations were not caused by data points that qualified simultaneously for more than one measure, since these were removed. Nor are the associations an artefact of the covariance of each individual measure with brain volume, body mass or correlated error variance in research effort: analyses using residuals of each cognitive measure from multiple regressions that included (i) relative brain volume, (ii) body mass, or (iii) with no correction for research effort, or (iv) with five independent measures of research effort, gave equivalent results (electronic supplementary material). To account for the possibility that observers may be more willing to ascribe behavioural flexibility to the great apes

Table 9.3 Correlation of cognitive and socio-ecological measures across primate species. Figures are correlation coefficients. EF, rate of extractive foraging; I, rate of innovation; SL, rate of social learning; TD, rate of tactical deception; TU, rate of tool use; DB, dietary breadth; %F, percentage of fruit in diet (typically measured as a percentage of foraging time); GS, social group size. EF, I, SL, TD and TU are corrected for research effort differences. Figures in bold are statistically significant correlations ($p < 0.025$). See the main text and the electronic supplementary material for details of measures

	EF	I	SL	TD	TU	DB	%F	GS
EF	1	0.60***	0.68***	0.54***	0.74***	0.42***	0.13	0.06
I		1	0.55***	0.51***	0.56***	0.18	0.08	0.12
SL			1	0.54***	0.69***	0.44***	0.32***	0.12
TD				1	0.58***	0.36***	0.21	0.30**
TU					1	0.28**	0.24	−0.05
DB						1	0.40***	0.25*
%F							1	0.14
GS								1

*$p < 0.025$.
**$p < 0.01$.
***$p < 0.001$.

than to other primates, we repeated the analysis with great apes removed, finding equivalent results (electronic supplementary material).

9.3.2 Extant genera variation

To address the concern that there may be error in individual species data, particularly in the case of species that have not been well studied, we repeated the PCA using the same procedures at the genera level. Once again, we found a single dominant component ($\chi^2 = 116.28$, $p < 0.0001$, variance contribution = 75%). The same pattern was observed when the analysis also incorporated Deaner *et al.*'s [28] genus-level composite index of performance in laboratory tests of cognition ($\chi^2 = 131.12$, $p < 0.0001$, variance contribution = 73%). Deaner *et al.*'s reduced model measure (inversed so that high scores represent high performance) loads heavily on g (loading = 0.73). This supports the argument that laboratory performance is reliant on general intelligence and demonstrates the covariation of six cognitive measures across extant primate genera.

9.3.3 Phylogenetic analysis

If the relationship between different measures of primate cognitive ability reflects an evolutionary history of coevolution, then the primate g_S component should remain when phylogeny is taken into account using independent contrasts for each measure. Repeated in this manner [44], the five-variable PCA revealed a single component on which all cognitive measures loaded, although innovation and tactical deception loaded less strongly than in the across-species analyses ($n = 57$, d.f. = 14, $\chi^2 = 70.20$, $p < 0.0001$, variance contribution = 0.53; extractive foraging, social learning and tool-use loadings = 0.76–0.84, innovation and tactical deception loadings = 0.66 and 0.55, respectively). The eight-variable PCA using independent contrasts revealed a degree of subdivision in the variance, with two components (χ^2 = 93.25, p < 0.0001), suggesting that some cognitive measures have coevolved more tightly than others. Social learning, tool use and extractive foraging all loaded heavily on the dominant component (loadings 0.79–0.84), which accounted for 38 per cent of the extracted variance, while innovation and tactical deception loaded somewhat more weakly, but still substantially, on this dominant component (loading = 0.59 and 0.51, respectively), as did diet breadth (loading = 0.56). Tactical deception also loaded on a second component together with group size, with percentage fruit loading negatively (variance contribution = 0.18; loading = 0.52, 0.73, −0.73 for tactical deception, group size, per cent fruit in diet, respectively). While it might be tempting to interpret this subdivision as indicative of correlated 'socio-technical' and 'Machiavellian' components of general intelligence, the loading of tactical deception on the dominant component of the eight-variable PCA, together with the absence of two components in the five-variable independent contrast PCA, or the aforementioned extant species five-variable and eight-variable PCAs, or the FAs, leaves us guarded against over-interpreting this finding.

9.3.4 The evolution of primate *g*

PCA can be used to calculate factor scores for each component it extracts, providing a composite score for the variables loading on a component. We calculated g_{S1} factor scores to provide a composite g_S measure for each species, which can be interpreted as a measure of comparative general intelligence. On average, the Hominoidea (excluding humans) out-scored other taxa, but no significant mean differences in g_{S1} scores were found between Cercopithecoidea, Ceboidea and Prosimii (Figure 9.1*a*).

To investigate the distribution of species' g_{S1} factor scores, we mapped them onto a primate phylogeny using MacClade v. 4.08. There was considerable overlap between primate superfamilies, and substantial variation within primate subfamilies (e.g. Cercopithecinae), which may represent measurement error, variation in evolutionarily labile cognitive abilities (i.e. independent evolutionary events) or phenotypic plasticity. To reduce measurement error, we pooled data for each genus (Figure 9.1*b*). The analysis revealed multiple convergent evolutionary events favouring high general intelligence across primate lineages, with four independent responses to selection in *Cebus, Papio, Macaca* and Hominoidea (Figure 9.1*b*). This interpretation involves fewer evolutionary events, and is thus more parsimonious, than all alternative scenarios, such as that high general intelligence evolved once in the common ancestors of apes and Old World monkeys and was then repeatedly lost. Some variance among genera is probably attributable to measurement error and error variance is expected to be highest in the least-studied taxa. Nonetheless, we note a correspondence between those primates with high g_{S1} scores and those renowned for complex cognition and rich behaviour (e.g. *Pan, Pongo, Cebus, Macaca* [3, 13, 27, 46–48], Figure 9.1*c*). Moreover, to address the concern that the data for

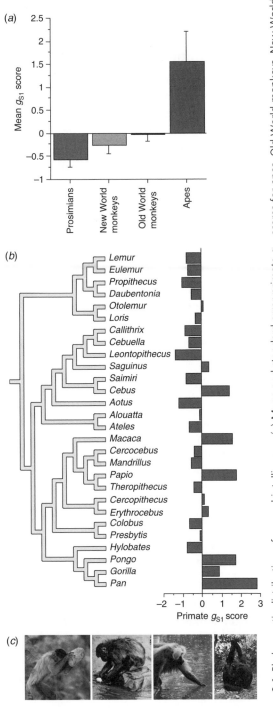

Figure 9.1 Phylogenetic distribution of general intelligence. (a) Mean and standard error primate g_{S1} scores for apes, Old World monkeys, New World monkeys and prosimians. Apes ($\bar{x} \pm$ s.e. = 1.55 $\pm$ 0.65) score more highly than other primate taxa, but no significant mean differences were found between Cercopithecoidea ($\bar{x} \pm$ s.e. = -0.02 ± 0.15), Ceboidea ($\bar{x} \pm$ s.e. = 1.26 $\pm$ 0.18) and Prosimii ($\bar{x} \pm$ s.e. = -0.48 ± 0.17) (ANOVA $F_{3, 56} = 8.17$, $p < 0.0001$; Fisher's PLSD, critical differences: ape versus prosimians = 0.93, versus New World = 0.81, versus Old World = 0.77, $p \leq 0.0001$). (b) Primate intelligence scores, as measured by primate g_{S1}, showing phylogenetic relatedness based on a composite tree [45]. Multiple convergent evolutionary events favoured high intelligence across primate lineages with independent responses to selection in Hominoidea, *Macaca*, *Cebus* and *Papio*. (c) Photographs illustrating examples of behavioural flexibility in the four high g_S lineages, covering foraging, technical and social domains (from left to right: *Cebus* nut-cracking (Copyright © L. Candisani/Minden Pictures), *Macaca* food washing, *Papio* fishing (Copyright © iStockphoto.com/R. Bursch), *Pan* handclasp grooming (a putative cultural tradition) (Copyright © M. Nakamura).

little-studied species may be unreliable, we repeated the phylogenetic reconstruction with the less well-studied species removed, finding similar results (electronic supplementary material).

9.3.5 Covariation with brain volume and laboratory performance

Table 9.4 and Table S2, electronic supplementary material illustrate the strong associations of g_{S1} with several measures of brain volume, while g_{S1} is also an effective predictor of the performance of primate species and genera in laboratory tests of cognition (Figure 9.2). These observations lend credence to the view that primate g_{S1} is a genuine measure of comparative intelligence. Moreover, PCA combining genus-level measures of cognitive performance in the laboratory with the aforementioned measures of behavioural flexibility again reveals a single dominant component (§9.2.2). The positive correlations of g_{S1} with brain size and laboratory performance, together with the steps taken to account for differences in research effort, and the finding that the results hold when the great apes are removed from the analyses (electronic supplementary material), undermine any suggestion that g_S is merely an artefact of reporting biases that flatter species deemed intelligent or that are easy to observe, or of over-reporting of intelligent behaviour in a small number of species. The finding that prosimians do not score significantly lower than New and Old World monkeys undermines the suggestion that g_S is an artefact of underreporting of prosimian behavioural flexibility. The weak loadings of group-size measures on g_{S1} rule out the potential artefact of more reports of behavioural flexibility in species with large groups.

Table 9.4 The relationship between primate general intelligence, g_S and brain volume. Regressions of four popular brain-size measures on g_{S1} scores, each conducted on both species values and independent contrasts. Figures in bold are statistically significant ($p < 0.05$). We find that g_{S1} is a significant predictor of brain size measured as neocortex ratio, executive brain ratio and neocortex size, but not residuals of neocortex on rest of brain. The latter uses a less than satisfactory reference variable, containing components that may coevolve with neocortex [16, 49], and is consistently more conservative than other measures [6, 12]. The relationships with measures 1–3 show a similar pattern but are weakened when the effect of body mass is statistically removed (electronic supplementary material, Table S2)

brain measure	analysis	r^2	F	p
1. neocortex ratio	across-species	0.35	14.88	**0.0006**
	independent contrasts	0.27	10.13	**0.003**
2. executive brain ratio	across-species	0.55	22.37	**0.0002**
	independent contrasts	0.25	5.86	**0.026**
3. ln (neocortex volume)	across-species	0.55	13.91	**0.0009**
	independent contrasts	0.19	6.39	**0.018**
4. residuals of neocortex on rest of brain	across-species	0.01	0.18	0.67
	independent contrasts	0.03	0.75	0.39

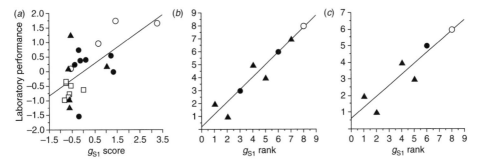

Figure 9.2 Primate g_{S1} covaries with performance of primate species in laboratory tests of comparative intelligence. g_{S1} score correlates strongly with three measures of performance, (a) Deaner et al.'s [28] measure compiled across multiple heterogeneous cognitive tasks ($n = 18$, $r^2 = 0.36$, $p = 0.009$; similar results are obtained using independent contrast analysis: $n = 17$, $r^2 = 0.23$, $p = 0.047$), (b) the combined performance across all learning tasks in the Riddell & Corl [50] dataset ('combined Riddell rank'; $\rho = 0.95$, $p = 0.012$), and (c) 'learning sets', the single task (from [50]) that provides the largest dataset ($\rho = 0.89$, $p = 0.048$). Deaner et al. [28] examined the sources contained within the Riddell & Corl [50] dataset, and thus these datasets are not fully independent. However, we include both since they represent different criteria and methodologies for data compilation. Regression lines are included for illustration. Open circles, apes; filled circles, Old World monkeys; triangles, New World monkeys; squares, prosimians.

9.3.6 Covariation of group size with g_S and laboratory performance

If social complexity is the prominent factor driving the evolution of intelligence in non-human primates [12–14, 20, 49, 51–54], then we would expect indicators of social complexity to be good predictors of g_S and of performance in laboratory tests of cognition. We explored the relationship between social group size and both g_{S1} and Deaner et al.'s [28] index of performance in laboratory tasks of cognition (reduced model), but found no significant relationships (g_{S1}: $n = 58$, $r^2 = 0.04$, $p = 0.12$; laboratory performance: $n = 16$, $r^2 = 0.002$, $p = 0.85$). This contrasts with the strong positive relationship between primate g and Deaner et al.'s measure (Figure 9.2a), and implies that general intelligence, rather than exclusively social intelligence, best explains the performance of primates in laboratory tests of cognition.

9.4 Discussion

Our analyses suggest that ecologically relevant cognitive abilities, from multiple domains, have coevolved in primates, revealing an across-species general intelligence, with general rather than purely social intelligence probably driving brain evolution. Seemingly, key cultural capabilities, notably social learning, tool use and behavioural innovation, form part of a highly correlated composite of cognitive traits. Thus, elements of cultural intelligence appear to be part of general intelligence. Our composite general intelligence measure correlates with brain volume measures and laboratory learning performance; nonetheless, general intelligence is not the result of a confounding effect of brain volume.

High levels of general intelligence evolved independently at least four times, with independent responses to selection favouring high g_S in capuchin, baboon, macaque and ape lineages.

Several hypotheses have been proposed concerning the factors favouring the evolution of the large primate brain and, since these have been presented as alternative explanations, concern has been expressed that seemingly conflicting findings have not been reconciled [38, 55, 56]. By suggesting that selection may have favoured general intelligence, rather than a single specialized domain, our analysis helps to alleviate such disquiet. Significantly, the analysis extends the finding that primate taxa consistently differ in performance across multiple domains from the laboratory [28] to ecologically valid natural contexts. Our analyses also extend comparative findings that link innovativeness (assessed on the basis of published reports or experimental tests) with asocial-learning performance, tool use and reduced neophobia (in birds and primates) and with social learning (in primates; reviewed in [37, 57, 58]). We note that primate g_S contains social (social learning, tactical deception), technical (tool use, innovation) and ecological (extractive foraging, diet breadth) intelligence components, supporting a battery of hypotheses regarding the factors driving brain evolution [6, 7, 12–17, 20, 26], but not the hypotheses that social or ecological intelligence is the sole cause of brain evolution. Indeed, social and ecological intelligence may be intrinsically linked in group-living animals [19, 21]. If social pressures are the major driving force behind primate cognitive evolution, our results suggest they have resulted in abilities extending beyond the social domain. Similarly, if a 'cultural drive' process has operated across primates, as envisaged by multiple authors [3, 4, 6, 7], it seemingly has also favoured non-cultural capabilities.

9.4.1 Sociality

Moreover, while our analysis (electronic supplementary material, Table S3) confirms the widely observed relationship between group size and brain size [12, 20], we find that group size does not covary with primate g_S, nor predict genera's performance in laboratory tests of cognition (laboratory data drawn from Deaner et al. [28]). Similarly, previous work has found weak or no correlations between primate group size and reported frequencies of social learning [23] and tactical deception [54], although our sample supported a correlation between tactical deception rate and group size. To the extent that group size measures social complexity, the group size findings are inconsistent with the view that social complexity selects for an intelligence applied to multiple domains. This raises the possibility that social complexity may not have been as important a driver of primate general intelligence as is widely believed. However, group size is 'at best a crude proxy' of social complexity [20, p. 649] and more sophisticated measures of social structure and complexity would be valuable. For example, it is plausible that rates of social learning may be predicted by factors such as tolerant gregariousness and the number of available individuals to learn from, rather than group size per se [7]. Moreover, our findings, since they concern non-human primates, do not conflict with the hypothesis that social factors differentially favoured intelligence in humans [2, 5]. Thus, our analyses do not preclude the possibility that adaptations to a cultural niche have been favoured in the lineage leading to humans [2, 5]. Indeed, high general intelligence, by allowing animals to construct a niche where behavioural flexibility provides advantages, may predispose subsequent evolution of specializations in particular abilities.

9.4.2 Experimental tests

Recently, the need for experimental verification of comparative results has been stressed [38, 55, 56]. Our analysis makes testable predictions, for example, that congeners' g-scores will be paralleled in experimental tests of cognition, and that high-g species should exhibit strong performance on all aspects of cognition. For instance, we predict that genera, such as *Cebus* and *Gorilla*, in which tool use is not widely observed, will be found to be capable of using tools in appropriate circumstances—as recently observed in wild individuals (e.g. [46, 59]). Ideally, experimental investigations of general intelligence should extend beyond the laboratory, since captive conditions may influence cognitive development and performance [7, 60, 61]. Species differences in general intelligence are likely to extend beyond primates. For example, rooks *Corvus frugilegus*, members of the large-brained and behaviourally flexible corvid par vorder [37], use tools in captivity but apparently not in the wild [62, 63], a finding consistent with the idea that such tool use can result from a generalized cognitive ability.

9.4.3 Comparisons with human intelligence

The strong correlation between distinct measures of primate cognitive performance is strikingly evocative of the correlations in performance on different IQ tests observed in humans. A possible explanation for this correspondence is that the g factor reported in humans reflects underlying general processes that evolved in common ancestors and are thus shared in our extant primate relatives. However, caution is warranted in interpreting this finding since here the observed associations occur across rather than within species [57]; in this respect, further within-species analyses would be valuable [30]. It is hard unequivocally to establish the nature of the correspondence between primate and human g measures given the very different measures and levels of analysis used, and the structure and level of human intelligence may be greatly reliant on language or another uniquely human capability. That said, primate g_S is highly consistent with current definitions of human intelligence that emphasize novel problem-solving abilities [1, 9]. For instance, high performers on our measure are species frequently reported to devise novel solutions, solve social and ecological problems, learn quickly and from experience, construct and manipulate tools and to learn from and deceive others [7, 27]: qualities attributed to intelligent humans. Moreover, primate g_S covaries with performance in laboratory tests.

9.4.4 Brain volume and cognition

Links between brain volume and cognitive capacity are controversial, both within humans and across animal species [1, 11, 38, 55, 64, 65]. Here, we show that primate g_S correlates with absolute forebrain volume measures and two of the three deployed relative measures, a result mirrored by analyses of laboratory-learning performance [42, 66]. Similarly, within humans, g shows a modest correlation with total brain and grey matter volumes [9, 11, 67, 68]. Our data, combined with the multiple studies linking various cognitive measures and brain volume across species [55], and recent findings demonstrating survival pay-offs to brain enlargement [37, 69, 70], suggests the 'volumetric stance' is warranted: brain component volumes are related to functionally relevant cognitive capacities.

In common with many human scientists and neuroscientists [1, 9, 11, 65], we note that the mechanisms behind the brain volume–cognition relationship are unknown and require study. It is important to establish if, how and why characteristics such as brain cell composition, connectivity, numerosity and diversity are linked to brain volume, why these characteristics vary across brain regions, how this variation is linked to cognitive function and whether common links between structure and function are found across taxa [65]. Adequate tests of cognitive function will be essential for this exercise. Note that comparisons across large taxonomic divides with very different brain architectures [64] will be problematic. For example, the scaling rules of brain enlargement may differ, even between mammalian orders [65], something that comparative studies analysing relationships within multiple orders should account for [70]. Common findings in different taxa strengthen confidence in the observed relationships. For example, similar relationships between innovation rate, tool-use rate, individual learning measures and relative forebrain volume are found in both birds and primates [37].

A variety of neural and cognitive mechanisms will underlie a particular act like innovation or social learning, and purportedly complex cognitive processes may in fact have simple underlying mechanisms [41, 64]. Accordingly, we envisage that such behaviour is unlikely to be the sole province of large-brained taxa [34, 64, 71]. However, our frequency data suggest that brain enlargement may facilitate more varied forms of behavioural flexibility, rather than simply the presence or absence of a broad category of behaviour such as social learning, extractive foraging or innovation. While our data do not allow us to examine the complexity of the processes underlying behavioural flexibility, it is possible that brain enlargement affords motor, processing or perceptual (especially visual) improvements that facilitate behavioural flexibility and are shared across cognitive domains, contributing to the correlated performance we observe. We suggest that brain enlargement facilitates improvements in the sophistication or efficiency of behavioural flexibility and the variety of problems to which it is applied, and that it may be necessary for some, but by no means all, advanced cognitive processes.

9.4.5 Underlying mechanisms

The coevolution of cognitive performance documented in this study suggests that conserved general processes, as opposed to specialized modules [24, 25], may be an important part of primate cognitive evolution, although we cannot exclude coevolution of distinct modules, modularity outside of the domains that we measure, or the evolution of modularity in the human lineage. For example, our data do not address whether spatial cognition varies independently from other cognitive measures [30, 33, 72]. While correlations between cognitive abilities cannot be used to demonstrate or disprove modularity [73], we can show the abilities we measure evolve together, and our data thus do not support the 'massively modular' view that cognitive abilities evolve independently [25]. Massive modularity is an extreme form of the modularity thesis, and more moderate views allow for coevolution of semi-independent modules. The general process view is arguably more parsimonious than even moderate modularity. We suspect the truth will lie somewhere in between, with shared general processes, themselves a product of evolution, sitting alongside adaptive specializations of aspects of cognition and perception. However, our results suggest that the view that components of intelligence and behavioural flexibility can evolve independently without constraint is untenable.

Our data are consistent with the increasingly accepted view that common processes are involved in both social and individual learning [74–76]. If much social learning is the result of general processes, then behaviour patterns acquired by social learning are expected to span multiple domains, a prediction supported by data from individual species such as the chimpanzee and the guppy *Poecilia reticulata* [71, 77]. Where social learning is an adaptive specialization, on the other hand, it might be expected to be restricted to a particular domain, such as learning about certain predators or foods.

Regarding the mechanisms underlying g_S, the observed correlations with brain volume suggest that differences in brain structure underlie g_S, but g_S could additionally plausibly be a product of positive feedback from niche construction [11, 78, 79]. For example, individuals from species with a slight g_S advantage may be able to inhabit more challenging environments, thus exposing themselves to circumstances favouring the expression of behavioural flexibility and to selection for further increases in flexibility.

Our analysis provides empirical confirmation of the assumption that primate species differ in their general intelligence, and that it covaries with brain encephalization and social-learning abilities. Our data are consistent with findings that great apes' social-learning abilities are superior to other primates [7, 77] and broadly consistent with van Schaik and Burkart's meta-analysis of taxonomic differences in primate cognition [7], although our data provide no evidence for a difference between prosimians and monkeys. However, only eight prosimian species are represented in our database, limiting the statistical power of comparisons with prosimians. Humans are located within the super-family with the highest g scores, but the analysis conflicts with a *Scala naturae* conception, suggesting instead that convergent selection may have repeatedly favoured intelligence in distant primate lineages.

9.4.6 Implications for the evolution of cultural transmission

The discussion above suggests numerous reasons to urge caution when discussing the evolution of social learning and the capacities underlying culture. Reconstruction of evolutionary patterns of social learning will require investigation of numerous and widespread taxa, and data on deficiencies in both social-learning mechanisms (such as imitation) and social-learning strategies (such as the capability for pay-off-based copying) will be important alongside positive data. The social-learning data we analyse compile the results of a considerable body of published work describing primate behaviour, but still represent an early step in reconstructing the evolution of social learning and other underlying cultural capabilities. In particular, much of our data comes from observational reports of social learning, carrying the problem that neither social learning nor the underlying social-learning process is experimentally established [61]. Statistical methods for detecting social learning in natural populations will enhance the reliability of observational reports [80, 81].

Since neither social learning nor culture is a unitary trait [77], but instead involve multiple processes, evolutionary reconstruction of social learning might usefully focus on particular mechanisms or capabilities (e.g. conformist social learning). In this respect, information on the developmental and neurocognitive mechanisms underlying social and individual learning is valuable, such as the compatibility of social and individual information-gathering processes, and understanding of the circumstances under which social learning is utilized [82].

If social-learning processes coevolve with, or even form part of, general cognitive processes, identifying a single factor as specifically favouring the evolution of social learning may prove challenging and perhaps even misguided. Positive feedback processes, such as social learning or cultural evolution, favouring further increases in cognitive flexibility, in turn facilitating enhanced social learning, will compound the problem of identification of a 'key' causal factor [3, 7, 83]. Social-learning efficacy may also change as a by-product of selection on another process, a consideration potentially important for theoretical models of the evolution of social learning. For example, selection favouring increased social tolerance or grouping may facilitate social learning [7, 84]. In principle, recently developed statistical methods may be able to select between alternative causal models [85], which would help establish to what extent the enhanced capacity for social learning was a key driver of primate intelligence or a by-product of some other driver. For the moment, we are unable to distinguish between these alternatives. However, we can, at least, confirm the existence of a positive relationship between the key capabilities underlying culture (e.g. enhanced social learning, behavioural innovation, tool use) and general intelligence across the primate order.

Acknowledgements

We are grateful to N. J. Boogert, G. R. Brown, R. O. Deaner, I. Deary, R. I. M. Dunbar, P. H. Harvey, L. Lefebvre, N. J. Mackintosh, K. Meacham, C. L. Nunn, M. Schipper, E. Visalberghi, A. Whiten, M. A. Zdebik and the University of St Andrews' *Social Evolution and Learning* and *Cognitive Discussion* groups for helpful conversation or comments on earlier drafts of this manuscript, to E. C. Bush, J. A. Kaufman, C. E. Macleod, J. Rilling and C. C. Sherwood for brain data and advice, to J. Jernvall for providing dietary breadth data for validation of our measure, to C. Chapman and H. A. C. Eeley for helpful advice on dietary categorization and to A. Oleksiak for preliminary analyses of deception frequency. S.M.R. thanks Utrecht University's High Potentials Programme and the

Netherlands Organisation for Scientific Research (NWO) Evolution and Behaviour Programme for funding. K.N.L. is partially funded by an ERC Advanced Investigator grant (EVOCULTURE, 232823).

References

1 Deary, I. J. 2001 *Intelligence: a very short introduction*. Oxford, UK: Oxford University Press.

2 Herrmann, E., Call, J., Hernàndez-Lloreda, M. V., Hare, B. & Tomasello, M. 2007 Humans have evolved specialized skills of social cognition: the cultural intelligence hypothesis. *Science* **317**, 1360–1366.

3 Whiten, A. & van Schaik, C. P. 2007 The evolution of animal 'cultures' and social intelligence. *Phil. Trans. R. Soc. B* **362**, 603–620.

4 Wilson, A. C. 1985 The molecular basis of evolution. *Sci. Am.* **253**, 148–157.

5 Boyd, R. & Richerson, P. J. 1985 *Culture and the evolutionary process*. Chicago, IL: University of Chicago Press.

6 Reader, S. M. & Laland, K. N. 2002 Social intelligence, innovation and enhanced brain size in primates. *Proc. Natl Acad. Sci. USA* **99**, 4436–4441.

7 van Schaik, C. P. & Burkart, J. M. 2011 Social learning and evolution: the cultural intelligence hypothesis. *Phil. Trans. R. Soc. B* **366**, 1008–1016.

8 Mackintosh, N. J. 1998 *IQ and human intelligence*. Oxford, UK: Oxford University Press.

9 Gray, J. R. & Thompson, P. M. 2004 Neurobiology of intelligence: science and ethics. *Nat. Rev. Neurosci.* **5**, 471–482.

10 Neisser, U. *et al.* 1996 Intelligence: knowns and unknowns. *Am. Psychol.* **51**, 77–101.

11 van der Maas, H. L. J., Dolan, C. V., Grasman, R. P. P. P., Wicherts, J. M., Huizenga, H. M. & Raijmakers, M. E. J. 2006 A dynamical model of general intelligence: the positive manifold of intelligence by mutualism. *Psychol. Rev.* **113**, 842–861.

12 Dunbar, R. I. M. 1995 Neocortex size and group size in primates: a test of the hypothesis. *J. Hum. Evol.* **28**, 287–296.

13 Byrne, R. W. & Whiten, A (eds). 1988 *Machiavellian intelligence: social expertise and the evolution of intellect in monkeys, apes and humans*. Oxford, UK: Oxford University Press.

14 Whiten, A. & Byrne, R. W (eds). 1997 *Machiavellian intelligence II. Extensions and evaluations*. Cambridge, UK: Cambridge University Press.

15 Harvey, P. H. & Krebs, J. R. 1990 Comparing brains. *Science* **249**, 140–146.

16 Barton, R. A. 2006 Primate brain evolution: integrating comparative, neurophysiological, and ethological data. *Evol. Anthropol.* **15**, 224–236.

17 Deaner, R. O., Nunn, C. L. & van Schaik, C. P. 2000 Comparative tests of primate cognition: different scaling methods produce different results. *Brain Behav. Evol.* **55**, 44–52.

18 Seyfarth, R. M. & Cheney, D. L. 2002 What are big brains for? *Proc. Natl Acad. Sci. USA* **99**, 4141–4142.

19 Cheney, D. L. & Seyfarth, R. M. 2007 *Baboon metaphysics: the evolution of a social mind*. Chicago, IL: University of Chicago Press.

20 Dunbar, R.I.M. &Shultz,S.2007 Understanding primate brain evolution. *Phil. Trans. R. Soc. B* **362**, 649–658.

21 Overington, S. E., Dubois, F. & Lefebvre, L. 2008 Food unpredictability drives both generalism and social foraging: a game theoretical model. *Behav. Ecol.* **19**, 836–841.

22 Cheney, D. L. & Seyfarth, R. M. 1988 Social and non-social knowledge in vervet monkeys. In *Machiavellian intelligence: social expertise and the evolution of intellect in monkeys, apes and humans* (eds R. W. Byrne & A. Whiten), pp. 255–270. Oxford, UK: Oxford University Press.

23 Reader, S. M. & Lefebvre, L. 2001 Social learning and sociality. *Behav. Brain Sci.* **24**, 353–355.

24 Cosmides, L. & Tooby, J. 1987 From evolution to behavior: evolutionary psychology as the missing link. In *The latest on the best: essays on evolution and optimality* (ed. J. Dupre), pp. 277–306. Cambridge, MA: MIT Press.

25 Carruthers, P. 2006 *The architecture of the mind: massive modularity and the flexibility of thought.* Oxford, UK: Oxford University Press.

26 Clutton-Brock, T. H. & Harvey, P. H. 1980 Primates, brain and ecology. *J. Zool., Lond.* **190**, 309–323.

27 Tomasello, M. & Call, J. 1997 *Primate cognition.* New York, NY: Oxford University Press.

28 Deaner, R. O., van Schaik, C. & Johnson, V. 2006 Do some taxa have better domain-general cognition than others? A meta-analysis of nonhuman primate studies. *Evol. Psychol.* **4**, 149–196.

29 Banerjee, K., Chabris, C. F., Johnson, V. E., Lee, J. J., Tsao, F. & Hauser, M. D. 2009 General intelligence in another primate: individual differences across cognitive task performance in a new world monkey (*Saguinus oedipus*). *PLoS ONE* **4**, e5883.

30 Herrmann, E., Hernández-Lloreda, M. V., Call, J., Hare, B. & Tomasello, M. 2010 The structure of individual differences in the cognitive abilities of children and chimpanzees. *Psychol. Sci.* **21**, 102–110.

31 Emery, N.J. & Clayton, N. S. 2004 The mentality of crows: convergent evolution of intelligence in corvids and apes. *Science* **306**, 1903–1907.

32 Matzel, L.D., Han, Y.R., Grossman, H.S., Karnik, M.S., Patel, D., Scott, N., Specht, S. M. & Gandhi, C. C. 2003 Individual differences in the expression of a 'general' learning ability in mice. *J. Neurosci.* **23**, 6423–6433.

33 Kolata, S., Light, K. & Matzel, L. D. 2008 Domain-specific and domain-general learning factors are expressed in genetically heterogeneous cd-1 mice. *Intelligence* **36**, 619–629.

34 Reader, S. M. & Laland, K. N. (eds) 2003 *Animal innovation.* Oxford, UK: Oxford University Press.

35 Byrne, R. W. 1992 The evolution of intelligence. In *Behaviour and evolution* (eds P. J. B. Slater & T.R. Halliday), pp. 223–265. Cambridge, UK: Cambridge University Press.

36 Lefebvre, L., Whittle, P., Lascaris, E. & Finkelstein, A. 1997 Feeding innovations and forebrain size in birds. *Anim. Behav.* **53**, 549–560.

37 Lefebvre, L., Reader, S. M. & Sol, D. 2004 Brains, innovations and evolution in birds and primates. *Brain Behav. Evol.* **63**, 233–246.

38 Lefebvre, L. 2011 Taxonomic counts of cognition in the wild. *Biol. Lett.* **7**, 631–633.

39 Gibson, K. R. 1986 Cognition, brain size and the extraction of embedded food resources. In *Primate evolution* (ed. J. G. Else), pp. 95–103. New York, NY: Cambridge University Press.

40 Byrne, R. W. & Whiten, A. 1990 Tactical deception in primates: the 1990 data-base. *Prim. Rep.* **27**, 1–101.

41 Reader, S. M. & MacDonald, K. 2003 Environmental variability and primate behavioural flexibility. In *Animal innovation* (eds S. M. Reader & K. N. Laland), pp. 83–116. Oxford, UK: Oxford University Press.

42 Shultz, S. & Dunbar, R. I. M. 2010 Species differences in executive function correlate with hippocampus volume and neocortex ratio across nonhuman primates. *J. Comp. Psychol.* **124**, 252–260.

43 Harvey, P. H. & Pagel, M. D. 1991 *The comparative method in evolutionary biology.* Oxford, UK: Oxford University Press.

44 Purvis, A. & Rambaut, A. 1995 Comparative analysis by independent contrasts (CAIC): an Apple Macintosh application for analysing comparative data. *Comp. Appl. Biosci.* **11**, 247–251.

45 Purvis, A. & Webster, A. J. 1999 Phylogentically independent comparisons and primate phylogeny. In *Comparative primate socioecology* (ed. P. C. Lee), pp. 44–70. Cambridge, UK: Cambridge University Press.

46 Moura, A. C., de, A. & Lee, P. C. 2004 Capuchin stone tool use in Caatinga dry forest. *Science* **306**, 1909.

47 van Schaik, C. P., Deaner, R. O. & Merrill, M. Y. 1999 The conditions for tool use in primates: implications for the evolution of material culture. *J. Hum. Evol.* **36**, 719–741.

48 Perry, S. 2011 Social traditions and social learning in capuchin monkeys (*Cebus*). *Phil. Trans. R. Soc. B* **366**, 988–996.

49 Keverne, E. B., Martel, F. L. & Nevison, C. M. 1996 Primate brain evolution: genetic and functional considerations. *Proc. R. Soc. B* **262**, 689–696.

50 Riddell, W. I. & Corl, K. G. 1977 Comparative investigation of the relationship between cerebral indices and learning abilities. *Brain Behav. Evol.* **14**, 385–398.

51 Humphrey, N. K. 1976 The social function of intellect. In *Growing points in ethology* (eds P. P. G. Bateson & R. A. Hinde), pp. 303–317. Cambridge, UK: Cambridge University Press.

52 Jolly, A. 1966 Lemur social behavior and primate intelligence. *Science* **153**, 501–506.

53 Dunbar, R. I. M. 1992 Neocortex size as a constraint on group size in primates. *J. Hum. Evol.* **20**, 469–493.

54 Byrne, R. W. & Corp, N. 2004 Neocortex size predicts deception rate in primates. *Proc. R. Soc. Lond. B* **271**, 1693–1699.

55 Healy, S. D. & Rowe, C. 2007 A critique of comparative studies of brain size. *Proc. R. Soc. B* **274**, 453–464.

56 Dechmann, D. K. N. & Safi, K. 2009 Comparative studies of brain evolution: a critical insight from the chiroptera. *Biol. Rev.* **84**, 161–172.

57 Reader, S. M. 2003 Innovation and social learning: individual variation and brain evolution. *Anim. Biol.* **53**, 147–158.

58 Overington, S. E., Morand-Ferron, J., Boogert, N. J. & Lefebvre, L. 2009 Technical innovations drive the relationship between innovativeness and residual brain size in birds. *Anim. Behav.* **78**, 1001–1010.

59 Breuer, T., Ndoundou-Hockemba, M. & Fishlock, V. 2005 First observation of tool use in wild gorillas. *PLoS Biol.* **11**, 2041–2043.

60 Laidre, M. E. 2008 Spontaneous performance of wild baboons on three novel food-access puzzles. *Anim. Cogn.* **11**, 223–230.

61 Reader, S. M. & Biro, D. 2010 Experimental identification of social learning in wild animals. *Learn. Behav.* **38**, 265–283.

62 Bird, C. D. & Emery, N. J. 2009 Rooks use stones to raise the water level to reach a floating worm. *Curr. Biol.* **19**, 1410–1414.

63 Lefebvre, L., Nicolakakis, N. & Boire, D. 2002 Tools and brains in birds. *Behaviour* **139**, 939–973.

64 Chittka, L. & Niven, J. 2009 Are bigger brains better? *Curr. Biol.* **19**, R995–R1008.

65 Herculano-Houzel, S., Collins, C. E., Wong, P. Y. & Kaas, J. H. 2007 Cellular scaling rules for primate brains. *Proc. Natl Acad. Sci. USA* **104**, 3562–3567.

66 Deaner, R. O., Isler, K., Burkart, J. & van Schaik, C. 2007 Overall brain size, and not encephalization quotient, best predicts cognitive ability across non-human primates. *Brain Behav. Evol.* **70**, 115–124.

67 Deary, I. J. 2000 *Looking down on human intelligence: from psychometrics to the brain.* Oxford, UK: Oxford University Press.

68 Schoenemann, P. T. 2006 Evolution of the size and functional areas of the human brain. *Annu. Rev. Anthropol.* **35**, 379–406.

69 Shultz, S., Bradbury, R. B., Evans, K. L., Gregory, R. D. & Blackburn, T. M. 2005 Brain size and resource specialization predict long-term population trends in British birds. *Proc. R. Soc. B* **272**, 2305–2311.

70 Sol, D., Bacher, S., Reader, S. M. & Lefebvre, L. 2008 Brain size predicts the success of mammal species introduced into novel environments. *Am. Nat.* **172**, S63–S71.

71 Laland, K. N., Atton, N. & Webster, M. M. 2011 From fish to fashion: experimental and theoretical insights into the evolution of culture. *Phil. Trans. R. Soc. B* **366**, 958–968.

72 Lefebvre, L. & Bolhuis, J. J. 2003 Positive and negative correlates of feeding innovations in birds: evidence for limited modularity. In *Animal innovation* (eds S. M. Reader & K. N. Laland), pp. 39–61. Oxford, UK: Oxford University Press.

73 Fodor, J. A. 1983 *The modularity of mind.* Cambridge, MA: MIT Press.

74 Heyes, C. M. 1994 Social learning in animals: Categories and mechanisms. *Biol. Rev.* **69**, 207–231.

75 Leadbeater, E. & Chittka, L. 2007 Social learning in insects—from miniature brains to consensus building. *Curr. Biol.* **17**, R703–R713.

76 Olsson, A. & Phelps, E. A. 2007 Social learning of fear. *Nat. Neurosci.* **10**, 1095–1102.

77 Whiten, A. 2011 The scope of culture in chimpanzees, humans and ancestral apes. *Phil. Trans. R. Soc. B* **366**, 997–1007.

78 Dickens, W. T. & Flynn, J. R. 2001 Heritability estimates versus large environmental effects: the IQ paradox resolved. *Psychol. Rev.* **108**, 346–369.

79 Odling-Smee, F. J., Laland, K. N. & Feldman, M. W. 2003 *Niche construction: the neglected process in evolution.* Princeton, NJ: Princeton University Press.

80 Hoppitt, W., Boogert, N. J. & Laland, K. N. 2010 Detecting social transmission in networks. *J. Theor. Biol.* **263**, 544–555.

81 Franz, M. & Nunn, C. L. 2009 Network-based diffusion analysis: a new method for detecting social learning. *Proc. R. Soc. B* **276**, 1829–1836.

82 Rieucau, G. & Giraldeau, L.-A. 2011 Exploring the costs and benefits of social information use: an appraisal of current experimental evidence. *Phil. Trans. R. Soc. B* **366**, 949–957.

83 Stout, D. 2011 Stone toolmaking and the evolution of human culture and cognition. *Phil. Trans. R. Soc. B* **366**, 1050–1059.

84 Lindeyer, C. M. & Reader, S. M. 2010 Social learning of escape routes in zebrafish and the stability of behavioural traditions. *Anim. Behav.* **79**, 827–834.

85 Shipley, B. 2002 *Cause and correlation in biology: a user's guide to path analysis, structural equations and causal inference.* Cambridge, UK: Cambridge University Press.

Chapter 10

The Origins of Stone Tool Technology in Africa: A Historical Perspective

Ignacio de la Torre

The search for the earliest stone tools is a topic that has received much attention in studies on the archaeology of human origins. New evidence could position the oldest traces of stone tool-use before 3.39 Myr, substantially earlier than previously documented. Nonetheless, the first unmistakable evidence of tool-making dates to 2.6 Ma, the period in which Oldowan assemblages first appear in the East African record. However, this is not an unchangeable time boundary, and considerations about the *tempo* and *modo* of tool-making emergence have varied through time. This chapter summarizes the history of research on the origins of stone knapping in Africa and places the current evidence in a historical perspective.

Keywords: stone tools; Oldowan; Africa; early Pleistocene; archaeology of human origins; history of palaeoanthropology

10.1 Introduction

The quest for the earliest evidence of culture is one of the main fields of research in human evolutionary studies and has occupied many scholars since the beginning of the discipline. During the last decade, there has been widespread consensus regarding 2.5–2.6 Myr—the age of the oldest Oldowan assemblages in Gona [1]—as the time period in which the earliest signs of human culture are traceable in the archaeological record. However, this chronological rubicon has changed during the two centuries of investigations on the archaeology of human origins. Indeed, the 2.5–2.6 Myr time barrier, in recent years considered as a consolidated threshold for the emergence of lithic technology, has just been shattered with new discoveries in Dikika, which if confirmed could push back the empirical evidence for stone tool use to before 3.39 Ma [2].

Given that a number of recent studies review the state of the art in Oldowan research and the origins of stone tool technology according to current archaeological evidence [3–6], this chapter adopts an alternative perspective, giving a double meaning to 'culture evolves' by examining not only the empirical record for the dawn of technology in Africa, but also the origins and evolution of ideas about this subject. The 'year zero' for the earliest cultural evidence, explanatory models for the emergence of technology and the possible makers of the first stone tools have varied substantially throughout the history of the discipline, according to theories and paradigms dominant in each research period. This chapter will consider the evolution of such ideas and place the current view of Oldowan technology in a historical perspective.

10.2 **Early perspectives on the origins of stone tool technology**

It was only at the end of the seventeenth century that stone tools ceased to be included within the general category of fossils and began to be considered as humanly made [7]. During the eighteenth and nineteenth centuries, lithic artefacts were classified and systematized into successive cultural phases, leading to highly influential models such as those developed by Thomsen and Boucher de Perthes, still used today as the basics of cultural classification in prehistory. The search for the earliest stone tools became a popular field of research from the beginning, and polemics soon arose; the question of the Eolithic came up in the 1860s, when Bourgeois announced the presence of flint tools in the Oligocene deposits of Thenay in France. Since then, alleged discoveries claimed the existence of 'Tertiary man' assemblages older than those of the Palaeolithic, made by humans living in a period—the Eolithic—in which stones were crudely worked or not knapped but used in their natural form. At the beginning of the twentieth century, Boule [8] attempted to demonstrate the dubious nature of the Eolithic industries claimed to have been discovered in Europe. However, despite the efforts of influential researchers (e.g. [8]), the Eolithic issue continued to be the subject of great controversies. Piltdown Man, for example, provided key support for the Eolith hypothesis until the 1940s and 1950s [9, 10], for it was assumed that, although Eolithic stones alone could be considered as natural, their association with a human fossil demonstrated their archaeological nature; in a tautological paradox, the dubious Piltdown Man provided support for the alleged stone tools it was associated with (and vice versa), and hence was used to prove the existence of the Eolithic culture in Europe.

In the meantime, researchers in Africa had started to develop the first cultural sequences, initially based on European referential frameworks. Leaving aside the polemic Eolithic, the Chellean was considered in Europe as the earliest handaxe culture, followed by the Acheulean, and then the Middle and Upper Palaeolithic. Although no absolute chronologies were available, Goodwin & Van Riet Lowe [11] proposed the Stellenbosch industry as the oldest in the African continent, which was paralleled to the European Chellean. However, new fieldwork led to the recognition of a culture even older than the Chellean, the Oldowan, named after the then-called Oldoway Gorge. In his first visit to the gorge in 1931, Louis Leakey discovered in the lower part of the sequence stone tools that seemed to exist before the emergence of handaxes and the Chellean. The first news of this novel industry was published in *Nature* on 26 December of that year [12], although the term Oldowan was still not employed (Table 10.1). A little later, a conference was organized in Cambridge by the Royal Anthropological Institute to discuss Leakey's [25] discoveries. At this meeting, Leakey reported the existence of a pebble industry in Oldoway Bed I, older than the Chellean from Bed II and the Acheulean from Bed III. Illustrious convenors,

Table 10.1 Some of the major events in the history of early stone tools in Africa

major events	reference
2009 cutmarked bones in Dikika reported to be older than 3.39 Myr	[2]
1999 sophisticated reduction sequences reported at Lokalalei 2C	[13]
1997 earliest stone tools dated at 2.5 Ma in Gona	[14]
1973 first archaeological discoveries in Hadar	[15]
1971 publication of excavations in Olduvai Beds I and II	[16]
1969 first lithics discovered in Omo	[17, 18]
1961 radiometric dating of the Oldowan at Olduvai	[19]
1960 discovery of *Homo habilis*, considered the first Oldowan toolmaker	[20]
1959 discovery of *Zinjanthropus boisei* associated with Oldowan tools	[21]
1934 formal description of the Oldowan	[22, 23]
1931 Louis Leakey reports 'pre-Chellean' artefacts in Olduvai	[12]
1913 Hans Reck reports fossiliferous beds in Olduvai	[24]

such as Gordon Childe, Burke, Bate and Smith Woodward, accepted that in Oldoway there was a gradual evolution from the pebble industry to handaxe cultures, and concluded that 'there is no reason to doubt that the series from East Africa is of at least equal antiquity with the European, and it may even begin somewhat earlier' [25, p. 67]. Although the term 'Oldowan' had not yet appeared in the proceedings of the Cambridge conference [25], this meeting was essential for the acceptance of such a culture [26].

Immediately afterwards, one of the earliest descriptions noted that 'the principal tool of the Oldowan culture is of very simple form. A rolled pebble or a nodule of chert, or a rough lump of almost any kind of rock is trimmed very roughly along one edge or side, so as to produce a jagged cutting edge' [22, p. 144], and a formal definition would follow, asserting that 'The Oldowan culture comprises a series of artefacts which are made either from water-worn pebbles or from lumps of rock. The piece of material to be made into a tool was then trimmed very roughly by striking off flakes in two directions so that the line of intersection of these flake scars gave a jagged cutting edge along one side of the pebble or lump of rock' [23, p. 40].

The Oldowan was not automatically accepted by all researchers as evidence of the earliest human culture in Africa. In 1919, Wayland had discovered another lithic industry, in the stone assemblages collected from the terraces of the Kafu River in Uganda. This culture, named Kafuan, consisted of fractured cobbles which were very archaic looking [27]. Although the characterization of the Kafuan and its sub-stages was based on dubious criteria such as the roundness or the elongation of pieces collected from river terraces with high-energy deposits [26], the fact remains that the term Kafuan became established in the archaeological literature of the 1930s–1950s (e.g. [28, 29]). Indeed, Leakey [23] even commented that he would have preferred to consider the assemblages of the lower beds at Olduvai as Developed Kafuan, but did not do so because Wayland argued that the Olduvai collections were more advanced than the most developed Kafuan culture.

Curiously, Leakey's renowned prescient skills failed for once when, referring to the Kafuan, he asserted that 'there is not really any justification for giving a separate culture name to the last stage of the 'pebble culture', and eventually the name 'Oldowan' will probably be dropped' [23, p. 40]. Eventually, it was the other way around, and by the end of the 1950s the Kafuan had almost disappeared from the literature; in a remarkably similar trajectory as the Eolithic in Europe [9], cumulative evidence led to the conclusion that the alleged assemblages from the higher terraces of African rivers were mere natural rocks [30, 31]. Tacitly, the Kafuan had ceased to exist.

Nonetheless, the Oldowan was not yet considered by all researchers as the earliest evidence of culture, and in the 1950s a new contender appeared. In the post-World War II scientific environment nearly all the academic community had accepted that the South African australopithecines were bipedal and somehow related to humans. In this context, it was suggested that australopithecine fossils were associated with cultural remains, the so-called osteodontokeratic industry [32]. Based on the Makapansgat assemblages, Dart proposed that australopithecines employed bones, teeth and horn in a variety of subsistence activities that included the killing and processing of animal carcasses.

Decades later, Brain [33] demonstrated that the australopithecines were the hunted rather than the hunters, whose remains had been accumulated alongside those of other animals by predators transporting carcasses to trees. Subsequently, the osteodontokeratic industry as defined by Dart [32] was largely discredited. Nevertheless, recent studies have provided new insights into the possible use of bone tools by South African australopithecines [34], which to some extent have revived credibility for Dart's original osteodontokeratic proposal.

10.3 Olduvai as a sequence of reference

With the settling of the Kafuan controversy [30, 31] and the ruling out of stratigraphic relationships between human fossils and lithic assemblages in the South African caves [35, 36], by the end of the 1950s there seemed to be consensus on the absence of links between australopithecines and stone tools. However, the 1959 discovery of the *Zinjanthropus* (now *Paranthropus*) *boisei* skull, spatially associated with a large lithic assemblage, sparked new controversies; according to Louis Leakey, the fact that the FLK Zinj site was located in the lower part of the Olduvai sequence proved the connection between the Oldowan culture and *Zinjanthropus boisei*.

Leakey's purpose was anything but innocuous, and it resembles Dart's attempts to provide South African australopithecines with some human traits by granting them the capacity for making the Osteodontokeratic culture. Leakey's consideration of the *boisei* skull as a new genus found considerable opposition, as many believed *boisei* could fit better within the South African genus *Paranthropus* named by Broom [37]—see review by Wood & Constantino [38]. However, Leakey [39] alleged that *Zinjanthropus* was ancestral to modern humans, the 'proof' being that *boisei* was a tool-maker; once again, cultural traits were used to justify phylogenetic links. Using a type of tautological reasoning, Leakey argued that the South African *Paranthropus* and *Australopithecus* were not 'real humans', for they did not make artefacts, whereas *Zinjanthropus* knapped stone tools and, therefore, was a human ancestor.

Despite controversies, the Oldowan was becoming central in the debate about the earliest cultural evidence in Africa. In fact, stone tools had adopted a pivotal role in explanatory mechanisms of human evolution. For example, Washburn [40] assumed that the adoption of bipedalism was directly related to tool-use. Along similar lines, Robinson [41] linked tool-making, brain size increase and bipedalism, although he rejected the idea that australopithecines—among which he included *Australopithecus, Paranthropus* and *Zinjanthropus*—made stone tools. Interestingly, Robinson [35, 41] distinguished between tool-use, which he accepted for australopithecines, and tool-making, exclusive to the genus *Homo*.

In this context, Olduvai (Figure 10.1) soon produced a new controversy with the discovery of *Homo habilis* [20]. More gracile and morphologically similar to humans than *Zinjanthropus boisei*, the very definition of *Homo habilis*, 'handy man', entailed that this hominin was seen as the author of the Oldowan. In a U-turn of earlier arguments, *Zinjanthropus boisei* became the prey of *Homo habilis* rather than the maker of the Oldowan tools [20]. It should be kept in mind that the anatomical arguments used by Leakey *et al.* [20] to include *habilis* within the genus *Homo* were highly controversial (see [42]), so once again cultural traits were tautologically employed to help justify taxonomic classifications; in this new reading of the evidence, the fact that *habilis* made stone tools 'proved' that it belonged to the genus *Homo* [20].

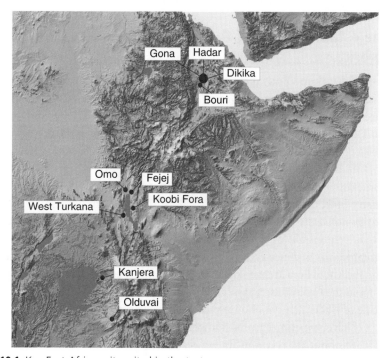

Figure 10.1 Key East African sites cited in the text.

The paradigm change caused by discoveries in Olduvai (Table 10.1) was also prompted by the radically new chronological framework developed for early archaeological assemblages; at the onset of the 1960s, most of the 'pre-Acheulean' evidence available corresponded to surface artefacts collected in river terraces all across Africa, plus some sparse archaeological remains from the South African caves. On the basis of the Pluvial theory originally proposed by Wayland (e.g. [27]), it was thought that the oldest stone tools corresponded to the end of the so-called First Pluvial or beginning of the Second Pluvial, no earlier than half a million years ago. However, the K/Ar dating of Olduvai Bed I [19] revolutionized temporal scales of human evolution; now shown to be older than 1.7 Myr, FLK Zinj placed stone tool-making more than 1 Myr earlier than had previously been considered.

In sum, by the mid-1960s, research on the earliest human cultures in Africa had undergone dramatic changes; it was now understood that typological sequences established in fluvial terraces across the entire continent had no chronological reliability and were of no use in differentiating techno-cultural stages. Furthermore, the inability to link the fossil-rich caves of South Africa with reliable radiometric and archaeological contexts made it difficult to use those sequences as a comparative reference. In contrast, Olduvai in East Africa yielded fluvio-lacustrine deposits with *in situ* assemblages, associations between stone tools and human fossils, and a reliable radiometric sequence. Consequently, by the mid-1960s there was consensus that the earliest cultural evidence was at least 1.8 Myr old, corresponded to the Oldowan (a culture defined three decades earlier), and had probably been made by hominins like the *Homo habilis* discovered in Olduvai Bed I.

10.4 The establishment of the modern chrono-stratigraphic framework

Success of fieldwork in Olduvai encouraged further research projects in East Africa, which in turn led to the discovery of new fossiliferous sequences throughout the Rift Valley. Two of the areas found during the late 1960s to early 1970s, Hadar and Koobi Fora (Figure 10.1), became particularly significant. The controversy over the dating of the Kay Behrensmeyer Site (KBS) industry—the oldest stone tools at Koobi Fora—(see summary in Brown [43]), resembled earlier attempts to link taxonomic classifications and archaeological contexts. Given the similarities between the Olduvai Bed I assemblages and the KBS industry [44], the original date for the Koobi Fora assemblages of 2.6 Myr was claimed to demonstrate an early emergence of the genus *Homo* which, by default, was assumed to be responsible for the stone tools. However, cumulative radiometric [45] and biostratigraphic [46] evidence eventually proved the original dating of the KBS tuff to be wrong, and the Koobi Fora archaeological sites were firmly established at around 1.8 Myr, the same age as the Olduvai Bed I assemblages.

In the case of Hadar, the paramount palaeontological implications of *Australopithecus afarensis* [47] have sometimes overshadowed the pivotal role this discovery also had in changing views about the relationship between tool-making and human evolution. As mentioned above, during the 1960s many considered that there was a close link between encephalization, adoption of bipedalism and emergence of stone tool-making [40, 41, 48]. However, the discovery of *Australopithecus afarensis*, a small-brained hominin dated to approximately 3.2 Myr, established a gap of almost 1.5 Myr between the oldest lithic assemblages in Olduvai and the earliest evidence of bipedalism in Hadar. Hence, *Australopithecus afarensis* proved that there was no cause-effect relationship between the emergence of bipedalism and stone tool-making; in a pendulum swing that revived pre-World War II paradigms [49], australopithecines were once again considered as little more than specialized apes. Therefore, it can be argued that, owing to the discoveries in Hadar and the ever-expanding chronological gap between the earliest hominins and the oldest stone tools, the 1970s and 1980s witnessed the separation of paradigms ruling human palaeontology and those related to the archaeology of human origins; cultural domains had ceased to be considered as a pivotal evolutionary mechanism driving the emergence of hominins.

Nonetheless, despite the increasing divergence between human palaeontology and archaeology, the Oldowan was firmly established as a term defining the earliest traces of human culture. The publication of excavations in Olduvai Beds I and II [16] provided a solid chrono-stratigraphic background and an unparalleled archaeological dataset, which became the empirical and methodological frame of reference for the rest of the Oldowan sequences in Africa [50]. By the 1970s, nearly all the scientific community agreed that the earliest evidence of culture was to be found in Africa, especially in the area of the Rift Valley. Continued fieldwork led to the discovery of even older assemblages than those in Olduvai and Koobi Fora; in Omo (Figure 10.1), lithic assemblages were discovered in the Shungura Formation [17, 18]. With a provisional age of 2.04 Myr—subsequently pushed back to 2.34 Myr [51]—the Omo sites provided some of the earliest evidence for stone tool-making. Also in the 1970s, early stone tools were reported in Gona/Hadar [15], for which a similar age to Omo was suggested. However, owing to the absence of precise radiometric and stratigraphic contexts for the Gona/Hadar material, Omo had the most reliable evidence for the earliest human culture during the 1970s and the 1980s.

Over the last two decades, there has been an exponential increase in evidence for early technologies; in the Gona area (Figure 10.1), recent fieldwork dated *in situ* assemblages to 2.5–2.6 Myr [14], making them the earliest stone tools yet known. Slightly younger are other lithic assemblages recently discovered in Hadar [52] and West Turkana [13], positioned in the same age interval as the Omo archaeological sites, at approximately 2.3 Myr. In short, the current archaeological record includes a number of well-dated lithic assemblages, which confirm that by 2.5 Myr stone tools were regularly made by some hominins. Given that the oldest fossils of early *Homo* [52, 53] are bracketed in the same age interval as the earliest stone tools, a common view has related the speciation event leading to the origins of *Homo* with the emergence of stone tools, whereas australopithecines usually have been depicted as lacking stone tool-making abilities. The increasingly larger gap between the earliest hominins—now dated at 6–7 Myr [54]—and the approximately 2.5 Myr date of the earliest stone tools [14], has maintained the rejection of causal connections between early phases of hominin evolution and the emergence of stone tool-making.

Nonetheless, there have been new attempts to link phylogenetic relationships with cultural evidence, such as in the case of *Australopithecus garhi* [55], for which an ancestral relation to *Homo* is proposed not only by chronological and anatomical similarities but also by its association with cut-marked bones [56].

The scenario is becoming increasingly complex; during the last two decades there has been agreement in positioning the earliest archaeological evidence at 2.5–2.6 Myr, and relating the appearance of stone tool-making to climatic changes, emergence of new hominin species and dietary shifts. Nonetheless, the recent discovery of cut-marked fossils in Dikika that could be older than 3.39 Myr [2], in a context where only *Australopithecus afarensis* may have existed, could force a reconsideration of some of the explanatory models traditionally proposed to explain the origins of stone tool-making.

10.5 Changing perspectives on the Oldowan

All modern conceptions of the earliest stone tools are based on the Oldowan technology and the monumental work of Leakey [16] in Olduvai. Nevertheless, views of the Oldowan have changed over the last few decades, due not only to empirical evidence available at the time, but also influenced by shifting dominant theories [50]. The chronological, stratigraphic and archaeological framework established by Leakey [16] was fundamentally typological and deeply rooted in the historical–cultural approach developed in Europe by Bordes [50]. From this perspective, the Oldowan and its variants were characterized by variable percentages of lithic types such as choppers, polyhedrons, discoids, different retouched types and others [16]. Inter-assemblage comparisons were based on tool-type frequencies, which were believed to have chrono-stratigraphic and cultural implications.

The advent of processualism in archaeology greatly influenced Oldowan studies (e.g. [57], N. Toth 1982, unpublished PhD thesis). This approach focused on function rather than typology of stone tools. Following a remarkably similar pattern as occurred in Middle Palaeolithic research [58], Oldowan morphological variability was considered to be the result of artefact reduction intensity, not the product of culturally designed shapes [57, 59]. In this perspective, the basic objective of Oldowan technology was the production of flakes (which in previous typological studies were considered as mere by-products), whereas core forms would vary according to cost–benefit strategies of raw material transport and use.

In recent years, integrative perspectives have been pursued and modern technological studies aim to combine processual views with the *chaîne opératoire*[1] approach [5, 50]. The importance of the study of reduction methods in the Oldowan is increasingly recognized and discussion of the technical abilities of early knappers is a key issue in Oldowan research. However, views on this topic have also changed through time, heavily influenced by their historical context.

Until the mid-1990s, it can be argued that the trend was to emphasize the archaism of earliest industries. Chavaillon [17], for example, coined the term 'Shungura facies' to describe the Omo assemblages, which, being considerably older than those at Olduvai and Koobi Fora, were thought to be also technologically more archaic. In a similar vein,

Roche [61] proposed that assemblages older than 2 Myr were made by hominins who did not control the basics of stone tool knapping and displayed poor technological skills. At that time, the term 'Pre-Oldowan' was frequently used to refer to assemblages older than those from Koobi Fora and Olduvai. Thus, it was proposed that assemblages earlier than 2 Myr were characterized by low density accumulations and poor management of lithic resources [62]. The term 'Nachukui industry' was coined for the West Turkana assemblages which, alongside the Shungura Facies [17], would constitute the Omo Industrial Complex [62]. In this context, the simplicity of early lithic technologies was emphasized, and it was proposed that the Oldowan as a whole showed the same level of skills as displayed by extant apes [63].

It is likely that the very limited evidence available in the 1970s and 1980s, alongside the unimpressive lithics of Omo and the reported simplicity of Lokalalei 1 in West Turkana, contributed to shape an 'ape's view' of the earliest industries. It could be argued, however, that such a perspective was also yet another expression of the dominant paradigm in Palaeolithic archaeology that, led by Binford [64, 65], emphasized the behavioural archaism of pre-modern humans. In response to this view, the last two decades have witnessed a steady paradigmatic change, through which the behavioural sophistication of pre-*sapiens* humans has become increasingly acknowledged [66]. New archaeological evidence in Middle and Lower Palaeolithic research has undoubtedly contributed to this changing view of previous interpretations, but it is also likely that the same record is now being considered from a different perspective.

Oldowan research exemplifies this theoretical shift, in which the discovery breakthroughs at Gona [14] and Lokalalei 2C [13] have been pivotal in shaping modern views about early technologies. The 2.6–2.5 Myr Gona assemblages [14] demonstrate that early knappers understood and controlled the principles of conchoidal fracture, i.e. they knew that certain rocks can be broken according to the direction and intensity of the force transmitted. Gona knappers applied this knowledge to successfully obtain series of flakes from cores exploited through a panoply of methods [67] on rocks that were preferentially selected from raw material sources [68]. This required complex grip coordination and developed perceptual abilities [69], probably beyond the range of skills displayed by extant apes [4, 6]. Along the same lines, the approximately 2.3 Myr site of Lokalalei 2C in West Turkana [13] has provided stunning evidence regarding the skills of early knappers; as at Gona, cobbles were preferentially selected from raw material sources and transported to the site [70]. Some of the conjoined sets account for more than 50 flakes [71], demonstrating that stone toolmakers were capable of systematically reducing cores. The Lokalalei 2C assemblage indicates knappers' ability to adapt to technical problems arising during the reduction sequence, displaying not only sophisticated know-how, but also considerable motor skills [71].

Preliminary data from pene-contemporary sites in Hadar [72] and reassessment of some of the Omo assemblages [73] also suggest that by 2.3 Myr hominins had already mastered the principles ruling stone knapping. Therefore, recent research on early technologies tends to emphasize the complexity of the first lithic assemblages, contradicting previous views on the alleged simplicity of the early Oldowan. Nonetheless, this new scenario prompts further questions on the evolutionary significance of the origins of stone tool-making, especially with regard to two issues: the processes that led to the emergence of stone knapping, and the evolutionary relationships between the earliest industries and the post-2 Myr Oldowan assemblages.

With respect to the evolutionary processes resulting in the emergence of the earliest archaeological sites, there was some perplexity when Gona showed that the first stone tools already demonstrated correct understanding of knapping principles [14, 74]. A gradualist evolutionary perspective expected that the earliest archaeological assemblages would represent poor attempts to obtain stone tools. However, the evidence from Gona and then Lokalalei 2C has provoked a reconsideration of this view; some now suggest that the emergence of stone tool production could have been an abrupt event slightly earlier than 2.6 Myr [74], whereas others have proposed the existence of an older than 2.5 Myr pre-archaeological phase, during which hominins experimented with stone tool manufacture [75]. According to the latter view, if in the period before 2.5 Myr knappers did not accumulate lithics at particular spots in the landscape, such behavioural patterns would not lead to the formation of sites, and therefore the earliest stone tools would be archaeologically invisible [59]. Interestingly, in the current paradigmatic cycle where alternative evolutionary mechanisms such as punctuated equilibrium and saltation have also become influential in archaeology (e.g. [66]), the 'pre-Gona' experimental stone tool-making hypothesis is still preferred by many, despite this theory of gradualist acquisition of technology advocating a pre-archaeological stage which is, by its own definition, empirically non-testable. In this context, studies combining primatological and archaeological evidence in order to trace the evolutionary origins of technology have proliferated [76, 77], although the limits of such comparisons have also been stated [4, 6].

Modern hypotheses will also have to accommodate the new evidence from Dikika; according to the discoverers [2], cut-marks on the pre-3.39 Myr bones could have been inflicted by naturally sharp-edged stone tools and not necessarily by intentionally knapped flakes. From this perspective, the 2.6 Myr sites at Gona remain the earliest documented evidence of intentional flaking. Nonetheless, now discoverers of the Dikika fossils claim that hominins were using sharp-edged tools 800 000 years earlier than at Gona. If confirmed, this proposal would provide new evidence to support the existence of a long process of experimentation with stone tool-making and/or use before hominins had mastered the principles of knapping by 2.6 Myr. Furthermore, it suggests that different hominin species could have been involved in that process.

Lastly, present evidence about the earliest Oldowan also prompts discussions on technological and cultural links between the earliest industries and the post-2 Myr Oldowan assemblages. There is now debate on the validity of considering the Oldowan as a single techno-complex during the approximately 1 Myr span from Gona to the emergence of the Acheulean around 1.7–1.6 Ma. With the demonstration of the technological sophistication of the earliest industries [13, 14], some authors prefer to include all the pre-Acheulean evidence within the Oldowan [74], whereas others propose a chronological meaning for the term 'Pre-Oldowan', reserved for sites older than 2 Myr [78]. Technological variability of the earliest sites has been the subject of recent debates [67, 73], but a systematic comparison with post-2 Myr Oldowan assemblages remains to be undertaken. Nonetheless, whereas two decades ago it was common to associate earlier sites with a more archaic technology, at present one could be tempted to do the reverse; Gona [67] and Lokalalei 2C [71] show more intense reduction sequences and more precise knapping skills than, for example, the classic Oldowan sequences at Olduvai Bed I [16, 79], which is more than 500 000 years younger. Accordingly, it is difficult to trace temporal trends within the Oldowan, and even more complicated to propose evolutionary progression.

This chapter assumes that a techno-complex is a group of cultures that share similar general traits but different specific types according to variable ecological and cultural features [80]. From this perspective and considering the current available evidence, it can be argued that the Oldowan techno-complex, based on the production of flakes through a variety of non-prepared methods of core reduction, shows significant inter-assemblage variability, conditioned by ecological, temporal and cultural parameters, and which most probably involved several species of hominins. Perhaps due to the unspecific traits defining the Oldowan as a technology, the mechanisms which lead to the emergence 1.7–1.6 Ma of a new techno-complex, the Acheulean, are still unclear.

10.6 A current view of the earliest stone tool-making

Current evidence could place the earliest use of stone tools in the Pliocene, at before 3.39 Ma [2]. This suggests that stone tool use has deep roots in our evolutionary lineage [75, 77], and could have played an instrumental role during some stages of human evolution. The oldest lithic assemblages discovered so far are substantially younger, with the earliest evidence at Gona dated at 2.6 Myr [1]. The Gona stone tools are followed by approximately 2.3 Myr lithic assemblages in West Turkana [78], Omo [17, 18] and Hadar [52]. Close to 2 Myr Oldowan assemblages are also documented in Kanjera [81], Koobi Fora [82] and Fejej [83], followed by the classic sequences at Olduvai [16], Koobi Fora [84] and others.

The earliest evidence of stone tool use and/or making seem to show spatial and chronological patterning; geographically (Figure 10.1), the oldest archaeological traces are limited to the northern part of the East African Rift Valley, with Bouri, Gona and arguably Dikika yielding evidence of tool use before 2.4 Myr. By approximately 2.3 Myr, toolmaking is also evidenced in the Lake Turkana basin (Omo, West Turkana), and by 2 Ma it had extended further to the south in the Lake Victoria region (e.g. Kanjera). The post-2 Myr Oldowan spread across the Rift Valley, eventually reaching South [85] and North Africa [86], and beyond [87].

All the earliest assemblages seem to share a number of features; Gona [14, 67], Hadar [72], Lokalalei 2C [71], Kanjera [81] and some of the Omo sites [73] indicate that early knappers controlled the mechanisms of conchoidal fracture and the basic principles of stone knapping. With regard to assemblage composition, all these sites show similar percentages in which cores and flakes predominate, standardized forms are absent and retouched tools are not abundant. Recurrent reduction of the same exploitation surfaces of cores is well attested, although there is substantial inter-assemblage variation regarding the use of unifacial, bifacial and multi-facial methods. Core striking platforms are usually unprepared and rejuvenation products aimed to reactivate flaking, although sometimes documented (e.g. Lokalalei 2C), are not abundant; once knapping surfaces lose the necessary convexities, cores are discarded. Raw material selectivity has been reported in most of the early sites [68, 70, 81, 88], and it is likely that raw material factors played a major role in the length of reduction sequences; the quality, large size and abundance of cobbles in areas such as Gona [68], West Turkana [70] and Hadar [88] could have facilitated long sequences of core exploitation, whereas the smaller size of raw materials available in Omo [73] and Kanjera [81] conditioned the number of flaking series. In short, the earliest assemblages show a well-reasoned technological process which began with the preferential selection of suitable raw materials, continued with an understanding of the volumetric concepts required to exploit such raw materials and a successful application of that know-how in the reduction of cores, followed by an optimal production of flakes.

10.7 **Conclusion**

At present, and coinciding with the first centenary of the scientific discovery of Olduvai Gorge by Kattwinkel in 1911, there is a considerable wealth of empirical data on the Oldowan and the origins of stone tool technology in Africa. There is also enough temporal distance to consider advances of the discipline from a historical perspective. This chapter has attempted to integrate both aspects, placing the current view of the Oldowan on historiographic grounds. Here, it has been argued that an early phase of research covered investigations until the late 1950s, which were characterized by poor stratigraphic control of assemblages and the absence of absolute dates for the early stone tools [11, 23, 27, 29]. The cascade of findings [19–21] in Olduvai Gorge since 1959 provided the Oldowan with a well-established stratigraphic sequence that pushed back stone tool-making to approximately 2 Myr, and sparked further discoveries in Africa, especially in the Rift Valley. Whereas in the 1960s it was common to associate hominin origins with stone tool-making [40, 41], the modern research period that began in the 1970s demonstrated that the first stages of hominization underwent an independent process that started much earlier than the Oldowan. During the 1970s and 1980s, the limited empirical evidence and the influence of the 'Binfordian' paradigm [64, 65] led to the portrayal of the Oldowan as a very simple and archaic technology, not too different from that displayed by extant apes [63]. Nevertheless, in the last 20 years this perspective has changed, owing in part to new discoveries [13, 14], but also influenced by a new theoretical environment which emphasizes the complexity of early human behaviour (see a summary in Whiten *et al.* [89]).

Today, earliest Oldowan assemblages are seen as indicative of the sophistication of the technology of early knappers. However, it is important to stress that this interpretation is rooted in contemporary paradigms and biased by the record currently available. The aim of this chapter has been to emphasize how variable perspectives are, especially when considered in their historical context. When Louis Leakey first reported the existence of an early industry in Olduvai, the conception of early technologies was very different from that of the present day. But there is no need to go back to 1931; only 1 year ago, the earliest evidence of stone tool use was 2.6 Myr. Now, this has been pushed back to 800 000 years earlier. As such, there is little doubt that new surprises await us in our future search for the earliest stone tools.

Acknowledgements

I wish to thank Norah Moloney, Chris Stringer, Andrew Whiten and two anonymous reviewers for their comments on earlier drafts of this chapter.

Note

1 See description of *chaîne opératoire* in the glossary to Goren-Inbar [60] (here, Chapter 11) in this collection.

References

1 Semaw, S. *et al.* 2003 2.6-Million-year-old stone tools and associated bones from OGS-6 and OGS-7, Gona, Afar, Ethiopia. *J. Hum. Evol.* **45**, 169–177.

2 McPherron, S. P., Alemseged, Z., Marean, C. W., Wynn, J. G., Reed, D., Geraads, D., Bobe, R. & Bearat, H. A. 2010 Evidence for stone-tool-assisted consumption of animal tissues before 3.39 million years ago at Dikika, Ethiopia. *Nature* **466**, 857–860.

3 Schick, K. & Toth, N. 2006 An Overview of the Oldowan industrial complex: the sites and the nature of their evidence. In *The Oldowan: case studies into the earliest Stone Age* (eds N. Toth & K. Schick), pp. 3–42. Gosport, IN: Stone Age Institute.

4 Toth, N. & Schick, K. 2009 The Oldowan: the tool making of early hominins and chimpanzees compared. *Annu. Rev. Anthropol.* **38**, 289–305.

5 Hovers, E. & Braun, D. R. (eds) 2009 *Interdisciplinary approaches to the Oldowan*. Dordrecht, The Netherlands: Springer.

6 Torre, I. de la 2010 Insights on the technical competence of the early Oldowan. In *Stone tools and the evolution of human cognition* (eds A. Nowell & I. Davidson), pp. 45–65. Boulder, CO: University Press of Colorado.

7 Grayson, D. K. 1983 *The establishment of human antiquity*. New York, NY: Academic Press.

8 Boule, M. 1905 L'origine des éolithes. *L'Anthropologie* **16**, 257–267.

9 Grayson, D. K. 1986 Eoliths, archaeological ambiguity, and the generation of 'middle-range' research. In *American archaeology past and future: a celebration of the Society for American Archaeology* 1935–1985 (eds D. J. Meltzer, D. D. Fowler & J. A. Sabloff), pp. 77–133. Washington, DC: Smithsonian Institution Press.

10 McNabb, J. 2006 The lying stones of Sussex: an investigation into the role of the flint tools in the development of the Piltdown forgery. *Archaeol. J.* **163**, 1–41.

11 Goodwin, A. J. H. & Van Riet Lowe, C. 1929 *The Stone Age cultures of South Africa*. Edinburgh: Annals of the South African Museum, nº XXVII.

12 Leakey, L. S. B., Hopwood, A. T. & Reck, H. 1931 New yields from the Oldoway bone beds, Tanganyika territory. *Nature* **128**, 1075.

13 Roche, H., Delagnes, A., Brugal, J.-P., Feibel, C., Kibunjia, M., Mourre, V. & Texier, J. 1999 Early hominid stone tool production and technical skill 2.34 Myr ago in West Turkana, Kenya. *Nature* **399**, 57–60.

14 Semaw, S., Renne, P., Harris, J. W. K., Feibel, C. S., Bernor, R. L., Fesseha, N. & Mowbray, K. 1997 2.5-million-year-old stone tool from Gona, Ethiopia. *Nature* **385**, 333–336.

15 Corvinus, G. K. 1976 Prehistoric exploration at Hadar, Ethiopia. *Nature* **261**, 571–572.

16 Leakey, M. D. 1971 *Olduvai Gorge: volume 3, excavations in Beds I and II, 1960–1963*. Cambridge, UK: Cambridge University Press.

17 Chavaillon, J. 1976 Evidence for the technical practices of early Pleistocene Hominids, Shungura Formation, Lower Omo Valley, Ethiopia. In *Earliest man and environments in the Lake Rudolf Basin* (eds Y. Coppens, F. C. Howell, G. L. Isaac & R. E. F. Leakey), pp. 565–573. Chicago, IL: University of Chicago Press.

18 Merrick, H. V., de Heinzelin, J., Haesaerts, P. & Howell, F. C. 1973 Archaeological occurrences of early Pleistocene Age from the Shungura Formation, Lower Omo Valley, Ethiopia. *Nature* **242**, 572–575.

19 Leakey, L. S. B., Evernden, J. F. & Curtis, G. H. 1961 The age of Bed I, Olduvai Gorge, Tanganyka. *Nature* **191**, 478–479.

20 Leakey, L. S. B., Tobias, P. V. & Napier, J. R. 1964 A new species of the genus *Homo* from Olduvai Gorge. *Nature* **202**, 5–7.

21 Leakey, L. S. B. 1959 A new fossil skull from Olduvai. *Nature* **184**, 491–493.

22 Leakey, L. S. B. 1934 The sequence of Stone Age cultures in east Africa. In *Essays presented to CG Seligman* (eds E. E. Evans-Pritchard, R. Firth, B. Malinowski & I. Schapera), pp. 143–146. London, UK: Kegan Paul, Trench, Trubner & Co. Limited.

23 Leakey, L. S. B. 1936 *Stone Age Africa. An outline of prehistory in Africa*. London, UK: Oxford University Press.

24 Reck, H. 1914 Erste Vorläufige Mitteilung über den Fund eines fossilen Menschenskelets aus Zentral-afrika. *Sitzungsberichte der Gesellschaft naturforschender Freunde* **3**, 81–95.

25 Woodward, A. S. *et al.* 1933 Early humans remains in east Africa. *MAN* **33**, 65–68.

26 O'Brien, T. P. 1939 *The prehistory of the Uganda protectorate*. Cambridge, UK: Cambridge University Press.

27 Wayland, E. J. 1937 The Stone Age cultures of Uganda. *MAN* **67**, 55–56.

28 Van Riet Lowe, C. 1953 The Kafuan culture in South Africa. *S. Afr. Archaeol. Bull.* **8**, 27–31.

29 Brain, C. K., Van Riet Lowe, C. & Dart, R. A. 1955 Kafuan Stone Artefacts in the post-Australopithecine breccia at Makapansgat. *Nature* **175**, 16–18.

30 Clark, J. D. 1958 The natural fracture of pebbles from the Bakota Gorge, Northern Rhodesia, and its bearing on the Kafuan Industries of Africa. *Proc. Prehistoric Soc.* **24**, 64–77.

31 Bishop, W. W. 1959 Kafu stratigraphy and Kafuan artifacts. *S. Afr. J. Sci.* **55**, 117–121.

32 Dart, R. A. 1957 The Makapansgat Australopithecine Osteodontokeratic culture. In *Third Pan-African congress on prehistory, Livingstone 1955* (ed. J. D. Clark), pp. 161–171. London, UK: Chatto & Windus.

33 Brain, C. K. 1981 *The Hunters or the hunted? An introducion to African cave taphonomy*. Chicago, IL: The University of Chicago Press.

34 d'Errico, F. & Backwell, L. R. 2003 Possible evidence of bone tool shaping by Swartkrans early hominids. *J. Archaeol. Sci.* **30**, 1559–1576.

35 Robinson, J. T. 1961 The australopithecines and their bearing on the origin of man and of stone tool-making. *S. Afr. J. Sci.* **57**, 3–13.

36 Mason, R. J. 1961 *Australopithecus* and the beginning of the Stone Age in South Africa. *S. Afr. Archaeol. Bull.* **16**, 8–14.

37 Broom, R. 1938 The Pleistocene anthropoid apes of South Africa. *Nature* **142**, 377–379.

38 Wood, B. & Constantino, P. 2007 *Paranthropus boisei*: fifty years of evidence and analysis. *Yearbook Phys. Anthropol.* **50**, 106–132.

39 Leakey, L. S. B. 1961 Africa's contribution to the evolution of man. *S. Afr. Archaeol. Bull.* **16**, 3–7.

40 Washburn, S. L. 1960 Tools and human evolution. *Sci. Am.* **203**, 63–75.

41 Robinson, J. T. 1964 Adaptative radiation in the Australopithecines and the origin of man. In
    African ecology and human evolution (eds F. C. Howell & F. Bourlière), pp. 385–416. London, UK:
    Methuen & Co. Limited.

42 Wood, B. & Collard, M. 1999 The changing face of genus *Homo*. *Evol. Anthropol.* **8**, 195–207.

43 Brown, F. H. 1994 Development of Pliocene and Pleistocene chronology of the Turkana basin, east
    Africa, and its relation to other sites. In *Integrative paths to the past paleoanthropological advances in
    honor of F Clark Howell* (eds R. S. Corruccini & R. L. Ciochon), pp. 285–312. New Jersey, NJ:
    Prentice Hall.

44 Leakey, M. D. 1970 Early artifacts from the Koobi Fora area. *Nature* **226**, 228–230.

45 McDougall, I., Maier, R., Sutherland-Hawkes, P. & Gleadow, A. J. W. 1980 K/Ar age estimate for the
    KBS tuff, east Turkana, Kenya. *Nature* **284**, 230–234.

46 Howell, F. C. 1972 Pliocene/Pleistocene *Hominidae* in Eastern Africa: absolute and relative ages. In
    *Calibration of hominoid evolution recent advances in isotopic and other dating methods as applicable to
    the origin of man* (eds W. W. Bishop & J. A. Miller), pp. 331–368. Edinburgh: Scottish Academic
    Press.

47 Johanson, D., White, T. D. & Coppens, Y. 1978 A new species of the genus *Australopithecus*
    (primates: hominidae) from the Pliocene of Eastern Africa. *Kirtlandia* **28**, 1–14.

48 Le Gros Clark, W. 1967 *Man-apes or ape-men? The story of discoveries in Africa*. New York, NY:
    Holdt, Rinehart and Winston, Inc.

49 Cartmill, M., Pilbeam, D. & Isaac, G. L. 1986 One hundred years of paleoanthropology. *Am. Sci.* **74**,
    410–420.

50 Torre, I. de la & Mora, R. 2009 Remarks on the current theoretical and methodological approaches
    to the study of early technological strategies in Eastern Africa. In *Interdisciplinary approaches to the
    Oldowan* (eds E. Hovers & D. R. Braun), pp. 15–24. Dordrecht, The Netherlands: Springer.

51 Howell, F. C., Haesaerts, P. & de Heinzelin, J. 1987 Depositional environments, archeological
    occurrences and hominids from members E and F of the Shungura Formation (Omo basin,
    Ethiopia). *J. Hum. Evol.* **16**, 665–700.

52 Kimbel, W. H. *et al.* 1996 Late Pliocene *Homo* and Oldowan tools from the Hadar formation (Kada
    Hadar member), Ethiopia. *J. Hum. Evol.* **31**, 549–561.

53 Schrenk, F., Bromage, T. G., Betzler, C. G., Ring, U. & Juwayeyi, Y. M. 1993 Oldest *Homo* and
    Pliocene biogeography of the Malawi Rift. *Nature* **365**, 833–836.

54 Brunet, M. *et al.* 2002 A new hominid from the Upper Miocene of Chad, Central Africa. *Nature*
    418, 145–151.

55 Asfaw, B., White, T., Lovejoy, O., Latimer, B., Simpson, S. & Suwa, G. 1999 *Australopithecus garhi*:
    a new species of early hominid from Ethiopia. *Science* **284**, 629–635.

56 Heinzelin, J. d., Clark, J. D., White, T., Hart, W., Renne, P., WoldeGabriel, G., Beyene, Y. & Vrba, E.
    1999 Environment and behavior of 2.5-million-year-old Bouri hominids. *Science* **284**, 625–629.

57 Isaac, G. L. 1986 Foundation stones: early artifacts as indicators of activities and abilities. In *Stone
    Age prehistory: studies in memory of Charles McBurney* (eds G. N. Bailey & P. Callow), pp. 221–241.
    Cambridge, UK: Cambridge University Press.

58 Dibble, H. L. 1987 The interpretation of Middle Paleolithic scraper morphology. *Am. Antiquity* **52**,
    109–117.

59 Potts, R. 1991 Why the Oldowan? Plio-Pleistocene tool-making and the transport of resources.
    J. Anthropol. Res. **47**, 153–176.

60 Goren-Inbar, N. 2011 Culture and cognition in the Acheulian industry: a case study from Gesher
    Benot Yaáqov. *Phil. Trans. R. Soc. B* **366**, 1038–1049.

61 Roche, H. 1989 Technological evolution in Early hominids. *Ossa* **14**, 97–98.

62 Kibunjia, M. 1994 Pliocene archaeological occurrences in the Lake Turkana Basin, Kenya. *J. Hum. Evol.* **27**, 157–171.

63 Wynn, T. & McGrew, W. C. 1989 An ape's view of the Oldowan. *MAN New Ser.* **24**, 383–398.

64 Binford, L. R. 1981 *Bones: ancient men and modern myths*. New York, NY: Academic Press.

65 Binford, L. R. 1985 Human ancestors: changing views of their behavior. *J. Anthropol. Archaeol.* **4**, 292–327.

66 d'Errico, F. & Stringer, C. B. 2011 Evolution, revolution or saltation scenario for the emergence of modern cultures? *Phil. Trans. R. Soc. B* **366**, 1060–1069.

67 Stout, D., Semaw, S., Rogers, M. J. & Cauche, D. 2010 Technological variation in the earliest Oldowan from Gona, Afar, Ethiopia. *J. Hum. Evol.* **58**, 474–491.

68 Stout, D., Quade, J., Semaw, S., Rogers, M. J. & Levin, N. E. 2005 Raw material selectivity of the earliest stone tool-makers at Gona, Afar, Ethiopia. *J. Hum. Evol.* **48**, 365–380.

69 Stout, D. 2011 Stone toolmaking and the evolution of human culture and cognition. *Phil. Trans. R. Soc. B* **366**, 1050–1059.

70 Harmand, S. 2009 Variability in raw material selectivity at the late Pliocene sites of Lokalalei, West Turkana, Kenya. In *Interdisciplinary approaches to the Oldowan* (eds E. Hovers & D. R. Braun), pp. 85–97. Dordrecht, The Netherlands: Springer.

71 Delagnes, A. & Roche, H. 2005 Late Pliocene hominid knapping skills: the case of Lokalalei 2C, West Turkana, Kenya. *J. Hum. Evol.* **48**, 435–472.

72 Hovers, E. 2001 Stone knapping in the Late Pliocene in Hadar, Ethiopia. *In* Knapping stone. A uniquely hominid behaviour? International workshop, 21–24 November. Pont-à-Mousson, Abstracts, pp. 11–12.

73 Torre, I. de la 2004 Omo revisited: evaluating the technological skills of Pliocene hominids. *Curr. Anthropol.* **45**, 439–465.

74 Rogers, M. J. & Semaw, S. 2009 From nothing to something: the appearance and context of the earliest archaeological record. In *Sourcebook of paleolithic transitions methods, theories, and interpretations* (eds M. Camps & P. Chauhan), pp. 155–171. New York, NY: Springer.

75 Panger, M. A., Brooks, A. S., Richmond, B. G. & Wood, B. 2002 Older than the Oldowan? Rethinking the emergence of hominin tool use. *Evol. Anthropol.* **11**, 235–245.

76 Whiten, A., Schick, K. & Toth, N. 2009 The evolution and cultural transmission of percussive technology: integrating evidence from palaeoanthropology and primatology. *J. Hum. Evol.* **57**, 420–435.

77 Haslam, M. *et al.* 2009 Primate archaeology. *Nature* **460**, 339–344.

78 Roche, H., Brugal, J.-P., Delagnes, A., Feibel, C., Harmand, S., Kibunjia, M., Prat, S. & Texier, J. 2003 Les sites archéologiques plio-pléistocènes de la formation de Nachukui, Ouest-Turkana, Kenya: bilan synthétique 1997–2001. *Comptes Rendus Palevol.* **2**, 663–673.

79 Torre, I. de la. & Mora, R. 2005 *Technological strategies in the lower Pleistocene at Olduvai Beds I & II*. Liege: ERAUL 112.

80 Clarke, D. L. 1968 *Analytical archaeology*. London, UK: Methuen.

81 Braun, D. R., Plummer, T., Ditchfield, P., Bishop, L. C. & Ferraro, J. V. 2009 Oldowan technology and raw material variability at Kanjera South. In *Interdisciplinary approaches to the Oldowan* (eds E. Hovers & D. R. Braun), pp. 99–110. Dordrecht, The Netherlands: Springer.

82 Braun, D. R., Harris, J. W. K., Levin, N. E., McCoy, J. T., Herries, A. I. R., Bamford, M. K., Bishop, L. C., Richmond, B. G. & Kibunjia, M. 2010 Early hominin diet included diverse terrestrial and aquatic animals 1.95 Ma in East Turkana, Kenya. *Proc. Natl Acad. Sci. USA* **107**, 10002–10007.

83 de Lumley, H. & Beyene, Y. (dirs) 2004 *Les sites préhistoriques de la région de Fejej, Sud-Omo, Ethiopie, dans leur contexte stratigraphique et paléontologique*. Paris: Editions Recherches sur les Civilisations (dirs).

84 Isaac, G. L. & Isaac, B. (eds) 1997 *Koobi Fora research project, volume 5: Plio-Pleistocene archaeology.* Oxford, UK: Oxford University Press.

85 Kuman, K. & Field, A. S. 2009 The Oldowan industry from Sterkfontein caves, South Africa. In *The cutting edge: new approaches to the archaeology of human origins* (eds K. Schick & N. Toth), pp. 151–169. Bloomington: Stone Age Institute Press.

86 Sahnouni, M. 1998 *The lower Paleolithic of the Maghreb: excavations and analyses at Ain Hanech, Algeria.* Oxford, UK: BAR International Series 689.

87 Gabunia, L., Antón, S. C., Lordkipanidze, D., Vekua, A., Justus, A. & Swisher III, C. C. 2001 Dmanisi and dispersal. *Evol. Anthropol.* **10**, 158–170.

88 Goldman-Neuman, T. & Hovers, E. 2009 Methodological considerations in the study of Oldowan raw material selectivity: insights from A.L. 894 (Hadar, Ethiopia). In *Interdisciplinary approaches to the Oldowan* (eds E. Hovers & D. R. Braun), pp. 71–84. Dordrecht, The Netherlands: Springer.

89 Whiten, A., Hinde, R. A., Laland, K. N. & Stringer, C. B. 2011 Culture evolves. *Phil. Trans. R. Soc. B* **366**, 938–948.

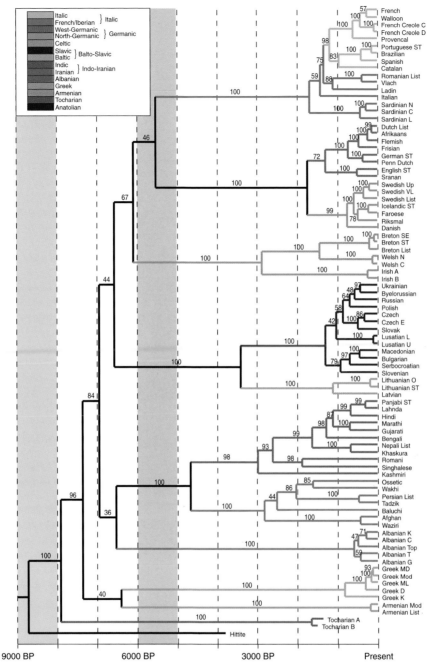

Colour Plate 1 (Also see Figure 16.1) A dated phylogenetic tree of 87 Indo-European languages. The tree is a consensus tree derived from the posterior samples of trees in the Bayesian analyses reported by Gray & Atkinson [32]. The values on the branches are the posterior probability of that clade. The root age of the tree is in the age range predicted by the Anatolian hypothesis. This figure also shows an interesting point that we had noted, but not emphasized, in our initial paper—while the root of the tree goes back around 8700 years, much of the diversification of the major Indo-European subgroups happened around 6000–7000 BP. This means that both the Anatolian and the Kurgan hypotheses could be simultaneously true. There was an initial movement out of Anatolia 8700 years ago and then a major radiation 6000–7000 years ago from southern Russia and the Ukraine. It also means that the intuition shared by many linguists that the Indo-European language family is about 6000 years old could be correct for the vast majority of Indo-European languages, just not the deeper subgroups.

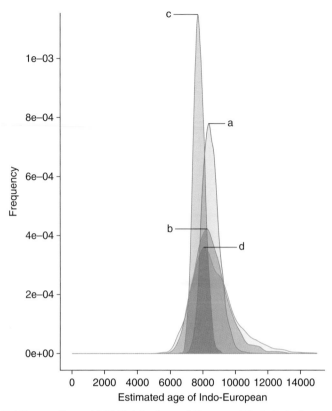

Colour Plate 2 (Also see Figure 16.2) Distributions of the age of Proto Indo-European estimated from the data of Ringe *et al.* [38]. Four different analyses were conducted using the program BEAST. Two analyses assumed equal rates of cognate gain and loss—one with a strict clock (light green) (a) and one with a lognormal relaxed clock (orange) (b). The other two analyses assumed that cognates could only be gained once but lost multiple times (stochastic Dollo). Again one implemented a strict clock (purple) (c) and one used a lognormal relaxed clock (light blue) (d). The date estimates obtained in all four analyses were consistent with the Anatolian hypothesis.

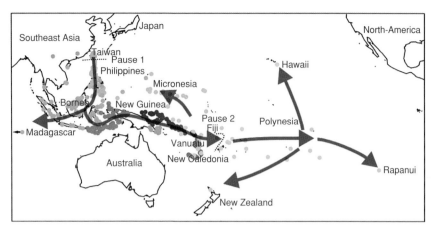

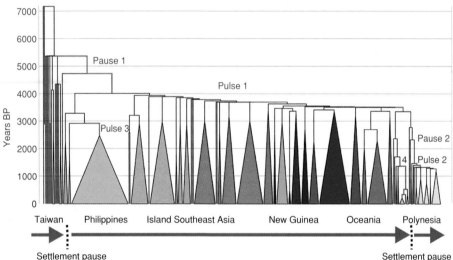

Colour Plate 3 (Also see Figure 16.4) Map and language family tree showing the settlement of the Pacific by Austronesian-speaking peoples. The map shows the settlement sequence and location of expansion pulses and settlement pauses. The tree is rooted with some outgroup languages (Buyang and Old Chinese) at its base. It shows an Austronesian origin in Taiwan around 5200 years ago, followed by a settlement pause (pause 1) between 5200 and 4000 years ago. After this pause, a rapid expansion pulse (pulse 1) led to the settlement of Island Southeast Asia, New Guinea and Near Oceania in less than 1000 years. A second pause (pause 2) occurs after the initial settlement of Polynesia. This pause is followed by two pulses further into Polynesia and Micronesia around 1400 years ago (pulses 2 and 4). A third expansion pulse occurred around 3000–2500 years ago in the Philippines.

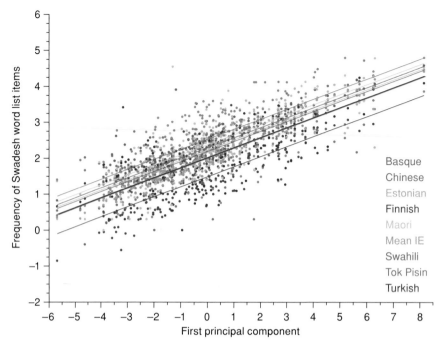

Colour Plate 4 (Also see Figure 17.2) Log-transformed frequency of use per million words for each of the eight languages plus the Indo-European mean vector of nine languages (see Table 17.1 and text) plotted against the first principal component factor scores of frequencies. The first principal component uses the mean IE-vector together with the other eight languages so as not to bias towards the Indo-European (see text). We fitted regression lines to each language, allowing different intercepts but constraining lines to be parallel simply for illustrative purposes. Fitted this way, the overall relationship accounts for 69.4% of the variance in the principal component. The positive slopes indicate that each language's frequencies of use correlate positively with the principal component that summarizes them. Allowing slopes to vary increases the percentage to 70.3% (not significantly different).

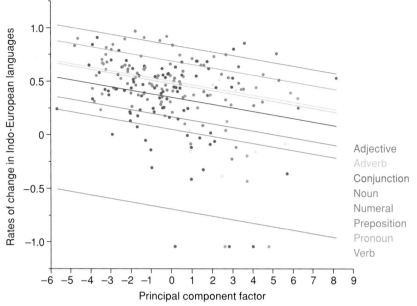

Colour Plate 5 (Also see Figure 17.3) Statistically estimated rates of lexical replacement for the Swadesh list in the Indo-European languages (from [6]) correlated with the first principal component loadings obtained from the frequency of use of the Swadesh list among 17 languages, and with part of speech. The relationship accounts for 46% of the variance in rates of lexical replacement ($p < 0.0001$), and holds separately within part-of-speech category: prepositions ('in', 'with'), conjunctions ('and', 'because'), adjectives ('white', 'thin'), verbs ('to throw', 'to eat'), nouns ('hand', 'hair'), special adverbs ('here', 'some'), pronouns ('I', 'they') and numerals ('one', 'five'). Regression lines were allowed to have separate intercepts but constrained to have the same slope. Allowing these slopes to vary increased the overall R^2 to 0.47, not a significant change.

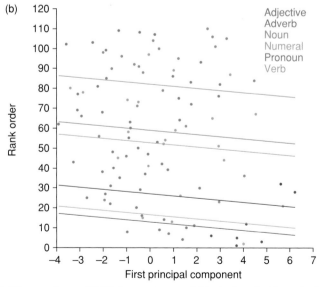

Colour Plate 6 (Also see Figure 17.4*b*) Regression model including the first principal component loadings and parts of speech $R^2 = 0.31$, $p < 0.0001$). Regression lines were allowed to have separate intercepts but were constrained to have the same slopes. Allowing separate slopes did not significantly increase the overall R^2.

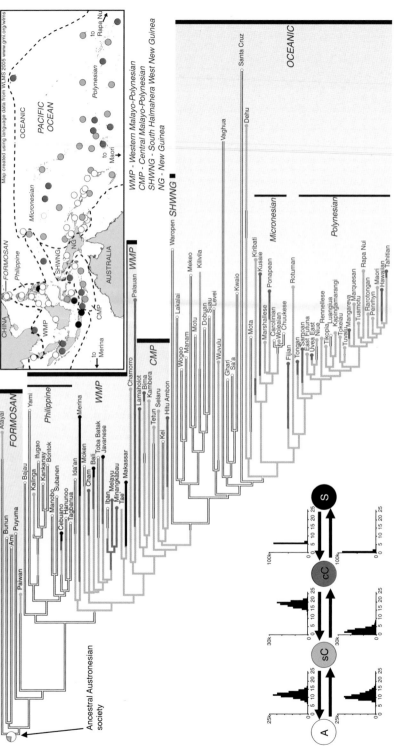

Colour Plate 7 (Also see Figure 18.1) Geographical distribution of the 84 Austronesian-speaking societies analysed in this study and their associated forms of political organization (top right). Data on political organization mapped on to a phylogeny of these societies (centre). This figure shows a single phylogenetic tree from the sample of 1000 most likely trees. Analyses in §18.2 were conducted using all 1000 trees. Colours along the branches indicate the inferred forms of organization from a single stochastic character mapping (SCM). Pie chart at the root of the tree represents the proportional probabilities of different forms of political organization in the ancestral Austronesian society inferred using maximum likelihood. Distributions of number of changes between states inferred using SCM (bottom left). Unfilled circle, Acephalous; blue circle, Simple Chiefdom; red circle, Complex Chiefdom; black circle, State.

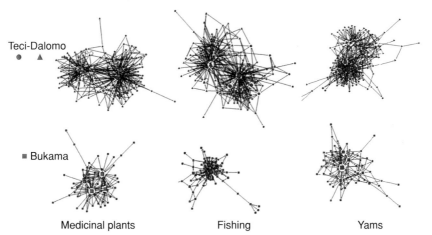

Teci-Dalomo
●　▲

■ Bukama

Medicinal plants　　　　　　　Fishing　　　　　　　Yams

Colour Plate 8 (Figure 21.1) Inferred cultural transmission networks for our three domains. The top row shows the networks for the villages of Teci and Dalomo while the bottom row shows Bukama. Each column represents one of the three domains. Nodes represent individuals. The lines and arrows point towards the selected model. Node sizes are proportional to the number of individuals who selected that person as a model. Node shapes and colours mark individuals' villages and sexes. Blue, males; red, females.

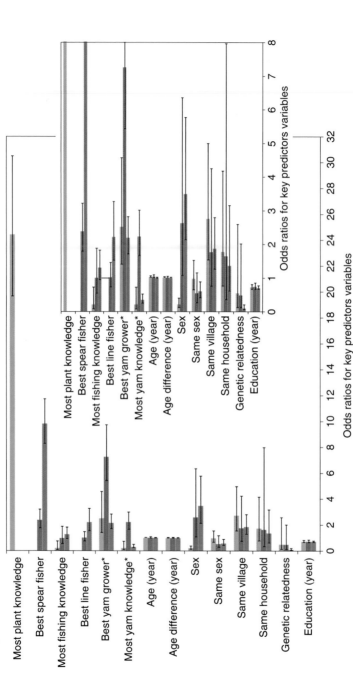

Colour Plate 9 (Also see Figure 21.2) Effect sizes and confidence intervals for our primary predictor variables in odds ratios. The inset plot is the same as the larger plot except that the axis is rescaled so the smaller odds ratios can be seen. The bars give the odds ratios for our estimated coefficients. Odds ratios greater than 1 indicate positive effects while those less than 1 indicate negative effects. The error bars are 95% CI estimated by resampling. The bar colours mark the different cultural domains. Green, Medicinal Plants odds ratio; red, Yams odds ratio; blue, Fishing odds ratio.

Chapter 11

Culture and Cognition in the Acheulian Industry: A Case Study from Gesher Benot Yaʿaqov*

Naama Goren-Inbar

The Acheulian presence in the Dead Sea Rift and its environs is characterized by the discontinuity of its cultural manifestations. Nevertheless, the long stratigraphic sequences of the Acheulian Technocomplex provide a unique opportunity for synergetic examination along a temporal trajectory. Hominin cognitive and cultural behaviour are studied at Gesher Benot Yaʿaqov through analyses of lithic, palaeontological and palaeobotanical assemblages, as well as the Early–Middle Pleistocene environment, ecology and climate. The study attempts to reconstruct reduction sequences of some major artefact groups at the site, which include raw material acquisition, production, technology, typology, usage and discard. Experimental archaeology illustrates artefact mobility on the palaeo-landscape. Strategies of biomass-exploitation are studied in detail, with other aspects yielding additional information on hominin subsistence and adaptive responses to their environment. The cultural marker of fire and the spatial association of selected categories of finds are integrated in the general synthesis, allowing reconstruction of the cultural and cognitive realm of Acheulian hominins. The synthesis attempts to reassess the abilities, social structure, subsistence and adaptability to the changing environment of hominins in the Levantine Corridor.

Keywords: Acheulian; Gesher Benot Yaʿaqov; Upper Jordan Valley; bifaces (handaxes and cleavers); cognitive abilities; Irian Jaya

11.1 Introduction

The unpredictability and low resolution of the archaeological findings dictate the extent of our knowledge of the Acheulian culture, accounting for our only partial success in reconstructing the cognitive abilities, cultural sophistication and complexity of the hominins of those times.

---

* Electronic supplementary material is available at http://dx.doi.org/10.1098/rstb.2010.0365 or via http://rstb.royalsocietypublishing.org.

The Acheulian Technocomplex [1] has the most extensive geographical distribution and the longest temporal duration of the Old World's prehistoric cultures [2], spanning some 1.6 Myr. Most of our knowledge of the Acheulian material culture and the abilities of its makers derive from the lithic marker of the Acheulian—the bifaces (handaxes and cleavers).[1] Other issues relating to hominin cognitive capacities are procurement and transportation of raw materials (e.g. [3–5]), technological abilities in general (e.g. [6–8]), variability of lithic assemblages [9–11], subsistence patterns [12], 'cultural zones' [13,14] and to a lesser extent symbolic aspects (e.g. [15]), as well as the hominin species/populations who were the bearers of the culture [16]. Clearly, the lithic artefacts are our main source of information on the culture, and hence the cognition, of the Acheulian hominins [17].

Here, we present various aspects of the Acheulian culture and cognitive abilities as currently known from the multi-disciplinary studies of the Acheulian site of Gesher Benot Ya'aqov (GBY). The Acheulian sequence of GBY is assigned to a phase, well known in Africa, which is characterized by the production of bifaces on large flakes [2]. The site's data allow us to study Acheulian communities within a discrete timeframe in the Early/ Middle Pleistocene in the Levantine Corridor. The present study focuses on issues related to the general theme of the present volume.

Discussion of the environment and ecology of the Acheulian provide the context for in-depth discussion of the complex system of Acheulian lithic production. The early production stages of bifaces contribute much to our knowledge of Acheulian abilities, and the Irian Jaya, present-day knappers producing bifacial tools, represent an analogous technological system. Matters other than lithics that touch on cultural and cognitive abilities will be integrated in a summary of our current knowledge of the GBY site.

11.2 The site, its location and its Acheulian characteristics

11.2.1 The evidence of the Levantine Corridor

The Levantine Corridor furnishes abundant information on the Acheulian Technocomplex. Over 360 find spots are known [18, fig. 4a,b] from an area of about 22 000 km², located in different phytogeographic and climatic zones. Yet, the antiquity of the Acheulian record, the massive impact of tectonic activity on the Dead Sea Rift and a variety of taphonomic processes make research of the Acheulian culture a difficult task. The Levantine Acheulian begins *ca* 1.5 Ma at the site of 'Ubeidiya [19] and ends *ca* 200 Ka as attested by the Acheulo-Yabrudian site of Qesem Cave [20, 21].

The identity of the hominins who produced the Levantine Acheulian culture remains unknown. The sites have furnished only scanty skeletal remains, including a few teeth from the Early Acheulian site of 'Ubeidiya [22, 23], a single right femur shaft (Layer Ea) and a molar tooth (Layer Eb) from the Acheulo-Yabrudian site of Tabun Cave [24, p. 67] and several teeth from the Acheulo-Yabrudian site of Qesem Cave [20]. The 'Galilee Man' skull found at Zuttiyeh Cave is attributed to an Acheulo-Yabrudian context [25]. One may speculate that in the Early and Middle Pleistocene more than one hominin species produced the Acheulian material culture, owing to the great temporal depth and the fact that different hominin types have been identified in association with Acheulian cultural remains [16]. Possible candidates are *Homo erectus* (*senso lato*), *Homo heidelbergensis*, 'Galilee Man', or other unknown fossil species. Furthermore, there is always the possibility of the temporal co-existence of several hominin types.

In this study, examples are drawn from the entire cultural sequence of the GBY site to illustrate a variety of issues, such as mobility and innovation, which are relevant to Acheulian subsistence, culture and cognitive abilities. The GBY site was selected as the reference base because of the outstanding preservation of its various assemblages (sealed rapidly after deposition in waterlogged conditions) and its meticulous excavation methods, which achieved high precision of the spatial configuration of the assemblages. The material culture, found in association with biological and geological material, allows in-depth and detailed examination of different behavioural and cognitive attributes of the resident hominins. Such a configuration, particularly with respect to organic preservation, is unmatched and hence places the studies of the GBY site in the forefront of studies of mankind's evolution.

11.2.2 The site

The Acheulian site of GBY is located 3.5 km south of the Hula Valley, bordered by the basaltic Korazim Saddle in the south, the Golan Heights in the east and the Galilee mountains in the west [26] (electronic supplementary material, Figure S1). The site has been exposed on both banks and within the course of the River Jordan. Excavations were carried out in 1989–1997 on the left bank of the river, exposing a 34 m thick depositional sequence of the Benot Yaákov Formation [27]. The sequence comprises a series of lake and lake-margin sediments tectonically deformed by the Dead Sea Transform [26, 28, 29]. The Acheulian archaeological horizons, reflecting hominin occupations on the lake margin, are bedded in these deposits [29], which are dated to the Early Pleistocene/early Middle Pleistocene [30]. Fifteen archaeological horizons are exceptionally rich in palaeontological, palaeobotanical and lithic assemblages, allowing us to study hominin abilities and track the southwest Asian continuum of a cultural phenomenon originating in Africa.

11.2.3 The characteristics of the Acheulian at GBY

The Levantine Acheulian material culture is very similar to that of the African record and is observed at GBY in the production of bifaces on volcanic materials (basalt and basanites) [31]. Similarities are also seen in the technological characteristics of biface production: thinning of the butt and minimal flaking on bifaces made on flakes. A further similarity is the presence of the cleaver, an African morphotype [30, 31]. It has been securely established that the lithic remains are associated with the floral and faunal finds (see below).

The continuous and long-lasting Acheulian cultural phenomenon at GBY is characterized both by techno-typological conservatism of artefact manufacture and by great variability of the frequencies of lithic types in different archaeological horizons [11].

11.2.4 **Background to the palaeoenvironment**

A high-resolution environment and habitat record of *ca* 100 Ka have been obtained from multi-disciplinary studies at the site (e.g. [32–35]). Those provide data on taxonomy, biodiversity, biogeography and taphonomy that permit a spatial and diachronic recon-struction of the background to hominin activities in the Upper Jordan Valley (UJV). Thousands of plant and faunal remains indicate an environment consisting of a fluctuat-ing freshwater lake and adjacent marshes. Lakeshore and offshore habitats are recorded, as well as riparian and grassland environments and, at a greater distance, field, woodland, parkland and forest environments, all typically Mediterranean in nature.

This reconstructed scenario, which integrates species of diverse origin [36, 37], is par-ticularly rich in food resources, both floral [38] and faunal [39]. The environmental and dietary data shed light on the ability of the local communities to forgo their ancestral African adaptations and to adjust to a Mediterranean environment with its particular ecology and habitats.

Clearly, the survival of the Acheulian communities in the UJV necessitated cognitive competence and extensive knowledge of the environment, landscape, ecological niches and their potential for continual existence. These have been investigated at GBY, result-ing in the identification of behavioural patterns that shed light on the cognitive abilities of the local hominins.

11.3 **Mapping the hominins' cognitive abilities**

11.3.1 **Exploitation of biological resources**

Skeletal animal remains found at the site reflect carcass processing of large and medium-sized animals, ranging from elephant, large bovids and rhinoceros to gazelle [36, 39, 40], together with smaller animals like fishes and crabs [32]. There are preferences for par-ticular species, with an emphasis on elephant (*Paleoloxodonta antiquus*) and fallow deer (*Dama* sp.) [41].

The detailed study of cut marks on fallow deer (*Dama* sp.) bones revealed that the processing of the fallow deer carcasses resembles that of the same species by the Upper Palaeolithic *Homo sapiens* of Hayonim Cave (Western Galilee, Israel) [41].

Processing of large game was associated with the production, manipulation and use of handaxes and cleavers [18, 42–44]. This entailed knowledge of animal behaviour together with a complex range of techno-morpho-typological expertise in stone tool production and manipulation (e.g. [45]).

Recently, a multi-faceted analysis of one archaeological horizon has provided the earli-est documentation of fish processing (Cyprinidae [carp] *Barbus* sp. nov.; [32, 46]). While fish processing and consumption have been considered a facet of modern human behav-iour (e.g. [47]), it is quite evident that at GBY hominins were already familiar with the process, enabling them to exploit yet another resource niche. There are indications that crustaceans too may have been part of the hominin diet at the site [32].

The exploitation of a wide spectrum of biomass undoubtedly involved knowledge and strategies that included insights into animal behaviour, their life cycles and seasonality, while incorporating other factors such as the mobility options and dietary preferences of the hominin communities.

Plant gathering is attested by the great variety of species identified, among them sub-merged species like prickly water lily (*Euryale ferox*) and water chestnut (*Trapa natans*) and remains of species that grow at some distance from the lake margin, like acorns, wild grape (*Vitis sylvestris*), olives, white beet (*Beta vulgaris*) and holy thistle (*Silybum marianum*).

The diachronic data relating to animal exploitation [36] clearly demonstrate the continued existence for millennia of the same breadth of ecological knowledge. The exploitation behaviours also relate to the abundant edible botanical remains documented throughout the GBY sequence, which include different parts (nuts, seeds, etc.) of the flora that grew in the vicinity of the site and in adjacent areas [32, 45, 48]. We interpret this continuity as reflecting hominin ability to transfer inter-generational information throughout the sequence of occupations. This is apparent in the material cultural as well (e.g. the techno-typology of lithic artefacts; [11]).

11.3.2 Fire and spatial organization

Each archaeological horizon at GBY holds evidence of fire. While the main source of information is burned flint microartefacts, burned flint macroartefacts and organic material occur as well [48–50]. Detailed analyses have concluded that the fire was an intentional and controlled phenomenon, indicative of developed technological abilities, rather than a natural occurrence [51]. Additional information derived from the detailed spatial analyses, which identified clusters of burned microartefacts ('phantom hearths') that had retained their original spatial location (e.g. [51, 52]). Further insight is derived from spatial analyses of other finds (faunal, floral and lithic) [32]. For example, in Layer II-6 Level 2, two main areas of activities were discerned, attesting to a variety of tasks (including stone knapping and modification, wood gathering and nut cracking). Further activities are indicated by the presence of fishes and crab clusters. Near the hearth were clusters of wood fragments, most probably firewood, as indicated by two burned pieces within the hearth itself. The hearth was undoubtedly a focal point of activity, as illustrated by the presence of lithic processing debris including *éclat de taille de biface*. Nut cracking is documented by the presence of several percussors[1] and pitted stones of basalt and limestone, also around the hearth. Most of the crab pincers are also associated with the hearth, indicating their potential as foodstuff. Other activities are located away from the hearth; they include flint knapping, as indicated by the large amount of microdebitage, and fish processing remains.

The control of fire in the UJV undoubtedly increased the number of exploitable niches and facilitated the exploitation of additional resources (e.g. *Euryale ferox*). It had a major impact on hominin subsistence and dietary behaviour. Thus, the association of the seeds and fruits with the hearth and the pitted stones confirms their association with the firing and heating process.

11.3.3 The lithic assemblages

The GBY Acheulian is associated primarily with two symmetrical and highly refined bifacial tools—handaxes and cleavers (electronic supplementary material, Figures S2 and S3). The site yielded large quantities of these tools as well as giant cores and other associated artefacts. The main products of giant core knapping were large flakes [2, 53], which were modified into bifaces. Detailed studies have enabled reconstruction of the *chaîne opératoire*[1] of the bifaces and facilitated understanding of the planning and execution of the bifacial tools by documenting different stages of the reduction process, unseen on the bifaces themselves. Previous analyses demonstrated that the Acheulians applied different core technologies to the production of large flakes. Recent in-depth analyses of the giant cores and their products [54] have revealed the following.

Giant cores were made on basalt and basanite (henceforth basalt) slabs that were extracted at some distance from GBY at unknown quarry sites in the volcanic bedrock in the vicinity of the site [55]. Quarrying the basalt slabs necessitated in-depth knowledge of the characteristics of the basaltic bedrock.

The quarrying technology involved several methods that we cannot reconstruct, although one method apparently left its traces on the slabs in the form of 'notches' (Figure 11.1). These could not have been produced by knapping as they lack the characteristic signature of its fracture mechanics. Rather, they may have been caused by the use of a lever. The slabs had a particular morphology that provided a natural sharp angle, facilitating knapping. A variety of additional steps were taken to reduce the size of the basalt slabs by fracturing, ensuring a more efficient reduction process (Figures 11.2 and 11.3).

All slabs were selected from non-vesicular and fine-grained basalts of the highest quality, demonstrating knowledge of the fracture-mechanics characteristics best suited for the production of the intended morphotypes. The knappers were familiar with the bedding plane[1] of the basalt and took it into account while exploiting the giant cores.

(a)

No. 5447

No. 7696

(b)

No. 5896

Figure 11.1 Three-dimensional scanning of notches (not to scale).

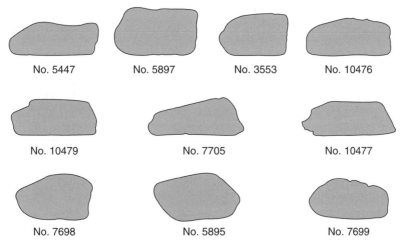

No. 5447   No. 5897   No. 3553   No. 10476

No. 10479   No. 7705   No. 10477

No. 7698   No. 5895   No. 7699

Figure 11.2 Three-dimensional scanning of slab sections (not to scale).

No. 10479
0 ━━━ 10 cm

No. 5897
0 ━━━ 10 cm

Figure 11.3 Three-dimensional scanning of fragmented slabs.

Detailed observation of the giant cores has enabled the identification of the bedding plane, and it can be demonstrated that the knappers evaluated each blank[1] for optimization of flaking by taking the bedding into consideration. This advanced type of knowledge and the manipulation of the blank to fit the knapper's requirements have been recognized and described in detail [56, figs. 5 and 6] in India (Figure 11.4).

Knapping involved percussors of different types and sizes, evidenced by various flake attributes and the recovery of hard and soft percussors. Basalt percussors range from boulders to fist-sized pebbles, limestone pebbles occur in all of the archaeological horizons and antler percussors have been reported [18, 45, 57, 58]. Although the production process reflects various technological strategies, the final large flakes were all

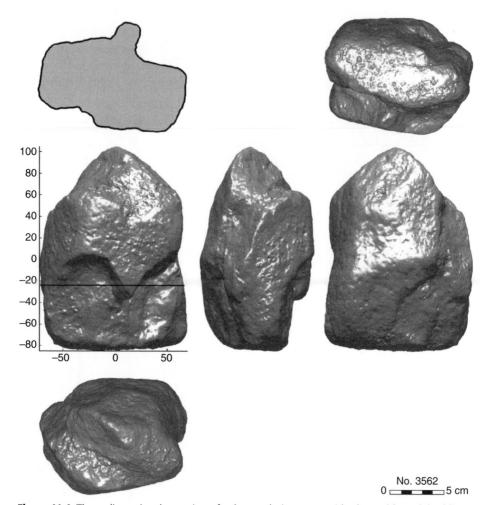

Figure 11.4 Three-dimensional scanning of exhausted giant core with observable rock bedding.

modified into extremely homogeneous bifacial tools of similar sizes and shapes [11, 31] (Figure 11.5). Some of the giant cores are exhausted (Figure 11.6), while others show only rudimentary treatment (fragmentation; Figure 11.3).

The above characteristics are represented in all of the archaeological horizons either by the complete set of traits or in different combinations, providing evidence for a particular cultural continuum over at least 50 000 years [11], and probably more. The high degree of variability in the *frequencies* of giant cores, waste products and bifacial tools may reflect different functions in the various archaeological horizons [11].

The reduction sequence[1] study yielded another behavioural insight into the 'mobility' of artefacts in the landscape. We have shown that handaxes and cleavers were produced

Figure 11.5 Three-dimensional scanning of large flakes.

Figure 11.6 Three-dimensional scanning of exhausted giant core.

in, used in and removed from the archaeological horizons. Madsen & Goren-Inbar [53] demonstrated that the number of giant cores present could not have produced the quantity of flakes and bifaces recovered from the archaeological horizons. This was supported by the observation that areas with high concentrations of bifaces were characterized by a marked deficit of waste products [53]. Further analyses provided data showing that basalt bifaces were modified and trimmed in particular areas, but the final products were lacking. The same behavioural mode was described for the production of flint bifaces, which are rare at the site. This helped in discerning a behavioural mode of bifacial reduction in which different raw materials were exploited [57, 58].

Further insight into behavioural modes was gained through the study of massive scrapers, tools that also derive from the knapping of giant cores. The hominins apparently used blanks whose morphology and other characteristics made them unsuitable for the production of bifaces for modification into massive scrapers with minimal investment of flaking [59]. It was suggested that these blanks were identified during knapping sessions and set aside to be used later. Present-day knappers use the same decision-making pattern: while using blanks for a particular tool type they may recognize a potential for making a quite different tool.

While the entire reduction process is not available to us, the archaeological record does furnish segments of this complex process. Further understanding of the complexity of the *chaîne opératoire* could be gained by several means, but for the purposes of the current study we selected an ethnographic analogy.

11.3.4 An ethnographic analogy

The production of bifacial tools is a complex system integrating long-term planning (using both working memory and planning memory) and its step-by-step implementation to obtain the desired end-product. This requires knowledge, experience, communication and the flexibility to change the procedure according to the circumstances. Complete reconstruction of such a complex system from the archaeological data is impossible, as information on many aspects is lacking.

As an attempt to fill in the gaps, an analogous ethnographic example is presented here. While the difficulties inherent in comparing the community behaviour of extant knappers with products knapped by the Acheulians are self-evident, the insights supplies by this analogy are remarkably instructive.

The detailed ethnographic description is drawn from the seminal work of Pétrequin & Pétrequin [60] in Irian Jaya, a study of the planning, production and distribution of bifacial tools. Among the Irian Jaya schemes we have selected those aimed at the production of bifaces made on volcanic rocks. This procedure requires a combination of knowledge in multiple fields, technological dexterity and know-how.

In the following paragraphs, we present side by side the segments of the *chaîne opératoire* of the Irian Jaya bifaces and those of GBY. The sub-headings bear cognitive titles drawn from ethnographic observations, using the terminology of Coolidge & Wynn [61].

11.3.4.1 'Large-scale spatial thinking', 'contingency' and 'long-term memory'

Knowledge of geography, environments, geology and the knapping properties (suitability) of a variety of rock types are all demonstrated in the behaviour of the Irian Jaya communities. Community members exploit different types of raw materials for the production of bifaces. The precise location of particular quarries has been known for generations and certain localities have been continuously exploited. Strategies shift from one type of quarrying activity to another according to need.

Observing the Irian Jaya knappers at work, it is fascinating to see their ability to produce similar objects from different raw materials by adjusting and modifying the technique (e.g. the selection of different percussors). The process entails lively discussion among the knappers while they confer on which strategy is best.

The archaeological finds at GBY provide unequivocal data that hominins had a similar spatial knowledge of where to find the quarries that supplied the different raw materials, knew how to procure the preferred material and adjusted their production methodology and technology to fit the particular raw material.

11.3.4.2 'Advanced planning', 'cooperative provisioning'

The planning and organization of quarrying expeditions by the Irian Jaya result from a communal/social decision driven by communal needs as part of an overall strategy rather than an individual decision. This activity is a traditional social event. While the GBY data clearly lack this kind of information, the data indicate a communal effort of procuring large quantities of heavy rocks—a task that cannot be accomplished by a single individual. Considering that the archaeological horizons were sealed very fast and their duration was not a very long one, the presence of giant cores, and the large quantities of their by-products, could be used to illustrate a communal activity.

11.3.4.3 'Spatial cognition' and 'procedural cognition'

The ethnographic quarrying activities employ a variety of techniques and technologies including construction of scaffolding and platforms, setting fires (in order to crack the face of the rock exposure) and producing percussors and levers of different materials and sizes. The Irian Jaya quarry at rock exposures where, after testing, the selected slabs undergo size reduction (fragmentation) on the spot, followed by the production of several preforms[1]. While little evidence of such activities is present at GBY, one might consider the large percussors (over 15 kg) as pertaining to quarrying activities. The peculiar 'notches' on some of the giant cores (Figure 11.1) indicate that there were other tools ('levers') used to dislodge the basalt slabs found at the site. A fragmentation stage clearly took place at GBY, as most of the items recovered at the site are slab fragments.

The preforms obtained through fragmentation by the Irian Jaya are transported to the village for further modification into the final bifacial form. In contrast with other raw materials, basalt preforms are handed over to experts because of the difficulty of knapping volcanic materials and the need for expertise in the later, more refined stages of their modification.

The complex pattern at GBY is rather different, in that beside preforms there are also unworked basalt slabs, giant cores and their by-products, as well as bifaces that were obviously produced elsewhere [57–59]. These differences may be explained to some extent by the fact that the economy and mode of life of the Acheulian communities differed greatly from those of the Irian Jaya village dwellers.

11.3.4.4 'Technical and procedural know-how', 'communication', 'specialization' and 'social cognition'

The expert basalt knappers of the Irian Jaya are extremely knowledgeable, and their information includes insight into the importance for flaking quality of the bedding of the volcanic rocks. This is crucial for the ultimate successful production of bifacial tools. The Acheulian knappers at GBY also had knowledge of rock bedding and the ability to exploit it (see above and Figure 11.4). Indeed, the knapping of basalt requires a high level of expertise. This is exemplified by the fact that among the Irian Jaya knappers, those who work basalt are considered the most expert. Knapping knowledge, which incorporates technical know-how as well as the properties of the raw material, is most probably transferred through both intra- and inter-generation communication (there is clear evidence for continuity in the exploitation of quarries of high-quality volcanic rocks for over two millennia). Teaching processes among the Irian Jaya involve learning through close observation, imitation and supervised experimentation, accompanied throughout by verbal guidance. This contradicts the assumption made by Coolidge & Wynn [61, p. 94] that tool cognition is primarily characterized by observation and minimal verbal exchange.

From the GBY data, it can be concluded that the Acheulian hominins were expert in basalt knapping and were able to overcome the obstacles of modifying an extremely hard-to-knap material. This knowledge was retained and transferred through the generations for at least 50 000 years, since comparison with the bifaces from the various layers demonstrates a very high degree of similarity. The main variations between the assemblages are in the frequencies and spatial distribution of the products of the biface *chaîne opératoire* [11]. These variations probably reflect different modes of behaviour responding to different demands, an issue that awaits further study. Unfortunately, the archaeological data are mute on the ways and means by which the lithic expertise was disseminated.

The GBY evidence clearly lacks the entire discourse: the discussion of the goal, the process of raw material procurement, the interaction between teachers and apprentices and the verbal exchanges between the experts during work are all missing. Still, the ethnoarchaeological comparison illustrates some great similarities.

11.3.5 Aspects of social interaction

Elements of social interaction are observed in many of the domains studied at GBY. Palaeontological, palaeobotanical and technological data provide evidence of cooperative group efforts such as that detailed above.

Although hunting is still debated (but see [45]), carcass processing is evidenced by the presence of bones of medium-sized and large mammals in all of the excavated archaeological horizons [36]. While perhaps only a few individuals were active in the hunt [62, 63] or the driving of the animal to the kill site, carcass processing requires the involvement of numerous individuals, as demonstrated ethnographically (e.g. [64–67]). At GBY this is evident through the reconstruction of carcass processing, as in the case of *Dama* sp. in both Layers V-5 and V-6 [41]. The concentration of large fish (*Barbus* sp.) in Layer II-6 Level 7 [32] also points to communal efforts.

The spatially structured co-occurrence of botanical, faunal and lithic finds in the archaeological horizons demonstrate that gathering of nuts and fruit (e.g. [49]), carcass processing, tool production and modification, as well as other activities, were an integral part of hominin activities carried out on the lake margin. Clearly, the Palaeolithic communities practised division of labour by age and gender, sharing the burden of communal survival. Although this social structure is merely implicit, it is widely supported by ethnographic analogies. The retention of cultural components for a long period indicates a shared cultural tradition.

Aspects of social cooperation are documented in the particulars of the spatial configurations of the archaeological horizons as well. Two cases have previously been reported in detail: the elephant kill site [45], and the 'biface pavement' [32]. Each case, but particularly the latter, illustrates a discrete activity area for a particular task, which most probably represents a short temporal event calling for multi-faceted social interaction and cooperation.

11.3.6 Innovation and creativity

The long duration of the Acheulian and, the consistently important role of the bifacial tools tend to produce a false impression of stagnation or stasis. 'The task, and the shape of the artefacts, remained essentially unchanged for over 1 million years. Innovation and creativity was not a component, and these are functions of modern working memory' [61, p. 122]. The archaeological record, however, furnishes a more complex scenario. There are diverse methods of biface production that clearly display flexibility of decision and creativity, all adhering to the same plan in achieving a predetermined goal. Furthermore, innovations were clearly made: evidence for the appearance of the soft hammer technique is mentioned above, and the beginnings of the Levallois technique that flourished during the Middle Palaeolithic can apparently be traced as well. Neither technique existed during the earlier part of the Levantine Acheulian record. These innovations, together with the creativity expressed in the full control of fire and its uses, clearly negate the notion of stagnation and/or stasis.

11.3.6.1 Language

Long-term planning and its implementation, which involve many aspects of social cooperation, demand an advanced form of communication. From examples like the reduction sequence of basalt bifaces, which involved know-how and expertise shown by the high quality (lack of knapping accidents) and precision (symmetry and refinement) of the end-products, it is thought that the GBY hominins had language abilities. Prolonged observations of modern-day knapping provide some insight into its teaching processes.

Knappers learn from each other and knapping sessions, which frequently take place in company, are accompanied by the exchange of ideas and tips. Knapping is not simply a repeated mechanical battering [61] but a blow-evaluation-blow procedure. Knappers strike a blow and then evaluate the results, frequently refitting the last flake removed to the core in order to evaluate the removal [60]. Interestingly, the knappers in Irian Jaya go through the same process; since their knapping sessions take place in a social context, the advantages and disadvantages of particular actions are thoroughly discussed. While the archaeological evidence will never supply evidence for verbal exchanges that took place while knapping, it is obvious that the Acheulian hominins did transmit knowledge and know-how, resulting in the production of similar artefacts by similar procedures. The dynamic decision-making and flexibility that characterize the reduction process of the bifaces is considered here to be an indication of the presence of language.

11.3.6.2 Concluding remarks

The most common approach to hominin abilities discerns phases in the evolution of cognitive abilities, marked primarily by distinct biological developments. Some scholars consider the prepared core technology and/or mass production of blades that appeared at some 300 Ka to be indicative of evolved planning 'suggesting a greater cognitive competence' [47, p. 3274], related to an increase in brain size. Coolidge & Wynn [61] claim that another leap in cognitive abilities resulted from a neural mutation that took place at *ca* 100–40 Ka, associated with the appearance of developed cognitive abilities that include working memory capacity (modern executive function).

This view of sequential neural evolution reflected in the growing complexity of hominin culture quite late in human history has been undermined by recent findings. These have revealed elaborate and sophisticated technological achievements (prepared core techniques and production of blades) from both East Africa and the Levant that date from a much earlier era, the Acheulian period (*ca* 0.5 Ma) [20, 68, 69].

Indeed, the record of GBY furnishes newly acquired data that are highly relevant to the extent of Acheulian cognitive abilities. It is clear that these cognitive abilities were quite developed, enabling them to use and exploit a variety of domains within their realm. Deep planning is especially apparent in the production sequence of bifaces and its by-products. The diverse methods of production observed on the site clearly demonstrate flexibility in decision-making as well as creativity in order to achieve the desired goal. In contrast to the view of the lithic reduction sequence as 'repetition and rhythm' [61, p. 93], the evaluation processes of each individual blow and the flexibility shown in selecting a particular method out of a varied repertoire, tailored to the specific circumstances at hand, are clearly indicative of advanced cognitive abilities. Moreover, the entire production system at GBY seems to be dependent on very precise communication, of which verbal language was the most probable means. Explaining bedrock bedding or evaluating the fineness and compactness of grain, crucial for attaining a successful end-result, would be impossible to achieve without language.

What is obvious is that the 'first appearance' of the cultural cognitive markers described here is to a large extent dependent on the archaeological resolution. The existence of these markers in GBY has been revealed through detailed studies. This intensity and scope of research are unfortunately rarely encountered, owing to differing circumstances and the poor archaeological record. Although the Acheulian cultural sequence lasted over 1.5 Myr, the pertinent information is fragmentary and extremely localized and can therefore provide only segments of its evolutionary history. This fragmentation undoubtedly masks the dynamics that are intrinsic to the Acheulian development. Clearly, the lack of information should not be interpreted as lack of change, innovation or cognitive ability. The recent discoveries concerning cognitive aspects of the Oldowan Technocomplex [70], which predates the Acheulian [71, 72], serve to illustrate the difficulty of obtaining data to assess hominin cognitive abilities.

There is still a long way for research to go before we will be able to correlate between biological and cultural evolution and make deductions about the one from the other. Still, the data from GBY show that the cognitive abilities of the Acheulian hominins were complex and highly 'modern', at least in the domains that we can explore through the archaeological record.

Acknowledgements

I am most grateful to the organizers, Andy Whiten, Robert Hinde, Chris Stringer and Kevin Laland, for inviting me to participate in the 'Culture evolves' conference and providing me with the opportunity to present some of my research results and views. This study was carried out with the support of an ongoing grant awarded by the Israel Science Foundation (grant no. 300/06) to the Centre of Excellence Project title: 'The effect of climate change on the environment and hominins of the UJV between *ca* 800 and 700 Ka ago as a basis for prediction of future scenarios'. The author wishes to thank the Israel Science Foundation and the Hebrew University of Jerusalem. My thanks to Gonen Sharon for his continuous research and help in deciphering the meaning behind the lithics, to Leore Grosman for producing the three-dimensional scanning images of the giant cores, Noah Lichtinger for improving the digitized graphics and Maya Oron for providing technological help. Anna Belfer-Cohen offered invaluable comments and corrections and improved the various drafts of this article. The three anonymous reviewers and Erella Hovers are thanked for their important comments and suggestions. Sue Gorodetsky edited the manuscript with her usual professionalism and dedication.

Note

1 Marks the first appearance of a term defined in the glossary.

References

1 Clarke, D. L. 1968 *Analytical archaeology*. London, UK: Methuen and Company Ltd.

2 Sharon, G. 2007 *Acheulian large flake industries: technology, chronology, and significance*. Oxford, UK: BAR International Series.

3 Ashton, N. & White, M. 2003 Biface and raw materials: flexible flaking in the British Early Palaeolithic. In *Multiple approaches to the Study of Bifacial Technology* (eds M. Soressi & H. Dibble), pp. 109–124. Philadelphia, PA: University of Pennsylvania Museum of Archaeology and Anthropology.

4 Callow, P. 1994 The Olduvai bifaces: technology and raw materials. In *Olduvai Gorge excavations in beds III, IV and the Masek beds 1968–1971* (eds M. D. Leakey & D. Roe), pp. 235–253. Cambridge, UK: Cambridge University Press.

5 Feblot-Augustins, J. 1990 Exploitation des matiers premieres dans l'Acheuleen d'Afrique: perspectives comportementales. *Paléo* **2**, 27–42.

6 Boëda, E. 2001 Techno-functional analysis of bifacial tools from the Acheulean layer C'3 at Barbas I (Dordogne, France). In *Les Industries a Outils Bifaciaux du Paléolithique Moyen d'Europe Occidentale* (ed. D. Cliquet), pp. 51–75. Liège, Belgium: Universite de Liège.

7 Boeda, É., Courty, M.-A., Federoff, N., Griggo, C., Hedley, I. G. & Muhesen, S. 2004 Le site Acheuléen d'El Meirah Syrie. In *From river to the sea: the Palaeolithic and the Neolithic on the Euphrates and in the Northern Levant* (eds O. Aurenche, M. L. Mière & P. Sanlaville), pp. 164–200. Oxford, UK: BAR International Series.

8 Jones, P. R. 1994 Results of experimental work in relation to the stone industries of Olduvai Gorge. In *Olduvai Gorge excavations in beds III, IV, and the Masek beds 1968–1971* (eds M. D. Leakey & D. A. Roe), pp. 254–298. Cambridge, UK: Cambridge University Press.

9 Kleindienst, M. R. 1961 Variability within the Late Acheulian assemblage in East Africa. *South African Archaeol. Bull.* **16**, 35–52.

10 Lycett, S. J. 2008 Acheulean variation and selection: does handaxe symmetry fit neutral expectations? *J. Archaeol. Sci.* **35**, 2640–2648.

11 Sharon, G., Alperson-Afil, N. & Goren-Inbar, N. 2011 Cultural conservatism against variability in the continual Acheulian sequence of Gesher Benot Yaàqov, Israel. *J. Hum. Evol.* **60**, 387–97.

12 Ungar, P. S., Grine, F. E. & Teaford, M. F. 2006 Diet in early *Homo*: a review of the evidence and a new model of adaptive versatility. *Annu. Rev. Anthropol.* **35**, 209–228.

13 Clark, D. J. 1975 A comparison of the Late Acheulian industries of Africa and the Middle East. In *After the Australopithecines: stratigraphy, ecology and culture change in the Middle Pleistocene* (eds K. W. Butzer & G. L. Isaac), pp. 605–659. Chicago, IL: Aldine.

14 Gamble, C. & Marshall, G. 2002 The shape of handaxes, the structure of the Acheulian world. In *A very remote period indeed: papers in the Palaeolithic presented to Derek Roe* (eds S. Milliken & J. Cook), pp. 19–27. Oxford, UK: Oxbow Books.

15 Kohn, M. & Mithen, S. 1999 Handaxes: products of sexual selection? *Antiquity* **73**, 518–526.

16 Rightmire, G. P. 2001 Patterns of hominid evolution and dispersal in the Middle Pleistocene. *Q. Int.* **75**, 77–84.

17 Gowlett, J. A. J. 1984 Mental abilities of early man: a look at some hard evidence. In *Hominid evolution and community ecology* (ed. R. Foley), pp. 167–192. London, UK: Academic Press.

18 Goren-Inbar, N. In press. Behavioral and cultural origins of Neanderthals: a Levantine perspective. In *150 Years of Neanderthal discoveries. Continuity and discontinuity* (eds S. Condemi & G.-C. Weniger). Berlin, Germany: Springer.

19 Bar-Yosef, O. & Goren-Inbar, N. 1993 The lithic assemblages of the site of 'Ubeidiya, Jordan Valley. Jerusalem, Israel: Hebrew University.

20 Hershkovitz, I., Smith, P., Sarig, R., Quam, R., Rodríguez, L., García, R., Arsuaga, J.-L., Barkai, R. & Gopher, A. 2011 Middle Pleistocene dental remains from Qesem Cave, Israel. *Am. J. Phys. Anthropol.* **144**, 575–592.

21 Frumkin, A., Karkanas, P., Bar-Matthews, M., Barkai, R., Gopher, A., Shahack-Gross, R. & Vaks, A. 2009 Gravitational deformations and fillings of aging caves: the example of Qesem karst system, Israel. *Geomorphology* **106**, 154–164.

22 Belmaker, M., Tchernov, E., Condemi, S. & Bar-Yosef, O. 2002 New evidence for hominid presence in the Lower Pleistocene of Southern Levant. *J. Hum. Evol.* **43**, 43–56.

23 Tobias, P. V. 1966 Fossil hominid from 'Ubeidiya, Israel. *Nature* **211**, 130–133.

24 Garrod, D. A. E. & Bate, D. M. A. 1937 *The Stone Age of Mount Carmel, excavation at Wadi Mughara.* Oxford, UK: Oxford University Press.

25 Turville-Petre, F. 1927 *Research in prehistoric Galilee, 1925–1926.* London, UK: British School of Archaeology in Jerusalem.

26 Belitzky, S. 2002 The structure and morphotectonics of the Gesher Benot Yaàqov area, Northern Dead Sea Rift, Israel. *Q. Res.* **58**, 372–380.

27 Goren-Inbar, N. & Belitzky, S. 1989 Structural position of the Pleistocene Gesher Benot Yaàqov site in the Dead Sea Rift Zone. *Q. Res.* **31**, 371–376.

28 Feibel, S. C. 2001 Archaeological sediments in lake margin environments. In *Sediments in archaeological contexts* (eds J. K. Stein & W. R. Farrand), pp. 127–148. Salt Lake City, UT: University of Utah Press.

29 Feibel, C. S. 2004 Quaternary lake margins of the Levant Rift Valley. In *Human paleoecology in the Levantine corridor* (eds N. Goren-Inbar & J. D. Speth), pp. 21–36. Oxford, UK: Oxbow Books.

30 Goren-Inbar, N., Feibel, C. S., Verosub, K. L., Melamed, Y., Kislev, M. E., Tchernov, E. & Saragusti, I. 2000 Pleistocene milestones on the out-of-Africa corridor at Gesher Benot Yaàqov, Israel. *Science* **289**, 944–974.

31 Goren-Inbar, N. & Saragusti, I. 1996 An Acheulian biface assemblage from the site of Gesher Benot Yaàqov, Israel: indications of African affinities. *J. Field Archaeol.* **23**, 15–30.

32 Alperson-Afil, N. *et al.* 2009 Hearth-related spatial patterning of hominins' activities at the Acheulian site of Gesher Benot Yaàqov, Israel. *Science* **326**, 1677–1680.

33 Ashkenazi, S., Klass, K., Mienis, H. K., Spiro, B. & Abel, R. 2009 Fossil embryos and adult Viviparidae from the Early–Middle Pleistocene of Gesher Benot Yaàqov, Israel: ecology, longevity and fecundity. *Lethaia* **43**, 116–127.

34 Goren-Inbar, N. & Spiro, B. In press. Early-middle Pleistocene paleoenvironments in the Levant. *J. Hum. Evol.* **60**, 319–522. *(Special Issue)*

35 Spiro, B., Ashkenazi, S., Mienis, H. K., Melamed, Y., Feibel, C., Delgado, A. & Starinsky, A. 2009 Climate variability in the Upper Jordan Valley around 0.78 Ma, inferences from time-series stable isotopes of Viviparidae, supported by mollusc and plant palaeoecology. *Palaeogeogr. Palaeoclimatol. Palaeoecol.* **282**, 32–44.

36 Rabinovich, R., Gaudzinski-Windheuser, S., Kindler, L. & Goren-Inbar, N. *The Acheulian site of Geshser Benot Yaàqov: mammal taphonomy - the assemblages of layers V-5 and V-6.* Dordrecht, The Netherlands: Springer.

37 Tchernov, E. 1988 The paleobiogeographical history of the southern Levant. In *The zoogeography of Israel* (eds Y. Yom-Tov & E. Tchernov), pp. 159–250. The Hague, The Netherlands: Dr. W. Junk Publishers.

38 Melamed, Y. 2003 Reconstruction of the Hula Valley vegetation and the hominid vegetarian diet by the Lower Palaeolithic botanical remains from Gesher Benot Yaàqov. PhD thesis, Bar-Ilan University, Israel.

39 Rabinovich, R. & Biton, R. Submitted. The Early-Middle Pleistocene faunal assemblages of Gesher Benot Yaàqov—taphonomy and paleoenvironment. *J. Hum. Evol.* **60**, 357–374.

40 Martínez-Navarro, B. & Rabinovich, R. 2011 The fossil Bovidae (Artiodactyla, Mammalia) from Gesher Benot Yaàqov, Israel: out of Africa during the Early-Middle Pleistocene transition. *J. Hum. Evol.* **60**, 375–86.

41 Rabinovich, R., Gaudzinski, S. & Goren-Inbar, N. 2008 Systematic butchering of fallow deer (*Dama*) at the early Middle Pleistocene Acheulian site of Gesher Benot Yaàqov, (Israel). *J. Hum. Evol.* **54**, 134–149.

42 Bello, S. M., Parfitt, S. A. & Stringer, C. 2009 Quantitative micromorphological analyses of cut marks produced by ancient and modern handaxes. *J. Archaeol. Sci.* **36**, 1869–1880.

43 Mitchell, J. C. 1997 Quantitative image analysis of lithic microwear on flint handaxe. *Microsc. Anal.* **26**, 15–17.

44 Mitchell, J. C. 1998 A use-wear analysis of selected British Lower Palaeolithic handaxes with special reference to the site of Boxgrove (West Sussex): a study incorporating optical microscopy, computer aided image analysis and experimental archaeology. PhD thesis, Oxford University, UK.

45 Goren-Inbar, N., Lister, A., Werker, E. & Chech, M. 1994 A butchered elephant skull and associated artifacts from the Acheulian site of Gesher Benot Yaàqov, Israel. *Paléorient* **20**, 99–112.

46 Zohar, I. & Biton, R. 2011 Land, lake, and fish: investigations of fish remains from Gesher Benot Yaàqov (paleo-Lake Hula). *J. Hum. Evol.* **60**, 343–56.

47 Foley, R. & Gamble, C. 2009 The ecology of social transitions in human evolution. *Phil. Trans. R. Soc. B* **364**, 3267–3279.

48 Goren-Inbar, N., Sharon, G., Melamed, Y. & Kislev, M. 2002 Nuts, nut cracking, and pitted stones at the Gesher Benot Yaàqov, Israel. *Proc. Natl Acad. Sci. USA* **99**, 2455–2460.

49 Goren-Inbar, N., Werker, E. & Feibel, C. S. 2002 *The Acheulian site of Gesher Benot Yaàqov: the wood assemblage*. Oxford, UK: Oxbow Books.

50 Goren-Inbar, N., Alperson, N., Kislev, M. E., Simchoni, O., Melamed, Y., Ben-Nun, A. & Werker, E. 2004 Evidence of hominin control of fire at Gesher Benot Yaàqov, Israel. *Science* **304**, 725–727.

51 Alperson-Afil, N. & Goren-Inbar, N. 2010 *The Acheulian site of Gesher Benot Yaàqov: ancient flames and controlled use of fire*. Dordrecht, The Netherlands: Springer.

52 Alperson-Afil, N. 2008 Continual fire-making by hominins at Gesher Benot Yaàqov, Israel. *Q. Sci. Rev.* **27**, 1733–1739.

53 Madsen, B. & Goren-Inbar, N. 2004 Acheulian giant core technology and beyond: an archaeological and experimental case study. *Eurasian Prehist.* **2**, 3–52.

54 Goren-Inbar, N., Grosman, L. & Sharon, G. In preparation. The record, technology and significance of the Acheulian giant cores of Gesher Benot Yaàqov, Israel. *J. Archaeol. Sci.* **38**, 1901–1917.

55 Weinstein, Y., Navon, O., Altherr, R. & Stein, M. 2006 The role of lithospheric mantle heterogeneity in the generation of Plio-Pleistocene alkali basaltic suites from NW Harrat Ash Shaam (Israel). *J. Petrol.* **47**, 1017–1050.

56 Petraglia, M., Porta, P. L. & Paddayya, K. 1999 The first Acheulian quarry in India: stone tool manufacture, bifaces morphology, and behaviors. *J. Anthropol. Res.* **55**, 39–70.

57 Goren-Inbar, N. & Sharon, G. 2006 Invisible handaxes and visible Acheulian biface technology at Gesher Benot Yaàqov, Israel. In *Axe age: Acheulian tool-making from quarry to discard* (eds N. Goren-Inbar & G. Sharon), pp. 111–135. London, UK: Equinox.

58 Sharon, G. & Goren-Inbar, N. 1999 Soft percussor use at the Gesher Benot Yaàqov Acheulian site? *Mitekufat Haeven* **28**, 55–79.

59 Goren-Inbar, N., Sharon, G., Alperson-Afil, N. & Laschiver, I. 2008 The Acheulian massive scrapers of Gesher Benot Yaàqov—a product of the biface *chaîne opératoire*. *J. Hum. Evol.* **55**, 702–712.

60 Pétrequin, P. & P'etrequin, A.-M. 1993 *Écologie d'un outil: la hache de pierre en Irian Jaya (Indonésie)*. Paris, France: CNRS.

61 Coolidge, F. L. & Wynn, T. 2009 *The rise of Homo sapiens—the evolution of modern thinking*. Chichester, UK: Wiley-Blackwell.

62 Janmart, J. 1952 Elephant hunting as practiced by the Congo Pygmies. *Am. Anthropol.* **54**, 146–147.

63 Movius, H. L. 1950 A wooden spear of Third Interglacial age from Lower Saxony. *Southwestern J. Anthropol.* **6**, 139–142.

64 Crader, D. C. 1983 Recent single-carcassbone scatter and the problem of 'butchery' sites in the archaeological record. In *Hunters and their prey* (eds J. Clutton-Brock & C. Grigson), pp. 107–141. Oxford, UK: BAR International Series.

65 Fisher, J. W. J. 1992 Observations on the Late Pleistocene bone assemblages from the Lamb Spring Site, Colorado. In *Ice Age hunters of the Rockies* (eds D. J. Stanford & J. S. Day), pp. 51–81. Boulder, CO: Denver Museum of Natural History and University Press of Colorado.

66 Fisher, J. W. J. 2001 Elephant butchery practices in the Ituri Forest, Democratic Republic of the Congo, and their relevance for interpreting human activities at prehistoric Proboscidean sites. In *Proc. of the Int. Conf. on Mammoth Site Studies* (ed. D. West), pp. 1–10. Lawrence, KS: University of Kansas.

67 Marks, S. A. 2005 *Large mammals and a brave people—subsistence hunters in Zambia*. New Brunswick, NJ: Transactions Publishers.

68 Bar-Yosef, O. & Kuhn, S. 1999 The big deal about blades: laminar technologies and human evolution. *Am. Anthropol.* **101**, 1–17.

69 Johnson, C. R. & McBrearty, S. 2010 500,000 year old blades from the Kapthurin Formation, Kenya. *J. Hum. Evol.* **58**, 193–200.

70 de la Torre, I. 2011 The origins of stone tool technology in Africa: a historical perspective. *Phil. Trans. R. Soc. B* **366**, 1028–1037.

71 Hovers, E. & Braun, D. R. 2009 Introduction: current issues in Oldowan research. In *Interdisciplinary approaches to the Oldowan* (eds E. Hovers & D. R. Braun), pp. 1–14. Dordrecht, The Netherlands: Springer.

72 Stout, D., Semaw, S., Rogers, M. J. & Cauche, D. 2010 Technological variation in the earliest Oldowan from Gona, Afar, Ethiopia. *J. Hum. Evol.* **58**, 474–491.

Glossary

Bedding plane A planar or near-planar surface that separates each successive layer of stratified rock (of the same or different lithology) from a preceding or following layer; a plane of deposition. In volcanic rocks: occurs as one of the cooling effects of the hot rock that lead to rock stratification upon consolidation; usually invisible to the naked eye.

Blank A piece of lithic raw material (either a natural pebble/cobble or a previously detached flake) that is suitable for further modification (mass extraction) by flaking or retouch.

Cleaver A tool shaped by bifacial removals whereby flakes are detached from both faces of the blank (and hence lenticular in cross section). Typically this tool is U-shaped with a straight distal edge (when viewed in plan view), presumably the tool's cutting edge.

Handaxe A tool shaped by bifacial removals from both faces of a cobble or large flake (and hence lenticular in cross section). Typically, this tool is distally pointed or teardrop-shaped (when viewed in plan view).

Percussor A hammer; may be a hard hammer, most commonly made of stone, or a soft hammer made of bone, antler or wood.

Preform A shaped lithic artefact especially prepared so that its surface and volume facilitate further modification towards its transformation into a tool with a pre-planned shape. Preforms are most often recognized in the context of producing bifacial tools.

Reduction sequence A series of removals, starting with the natural form of the lithic raw material and ending with a predetermined blank or a retouched tool. In the context of making Acheulian bifaces, the sequence is shaping of the natural piece, removal of the rind (cortex) on the outer surface of the natural form, preparing the appropriate angles that are essential for flaking, preparing the surface for the following mass removal, extracting a sizable flake and shaping the end product, which is the pre-planned tool.

Chaîne opératoire (operational sequence) The technological process of making an object: a sequence that consists of focusing on a mental template (the pre-planned shape of a lithic object), selecting sets of actions needed for its execution, and actualizing them through physical action upon matter. In lithic studies it is used sometimes interchangeably with the term 'reduction sequence'.

Chapter 12

Stone Toolmaking and the Evolution of Human Culture and Cognition

Dietrich Stout

Although many species display behavioural traditions, human culture is unique in the complexity of its technological, symbolic and social contents. Is this extraordinary complexity a product of cognitive evolution, cultural evolution or some interaction of the two? Answering this question will require a much better understanding of patterns of increasing cultural diversity, complexity and rates of change in human evolution. Palaeolithic stone tools provide a relatively abundant and continuous record of such change, but a systematic method for describing the complexity and diversity of these early technologies has yet to be developed. Here, an initial attempt at such a system is presented. Results suggest that rates of Palaeolithic culture change may have been underestimated and that there is a direct relationship between increasing technological complexity and diversity. Cognitive evolution and the greater latitude for cultural variation afforded by increasingly complex technologies may play complementary roles in explaining this pattern.

Keywords: Palaeolithic; technology; hierarchical behaviour; cumulative culture; Oldowan; Acheulean

12.1 Introduction

Humans display evolved capacities for complex technological, symbolic and social action that are unique among extant species. But what exactly has evolved to produce these capacities? A prime candidate is the human brain, long viewed as the source of our distinctive 'mental powers' and the *sine qua non* of human uniqueness [1]. However, early evolutionary theorists also recognized the importance of culture [2, 3] in accounting for the complexity of modern human behaviour. More recently, it has been suggested that the full range of modern human behaviour may be explicable as a product of cumulative cultural evolution [4], and that key behavioural transitions in human prehistory reflect the dynamics of cultural, rather than biological, evolution [5]. To further dissect the complex interaction of human cognitive and cultural evolution, it will be necessary to better understand these patterns of prehistoric culture change.

There is general agreement that human and animal 'cultures' are distinguished by the much greater diversity and complexity of the former. What remains unclear is whether this difference arises from the increased fidelity of human cultural transmission [4, 6], from the greater cognitive capacity of individual humans [7] or from some complex interaction of the two [8]. This is a difficult question to address because modern humans differ from even our closest living relatives on a wide array of interdependent somatic, cognitive and cultural dimensions. The question of which trait(s) may have had evolutionary/causal priority in human evolution is a historical one regarding developments that appear simultaneous from a comparative perspective.

Archaeological evidence provides a complementary data source that is better positioned to answer questions about developments since the last common ancestor with *Pan*. Palaeolithic stone tools offer a relatively abundant and continuous record of technological change over the past 2.5 Myr, documenting the gradual expression of new behavioural capabilities. Exploitation of this evidence will depend on the development of increasingly robust inferential links between archaeological remains, past behaviours, and the necessary cognitive and cultural mechanisms supporting these behaviours. High on the list of tools needing to be developed is a systematic method for describing the complexity and diversity of Palaeolithic technologies.

It might be supposed that 150 years of Palaeolithic archaeology had already solved this problem, and that the wealth of named cultures, 'industries' and 'modes' in the literature would be sufficient for comparison. Indeed, it has been argued that the longevity of the Oldowan and Acheulean Industries reflects an absence of cumulative cultural evolution in the Lower Palaeolithic [7, 9]. However, the nature of cultural variation in the Oldowan is a matter of ongoing debate [10, 11] and many researchers do see evidence of progressive technological change within the Acheulean (e.g. [12–14]). One difficulty with classical archaeological approaches to technological variation has been a tendency to focus on the form of artefacts rather than on the processes that produced them. This is problematic because it conflates many potential sources of variation [15] and because it is biological capacities and cultural 'recipes' [16] that evolve, not artefact morphologies. Analysis of the hierarchical organization of toolmaking action sequences may provide a better foundation for inferences about culture and cognition.

12.2 Stone toolmaking action hierarchies

Analysis of toolmaking action sequences is not new in archaeology. For over 30 years, the *châine opértoire* approach has focused on describing the processes of Palaeolithic tool production, based on insights gained from experimental replication and the 'reading' of production scars left on tools (e.g. [12, 17]). However, this approach has yet to be fully integrated with theoretical and methodological insights from other disciplines. As the name implies, the *châine opértoire* approach involves the reconstruction of action 'chains' or sequences, commonly represented as flow charts. This sequential approach has been useful in reconstructing the details of particular past technologies, but is less suitable for generalizing comparisons or cognitive analyses. The presence of hierarchical as well as sequential structure in human action has been a cornerstone of cognitive science since the demise of behaviourism [18–20], and is especially relevant to understanding the goal-oriented flexibility [18] of behaviours like stone toolmaking, in which consistent products are generated from inherently variable raw materials and action outcomes [17]. Elements of hierarchical analysis are implicit in many technological descriptions produced by the *châine opértoire* approach, but the formal description of Palaeolithic technologies in these terms should help provide a more uniform framework for comparison and promote better integration with research on the hierarchical structure in motor control [21], functional neuroanatomy [22, 23] and social transmission [16, 24–26].

In a hierarchy, individual elements are grouped into increasingly inclusive nested categories. This is commonly depicted using tree diagrams, with multiple nodes at lower (subordinate) levels being linked to single nodes at the next higher (superordinate) level, culminating in a single node at the top of the diagram. In action hierarchies, superordinate levels correspond to more abstract goals and/or temporally extended processes, from the overall objective (e.g. 'make coffee') down through more particular sub-goals and operations ('add sugar') to highly specific motor acts ('grasp spoon'). This multi-level organization provides flexibility by allowing context-specific adaptive variation at subordinate levels to be combined with more global stability at superordinate levels. For example, 'turn on light' is a coherent goal that might be accomplished by flipping a switch, twisting a knob or pulling a cord [23]. Critically, information can flow both up and down within hierarchies so that superordinate goals determine subordinate action selection ('top-down' influence) but are themselves driven by subordinate action outcomes ('bottom-up' influence). This bi-directional interaction is an important mechanism supporting the learning and adaptability of complex behaviours [21] like stone toolmaking.

Hierarchical structure is interesting from a cognitive perspective because it implies the existence of superordinate representations abstracted from, and maintained over, the course of multiple subordinate events [23]. As such, it implicates processes of stimulus generalization, relational integration, temporal abstraction and goal abstraction associated with the distinctive response properties and anatomical connections of prefrontal cortex [22]. Hierarchical structure is also interesting with respect to cultural evolution because it relates to questions about the 'level' of copying [6] and potential biases in transmission [25].

Early hierarchical analyses of stone toolmaking action sequences were developed by Holloway [27] and Gowlett [28]. More recently, the hierarchical structure of toolmaking has been described in relation to models from cognitive neuroscience and developmental psychology [29–31]. Moore [30] presented a tree structure notation, adapted from Greenfield [32], which is further modified here to describe the organization of major Lower Palaeolithic toolmaking methods as inferred from modern experiments and the analysis of archaeological materials.

12.2.1 Oldowan (*ca* 2.6–1.4 Ma; Figure 12.1*a*)

The earliest known stone tools [33] are assigned to the Oldowan Industry and consist of sharp stone flakes struck from cobble 'cores' by direct percussion with another stone (the 'hammerstone'). Experimentally, Oldowan flake production minimally involves: (i) procurement

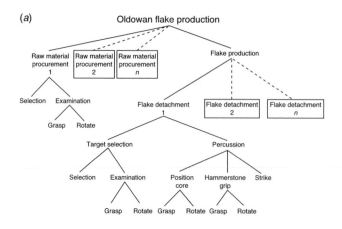

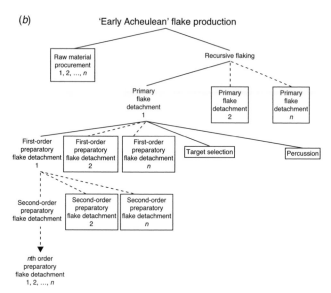

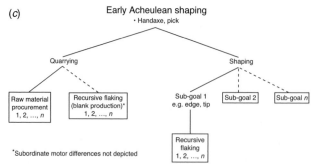

Figure 12.1 Lower Palaeolithic action hierarchies. Lines connect subordinate elements with the superordinate element they instantiate. Dashed lines indicate optional elements, numbers indicate duplications of action elements and boxes enclose 'collapsed' action chunks whose subordinate elements have been omitted to avoid crowding. For example, in (c) 'recursive flaking (blank production)' is an optional element of 'quarrying' that might be duplicated an unspecified number of times (1, 2, ..., n). The subordinate elements of 'recursive flaking' are depicted in (b) and omitted in (c). (d) Dagger, soft hammer production not included in model; asterisk, typically includes complex flake detachments.

(Continued)

(d)

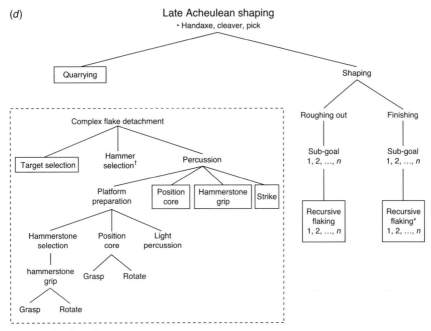

Figure 12.1 *Continued.*

of raw materials (both core and hammerstone) of appropriate size, shape and composition and (ii) actual flaking, including core examination, target selection, core positioning/support, hammerstone grip selection and accurate percussion. This may be represented by a tree diagram (Figure 12.1*a*) with six nested levels, ranging from the overall goal of flake production to specific manipulations of the core and hammerstone. Within this structure, certain discrete action 'chunks' can be repeated an indefinite number of times, as indicated by numbers 1, 2, …, *n* (dashed lines indicate optional elements, boxes enclose 'collapsed' action chunks where subordinate elements have been omitted to avoid crowding). For example, previous authors have identified a 'basic flake unit' [30] or 'flake loop' [28] (here termed 'flake detachment'), which is duplicated until some superordinate goal (e.g. desired numbers of flakes of appropriate size and sharpness) is achieved. Similarly, a basic 'raw material procurement' chunk may be repeated until quality and quantity criteria are met. Such modular structure is an efficient and productive characteristic of hierarchical organization that has received much attention in the study of language under the heading of 'discrete infinity' [34]. It is made possible by the combination at a superordinate level of units that remain distinct at the subordinate level, a possibility that would be absent in a 'flat' behavioural chain.

In this way, basic core manipulations (grasp, rotate) are combined in a superordinate process of core positioning, which is combined with an appropriate hammerstone grip and striking movement in the larger process of percussion, which is combined with the selection of an appropriate target in the process of flake detachment. At this level, it is possible that individual flake detachments might form a simple linear chain, with the location of each detachment being selected purely on the basis of current core affordances (produced in part by the immediately preceding detachments [30]). However, it is now clear from the archaeological record that some early Oldowan assemblages exhibit systematically biased patterns of flake detachment that are underdetermined by the morphological variability of Oldowan cores. Examples [10, 11] include removal of flakes predominantly from a single core surface ('unifacially') or alternately from two intersecting surfaces ('bifacially'). This patterning implies some superordinate relationship between individual flake detachments, perhaps in the form of relatively complex 'technological rules' and conscious planning [11], but minimally involving a learned tendency to select targets in relation to the position of previous detachments (e.g. laterally adjacent, alternate face, same plane, etc.). This superordinate relationship between flake detachments is represented in Figure 12.1a by the node labelled 'flaking'. This added level of hierarchical organization allows for some diversity in Oldowan flake production patterns, however, the relation of such variation to ecological, functional and/or cultural factors remains to be further explored [10].

12.2.2 Early Acheulean (ca 1.6–0.9 Ma)

Around 1.6 Ma, a number of technological innovations begin to appear in the archaeological record. These include more elaborate methods of flake production, such as 'hierarchical centripetal' [35] flaking and single-platform 'Karari scraper' cores [36], as well as the production of intentionally shaped Acheulean tools including 'handaxes' and 'picks'. The new flake production methods are not technically considered part of the Acheulean, however, they are contemporaneous with the Early Acheulean [37] and are considered here as part of the same general phenomenon of Lower Pleistocene technological change.

12.2.2.1 Elaborate flake production (Figure 12.1b)

Karari scrapers are a distinctive artefact type known from the basal Okote Member (1.6–1.5 Ma) at Koobi Fora, Kenya, and are produced by removing flakes from around the circumference of large flake or fractured cobble. This is thought to be a particularly efficient way to generate useful flakes and to require a 'higher degree of planning' insofar as a morphologically suitable large flake or cobble fragment must first be produced with the intent for subsequent use as a core [38]. The hierarchical centripetal method reported from the ST Site Complex (1.2–1.1 Ma) at Peninj, Tanzania, also appears to be aimed at the efficient production of useful flakes and similarly involves preparatory operations [35]. In this case, one or more subordinate 'preparatory' flakes are removed from a lateral 'preparation surface' in order to establish an advantageous morphology for the removal of desired 'primary' flake from the 'main surface'.

These different forms of elaborate flake production reflect a similar underlying innovation in action organization: modification of the core specifically in order to enable subsequent flake detachments. This differs from bifacial and unifacial flaking patterns seen in the Oldowan in that modification, as an explicitly preparatory action, is actually embedded within the process of primary flake detachment. As depicted in Figure 12.1b, this involves inserting at least one subordinate instance of preparatory flake detachment within the primary flake detachment tree, much as in the 'complex flake unit' of Moore [30]. This results in an increase from six to seven nested levels. In the case of Karari scraper cores, a single subordinate detachment is involved in the production of the initial large flake or split cobble, which is then iteratively flaked according to a particular (circumferential) pattern. In hierarchical centripetal flaking, one or more subordinate flakes are removed in order to alter the configuration of the core prior to primary flake detachment.

In view of recent interest in the evolution of recursive cognition (e.g. [39]), it is interesting to note that this embedding of flake detachments within flake detachments is formally recursive, with the theoretical potential to embed an infinite number of subordinate detachments (i.e. detach a flake to prepare to detach a flake to prepare to detach a flake…). This is depicted in Figure 12.1*b* as optional nodes corresponding to second through *n*th-order embedded detachments. As in recursive linguistic syntax, however, there are pragmatic limits to the actual number of embedded nodes in recursive flaking, including both physical and cognitive constraints. Karari and hierarchical centripetal methods, at least as described here, need not involve more than one level of recursive embedding.

12.2.2.2 Large cutting tools (Figure 12.1c)

The production of Early Acheulean 'large cutting tools' (LCTs) involves both structured flaking and intentional shaping. Two LCT forms typical of the earliest Acheulean sites are pointed handaxes produced on large (greater than 10 cm) flakes and relatively thick, pointed picks typically produced from cobbles [37]. The production of large flakes (called 'blanks') suitable for shaping into a handaxe was a key innovation [15] of the Early Acheulean, and involves an elaboration of raw material procurement into a multi-component quarrying process, depicted to the left of Figure 12.1*c*. Raw material selection criteria must now privilege size over composition, allowing for the production of large flakes. Even given an adequately sized core, however, the consistent production of suitable blanks is quite challenging [40]. Blank production requires a heavier hammerstone and much greater force than Oldowan flake production, and the largest cores would have necessarily been supported on the ground instead of in the hand. This requires the use of additional small boulders or cobbles to brace the core in an appropriate position [41]. Manipulation and rotation of both core and hammerstone may have required two hands and a variety of new body postures. These fundamental differences in perceptual-motor organization, not depicted in Figure 12.1*c*, make Acheulean blank production qualitatively different from Oldowan flaking [37].

At a higher level of organization, however, there are important structural similarities. The earliest blank production strategy may have been a simple iteration of flake detachments, leaving behind a 'casual core' resembling a large Oldowan core [41]. Adoption of a bifacial flaking pattern, which helps to maintain adequate edge angles during sequential blank removals, was also common [41]. This may have been an explicit strategy but, as in the Oldowan, can be minimally modelled as a simple target selection bias. Even in these simple strategies, however, recursive flaking would sometimes have been necessary to 'open' the boulder core by removing a subordinate flake, itself too small to serve as a blank, intended to establish the first viable striking surface. By 1.2–1.1 Ma, de la Torre *et al.* [42] report evidence of more extensive recursive flaking to establish core edge angles and surface morphology during blank production at the sites of RHS-Mugulud and MHS-Bayasi from Peninj. These blank production strategies can be compared with the elaborate flake production methods described above, and are diagrammed as repeated instances (1, 2, …, *n*) of recursive flaking in Figure 12.1*c*.

The production of an LCT directly from a cobble involves different raw material criteria (smaller size, oblong shape), omission of the entire blank production sequence, and more extensive shaping [40]. This coordination of production elements requires that the top node of the model contains some stable representation of intended tool form (e.g. handaxe or pick; importantly, these forms co-occur at single sites) and associated lower level actions. As has long been recognized, the production of standard forms from variable materials requires some such higher order representation [15, 27]. This need not be a fully specified geometric archetype and, especially in the early record, seems more likely to comprise certain learned characteristics of effective tools.

Desired tool characteristics were achieved through 'shaping': a sequence of flake detachments that result in a particular core form. In the case of a pick, for example, removal of one or more rows of flakes from two parallel sides of an oblong cobble would result in a thick pointed form with a triangular cross section. This might be modelled as a massively recursive sequence with each flake detachment enabling subsequent detachments culminating in the final removal required to achieve a pre-specified form. However, this depth of structure and planning is unnecessary and unlikely. Modern toolmakers (e.g. [17]) describe shaping in terms of the pursuit of local sub-goals resulting in the successive approximation of an overall target form. For example, a short series of flakes might be aimed at creating an edge, followed by a reappraisal of the overall form, selection of the next appropriate sub-goal and so on. This is depicted to the right of Figure 12.1*c*, with multiple duplications of (potentially) recursive flaking action chunks being combined to achieve local sub-goals which are themselves combined to achieve overall shaping goals. The result is a further increase in the hierarchical complexity of the associated tree, which now includes nine nested levels.

This multi-level goal structure adds flexibility, reduces the requirement for extended contingency planning, and takes advantage of the core itself as a continuously available external resource structuring behaviour. It also provides latitude for substantial technological variation in that similar forms may be achieved from different raw materials using different subordinate goal structures. For example, at the Olduvai site of TK (1.33 Ma) LCTs were produced using a consistent 'rhomboidal' strategy of unifacial removals from opposite sides of tabular quartz blocks [43], while at sites OGS-12 and BSN-17 from Gona, Ethiopia (approx. 1.6 Ma) [37] and Kokiselei 4, from West Turkana, Kenya (approx. 1.7 Ma) [12], variable combinations of unifacial and bifacial removals from two or three worked edges were used to fashion trihedral picks from lava cobbles.

12.2.3 **Late Acheulean (*ca* 0.7–0.25 Ma; Figure 12.1*d*)**

Although the Acheulean has been characterized as a monolithic, unchanging industry (e.g. [9]), this may in part reflect the fact that the earliest well-known European Acheulean sites date to only about 0.5 Ma (e.g. [44]) (although sites dating to 0.6–0.8 Ma have been reported in southern Europe [45, 46]). African archaeologists have long recognized an important technological transition between the Early and Late Acheulean, occurring sometime before 0.5 Ma [13]. Classically, this transition involves the appearance of smaller, thinner, more regular and symmetrical LCTs thought to require the use of a 'soft hammer' technique during production. Less-refined forms persist after this time, and may dominate some assemblages or even entire regions [47, 48], however, it is clear that the global range of Acheulean variation expanded to include new forms. The 0.7 Ma of Isenya in Kenya [12] is currently one of the earliest reported examples of such tools. The site also provides examples of 'cleavers', a typical Late Acheulean LCT form involving the production of morphologically predetermined blanks.

12.2.3.1 Predetermined blank production

In a typological sense, cleavers have been defined as LCTs with a transverse, blade-like 'bit' more than half the width of the tool [49], however, this is recognized as an arbitrary division of a morphological continuum. In the technological sense [12] followed here, cleavers are the product of a predetermined blank production process designed to yield a long, sharp cleaver bit on the blank prior to any shaping. Strategies documented at Isenya include a 'unipolar' method in which a subordinate, preparatory flake parallel to the objective flake shapes the cleaver bit, and the surprising 'Kombewa' method in which a primary blank is produced and a secondary blank then removed from it, yielding a biconvex shape with a sharp edge around almost the entire perimeter. These predetermination strategies represent an elaboration of Early Acheulean recursive blank production, involving an increase in the number of subordinate detachments required, and are included within the superordinate node 'quarrying' to the left of Figure 12.1*d*. Fully predetermined blank production is clearly documented at Isenya 0.7 Ma and may even date to greater than 1.0 Ma in South Africa [50]. Certainly, by *ca* 0.4–0.3 Ma, it is widespread and includes a range of variants like the 'Victoria West' and 'Tabel-bala-Tachengit' methods [13, 51].

Late Acheulean 'proto-Levallois' methods are widely seen as transitional to subsequent Middle Stone Age (MSA) 'Levallois' prepared core flake production strategies [51], with the main shifts being a reduction in size (probably related to the introduction of hafting in the MSA) and a further diversification of methods (e.g. preferential, centripetal, convergent, etc.). In fact, production of diverse small tools in 'Late Acheulean' times may have been underestimated (cf [50]), and standardized blade production (long considered a hallmark of modern humans) has been reported from two 0.5 Ma sites in the Kapthurin Formation, Kenya [52].

12.2.3.2 Late Achuelean shaping (Figure 12.1d)

Production of the thinner, more regular LCTs characteristic of the Late Acheulean requires a more elaborate shaping process. Cross-sectional thinning is one of the most distinctive and technically demanding characteristics of the process [14, 53, 54], requiring the reliable production of flakes that travel more than half-way across the surface of the piece without removing large portions of the edge. Examples of well-thinned Late Acheulean LCTs have been described from Europe (e.g. [55]), Western Asia (e.g. [56]) and Africa (e.g. [54]) in a variety of raw materials.

Experimentally, thinning flakes are often achieved using a soft hammer of bone or antler that can initiate fracture without gouging the edge, and such hammers have been found in Late Acheulean contexts [44]. However, it is possible to achieve similar results with a hammerstone if the surface to be struck (the 'striking platform') is properly prepared [57]. Indeed, some such 'platform preparation' is also required for the effective use of a soft hammer. This preparation involves the small-scale chipping and/or abrasion of edges to alter their sharpness, bevel and placement relative to the midline [53] and can take place on both striking and release surfaces [54]. Small-scale chipping is usually accomplished with light, glancing blows of a smaller, specifically selected hammerstone held in a more flexible grip. Whether or not a soft hammer is used, various different sized hammerstones may be required for different sub-goals within the shaping process.

Following Moore [30], platform preparation is modelled as a subordinate process within percussion. This adds a further level of hierarchical structure, as well as qualitatively different perceptual-motor elements. Together with selection of a hammer appropriate to the intended percussion, platform preparation becomes part of a new structural unit, 'complex flake detachment', which is depicted in the inset box to the left of Figure 12.1d. Complex flake detachment constitutes an action 'chunk' may be substituted for simple flake detachment and combined iteratively and/or recursively to achieve sub-goals during shaping and especially thinning (marked by asterisk in Figure 12.1d).

Archaeologists generally recognize at least two major stages of Late Acheulean LCT shaping: 'roughing-out' and 'finishing', depicted to the right of Figure 12.1d. Roughing-out is somewhat comparable with Early Acheulean shaping, but involves the specific aim of establishing a centred, bifacial edge with adequate geometry to support subsequent thinning operations. This superordinate goal is implemented through various sub-goals addressing particular portions of the core through structured complex flaking. Roughing-out generally involves hard hammer percussion, large flake production and little or no platform preparation. Finishing involves the detachment of thinning flakes and small marginal flakes in order to achieve sub-goals of thinning and regularizing the core, through localized episodes of recursive (often complex) flaking. Smaller and soft hammers may be used, and platform preparation can be extensive. The result is a relatively thin, lightweight tool with sharp, regular bifacial edges, associated with the most complex action tree considered so far, comprising 10 nested levels.

12.3 Lower Palaeolithic culture change

This chapter examines one of the best known, widely accepted and well-documented characteristics of the Lower Palaeolithic record: the increase over time in the upper limits of variation in technological complexity on a global scale. Fine-grained patterns of change are of course more complicated, yet there can be little doubt that the most complex technologies known from 0.25 Ma far exceed those of 2.5 Ma. What remains controversial is the tempo, mode and magnitude of this change, and whether it is more consistent with biological or cultural explanation. One prevalent view emphasizes the 'remarkable conservatism' of Acheulean technology [58], which is thought to reflect punctuated rather than gradual change and to exemplify a dearth of cumulative cultural evolution in the Lower (and even Middle) Palaeolithic [7, 9]. It has been argued that this slow, punctuated pattern of Palaeolithic technological change is best explained in terms of underlying cognitive constraints (i.e. biological evolution) [9, 59]. Analysis of the hierarchical structure of toolmaking action sequences provides a standard format for technological comparison, which may be useful in assessing these arguments.

The most obvious result of the preceding analysis is that Lower Palaeolithic technological change is indeed cumulative. Elaborate flake production and shaping methods build on previously established technologies by adding levels of hierarchical structure and/or modifying the content of existing sub-processes. However, it might still be argued that the *rate* of change is slow enough to imply cognitive differences from modern humans. This leads to questions of how to quantify culture change, and what exactly a 'modern' rate would be. Neolithic rates of change would surely dwarf those of the Lower Palaeolithic, but pale in comparison to the twentieth century. Simply assigning a value of '1' to each of the technological innovations discussed above produces a similar pattern of increasing rate of change over time (Figure 12.2), suggesting that the entire history of human technological evolution might follow a single exponential curve. This heuristic exercise remains far too crude, and the evidence too sporadic, to rule out major discontinuities and inflections owing to biological change and/or other extrinsic factors. For example, the absence of incremental change 1.6–2.6 Ma constitutes an Oldowan 'stasis' [10, 33], however, it is not inherently obvious whether this represents a discontinuity or merely the long tail of an exponential curve. In any case, the apparent pattern does provide a case for more seriously considering intrinsic factors that might tend to produce a uniform curve at this coarse level of analysis. One such factor is the intrinsic relationship between technological complexity and diversity.

The action hierarchy analysis suggests that complexity constrains diversity. Simply put, there just is not that much potential for variation in Oldowan flake production. It is only with more complicated technologies that multiple variants become possible, because more choices are possible. Technical innovations like recursive flaking and platform preparation alleviate raw material constraints, allowing for the emergence of more hierarchically complex strategies with multiple, differentiated end-products. Increasing hierarchical complexity in turn favours the emergence of technical innovations by providing greater latitude for the recombination of action elements and sub-assemblies. Across such diverse disciplines as physics, chemistry, genetics and linguistics, hierarchical recombination has been recognized as a fundamental process driving 'self-diversification' [34]. For example, there is an analogy [16] to be made with the way in which genetically regulated developmental hierarchies enable evolutionarily productive processes of segmental

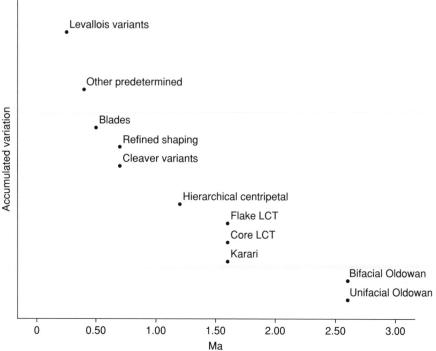

Figure 12.2 Accumulation of Palaeolithic technological variations discussed in the text. Each innovation adds an increment of '1' on the *y*-axis; some points (e.g. 'cleaver variants') correspond to more than one innovation.

duplication and differentiation. In much the same way, increasing technological complexity might become autocatalytic, contributing to the apparently exponential pattern of human technological evolution seen at the largest scale of analysis.

All of this implies that Lower Palaeolithic hominins possessed adequate cognitive substrates for some degree of cumulative cultural evolution, an unsurprising result considering the transmission capacities of modern chimpanzees [60]. Nevertheless, significant evolutionary elaborations of these shared capacities might have occurred during the Lower Palaeolithic, relaxing constraints on the complexity of transmitted techniques and allowing for increasing rates of change. One candidate for such cognitive evolution is the modern human propensity for detailed copying of behavioural means (*imitation*) as opposed to ends (*emulation*) [6, 60]. However, consideration of the action hierarchies presented above immediately raises a question as to what exactly counts as a means and what as an end. How far down the hierarchy must one go to be engaged in imitation, and how far up for emulation?

Studies of imitation in children suggest that copying is better understood in terms of goal hierarchies rather than a strict means/ends dichotomy [26]. Thus, a specific arm movement trajectory would be a subordinate goal to the superordinate goal of displacing an external object rather than a qualitatively different 'behavioural means'. When cognitive resources are limited and multiple goals compete for attention, children tend to reproduce superordinate goals at the expense of subordinate goals [26], paralleling a similar hierarchical bias in adults' selective perception, memory and transmission of narrative event information [25]. When competing superordinate goals are removed, children are more successful at copying 'low-level' goals, including movement trajectories [26]. In apes, similar capacities for low-level copying are illustrated by the 'Do-as-I-do' imitation of specific bodily actions [60], whereas in more complex, instrumental tasks the subordinate 'means' are often omitted [6]. For both apes and children, it would seem that the fidelity of imitation is constrained more by the complexity (especially, the number of hierarchical levels) of behaviour to be copied rather than by the level of copying *per se*.

At a given processing capacity, we should thus expect copying fidelity to be negatively correlated with hierarchical complexity. Insofar as copying errors introduce variation, this would again contribute to the intrinsic relationship between complexity and diversification in cultural evolution. At relatively high levels of behavioural complexity, however, copying fidelity would decrease to the point that transmission might fail entirely. For example, Late Acheulean shaping is the most complex Lower Palaeolithic technology analysed here and a failure in its transmission (cf [61]) might help to explain the greater thickness of LCTs in eastern Asia [47, 48].

From this perspective, successful transmission of complex technological behaviours would depend on two factors: individual capacities for hierarchical information processing (cf [7]) and social mechanisms of skill acquisition [62]. Neither of these need remain constant, and both are likely to have been influenced by the biological evolution of hominin brains [63], which nearly tripled in size during the Lower Palaeolithic. Hierarchical cognition is supported by lateral frontal cortex [22], the more anterior portions of which are disproportionately expanded in humans [64]. Increasing levels of abstraction in action organization place demands on increasingly anterior portions of frontal cortex [22] and precisely this pattern of increased anterior activation has been observed in a brain imaging study comparing Late Acheulean versus Oldowan toolmaking [29]. This is consistent with the possibility that evolving neural substrates for complex action organization could have interacted with autocatalytic increases in technological complexity to produce a 'runaway' process of biocultural evolution [8, 65].

Complex hierarchical cognition is not, however, sufficient for the reproduction of Palaeolithic technological behaviours. Stone toolmaking, from the Oldowan on, requires bodily skills [29, 66] that cannot be acquired directly through observation. These pragmatic skills can only be developed through deliberate practice and experimentation leading to the discovery of low-level dynamics that would remain 'opaque' (cf [67]) to observation alone. Available evidence indicates that it takes more than a few hours of practice for modern humans to master even simple Oldowan flake production [68], and personal experience suggests that Late Acheulean skill may demand hundreds of hours.

In the modern community of Langda in Papua Provence, Indonesia, traditional stone toolmaking skills are transmitted through semi-formal apprenticeships that can last

10 years or more [62]. Motivation and commitment through this extended period are promoted by the social context of toolmaking, which occurs in a supportive group setting and is a source of pride, pleasure and personal identity for practitioners. Central to the learning process is a heavy investment in the individual practice needed to consolidate basic perceptual-motor skills. This is encouraged by the positive social value placed on practice and is supported by instruction, demonstration, intervention and assistance from more experienced toolmakers, all of which acts as a social 'scaffold' promoting individual skill acquisition.

Experimental studies similarly show that, while novice toolmakers rapidly learn to identify and select appropriate targets [68], it takes much longer to develop the perceptual-motor skill needed to predict and control flake detachments [29, 69, 70]. Such skill development requires the discovery of appropriate techniques through behavioural experimentation [71] with various different grips, postures and angles of percussion, as well as with hammerstones of varying size, shape and density. Discovery of optimal techniques might be facilitated by social scaffolding [62], explicit instruction or high-fidelity imitation of an expert model, but minimally requires focused attention, self-monitoring and the inhibition of automatic reactions during repetitious practice [71, 72]. Social motivation and support for such protracted practice are important contributing factors that appear to be uniquely developed in humans [6, 73] and may reflect further interactions between biologically evolving neural and endocrine substrates of prosocial behaviour [63, 65, 74] and culturally evolving hominin technologies.

12.4 **Conclusions**

Stone toolmaking action analyses presented here demonstrate the presence of cumulative cultural evolution in the Lower Palaeolithic and suggest that this accumulation displays an accelerating rate of change continuous with that seen in later human history. This should encourage interest in intrinsic processes of cultural evolution that might tend to produce such a uniform curve, including the potentially autocatalytic effects of increasing technological complexity. As illustrated here, Lower Palaeolithic technologies clearly do increase in hierarchical complexity through time, raising the possibility of important interactions with the evolution of human cognitive control [63] and socially supported skill acquisition [6, 62]. Analyses developed here have attempted to build on previous contributions [12, 17, 27, 28, 30, 32] but remain quite limited in scope. For example, they are semi-arbitrarily bounded at the lower end by relatively large-scale and under-specified reaching, grasping and manipulating actions and at the upper end by the articulation with other major domains of hominin behaviour, especially including tool use. Continued efforts in these directions will be needed to adequately characterize the pattern, mechanisms and rate of Lower Palaeolithic technological change.

References

1 Owen, R. 1857 On the characters, principles of division and primary groups of the class Mammalia. *J. Proc. Linn. Soc.* **2**, 1–37.

2 Wallace, A. R. 1870 *Contributions to the theory of natural selection, a series of essays*. London, UK: Macmillan.

3 Darwin, C. 1871 *The descent of man: and selection in relation to sex*. London, UK: John Murray.

4 Tomasello, M. 1999 *The cultural origins of human cognition*. Cambridge, MA: Harvard University Press.

5 Powell, A., Shennan, S. & Thomas, M. G. 2009 Late Pleistocene demography and the appearance of modern human behavior. *Science* **324**, 1298–1301.

6 Tennie, C., Call, J. & Tomasello, M. 2009 Ratcheting up the ratchet: on the evolution of cumulative culture. *Phil. Trans. R. Soc. B* **364**, 2405–2415.

7 Whiten, A., Horner, V. & Marshall-Pescini, S. 2003 Cultural panthropology. *Evol. Anthropol.* **12**, 92–105.

8 Whiten, A. & van Schaik, C. 2006 The evolution of animal 'cultures' and social intelligence. *Phil. Trans. R. Soc. B* **362**, 603–620.

9 Mithen, S. 1999 Imitation and cultural change: a view from the Stone Age, with specific reference to the manufacture of handaxes. In *Mammalian social learning: comparative and ecological perspectives* (eds H. O. Box & K. R. Gibson), pp. 389–413. Cambridge, MA: Cambridge University Press.

10 Stout, D., Semaw, S., Rogers, M. J. & Cauche, D. 2010 Technological variation in the earliest Oldowan from Gona, Afar, Ethiopia. *J. Hum. Evol.* **58**, 474–491.

11 Delagnes, A. & Roche, H. 2005 Late Pliocene hominid knapping skills: the case of Lokalalei 2C, West Turkana, Kenya. *J. Hum. Evol.* **48**, 435–472.

12 Roche, H. 2005 From simple flaking to shaping: stone knapping evolution among early hominins. In *Stone knapping: the necessary conditions for a uniquely hominin behaviour* (eds V. Roux & B. Bril), pp. 35–48. Cambridge, MA: McDonald Institute for Archaeological Research.

13 Clark, J. D. 2001 Variability in primary and secondary technologies of the Later Acheulian in Africa. In *A very remote period indeed: papers on the Palaeolithic presented to Derek Roe* (eds S. Miliken & J. Cook), pp. 1–18. Oakville, CT: Oxbow Books.

14 Schick, K. D. & Toth, N. 1993 *Making silent stones speak: human evolution and the dawn of technology*. New York, NY: Simon & Schuster.

15 Isaac, G. L. 1986 Foundation stones: early artefacts as indicators of activities and abilities. In *Stone age prehistory: studies in honor of Charles McBurney* (eds G. N. Bailey & P. Callow), pp. 221–241. London, UK: Cambridge University Press.

16 Mesoudi, A. & O'Brien, M. J. 2008 The learning and transmission of hierarchical cultural recipies. *Biol. Theory* **3**, 63–72.

17 Pelegrin, J. 1990 Prehistoric lithic technology: some aspects of research. *Archaeol. Rev. Cambridge* **9**, 116–125.

18 Lashley, K. 1951 The problem of serial order in behavior. In *Cerebral mechanisms in behavior* (ed. L. A. Jeffress), pp. 112–136. New York, NY: John Wiley.

19 Chomsky, N. 1957 *Syntactic structures*. The Hague, The Netherlands: Mouton.

20 Miller, G. A., Pribram, K. H. & Galanter, E. 1960 *Plans and the structure of behavior*. New York, NY: Holt, Reinhart and Winston.

21 Wolpert, D., Doya, K. & Kawato, M. 2003 A unifying computational framework for motor control and social interaction. *Phil. Trans. R. Soc. Lond. B* **358**, 593–602.

22 Badre, D. & D'Esposito, M. 2009 Is the rostro-caudal axis of the frontal lobe hierarchical? *Nat. Rev. Neurosci.* **10**, 659–669.

23 Botvinick, M. M. 2008 Hierarchical models of behavior and prefrontal function. *Trends Cogn. Sci.* **12**, 201–208.

24 Byrne, R. & Russon, A. E. 1998 Learning by imitation: a hierarchical approach. *Behav. Brain Sci.* **21**, 667–721.

25 Mesoudi, A. & Whiten, A. 2004 The hierarchical transformation of event knowledge in human cultural transmission. *J. Cogn. Cult.* **4**, 1–24.

26 Bekkering, H. & Prinz, W. 2002 Goal representations in imitative actions. In *Imitation in animals and artifacts* (eds K. Dautenhahn & C. Nehaniv), pp. 553–572. Cambridge, MA: MIT Press.

27 Holloway, R. 1969 Culture: a human domain. *Curr. Anthropol.* **10**, 395–412.

28 Gowlett, J. A. J. 1984 Mental abilities of early man: a look at some hard evidence. In *Hominid evolution and community ecology* (ed. R. Foley), pp. 167–192. New York, NY: Academic Press.

29 Stout, D., Toth, N., Schick, K. D. & Chaminade, T. 2008 Neural correlates of Early Stone Age tool-making: technology, language and cognition in human evolution. *Phil. Trans. R. Soc. B* **363**, 1939–1949.

30 Moore, M. W. 2010 'Grammars of action' and stone flaking design space. In *Stone tools and the evolution of human cognition* (eds A. Nowell & I. Davidson), pp. 13–43. Boulder, CO: University Press of Colorado.

31 Stout, D. 2010 Possible relations between language and technology in human evolution. In *Stone tools and the evolution of human cognition* (eds A. Nowell & I. Davidson), pp. 159–184. Boulder, CO: University Press of Colorado.

32 Greenfield, P. M. 1991 Language, tools, and brain: the development and evolution of hierarchically organized sequential behavior. *Behav. Brain Sci.* **14**, 531–595.

33 Semaw, S. 2000 The world's oldest stone artefacts from Gona, Ethiopia: their implications for understanding stone technology and patterns of human evolution 2.6–1.5 million years ago. *J. Archaeol. Sci.* **27**, 1197–1214.

34 Studdert-Kennedy, M. & Goldstein, L. 2003 Launching language: the gestural origins of discrete infinity. In *Language evolution* (eds M. H. Christiansen & S. Kirby), pp. 235–254. Oxford, UK: Oxford University Press.

35 de la Torre, I., Mora, R., dominguez-Rodrigo, M., de Luque, L. & Alcala, L. 2003 The Oldowan industry of Peninj and its bearing on the reconstruction of the technological skills of Lower Pleistocene hominids. *J. Hum. Evol.* **44**, 203–224.

36 Isaac, G. L., Harris, J. W. K. & Kroll, E. 1997 The stone artifact assemblages: a comparative study. In *Koobi Fora research project, volume 5: Plio-Pleistocene archaeology* (eds G. Isaac & B. Isaac), pp. 262–299. Oxford, UK: Clarendon Press.

37 Semaw, S., Rogers, M. & Stout, D. 2009 The Oldowan–Acheulian transition: is there a 'developed Oldowan' artifact tradition? In *Sourcebook of Paleolithic transitions: methods, theories, and interpretations* (eds M. Camps & P. Chauhan), pp. 173–193. New York, NY: Springer.

38 Ludwig, B. V. & Harris, J. W. K. 1998 Towards a technological reassessment of East African Plio-Pleistocene lithic assemblages. In *Early human behavior in global context. The rise and diversity of the Lower Palaeolithic record* (eds M. D. Petraglia & R. Korisettar), pp. 84–107. London, UK: Routledge.

39 Hauser, M. D., Chomsky, N. & Fitch, W. T. 2002 The faculty of language: what is it, who has it and how did it evolve? *Science* **298**, 1569–1579.

40 Jones, P. R. 1994 Results of experimental work in relation to the stone industries of Olduvai Gorge. In *Olduvai Gorge volume V: excavations in Beds IV, V and the Masek Beds 1968–1971* (eds M. D. Leakey & D. Roe), pp. 254–298. Cambridge, MA: Cambridge University Press.

41 Toth, N. 2001 Experiments in quarrying large flake blanks at Kalambo Falls. In *Kalambo Falls prehistoric site, volume 3: the earlier cultures: Middle and Earlier Stone Age* (ed. J. D. Clark), pp. 600–604. Cambridge, MA: Cambridge University Press.

42 de la Torre, I., Mora, R. & Martinez-Moreno, J. 2008 The Early Acheulean in Peninj (Lake Natron, Tanzania). *J. Anthropol. Archaeol.* **27**, 244–264.

43 de la Torre, I. & Mora, R. 2005 *Technological strategies in the Lower Pleistocene at Olduvai Beds I & II*. Liège, France: Université de Liège. (ERAUL (112)).

44 Roberts, M. B. & Pope, M. I. 2009 The archaeological and sedimentary records from Boxgrove and Slindon. In *The quaternary of the Solent Basin and the Sussex raised beaches* (eds R. M. Briant, R. T. Hosfield & F. F. Wenban-Smith), pp. 96–122. London, UK: Quaternary Research Association.

45 McNabb, J. 2007 *The British Lower Palaeolithic: stones in contention*. London, UK: Routledge.

46 Scott, G. R. & Gibert, L. 2009 The oldest hand-axes in Europe. *Nature* **461**, 82–85.

47 Norton, C. J. & Bae, K. 2008 The Movius Line sensu lato (Norton *et al.* 2006) further assessed and defined. *J. Hum. Evol.* **55**, 1148–1150.

48 Petraglia, M. D. & Shipton, C. 2008 Large cutting tool variation west and east of the Movius Line. *J. Hum. Evol.* **55**, 962–966.

49 Leakey, M. D. & Roe, D. A. 1994 *Olduvai Gorge. Vol. 5, excavations in beds III, IV and the Masek beds, 1968–1971*. Cambridge, MA: Cambridge University Press. editors.

50 Beaumont, P. B. & Vogel, J. C. 2006 On a timescale for the past million years of human history in central South Africa. *S. Afr. J. Sci.* **102**, 217–228.

51 Tryon, C., McBrearty, S. & Texier, J. 2005 Levallois Lithic technology from the Kapthurin Formation, Kenya: Acheulian origin and Middle Stone Age diversity. *Afr. Archaeol. Rev.* **22**, 199–229.

52 Johnson, C. R. & McBrearty, S. 2010 500000 year old blades from the Kapthurin formation, Kenya. *J. Hum. Evol.* **58**, 193–200.

53 Callahan, E. 1979 The basics of biface knapping in the Eastern Fluted Point Tradition: a manual for flintknappers and lithic analysts. *Archaeol. East. N. Am.* **7**, 1–172.

54 Edwards, S. W. 2001 A modern knapper's assessment of the technical skills of the Late Acheulean biface workers at Kalambo Falls. In *Kalambo Falls prehistoric site, volume 3: the earlier cultures: Middle and Earlier Stone Age* (ed. J. D. Clark), pp. 605–611. Cambridge, MA: Cambridge University Press.

55 Roberts, M. B. & Parfitt, S. A. 1999. English Heritage Archaeological Report 17. A Middle Pleistocene hominid site at Eartham Quarry, Boxgrove, West Sussex.

56 Gilead, D. 1970 Handaxe industries in Israel and the Near East. *World Archaeol.* **2**, 1–11.

57 Bradley, B. & Sampson, C. G. 1986 Analysis by replication of two Acheuleian artefact assemblages from Caddington, England. In *Stone Age prehistory: studies in memory of Charles McBurney* (eds G. N. Bailey & P. Callow), pp. 29–46. Cambridge, MA: Cambridge University Press.

58 Klein, R. G. 1999 *The human career: human biological and cultural origins*. Chicago (Ill.), IL: University of Chicago Press.

59 Wynn, T. & Coolidge, F. L. 2004 The expert Neandertal mind. *J. Hum. Evol.* **46**, 467–487.

60 Whiten, A., McGuigan, N., Marshall-Pescini, S. & Hopper, L. M. 2009 Emulation, imitation, over-imitation and the scope of culture for child and chimpanzee. *Phil. Trans. R. Soc. B* **364**, 2417–2428.

61 Schick, K. D. 1994 The Movius Line reconsidered: perspectives on the earlier Paleolithic of eastern Asia. In *Integrative paths to the past: Paleoanthropological advances in honor of F. Clark Howell* (eds R. S. Corruccini & R. L. Ciochon), pp. 569–595. Englewood Cliffs, NJ: Prentice Hall.

62 Stout, D. 2005 The social and cultural context of stone-knapping skill acquisition. In *Stone knapping: the necessary conditions for a uniquely hominin behaviour* (eds V. Roux & B. Bril), pp. 331–340. Cambridge, MA: McDonald Institute for Archaeological Research.

63 Stout, D. 2010 The evolution of cognitive control. *Top. Cogn. Sci.* **2**, 614–630.

64 Passingham, R. E. 2008 *What is special about the human brain?* Oxford, UK: Oxford University Press.

65 Holloway, R. L. 1967 The evolution of the human brain: some notes toward a synthesis between neural structure and the evolution of complex behavior. *Gen. Syst.* **12**, 3–19.

66 Bril, B., Roux, V. & Dietrich, G. 2000 Habilites impliquees dans la taille des perles en roches dure: characteristiques motrices et cognitives d'une action situee complexe. In *Les perles de cambay: des practiques techniques aux technosystemes de l'orient ancien* (ed. V. Roux), pp. 211–329. Paris, France: Editions de la MSH.

67 Gergely, G. & Csibra, G. 2006 Sylvia's recipe: the role of imitation and pedagogy in the transmission of cultural knowledge. In *Roots of human sociality: culture, cognition and human interaction* (eds N. J. Enfiled & S. C. Levenson), pp. 229–255. Oxford, UK: Berg Publishers.

68 Stout, D. & Chaminade, T. 2007 The evolutionary neuroscience of tool making. *Neuropsychologia* **45**, 1091–1100.

69 Bril, B., Rein, R., Nonaka, T., Wenban-Smith, F. & Dietrich, G. 2010 The role of expertise in tool use: skill differences in functional action adaptations to task constraints. *J. Exp. Psychol. Hum. Percept. Perform.* **36**, 825–839.

70 Nonaka, T., Bril, B. & Rein, R. 2010 How do stone knappers predict and control the outcome of flaking? Implications for understanding early stone tool technology. *J. Hum. Evol.* **59**, 155–167.

71 Ericsson, K. A., Krampe, R. T. & Tesch-Romer, C. 1993 The role of deliberate practice in the acquisition of expert performance. *Psychol. Rev.* **100**, 363–406.

72 Rossano, M. J. 2003 Expertise and the evolution of consciousness. *Cognition* **89**, 207–236.

73 Burkart, J. M., Hrdy, S. B. & Schaik, C. P. V. 2009 Cooperative breeding and human cognitive evolution. *Evol. Anthropol.* **18**, 175–186.

74 Heinrichs, M., von Dawans, B. & Domes, G. 2009 Oxytocin, vasopressin, and human social behavior. *Front. Neuroendocrinol.* **30**, 548–557.

Chapter 13

Evolution, Revolution or Saltation Scenario for the Emergence of Modern Cultures?

Francesco d'Errico and Christopher B. Stringer

Crucial questions in the debate on the origin of quintessential human behaviours are whether modern cognition and associated innovations are unique to our species and whether they emerged abruptly, gradually or as the result of a discontinuous process. Three scenarios have been proposed to account for the origin of cultural modernity. The first argues that modern cognition is unique to our species and the consequence of a genetic mutation that took place approximately 50 ka in Africa among already evolved anatomically modern humans. The second posits that cultural modernity emerged gradually in Africa starting at least 200 ka in concert with the origin of our species on that continent. The third states that innovations indicative of modern cognition are not restricted to our species and appear and disappear in Africa and Eurasia between 200 and 40 ka before becoming fully consolidated. We evaluate these scenarios in the light of new evidence from Africa, Asia and Europe and explore the mechanisms that may have led to modern cultures. Such reflections will demonstrate the need for further inquiry into the relationship between climate and demographic/cultural change in order to better understand the mechanisms of cultural transmission at work in Neanderthals and early *Homo sapiens* populations.

Keywords: symbolism; Neanderthals; anatomically modern humans; modernity; Middle Stone Age; Mousterian

13.1 **Introduction**

It is too easy to argue that since we are the only hominin species left on the planet we must be unique and special in some respect. This proposition does not tell us what were the paths that our ancestors took to become so distinctive and to what extent we share partially, or entirely, this supposed uniqueness with our present or past relatives.

The question of the origin of the attributes that define us as humans is the subject of a lively debate among scholars from disciplines such as primatology, archaeology, palaeoanthropology, genetics, evolutionary psychology and linguistics. Ongoing gradual integration of results from these disciplines enables researchers to ask the old questions about who we are and from where do we come on new bases, and hopefully providing more informed answers. Once firmly separating us from the remainder of present and past hominids, genetic and behavioural boundaries are becoming less and less well defined. Depending on the exact comparison made, chimpanzees share about 95–98% of our genes [1], and have the capacity to develop cultural variants—for example in gathering or processing food—which are largely independent of environmental opportunities and genetic differences between groups [1]. We now know that symbolic thinking—the capacity to attribute specific meaning to conventional signs—is not peculiar to us and that we share that capacity with a growing number of primate and non-primate species [1]. The recent finding that significant interbreeding occurred between Neanderthals and modern populations [2] refutes the long-standing model that proposes all living humans trace their ancestry exclusively back to a small African population that expanded and completely replaced archaic human species, without any interbreeding. These discoveries raise again, but in a more cogent way, the question of what factors drove cultural evolution in our lineage, how these factors interacted, and what was the timing of the emergence of quintessential human features such as modern cognition, language, imagination, art, religious beliefs and so forth. A number of different explanations have been proposed to account for the origin of cultures comparable to ours. Some authors consider that a genetic mutation in the functioning of the brain is the most probable prime mover and have argued that such a mutation, leading to a sudden diffusion of modern traits, must have occurred approximately 50 000 years ago (50 ka) among African anatomically modern humans (AMH) [3]. Others situate this neurological switch between 60 and 80 ka and associate it with cultural innovations recorded at this time in southern Africa [4]. These views have been strongly challenged by authors supporting the scenario of a gradual emergence of modern cultural traits in Africa as a consequence of the selection processes that have led to the emergence of our species in that continent [5, 6]. Other authors share the view of the three previous models that modern cultural traits may have arisen among AMH populations in Africa, but consider that population size rather than a speciation more plausibly accounts for the spread, episodic disappearance, and re-emergence of innovations in Africa [7–9]. Finally, partisans of what could be called the 'cultural' model argue that the cognitive prerequisites of modern human behaviour were already largely in place among the ancestors of Neanderthals and modern humans and cite social and demographic factors, arguably triggered by climate change, to explain the asynchronous emergence, disappearance and re-emergence of modern cultural traits among both African 'modern' and Eurasian 'archaic' populations [10–15]. In such a scenario, 'modernity' and its corollary 'cumulative culture' is the end product of a saltational cultural evolution within human populations that were to a large extent, and irrespectively of their taxonomic affiliation, cognitively modern. The main driving force in this last scenario is long-term climatic and environmental variability and its effect on population dynamics.

How can we test these scenarios? Many behavioural features considered as keys to crossing the Rubicon towards cultural modernity, such as altruism, enhanced memory, complex language and increased social learning leading to cumulative cultures [8], leave little direct archaeological traces behind them, and we are forced to infer their emergence in ancient human populations from the occurrence of elements of material culture that may signal their acquisition. Thus, evaluating the pertinence of the above models depends on the cultural traits we label as 'modern', the chance that they leave a durable and unambiguous trace in the archaeological record, and reliable dating. It also hinges on the abilities of the various schools of thought to convincingly link a favoured mechanism (genetic mutation, speciation, demography, climate, etc.) to a predicted outcome (stochastic event, gradual emergence, punctuated equilibrium, saltational evolution, etc.), and to demonstrate that the favoured mechanism was at work during the entire time span that led to the emergence of cultures comparable to ours. Ideally, we would also expect the preferred mechanism(s) to account for the cultural variability observed among historically known human societies, and the societies of our extant and extinct closest relatives.

The criteria used to identify modern cultures in the archaeological record—or degrees of cultural modernity in the case of gradual scenarios—vary according to the authors [3, 5, 11, 13, 14], and are far from unanimously accepted. Exploitation of coastal environments; greater complexity of food gathering procedures, such as the use of nets, traps, fishing gear; complex use of fire for cooking, food conservation; ecosystem management; producing and hafting stone tools; invention of specialized tool-kits to adapt to extreme environments; higher population densities approaching those of modern hunter–gatherers; complex tools, the styles of which may change rapidly through time and space; structures such as huts that are organized for different activities; long-distance transport of valued materials; formal artefacts shaped from bone, ivory, antler, shell; musical traditions; sea crossing and navigation technology; personal ornamentation in the form of body painting and personal ornaments; art, including abstract and figurative representations; evidence for ceremonies or rituals; complex treatment of the dead: the more the 'checklist' of modern traits has expanded in the last decade, the more it appears that preferences in the selection made were largely dictated by the conscious or unconscious intention of favouring one scenario over another. Additionally, many historically known modern human societies were either lacking a consistent number of these features or, while displaying them, would have left little evidence of them behind for recognition by future archaeologists. However, some consensus exists on the fundamental role played by symbolically mediated behaviours in the creation of modern cultures [16]. This innovation, which demonstrated the ability of sharing, storing and transmitting coded information within and across groups, has played a crucial role in creating and maintaining technical and social conventions, beliefs and identities that characterize all known human societies. Chimpanzees clearly have the capacity to develop and transmit cultural traditions [1], but they have never been observed creating systems of symbols in the wild, embodying them in their material culture or displaying them on their bodies. In this chapter, we will evaluate the scenarios proposed to account for the origin of modern cultures in the light of the earliest archaeological evidence for crucial cultural innovations, including symbolically mediated behaviours, in Africa, Asia and Europe. Such reflections demonstrate the need for further inquiry into the relationship between climate and demographic/cultural change, in order to better understand the mechanisms of cultural transmission at work within Neanderthal and early *Homo sapiens* populations.

13.2 Archaeological evidence for the origin of modern cultures

13.2.1 Subsistence strategy and technology

Recent discoveries have dramatically changed our knowledge concerning the chronology of the emergence of modern traits, and the fossil human populations with which they were associated. For most of the last century, the astonishing evidence of the complexity of Cro-Magnon behaviour in Europe convinced a large part of the scientific community that modern features had a sudden origin, coinciding with the beginning of the Upper Palaeolithic in Europe, approximately 40 ka. This perception was to a large extent determined by a lack of information on Africa and Asia, and a reductive view of Neanderthal cultural achievements. Research conducted in southern Africa has challenged the idea [3] that the reduction in prey size, in high ranking prey abundance, and shift to fast moving creatures such as birds or hares, recorded at Later Stone Age (LSA) sites, results from the lack of suitable technology and cognition in preceding Middle Stone Age (MSA) populations. Data now show that MSA people were competent hunters with a focus on large ungulate prey, but who also opportunistically exploited smaller ungulates, tortoises and small mammals, probably using traps and snares [17]. Fishing and shellfish exploitation are attested at coastal sites [6] but were, apparently, strictly controlled by changes in coastline configuration determined by sea-level fluctuations [18]. Demographic pulses are now seen as a best-fit explanation to account for changes in hunting strategies between the MSA and the LSA but also within each of these periods [17, 19]. It has also become clear, as more data have become available, that there are both time related and geographical variations among MSA faunal assemblages, suggesting that subsistence strategies were both complex and adaptable [17]. Technology during the Middle Stone Age shows a pattern of innovation followed by disappearance. Blade technology and formal stone tools in the form of backed pieces—tools modified by retouch on a side—are signalled at sites such as Twin Rivers and Kalambo Falls, Zambia, dated at approximately 300 ka [20], but absent at many others. Uncertain instances of small blade production come from a Pinnacle Point cave dated at approximately 160 ka [6]. Although changes in lithic technology are recognized between the MSA I (approx. 110–115 ka) and the MSA II (approx. 94–85 ka) at Klasies [21], no formal stone tools nor a dedicated knapping technology to produce them are recorded before the Still Bay. Characterized by foliate bifacial points used as spear tips (Figure 13.1*a*), this technocomplex apparently spans only 1–3 ka, and disappears near the transition between the end of the last interglacial (*sensu lato*) and the downturn to Marine Isotope

Stage (MIS) 4 (approx. 70 ka). After a possible gap corresponding to the peak of this isotopic stage, interpreted as a phase of depopulation or low population density [22], lithic technology became characterized by the production of small blades retouched into segments [23], and other backed pieces (Figure 13.1*b*), called Howiesons Poort (HP), spanning between approximately 65 ka and 59 ka. This gives way, during the following post-Howiesons Poort, to unifacial points on flakes (Figure 13.1*c*), similar to the Mousterian points made by Neanderthals in Europe [23, 24], and subsequently to unstandardized microlithic tools produced by the bipolar technique during the early LSA. A precocious emergence of technical innovation is also observed in north Africa, where new dating situates the earliest occurrences of the distinctive pedunculate point forms typical of the Aterian at 145 ka [25].

Evidence for a controlled use of fire to increase the quality and efficiency of stone tool manufacturing processes has been reported from Pinnacle Point, Mossel Bay, approximately 72 ka [26]. Laborious heat treatment to produce compound glues combining plant gum and ochre is attested in the Howiesons Poort layers of Sibudu Cave [27]. Location of such adhesives on small HP backed pieces indicates the latter were used as barbed spear [23] or arrow points [28]. One of the major discoveries of MSA archaeology in the last decades has been the identification of a varied and relatively complex bone technology, previously seen by many authors as an innovation directly stemming from the spread of AMH across Europe at the beginning of the Upper Palaeolithic. Large harpoons made from substantial mammals limb bones (Figure 13.1*d*), found at Katanda, central Africa, may possibly go back to approximately 90 ka [29]. Fully shaped bone tools (projectile points, awls and spatulas) are found at southern African Still Bay and HP sites such as Blombos and Sibudu [30, 31]. The careful deliberate polishing of the approximately 75 ka Blombos bone projectile points (Figure 13.1*e*) has no apparent functional reason and, rather, seems a technique used to give a distinctive appearance and/or an "added value" to this category of artefacts. This may imply that symbolic meaning was attributed to bone tools. Reduction in size between the Still Bay and HP projectile points (Figure 13.1*f*) has been tentatively interpreted as a shift from the use of hand-delivered bone spear heads to bow and bone arrow technology, possibly with the use of poison [28]. This hypothesis is now reinforced by the morphometric and microscopic analysis of HP segments [28]. However, it is unclear why, if they represented an advantageous innovation, bone tools occur only at a few MSA sites and are absent or rare after the HP. It is equally unclear why no evidence for the use of bows and arrows is found among modern human populations during their expansion in Asia and Europe.

New discoveries and reappraisal of key Mousterian sequences in Europe and the Near East identify trends in Neanderthal subsistence strategies and technology that parallel in many respects the pattern of innovation followed by disappearance described for Africa. Very few scholars would argue now, as was routine in the early 1980s and 1990s, that contrary to Upper Palaeolithic Cro-Magnons, Neanderthal subsistence strategies were based on scavenging large mammal carcasses, constrained to favourable biotopes, that these populations had limited planning capacities, and were only able to develop expedient technologies involving a low degree of conceptualization. Now we know from prey hunted that Neanderthals were effective, flexible hunters, at a number of sites they were able to live in cold inhospitable environments, and at times they also exploited a broad range of terrestrial and marine resources [32–35]. Ongoing research on the technological variability of the Mousterian in Europe identifies variations in time and space in lithic technology and tool types interpreted as discrete cultural adaptations, comparable to those observed in contemporary African populations. As with Africa, in Europe we observe the punctuated emergence and disappearance of blade technology (Figure 13.1*g*) and more 'formal' stone tools (Figure 13.1*h*) since 200 ka, with an apparent acceleration in the turnover of types of *débitage* and tools after the last interglacial [36]. This culminated in a clear regionalization of cultural features during the millennia that immediately preceded the recognized arrival of modern humans in Europe. Research conducted in the Levant reveals that at sites with diagnostic Neanderthal and modern human remains, the two populations hunted the same species, produced their tool kits by applying Levallois flaking and manufactured a comparable range of tool types [37]. Differences between the Middle and Upper Palaeolithic of Europe in lithic raw material procurement strategies [38] have been interpreted as evidence for more reduced Neanderthal geographical ranges and social networks. However, such distances are extremely variable within the Mousterian, for example reaching figures comparable with those recorded in the Upper Palaeolithic in eastern Europe [39]. On the other hand, very local procurement strategies are recorded at many MSA sites in South Africa, including HP sites [23, 24].

Recent research has shown that Neanderthal hunting weapons were comparable to those used by broadly contemporaneous Middle Stone Age populations in southern Africa. Wooden spears over 2 m long, made of spruce and pine, have been discovered at Schöningen in Germany, dating from approximately 300 to 400 ka. These were probably used as thrusting spears but might also have been javelins, as suggested by their forward centre of gravity [40]. This has been contested [41] on the basis of the upper limb morphology associated with projectile-throwing Upper Palaeolithic humans (but absent in Neanderthals), on the too-close range of hand-thrown spears to hunt large animals and the fact that the Schöningen spears are too heavy to be thrown. However, it has been shown contra [41] that the Romans and Greeks used long and quite heavy javelins in war, and for hunting wild animals, and that over-arm throwing was not necessarily an habitual activity until the late Upper Palaeolithic [42]. Moreover, a large literature now supports the view that the hunting equipment of Neanderthals was not limited to simple wooden spears. Tip morphology, evidence of hafting and the presence of diagnostic impact scars indicate that at a number of sites from Europe and the Levant, going back at least to early MIS 6 (approx. 186 ka), Levallois and retouched Mousterian points were used as weapon armatures [42].

As far as hafting and the production of composite tools are concerned, the level of technical development of Neanderthals seems comparable to that recently identified at HP sites from South Africa. At the Italian site of Campitello, dated to MIS 6, Neanderthals heated birch bark in a reductive environment to temperatures of *ca* 350° in order to obtain pitch for hafting flint flakes, found associated with elephant bone [43]. A similar

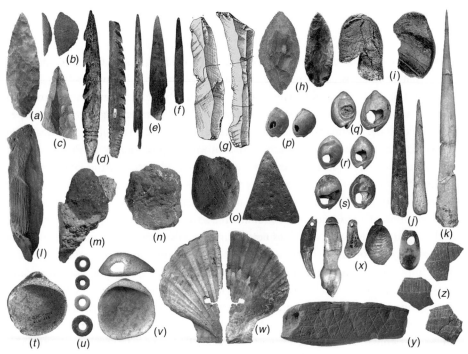

Figure 13.1 Archaeological material cited in the text: (a) Still Bay bifacial point from Blombos Cave, Cape Province, South Africa, (b) Howiesons Poort segment from South Africa, (c) Post-Howiesons Poort point from Sibudu Cave, (d) bone harpoons from Katanda, Democratic Republic of Congo, (e) bone projectile points from Blombos Cave, (f) possible bone projectile point from Sibudu Cave, (g) flint blades from the Mousterian site of Etouville, Normandy, France, (h) Mousterian stone tools from Haldenstein-Höle (left) and Königsaue (right) (i) birch bark pitches from Königsaue, Germany, (j) Châtelperronian bone awls from Grotte du Renne, France, (k) Uluzzian bone awl from Castelcivita Cave, Italy, (l–o) pigmental material from Blombos Cave (l), Skhul, Israel (m, n), Pech de l'Azé, Dordogne, France (o), marine shell beads from Blombos (p), Oued Djebbana, Algeria (left) and Skhul, Israel (right) (q), Grotte des Pigeons, Morocco (r), Rhafas (left) and Ifri N'Ammar (right), Morocco (s), (t) Glycimeris shell with a natural perforation and traces of red pigment from Qafzeh, (u) ostrich egg shell beads from Mumba rock shelter, Tanzania, (v) Glycimeris shell with a natural perforation from Cueva de Los Aviones, Spain, (w) Pecten bearing residues of red pigment on its external white aspect from Cueva Anton, Spain, (x) Châtelperronian personal ornaments from Grotte du Renne (from the left perforated fox canine, grooved bovid incisor, perforated rein deer phalange, grooved Rynconella fossil bivalve) and Quinçay (perforated red deer canine), (y) engraved haematite slab from the Still Bay layers of Blombos Cave and (z) fragments of engraved ostrich egg shell from the Howiesons Poort layers of Diepkloof, Cape Region, South Africa. Credit for images: (a, d–f, j, k–s, v, w, y), photos F. d'Errico; (b, x), © Marian Vanhaeren, 2011; (c), © Paola Villa, 2011. (g), modified from [79]; (h, right), © Landesamt für Denkmalpflege und Archäologie Sachsen-Anhalt, Juraj Lipták, 2011; (h, left) © University of Tübingen, 2011; (i), © LDA Sachsen-Anhalt, J. Lipták; (t), Reprinted from *Journal of Human Evolution*, **56**(3), Daniella E. Bar-Yosef Mayer, Bernard Vandermeersch, and Ofer Bar-Yosef, Shells and ochre in Middle Paleolithic Qafzeh Cave, Israel: indications for modern behavior, pp. 307–314, Copyright (2009), with permission from Elsevier; (u), © University of Tübingen, 2011. (z), Reproduced from Texier, J.-P. *et al.*, *Proc. Natl Acad. Sci. USA*, **107**, A Howiesons Poort tradition of engraving ostrich egg shell containers dated to 60,000 years ago at Diepkloof Rock Shelter, South Africa, © 2010, pp. 7621–7622 with permission from PNAS.

treatment is attested at the Middle Palaeolithic site of Königsaue in Germany, dated to approximately 48 ka, where two fragments of birch-bark pitch (Figure 13.1*i*) still show the imprint of the bifacial tool once adhering to them [44]. Heat treatment of lithic raw material to facilitate knapping is so far unrecognized among Neanderthals, Upper Palaeolithic modern humans before the Solutrian (approx. 22 ka), and most African and non-African modern humans contemporaneous with or posterior to the Pinnacle Point instances of this technique. An alternative 'ecological' explanation to the 'cognitive' one, favoured by Brown *et al.* [26], might better account for this pattern: heat treatment may be an innovation that occurs in situations in which ecological constraints exert pressure for the creation of specialized stone tool kits made of highly anisotropous raw material, thereby creating something that does not occur naturally in the environment.

The most common use of bone during the Eurasian Lower and Middle Palaeolithic is that of long-bone shaft fragments to retouch lithic tools [45]. Knapped handaxes and scrapers were also occasionally produced at Acheulian and Mousterian sites. Bone industries showing a level of technological complexity equivalent to that normally associated with Upper Palaeolithic cultures are only found in 'transitional' technocomplexes such as the Châtelperronian in France (Figure 13.1*j*) and the Uluzzian in Italy (Figure 13.1*k*). The former technocomplex is now firmly attributed to Neanderthals [46] while such an attribution is still tentative for the latter due to the scarcity and undiagnostic character of the human remains associated with those layers. The interpretation of the Châtelperronian bone tools and, as we will see later, personal ornaments, in particular those from the Grotte du Renne, Arcy-sur-Cure, is controversial [10]. Their presence in Châtelperronian layers has been interpreted as the result of independent Neanderthal innovation, as reflecting trade or scavenging from abandoned contemporary Aurignacian sites, as intrusion from overlying Aurignacian layers or, more recently, to the fact that the Châtelperronian makers of those tools may have well been modern humans [47]. A number of factors, linked to the stratigraphic distribution of the bone tools, personal ornaments, human remains and diagnostic Châtelperronian tools, as well as to the presence of by-products of bone tool manufacture, indicate that Châtelperronian Neanderthals were the makers and the users of the bone tools [10, 48]. This conclusion is further supported by similar finds from the Châtelperronian site of Quinçay, Vienne region, where contamination from later AMH occupation can be excluded, as none exists. The conclusion that Châtelperronian bone tools were made by Neanderthals does not resolve the contentious problem of whether this technology was independently invented prior to the arrival of AMH in western Europe or if it was in some way adopted or re-elaborated as a result of contact with the latter [10, 49]. To address this question, we need a consensual stratigraphic, chronological and palaeoclimatic framework for the early Upper Palaeolithic technocomplexes [50] and a refined knowledge of the material culture associated with them.

Archaeozoological, technological and microscopic analyses of Châtelperronian and Uluzzian bone tools [48, 51] demonstrate that they are not expedient tools used in single instances to fulfil immediate needs, but rather are the result of planned chains of complex technological actions, shared by groups belonging to the same cultural tradition. This is demonstrated by the consistency that we have identified in the choice of the species and bone type, technique of manufacture, overall tool morphology and resharpening techniques. Such know-how does not appear qualitatively different from that recorded at more recent Upper Palaeolithic sites. This indicates that even if it was demonstrated that the use of bone tools or personal ornaments by Neanderthals was the result of cultural contact with moderns, this would in fact reinforce rather than dismiss the modern character of their cognition, as it would show their ability, as observed in many historical instances among modern human populations, to incorporate external stimuli and reshape those influences in order to make them an integral part of their own culture.

13.2.2 Symbolic mediated behaviour

What is the earliest evidence for symbolic behaviour in the archaeological record? Although inhumation and treatment of the dead are generally regarded as quintessential features of modern humanity, carrying of infant corpses—in one case for 68 days—and attention paid to corpses of adults has been reported from a number of primates in the wild [52]. We ignore the meaning of these practices and whether they are to some extent symbolic in nature, but they suggest that chimpanzees may have a greater awareness of death and dying than previously thought. A second problem when searching for early funerary practices is, of course, their variable archaeological visibility: burials will leave more traces than exposure in the open. A rapid survey of the evidence reveals that this reason can account for the patchiness of the archaeological record, and that both Neanderthals and modern humans probably engaged very early in a variety of funerary practices. The claim for a polish suggestive of curation of a skull at the approximately 160 ka old site of Herto in Ethiopia has not, so far, been supported by further data [53]. At present, the approximately 115 ka cave occupation of Skhul in Israel has the oldest known symbolic burial, an early modern male interred clasping the lower jaw of a massive wild boar [54]. The 100 ka occupation of Qafzeh Cave near Nazareth also has a number of modern human burials, one of which was a child whose body was covered by deer antlers [55]. However, we hardly pick up this practice again in modern humans for more than 40 ka. Only three MSA burials are known, that of the Border Cave, with a possible age of 70 ka, and those of Nazlet Khater [56], and Taramsa, Egypt [57] dated, respectively, to 40 ka and 68 ka. In Europe the oldest Upper Palaeolithic burials are Gravettian and date to approximately 30 ka. The bodily traces of earlier moderns in Europe, the Aurignacians, are mainly in the form of pierced human teeth [58] suggesting that they preferred to carry traces of their enemies or their ancestors with them rather than burying them. Around 40 ka two individuals were interred separately at Mungo [59] in south eastern Australia—a woman was cremated at high temperature and another adult (sex uncertain) was buried stretched out and with a covering of haematite pigment (perhaps originally on the skin, or perhaps on some covering material such as a hide or bark). Neanderthal burials in the Levant are as old or might be even older than those of moderns, if one accepts the most ancient date for the Tabun C1 burial [60].

Neanderthal burials in Europe are numerous but concentrated in a few areas, suggesting that Neanderthals, as modern humans in Africa, may have engaged in funerary practices leaving no traces in the archaeological record. Although in a number of cases this information is difficult to verify now, grave goods consisting of stone tools, bone retouchers, engraved bone and a rock slab engraved with cupules were reported at Neanderthal burials such as La Ferrassie, La Chapelle-aux-Saint, Le Moustier in France, Amud and Dederiyeh in the Middle East [61]. The oldest known human bone used as a tool is a fragment of Neanderthal skull from La Quina in the Charentes region of France [62].

Although systematic exploitation of pigmental material is generally interpreted as the archaeological expression of symbolic behaviour, this view remains controversial. Supporters of the symbolic interpretation stress deliberate choice for intense red hues, preference for pigment from far away sources, deliberate heating to change pigment colour, presence on just one side of an object, coloration of shell beads, and the inferred light colour of Neanderthal skin appropriate to receive black painting [63–65]. Supporters of the functional interpretation often do not deny that pigment may have also been used for symbolic purposes, but they stress the difficulty of firmly demonstrating such an interpretation. They rely on the attested ethnographic use of pigmental material to propose alternative functions such as skin protection from sun or insects, as medicine, for tanning hides, or as a binding agent to facilitate hafting [27]. The debate between the two sides has probably become unnecessarily polarized. Ethnographically, the symbolic/functional divide would be an alien concept to most contemporary hunter–gatherer societies, who do not perceive such distinctions between material, actions and causality. Symbol use and its material expressions are ultimately functional in the sense of creating or marking individual and group identities and as such, have potential adaptive value by enhancing group cohesiveness. In other words, a systematic and purely functional use of pigments is difficult to conceive. Red pigmental material, attested in Africa at archaeological sites dated to approximately 160 ka [6] and possibly at sites dated to approximately 280 ka [5] becomes a common feature of approximately 100 ka (Figure 13.1*l*) and younger MSA sites [5, 63]. In the Middle East the oldest evidence for systematic use of pigments dates back to approximately 100 ka (Figure 13.1*m, n*) and comes from Qafzeh [66] and Skhul [65]. Clear evidence of heating, probably to change the colour of the pigmental material, is attested at these two sites [65]. Pigments, mostly black but also red, have been used by Neanderthals in Europe (Figure 13.1*o, w*) since approximately 300 ka [64], but their use became systematic only after approximately 60 ka [64]. The last-known Neanderthals in France made intensive use of both black and red pigments. A case in point is the 18 kg of red and black pigments, often bearing traces of use, found in the Châtelperronian layers of the Grotte du Renne, Arcy-sur-Cure [50], the largest quantity of pigmental material found so far at a Palaeolithic site.

Convincing evidence for the use of personal ornaments, consisting of perforated marine shells belonging to a single species at each site, is found from caves in south Africa, north Africa and the Middle East dated to between 120 and 70 ka [67]. At Blombos Cave, 49 deliberately perforated *Nassarius kraussianus* shell beads (Figure 13.1*p*) with clear evidence of use-wear, some bearing traces of ochre come from approximately 75 ka old levels. The perforated *Conus* shell from Border Cave, associated with the burial of a young individual may be as old as 76 ka according to the recent chronological attribution of this burial [68]. Perforated *Nassarius gibbosulus* shells were recovered at the Aterian site of Oued Djebbana, Algeria (Figure 13.1*q*), and Skhul from approximately 100 ka levels that include 10 *Homo sapiens* burials. Perforated shells of the same species (Figure 13.1*r, s*) showing traces of intentional modifications, possible deliberate heating to change the colour of the bead, use-wear and traces of red ochre were recovered from approximately 80–70 ka levels at Grotte des Pigeons, Rhafas, Ifri n'Ammar and Contrebandiers in Morocco [67]. Other marine shells interpreted as beads (Figure 13.1*t*) come from the approximately 90 ka Mousterian levels at Qafzeh Cave in Israel [69]. They consist of 10 naturally perforated *Glycymeris insubrica* shells. The only Neanderthal site that has yielded possible evidence for the use of shell beads by Neanderthals is the Cueva de los Aviones in southern Spain [12]. The Mousterian layers of this site, dated to approximately 45–50 ka BP, contained a marine shell assemblage including three valves of *Acanthocardia* and *Glycymeris*, bearing natural perforations (Figure 13.1*v*). One of the latter contained a residue of red pigment identified as haematite. Beads seemingly disappeared in Africa and the Levant between approximately 70 ka and approximately 40 ka [67], and reappeared almost everywhere in Africa and Eurasia after this time span; approximately 40 ka old beads from Europe are associated with both Neanderthals and AMH [64]. They differ from their approximately 120–70 ka antecedents in that they take the form of hundreds of discrete types, identifying regional patterns [58]. As with formal bone tools (see above), the minimalistic consensual interpretation of personal ornament use by Neanderthals (Figure 13.1*x*) is that they were fully able to incorporate new categories of symbolic items in their own culture. At approximately 40 ka, beads in Africa were made on ostrich egg shells (Figure 13.1*u*), and only later are diverse ranges of raw material introduced for bead manufacture. In southeast Asia, the oldest documented ornament is a perforated tiger shark tooth found in New Ireland, New Guinea at a site dated between 39.5 and 28 ka [70]. The earliest evidence for bead use in Australia comes from the site of Mandu Mandu, Cape Range of Western Australia, where 22 *Conus* sp. shell beads were recovered in a layer radiocarbon dated to *ca* 32 ka [71].

The earliest secure abstract designs, engraved on bone and ochre, are found in South Africa and are dated to ca 100 ka [72]. Examples are the complex geometric patterns on ochre (Figure 13.1*y*) from approximately 100 to 70 ka levels at Blombos Cave and from MSA layers at Klein Kliphuis in the Western Cape, and approximately 73 ka old notched and engraved bone from Blombos and Klasies [30]. Abstract designs on artefacts seem to disappear in southern Africa between approximately 70 ka and 55 ka, after which they reappear at Diepkloof shelter (Figure 13.1*z*) in the form of engraved ostrich eggshells [73]. Evidence from the Middle East includes an engraved cortex dated at approximately 50 ka from the Mousterian site of Quneitra that could be associated with *H. sapiens* or Neanderthals, and an engraved lithic core from approximately 90 ka levels at Qafzeh. A number of objects bearing putative engravings have also been reported from Lower and

Middle Palaeolithic sites in Europe. Some of these 'engravings' resulted from natural phenomena and carcass processing. Others were deliberate engravings [64], but still need detailed publication. Figurative representations consisting of painted, engraved and carved animals, are so far only well dated to much later, at approximately 31 ka in Africa, at Apollo 11 shelter [74], Namibia, and at approximately 35 ka in Europe, for example at Chauvet, Fumane and in southern Germany [75]. The oldest known carved musical instruments, consisting of flutes made of bird bone and mammoth ivory decorated with notches, are found in Europe and also date back to approximately 35 ka [76]. No convincing musical instruments are associated with Neanderthals, so far [77].

13.3 **Discussion and conclusion**

Our review of the evidence contradicts the idea that the emergence of crucial technological innovations and symbolic material culture was the result of a sudden change in human cognition occurring in Europe or Africa approximately 40–50 ka, or just in Africa approximately 60–80 ka. Possible differences in subsistence strategies and technology between anatomically modern and late archaic humans, as well as their variations in time and space, do not prove the case for an inherent incapacity of the latter to reach the degree of fitness that we observe in their penecontemporaneous modern counterparts. Although comparisons between cultural adaptations in very different and changing environmental settings are obviously difficult to draw, it is clear that in some instances European Neanderthals developed knapping techniques and tool types that were more 'advanced' than those of some African Middle Stone Age groups, that the opposite also occurred, and that in other situations, such as in the Levant, technology was virtually identical. Instances of symbolically mediated behaviours comparable to those observed in historically known human populations are recorded by at least 100 ka, probably before, in Africa, by approximately 120–100 ka in the Middle East and probably by at least 60 ka in Europe. This contradicts the assumption that the crucial innovations that have made us as we are can only have come from, or have been assimilated from an anatomically modern humanity, and counters the simplest versions of the Out of Africa model for the origin of modern cultures that directly link the origin of these innovations to events taking place in Africa at about 200 ka, or between 40 and 80 ka. Evidence also shows that no uninterrupted accretion of innovations or exponential growth, as predicted by this model, is observed in Africa (or in Europe). During the period between approximately 160 ka and 20 ka complex technologies, adaptation to hostile environments, engravings, pigments, personal ornaments, formal bone tools and burial practices apparently appear, disappear and reappear in different forms, suggesting major discontinuities in cultural transmission. The discontinuous nature in time and space of this process, and the commonalities found in both hemispheres, indicate that local conditions must have played a role in the emergence, diffusion and the eventual disappearance or continuity of crucial innovations in different regions. These local conditions must have been closely linked to the size and organization of cultural systems and ecological settings in which these populations evolved, and sometimes probably disappeared.

A string of recent papers [8, 9] following the seminal work of Cavalli-Sforza, Feldman and Boyd and Richerson have explored the role of demography in the emergence and loss of cultural innovations through modelling.

Powell *et al.* [9] reach the conclusion that the number and size of subpopulations and the degree of interaction between them are key factors in the emergence, maintenance, spread and loss of innovations. They speculate that population size in Africa could have reached a critical threshold about 100 000 years ago, when population density and enhanced contact between groups could have allowed the rate of accumulation of innovations to significantly overtake their loss. Thus, cultural change in the Middle Stone Age greatly accelerated and the increased store of learning was beneficial to the survival of individuals and their groups. In turn this would have started a feedback mechanism, leading to a further increase in population density and contacts and so on. Their results are significant because they provide a sound explanation for the emergence and loss of innovations without invoking speciation as a prime mover. However, one may argue, particularly after the publication of the preliminary results of the Neanderthal Genome Project, that the model they develop could equally be applied to explain the emergence and loss of similar innovations among Neanderthals and the asynchronous emergence of innovations in other regions of the planet. Behavioural differences between Neanderthals and modern humans, as well as between different subpopulations belonging to these human types, may largely depend, following the logic of Powell *et al.*'s own conclusions, on group size and cultural exchange rate rather than on in-built differences in cognition. Also, the predictions of Powell *et al.* rather leave open the question of what stimulated demographic growth in the first place. For example, they evoke the climatic deterioration of MIS 4 as a possible factor leading to population decline and the loss of cultural innovation that we observe in north and south Africa after approximately 70 ka, but no clear mechanism is proposed to explain how this deterioration might have produced a similar demographic demise in areas of the planet where this climatic deterioration certainly had very different impacts. This suggests to us that in order to make further progress in this field, we need a research strategy that allows us to model and quantify the link between environment and a particular past cultural adaptation, predict the response of that adaptation to climatic change and verify whether the rise and spread of innovations result in an expansion or contraction of the eco-cultural niche of a given population. Assumptions about cognition based on taxonomic affiliation should play no *a priori* role, and the key tools would then be archaeology, palaeoenvironmental studies, climate modelling and methods to integrate results from these disciplines. At present this appears to us to be the best way to reconstruct the timing and mode of emergence of key innovations in material culture in Eurasia and Africa, to identify whether and how climatic changes have influenced the distribution of Neanderthal and modern human populations and behavioural patterns in these two regions, and to understand the mechanisms that have governed cultural transmission and social learning during this crucial time span for the evolution of human cultures. The predominance of Africa in the story of modern human origins was probably primarily because of its larger geographical and human population size, which gave greater opportunities for morphological and behavioural variations, and for innovations to both develop and be conserved, rather than the result of a special evolutionary pathway. Exactly as with our present genetic diversity, 'modernity' was not a package that had a unique African origin in one time, place and population, but was a composite whose elements appeared at different times and places, including some outside the African continent, either shared or developed in parallel. These were then gradually assembled through a variety of paths and processes to assume the form that we recognize as behavioural modernity today. However, the Neanderthal Genome Project adds another level of complexity to the issues that we have attempted to unravel in this chapter in that it has identified a number of genes that appear to be unique to the modern humans sampled, and some of these appear to have as yet unresolved cognitive and physiological functions. The likelihood that modern humans both within and outside of Africa have small but different suites of 'archaic' genes acquired through introgression [78] and that archaic populations might in return have received varying 'modern' components, may shed further light on the complex issue of the emergence of 'behavioural modernity'. Increases in archaeological resolution—most of the evidence presented here was unknown a decade ago—and new insights into our genetic history may aid in unravelling the mechanisms that have driven our ancestors' genetic-cultural coevolution.

Acknowledgements

The authors thank two anonymous reviewers for their constructive comments. Francesco d'Errico acknowledges financial support from the European Research Council (FP7/2007/2013)/ERC Grant TRACSYMBOLS n°249 587) and the Programme PROTEA of the French Ministry of Higher Education and Research. Chris Stringer is a Member of the Ancient Human Occupation of Britain project, funded by the Leverhulme Trust.

References

1 Whiten, A. 2011 The scope of culture in chimpanzees, humans and ancestral apes. *Phil. Trans. R. Soc. B* **366**, 997–1007.

2 Green, R. E. *et al.* 2010 A draft sequence of the Neandertal genome. *Science* **328**, 680–684.

3 Klein, R. G. 2009 *The human career: human biological and cultural origins*. Chicago, IL: The University of Chicago Press.

4 Mellars, P. 2006 Why did modern human populations disperse from Africa *ca* 60,000 years ago? A new model. *Proc. Natl Acad. Sci. USA* **103**, 9381–9386.

5 McBrearty, S. & Brooks, A. 2000 The revolution that wasn't: a new interpretation of the origin of modern human behavior. *J. Hum. Evol.* **39**, 453–563.

6 Marean, C. W. *et al.* 2007 Early human use of marine resources and pigment in South Africa during the Middle Pleistocene. *Nature* **449**, 905–908.

7 Stringer, C. 2007 The origin and dispersal of *Homo sapiens*: our current state of knowledge. In *Rethinking the human revolution: new behavioural and biological and perspectives on the origins and dispersal of modern humans* (eds P. Mellars, K. Boyle, O. Bar-Yosef & C. B. Stringer), pp. 15–20. Cambridge, UK: McDonald Institute.

8 Richerson, P. J., Boyd, R. & Bettinger, R. L. 2009 Cultural innovations and demographic change. *Hum. Biol.* **81**, 211–235.

9 Powell, A., Shennan, S. & Thomas, M. 2009 Late Pleistocene demography and appearance of modern human behavior. *Science* **324**, 1298–1301.

10 d'Errico, F., Zilhão, J., Julien, M., Baffier, D. & Pélegrin, J. 1998 Neanderthal acculturation in Western Europe? A critical review of the evidence and its interpretation. *Curr. Anthropol.* **39**, 1–44.

11 d'Errico, F. 2003 The invisible frontier. A multiple species model for the origin of behavioral modernity. *Evol. Anthropol.* **12**, 188–202.

12 Zilhão, J. *et al.* 2009 Symbolic use of marine shells and mineral pigments by Iberian Neandertals. *Proc. Natl Acad. Sci. USA* **107**, 1023–1028.

13 Hovers, E. & Belfer-Cohen, A. 2006 'Now you see it, now you don't'—modern human behavior in the Middle Paleolithic. In *Transitions before the transition: evolution and stability in the Middle Paleolithic and Middle Stone Age* (eds E. Hovers & S. L. Kuhn), pp. 295–304. New York, NY: Springer.

14 Conard, N. 2008 A critical view of the evidence for a southern African origin of behavioral modernity. *South Afr. Archaeol. Soc.* **10**, 175–179.

15 Goren-Inbar, N. 2011 Culture and cognition in the Acheulian industry: a case study from Gesher Benot Yaàqov. *Phil. Trans. R. Soc. B* **366**, 1038–1049.

16 Rossano, M. J. 2010 Making friends, making tools, and making symbols. *Curr. Anthropol.* **51**, 89–98.

17 Wadley, L. 2009 Were snares and traps used in the Middle Stone Age and does it matter? A review and a case study from Sibudu, South Africa. *J. Hum. Evol.* **58**, 179–192.

18 Fisher, E. C., Bar-Matthews, M., Jerardino, A. & Marean, C. W. 2010 Middle and Late Pleistocene paleoscape modeling along the southern coast of South Africa. *Quat. Sci. Rev.* **29**, 1382–1398.

19 Stiner, M. C., Munro, N., Surovell, T. A., Tchernov, E. & Bar-Yosef, O. 1999 Paleolithic growth pulses evidenced by small animal exploitation. *Science* **283**, 190–194.

20 Barham, L. S. 2001 Central Africa and the emergence of regional identity in the Middle Pleistocene. In *Human roots: Africa and Asia in the Middle Pleistocene* (eds L. S. Barham & K. Robson-Brown), pp. 65–80. Bristol, UK: Western Academic and Specialist Press.

21 Wurz, S., le Roux, N. J., Gardner, S. & Deacon, H. J. 2003 Discriminating between the end products of the earlier Middle Stone Age sub-stages at Klasies River using biplot methodology. *J. Archaeol. Sci.* **30**, 1107–1126.

22 Jacobs, Z., Roberts, R. G., Galbraith, R. F., Deacon, H. J., Grun, R., Mackay, A., Mitchell, P., Vogelsang, R. & Wadley, L. 2008 Ages for the Middle Stone Age of Southern Africa: Implications for Human Behavior and Dispersal. *Science* **322**, 733–735.

23 Villa, P., Soriano, S., Teyssandier, N. & Wurz, S. 2010 The Howiesons Poort and MSA III at Klasies River main site, Cave 1A. *J. Archaeol. Sci.* **37**, 630–655.

24 Soriano, S., Villa, P. & Wadley, L. 2007 Blade technology and tool forms in the Middle Stone Age of South Africa: the Howiesons Poort and post-Howiesons Poort at Rose Cottage Cave. *J. Archaeol. Sci.* **34**, 681–703.

25 Richter, D., Moser, J., Nami, M., Eiwanger, J. & Abdeslam Mikdad, A. 2010 New chronometric data from Ifri n'Ammar (Morocco) and the chronostratigraphy of the Middle Palaeolithic in the Western Maghreb. *J. Hum. Evol.*

26 Brown, K. S., Marean, C. W., Herries, A., Jacobs, Z., Tribolo, C., Braun, D., Roberts, D. L., Meyer, M. C. & Bernatchez, J. 2009 Fire as an engineering tool of early modern humans. *Science* **325**, 859–862.

27 Wadley, L., Hodgskiss, T. & Grant, M. 2009 Implications for complex cognition from the hafting of tools with compound adhesives in the Middle Stone Age, South Africa. *Proc. Natl Acad. Sci. USA* **106**, 9590–9594.

28 Lombard, M. & Phillipson, L. 2010 Indications of bow and stone-tipped arrow use 64000 years ago in KwaZulu-Natal, South Africa. *Antiquity* **84**, 1–14.

29 Yellen, J. E., Brooks, A.S., Cornelissen, E., Mehlman, M.& Stewart, K. 1995 A Middle Stone Age worked bone Industry from Katanda, Upper Semliki Valley, Zaire. *Science* **268**, 553–556.

30 d'Errico, F. & Henshilwood, C h. 2007 Additional evidence for bone technology in the southern African Middle Stone Age. *J. Hum. Evol.* **52**, 142–163.

31 Backwell, L. R., d'Errico, F. & Wadley, L. 2008 Middle Stone Age bone tools from the Howiesons Poort layers, Sibudu Cave, South Africa. *J. Archaeol. Sci.* **35**, 1566–1580.

32 Costamagno, S., Meignen, L., Beauval, C., Vandermeersch, B. & Maureille, B. 2006 Les Pradelles (Marillac-le-Franc, France): a Mousterian reindeer hunting camp? *J. Anthropol. Arch.* **25**, 466–484.

33 Stringer, C. B. *et al.* 2008 Neanderthal exploitation of marine mammals in Gibraltar. *Proc. Natl Acad. Sci. USA* **105**, 14319–14324.

34 Rendu, W. 2010 Hunting behavior and Neanderthal adaptability in the Late Pleistocene site of Pech-de-l'Azé I. *J. Archaeol. Sci.* **37**, 1798–1810.

35 Mussi, M. & Villa, P. 2008 Single carcass of *Mammuthus primigenius* with lithic artifacts in the Upper Pleistocene of northern Italy. *J. Arch. Sci.* **35**, 2606–2613.

36 Delagnes, A. & Meignen, L. 2006 Diversity of Lithic Production Systems During the Middle Paleolithic in France. In *Transitions Before the Transition. Evolution and Stability in the Middle Paleolithic and Middle Stone Age* (eds E. Hovers & S. L. Kuhn), pp. 85–107. New York, NY: Springer.

37 Yeshurun, R., Bar-Oz, G. & Weinstein-Evron, M. 2007 Modern Hunting Behavior in the Early Middle Paleolithic: Faunal Remains from Misliya Cave, Mount Carmel, Israel. *J. Hum. Evol.* **53**, 656–677.

38 Feblot-Augustins, J. 1999 Raw material transport patterns and settlement systems in the European Lower and Middle Palaeolithic: continuity, change and variability. In *The Middle Palaeolithic occupation of Europe* (eds W. Roebroeks & C. Gamble), pp. 193–214. Leiden, The Netherlands: University of Leiden.

39 Jaubert, J., Delagnes, A. & Meignen, L. 2007 De l'espace parcouru à l'espace habité au Paléolithique Moyen. In *Les Néandertaliens. Biologie et cultures* (eds B. Vandermeersch & B. Maureille), pp. 263–281. Paris, France: CTHS.

40 Thieme, H. 1997 Lower Palaeolithic hunting spears from Germany. *Nature* **385**, 807–810.

41 Churchill, S. E. & Rhodes, J. A. 2009 The evolution of the human capacity for 'killing at a distance'. In *The evolution of hominin diets: integrating approaches to the study of Palaeolithic subsistence* (eds J. Hublin & M. P. Richards), pp. 201–210. Dordrecht, The Netherlands: Springer.

42 Villa, P. & Soriano, S. 2010 Hunting weapons of neanderthals and early modern humans in South Africa. *J. Anthrop. Res.* **66**, 5–38.

43 Mazza, P. *et al.* 2006 A new Palaeolithic discovery: tar-hafted stone tools in a European Mid-Pleistocene bone-bearing bed. *J. Archaeol. Sci.* **33**, 1310–1318.

44 Koller, J., Baumer, U. & Mania, D. 2001 High-tech in the Middle Palaeolithic: Neandertal manufactured pitch identified. *Eur. J. Archaeol.* **4**, 385–397.

45 Patou-Mathis, M. 2002 *Retouchoirs, compresseurs, percuteurs … os a impressions et eraillures.* Paris, France: Société Préhistorique Française.

46 Bailey, S. E. & Hublin, J. 2006 Dental remains from the Grotte du Renne at Arcy-sur-Cure (Yonne). *J. Hum. Evol.* **50**, 485–508.

47 Bar-Yosef, O. & Bordes, J. G. 2010 Who were the makers of the Châtelperronian culture? *J. Hum. Evol.* **59**, 586–93.

48 d'Errico, F., Julien, M., Liolios, D., Vanhaeren, M. & Baffier, D. 2003 Many awls in our argument. Bone tool manufacture and use in the Châtelperronian and Aurignacian levels of the Grotte du Renne at Arcy-sur-Cure. In *The chronology of the Aurignacian and of the transitional technocomplexes. dating, stratigraphies, cultural implications* (eds J. Zilhão & F. d'Errico), pp. 247–271. Lisbon, Portugal: Instituto Português de Arqueologia.

49 Zilhão, J. 2006 Neandertals and moderns mixed, and it matters. *Evol. Anthropol.* **15**, 183–195.

50 Salomon, H. 2009. Les matières colorantes au début du Paléolithique supérieur: sources, transformations et fonctions, PhD dissertation, University of Bordeaux.

51 d'Errico, F., Borgia, V. & Ronchitelli, G. In press. Uluzzian bone technology and its implications for the origin of behavioural modernity. *Quat. Intern.*

52 Anderson, J. R., Gillies, A. & Lock, L. C. 2010 *Pan* thanatology. *Curr. Biol.* **20**, 349–351.

53 Clark, D. J., Beyene, Y., Wolde, G., Asfaw, W. H. B. & White, T. D. 2003 Stratigraphic, chronological and behavioral contexts of Pleistocene *Homo sapiens* from the Middle Awash, Ethiopia. *Nature* **423**, 747–752.

54 Grün, R. *et al.* 2005 U-series and ESR analyses of bones and teeth relating to the human burials from Skhul. *J. Hum. Evol.* **49**, 316–334.

55 Vandermeersch, B. 1970 Une sépulture moustérienne avec offrandes decouverte dans la grotte de Qafzeh. *CR Acad. Sci.* **268**, 298–301.

56 Crevecoeur, I. 2006 *Etude anthropologique du squelette du Paléolithique supérieur de Nazlet Khater 2* (Egypte). Leuven, Belgium: Leuven University Press.

57 Van Peer, P h., Vermeersch, P. & Paulissen, E. 2010 *Chert quarrying, lithic technology and a modern human burial at the Palaeolithic site of Taramsa 1. Upper Egypt.* Leuven, Belgium: Leuven University Press.

58 Vanhaeren, M. & d'Errico, F. 2006 Aurignacian ethnolinguistic-geography of Europe revealed by personal ornaments. *J. Archaeol. Sci.* **33**, 1105–1128.

59 Olley, J. M., Roberts, R., Yoshida, H. & Bowler, J. M. 2006 Single-grain optical dating of grave-infill associated with human burials at Lake Mungo, Australia. *Quat. Sci. Rev.* **25**, 2469–2474.

60 Grün, R. & Stringer, C. B. 2000 Tabun revisited: revised ESR chronology and new ESR and U-series analyses of dental material from Tabun C1. *J. Hum. Evol.* **39**, 601–612.

61 Maureille, B. & Vandermeersch, B. 2007 Les sépultures néandertaliennes. In *Les Néandertaliens, biologie et cultures* (eds B. Vandermeersch & B. Maureille), pp. 311–322. Paris, France: C.T.H.S.

62 Verna, C. & d'Errico, F. 2011. The oldest evidence for the use of human bone as a tool. *J. Hum. Evol.* **60**, 145–157.

63 Watts, I. 2009 Red ochre, body painting and language: interpreting the Blombos ochre. In *The cradle of language* (eds R. Botha & C. Knight), pp. 62–92. Oxford, UK: Oxford University Press.

64 d'Errico, F., Vanhaeren, M., Henshilwood, C h., Lawson, G., Maureille, B., Gambier, D., Tillier, A.-M., Soressi, M. & van Niekerk, K. 2009 From the origin of Language to the Diversification of Language. What can archaeology and palaeoanthropology say ? In *Becoming eloquent. Advances on the emergence of language, human cognition, and modern culture* (eds F. d'Errico & J.-M. Hombert), pp. 13–68. Amsterdam, The Netherlands: Benjamins.

65 d'Errico, F., Salomon, H., Vignaud, C. & Stringer, C. 2010 Pigments from the Middle Palaeolithic levels of Es-Skhul (Mount Carmel, Israel). *J. Arch. Sci.* **37**, 3099–3110.

66 Hovers, E., Ilani, S., Bar-Yosef, O. & Vandermeersch, B. 2003 An Early Case of Color Symbolism. Ochre Use by Modern Humans in Qafzeh Cave. *Cur. Anthr.* **44**, 492–522.

67 d'Errico, F. *et al.* 2009 Additional evidence on the use of personal ornaments in the Middle Paleolithic of North Africa. *Proc. Natl Acad. Sci. USA* **106**, 16051–16056.

68 Bird, M. I., Fifield, L. K., Santos, G. M., Beaumont, P. B., Zhou, Y., di Tada, M. L. & Hausladen, P. A. 2003 Radiocarbon dating from 40 to 60 ka BP at Border Cave, South Africa. *Quat. Sci. Rev.* **22**, 943–947.

69 Bar-Yosef Mayer, D., Vandermeersch, B. & Bar-Yosef, O. 2009 Shells and ochre in Middle Paleolithic Qafzeh Cave, Israel: indications for modern behavior. *J. Hum. Evol.* **56**, 307–314.

70 Leavesley, M. G. 2007 A shark-tooth ornament from Pleistocene Sahul. *Antiquity* **81**, 308–315.

71 Morse, K. 1993 Shell beads from Mandu Mandu Creek rock-shelter, Cape Western Australia, dated before 30000 ka BP. *Antiquity* **67**, 877–883.

72 Henshilwood, C. S., d'Errico, F. & Watts, I. 2009 Engraved ochres from the Middle Stone Age levels at Blombos Cave, South Africa. *J. Hum. Evol.* **57**, 27–47.

73 Texier, J.-P. *et al.* 2010 A Howiesons Poort tradition of engraving ostrich eggshell containers dated to 60,000 years ago at Diepkloof Rock Shelter, South Africa. *Proc. Natl Acad. Sci. USA* **107**, 7621–7622.

74 Wendt, W. E. 1976 Art mobilier from the Apollo 11 Cave, southwest Africa: Africa's oldest dated works of art. *South African Archaeol. Bull.* **31**, 5–11.

75 Conard, N. 2009 A female figurine from the basal Aurignacian of Hohle Fels Cave in southwestern Germany. *Nature* **459**, 248–252.

76 Conard, N. J., Malina, M. & Münzel, S. 2009 New flutes document the earliest musical tradition in southwestern Germany. *Nature* **460**, 737–740.

77 d'Errico, F. & Lawson, G. 2006 The Sound Paradox. How to assess the acoustic significance of archaeological evidence? In *Archaeoacustics* (eds C. Scarre & G. Lawson), pp. 41–57. Cambridge, UK: McDonald Institute.

78 Stringer, C. 2011 *The origin of our species*. London, UK: Penguin.

79 Delagnes, A. & Ropars, A. 1996 *Paléolithique moyen en Pays de Caux (Haute-Normandie). Le Pucheuil, Etoutteville: deux gisement de plein air en milieu Loessique*. Paris, France: Maison des Sciences de l'Homme.

Chapter 14

Descent with Modification and the Archaeological Record

Stephen Shennan

Recent years have seen major advances in our understanding of the way in which cultural transmission takes place and the factors that affect it. The theoretical foundations of those advances have been built by postulating the existence of a variety of different processes and deriving their consequences mathematically or by simulation. The operation of these processes in the real world can be studied through experiment and naturalistic observation. In contrast, archaeologists have an 'inverse problem'. For them the object of study is the residues of different behaviours represented by the archaeological record and the problem is to infer the microscale processes that produced them, a vital task for cultural evolution since this is the only direct record of past cultural patterns. The situation is analogous to that faced by population geneticists scanning large number of genes and looking for evidence of selection as opposed to drift, but more complicated for many reasons, not least the enormous variety of different forces that affect cultural transmission. This chapter reviews the progress that has been made in inferring processes from patterns and the role of demography in those processes, together with the problems that have arisen.

Keywords: meme's eye-view; cultural drift; functional and neutral variation; transmission of complex technologies; demography and cultural complexity; archaeological record

14.1 Introduction

Over the last 30 years, the idea that the processes producing cultural stability and change are analogous in important respects to those of biological evolution has become increasingly popular. On this view, just as biological evolution is characterized by changing frequencies of genes in populations through time as a result of such processes as natural selection, so cultural evolution refers to the changing distributions of cultural attributes in populations, likewise affected by processes such as natural selection but also by others that have no analogue in genetic evolution. Since the presentation of the fundamental mathematically based theory by Cavalli-Sforza & Feldman [1] and Boyd & Richerson [2], the development of what has come to be called 'dual inheritance theory' or 'gene–culture coevolution theory' has continued (e.g. [3, 4]) and it has been accompanied by a slowly growing number of empirical case studies, applying the ideas to understanding patterned variation in cultural data (e.g. [5]).

The processes involved are complex and subtle. In the case of culture, the inheritance mechanism is social learning. Of course, the routes through which culture is inherited are much more diverse than those for genes and different routes have different consequences for the patterning of cultural change through time [1]. Variation in what is inherited is generated by innovations. These may be unintended copying errors, but they can also be intentional changes, perhaps arising from trial-and-error experimentation, which leads an individual to stop doing what they had previously learned and to start doing it differently, or even to do something different altogether. Whether this will be widely adopted depends on a range of selection and bias mechanisms, many of which have no equivalent in genetic evolution but whose existence and importance have formed the subject of major developments in the theory of cultural evolution over the last 30 years.

Natural selection in the narrowest sense affects humans as it does members of all other species. However, natural selection can also act on cultural attributes, in the sense that those individuals who inherit or acquire certain cultural attributes may have a greater probability of surviving and/or reproducing than those who do not; as a result those cultural attributes will become increasingly prevalent. For example, it is clear that in many parts of the world adopting an agricultural rather than a hunting-and-gathering way of life led to greater reproductive success; as a result, the cultural traits that characterize agriculture spread and, in some cases, subsequently influenced genetic evolution (e.g. the ability to digest lactose [6]). An analogous process of *cultural selection* can also operate if individuals with certain cultural traits are more likely to be taken as models for imitation than others, by virtue of those traits, and these in turn become successful models as a result. The traits concerned will become more prevalent even if they have no bearing on reproductive success whatsoever, and indeed, even if they are deleterious to it. This is because if an attribute is passed on other than by parents to children there is no reason for its success to depend on the reproductive success of the individuals concerned. For example, if celibate priests are more likely than other adults to be teachers and if, as a result of what they teach, their pupils are more likely to become celibate priests and teachers, then the values they teach will increase in frequency relative to others [2, ch. 6].

In addition to these selection mechanisms, it has been shown that a number of 'bias' processes can affect what is transmitted; these refer to factors that affect what and who people try to copy when they are learning from others [2, 3]. Thus, 'results bias' refers to the situation where people look at what other people do, for example, the crops they plant, compare the results with what they are doing themselves, and then change what they do because the other way of doing things seems to be more effective. 'Content biases' are affected by features of transmissible phenomena that make them intrinsically more or less memorable for reasons relating to the structure of the mind or the strong reactions they provoke; examples might be fairy tales or so-called urban myths. 'Context biases' are aspects of the context of learning that affect what is transmitted; thus, something may be copied simply because the person initially doing it is prestigious ('prestige bias') or because it is what most people locally do ('conformist bias'). In these latter two cases, whether a particular cultural attribute or practice becomes more prevalent in a population has nothing to do with its intrinsic properties but only with the context of learning.

Finally, there is the cultural equivalent of genetic drift [1, ch. 3]. In other words, the frequencies of particular cultural attributes can change for essentially chance reasons not involving any preference for a particular attribute. Who or what you copy may simply be a random choice dependent on who or what you meet. Thus, variants that occur more frequently in a population will have a greater chance of being copied purely by virtue of their greater frequency, but in any finite population there will also be an element of chance in what specific variants are copied, and when populations are small the role of chance will be important. If there is no innovation, the outcome will be that a single variant becomes fixed; the time taken for this depends on the population size.

14.2 **The 'meme's eye-view'**

However, as just described, all these processes focus on the people involved in the processes. This is obviously an extremely important perspective but it is not the only one. It is also important to look at the processes from the meme's eye-view [7, 8], the perspective of the cultural attributes themselves. This perspective matters because these culturally transmitted features are the only data accessible to archaeologists, and often all that anthropologists have as well. In fact, they are the only direct data about past cultural traditions and the forces affecting them that we have available. Moreover, the agent-centred cultural evolutionary processes described above are microscale ones: they occur at short time scales, at most a human generation but very often on a virtually day-to-day basis, and between individuals or small groups. The question then becomes, to what extent is it possible to identify the action of the various cultural evolutionary processes outlined above on the basis of distributions of through-time variation in the past, given the often poor temporal resolution of the archaeological record and the enormous range of complex processes that have affected it? This is a classic 'inverse problem' of a type very familiar to archaeologists: inferring the microscale processes producing a pattern from the pattern itself, as opposed to carrying out designed experiments or making naturalistic observations of processes in the field and examining their consequences. The problems are analogous to those faced by population geneticists in identifying the operation of selection and other processes given the evidence of gene distributions, but in that case the problems are less complex, the amounts of data available are now enormous and very powerful methods have been developed with a strong and well-justified theoretical background. However, as with the development of the theoretical models that created the basis for the field of cultural evolution, the existence of these methods is something from which empirical cultural evolutionary studies can benefit.

In fact, even to demonstrate that a pattern of contemporary variation or one of continuity through time results from the operation of a cultural inheritance process (i.e. is a 'meme'), as opposed to being a contingent response to local environmental conditions, is not straightforward. Going on to make inferences about the processes acting on the cultural lineages identified is even more difficult, and they look different from the 'meme's' perspective than from the agent's. Thus, in a recent paper on the evolution of Polynesian canoes, Rogers & Ehrlich [9] refer to the process acting on those canoe traits that have a functional significance as natural selection, and so it is from the perspective of the traits themselves, in that particular traits survive and are copied preferentially as a result of their greater functional effectiveness (cf [10])—something that could in principle be tested experimentally. What the results do not do as they stand is distinguish between *natural selection operating on human agents via cultural traits, and thus on the future frequency of those traits* and *results bias*, as defined above. In other words, the process could have operated as a result of the makers and users of ineffective canoes drowning more frequently, thus leading to the demise of those designs, while groups with better-designed canoes, perhaps different communities, survived and colonized new islands. Alternatively, it could have worked through people observing the performance of different canoe designs and preferentially copying those they perceived as more effective. The latter would potentially be far faster and the implied time-scale difference could provide a basis for distinguishing between the two processes. Making this sort of distinction is actually at the root of some of the most long-standing debates in archaeology, for example, whether the spread of farming into Europe was a process of indigenous adoption (involving results bias) or demographic expansion and extinction (natural selection acting on the bearers of cultural traditions). Note that despite the numerous attacks on the idea of memes as replicators encouraging their own reproduction, it is emphatically the case in both the above scenarios that whether or not people reproduce particular traits depends on the specific characteristics of the traits themselves.

In fact, the basic procedures of an evolutionary archaeology of cultural traditions are now clear [11]. It is necessary to identify the histories of transmission to show that an ancestor–descendant relationship exists, if indeed it does [12], and then attempt to understand the forces shaping it, all on the basis of patterned variation in the archaeological record. In practice, however, these two operations, identifying a transmission history and characterizing the forces affecting it, are not necessarily sequential, and the information to make the distinctions required may simply not exist. Thus, if a particular cultural attribute, for example, the sharpness of a lithic cutting edge, is very strongly determined by its function, then it will contain no signal of its transmission history as a particular technique of stone tool production, even though it is likely that it had one (as opposed to being discovered anew by every novice flint knapper through trial-and-error learning).

Clearly, transmission implies continuity but continuity does not necessarily imply transmission. It might arise, for example, from the continuity of environmental conditions or of a particular function. In practice, probably the most important method for characterizing transmission in archaeology has been seriation. This is a very well-known technique developed in the late nineteenth and early twentieth centuries for the purpose of building artefact chronologies in the absence of absolute dates; it involves putting phenomena in a sequential order on the basis of some measure of their similarity to one another [12, 13]. If we have independent evidence of the chronological order, we can test whether the phenomena that are most similar to one another are indeed closest to one another in time. To the extent that they are, continuity is implied. Thus, if successive

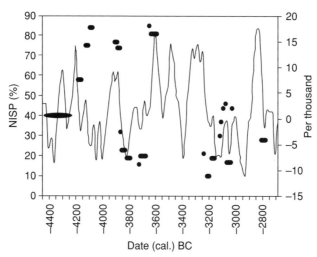

Figure 14.1 Fluctuations in the proportion of wild animals through time in faunal assemblages (filled circles) from the Swiss Neolithic between 4400 and 2800 cal. BC. Percentage of number of identified specimens (left-hand axis), against a climatic indicator, the delta ^{14}C value (right-hand axis); higher values indicate cooler, wetter conditions. (Reproduced from Huester-Plogmann, H., Schibler, J., and Steppan, K. 1999 The relationship between wild mammal exploitation, climatic fluctuations, and economic adaptations. A trans disciplinary study on Neolithic sites from Lake Zurich region, Southwest Germany and Bavaria. In *Historia animalium ex ossibus. Festschrift fur Angela von denDriesch* (eds C. Becker, H. Manhart, J. Peters, and J. Schibler), pp.189–200. Rahden, Germany: Verlag Marie Leidorf (Figure1) with permission from the publisher and the author.)

pottery assemblages linked by transmission, characterized by counts of different ceramic types, are put in order, then the changing frequencies of the types will show a characteristic pattern of first appearance, increasing popularity and decline. Ultimately, however, our conviction that cultural transmission is the predominant force accounting for the pattern is also based on other knowledge, for example, that the making of pottery is an activity acquired by social learning. Other situations are *a priori* less clear cut. Thus, Huester-Plogmann and colleagues [14] showed graphically that through-time fluctuations in the proportional and absolute frequencies of wild and domestic animal bones at Neolithic sites in Switzerland probably did not relate to changing cultural preferences for hunting or keeping domestic animals but to climatic fluctuations, because hunting became predominant at times of a cool, wet climate, which could be demonstrated by independent evidence (Figure 14.1).

14.3 **Characterizing cultural drift**

The main single topic on which the characterization of processes has focused in archaeology is the identification of cultural drift and departures from it. The idea that cultural phenomena could be subject to drift processes goes well back into the mid-twentieth century and before (e.g. [15]). In his early expositions of evolutionary archaeology, Dunnell (e.g. [10]) suggested that the attributes of material culture assemblages could be divided into those influenced by selection (functional attributes) and those that were not (stylistic attributes). However, the key development in linking material culture attributes to evolutionary theory was Neiman's [16] demonstration of the way the mathematics of the neutral theory of evolution could be used to generate quantitative expectations of what a distribution of artefact frequencies should look like if drift and innovation were the only factors affecting it, rather than simply making *a priori* judgements about what is likely to have been functional and what stylistic, as previous authors had done.

Specifically, he made use of the fact that at mutation/innovation-drift equilibrium, when the mutation rate is very low, the homogeneity of a population made up of variants whose distribution is only affected by drift and innovation is proportional to twice the effective population size times the innovation rate ($2N_e/\mu$) [16]. As this quantity (designated θ) increases, the homogeneity of the population decreases. This may be compared with the value of θ obtained from a given set of data:

$$\theta = \frac{1}{\sum_i p_i^2} - 1,$$

where p_i is the relative frequency of the ith member of a population of k variants.

However, as Neiman pointed out, there is a preliminary issue that needs to be taken into account if we are to use our archaeological data for this purpose. We cannot necessarily assume that the frequency of decorative types in an archaeological assemblage corresponds to the frequency of variants in the past population; it will have been governed, among other things, by discard rates. Nevertheless, Neiman showed by simulation that where assemblages are the product of multiple transmission episodes and multiple discard events, then the assemblage frequency distribution of types/variants will closely correspond to that of the frequency of the variants in the population from which the assemblage is drawn.

However, we still need to obtain an estimate of the neutral expected variation in a sample of a given size. For this Neiman made use of an equation from Ewens [17] who showed that, if the neutrality assumption holds, then the expected number of different variants in a sample ($E(k)$) is a function of the sample size (n) and the parameter θ, based on the effective population size and the mutation rate, presented above [16, eqn (9)]:

$$E(k) = \sum_{i=0}^{n-1} \frac{\theta}{\theta + i}.$$

Since in a given case we know the observed number of variants (k) and the sample size (n), we can use this equation to obtain an estimate of θ [16].

Following the logic of genetic drift, in cultural drift variation is the result of random copying of cultural attributes, with some possibility of innovation, and the results of the process depend solely on the innovation rate and the effective population size, itself dependent on the scale of interaction. It is very unlikely that any individual act of copying, for example, of a ceramic decorative motif, will be random in terms of the model copied, but if everyone has their own reasons for copying one person rather than another, the result will be that there are no directional forces affecting what or who is copied. Neiman's original case study indicated that patterning in the rim attributes of eastern North American Woodland period pottery was a result of drift, and on this basis he was able to go on to argue that the Woodland period was one of large-scale human interaction, a view that had been held by earlier scholars but had subsequently been rejected, for reasons that Neiman was able to show were erroneous. In contrast, Shennan & Wilkinson [18] showed that patterning in the frequency through time of decorative attributes of Early Neolithic pottery from a small region of Germany indicated a more even distribution of variants than expected under drift, in the later phases of the sequence studied; i.e. there was an 'anti-conformity' bias, with many different types being relatively frequent (Figure 14.2). Conversely, Kohler *et al.* [19] in a case study of decorative designs on

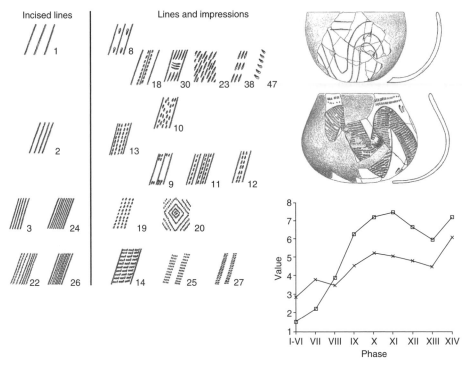

Figure 14.2 Plot of actual diversity (squares) and neutral predicted diversity (crosses) of the decorative variation on Early Neolithic ceramic vessels from a site in Germany against the sequence of chronological phases from the site (lower right). From phase IX onwards the diversity values are greater than those predicted by the neutral model. Examples of Early and Late vessels (upper right). The diversity values were calculated on the basis of the frequencies of the decorative motifs shown on the left. Adapted from Shennan & Wilkinson [18, fig. 4c]; Luening, J. & Stehli, P. 1994 *Die bandkeramik im Merzbachtal auf der Aldenhovener platte*. Bonn: Habelt, plates 6.3 and 29.7, pp. 207–394; Frirdich, C. 1994 kulturgeschichtliche betrachtungen zur bandkeramik im Merzbachtal, fig. 10, respectively. © Institut für Archäologische Wissenschaften, Abt. Vor- und Frühgeschichte, Johann Wolfgang Goethe-Universität Frankfurt am Main. Reproduced by permission of the Society for American Archaeology from Shennan, S. J. and Wilkinson, J. R. 2001, Ceramic style and change and neutral evolution: a case study from Neolithic Europe. *American Antiquity*, **66**, pp. 577–93.

pottery from the southwest USA, were able to show a departure in the direction of conformity. Thus, these methods do provide a potential basis for distinguishing some of the transmission forces outlined above, although the statistical methods used to test for departures from drift in these cases were very weak.

The above studies followed Neiman in using an assemblage diversity measure to identify drift. Subsequently, Bentley and colleagues [20] took another aspect of predictions of the neutral theory as their focus, the proportion of variants having a given frequency, and used computer simulation to explore the implications of the neutral model in terms of the relative frequency distribution of individual variants accumulated over time. They showed that the result was a power law, with a small number of the variants attaining very high frequencies but most occurring only very few times, so long as $N\mu$ is not too large. Clearly, if the mutation rate is high then no variant is going to achieve high frequencies because variants are constantly being replaced.

They explored the implications of this model by analysing a number of datasets, including the distribution of baby names represented in the 1990 US census and in a series of sample datasets for each decade of the twentieth century. They found an extremely good fit to a power law distribution in all cases, although this was not statistically tested, and therefore suggested that the distributions were governed by a process of random copying. In such cases, although one can predict that a small number of variants will attain very high frequencies, it is impossible to predict which ones.

Mesoudi & Lycett [21] took this approach further by simulating the frequency distributions produced by biased transmission processes distinct from the drift model of random copying. They showed that conformist and anti-conformist transmission produced log–log frequency distributions with markedly distinctive features different from those produced by random copying, and confirmed Bentley & Shennan's [22] result that if copying is independent of the frequency of the models available to be copied then the distribution of frequencies will be exponential. However, they also showed that processes of 'frequency-dependent trimming', in which there is a bias against copying either the most popular or the least popular variants, are not easy to distinguish from simple random copying. However, in no case did they attempt to test statistically the extent of the departure from random copying that would be required to reject this model.

All these studies addressed the frequencies of discrete traits. Eerkens & Lipo [23] developed a similar approach to the characterization of neutral variation in continuous measurements and the measurement of departures from it. Studies of drift in discrete attributes have not addressed the processes that generate variation in those attributes, whether copying error or the intentional creation of, e.g. new decorative motifs, but have simply explored the effects of different innovation rates. In contrast, in the case of variation in continuous attributes there has been a focus on precisely what is involved in the generation of small errors and what the consequences are for the outcome of those errors over repeated transmission episodes, because in this case we have some knowledge about what the relevant processes are. Specifically, psychological studies have shown that below a certain threshold (the so-called Weber fraction), people are incapable of distinguishing differences in physical dimensions; the threshold is relative to the scale of the dimension. Thus, lines that are within 3 per cent of each other in terms of their length cannot be distinguished [23]. Over multiple transmission episodes, and assuming that no other processes are operating, the errors generated by this sub-perceptual copying error will accumulate, although the accumulation rate will gradually slow down (Figure 14.3a). On the other hand, if individuals tend to conform to the mean of the population at any given

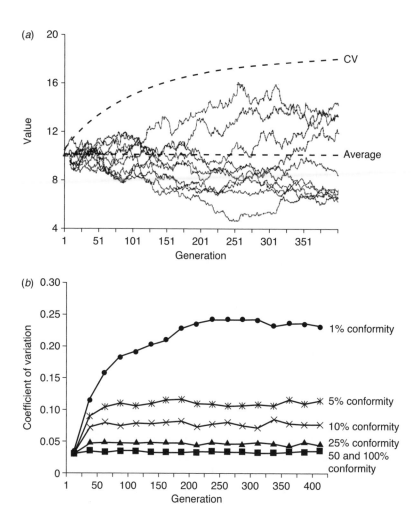

Figure 14.3 (a) Results of simulations of 10 transmission chains of a continuous measurement with sub-perceptual error at each transmission step, under conditions of unbiased transmission, showing the mean and the coefficient of variation (CV). (b) The effect of different intensities of conformist transmission. Here, the data points represent average CV values calculated over 10 simulations. Reprinted from *Journal of Anthropological Archaeology*, **24**(4), Jelmer W. Eerkens and Carl P. Lipo, Cultural transmission, copying errors, and the generation of variation in material culture and the archaeological record, pp. 316–334, Copyright (2005), with permission from Elsevier.

transmission episode then the variation in the measurement concerned will reach an equilibrium level, with a range dependent on the strength of the conformity (Figure 14.3b). Prestige bias also acts to reduce variation over repeated transmission episodes but its effects will vary depending on the proportion of individuals that are taken to be prestigious for the attribute in question [23]. The authors applied the theory to explaining variation in projectile point dimensions in the western US Owens Valley and in Illinois Woodland ceramic vessel diameters. They showed that drift was sufficient to explain the variation in projectile point thickness, but base width showed less variation than expected, so some biasing process leading to a reduction in variation over time must have been operating while, in the case of the pottery vessel diameters, variation increasing mechanisms were at work.

Lycett & von Cramon-Taubadel [24] have recently also explored the use of continuous measurements to explore questions of drift. In just the same way as recent results have shown that genetic variation in modern human populations declines in a regular fashion with distance from east Africa as a result of serial bottle-necking or founder effects [25], they postulated that there should be similar effects on variation in the dimensions of Acheulean handaxes if the main factor affecting them was drift as populations of handaxe uses spread out of Africa. Their results indicated that handaxe variation did indeed decrease in the manner predicted.

Recently, Hamilton & Buchanan [26] have used both these approaches in an analysis of the role of drift in affecting variation in the dimensions of the projectile points of early hunter–gatherers in North America. They showed that over time accumulated copying error (ACE) in a given dimension as a result of the Weber fraction will lead to a decrease in the mean of the dimension concerned because smaller values will be copied with less error, as the errors are proportional rather than absolute, while larger values will be copied with greater error and sometimes that error will be in the direction of smaller values; the variance, however, will increase through time in a linear fashion. They then investigated the effect of introducing biased transmission into the system, for example, that generated by copying the most prestigious individual available or conformist copying of the local mean. They show that whereas these biases and ACE have no effect on the mean, which still decreases with the number of copying episodes, they do have an effect on the variance, which increases to a limit determined by the strength of the bias and then stabilizes. They went on to examine the role of both founder effects, indicated as above by changes in within-assemblage variation, and ACEs in accounting for variation in the sizes of Clovis-type projectile points through time. Time was measured by using radiocarbon dates.

They found no evidence of multiple founder effects in this case but did find that the mean size of projectile points decreased through time and that the variance in size was constant, suggesting that the key factor affecting the size of the points was strongly biased transmission with ACE. They noted that a decrease in mean point size over time greater than that expected by drift, or any increase in size, would be indicative of directional selection.

Clearly, in all these studies, the key issue is to have strong methods for distinguishing the effects of different processes and few if any of the studies described above have really attempted to do this in a rigorous fashion. This point has been developed in a recent paper by Steele *et al.* [27]. In the case of the discrete trait drift models, for example, they point out that if the standard methods are being used it is important to be sure that the system being studied is at mutation-drift equilibrium, otherwise it cannot be assumed that apparent departures from drift are real. More generally, they argue that simply comparing an empirical to a theoretically based frequency distribution is insufficient even when it is done using an appropriate statistical test, and earlier work by and large has not even done that. It is necessary, they argue, to go further and consider the effects of other variables that there are grounds for thinking might be having at least some influence on the distribution in question. The authors develop this argument through an analysis of the factors affecting the frequency distribution of different rim shapes in ceramic bowls from the Hittite Bronze Age capital of Bogazkoy. They found that although statistical tests on the diversity of rim types did not indicate a departure from neutrality, in fact the frequency of different types was affected by the functionally significant variable of ware type—the coarseness of the vessel fabric—which was influencing potters' decision making. They also found a trend in bowl sizes that did not correspond to the ACE model described above. This was not revealed by simply testing for the departure of the bowl rim frequency distribution from neutrality, which did not produce a statistically significant result.

This example brings home the point that the real issue in most cases of trying to understand the factors affecting variation in archaeological assemblages is less likely to be the question of whether the variation is neutral or not, but what is the relative importance of various selective and stochastic factors in accounting for it. The way this can be done has been shown by Brantingham [28] using the Price equation, on the basis of a study of variation in the relative frequency of ceramic decoration in an artificial dataset where different households in a village decorate their ceramics with different frequencies. He distinguishes payoff-correlated from payoff-independent variation, corresponding to 'functional' and 'stylistic' variation, respectively, where the functional aspect of decoration could refer, for example, to social benefits to be gained by conforming to the usage of the local majority or penalties for not conforming. Stylistic, or non-functional, variation might arise, on the other hand, as a result of copying errors in producing the correct proportion of decorated vessels, or individual experimentation.

As Brantingham describes, on the assumption that any real process of change potentially involves an aspect related to payoffs and an aspect that is payoff independent, an equation can be written bringing the two together. Thus, in the case of his artificial example,

$$p_i^t z_i^t = p_i \frac{W_i}{W}(z_i + \delta_i),$$

where p_i is the proportion of all vessels made by household i in the previous time step, z_i is the relative frequency of ceramic decoration in household i, w_i is the payoff to household *i*, given ceramic decoration at proportional frequency z_i, w is the mean payoff to all households given a mean proportion of ceramic decoration, δ_i is the stochastic fluctuation in the frequency of decoration in household *i*, the equation states that the contribution of household *i* to the new frequency of ceramic decoration at the next time step, depends on change in its contribution to the total number of vessels from the previous step, which is payoff related, and in the frequency with which the vessels are decorated. He goes on to show that the general formula for the total evolutionary change in the frequency of ceramic decoration (Δz) corresponds to the sum of payoff-related and payoff-independent variations as given by the Price equation:

$$\Delta z = \mathrm{COV}\left(\frac{w_i}{w}, z_i\right) + E\,(\delta_i),$$

where $\mathrm{COV}\,(w_i/w, z_i)$ is the covariance between the relative payoffs and relative frequency of decorated ceramics, the functional variation and $E\,(\delta_i)$ is the expected value of stochastic fluctuations in the relative frequency of ceramic variation, the stylistic variation. As Brantingham points out, this formulation, in which change in any given attribute over time can be affected to different degrees by both functional and stylistic variation, contradicts Dunnell's argument that style and function are mutually exclusive.

The implications of the approach are then illustrated by analysis of a simulated dataset made up of 50 households, with 2000 pottery-making generations, a small positive payoff to decorating vessels ($\beta = 0.005$) and a very slight tendency ($\mu = 0.0001$) for the variation introduced in each generation to increase the proportion of decorated vessels, the two relevant parameters for the Price equation. Analysis of the frequency patterns in the data generated by the simulations recovered the known payoff value and the value for novel variation introduced in each generation with a high degree of accuracy, confirming the potential for inferring the strength and nature of functional and stylistic processes from real archaeological data. The Price equation method has now been taken further by Brantingham & Perreault [29].

14.4 **The evolution of complex technologies**

The examples above have been largely concerned with distinguishing drift from other evolutionary forces in the case of situations where we have very little information about the specific goals the makers and users of the artefacts were trying to achieve and the relevant constraints, except for our knowledge of the Weber fraction and its implications in the case of continuous measurements. In cases where we know a lot more about these goals and constraints, hypotheses can be more closely framed and at least in principle more readily tested. Recently, Charlton and colleagues [30, 31] have taken an evolutionary approach to understanding iron-smelting technology in a case study from northwest Wales. Here, there can be no doubt about the goal (at least in general terms) and the conditions required to successfully smelt iron are well understood, arising as they do from universal properties of the materials involved.

Once again though, the issue is first to identify patterns of cultural descent in the methods used and to distinguish variation arising from transmission from that relating, for example, to the local ore or fuel type; and then to characterize the forces affecting that variation, in a situation where, by the very nature of the process there are only a limited number of successful solutions. The most informative source of information on the processes involved in past episodes of early iron production is chemical variation in the slags produced as a waste product. In this case then the data are quantitative variations in the chemistry of chronologically ordered slag deposits and the inverse problem is as above: can we establish whether or not there is a signal of cultural descent in the chemical variation; if so, what can we infer about the factors affecting transmission processes that produced it?

Charlton [30] showed convincingly that a transmission signal could be identified. In terms of the forces acting on the technical knowledge and practices passed on from one iron producer to another, it is easy to imagine that there might be some more or less random variation in exactly what was done each time. It is also likely that there would be strong selection for those practices that were successful, though, given the complexity of the process and its many stages, it would not necessarily be easy to identify precisely what produced a successful smelt on any given occasion. From the point of view of the agents, it is thus likely that transmission would be affected by results bias; from the point of view of the smelting recipes, this would be a process of natural selection, since recipes would be differentially reproduced depending on their ability to successfully smelt iron. The results of Charlton *et al.* [31] showed that all changes related to furnace operation could be accounted for by a drift process but that at a certain point a second effective procedure was more or less accidentally discovered and a decision was taken to use make use of the two distinct procedures, visible in different slag signatures (Figure 14.4). At the same time, there were clear trends in the use of manganese-rich ores with better fluxing capabilities, and evidence of decreased variability in reducing conditions related to results bias: that is to say the iron makers consistently reproduced the airflow conditions that gave the best results for a given recipe. Ore variability, on the other hand, did not decrease through time and probably simply reflects the properties of the bog ore available.

14.5 **Drift, demography and the adaptive role of culture**

Most of the work described above has focused on looking for evidence of pure drift or departures from it, and considering the implications for the processes believed to be operating in particular cases, but there has been another strand of more theoretical work which has considered the implications of drift or sampling processes under different demographic conditions. Even in cases where selection or bias are strong in principle they can be overwhelmed by the effects of chance if the effective size of the relevant population is very small. If some functionally useful knowledge, for example, is only held by a small number of old men and they all die suddenly in a disease outbreak, the knowledge will be lost regardless of its usefulness. This phenomenon has been known since the earlier twentieth century [32].

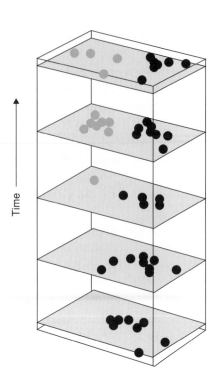

Figure 14.4 Chemistry of slags from the medieval Welsh iron-smelting site of Llwyn Du projected into PC space and arranged in stratigraphic order. Group 1 slag is plotted in dark grey and group 2 slag is plotted in light grey. The two groups are close to two distinct optima for successful iron production under different smelting conditions. Reprinted from *Journal of Anthropological Archaeology*, **29**(3), Michael F. Charlton, Peter Crew, Thilo Rehren, and Stephen J. Shennan, Cultural transmission, Explaining the evolution of ironmaking recipes – An example from northwest Wales, pp. 352–367, Copyright (2010), with permission from Elsevier.

Shennan [33] suggested that this sort of process might be relevant to explaining why so-called modern human symbolic culture might have taken so long to appear on a large scale after the emergence of anatomically modern humans *ca* 200 ka. Some of its characteristics appear and disappear sporadically in Africa over a long period but it does not appear to take off on a large scale anywhere until after 50 ka, when there is both genetic and archaeological evidence for major population increase. Shennan argued that this was a result of population levels being kept low by adverse climate conditions in Africa. On the basis of a genetic model [34], modified to include oblique transmission of cultural traits, he showed by simulation that larger populations can evolve to a higher average fitness than smaller ones because they carry a smaller drift load of deleterious cultural traits. Subsequently, Powell *et al.* [35] used an analytical model created by Henrich [36] to address the same issue (Figure 14.5). On this model, individuals learn a new skill by attempting to copy the best individual of the senior generation in their group. Most people are not as good as the best, reflected in the group modal value for the skill. However, there will always be some random variation between the individuals in their attempts to innovate and occasionally someone may exceed the current best. This will then become the example to follow, and as a result, even though most people are not as good as the best, the modal value will be pulled in a positive direction. However, the probability of exceeding the current best depends on the cultural effective population size. If population size decreases then no one in the new generation may even match the current best so the maximum level of achievement will decline. Powell *et al.*'s simulation based on this

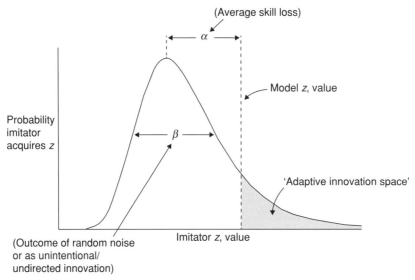

Figure 14.5 Henrich's model for result-biased transmission with error using the Gumbel distribution. Adapted from Henrich [36, fig. 1]. Reproduced by permission of the Society for American Archaeology from Henrich, J. 2004, Demography and cultural evolution: why adaptive cultural processes produced maladaptive losses in Tasmania, *American Antiquity*, **69**, pp. 197–214.

model showed that greater population densities or increased migration rates between groups would lead to the kind of cultural accumulation that modern human symbolic culture represents (cf [37]; Figure 14.6). Kline & Boyd [38] have shown that there is ethnographic evidence for the predictions of this model in Polynesia, with larger/ well-connected islands having more complex technologies than smaller ones (though contrast [39]).

14.6 Discussion

It has taken a long time to start developing methods of empirical data analysis to solve the inverse problem of making inferences from archaeological frequency distributions in order to arrive at explanations of their form and inter-relationships in terms of cultural evolutionary processes, and it seems reasonable to suggest that the work has barely begun. For example, it can be argued that the methods described here are much more appropriate for cases where a reasonably high degree of chronological resolution is available, likely to be more frequent in more recent periods. Thus, Richerson & Boyd [40] have expressed some doubt about attempting to fit micro-evolutionary models of process to archaeological data given their normally coarse chronological resolution and the lack of information available for parametrizing such models, and in particular about using a 'null' model of drift as a starting point, since other more complex models might well give the same result. They point out that what appears as drift may simply be the result of short-term selection pressures that push in opposite directions from one short time

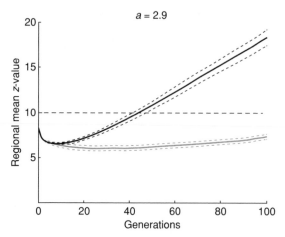

Figure 14.6 Simulated regional mean z-values (averaged over 100 iterations) over 100 generations in a world containing randomly distributed groups at a given density, divided into two halves, one with a high and one with a low migration rate, but with no barrier between them. The 95% CI for each region are given as dotted lines. Msd is the migratory range expressed as a proportion of the mean nearest neighbour distance. Black line, Msd = 1; light grey line, Msd = 0.1. From *Science*, **324**(5932), Adam Powell, Stephen Shennan, and Mark G. Thomas, Late pleistocene demography and the appearance of modern human behavior, pp. 1298–1301, figure S2. Reprinted with permission from AAAS.

period to the next, and thus are not resolvable. This is certainly true but it is questionable how much distinguishing 'real' drift from 'pseudo' drift matters, certainly when data are available that have a human-generation level of resolution. What matters is identifying the presence of selection/bias forces pushing the choices people make in some consistent direction over time, and attempting to explain them. Similarly, they argue that it is better to build models incorporating theoretical concepts, for example, 'neophilia', a preference for things that are slightly different, in the stylistic sphere. However, there are dangers in rather vague concepts like this, whose values could potentially be fine-tuned to fit whatever pattern we find. The view taken here is that we are better off obtaining estimates of innovation rates from our data. As always, it is certainly true that the more information we have in any given case and the more we have independent grounds for inferring the probable selection pressures operating, as in the case of iron production, the better our models are likely to be. Equally, the cumulative development of the methods described in this chapter offers increasing potential for distinguishing the role of different evolutionary forces. Finally, it is becoming increasingly clear that demographic factors play an important role in the processes discussed in this chapter and that if we can obtain independent evidence of prehistoric demographic patterns we will be in a much better position to build models that are appropriate for particular cases.

References

1 Cavalli-Sforza, L. L. & Feldman, M. W. 1981 *Cultural transmission and evolution: a quantitative approach.* Princeton, NJ: Princeton University Press.

2 Boyd, R. & Richerson, P. J. 1985 *Culture and the evolutionary process*. Chicago, IL: University of Chicago Press.

3 Henrich, J. & McElreath, R. 2003 The evolution of cultural evolution. *Evol. Anthropol.* **12**, 123–135.

4 Henrich, J., Boyd, R. & Richerson, P. J. 2008 Five misunderstandings about cultural evolution. *Hum. Nat.* **19**, 119–137.

5 Bettinger, R. L. & Eerkens, J. 1999 Point typologies, cultural transmission, and the spread of bow-and-arrow technology in the prehistoric Great Basin. *Am. Antiq.* **64**, 231–242.

6 Feldman, M. W. & Cavalli-Sforza, L. L. 1989 On the theory of evolution under genetic and cultural transmission with application to the lactose absorption problem. In *Mathematical evolutionary theory* (ed. M. W. Feldman), pp. 145–173. Princeton, NJ: Princeton University Press.

7 Dawkins, R. 1976 *The selfish gene*. Oxford, UK: Oxford University Press.

8 Dennett, D. C. 1995 *Darwin's dangerous idea: evolution and the meanings of life*. London, UK: Allen Lane.

9 Rogers, D. S. & Ehrlich, P. R. 2008 Natural selection and cultural rates of change. *Proc. Natl Acad. Sci. USA* **105**, 3416–3420.

10 Dunnell, R. C. 1978 Style and function: a fundamental dichotomy. *Am. Antiq.* **43**, 192–202.

11 Shennan, S. J. 2008 Evolution in archaeology. *Annu. Rev. Anthropol.* **37**, 75–91.

12 O'Brien, M. J. & Lyman, R. L. 2000 *Applying evolutionary archaeology*. New York, NY: Plenum.

13 Lyman, R. L. & O'Brien, M. J. 2006 Seriation and cladistics: the difference between anagenetic and cladogenetic evolution, 2006. In *Mapping our ancestors: phylogenetic approaches in anthropology and prehistory* (eds C. P. Lipo, M. J. O'Brien, M. Collard & S. J. Shennan), pp. 65–88. New Brunswick, NJ: AldineTransaction.

14 Hüester-Plogmann, H., Schibler, J. & Steppan, K. 1999 The relationship between wild mammal exploitation, climatic fluctuations, and economic adaptations. A trans-disciplinary study on Neolithic sites from Lake Zurich region, Southwest Germany and Bavaria. In *Historia animalium ex ossibus. Festschrift für Angela von den Driesch* (eds C. Becker, H. Manhart, J. Peters & J. Schibler), pp. 189–200. Rahden, Germany: Verlag Marie Leidorf.

15 Binford, L. R. 1963 'Red Ocher' caches from the Michigan area: a possible case of cultural drift. *Southwest J. Anthropol.* **19**, 89–108.

16 Neiman, F. D. 1995 Stylistic variation in evolutionary perspective: inferences from decorative diversity and inter-assemblage distance in Illinois Woodland ceramic assemblages. *Am. Antiq.* **60**, 7–36.

17 Ewens, W. J. 1972 The sampling theory of selectively neutral alleles. *Theor. Popul. Biol.* **3**, 87–112.

18 Shennan, S. J. & Wilkinson, J. R. 2001 Ceramic style change and neutral evolution: a case study from Neolithic Europe. *Am. Antiq.* **66**, 577–593.

19 Kohler, T. A., VanBuskirk, S. & Ruscavage-Barz, S. 2004 Vessels and villages: evidence for conformist transmission in early village aggregations on the Pajarito Plateau, New Mexico. *J. Anthropol. Archaeol.* **23**, 100–118.

20 Bentley, R. A., Hahn, M. W. & Shennan, S. J. 2004 Random drift and culture change. *Proc. R. Soc. Lond. B* **271**, 1443–1450.

21 Mesoudi, A. & Lycett, S. J. 2009 Random copying, frequency-dependent copying and culture change. *Evol. Hum. Behav.* **30**, 41–48.

22 Bentley, R. A. & Shennan, S. J. 2003 Cultural evolution and stochastic network growth. *Am. Antiq.* **68**, 459–485.

23 Eerkens, J. W. & Lipo, C. P. 2005 Cultural transmission, copying errors, and the generation of variation in material culture in the archaeological record. *J. Anthropol. Archaeol.* **24**, 316–334.

24 Lycett, S. J. & von Cramon-Taubadel, N. 2008 Acheulean variability and hominin dispersals: a model-bound approach. *J. Archaeol. Sci.* **35**, 553–562.

25 Liu, H., Prugnolle, F., Manica, A. & Balloux, F. 2006 A geographically explicit genetic model of worldwide human-settlement history. *Am. J. Hum. Genet.* **79**, 230–237.

26 Hamilton, M. J. & Buchanan, B. 2009 The accumulation of stochastic copying errors causes drift in culturally transmitted technologies: quantifying Clovis evolutionary dynamics. *J. Anthropol. Archaeol.* **28**, 55–69.

27 Steele, J., Glatz, C. & Kandler, A. 2010 Ceramic diversity, random copying, and tests for selectivity in ceramic production. *J. Archaeol. Sci.* **37**, 1348–1358.

28 Brantingham, P. J. 2007 A unified evolutionary model of archaeological style and function based on the Price equation. *Am. Antiq.* **72**, 395–416.

29 Brantingham, P. J. & Perreault, C. 2010 Detecting the effects of selection and stochastic forces in archaeological assemblages. *J. Archaeol. Sci.* **37**, 3211–3225.

30 Charlton, M. F. 2009 Identifying iron production lineages: a case-study in north-west Wales. In *Pattern and process in cultural evolution* (ed. S. J. Shennan), pp. 133–144. Berkeley, CA: University of California Press.

31 Charlton, M. F., Crew, P., Rehren, T. & Shennan, S. J. 2010 Explaining the evolution of ironmaking recipes—an example from northwest Wales. *J. Anthropol. Archaeol.* **29**, 352–367.

32 Rivers, W. H. R. 1926 *Psychology and ethnology*. London, UK: Kegan Paul, Trench, Trubner.

33 Shennan, S. J. 2001 Demography and cultural innovation: a model and some implications for the emergence of modern human culture. *Camb. Archaeol. J.* **11**, 5–16.

34 Peck, J. R., Barreau, G. & Heath, S. C. 1997 Imperfect genes, Fisherian mutation and the evolution of sex. *Genetics* **145**, 1171–1199.

35 Powell, A., Shennan, S. J. & Thomas, M. G. 2009 Late Pleistocene demography and the appearance of modern human behavior. *Science* **324**, 1298–1301.

36 Henrich, J. 2004 Demography and cultural evolution: why adaptive cultural processes produced maladaptive losses in Tasmania. *Am. Antiq.* **69**, 197–214.

37 d'Errico, F. & Stringer, C. B. 2011 Evolution, revolution or saltation scenario for the emergence of modern cultures? *Phil Trans R. Soc. B* **366**, 1060–1069.

38 Kline, M. A. & Boyd, R. 2010 Population size predicts technological complexity in Oceania. *Proc. R. Soc. B* **277**, 2559–2564.

39 Collard, M., Buchanan, B., Morin, J. & Costopoulos, A. 2011 What drives the evolution of hunter–gatherer subsistence technology? A reanalysis of the risk hypothesis with data from the Pacific Northwest. *Phil. Trans. R. Soc. B* **366**, 1129–1138.

40 Richerson, P. J. & Boyd, R. 2008 Response to our critics. *Biol. Phil.* **23**, 301–315.

Chapter 15

The Evolution of the Diversity of Cultures

R. A. Foley and M. Mirazón Lahr

The abundant evidence that *Homo sapiens* evolved in Africa within the past 200 000 years, and dispersed across the world only within the past 100 000 years, provides us with a strong framework in which to consider the evolution of human diversity. While there is evidence that the human capacity for culture has a deeper history, going beyond the origin of the hominin clade, the tendency for humans to form cultures as part of being distinct communities and populations changed markedly with the evolution of *H sapiens*. In this chapter, we investigate 'cultures' as opposed to 'culture', and the question of how and why, compared to biological diversity, human communities and populations are so culturally diverse. We consider the way in which the diversity of human cultures has developed since 100 000 years ago, and how its rate was subject to environmental factors. We argue that the causes of this diversity lie in the distribution of resources and the way in which human communities reproduce over several generations, leading to fissioning of kin groups. We discuss the consequences of boundary formation through culture in their broader ecological and evolutionary contexts.

Keywords: culture; human evolution; human diversity; cultural evolution

15.1 **Introduction**

In evolutionary terms, if culture is the way in which humans deploy their behaviour through socially learned means, then it could be said that there is only one culture. As other papers in this collection show, the capacity to be at least a limited culture-bearing animal has deep roots in the hominoid clade, probably evolved convergently in other mammalian species, and evolved during the course of hominin evolution over a period of several million years [1]. The concept of culture has become increasingly part of the evolutionary toolbox [2], but the use of 'culture' by evolutionary biologists remains only a fragment of the anthropological range. While 'culture' is the cognitive system which enables us to generate much of our behaviour, and presumably ultimately involves a set of biologically based cognitive processes, the product is something else entirely.

The human capacity for culture has resulted in enormous diversity at the population level, so that we can recognize that the way in which humans form cultures is as important, in evolutionary terms, as the capacity for culture itself. So, while at the species level there may have been the 'evolution of culture', once in place we need to consider an entirely different question—why are there so many different 'cultures'? The answer we will propose is that cultures were and are the outcome of the way in which kin-based human communities reproduce themselves over generations, and in doing so fission; that the rate of fissioning is strongly influenced by ecological and geographical factors; and that humans have a unique cognitive capacity to generate socially transmissable behaviours which structure the outcome of the fissioning. The result is the formation of boundaries between human communities; cultures are the consequence of these group boundaries, and boundary formation is perhaps the central and most important element of the evolutionary ecology of culture. The diversity of cultures derives from the intersection of species-specific cognitive capacities with demographic and ecological conditions over the past 100 000 years. In particular—in contrast to biological processes—it is the way in which that capacity for culture generates behaviours with low within-group variation and high between-group variation that has underpinned the success of the species.

15.2 **Culture and cultures**

We consider, following Boyd and Richerson [3], the capacity for culture to be a species-specific trait, in which the human brain produces mental states which process, transmit and receive information 'capable of affecting individuals' behaviour that they acquire from other members of their species through teaching, imitation, and other forms of social transmission'. One of the primary outcomes of the capacity for culture is particular sets of behaviour, mostly homogeneous within populations, and different between them. Culture, therefore, produces 'cultures'. Individuals in close social proximity adopt behaviours which are similar to each other and different from others. Cultures, for the purpose of this chapter, therefore, are communities with shared behaviours, and we would argue that although other types of cultures can and do occur, they have in evolutionary terms been isomorphic with kin-based reproductive communities, and thus populations in the biological sense [4]. In contrast to other discussions about cultural diversity [5–7], we are interested in the diversity of these communities, as ethno-linguistic groups in all probability, rather than the cultural traits which define them and are propagated by them. We therefore distinguish between cultural diversity (which refers to the way in which socially learned traits diversify and spread), and the diversity of cultures, which refers to the populations or communities which are the reproductive vehicles for cultural traits, and which are the evolutionary beneficiaries (or, conversely, losers) of their adaptive values. In this context, this chapter is more concerned with the communities as social and biological units (diversity of cultures), than the specifics of their cultural attributes (cultural diversity).

Communities are, of course, notoriously difficult to define, and have few fixed boundaries. For many reasons, individuals move from community to community during their lifetime, and may belong to more than one. Communities may also be nested one within another. We may consider Kenya to be a community as a nation, but it is also a series of communities defined ethno-linguistically—Kikuyu, Turkana, etc.—and even within those, further kin-based clans and groups occur. Fissioning and subdividing seems to be an integral part of the process of culture formation, and so cultures must also be defined as multiscalar.

Cultural communities form the bedrock of human organization and diversity [8], and it is our argument here that the process of the diversification of human communities involving cultural behaviours is an essential part of the human evolutionary story. Structured, comparatively invariant, human cultures provide many of the great strengths of human adaptation—the products of the processes of conformity; they also often lie at the heart of human conflict. In summary, an aim of this chapter is to ask why are there so many human cultures and how did they come to develop?

15.3 Human diversity: a biological and cultural paradox

One obvious answer to the question about the scale of the diversity of human cultures is to posit that it reflects the scale of biological diversity. Humans are a vast population, spread across the whole globe, and living in many different environments. It could therefore be expected that large numbers of human cultures would reflect high levels of biological—or more specifically, genetic—diversity. However, this is not the case. The human species is a young one, descended from a small population that lived in Africa between 150 and 200 kyr ago. As a result, the human species is genetically not very diverse. Measuring genetic diversity can be done in a number of ways, but a simple one is to compare sequence diversity in mitochondrial DNA across species. Figure 15.1 shows for species and subspecies of great apes and humans that the latter have the lowest level of diversity, reflecting the short time-depth of human populational origins [9].

Any attempt to compare cultures across species in a similar way is doomed, as the scale of difference is too vast. Humans are genuinely unique in the rate at which they can generate differences between communities, even if there are primate homologues for the capacity. The Ethnologue records some 6909 extant languages [10]. Price's Atlas of Ethnographic Societies [11] records over 3814 distinct cultures having been described by anthropologists, certainly a major underestimate. In practice, given definitional problems and a state of constant flux, a precise number cannot be calculated. However, another way of considering the problem is to calculate that if all the world's languages were evenly distributed across the habitable world, then, on average, a journey of only 78 km would bring a traveller from the centre of their language territory to a language boundary. A journey of 1000 km would, on average, pass through over six language territories. The traveller across the same distance would be less able to distinguish major phenotypic differences, and would see few marked boundaries. Languages are more widespread than cultures, in most cases, so the rate of changing culture would be even faster. These areas and distances are well below the resolution for geographical ancestry estimates based on genetics.

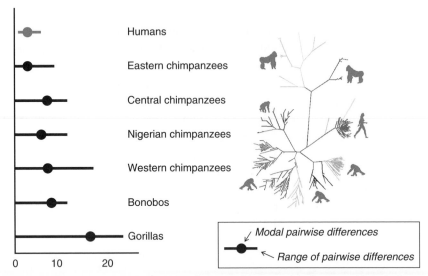

Figure 15.1 Comparative genetic diversity of apes and humans. The horizontal bars indicate the range and average pairwise difference between individuals in mtDNA sequence; the cartoon on the right is an unrooted tree of the ape/human clade, based on mtDNA, in which the branch lengths are equivalent to sequence divergence. Modified from Gagneux *et al.* [9].

These are gross generalizations, and exceptions can be found where biological boundaries are abrupt and clear-cut, and cases where cultural boundaries are diffuse. Also, the areas occupied by cultures vary environmentally [12–15], and so the distances may well be smaller or larger. Nonetheless, this broad generalization is sufficiently true to allow us to explore the paradox of low biological diversity and high numbers of cultures, in terms of the processes of cultural diversification.

The relationship between biological and cultural diversity can be examined through its structure. According to Lewontin [16], approximately 85 per cent of the genetic variation observed in human populations occurs within, rather than between populations [16]. Although out of date, Lewontin's analysis of variance remains a relevant observation about genetic variance. His analysis was pre-genomic, and based on single loci considered independently. Molecular data and multiple loci have greatly modified Lewontin's observation [17, 18], but it remains the case that there is considerable variation within all human populations and communities, certainly at larger geographical scales.

What happens when we turn to cultural diversity and ask the same question about intra- and inter-population variation? It is obvious that cultural variation should be partitioned very differently, for what constitutes a culture is the sharing of behavioural, social and material traits, and these are different between cultures [19]. Cultural diversity can virtually be defined as between populational behavioural variation (Figure 15.2). Of course, it is not the case that every member of a culture is behaviourally identical, and in practice a culture is made up of individuals each of whom has a different combination of behaviours, in the same way as each individual in a population has a unique combination of genes.

	Intra-population variation	Inter-population variation
Human genetic diversity	High	Variable
Human cultural diversity	Low	Normally high, but can be low

Figure 15.2 Characterizing the structure of human diversity. Genetic, and to some extent phenotypic biological, variation has been shown to be highly variable within populations, and less so between them; in contrast, the key trait for cultural variation is that it is normally very low within a population, but high between.

One of the main differences between genes and cultural traits is the within-populational frequency of variants, with cultural variants being mostly more homogeneous within than between groups in their expression. It is this difference that allows us to draw cultural maps as territories far more easily than we could with biological markers.

The key point is that both biological and cultural traits reside in individuals, but take on a population-level character which is both shaped by and shapes evolution. Both types of trait vary within and between populations, and can be described in frequency terms, but their structure is very different, and so acts differently in adaptive terms. Selection for generating and/or maintaining different cultures is nothing more, in a way, than strong pressure for fixation of behaviour within groups. The remainder of this chapter will consider how this diversity of cultures has developed—the pattern—and the processes by which it is structured.

15.4 Prehistory of the diversity of human cultures

15.4.1 Evolution of *Homo sapiens*: constraining cultural evolution

The paradox of low biological diversity and high cultural diversity among humans can be used to provide us with a basis for considering the origins of community-based cultural diversity. A variety of genomic markers place the demographic origin of *H. sapiens* towards the end of the Middle Pleistocene, somewhere between 200 and 150 kyr ago [20]. Different genetic markers provide slightly different estimates, but this is a broadly robust conclusion [21]. For mitochondrial DNA, the older genetic lineages (i.e. haplogroups such as L in the current terminology) have an origin (i.e. coalesce) at around 100 kyr ago [20], and there is a suggestion that the genetic diversification of the major geographical groupings of the human population known today occurred between then and 60 kyr ago [22]. This does not exclude other and earlier populational lineages, none of which have persisted through to the present day. These results indicate an African origin for the species, with most current human diversity developing after 100 kyr ago.

This information is broadly consistent with the fossil record, although the latter is despairingly sparse for much of the period [23]. Omo Kibbish, in Ethiopia, shows a 'modern' if very robust morphology at 190 kyr ago [24]; Herto, also in Ethiopia, at 160 kyr ago [25], is also 'modern' in certain key anatomical attributes, although does not fit obviously within extant variation. Apart from these early specimens, the African fossil record is scant; Klasies River Mouth (South Africa), Skhul and Qafzeh (Israel, but biogeogra-phically African) occur around 100 kyr ago; and until the end of the Pleistocene the only African specimens of note are Aduma (Ethiopia) and Hoffmeier (South Africa); these are either not very informative, or else do not relate strongly to extant regional populations. Outside Africa, modern human fossils are present from at least 40 kyr ago in Australia, 45 kyr ago in South-East Asia, and at roughly similar times in North Africa, the Middle East and Europe (see [26] for summary of later Pleistocene record). Overall, the fossil record indicates a much earlier presence of modern humans in Africa than elsewhere, weak links with local recent populations, and a much later appearance outside Africa.

In terms of evolutionary population history and the diversity of cultures, the genetic and fossil evidence allows us to say that the clock essentially starts no more than 200 kyr ago, and most probably at a much younger date (less than 100 kyr ago).

15.4.2 Phases in the evolution of the diversity of cultures

From this starting point towards the end of the Middle Pleistocene a number of informal phases can be identified, which provide some insights onto the way in which human populations diversified culturally.

15.4.2.1 Phase 1: anatomical modernity and cultural continuity

Although the earliest fossil specimens which have been referred to as anatomically modern occur between 200 and 150 kyr ago, on the basis of archaeological evidence one would be hard pressed to identify any change in the patterns of cultural diversity or the propensity for cultural differentiation at this time. The transition from archaic to modern humans is characterized by the continuation of Mode 3 technologies (i.e. the prepared core technology which defines the Middle Stone Age (MSA) of Africa and the Middle Palaeolithic of Europe, as found in both European and African lineages [27]). Prepared core/flake technologies occur considerably earlier, possibly as old as 300 kyr ago, and possibly involve a number of innovations in behaviour (use of ochre, for example) [28], but continue unchanged throughout the anatomical transition [27]. The implication is not necessarily that there is no diversification of community-based cultures, as it can be argued that these are of considerable antiquity and existed in some form in the last common ancestor with *Pan* [29], but that the rate and material group marking do not change substantially. Anatomy precedes evidence for changes in cultural diversification.

15.4.2.2 Phase 2: the African MSA, ephemerality and regionality

Contrary to much earlier writing, it is now fully recognized that the evolution of modern humans is associated with the MSA or Mode 3 technology, rather than the Upper Palaeolithic and Mode 4 or blade industries [27]. However, it is also becoming clear that the MSA is not itself homogeneous. The early parts are very poorly dated and understood, but recent research has shown that what can be considered the classic or later MSA probably occurs from approximately 120 kyr ago. This phase of the MSA is characterized by a much greater degree of regional variation, shown in the presence of both particular patterns of lithic reduction—for example, the microliths of the Howieson's Poort industry—and particular end forms or tool types (the Aterian tanged points of North Africa, the delicate Stillbay bifacial points in South Africa, for example). Associated with this phase is also the first evidence for body decoration (beads) [30–33] and for intentional marking which has been interpreted as 'symbolic' [34]. It can plausibly be argued that what is emerging here is a greater pattern of populational differentiation based on behaviour. Stone tools can probably only be a crude reflection of this, but this phase (from 120 to 50 kyr ago) reflects the cultural differentiation of the first modern human populations as they dispersed across Africa.

More detailed chronological studies have added a further twist to our understanding of this period. Jacobs *et al.* have shown that the Howieson's Poort is in fact a short-lived (5 kyr) flourishing of a particular cultural entity, not part of any prolonged trend [35]. This ephemerality, most probably also for the Stillbay, could indicate the sort of short-lived rapid expansion and decline associated with cultural markers and their host populations which is central to notions of cultural evolution and diversity.

15.4.2.3 Phase 3: the diversification of human populations in the Old World

Prior to approximately 50 kyr ago there is no substantial evidence for modern humans outside Africa (with the exception of the sites of Skhul and Qafzeh in the Levant, and there are grounds for considering this to have been part of the within-African dispersals, and ephemeral). Beyond this date, human populations were clearly larger, genetically more diverse, and became widespread in Eurasia, and, indeed, had dispersed into Australia [22, 36]. By this stage, evidence for the 'diversity of cultures' is substantial. The existence of regional traditions noted in the African MSA becomes even more marked in the Upper Palaeolithic and LSA; this is typified by the marked increase in the number of regional 'cultures' (in archaeological terms) which appear, and are characterized by differences in both lithics and more stylistic features—figurines, bone points, harpoons, beads and so on. These persist for only a few thousand years (much shorter than those of the MSA). The best known of these are units such as the Aurignacian, Gravettian, Solutrean, Wilton, Kenya Capsian and Eburran, but in all probability there are many more. There seems to be little doubt that by 40 kyr ago, in Europe at least, culture-based community differentiation was occurring, probably in ways very similar to those observed ethno-graphically. Vanhaeren and D'Errico have demonstrated in a very elegant and detailed analysis of the morphology of Aurignacian beads that the pattern of variation is best interpreted as ethno-linguistic groups across Europe [37]. Sadly, other parts of the world do not have a sufficiently complete record to recognize similar patterns. Beads and stylized decoration on ostrich eggshells in Africa during Phase 2 [38] may indicate that, albeit demo-graphically less stable, Phase 3 of cultural differentiation only represents the Eurasian magnification of what was already taking place in Africa.

15.4.2.4 Phase 4: climate, environment and fragmentation

There is little evidence to suppose that after 50 kyr ago there has been a significant genetically based change in the capacity for humans to express themselves culturally, and so in one sense one might expect that the pattern in place by Phase 3 simply continues. To some extent, in terms of process, it does. However, the period after 25 kyr ago shows a new intensification. Again, Europe, with its much richer archaeological record, provides the clearest evidence. The archaeological evidence shows an increase in the level of regionalization, and also a much greater elaboration of traits which can be described as having a primarily social function (e.g. cave art). One example is burials from Sunghir, where the three corpses were covered with more than 13 000 beads; another would be the extraordinary proliferation of art in the Magdalenian; and yet another is the existence of epi-Palaeolithic social territories in the North German plain in the Late Pleistocene [39]. The most probable explanation is that this is an effect of climatic deterioration (the last glacial maximum), leading to fragmentation of populations, isolation and intensification of group-based processes and identity [40]. In effect, this phase shows that the diversity of cultures is likely to reflect demographic and ecological processes [41], and possibly ones where the option of spreading risk by reducing boundaries [12] is not viable because there may have been genuine isolation of small populations. However, major resource pressure can also lead to opposite strategies—the formation of very low density, very mobile groups which cover very large territories. These latter would benefit from decreased cultural boundedness and increased small community inclusivity, and may underlie the homogeneity of the Australian prehistoric record of the time [42]. These regional cultural trajectories set the different starting points for the subsequent phase of economic intensification.

15.4.2.5 Phase 5: post-Pleistocene complexity and the growth of intensive economies, cities and empires

The end of the Pleistocene was shaped by climatic amelioration which started around 14 kyr ago, and with this came innumerable changes in human demography and adaptation. The first changes were the dispersals of hunter–gatherers, seen worldwide (e.g. the African LSA, the European Mesolithic or the colonization of America) in response to warmer conditions, which in parts of the world, led to the development of food production and domestication. At this point evidence for the diversity of cultures increases very significantly. This is a mixed pattern; on the one hand, some of the dispersals associated with agriculture led to a homogenization in the first instance, with closely related cultural and linguistic communities spreading widely—in Africa (Bantu), in Europe (Indo-European) and across the Pacific (Austronesian) [43]. On the other hand, this also resulted in the fragmentation of indigenous groups, with highly diverse communities existing in a complex palimpsest in many parts of the world. Large-scale population dispersals and subsequent reduced contact resulted in rapid and extensive differentiation (1231 Austronesian languages developed in less than 5000 years, and 522 Bantu ethno-linguitic groups in Africa) [10]. The development of cities, states and empires both enhanced this process, but also, with growing economic and military differentiation, led to a reduction in diversity through extinction and absorption. The result is human land-scapes which are complex, with diverse communities existing in a patchwork of overlapping territories or cultural units.

15.4.3 Pattern of cultural evolution

What does this brief review of the history of the diversification of cultures show? It can certainly be argued that there is, in the human phenotype, an inherent capacity for communities to diversify and to mark this culturally. There is no reason to suppose that non-modern communities may not also have shared this capacity. However, we would be hard pressed to identify this in the earliest phase of *H. sapiens*. From very approximately 120 kyr ago, we see much greater evidence for the process of the diversification of cultures, first in Africa, and then elsewhere. The rate, however, is not constant, neither through time, nor in relation to climate, environment and demography. Furthermore, we would argue that this early process of diversification is intimately related to the diversification of biological populations, and so language and culture do map broadly on to genetic diversity, but that later dispersals and extinctions have blurred this correlation. However, as discussed above, the structure of this diversity is very different, and this allows us to consider in more detail the processes through which the evolution of the diversity of cultures takes place.

15.5 Determinants and outcomes of the diversity of cultures

Having briefly considered the history of patterns of cultural differentiation, two broad issues emerge: the first is the question of what the underlying causes of community differentiation based on cultural traits are, and the second, the consequences for human populational structure.

15.5.1 What leads to the diversification of culturally defined communities?

Determining causality in evolution, especially where humans are concerned, is never simple or uncontroversial, partly because one has to be precise about the nature of the causality proposed (proximate versus ultimate mechanisms, for example), and partly because of a reluctance among anthropologists to accept causal relationships of large issues such as culture. We are concerned here with two very precise elements. One of these is the way in which ecology and the environment more broadly affect the rate of community differentiation—in effect, closely related to Tinbergen's functional question; the second is that cultural diversification arises, almost inevitably, from the reproductive life history of communities. We do not address here, although inevitably assume, that there are underlying proximate cognitive mechanisms which interact with these broader demographic and ecological factors.

15.5.1.1 Resources, ecology and environment

The distribution of human cultures has been the subject of considerable recent research; a number of studies have shown that, both regionally and globally, the distribution is not random, but rather strongly influenced by environment. Birdsell [44] was among the first to show this for Australia; in the past decade or so, similar patterns have been shown for languages globally [12], within Africa [15], in North America [13], and for cultures globally [14] and in relation to political complexity [45]. In broad terms, the pattern found is one that replicates many of the species–area relationships for other mammals, with greater diversity in tropical regions and in areas with high productivity. Latitude, temperature and rainfall are all good predictors of the ethnographically observed diversity of cultures (Figure 15.3). A number of proximate mechanisms have been proposed— for example, that the formation of boundaries between groups is promoted by resource

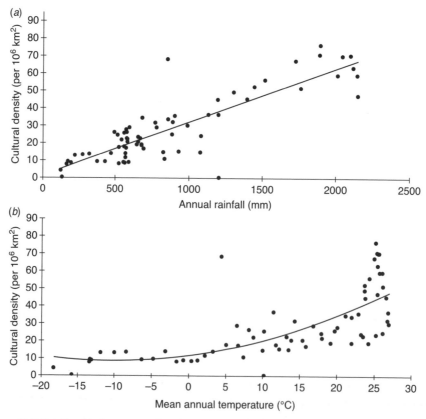

Figure 15.3 Relationship between cultural density (the number of populational cultures per unit area) and rainfall (top) and temperature (bottom). Modified from Collard & Foley [14].

reliability and reduced where variability and associated risk is such that it pays to maintain relationships across communities.

There are a number of ways of phrasing a resource-based hypothesis for the diversity of human cultures. The most parsimonious is to think in terms of the probability of boundary formation. Human cultures, as communities of individuals, form when boundaries begin to occur within such communities, and when, through both adaptive and neutral mechanisms, the traits of each community—from language to decoration to technology— begin to diverge. Where individuals and ideas can flow across such potential boundaries, then the probability of divergence is reduced. In essence, the formation of boundaries, and so different cultures, is an outcome of the context; this may be the natural context, where there are real geographical barriers, or demographic ones, where there may be competition. In either case, diversity of cultures is basically being driven by resource availability and its social and economic context [46]. The boundary formation, or lowering of interaction rates, results in a (rapid?) move towards fixation of some cultural traits in each daughter community. If we turn back to the evidence for the development of this pattern during the Pleistocene, we can note that the changing climatic and demographic conditions of the past 120 kyr are likely to have influenced the rate of boundary formation, and thus produced geographical patterns different from those seen today. The underlying ecological causality, however, would remain the same. This is a simple proposal which would hold for the longer phases of expansion of human populations and major dispersals; however, under some circumstances, there may be intense boundary formation as part of a process of local intensification, despite there being continued interaction [47].

15.5.1.2 The life history of a community: kinship and reproduction

If ecology and resource distribution shape the variation in rate and probability of boundary formation, other factors which make it probable that communities will diverge, even in the most unfavourable of conditions, need to be considered.

It was asserted at the outset that a culture was multiscalar, and can be anything from a nation to a local clan. Much recent theory has focused on how virtually any group may form a subculture or a cultural variant. However, for the largest proportion of human history and prehistory, and certainly for the context in which humans evolved, communities would have been local reproductive units, based on kinship, probably built around a descent group. We have argued elsewhere that this form of community is likely to be the fundamental unit of human sociality, and probably homologous with the chimpanzee community [4, 8]. When we talk, therefore, of the evolution of the diversity of cultures, what we are interested in is communities such as these, and how they develop their own identity.

If most aboriginal human communities were based broadly on descent groups, then descent traced from a single ancestor community would be tree-like through the generations. Over a relatively small number of generations, such a community would have more and more descendent reproductive units, less and less closely related to each other. Fissioning of these communities, and often physical movement into other areas, is an inevitable consequence of the life history of any descent groups and has been central to classic anthropology. Over time, descent and divergence will lead to the fissioning of communities and the formation of separate ones, with adaptive and demographic consequences [48]. As this process occurs, cultural norms and behaviours develop which hold these communities together, such that the outcome will be both cultural and biological diversity. This process—what we are referring to here as the life history of descent groups—underpins the diversity of cultures.

15.5.2 What are the outcomes of a tendency to form cultures?

Given three key elements of the process of cultural differentiation—(i) that human communities have a tendency to diverge as a product of how biological and social reproduction develops over several generations, (ii) that the species as a whole exploits this tendency through cognitive systems which mark differences between communities, and (iii) that the rate of such fissioning is ecologically and demographically sensitive—we can ask a further question, namely how these processes, operating together, have structured the diversity of culture on regional and global scales.

15.5.2.1 Phylogenetic relatedness in culture and biology

Perhaps the most significant outcome of the processes described here is that, for the most part, the more similar two cultures are, the greater their geographical proximity. There has been some debate about the role of ethnogenesis versus phylogenesis in the formation of new communities [49], but, as described above, the overall pattern, the broad regional social areas, would indicate that the formation of new cultures normally occurs through two communities fissioning adjacent to each other. Subsequent dispersals, extinction and other such processes, may well blur this pattern, but phylogenesis is the basis for the fact that linguistically and culturally it is possible to identify affinities across continents at least. As, by definition, genetic systems must descend and diverge in this way, and as reproduction will, even for autosomal genes, tend to follow this pattern, then there should always be a strong pattern of co-variation between biological and cultural relatedness at this broad level [50]. To that extent, the history of the diversity of human cultures will also be the history of human populations as they have formed, moved and died out, and there will be a relationship between biological and cultural phenotypes.

15.5.2.2 Regional diversity

If phylogenesis drives the diversificiation of communities, and with it biological and cultural differences, then patterns of regional diversity are the outcome. However, these are not the same across the globe. The frequency of cultural and populational differentiation relates to the probability of a boundary, natural or social, forming between two communities. Elsewhere we have shown this to be strongly influenced by two factors—the probability of isolation, and the variance in resource availability between habitats [46]. High levels of diversity of cultures are more likely to occur where there is a high probability of geographical isolation, and where there is a high gradient in resource availability between habitats, or both (Figure 15.4).

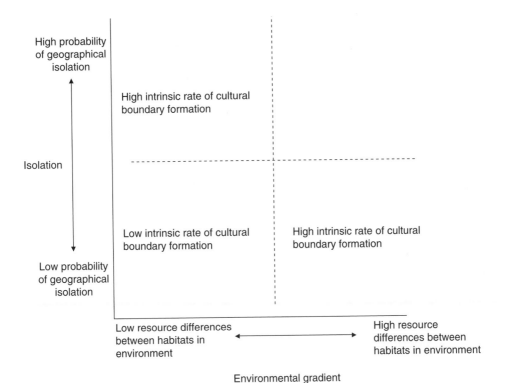

Figure 15.4 Relationship between environmental gradients and isolation in rates of group-boundary formation (i.e. formation of diversity in cultural units). Environments may have high or low probabilities of forcing populations to become isolated, and they may also have either large or small habitat differences in resource availability and richness. The former will determine the rate of boundary formation due to drift and isolation; the latter the rate of boundary formation due to competitive fissioning. Reproduced from Foley, R.A. 2004 The evolutionary ecology of linguistic diversity in human populations. In *Traces of ancestry: studies in honour of Colin Renfrew* (ed. M. Jones) with permission from McDonald Institute for Archaeological Research.

15.5.2.3 Extinction

In developing the ideas here about the diversity of cultures, emphasis has been on the inevitable proliferation of cultures as communities reproduce, grow and adapt. It might be expected that there would simply be a continuous and endless process of cultural expansion; however, the recurrent recognition that there are environmentally driven patterns across many regions suggests that actually there is at least a partial state of equilibrium in the diversity of cultures. For an equilibrium to occur then there must be a balancing process of 'extinction'. Archaeologists have done much to map the comings and goings of archaeological cultures, but much remains to be done to see how these relate to the processes described here; however, the expansion of western populations in the past 500 years, with the consequent loss of languages, cultures and populations, shows that it is a powerful force.

However, it is not the rate or power that concern us here, but the impact on the structure of diversity. According to the model of gradual phylogenesis by fissioning proposed above, across a landscape there should be a general pattern of continuity between communities, cultures and populations; however, should extinction occur at points along this continuity, and should there be subsequent expansions, then the overall structure will consist of a series of related communities, with a few outliers occurring. In practice, this is a situation seen very frequently throughout the world—non-Bantu in a sea of Bantu-speaking cultures in Africa; Papuan isolates in a continuum of Austronesian speakers; Basques among the Indo-Europeans, and so on. The extinction of groups, with their languages and their cultural traditions, structure regional diversity.

What is perhaps most significant, however, is that this is where mismatches between genetics and culture will begin to occur; cultures may well disappear, because they are complex, made up of multiple traits and require large groups to survive; genes, on the other hand, can slip through such events on an individual basis and as part of a survival strategy of the individuals themselves. Genetic lineages, therefore, are likely to be older and more persistent than cultural ones.

15.6 Conclusions

15.6.1 Individual strategies, group norms, biology and culture

The evidence summarized here suggests that the diversity of human cultures is a specific outcome of the way in which human populations have expanded and dispersed since the origin of the species. Lineage-based communities will fission over time, and the result will be divergence and the formation of boundaries. The rate of fissioning and boundary formation will be ecologically and environmentally sensitive, and local demography will play a major role. While this process is likely to occur in many species, humans bring to it a particular cognitive ability, namely a very high rate of socially transmitted behaviours across a whole realm of activities. The adaptive nature of many of these is one element, but both adaptive and neutral components will have consequential effects on diversification of populations. In particular, it is the capacity of socially transmitted behaviours to retain within group homogeneity—and between group differences—that underlies the links between biological and cultural differentiation.

Two points might seem to emerge from this discussion—one, that culture is simply tracking biological diversity, and the second, that while genes belong to individuals, cultures belong to groups. While there is an element of truth in both these points, it is the differences from them which are more interesting. First, while there is a regional co-variation between culture and biology, phylogenetically, ecologically and demographically, it is more probable that patterns of genetic diversification are following cultural packages, rather than the other way around. Culture, in this sense, constrains biological diversity. Language, beliefs and other customs strongly influence mate choice, and so the transmission of genes. Second, while it can clearly be demonstrated that genes belong to individuals, the converse—that cultural traits belong to groups—does not necessarily follow. In practice, each individual carries around a suite of cultural traits, usually in the context of many other individuals who will share them. However, an individual can deploy his or her suite of such traits in many different ways, including abandoning them completely in favour of others. As such, individuals can further their genetic interest by manipulating their cultural traits—hence confusing further the relationships between biology and culture. Individuals exploit 'cultures' for Darwinian purposes.

15.6.2 What advice should we give the culturally ambitious chimpanzee?

Finally, this chapter has focused entirely on humans, and more specifically modern humans, with no references to a broader hominin or hominoid comparative context. Given the presence of many aspects of 'culture' in pre-human hominins, and among some of the anthropoid apes, it might be asked why do these species not diversify at the same rates, and create the same rich patchwork of culturally diverse communities? The odd variation in chimpanzee handshakes does not compete with more than 6000 different ways of saying hello [51]. To answer that question would be to specify the conditions under which human evolution took on its unique trajectory.

On the basis of the argument developed in this chapter, there are three avenues to be explored. One could be that chimpanzees and early hominins simply lack the cognitive capacity to generate sufficient behavioural variation which can be transmitted, retained and observed. Without that cognitive skill, the persistence of cultural traits, their maintenance within lineages, might not be possible and so 'cultures' die out at a faster rate than they are generated.

A second possibility is that diversity of cultures requires certain environmental and ecological conditions. A high rate of boundary formation required a high gradient of environmental difference, and also a potential for isolation by distance. It is possible that chimpanzees and early hominins inhabit environments lacking the conditions necessary for such diversification, or, as Shennan has suggested, habitats which do not support sufficiently high population densities.

The third proposition lies in the way in which communities developed and fissioned. In practice, human communities will make contacts and alliances even after divergence, often through marriage, and often to maintain sufficient military strength. There is increasing evidence that chimpanzee males are unremittingly hostile to members of other communities [52], and this lack of ability to moderate conditionally inter-group encounters may, ironically, be what inhibits high levels of chimpanzee cultural diversity.

Whichever is the case, the similarities and the contrasts between humans and chimpanzees are essential for understanding the conditions under which humans have proved to be capable of generating diversity of community behaviours on an unprecedented rate.

Acknowledgements

The research reported here was partially supported through many research grants from NERC, UKIERI, Eurocores, the Isaac Newton Trust, the King's College Human Diversity Project, and the Leverhulme Trust. We thank Federica Crivellaro for discussions.

References

1 Whiten, A., Hinde, R. A., Laland, K. N. & Stringer, C. B. 2011 Culture evolves. *Phil. Trans. R. Soc. B* **366**, 938–948.

2 Bonner, J. T. 1980 *The evolution of culture in animals*. Princeton, NJ: Princeton University Press.

3 Richerson, P. & Boyd, R. 2005 *Not by genes alone: how culture transformed human evolution*. Chicago, IL: University of Chicago Press.

4 Foley, R. A. 2001 Evolutionary perspectives on the origins of human social institutions. *Proc. Br. Acad.* **110**, 171–195.

5 Collard, M., Buchanan, B., Morin, J. & Costopoulos, A. 2011 What drives the evolution of hunter–gatherer subsistence technology? A reanalysis of the risk hypothesis with data from the Pacific Northwest. *Phil. Trans. R. Soc. B* **366**, 1129–1138.

6 Currie, T. E. & Mace, R. 2011 Mode and tempo in the evolution of socio-political organization: reconciling 'Darwinian' and 'Spencerian' evolutionary approaches in anthropology. *Phil. Trans. R. Soc. B* **366**, 1108–1117.

7 Shennan, S. 2011 Descent with modification and the archaeological record. *Phil. Trans. R. Soc. B* **366**, 1070–1079.

8 Foley, R. A. & Lahr, M. M. 2001 The anthropological, demographic and ecological context of human evolutionary genetics. In *Genes, fossils and behavior: an integrated approach to modern human origins* (eds P. Donnelly & R. A. Foley), pp. 223–245. Omaha, NE: IOS Press.

9 Gagneux, P. *et al.* 1999 Mitochondrial sequences show diverse evolutionary histories of African hominoids. *Proc. Natl Acad. Sci. USA* **96**, 5077–5082.

10 Lewis, M. P. 2009 *Ethnologue: languages of the world*, 16th edn. Dallas, TX: SIL International.

11 Price, D. 1990 *Atlas of world cultures*. London, UK: Sage.

12 Nettle, D. 1998 Explaining global patterns of language diversity. *J. Anthropol. Archaeol.* **17**, 354–374.

13 Mace, R. & Pagel, M. 1995 A latitudinal gradient in the density of human languages in North America. *Proc. R. Soc. Lond. B* **261**, 117–121.

14 Collard, I. F. & Foley, R. A. 2002 Latitudinal patterns and environmental determinants of recent human cultural diversity: do humans follow biogeographical rules? *Evol. Ecol. Res.* **4**, 371–383.

15 Moore, J. L., Manne, L., Brooks, T., Burgess, N. D., Davies, R., Rahbek, C., Williams, P. & Balmford, A. 2002 The distribution of cultural and biological diversity in Africa. *Proc. R. Soc. Lond. B* **269**, 1645–1653.

16 Lewontin, R. C. 1972 The apportionment of human diversity. *Evol. Biol.* **6**, 391–398.

17 Edwards, A. 2003 Human genetic diversity: Lewontin's fallacy. *Bioessays* **25**, 798–801.

18 Rosenberg, N. A., Pritchard, J. K., Weber, J. L., Cann, H. M., Kidd, K. K., Zhivotovsky, L. A. & Feldman, M. W. 2002 Genetic structure of human populations. *Science* **298**, 2381–2385.

19 McElreath, R., Boyd, R. & Richerson, P. J. 2003 Shared norms and the evolution of ethnic markers. *Curr. Anthropol.* **44**, 122–129.

20 Gonder, M. K., Mortensen, H. M., Reed, F. A., de Sousa, A. & Tishkoff, S. A. 2007 Whole-mtDNA genome sequence analysis of ancient African lineages. *Mol. Biol. Evol.* **24**, 757–768.

21 Underhill, P. & Kivisild, T. 2007 Use of Y chromosome and mitochondrial DNA population structure in tracing human migrations. *Annu. Rev. Genet.* **41**, 539–564.

22 Atkinson, Q. D., Gray, R. D. & Drummond, A. J. 2008 mtDNA variation predicts population size in humans and reveals a major southern Asian chapter in human prehistory. *Mol. Biol. Evol.* **25**, 447–468.

23 Lahr, M. M. & Foley, R. A. 2001 Genes, fossils and behavior: when and where do they fit? In *Genes, fossils and behavior: an integrated approach to modern human origins* (eds P. Donnelly & R. A. Foley), pp. 13–48. Omaha, NE: IOS Press.

24 McDougall, I., Brown, F. & Fleagle, J. 2005 Stratigraphic placement and age of modern humans from Kibish, Ethiopia. *Nature* **433**, 733–736.

25 White, T. D., Asfaw, B., DeGusta, D., Gilbert, H., Richards, G. D., Suwa, G. & Howell, F. C. 2003 Pleistocene *Homo sapiens* from Middle Awash, Ethiopia. *Nature* **423**, 742–747.

26 Klein, R. G. 2009 *The human career*. Chicago, IL: Chicago University Press.

27 Foley, R. A. & Lahr, M. M. 1997 Mode 3 technologies and the evolution of modern humans. *Cambr. Archaeol. J.* **7**, 3–36.

28 Barham, L. S. 1998 Possible early pigment use in South-Central Africa. *Curr. Anthropol.* **39**, 703–710.

29 Whiten, A., Goodall, J., McGrew, W. C., Nishida, T., Reynolds, V., Sugiyama, Y., Tutin, C. E. G., Wrangham, R. W. & Boesch, C. 1999 Cultures in chimpanzees. *Nature* **399**, 682–685.

30 d'Errico, F., Henshilwood, C., Vanhaeren, M. & Karen van Niekerk, K. 2005 *Nassarius kraussianus* shell beads from Blombos Cave: evidence for symbolic behaviour in the Middle Stone Age. *J. Hum. Evol.* **48**, 3–24.

31 Bouzouggar, A. *et al.* 2007 82,000-Year-old shell beads from North Africa and implications for the origins of modern human behavior. *Proc. Natl Acad. Sci. USA* **104**, 9964–9969.

32 d'Errico, F., Vanhaeren, M., Barton, N., Bouzouggar, A., Mienis, H., Richter, D., Hublin, J.-J., McPherron, S. P. & Lozouet, P. 2009 Additional evidence on the use of personal ornaments in the Middle Paleolithic of North Africa. *Proc. Natl Acad. Sci. USA* **106**, 16051–16056.

33 Henshilwood, C. S., d'Errico, F. & Watts, I. 2009 Engraved ochres from the Middle Stone Age levels at Blombos Cave, South Africa. *J. Hum. Evol.* **57**, 27–47.

34 Henshilwood, C. S. *et al.* 2002 Emergence of modern human behavior: Middle Stone Age engravings from South Africa. *Science* **295**, 1278–1280.

35 Jacobs, Z., Roberts, R. G., Galbraith, R. F., Deacon, H. J., Grün, R., Mackay, A., Mitchell, P., Vogelsang, R. & Wadley, L. 2008 Ages for the Middle Stone Age of southern Africa: implications for human behavior and dispersal. *Science* **322**, 733–735.

36 O'Connell, J. F. & Allen, J. 2004 Dating the colonization of Sahul (Pleistocene Australia–New Guinea): a review of recent research. *J. Archaeol. Sci.* **31**, 835–853.

37 Vanhaeren, M. & d'Errico, F. 2006 Aurignacian ethnolinguistic geography of Europe revealed by personal ornaments. *J. Archaeol. Sci.* **33**, 1105–1128.

38 Texier, P. J. *et al.* 2010 A Howiesons Poort tradition of engraving ostrich eggshell containers dated to 60,000 years ago at Diepkloof Rock Shelter, South Africa. *Proc. Natl Acad. Sci. USA* **107**, 6180–6185.

39 Kuzmin, Y. V., Burr, G. S., Jull, A. J. T. & Sulerzhitsky, L. D. 2004 AMS C-14 age of the Upper Palaeolithic skeletons from Sungir site, Central Russian Plain. *Nucl. Instrum. Meth. B* **223-224**, 731–734.

40 Bouquet-Appel, J.-P. & Demars, P. Y. 2000 Population kinetics in the Upper Palaeolithic in Western Europe. *J. Archaeol. Sci.* **27**, 551–570.

41 Powell, A., Shennan, S. & Thomas, M. G. 2009 Late Pleistocene demography and the appearance of modern human behavior. *Science* **324**, 1298–1301.

42 Veth, P. M. 1993 *Islands in the interior*. Ann Arbor, MI: International Monographs in Prehistory.

43 Bellwood, P. & Renfrew, A. C. 2003 *Examining the farming/language dispersal hypothesis*. Cambridge, UK: McDonald Institute for Archaeological Research.

44 Birdsell, J. B. 1953 Some environmental and cultural factors influencing the structure of Australian aboriginal populations. *Am. Nat.* **87**, 171–207.

45 Currie, T. E. & Mace, R. 2009 Political complexity predicts the spread of ethnolinguistic groups. *Proc. Natl Acad. Sci. USA* **106**, 7339–7344.

46 Foley, R. A. 2004 The evolutionary ecology of linguistic diversity in human populations. In *Traces of ancestry: studies in honour of Colin Renfrew* (ed. M. Jones). Cambridge, UK: McDonald Institute for Archaeological Research.

47 Hodder, I. 1977 The distribution of material culture items in the Baringo Distrct, Western Kenya. *Man* **12**, 239–269.

48 Sahlins, M. 1961 The segmentary lineage: an organization of predatory expansion. *Am. Anthropol.* **63**, 322–345.

49 Collard, M., Shennan, S. J. & Tehrani, J. J. 2006 Branching, blending, and the evolution of cultural similarities and differences among human populations. *Evol. Hum. Behav.* **27**, 169–184.

50 Cavalli-Sforza, L. L., Piazza, A., Menozzi, P. & Mountain, J. 1988 Reconstruction of human evolution: bringing together genetic, archaeological and linguistic data. *Proc. Natl Acad. Sci. USA* **85**, 6002–6006.

51 Whiten, A. 2011 The scope of culture in chimpanzees, humans and ancestral apes. *Phil. Trans. R. Soc. B* **366**, 997–1007.

52 Mitani, J., Watts, D. & Amsler, S. 2010 Lethal intergroup aggression leads to territorial expansion in wild chimpanzees. *Curr. Biol.* **20**, R507–R508.

Chapter 16

Language Evolution and Human History: What a Difference a Date Makes

Russell D. Gray, Quentin D. Atkinson
and Simon J. Greenhill

Historical inference is at its most powerful when independent lines of evidence can be integrated into a coherent account. Dating linguistic and cultural lineages can potentially play a vital role in the integration of evidence from linguistics, anthropology, archaeology and genetics. Unfortunately, although the comparative method in historical linguistics can provide a relative chronology, it cannot provide absolute date estimates and an alternative approach, called glottochronology, is fundamentally flawed. In this chapter we outline how computational phylogenetic methods can reliably estimate language divergence dates and thus help resolve long-standing debates about human prehistory ranging from the origin of the Indo-European language family to the peopling of the Pacific.

Keywords: linguistics; glottochronology; Indo-European; Austronesian; cultural evolution

16.1 Introduction

Historical inference is hard. Trying to work out what happened 600 years ago is difficult enough. Trying to make inferences about events 6000 years ago may seem close to impossible. As W. S. Holt observed, the study of human history is 'a damn dim candle over a damn dark abyss'. And yet evolutionary biologists routinely make inferences about events millions of years in the past. Our ability to do this was revolutionized by Zuckerkandl & Pauling's [1] insight that molecules are 'documents of evolutionary history'. Molecular sequences have inscribed in their structure a record of their past. Similarities generally reflect common ancestry. Today, computational phylogenetic methods are routinely used to make inferences about evolutionary relationships and processes from these sequences. These inferences are more powerful when independent lines of evidence, such as information from studies of morphology, geology and palaeontology, are brought to bear on a common problem.

Languages, like genes, are also 'documents of history'. A vast amount of information about our past is inscribed in the content and structure of the approximately 7000 languages that are spoken today [2]. Historical linguists have developed a careful set of procedures termed the 'comparative method' to infer ancestral states and construct language family trees [3, 4]. Ideally, as Kirch & Green [5] and Renfrew [6] have argued, independent evidence from anthropology, archaeology and human genetics are used to 'triangulate' inferences about human prehistory and cultural evolution. From anthropology comes an understanding of social organization, from archaeology comes an absolute chronology of changes in material culture, and from genetic studies we get information about the sequence of population movements and the extent of admixture. Traditionally, historical linguistics has contributed inferences about ancestral vocabulary and a relative cultural chronology to this synthesis.

While this 'new synthesis' [7] is a worthy aim, it is often very difficult to link the different lines of evidence together. Archaeological remains do not speak. Genes and languages can have different histories or appear spuriously congruent. The one thing that is critically important to successfully triangulating the different lines of evidence together is timing. If archaeological, genetic and linguistic lines of evidence show similar absolute dates for a common sequence of events, then our confidence that a common process is involved would be hugely increased, and the 'damn dark abyss' of human history greatly illuminated. Sadly, the absence of appropriate calibration points and systematic violations of the molecular clock mean that there are large sources of error associated with most genetic dates for human population history [8]. Sadder still, although the comparative method in linguistics can provide a relative chronology, it cannot provide absolute date estimates. In the words of April MacMahon & Rob MacMahon [9] 'linguists don't do dates'. We are not so pessimistic. In what follows we will outline why dating linguistic lineages is a difficult, but not impossible, task.

16.2 Dating difficulties

A quick glance at an Old English text, such as the epic poem *Beowulf*, should be enough to convince anyone of two facts. Languages evolve and they evolve rapidly. New words arise and others are replaced. Sounds change, grammar morphs and speech communities split into dialects and then distinct languages. Given this linguistic divergence over time, one plausible intuition is that it might be possible to use some measure of this divergence to estimate the age of linguistic lineages in much the same way that biologists use the divergence of molecular sequences to date biological lineages. 'Glottochronology' attempts to do just that. In the early 1950s, a full decade before Zuckerkandl & Pauling introduced the idea of a molecular clock to biology, Swadesh [10, 11] developed an approach to historical linguistics termed lexicostatistics and its derivative 'glottochronology'. This approach used lexical data to determine language relationships and to estimate absolute divergence times. Lexicostatistical methods infer language trees on the basis of the percentage of shared cognates between languages—the more similar the languages, the more closely they are related. Cognates are words in different languages that have a common ancestor. In biological terminology they are homologous. Words are judged to be cognate if they have a pattern of systematic sound correspondences and similar meanings. Glottochronology is an extension of lexicostatistics that estimates language divergence times under the assumption of a 'glottoclock', or constant rate of language change. The following formulae can be used to relate language similarity to time along an exponential decay curve:

$$t = \frac{\log C}{2 \log r},$$

where t is time depth in millennia, C is the percentage of cognates shared and r is the 'universal' constant or rate of retention (the expected proportion of cognates remaining after 1000 years of separation). Usually analyses are restricted to the Swadesh word list—a collection of 100–200 basic meanings that are thought to be relatively culturally universal, stable and resistant to borrowing. These include kinship terms (e.g. mother, father), terms for body parts (e.g. hand, mouth, hair), numerals and basic verbs (e.g. to drink, to sleep, to burn). For the Swadesh 200-word list, the retention rate (r) was estimated from cases where the divergence date between languages was known from historical records. This rate was found to be approximately 81 per cent.

Unfortunately, this apparently simple and elegant solution to the important problem of dating linguistic lineages encountered some major obstacles [12, 13], and thus most historical linguists now view glottochronological calculations with considerable scepticism. The most fundamental obstacle encountered by glottochronology is the fact that languages, just like genes, often do not evolve at a constant rate. In their classic critique of glottochronology, Bergsland & Vogt [12] compared present-day languages with their archaic forms. They found considerable evidence of rate variation between languages. For example, Icelandic and Norwegian were compared with their common ancestor, Old Norse, spoken roughly 1000 years ago. Norwegian has retained 81 per cent of the vocabulary of Old Norse, correctly suggesting an age of approximately 1000 years. However, Icelandic has retained over 95 per cent of the Old Norse vocabulary, falsely suggesting that Icelandic split from Old Norse less than 200 years ago. This is not an isolated example. In a survey of Malayo-Polynesian languages, Blust [13] documented variations in the retention of basic vocabulary driven by factors such as language contact and large changes in population size that ranged from 5 to 50 per cent in the approximately 4000 years from Proto Malayo-Polynesian to the present. Blust argued that these huge differences in retention rates inevitably distorted both the trees obtained by lexicostatistics and the glottochronological dates.

It is ironic that over the past half-century, computational methods in historical linguistics have fallen out of favour while in evolutionary biology computational methods have blossomed. Rather than giving up and saying, 'we don't do dates', computational biologists have developed methods that can accurately estimate phylogenetic trees and divergence dates even when there is considerable lineage-specific rate heterogeneity. Evolutionary biologists today typically use likelihood and Bayesian methods to explicitly model all the substitution events, instead of building trees from pairwise distance matrices [14, 15]. The development of these more powerful computational methods has been facilitated by both a spectacular increase in the availability of molecular sequences and dramatic increases in computational power in the past 20 years [16]. The use of all the sequence information, and more complex and realistic models of the substitution process, mean that likelihood and Bayesian methods outperform the simple clustering methods, especially when rates of molecular change are not constant [17]. In addition to developing methods to build more accurate trees, evolutionary biologists have recently developed methods to obtain more accurate date estimates, even when there are departures from the assumption of a strict molecular clock.

One popular approach pioneered by Sanderson [18, 19] involves two steps. First, a set of phylogenetic trees and their associated branch lengths are estimated. In Bayesian phylogenetic analyses of molecular evolution, the branch lengths are proportional to the number of substitutions along a branch given the data, the substitution model and the priors. The second step involves converting the relative branch lengths into time. Calibration points are required to do this. These are places where nodes (branching points) on the trees can be constrained to a known date range. These known node ages are then combined with the branch-length information to estimate rates of evolution across each tree. A penalized-likelihood model is used to allow rates to vary across the tree while incorporating a 'roughness penalty'. The more the rates vary from branch-to-branch, the greater the cost (see [18, 19] for more detail). The algorithm allows an optimal value of the roughness penalty to be selected. In this way, the combination of calibrations, branch-length estimates and the rate-smoothing algorithm enables dates to be estimated without assuming a strict clock. An alternative 'relaxed phylogenetics' approach, in which the tree and the dates are simultaneously estimated, has recently been developed by Drummond *et al.* [20]. In 'relaxed phylogenetics', the assumption of a strict clock can be eased by modelling the rate variation using lognormal or exponential distributions (see [20] for more detail). In the sections that follow, we will explore how these computational phylogenetic methods can be used to illuminate the linguistic and cultural history of people both in Europe and in the Pacific.

16.3 The origin of the Indo-European languages

The origin of the Indo-European languages has recently been described as 'one of the most intensively studied, yet still most recalcitrant problems of historical linguistics' [21, p. 601]. Despite over 200 years of scrutiny, scholars have been unable to locate the origin of Indo-European definitively in time or place. Theories have been put forward advocating ages ranging from 4000 to 23 000 years, with hypothesized homelands including Central Europe, the Balkans and even India. Mallory [22] acknowledges 14 distinct homeland hypotheses since 1960 alone. He rather colourfully remarks that, 'the quest for the origins of the Indo-Europeans has all the fascination of an electric light in the open air on a summer night: it tends to attract every species of scholar or would-be savant who can take pen to hand' [22, p. 143].

Of all the diverse theories about the origin of Indo-Europeans there are currently two that receive the most attention. The first, put forward by Gimbutas [23, 24] on the basis of linguistic and archaeological evidence, links Proto-Indo-European (the hypothesized ancestral Indo-European tongue) with the Kurgan culture of southern Russia and the Ukraine. The Kurgans were a group of semi-nomadic, pastoralist, warrior-horsemen who expanded from their homeland in the Pontic steppes during the fifth and sixth millennia BP, conquering Danubian Europe, Central Asia and India, and later the Balkans and Anatolia. This expansion is thought to roughly match the accepted ancestral range of Indo-European [25]. As well as the apparent geographical congruence between Kurgan and Indo-European territories, there is linguistic evidence for an association between the two cultures. Words for supposed Kurgan technological innovations are consistent across widely divergent Indo-European sub-families. These include terms for 'wheel' (*rotho-, *k^W(e)k^Wl-o-), 'axle' (*aks-lo-), 'yoke' (*jug-o-), 'horse' (*ekwo-) and 'to go, transport in a vehicle' (*wegh- [14, 15]): it is argued that these words and associated technologies must have been present in the Proto-Indo-European culture and that they were likely to have been Kurgan in origin. Hence, the argument goes, the Indo-European language family is no older than 5000–6000 BP. Mallory [22] argues for a similar time and place of Indo-European origin—a region around the Black Sea about 5000–6000 BP (although he and many linguists are more cautious and refrain from identifying Proto-Indo-European with a specific culture such as the Kurgans).

The second theory, proposed by the archaeologist Renfrew [26], holds that Indo-European languages spread, not with marauding horsemen, but with the expansion of agriculture from Anatolia between 8000 and 9500 years ago. Radiocarbon analysis of the earliest Neolithic sites across Europe provides a fairly detailed chronology of agricultural dispersal. This archaeological evidence indicates that agriculture spread from Anatolia, arriving in Greece at some time during the ninth millennium BP and reaching as far as the British Isles by 5500 BP [27]. Renfrew maintains that the linguistic argument for the Kurgan theory is based only on limited evidence for a few enigmatic Proto-Indo-European word forms. He points out that parallel semantic shifts or widespread borrowing can produce similar word forms across different languages without requiring that an ancestral term was present in the proto-language. Renfrew also challenges the idea that Kurgan social structure and technology was sufficiently advanced to allow them to conquer whole continents in a time when even small cities did not exist. Far more credible, he argues, is that Proto-Indo-European spread with the spread of agriculture.

The debate about Indo-European origins thus centres on archaeological evidence for two population expansions, both implying very different timescales—the Kurgan theory with a date of 5000–6000 BP, and the Anatolian theory with a date of 8000–9500 BP. One way of potentially resolving the debate is to look outside the archaeological record for independent evidence, which allows us to test between these two time depths. Does linguistics hold the key? Well, not if linguists do not do dates. However, if we could reliably date the origin of the Indo-European languages, then it would make a huge difference to this 200-year old debate.

We set about this rather daunting task by building on what Darwin dubbed the 'curious parallels' between biological and linguistic evolution (see [28] for an analysis of the history of these parallels). If languages, like biological species, are also 'documents of history', then perhaps they could be analysed using the same computational evolutionary methods. Maybe the solutions biologists have found to violations of the molecular clock could be used to overcome problems with glottochronology. It requires a large amount of data to estimate tree topology and branch lengths accurately. Our data were taken from the Dyen *et al.* [29] Indo-European lexical database, which contains expert cognacy judgements for 200 Swadesh list terms in 95 languages. Dyen *et al.* [29] identified 11 languages as less reliable and hence they were not included in the analysis presented here. We added three extinct languages (Hittite, Tocharian A and Tocharian B) to the database in an attempt to improve the resolution of basal relationships in the inferred phylogeny. For each meaning in the database, languages were grouped into cognate sets. By restricting analyses to basic vocabulary, such as the Swadesh word list, the influence of borrowing can be minimized. For example, although English is a Germanic language, it has borrowed around 60 per cent of its total lexicon from French and Latin. However, only about 6 per cent of English entries in the Swadesh 200-word list are clear Romance language borrowings [30]. Known borrowings were not coded as cognate in the Dyen *et al.* database. The cognate sets were binary-coded—that is in a matrix a column was set up for each cognate set in which the presence of a cognate for a language was denoted with a '1' and an absence with a '0'. This produced a matrix of 2449 cognate sets for 87 languages. This matrix was analysed in the Bayesian phylogenetics package MRBAYES [31] using a simple model that assumed equal rates of cognate gains and losses to produce a sample of trees from the posterior probability distribution of the trees (the set of trees found in the Markov chain Monte Carlo runs post 'burn in' given the data, model of cognate evolution and priors on variables such as the parameters of the model and branch lengths). In order to infer divergence dates, we needed to calibrate the rates of evolution by constraining the age of nodes on each tree in accordance with historically attested dates. For example, the Romance languages probably began to diverge prior to the fall of the Roman Empire. The last Roman troops were withdrawn south of the Danube in AD 270. Thus, we constrained the age of the node corresponding to the most recent common ancestor of the Romance languages to AD 150–300. We constrained the age of 14 nodes on the trees. The penalized rate-smoothing algorithm was then used to covert the set of trees into dated 'chronotrees' (see [32] for more details on the methods and calibrations used).

Our initial analyses provided strong support for the time-depth predictions of Anatolian hypothesis. The date estimates for the age of Proto Indo-European centred around 8700 BP (Figure 16.1). None of our sample of chronotrees was in the 5000–6000 years BP age range predicted by the Kurgan hypothesis. A key part of any Bayesian phylogenetic analysis is an assessment of the robustness of the inferences. We did our best to try and 'break' the initial result. We examined the impact of altering the branch length priors in our analysis, of throwing out cognates Dyen *et al.* had dubbed 'dubious', of removing some calibrations, of trimming the data to the most stable items and rerooting

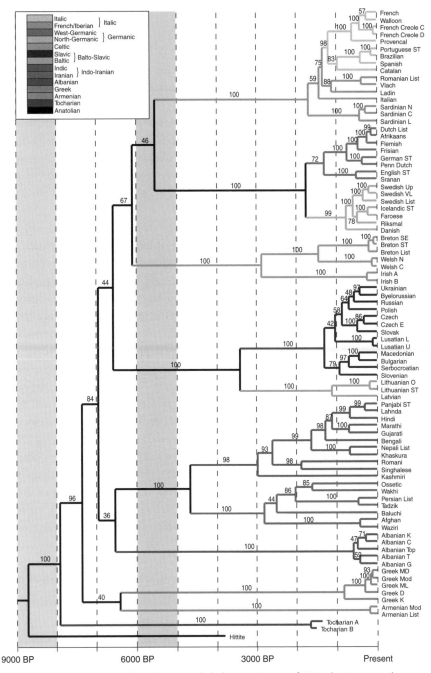

Figure 16.1 (Also see Colour Plate 1) A dated phylogenetic tree of 87 Indo-European languages. The tree is a consensus tree derived from the posterior samples of trees in the Bayesian analyses reported by Gray & Atkinson [32]. The values on the branches are the posterior probability of that clade. The root age of the tree is in the age range predicted by the Anatolian hypothesis. This figure also shows an interesting point that we had noted, but not emphasized, in our initial paper—while the root of the tree goes back around 8700 years, much of the diversification of the major Indo-European subgroups happened around 6000–7000 BP. This means that both the Anatolian and the Kurgan hypotheses could be simultaneously true. There was an initial movement out of Anatolia 8700 years ago and then a major radiation 6000–7000 years ago from southern Russia and the Ukraine. It also means that the intuition shared by many linguists that the Indo-European language family is about 6000 years old could be correct for the vast majority of Indo-European languages, just not the deeper subgroups.

the trees. None of these changes substantially altered our date estimates of the age of Proto Indo-European. If anything, they often tended to make the distribution older, not younger [32, 33].

The response to our paper was rather mixed. While some linguists were positive, many simply failed to understand that the methods we had used were substantially different from traditional glottochronology [34]. A small number of critics raised concerns about the data we had used, the binary coding of the cognate sets, the simple model of cognate evolution and the impact of undetected borrowing. Let us deal with each of these potentially valid concerns in turn.

First, although the cognate coding in the Dyen *et al.* dataset was conducted by experienced linguists, it may well contain some errors [35]. While these errors are likely to be a relatively small proportion of the total data, it is possible that they might have biased our date estimates. It is also possible that the simple stochastic model of cognate evolution we used led to inaccurate results because the model assumed that the rates of cognate gain and loss were equal—an assumption that is not realistic. It is rare for very similar words with similar meanings to be independently invented [36]. A more realistic model would thus allow cognates to be gained only once but lost multiple times. This mirrors the principle in evolution biology known as Dollo's Law, which suggests that once complex structures are lost they are unlikely to be evolved again. While simple models do not necessarily produce inaccurate results [33], in Bayesian analyses it is important to assess the robustness of the conclusions to any model misspecification. For this reason, Geoff Nicholls and R.G. developed a stochastic 'Dollo' model of cognate evolution [37]. We used this model to analyse an independent dataset [38], predominantly comprising ancient Indo-European languages. These analyses of a separate dataset with an entirely different model produced almost identical results to our initial analyses of the Dyen data [37, 39]. Not content with this proof of the robustness of our analyses, we recently re-analysed the Ringe *et al.* data using the lognormal relaxed clock and the stochastic Dollo model implemented in the package BEAST [40]. Yet again the date estimates for Proto Indo-European fell into the age range predicted by the Anatolian hypothesis (Figure 16.2). Re-analysing the Dyen *et al.* data with the lognormal relaxed clock and the stochastic Dollo model also produced results that are highly congruent with the initial results of Gray & Atkinson.

If neither problems with the data nor the model of cognate evolution appear to have biased our results, what about the binary coding of the cognate sets? Evans *et al.* [41] claim that our coding is 'patently inappropriate' because it assumes independence between the cognate sets. Our sets are clearly not independent because one form will often replace another within a meaning class (although some polymorphism does occur). On the surface this is a plausible argument. However, Evans *et al.* provide no argument for why the lack of independence will bias the time- depth estimates to be too old (rather than merely underestimating the variance). On the contrary, we have simulated totally dependent cognate evolution and shown that it does not bias the date estimates [39]. Others have found empirically that binary and multi-state codings of the same lexical data produce virtually identical results [42]. Furthermore, Pagel & Mead [43] demonstrated

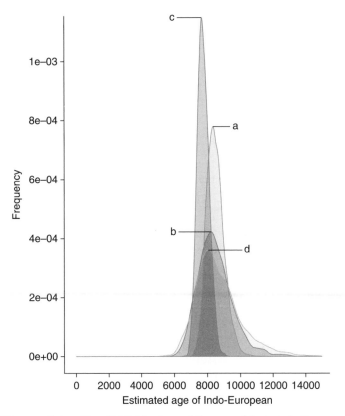

Figure 16.2 (Also see Colour Plate 2) Distributions of the age of Proto Indo-European estimated from the data of Ringe *et al.* [38]. Four different analyses were conducted using the program BEAST. Two analyses assumed equal rates of cognate gain and loss—one with a strict clock (light green) (a) and one with a lognormal relaxed clock (orange) (b). The other two analyses assumed that cognates could only be gained once but lost multiple times (stochastic Dollo). Again one implemented a strict clock (purple) (c) and one used a lognormal relaxed clock (light blue) (d). The date estimates obtained in all four analyses were consistent with the Anatolian hypothesis. *Note: this caption refers to the version of the figure in the Colour Plate Section.*

that, at least when the number of states is constant, binary and multi-state-coded data produce trees that differ only in length by a constant proportionality. In other words, the binary and multi-state trees are just scaled versions of one another and therefore the date estimates will not be biased. This result is also likely to hold when the number of states varies (M. Pagel 2010, personal communication).

Removing all the borrowed cognates from a dataset can be difficult. While irregular sound correspondences might make some easy to identify, others may be difficult to detect. Garrett [44] argues that borrowing of lexical terms, or advergence, within the major Indo-European subgroups could have distorted our results. To assess this possibility, we examined the impact of different borrowing scenarios by simulating cognate evolution [45]. The results showed that tree topologies constructed with Bayesian phylogenetic methods were robust to realistic levels of borrowing in basic

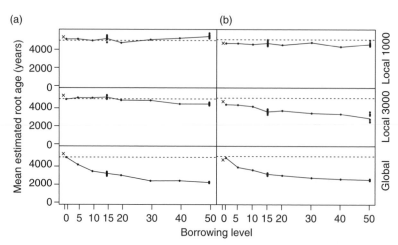

Figure 16.3 Mean reconstructed root time for each simulation under three borrowing scenarios: (i) local borrowing within 1000 years, (ii) local borrowing within 3000 years, and (iii) global borrowing. Two different tree topologies were used in the simulations: (a) tree 1 and (b) tree 2. The dotted line marks the true root age and the cross marks the root age under the no borrowing scenario.

vocabulary (0–15%). Inferences about divergence dates were slightly less robust and showed a tendency to *underestimate* dates (Figure 16.3). The effect is pronounced only when there is global rather than local borrowing on the tree. This is the least likely scenario we simulated and suggests that if our estimates for the age of Indo-European are biased by undetected borrowing at all, they are likely to be too young, rather than too old.

While all these re-analyses and simulation studies demonstrate the reliability of our estimates for the age of Indo-European, perhaps the most compelling refutation of our critics' arguments comes from the model validation analyses we recently conducted. Nicholls & Gray [46] sequentially removed calibration points from some analyses conducted using the stochastic Dollo model implemented in the program TRAITLAB. We then re-ran the analysis and examined the date estimates of these nodes. If model misspecification meant that our age estimates were systematically too old, then the estimated ages should be systematically older than the known ages of the nodes in the trees that we removed the calibrations from. This was not the case. Overwhelmingly, the estimates were congruent with the known node ages.

16.4 **The Austronesian expansion**

The Austronesian settlement of the vast Pacific Ocean has been a topic of enduring fascination. It is the greatest human migrations in terms of the distance covered and the most recent. There are two major hypotheses for the Austronesian settlement of the Pacific. The first hypothesis is the 'pulse–pause' scenario [5, 47–49]. This scenario argues that the ancestral Austronesian society developed in Taiwan around 5500 years ago. Around 4000–4500 years ago, there was a rapid expansion pulse across the Bashii channel into the Philippines, into Island Southeast Asia, along the coast of New Guinea, reaching Near Oceania by around 3000–3300 years ago [50]. As the Austronesians travelled this route, they integrated with the existing populations in the area (particularly in New Guinea), and innovated new technologies. After reaching Western Polynesia (Fiji, Tonga and Samoa) approximately 3000 years ago, the Austronesian expansion paused for around 1000–1500 years, before a second rapid expansion pulse spread Polynesian languages as far afield as New Zealand, Hawaii and Rapanui.

The second hypothesis of Pacific settlement—the 'slow boat' scenario—argues for a much older origin in Island Southeast Asia [51–53]. According to this scenario, date estimates from mitochondrial DNA lineages suggest that Austronesian society developed around 13 000–17 000 years ago in an extensive network of sociocultural exchange in the Wallacean region around Sulawesi and the Moluccas. Proponents of this scenario propose that the submerging of the Sunda shelf at the end of the last ice-age triggered the Austronesian expansion [53]. This 'flood' led to a two-pronged movement of people, north into the Philippines and Taiwan, and east into the Pacific. Significantly, they argue that this movement of people was paralleled by the spread of Austronesian languages (i.e. Austronesian genes and languages have a common history). 'The Austronesian languages originated within island Southeast Asia during the Pleistocene era and spread through Melanesia and into the remote Pacific within the past 6000 years' [54, p. 1236].

These two scenarios of Pacific settlement make quite different predictions about the origin, age and sequence of the Austronesian expansion. The pulse–pause model predicts that a phylogenetic tree of Austronesian languages should be rooted in Taiwan and show a chained topology that mirrors the generally eastwards spread of the languages. According to this model, the Austronesian language family should be about 5500 years old. Most boldly, the model predicts that there should be a long pause between the Taiwanese languages and the rest of Austronesian, followed by a rapid diversification pulse and then another long pause in Polynesia. In contrast, the slow boat model predicts that any language family tree should be rooted in the Wallacean region, be between 13 000 and 17 000 years old and have a two-pronged topology, with one branch going north to the Philippines and Taiwan and the other eastwards along the New Guinea coast out into Oceania.

Clearly, a robustly dated language phylogeny would be an ideal way to test between the pulse–pause and slow boat models of Austronesian expansion. However, the construction of an accurate, dated language phylogeny for the Austronesian languages provides numerous challenges for any would be language phylogenticist. First, the rapid expansion of the Austronesian family means that it is likely to be difficult to resolve the fine branching structure of the Austronesian language tree as there is little time for the internal branches on the tree to develop numerous shared innovations [55]. Second, as these languages moved across the Pacific, they encountered new environments and the consequent need for new terminology may have increased the rates of language replacement.

This acceleration in rates is likely to be exacerbated by the effects of language contact—particularly within Near Oceania [56]. Additionally, many Austronesian languages have small speech communities, which are also likely to speed up the rates of language evolution [57]. The effects of these factors can be seen in the 10-fold variation in cognate retention rates in Austronesian languages [13].

Successful phylogenetic analyses require data with sufficient historical information to resolve the aspects of the phylogeny we are interested in. Over the past 7 years we have compiled a large web-accessible database of cognate-coded basic vocabulary for over 700 Austronesian languages [16]. This database was initially based on 230 language word lists we obtained from Bob Blust, but by placing it on the web we have been able to grow and refine the database and cognate coding with the generous assistance of linguists around the globe. In the 400-language dataset reported in Gray *et al.* [49], the 210 items of basic vocabulary produced a matrix of 34 440 binary-coded cognate sets.

The first prediction we tested with the Bayesian phylogenetic analyses of this data concerned the origin and sequence of Austronesian expansion. Under the pulse–pause scenario, the Austronesians originated in Taiwan and had a single-chained expansion down through the Philippines, through Wallacea, along New Guinea into Near Oceania and Polynesia. In contrast, the slow boat scenario posits a two-pronged expansion from a Wallacean origin. Our set of trees placed the root of trees in Taiwan, and followed it with the sequence predicted by the pulse–pause scenario (Figure 16.4).

The second key prediction of the two Pacific settlement scenarios concerned the age of the expansion. To test this prediction, we estimated the age at the root of our trees. To begin with, we calibrated 10 nodes on the trees with archaeological date estimates and known settlement times. For example, speakers of the Chamic language sub-group were described in Chinese records around 1800 years ago and probably entered Vietnam around 2600 years ago [58]. We can therefore calibrate the appearance of the Chamic node on our tree to between 2000 and 3000 years ago. A second calibration, based on archaeological evidence, constrains the age of the hypothesized ancestral language spoken by all the languages of Near Oceania, Proto Oceanic. The speakers of Proto Oceanic arrived in Oceania around 3000–3300 years ago and brought with them distinctively Austronesian societal organization and cultural artefacts. These artefacts have been identified and dated archaeologically, and include the Lapita adze/axe kits, housing types, fishing equipment (such as the one-piece rotating fishhooks, and one-piece trolling lure), as well as common food plants and domesticated animals from Southeast Asia.

To estimate the age of the Austronesian family without assuming a strict glottoclock, we used the penalized likelihood approach outlined above. The results unequivocally supported the younger age of the pulse–pause scenario, with an origin of the Austronesian family around 5200 years ago (Figure 16.5a). Like the Indo-European analyses, the results were robust to assumptions about specific calibration points. For example, when we removed all the calibration points, apart from the Proto Oceanic constraint and the three ancient languages [59], the estimated age of Proto Austronesian was virtually identical (Figure 16.5b).

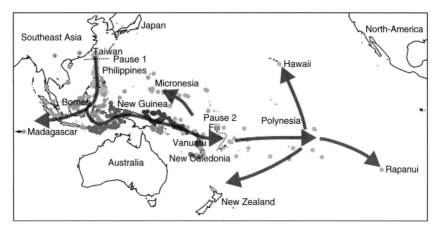

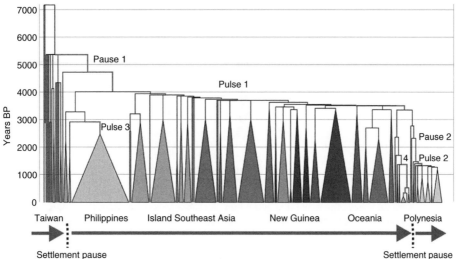

Figure 16.4 (Also see Colour Plate 3) Map and language family tree showing the settlement of the Pacific by Austronesian-speaking peoples. The map shows the settlement sequence and location of expansion pulses and settlement pauses. The tree is rooted with some outgroup languages (Buyang and Old Chinese) at its base. It shows an Austronesian origin in Taiwan around 5200 years ago, followed by a settlement pause (pause 1) between 5200 and 4000 years ago. After this pause, a rapid expansion pulse (pulse 1) led to the settlement of Island Southeast Asia, New Guinea and Near Oceania in less than 1000 years. A second pause (pause 2) occurs after the initial settlement of Polynesia. This pause is followed by two pulses further into Polynesia and Micronesia around 1400 years ago (pulses 2 and 4). A third expansion pulse occurred around 3000–2500 years ago in the Philippines.

The pulse–pause scenario makes a third key prediction by proposing a sequence of expansion pulses and pauses. Under this scenario, there were two pauses in the great expansion—the first occurred before the Austronesians entered the Philippines around 5000–4000 years ago, and the second occurred after the settlement of Western Polynesia (Fiji, Samoa, Tonga) starting around 2800 years ago. We tested this prediction in two

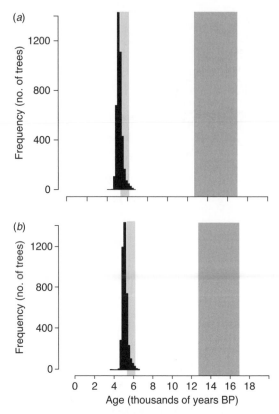

Figure 16.5 Histograms of the Bayesian phylogenetic estimates for the age of Proto Austronesian. (*a*) Shows the estimated age when all calibrations were used. (*b*) Shows the estimates when only Proto Oceanic and three ancient languages were used as calibrations.

ways. First, we identified the branches on our trees corresponding to these two pauses (Figure 16.4). The length of the branches again represents the number of changes in cognate sets. If these pauses did occur, then those branches should be much longer than others owing to the increased amount of time for linguistic change. Indeed, the length of these branches was significantly longer than the overall branch-length distribution, providing good evidence that pauses did occur in the predicted locations.

The pulse–pause scenario predicts pulses as well as pauses. If there were expansion pulses in language change, then we would expect to see increases in language diversification rates after the predicted pauses. To test this prediction, we modelled language diversification rate over our set of language trees. This method identified a number of significant increases in language diversification rates (branches coloured red in Colour Plate 4). Two of these increases occurred as predicted on the branches just after the two pauses. Intriguingly, we identified some unpredicted pulses as well. The third pulse we identified suggested a more recent population expansion in the Philippines around 2000–2500 years ago as one language subgroup expanded at the expense of others. The fourth pulse occurred in the Micronesian languages and appears to be linked to the second pulse into Polynesia.

What insights can these language dates give us about the great Austronesian expansion? It has been suggested that the first pause might be linked to an inability of the Austronesians to cross the 350 km Bashi channel separating the Philippines from Taiwan [47, 48]. Terms for outrigger canoes and sails can only be reconstructed back to the languages occurring after the first pause [47, 48]. It seems likely therefore that the invention of the outrigger enabled the Austronesians to cross the channel and spread rapidly across the rest of the Pacific. After travelling 7000 km in 1000 years, what might have caused the Austronesians to stop in Western Polynesia? Expanding into Eastern Polynesia presented the Austronesians with a new range of challenges that would have also required technological or social solutions including: the ability to estimate latitude from the stars, the ability to sail across the prevailing easterly tradewinds, double-hulled canoes for greater stability and carrying capacity, and social strategies for handling the greater isolation [60].

The results reveal the rapidity of cultural spread. The Austronesians travelled—and settled—the 7000 km between the Philippines and Polynesia in around 1000 years. During this relatively short time, the Austronesian culture not only spread, but developed the collection of technologies known as the Lapita cultural complex [5]. This complex includes distinctive and elaborately decorated pottery, adzes/axes, tattooing, bark-cloth and shell ornamentation. Our results suggest that either this complex was generated in a very short time-window (four or five generations), or there was substantial post-settlement contact between Near Oceania and the pre-Polynesian society. One possibility is that there is a more complex history in this region. The languages of New Caledonia and Vanuatu show some strikingly non-Austronesian features such as serial verb constructions, and the cultures there show some unusual similarities with some cultures from highland New Guinea—including nasal septum piercings, penis sheathes and mop-like headdresses [61]. It has recently been suggested that one explanation for these similarities might be two waves of settlement into Remote Oceania, with a first wave of Austronesian-speaking settlers being rapidly followed by a second wave of Papuan peoples who had acquired Austronesian voyaging technology [61].

16.5 **Conclusion**

Some scholars are rather sceptical that anything of substance can come out of attempts to 'Darwinize culture'. They concede that some loose analogies can be found, but claim that these are rather superficial and unlikely to yield substantive insights into complex cultural processes. In the words of Fracchia & Lewontin [62, p. 14], Darwinian approaches to culture do not 'contribute anything new except a misleading vocabulary that anesthetises history'. The focus of Fracchia & Lewontin's critique is on selectionist, memetic accounts of historical change. Elsewhere, we have argued that phylogenetic or 'tree thinking' provides another way of Darwinizing culture that does not require a commitment to problematic aspects of memetics such as particulate cultural inheritance and tidy lineages of directly copied replicators [63]. One aspect of phylogenetic inference is the estimation of divergence dates. The accurate estimation of divergence dates is a tricky business. Care needs to be taken to ensure that the calibrations are valid and the inferences are robust to possible model misspecification and undetected borrowing. However, the central theme of this chapter has been that when it comes to understanding our past these carefully estimated dates really do make a difference. Robust phylogenetic estimates of linguistic divergence dates give us a powerful tool for testing hypotheses about human prehistory. They enable us to integrate linguistic, archaeological and genetic data, and link major population expansions to innovations in culture such as the development of farming and the invention of the outrigger canoe. In short, a phylogenetic approach to culture illuminates rather than anaesthetizes history.

Acknowlegements

We would like to thank Lyle Campbell, Kevin Laland, April McMahon, Robert Ross, Andy Whiten and an anonymous referee for their helpful comments on this manuscript. Figures are reprinted with permission from *Proceedings of the Royal Society B* (Figure 16.3) and *Science* (Figure 16.4). This work was funded by Marsden grants from the Royal Society of New Zealand.

References

1 Zuckerkandl, E. & Pauling, L. 1965 Molecules as documents of evolutionary history. *J. Theor. Biol.* **8**, 357–366.

2 Evans, N. 2010 *Dying words: endangered languages and what they have to tell us.* Oxford, UK: Blackwell.

3 Durie, M. & Ross, M. 1996 *The comparative method reviewed: regularity and irregularity in language change.* New York, NY: Oxford University Press.

4 Campbell, L. & Poser, W. J. 2008 *Language classification: history and method.* Cambridge, UK: Cambridge University Press.

5 Kirch, P. V. & Green, R. C. 2001 *Hawaiki, Ancestral Polynesia. An essay in historical anthropology.* Cambridge, UK: Cambridge University Press.

6 Renfrew, C. 2002 The 'emerging synthesis': the archaeogenetics of farming/language dispersals and other spread zones. In *Examining the farming/language dispersal hypothesis* (eds P. Bellwood & C. Renfrew). Cambridge, UK: McDonald Institute for Archaeological Research.

7 Renfrew, C. 2010 Archaeogenetics: towards a 'new synthesis'? *Curr. Biol.* **20**, R162–R165.

8 Ho, S. Y. W. & Larson, G. 2006 Molecular clocks: when times are a-changin'. *Trends Genet.* **22**, 79–83.

9 McMahon, A. & McMahon, R. 2006 Why linguists don't do dates: evidence from Indo-European and Australian languages. In *Phylogenetic methods and the prehistory of languages* (eds P. Forster & C. Renfrew), pp. 153–160. Cambridge, UK: McDonald Institute for Archaeological Research.

10 Swadesh, M. 1952 Lexicostatistic dating of prehistoric ethnic contacts. *Proc. Am. Phil. Soc.* **96**, 452–463.

11 Swadesh, M. 1955 Towards greater accuracy in lexicostatistic dating. *Int. J. Am. Linguist.* **21**, 121–137.

12 Bergsland, K. & Vogt, H. 1962 On the validity of glottochronology. *Curr. Anthropol.* **3**, 115–153.

13 Blust, R. 2000 Why lexicostatistics doesn't work: the 'universal constant' hypothesis and the Austronesian languages. In *Time depth in historical linguistics* (eds C. Renfrew, A. McMahon & L. Trask), pp. 311–332. Cambridge, UK: McDonald Institute for Archaeological Research.

14 Pagel, M. 1999 Inferring the historical patterns of biological evolution. *Nature* **401**, 877–884.

15 Huelsenbeck, J. P., Ronquist, F., Nielsen, R. & Bollback, J. P. 2001 Bayesian inference of phylogeny and its impact on evolutionary biology. *Science* **294**, 2310–2314.

16 Greenhill, S. J., Blust, R. & Gray, R. D. 2008 The Austronesian Basic Vocabulary Database: from bioinformatics to lexomics. *Evol. Bioinformatics* **4**, 271–283.

17 Huelsenbeck, J. P. 1995 Performance of phylogenetic methods in simulation. *Syst. Biol.* **44**, 17–48.

18 Sanderson, M. 2002 R8s, analysis of rates of evolution, version 1.50. See http://ginger.ucdavis.edu/r8s/.

19 Sanderson, M. 2002 Estimating absolute rates of evolution and divergence times: a penalized likelihood approach. *Mol. Biol. Evol.* **19**, 101–109.

20 Drummond, A. J., Ho, S. Y. W., Phillips, M. J. & Rambaut, A. 2006 Relaxed phylogenies and dating with confidence. *PLoS Biol.* **4**, e88. 699–710.

21 Diamond, J. & Bellwood, P. 2003 Farmers and their languages: the first expansions. *Science* **300**, 597–603.

22 Mallory, J. P. 1989 *In search of the Indo Europeans: language, archaeology and myth*. London, UK: Thames and Hudson.

23 Gimbutas, M. 1973 Old Europe c. 7000–3500 BC, the earliest European cultures before the infiltration of the Indo-European peoples. *J. Indo-Eur. Stud.* **1**, 1–20.

24 Gimbutas, M. 1973 The beginning of the Bronze Age in Europe and the Indo-Europeans 3500–2500 BC. *J. Indo-Eur. Stud.* **1**, 163–214.

25 Trask, L. 1996 *Historical linguistics*. New York, NY: Arnold.

26 Renfrew, C. 1987 *Archaeology and language: the puzzle of Indo-European origins*. London, UK: Cape.

27 Gkiasta, M., Russell, T., Shennan, S. & Steele, J. 2003 Neolithic transition in Europe: the radiocarbon record revisited. *Antiquity* **77**, 45–62.

28 Atkinson, Q. & Gray, R. D. 2005 Curious parallels and curious connections: phylogenetic thinking in biology and historical linguistics. *Syst. Biol.* **54**, 513–526.

29 Dyen, I., Kruskal, J. B. & Black, P. 1997 FILE IE-DATA1. See http://www.ntu.edu.au/education/langs/ielex/IE-DATA1.

30 Embleton, S. 1986 *Statistics in historical linguistics*. Bochum, Germany: Brockmeyer.

31 Huelsenbeck, J. P. & Ronquist, F. 2001 MRBAYES: Bayesian inference of phylogeny. *Bioinformatics* **17**, 754–755.

32 Gray, R. D. & Atkinson, Q. D. 2003 Language-tree divergence times support the Anatolian theory of Indo-European origin. *Nature* **426**, 435–439.

33 Atkinson, Q. D. & Gray, R. D. 2006 How old is the Indo-European language family? Progress or more moths to the flame? In *Phylogenetic methods and the prehistory of languages* (eds P. Forster & C. Renfrew), pp. 91–109. Cambridge, UK: McDonald Institute for Archaeological Research.

34 Balter, M. 2003 Early date for the birth of Indo-European languages. *Science* **302**, 1490–1491.

35 Johnson, K. 2008 *Quantitative methods in linguistics*. Malden, MA: Blackwell.

36 Campbell, L. 2004 *Historical linguistics: an introduction*, 2nd edn. Edinburgh, UK: Edinburgh University Press.

37 Nicholls, G. K. & Gray, R. D. 2006 Quantifying uncertainty in a stochastic Dollo model of vocabulary evolution. In *Phylogenetic methods and the prehistory of languages* (eds P. Forster & C. Renfrew), pp. 161–171. Cambridge, UK: McDonald Institute for Archaeological Research.

38 Ringe, D., Warnow, T. & Taylor, A. 2002 Indo-European and computational cladistics. *Trans. Phil. Soc. B* **100**, 59–129.

39 Atkinson, Q., Nicholls, G. & Gray, R. D. 2005 From words to dates: water into wine, mathemagic or phylogenetic inference? *Trans. Phil. Soc.* **103**, 193–219.

40 Drummond, A. J. & Rambaut, A. 2007 BEAST: Bayesian evolutionary analysis by sampling trees. *BMC Evol. Biol.* **7**, 214.

41 Evans, S. N., Ringe, D. & Warnow, T. 2006 Inference of divergence times as a statistical inverse problem. In *Phylogenetic methods and the prehistory of languages* (eds P. Forster & C. Renfrew), pp. 119–129. Cambridge, UK: McDonald Institute for Archaeological Research.

42 Kitchen, A., Ehret, C., Assefa, S. & Mulligan, C. J. 2009 Bayesian phylogenetic analysis of Semitic languages identifies an Early Bronze Age origin of Semitic in the Near East. *Proc. R. Soc. B* **276**, 2703–2710.

43 Pagel, M. & Meade, A. 2006 Estimating rates of lexical replacement on phylogenetic trees of languages. In *Phylogenetic methods and the prehistory of languages* (eds P. Forster & C. Renfrew), pp. 173–182. Cambridge, UK: McDonald Institute for Archaeological Research.

44 Garrett, A. 2006 Convergence in the formation of Indo-European subgroups: phylogeny and chronology. In *Phylogenetic methods and the prehistory of languages* (eds P. Forster & C. Renfrew), pp. 139–152. Cambridge, UK: McDonald Institute for Archaeological Research.

45 Greenhill, S. J., Currie, T. E. & Gray, R. D. 2009 Does horizontal transmission invalidate cultural phylogenies? *Proc. R. Soc. B* **276**, 2299–2306.

46 Nicholls, G. K. & Gray, R. D. 2008 Dated ancestral trees from binary trait data and its application to the diversification of languages. *J. R. Stat. Soc. B* **70**, 545–566.

47 Blust, R. 1999 Subgrouping, circularity and extinction: some issues in Austronesian comparative linguistics. In *Selected papers from the Eighth International Conference on Austronesian Linguistics* (eds E. Zeitoun & P. J. K. Li), pp. 31–94. Taipei, Taiwan: Academia Sinica.

48 Pawley, A. 2002 The Austronesian dispersal: languages, technologies and people. In *Examining the farming/language dispersal hypothesis* (eds P. Bellwood & C. Renfrew), pp. 251–274. Cambridge, UK: McDonald Institute for Archaeological Research.

49 Gray, R. D., Drummond, A. J. & Greenhill, S. J. 2009 Language phylogenies reveal expansion pulses and pauses in Pacific settlement. *Science* **323**, 479–483.

50 Spriggs, M. 2010 'I was so much older then, I'm younger than that now': why the dates keep changing for the spread of Austronesian languages. In *A journey through Austronesian and Papuan linguistic and cultural space: papers in honour of Andrew K. Pawley* (eds J. Bowden, N. Himmelmann & M. Ross), pp. 113–140. Canberra, Australia: Pacific Linguistics.

51 Oppenheimer, S. & Richards, M. 2001 Fast trains, slow boats and the ancestry of the Polynesian islanders. *Sci. Prog.* **84**, 157–181.

52 Hill, C. *et al.* 2007 A mitochondrial stratigraphy for island southeast Asia. *Am. J. Hum. Genet.* **80**, 29–43.

53 Soares, P. *et al.* 2008 Climate change and postglacial human dispersals in southeast Asia. *Mol. Biol. Evol.* **25**, 1209–1218.

54 Richards, M., Oppenheimer, S. & Sykes, B. 1998 mtDNA suggests Polynesian origins in eastern Indonesia. *Am. J. Hum. Genet.* **63**, 1234–1236.

55 Pawley, A. 1999 Chasing rainbows: implications of the rapid dispersal of Austronesian languages for subgrouping and reconstruction. In *Selected papers from the Eighth International Conference on Austronesian Linguistics*, vol. 1 (eds E. Zeitoun & P. J. K. Li), pp. 95–138. Taipei, Taiwan: Academia Sinica.

56 Ross, M. 1996 Contact-induced change and the comparative method: cases from Papua New Guinea. In *The comparative method reviewed: regularity and irregularity in language change* (eds M. Durie & M. D. Ross), pp. 180–217. New York, NY: Oxford University Press.

57 Nettle, D. 1999 Is the rate of linguistic change constant? *Lingua* **108**, 119–136.

58 Thurgood, G. 1999 *From ancient Cham to modern dialects: two thousand years of language contact and change.* Hawaii: University of Hawaii Press.

59 Greenhill, S. J., Drummond, A. J. & Gray, R. D. 2010 How accurate and robust are the phylogenetic estimates of Austronesian language relationships? *PLoS ONE* **5**, e9573.

60 Irwin, G. 1998 The colonization of the Pacific: chronological, navigational and social issues. *J. Polynesian Soc.* **107**, 111–144.

61 Blust, R. 2008 Remote Melanesia: one history or two? An addendum to Donohue and Denham. *Oceanic Linguist.* **47**, 445–459.

62 Fracchia, J. & Lewontin, R. C. 2005 The price of metaphor. *History Theory* **44**, 14–29.

63 Gray, R. D., Greenhill, S. J. & Ross, R. M. 2007 The pleasures and perils of Darwinzing culture (with phylogenies). *Biol. Theory* **2**, 360–375.

Chapter 17

How Do We Use Language? Shared Patterns in the Frequency of Word Use Across 17 World Languages

Andreea S. Calude and Mark Pagel

We present data from 17 languages on the frequency with which a common set of words is used in everyday language. The languages are drawn from six language families representing 65 per cent of the world's 7000 languages. Our data were collected from linguistic corpora that record frequencies of use for the 200 meanings in the widely used Swadesh fundamental vocabulary. Our interest is to assess evidence for shared patterns of language use around the world, and for the relationship of language use to rates of lexical replacement, defined as the replacement of a word by a new unrelated or non-cognate word. Frequencies of use for words in the Swadesh list range from just a few per million words to 191 000 or more. The average inter-correlation among languages in the frequency of use across the 200 words is 0.73 ($p < 0.0001$). The first principal component of these data accounts for 70 per cent of the variance in frequency of use. Elsewhere, we have shown that frequently used words in the Indo-European languages tend to be more conserved, and that this relationship holds separately for different parts of speech. A regression model combining the principal factor loadings derived from the worldwide sample along with their part of speech predicts 46 per cent of the variance in the rates of lexical replacement in the Indo-European languages. This suggests that Indo-European lexical replacement rates might be broadly representative of worldwide rates of change. Evidence for this speculation comes from using the same factor loadings and part-of-speech categories to predict a word's position in a list of 110 words ranked from slowest to most rapidly evolving among 14 of the world's language families. This regression model accounts for 30 per cent of the variance. Our results point to a remarkable regularity in the way that human speakers use language, and hint that the words for a shared set of meanings have been slowly evolving and others more rapidly evolving throughout human history.

Keywords: language evolution; frequency of use; word evolution

17.1 **Introduction**

There is now a growing feeling among researchers that elements of human language can be studied as discrete entities that are transmitted from mind to mind and evolve by a process of descent with modification [1]. Languages can be transmitted with a surprising degree of fidelity, and the many parallels between linguistic and genetic evolution mean that approaches drawn from the fields of phylogenetics and comparative biology are increasingly being applied to study languages. Phylogenies of languages chart the history and movement of human cultures [2–5], and elements of language can be studied to understand the social, cultural and linguistic factors that govern their rates and patterns of change through time [1]. Our interest here is to examine the generality of one force known from previous work [6] to influence rates of lexical evolution, that being the frequency with which words are used in everyday language.

If words are thought of as one of the discrete units of a language, they show what molecular geneticists would refer to as rate heterogeneity, with some evolving at high rates and others at far slower rates. For example, among a sample of 87 Indo-European languages, all speakers use a related group of sounds or words to describe 'two' (we use the symbol <'> to denote a given meaning, or concept, and the symbol <"> to refer to a word form) objects but use 45 or more different and unrelated words to describe something as 'dirty' [6, 7]. The related sounds for the word "two" are all homologues or what linguists would refer to as cognates—words that derive by descent with modification from a common ancestral word. The 45 different ways of expressing the idea of 'dirty' thus represent at least 45 newly produced or non-cognate words in the 9000 or so years since the Indo-European languages descended from their common proto-language. The rate at which new non-cognate words arise can be studied phylogenetically using language phylogenies and appropriate statistical models [1, 6, 8]. Applied to a sample of Indo-European language trees, we have found that the quantitative rates of change for "two" and "dirty" differ about 100-fold [6].

Why do the words for some meanings evolve so rapidly and others slowly? In a previous report [6], we described a general evolutionary law relating the frequency with which words are used in everyday speech to rates of lexical replacement, defined as the replacement of a word by a new unrelated or non-cognate word. Measured across the Indo-European languages, frequently used words have slower rates of lexical replacement than infrequently used words. We reached this conclusion from studying linguistic corpora for four phylogenetically widely spaced Indo-European languages: Greek, Russian, Spanish and English. Linguistic corpora record, among other things, the frequencies with which speakers use a wide range of words in their everyday speech (Tables 17.1 and 17.2). Greek is a basal member of the Indo-European language tree, Russian is part of the Slavic language family, Spanish is one of the Romance languages and English is a Germanic language.

We studied the frequencies of use in each of these languages for the 200 words that make up the Swadesh fundamental vocabulary word list [10]. The list comprises 200 common meanings, such as 'mother', 'lake', 'mountain', 'three', 'red', 'green', 'to vomit', 'to kill', 'dirty' and 'dull', that Swadesh thought would be present in all languages, much

Table 17.1 Language corpora consulted by language family. The corpus size is given from the documentation of each of the corpora used. The language classification is given from the online Ethnologue database [9]

language family	language	size (no. of words)
Indo-European	English	100 million
	Russian	140 million
	Greek	47 million
	Portuguese	45 million
	Spanish	1 million
	Chilean Spanish	450 million
	French	31 390 000
	Czech	100 million
	Polish	450 million
Sino-Tibetan	Chinese	1 million
Uralic	Finnish	21 329 990
	Estonian	1 million
Niger-Congo	Swahili	2 million
Altaic	Turkish	2 million
Austronesian	Māori	1 million
unclassified languages	Basque	5 million
Creole	Tok Pisin	864 900

like one might expect there to be a universal set of genes among biological organisms. The list avoids technical terms and specific environmental terms. It would be possible to construct a different list, but the Swadesh list has formed the principal basis for pursuing historical reconstructions and for investigating language history for the past 60 years. The list is commonly used to infer linguistic phylogenies, and it is the set of words that we used to measure rates of lexical replacement in our earlier work.

Despite being separated by thousands of years of linguistic evolution, the average inter-correlation among the four languages in the frequency with which they used these common words was 0.85. This very high average inter-correlation suggests that speakers of different languages use language in the same way and probably for the same purpose. The phylogenetic placement of the four languages we studied further suggests that frequency of use is a stable trait, leading to the speculation that the frequencies we observe in these extant languages are representative of the ancestral or proto-Indo-European languages. If word-use frequencies are a stable and fundamental feature of human language use in general, this leads to the intriguing possibility that the words for a shared set of meanings will be slowly evolving and others more rapidly evolving in all of the world's languages, and that this will probably have been true throughout human history. This is to say that both the frequencies of use and the rates of lexical replacement we found for the Indo-European languages might be representative more broadly of human language evolution.

Table 17.2 Sources of the corpora

Basque	twentieth Century Corpus of Basque, http://www.uzei.com/
Chilean Spanish	Scott Sadowsky, LIFCACH, http://www2.udec.cl/~ssadowsky
Chinese (Mandarin)	Lancaster Corpus of Mandarin Chinese, http://corpus.leeds.ac.uk
Czech	Czech National Corpus, http://ucnk.ff.cuni.cz/english/kdejsme.php
English	BNC, http://www.natcorp.ox.ac.uk
Estonian	Corpus of Written Estonian, http://www.cl.ut.ee/korpused
Finnish	Parole Corpus of Finnish, http://kaino.kotus.fi/sanat/taajuuslista/parole_5000. html
French	Frantext, http://www.atilf.fr/frantext.htm
Greek	HNC, http://hnc.ilsp.gr/en
Māori	Māori Broadcasting Corpus, Boyce, M. T. 2006 A corpus of modern spoken Māori. Unpublished PhD thesis available in the library at Victoria University of Wellington.
Polish	Polish National Corpus, http://nkjp.pl
Portuguese	Mark Davies, http://www.corpusdoportugues.org/x.asp
Russian	Sharoff, S. Corpus linguistics around the world (eds Archer, D., Wilson, A. & Rayson, P.), pp. 167–180 (Rodopi, Amsterdam, 2005), http://www.ruscorpora.ru/
Spanish	Mark Davies, http://www.corpusdelespanol.org
Swahili	Helsinki Corpus of Swahili, http://www.aakkl.helsinki.fi/cameel/corpus
Tok Pisin	Slone Wantok Corpus, http://www.tokpisin.org
Turkish	METU Turkish Corpus, http://www.ii.metu.edu.tr/corpus

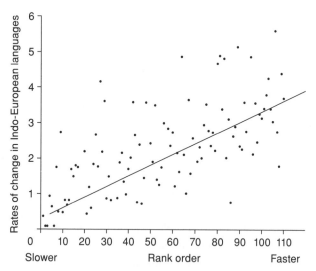

Figure 17.1 Data from Pagel [1]. Statistically estimated rates of lexical replacement for 110 words in the Swadesh list in the Indo-European languages (from [6]) correlated with rank-ordering of subjectively assessed rates of change for the same words in a worldwide sample of 14 language families [11]. The correlation $r = 0.65$. The language families include Sino-Tibetan, Austroasiatic, Altaic, Austronesian, Australian, Khoisan, North Caucasian, Dravidian, Indo-European, Kartvelian, Afroasiatic, Tai, Uralic and Yenisan.

Pagel [1] reports some evidence in support of this speculation. Figure 17.1 (data from [1]) plots the rates of lexical replacement for the Indo-European languages [6] against a list of 110 words that the late Russian comparative linguist Sergei Starostin identified as among the most stable in 14 language families from around the world [11]. Starostin's list is a subjective rank-ordering based on his work with these language families from the most stable (rank = 1) or slowly evolving to less stable (rank = 110). The figure shows that slowly evolving words in Indo-European languages are also slowly evolving in the world's other language families, and vice versa: rates of evolution might indeed have been conserved throughout human history.

Here, we wish to examine these ideas further by collecting data on frequencies of word use from languages around the world, and relating those frequencies to rates of lexical replacement and to Starostin's list.

17.2 **Data and methods**

We collected data on the frequency of word use for the 200 Swadesh word list items from linguistic corpora describing 17 languages (Table 17.1). The languages derive from six language families (Austronesian, Altaic, Indo-European, Niger-Congo, Sino-Tibetan and Uralic), plus one unclassified language (Basque), and a creole language (Tok Pisin). The families are widely geographically spaced and represent 65 per cent of the world's 7000 or so extant languages [9]. The corpora range in size from one million recorded words (Chinese, Estonian, Māori and Spanish) to 450 million words (Chilean Spanish and Polish; Table 17.1). The corpora include spoken and written language use from a variety of genres, including spontaneous conversation, academic writing, newspaper articles and radio transcripts. The Tok Pisin corpus is smaller and less balanced than the others, but we include it here for its interest as a creole.

We normalized all frequency-of-use data from Table 17.1 to a common basis of frequency of use per one million words. The Indo-European languages are disproportionately represented, so we calculated a mean Indo-European frequency-of-use score for the nine Indo-European languages (treating Chilean Spanish as Indo-European). There were 70 words out of the 17 languages × 200 Swadesh list items, or 2 per cent of the total, for which frequency data were not available. We replaced these missing data with the mean frequency calculated from the other languages and again using the mean Indo-European frequency rather than the separate Indo-European data points. If a word was missing from one of the Indo-European languages, we used the others to calculate the IE mean.

We added to these frequency data, information from our previous work [6] on the rates of lexical replacement in the Indo-European languages for each of the meanings in the Swadesh word list. These rates were estimated using a statistical likelihood model of word evolution [7] applied to phylogenetic trees derived from 87 Indo-European languages. The number of cognate classes (the number of distinct unrelated sets of words) for a given meaning varied from 1 (e.g. 'two') to 46 (e.g. 'dirty'). For each of the 200 meanings, we calculated the mean of the posterior distribution of rates as derived from a Bayesian Markov chain Monte Carlo model that simultaneously accounts for uncertainty in the parameters of the model of cognate replacement and in the phylogenetic tree of the languages. Rate estimates were scaled to represent the expected number of cognate replacements per 10 000 years, assuming an 8700 year age for the Indo-European language family [2]. We used these Indo-European rates because they are as yet the only published rates based on statistical modelling applied to phylogenies.

The Indo-European rates of lexical replacement vary roughly 100-fold. At the slow end of the distribution, the rates predict 0–1 cognate replacements per 10 000 years for words such as 'two', 'who', 'tongue', 'night', 'one' and 'to die'. By comparison, for the faster evolving words such as 'dirty', 'to turn', 'to stab' and 'guts', we predict up to nine cognate replacements in the same time period. In the historical context of the Indo-European language family, this range yields an expectation of between 0–1 and 43 lexical replacements throughout the 130 000 language-years of evolution the linguistic tree represents, very close to the observed range in the fundamental vocabulary of 1–46 distinct cognate classes among the different meanings. These rates can be converted to estimates of the linguistic half-life [6, 12], or the time in which there is a 50 per cent chance the word will be replaced by a different non-cognate form. These times vary from 750 years for the fastest evolving words to over 10 000 years for the slowest.

17.3 **Results**

17.3.1 **Frequency of use**

We logarithmically transformed the frequency data prior to analyses. The average inter-correlation among the languages in the frequencies of use across the 200 word meanings is 0.73 ($p < 0.0001$), using the single Indo-European mean. Previously, we found an average inter-correlation of 0.85 for English, Russian, Greek and Spanish [6], and here we find an average inter-correlation among the nine Indo-European languages of 0.82. To summarize these correlations, we derived the first principal component of the frequency data again using a single vector of the mean frequencies for the nine Indo-European languages. The first principal component was the only principal factor with an eigenvalue greater than 1.0 and accounts for 70.4 per cent of the variance. This figure includes several large outliers with plausible explanations (see discussion below as to what these might be) and so is probably conservative.

The individual languages each fit the first principal component (Figure 17.2) as we would expect from their high average inter-correlations. The different 'elevations' or y-axis intercepts of the languages are statistically different and might be of interest, but we cannot know whether they are artefacts of the reported size of each corpus. A corpus might report being based on 45 million utterances, but we cannot independently verify this. However, these mean differences do not influence correlations or the principal component. Where there are outliers on the plot, they are often specific to a particular language rather than to a set of languages and therefore probably arise from idiosyncratic language-specific factors. For example, the word "rotten" is used at a relatively high frequency in Finnish, but not in the other Uralic languages. The Finnish corpus is drawn principally from newspaper and magazine texts, and literature. Because much of Finland

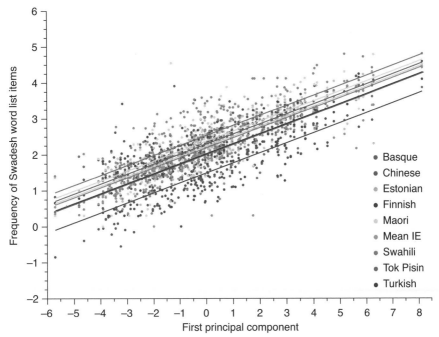

Figure 17.2 (Also see Colour Plate 4) Log-transformed frequency of use per million words for each of the eight languages plus the Indo-European mean vector of nine languages (see Table 17.1 and text) plotted against the first principal component factor scores of frequencies. The first principal component uses the mean IE-vector together with the other eight languages so as not to bias towards the Indo-European (see text). We fitted regression lines to each language, allowing different intercepts but constraining lines to be parallel simply for illustrative purposes. Fitted this way, the overall relationship accounts for 69.4% of the variance in the principal component. The positive slopes indicate that each language's frequencies of use correlate positively with the principal component that summarizes them. Allowing slopes to vary increases the percentage to 70.3% (not significantly different).

is low lying and makes contact with the Baltic, the Finnish corpus team suggested that many articles in the Finnish media focus on the consequent problems of rotting wood and damage caused to housing because of dampness. Similarly, in Māori, the word "ngā" meaning 'to breathe', is also used as a noun meaning 'breath' but it occurs in expressions such as "ngā ... nā" ('those near you'), "ngā ... nei" ('those near me') and "ngā ... rā" ('those away from both speaker and listener'), and even as a definite plural article, meaning 'the'. The English verb "to know" is distributed across two finer grained distinctions in French, namely, "connaître" ('to know a person') and "savoir" ('to know a thing/fact/theory'). The word "louse" might have been used at a relatively high frequency by our hunter–gatherer ancestors, but now its frequency varies considerably among languages.

Other outliers might arise from issues of how to code some words. The Swadesh list item "day" refers to the period of daytime as opposed to the period of darkness that

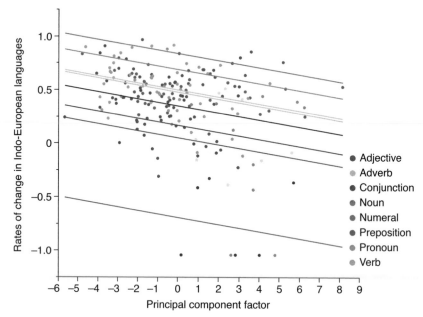

Figure 17.3 (Also see Colour Plate 5) Statistically estimated rates of lexical replacement for the Swadesh list in the Indo-European languages (from [6]) correlated with the first principal component loadings obtained from the frequency of use of the Swadesh list among 17 languages, and with part of speech. The relationship accounts for 46% of the variance in rates of lexical replacement ($p < 0.0001$), and holds separately within part-of-speech category: prepositions ('in', 'with'), conjunctions ('and', 'because'), adjectives ('white', 'thin'), verbs ('to throw', 'to eat'), nouns ('hand', 'hair'), special adverbs ('here', 'some'), pronouns ('I', 'they') and numerals ('one', 'five'). Regression lines were allowed to have separate intercepts but constrained to have the same slope. Allowing these slopes to vary increased the overall R^2 to 0.47, not a significant change.

English speakers at least call "night". But languages including English, German and Māori also use the form meaning 'day' in the common greeting "Good day!". This formulaic use greatly increases the frequency of "day" in any corpus containing conversational data, or any dialogue (whether actual or fictional). In contrast, in Chinese, there are three choices for 'day': the formal version, "日" (which also means 'Japan', 'date' and 'sun'), the more informal character "禾" (but this can also be used to mean 'sky', 'heavens', 'God', 'weather', 'nature', 'season') or the form "白禾" (which actually means 'daytime'). The latter fits best the Swadesh word meaning intended; however, this is going to be much less frequently used in Chinese, in comparison to its cross-linguistics given that 'Good day!' in Chinese involves the "禾" character, and not "白禾".

17.3.2 Rates of lexical replacement

If frequencies of use are a shared feature of human language and if frequencies predict rates of lexical replacement, then the principal component of frequencies from the worldwide sample should predict the rates of lexical replacement for the Indo-European languages. We predicted Indo-European rates from first factor loadings in a two-factor linear regression model including parts of speech coded as discrete categories. As expected, higher principal factor loadings are associated with lower rates of lexical replacement, and this relationship holds separately within parts of speech ($R^2 = 0.46$, $p < 0.0001$, Figure 17.3). This result is comparable to the percentage of variance in rates of lexical replacement we were able to account for using the Greek, Spanish, Russian and English frequencies in our earlier study [6].

We repeated this analysis using a different principal component calculated from a dataset from which we had deleted the Indo-European languages. This removes any possibility of a correlation arising between the rates of replacement and frequency of use that might be true only of the Indo-European languages. This new principal component accounted for 67 per cent of the variance and returned an R^2 value in the multiple regression of 0.46 per cent ($p < 0.0001$), unchanged from the previous analysis.

17.3.3 Rank-order rates of change from a worldwide sample

We repeated the regression model above, this time predicting Starostin's rank-order subjective ratings of stability for 110 words from the Swadesh word list. The first principal component is a significant predictor of rank order, and the overall model accounts for 30 per cent of the variance ($R = 0.54$, $p < 0.001$). Repeating this analysis using the modified principal component from which the Indo-European languages had been removed also returns an R^2 of 0.31 ($p < 0.0001$, Figure 17.4).

17.4 Discussion

Our results confirm our earlier speculation that the frequency with which a common set of words is used in everyday speech is a shared feature of human languages: to a reasonable first approximation, this appears to suggest that all human groups use language in a similar way, and probably for the same purpose. Pagel [13] has argued elsewhere that human language evolved to allow people to vary how they are perceived in the social phenotype of human culture in a manner analogous to the ways that genes use gene regulation to vary their expression in organismal phenotypes. In both cases, a form of digital communication—language or gene regulation—is used to influence how a replicating entity is exposed to the outside world. Unlike all other animal societies, human culture is based on elaborate specialization, exchange and division of labour among unrelated people. These complex reciprocal relationships are inherently laced with commonalities and conflicts of interest.

Language is the means by which we achieve a precise and nuanced communication system to manage how we are seen by others, and to influence how others are seen. Language permits people to enhance their own contributions to relationships or exchanges, and perhaps gently to denigrate those of others, and more generally to keep track of who did what to whom, at what time and how often. Our cooperative societies depend on language to transmit this information about others' reputations as a way of promoting

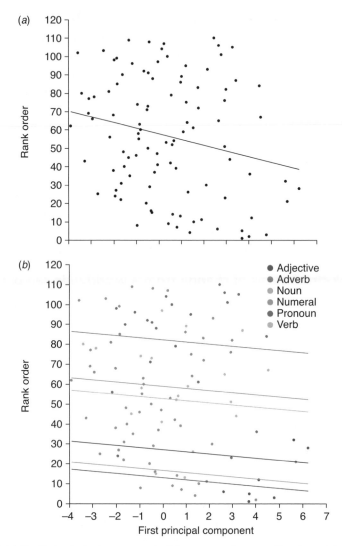

Figure 17.4 (a) The first principal component of frequency of use predicts the subjective rank-order rate of change for 110 words as judged in a worldwide sample of 14 language families [11], correlation $r = 0.22$, $p < 0.0263$. The language families are described in Figure 17.1. (b) (Also see Colour Plate 6) Regression model including the first principal component loadings and parts of speech $R^2 = 0.31$, $p < 0.0001$). Regression lines were allowed to have separate intercepts but were constrained to have the same slopes. Allowing separate slopes did not significantly increase the overall R^2.

exchanges among unrelated people. Frequently used words in the Swadesh list include the pronouns and number words and the so-called special adverbs or "who", "what", "where", "why" and "when". The shared high frequency of use of these socially relevant words is consistent with this idea of language as a device for social regulation.

No one, of course, doubts that language is for communicating. Its value in transmitting knowledge, making plans and in teaching is obvious. But from a gene's eye view, communication is only valuable insofar as it influences another animal's behaviour in a way that serves the communicator. One problem with thinking of language as merely a system for transmitting information is that much of what we might share with someone else could benefit them, without returning any benefit to ourselves, or worse it might disadvantage us. If someone reveals where their favourite source of water is, they might then find themselves having to compete for that resource. This tells us to look for clues in the nature and use of language that point to how it benefits the speaker. Transmitting information can benefit speakers, but this benefit might often have less to do with the information itself than the cooperative or reciprocal relationship that an act of potential altruism encourages. On this view, being in a position to share information is an act with the potential to enhance one's value and prestige in other's eyes.

We find it remarkable that frequency of use and a word's part of speech can together account for close to half of the variation in rates of lexical replacement. The results using Starostin's rank-order list are encouraging that this might be a very general effect, and we look forward to testing whether our results predicting rates of lexical replacement hold in new samples using rates derived from other language families. Frequency of use might affect rates of lexical replacement by altering 'production errors'—akin to the mutation rate in genetics—or by altering the rate at which a new form is adopted in a speech community (akin to selection) or both [6, 14]. Word use may be under strong purifying selection within populations of speakers, if only through the rule 'speak as most others do'. It is difficult to understand how entire populations of speakers could otherwise agree on a single or a small number of mostly arbitrary sounds to represent a given meaning. Such a rule would have been advantageous in our history if speakers who make mistakes are disadvantaged.

Some words may acquire connections in the cognitive or semantic space [15], connections the strength or size of which may influence how rapidly words evolve. For example, the Old English "gebed" meaning "prayer" (from the Old Proto-Indo-European root "*gwedh") became shortened to the form "bede" meaning "prayer bead" or rosaries used for prayer, from which we now have the modern English word "bead" (used widely in any necklaces and other cultural artefacts). This may suggest a third route by which frequency effects operate, that being to increase the chance that a word acquires connections to other words or meanings by virtue of being used in a variety of settings and situations.

Linguists are well aware that linguistic behaviour, sociolinguistic variation and language change are moderated to a great extent by the frequency with which words are used [14, 16, 17], but these studies have not investigated the link between frequency and rates of lexical replacement over periods of thousands of years. Language evolution and change are highly sensitive to frequency of use [6, 18, 19]. Frequency effects begin to play a role in building up of linguistic categories and sequential patterns right from the language development stage, as children acquire language through repetition [20], and continue through adulthood (adults are good at estimating the frequency of words in a given list, cf. [21]), as well as through the process of learning a second/foreign language [14]. High-frequency items behave differently and possess different characteristics from low-frequency items across all linguistic levels, from the graphic symbols used to write down texts, to the sound patterns involved in uttering them and the morphemes used to make up words, and including the grammatical structures observed [22].

17.5 Concluding remarks

Our results point to a surprising regularity in the way that human speakers use language. It might be that the way we use language and its structure means that some words inevitably will be used more than others. If so, then this leads to the intriguing possibility that the words for a shared set of meanings will be slowly evolving and others more rapidly evolving in all of the world's languages, and that this will probably have been true throughout human history.

Other elements of language and culture might also be studied to try to understand the factors that influence their rates of change. An obvious next step for studying how frequency of use affects lexical replacement is to move 'down' one level to phonemes. Do these building-block sounds get replaced within words as part of the normal progress of lexical change, and is their rate of replacement influenced by how often they are used in language as a whole? Moving outside of language, what factors influence the rates of change of technological innovations or styles of fashion and art? It is less clear how to apply the idea of frequency of use in these examples, but there might be analogues. For example, how often a piece of technology is used, its contribution to a society's wealth or how widely adopted it is, might be related to the rate at which it evolves or adapts to societies' changing needs or whims.

Acknowledgements

We thank the Leverhulme Trust and the European Research Council (M.P.) and the New Zealand Foundation for Research, Science and Technology (A.S.C.) for supporting this work. We are grateful to Heiki-Jaan Kaalep, Bilge Say, Scott Sadowsky, Arvi Hurskainen, Michal Kren, Piotr Pezik, Katherine Cao and Miriam Urkia for help with the corpus data. Chris Venditti and Andrew Meade helped with analyses.

References

1 Pagel, M. 2009 Human language as a culturally transmitted replicator. *Nat. Rev. Genet.* **10**, 405–415.

2 Gray, R. D. & Atkinson, Q. D. 2003 Language-tree divergence times support the Anatolian theory of Indo-European origin. *Nature* **426**, 435–439.

3 Gray, R., Drummond, A. & Greenhill, S. 2009 Language phylogenies reveal expansion pulses and pauses in Pacific settlement. *Science* **323**, 479–483.

4 Holden, C. 2002 Bantu language trees reflect the spread of farming across sub-Saharan Africa: a maximum-parsimony analysis. *Proc. R. Soc. Lond. B* **269**, 793–799.

5 Kitchen, A., Ehret, C., Assefa, S. & Mulligan, C. 2009 Bayesian phylogenetic analysis of Semitic languages identifies an Early Bronze Age origin of Semitic in the Near East. *Proc. R Soc. B* **276**, 2703–2710.

6 Pagel, M., Atkinson, Q. & Meade, A. 2007 Frequency of word-use predicts rates of lexical evolution throughout Indo-European history. *Nature* **449**, 717–720.

7   Pagel, M. & Meade, A. 2006 Estimating rates of lexical replacement on phylogenetic trees of languages. In *Phylogenetic methods and the prehistory of languages* (eds P. Forster & C. Renfrew), McDonald Institute Monographs, pp. 173–182. Cambridge, UK: McDonald Institute of Archaeology.

8   Pagel, M. 2000 Maximum likelihood models for glottochronology and for reconstructing linguistic phylogenies. In *Time-depth in historical linguistics* (eds C. Renfrew, A. MacMahon & L. Trask), pp. 189–207. Cambridge, UK: McDonald Institute of Archaeology.

9   Lewis, M. P. (ed.) 2009 *Ethnologue: languages of the world*, 16th edn. Dallas, TX: SIL International.

10 Swadesh, M. 1952 Lexicostatistic dating of prehistoric ethnic contacts. *Proc. Am. Phil. Soc.* **96**, 452–463.

11 Starostin, S. A. 2007 Languages of the Slavic culture. In *Works on linguistics* (ed. S. A. Starostin), pp. 827–839. Moscow: Nauka.

12 Pagel, M. 2000 The history, rate, and pattern of world linguistic evolution. In *The evolutionary emergence of language* (eds C. Knight, M. Studdert-Kennedy & J. Hurford), pp. 391–416. Cambridge, UK: Cambridge University Press.

13 Pagel, M. 2008 Rise of the digital machine. *Nature* **452**, 699.

14 Ellis, N. 2002 Frequency effects in language processing: a review with implications for theories of implicit and explicit language acquisition. *Stud. Sec. Lang. Acquis.* **24**, 143–188.

15 Huettig, F., Quinlan, P. T., McDonald, S. A. & Altmann, G. T. M. 2006 Models of high-dimensional semantic space predict language-mediated eye movements in the visual world. *Acta Psychol.* **121**, 65–80.

16 Bybee, J. 2007 *Frequency of use and the organisation of language*. Oxford, UK: Oxford University Press.

17 Bybee, J. & Hopper, P. (eds) 2001 *Frequency and the emergence of linguistic structure*. Amsterdam, The Netherlands: Benjamins.

18 Croft, W. 2000 *Explaining language change: an evolutionary approach*. London, UK: Longman.

19 Kemmer, S. & Israel, M. 1994 Variation and the usage-based model. *In Papers from the thirtieth regional meeting of the Chicago Linguistics Society: Para-session on variation and linguistic theory*, vol. 2 (eds K. Beals, J. Denton, R. Knippen, L. Melnar, H. Suzuki & E. Zeinfeld), pp. 165–179. Chicago, IL: Chicago Linguistics Society.

20 Tomasello, M. 2003 *Constructing a language*. Cambridge, MA: Harvard University Press.

21 Shapiro, B. J. 1969 The subjective estimate of relative word frequency. *J. Verb. Learn. Verb. Behav.* **8**, 248–251.

22 Bybee, J. & Thompson, S. 2000 Three frequency effects in syntax. *Berkeley Linguist. Soc.* **23**, 65–85.

Chapter 18

Mode and Tempo in the Evolution of Socio-Political Organization: Reconciling 'Darwinian' and 'Spencerian' Evolutionary Approaches in Anthropology*

Thomas E. Currie and Ruth Mace

Traditional investigations of the evolution of human social and political institutions trace their ancestry back to nineteenth-century social scientists such as Herbert Spencer, and have concentrated on the increase in socio-political complexity over time. More recent studies of cultural evolution have been explicitly informed by Darwinian evolutionary theory and focus on the transmission of cultural traits between individuals. These two approaches to investigating cultural change are often seen as incompatible. However, we argue that many of the defining features and assumptions of 'Spencerian' cultural evolutionary theory represent testable hypotheses that can and should be tackled within a broader 'Darwinian' framework. In this chapter we apply phylogenetic comparative techniques to data from Austronesian-speaking societies of Island South-East Asia and the Pacific to test hypotheses about the mode and tempo of human socio-political evolution. We find support for three ideas often associated with Spencerian cultural evolutionary theory: (i) political organization has evolved through a regular sequence of forms, (ii) increases in hierarchical political complexity have been more common than decreases, and (iii) political organization has coevolved with the wider presence of hereditary social stratification.

Keywords: social evolution; phylogenetic comparative methods; cultural evolution; cultural phylogenetics; evolutionism; evolutionary trend

* Electronic supplementary material is available at http://dx.doi.org/10.1098/rstb.2010.0318 or via http://rstb.royalsocietypublishing.org.

18.1 **Introduction**

The application of evolutionary theory to investigate human cultural diversity goes back to at least the founding of Anthropology in the latter half of the nineteenth century [1]. However, there has been considerable debate as to the most appropriate intellectual framework for understanding how human societies and cultures change over time [1–5].[1] In this chapter we draw a distinction between two research traditions (which we label 'Spencerian' and 'Darwinian'), which show differences in their method and focus of investigations, and their concept of evolution. While these two approaches are often seen as incompatible, we argue that many of the defining features and assumptions of Spencerian evolutionary theories represent testable hypotheses that can be reconciled with an explicitly Darwinian view of cultural evolution. In this chapter we demonstrate how these ideas can be tested using phylogenetic comparative analyses.

The archaeological record indicates that since the end of the last ice age there has been an overall increase in the scale and complexity of human groups. This trend has been described as *'history's broadest pattern'* [6, p. 267], and *'the most salient feature in human history'* [1, p. 288]. The idea of directionality is central to the concept and definition of evolution traditionally employed in Anthropology, particularly in studies of social and political organization: '…by evolved we mean—as I believe most anthropologists do—advanced along a trajectory of increasing complexity.' [1, p. 276]. Other defining features of traditional social evolutionary hypotheses have been that human societies can be classified as falling into a few discrete forms of organization, and that societies pass through these different forms (or 'stages') in the same order across cultures [1, 2, 7–10]. For example, in Service's influential scheme of Band, Tribe, Chiefdom and State, small family groups of foragers ('Bands') evolve into larger, yet still essentially, egalitarian kinship-based, agricultural groups ('Tribes'). Tribes evolve into societies where political leadership over a collection of local groups is centralized in a hereditary office of paramount chief. Chiefdoms finally evolve into States, characterized by a centralized political bureaucracy that contains specialized offices for decision-making and control functions [7, 9]. To distinguish them from the research into cultural evolution described below, we label such studies *Spencerian*, acknowledging the influence of Herbert Spencer in the development of these ideas [1, 11, 12].

More recent evolutionary theories of cultural and social change draw their inspiration from the neo-Darwinian synthesis in Biology and apply the term 'evolution' in the same way that biologists do: to mean 'descent with modification' [3, 4, 12–16]. Studies within this framework are thus part of a larger movement in the social sciences to apply theories and methods developed originally in Evolutionary Biology to understand human behaviour and evolution [4, 15]. *Darwinian* cultural evolutionary theory, sometimes labelled dual-inheritance theory, takes as its starting point the fact that humans inherit not only genetic information from their parents but also cultural information from a variety of sources, both of which affect the phenotype of an organism [4, 13]. A key feature of such investigations is the use of techniques from population genetics to model the transmission of traits to help make sense of the complex interactions between genes and culture, and to examine how processes such as natural selection (working on both individuals and groups), cognitive biases and non-selective processes such as drift affect the maintenance and spread of cultural or genetic variants [3, 15]. Thus far, this approach has been predominantly theoretical with the focus on the construction of mathematical models, which demonstrate how cultural evolutionary process can work [4, 13, 17]. Recently, methods from cultural psychology have also been applied to examine cultural transmission processes in experimental situations [18].

Spencerian evolutionary hypotheses have been criticized for trying to pigeon-hole societies into evolutionary types. These critics argue that the forms of social and political organization, and contingent historical pathways, are too numerous to fit easily within the proposed evolutionary sequences [19–22]. Furthermore, there has been a tendency to focus on changes towards increased socio-political complexity, yet there are many examples of societies that have decreased in complexity [22, 23]. It also argued that these theories are deeply ethnocentric and that the perceived move towards more 'civilized' societies was seen as being universal, and indicative of progress in human affairs, i.e. 'things were getting better' [12, 24]. Particularly in the earliest writings, 'Civilized' societies (as typified by the kind of Western nation states in which the theorists lived) were deemed to be superior to other kinds of societies. In the most extreme arguments, differences in 'cultural attainment' were put down to biological differences between societies and used as a justification for domination and colonization of traditional societies by European powers [24].

Darwinian researchers have often sought to distance themselves from these Spencerian hypotheses. For example, Richerson and Boyd state 'The progressive evolutionary theories debated by generations of anthropologists have almost nothing in common with … [the] Darwinian notion of evolution' [3, p. 59], and Mesoudi et al. contrast Darwinian theories of cultural evolution with the 'progressive, unilinear theories … in which human societies were seen as progressing through a fixed set of stages, from 'savagery' through 'barbarism' to 'civilisation', which they describe as 'erroneous' and 'flawed' [15, p. 331]. While the Darwinian perspective offers a powerful way of investigating cultural evolution, this has not always been appreciated by Spencerians (e.g. [1, 11]). This has partly been due to *some* researchers under the Darwinian banner wishing to draw too close an analogy between the *mechanisms* of genetic and cultural evolution. However, the true defining characteristic of Darwinian evolution is the notion of descent with modification, i.e. that *heritable* traits change over time. It does not matter whether innovations are accidental or purposefully acquired, or whether cultural traits are discrete, replicating entities, analogous to genes: the important point is that these traits are passed on with sufficient fidelity [25]. Furthermore, many interesting aspects of cultural evolution are the results of differences between biological and cultural systems such as modes of transmission other than parent-to-offspring [13], and the possibility of the widespread adoption of behaviours that are maladaptive from a biological perspective [4].

In many respects, the focus of research of these two approaches has been very different. Darwinian cultural evolutionists tend to examine the micro-evolutionary processes affecting the frequencies of cultural traits within populations of individuals [15]. Unlike the Spencerians, these researchers have generally not tackled questions relating to long-term macro-evolutionary patterns and processes in the evolution of social and political organization since the last ice age. Also, it is important to separate out the normative critiques that Spencerian evolutionary theory is ethnocentric, racist or progressive, from the many empirical questions relating to these topics which remain unresolved and could benefit from being addressed within an explicitly Darwinian framework. We argue that many of the assumptions and defining features of Spencerian theories represent testable hypotheses about the mode and tempo of social and cultural evolution, and that, thus far, there has been a distinct lack of quantitative tests of many of these ideas.

While archaeological information has an important role to play in addressing these questions [10], data may not always be available in sufficient detail for a large enough number of sites to allow a rigorous test of competing hypotheses. This is a common problem in investigations of prehistory, and in such cases it is important to supplement the insights from archaeology with those of other disciplines [26]. Recently, researchers interested in cultural evolution have begun to apply phylogenetic methods, originally developed in Evolutionary Biology, to empirically investigate questions relating to the pattern and process of human cultural evolution within a Darwinian framework [5]. These techniques have been used to address questions about general evolutionary processes such as whether rates of linguistic change are linked to such factors as the frequency with which words are used [27], as well more specific questions relating to the *longue durée* of human history such as the dispersal and diversification of widespread language families [28], the ancestral forms of residence practices in South-East Asia and the Pacific [26], and the adoption of cattle and changes in inheritance systems in sub-Saharan Africa [29]. In this chapter, we show how a particular type of phylogenetic analysis, Phylogenetic Comparative Methods (PCMs) [5], can be used to test hypotheses relating to three aspects of socio-political evolution that have been key features of Spencerian hypotheses, but which have often been questioned: (i) the *sequence* of evolution of human groups (do changes in political organization follow a regular sequence?), (ii) the *direction* of evolution (have societies increased in the scale and complexity of their organization over time, and if so, have increases tended to be more common than decreases?), and (iii) the coevolution of social traits (do different aspects of social organization tend to change together?).

18.2 **Analyses**

A phylogenetic tree (or sample of trees) represents a hypothesis about the historical relationships between the units of analysis. PCMs make statistical inferences about evolutionary processes by mapping traits onto the tips of these trees. These techniques are based on the logical proposition that given data about the present distribution of traits across taxa and knowledge about the historical relationships between these taxa, it is possible to infer what the traits were like in the past and how they have changed to give rise to their present distribution [30]. These methods therefore offer a principled way of investigating the long-term patterns and processes of cultural evolution. Here we combine ethnographic data from Austronesian-speaking societies of Island South-East

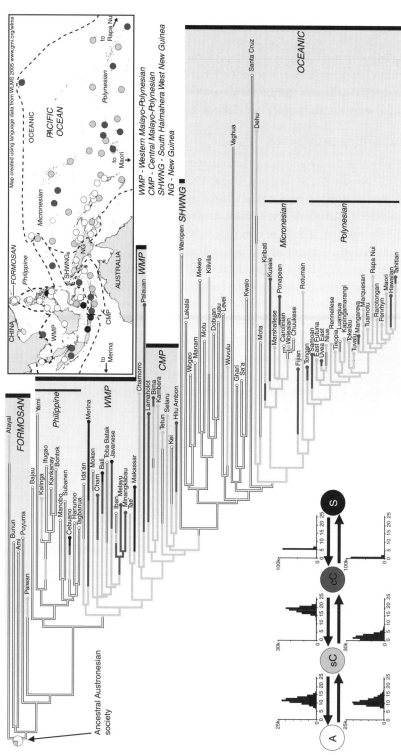

Figure 18.1 (Also see Colour Plate 7) Geographical distribution of the 84 Austronesian-speaking societies analysed in this study and their associated forms of political organization (top right). Data on political organization mapped on to a phylogeny of these societies (centre). This figure shows a single phylogenetic tree from the sample of 1000 most likely trees. Analyses in §18.2 were conducted using all 1000 trees. Colours along the branches indicate the inferred forms of organization from a single stochastic character mapping (SCM). Pie chart at the root of the tree represents the proportional probabilities of different forms of political organization in the ancestral Austronesian society inferred using maximum likelihood. Distributions of number of changes between states inferred using SCM (bottom left). Unfilled circle, Acephalous; blue (light grey) circle, Simple Chiefdom; red (dark grey) circle, Complex Chiefdom; black circle, State. *Note: this caption refers to the version of the figure in the Colour Plate section.*

Asia and the Pacific with a sample of phylogenetic trees, which have previously been constructed using linguistic data (Figure 18.1) to perform phylogenetic comparative analyses using Maximum Likelihood and Stochastic Character Mapping techniques in the software packages BAYESTRAITS (http://www.evolution.rdg.ac.uk/BayesTraits.html) and SIMMAP (http://www.simmap.com/) (see electronic supplementary material).

18.2.1 Evolutionary sequences

A key feature of Spencerian hypotheses is that changes in human socio-political organization follow evolutionary sequences (e.g. Band, Tribe, Chiefdom and State discussed earlier). Such classificatory schemes contain two logically distinct elements: (i) societies are grouped together based on observed similarities in the way they are organized, (ii) the categories are arranged on a scale of complexity with societies hypothesized to pass through adjacent stages of organization in the direction of increasing socio-political complexity. Therefore, it is perfectly possible to classify societies according to some criteria without this classification representing an evolutionary sequence, and societies could evolve without having to pass through the same stages in the same order. For our present purposes we can classify political organization into four categories of increasing complexity based on the number of hierarchical decision-making levels in a society. Acephalous societies are organized politically only at the level of the local community (e.g. the village). Simple Chiefdoms have one permanent level of leadership uniting several villages, while Complex Chiefdoms have two levels. Societies with more than two hierarchical decision-making levels above the local community are labelled 'States' (see electronic supplementary material). Whether this classification does in fact represent an evolutionary sequence is an empirical question on which suitable lines of evidence must be brought to bear.

PCMs can be used to examine the support for evolutionary sequences, and are commonly used to address questions about evolutionary pathways in biological evolution (e.g. the evolution of Carnivore social systems [31]). We have previously evaluated six different models of the evolution of political organization [32] (Figure 18.2), which are derived from discussions in the literature. Three of these models reflect the Spencerian hypothesis that change in political organization has been *sequential* in the direction of increasing hierarchical complexity (i.e. the transitions Acephalous society to Simple Chiefdom, Simple Chiefdom to Complex Chiefdom, Complex Chiefdom to State have occurred, but the larger, direct increases Acephalous society to Complex Chiefdom, Acephalous society to State and Simple Chiefdom to State have not). The RECTILINEAR model reflects the idea that only sequential increases in complexity can occur. This view is often attributed to the classical evolutionists such as Spencer and Morgan [1]. We also specified two models in which increases are sequential but decreases are also possible. In the UNILINEAR model, decreases occur only to adjacent levels of complexity, while in the RELAXED UNILINEAR model, decreases can occur to any lower level. In contrast, in the other three models increasing political complexity does not follow a regular sequence. We specified two models based on the idea that different forms or organization have developed along separate evolutionary pathways having evolved from an acephalous

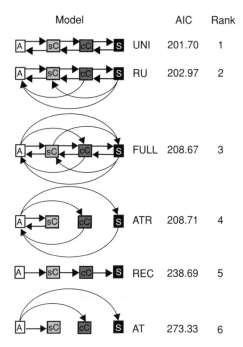

Figure 18.2 Support for different models of political evolution based on the Akaike Information Criterion (AIC) (REC, Rectilinear; UNI, Unilinear; RU, Relaxed Unilinear; FULL, Full model; AT(R), Alternative Trajectories (Reversible)). Adapted with permission from Macmillan Publishers Ltd: *Nature*, **467**(7317), Thomas E. Currie, Simon J. Greenhill, Russell D. Gray, Toshikazu Hasegawa, and Ruth Mace, Rise and fall of political complexity in island South-East Asia and the Pacific, pp. 801–804, copyright (2010).

form of organization [22]: ALTERNATIVE TRAJECTORIES (only increases possible) and ALTERNATIVE TRAJECTORIES (REVERSIBLE) (decreases also possible). Finally, in the FULL model any change is possible, representing the idea that political organization has been completely unconstrained.

Analyses show the UNILINEAR model to be the best supported, closely followed by the RELAXED UNILINEAR model (Table 18.1). The FULL model and the reversible version of the ALTERNATIVE TRAJECTORIES model are less well supported, while those models that do not allow declines in political complexity (i.e. RECTILINEAR and non-reversible ALTERNATIVE TRAJECTORIES model) are even poorer fits to the data. Overall, the analyses provide strong support for the type of sequences of political evolution that have formed a core feature of the Spencerian hypotheses of cultural evolution. Importantly, they highlight that change has not always been in the direction of increasing complexity. Whether increases in complexity have been more common than decreases is dealt with in the next section.

18.2.2 **Direction of evolution**

Another defining feature of the Spencerian hypotheses is that there is a direction to cultural evolution, i.e. the complexity of socio-political organization increases over time.

Table 18.1 Percentage of Stochastic Character Mappings in which increases or decreases in complexity are more common, and comparisons of inferred number of changes between different forms of organization using paired sample t-tests (d.f. = 99 998). In all comparisons, the number of changes towards the more complex form of organization is significantly higher than the number of changes towards less complex forms

comparison	% increases	% decreases	% equal	mean increases	mean decreases	mean difference	s.d.	t	p
A → sC versus sC → A	60.3	27.0	12.7	11.1	10.6	0.6	3.15	55.98	<0.001
sC → cC versus cC → sC	99.9	<0.1	<0.1	17.9	2.0	15.9	3.23	1561.99	<0.001
cC → S versus S → cC	100	0	0	5.1	0.1	5.0	0.05	34 107.00	<0.001
sC → cC versus sC → A	98.2	0.9	0.8	17.9	10.6	7.4	2.81	828.38	<0.001
cC → S versus cC → sC	93.0	3.7	3.3	5.1	2.0	3.1	1.72	569.15	<0.001

That the archaeological record indicates an overall increase in complexity since the end of the last ice age is not in dispute [33]. Yet, the archaeological and historical records also indicate periods when societies have decreased in complexity [23], which is supported by the findings described in §18.2.1, and it is unclear if increases have generally been more common than decreases. Additionally, it is important to understand how such a macro-evolutionary trend can arise if cultural evolution, like biological evolution, is not goal directed.

Although Spencerian cultural evolutionary theories have been characterized as assuming that increases in complexity have dominated, there has, in fact, been a lack of consensus on this issue [1]. For example, Tylor proposed that human history 'is not the history of a course of degeneration, or even of equal oscillations to and fro, but of a movement which, in spite of frequent stops and relapses, has on the whole been forward' (Tylor 1870, p. 193 cited in [1, p. 28]), while Spencer argued that 'the theory of progression, in its ordinary form, seems to me to be untenable…It is possible, and, I believe, probable, that retrogression has been as frequent as progression' (Spencer 1890, p. 93, cited in [1, p. 27]). More recently, Diamond states that increasing complexity is 'no more than an average long-term trend, with innumerable shifts in either direction: 1000 amalgamations for 999 reversals' [6, p. 281]. Richerson & Boyd [33], while acknowledging that decreases in complexity can and have occurred, clearly see increases in complexity as more common, arguing that complex social organization is compulsory in the long run, owing to the competitive advantage that societies hold in competition between groups.

Despite the fact that biological evolution is not goal-directed, there are a number of large-scale trends that can be witnessed over evolutionary time. A trend here is defined as a directional shift in a measurement value of some attribute over time (e.g. the extreme of a distribution, or a measure of its central tendency) [34]. Some trends are present only in certain clades and over certain time scales, while others seem to hold over the entire history of life on earth (e.g. increases in the maximum degree of biological complexity, and body size—see ref. [35] for a summary of the proposed macro-evolutionary trends). In our own lineage, the trend of increasing brain size in homonins is well-established even if there is much discussion as to the reasons for it [36].

One explanation for such macro-evolutionary trends is that selection has favoured a consistent directional shift in the trait in question. For example, it has been argued that selection acts as a driving force favouring increased body size owing to the potential advantages that are gained from being large (e.g. more efficient metabolism and homeostasis, advantage in competition over resources, greater mobility, and decreased predation) [37]. However, it also possible for trends to occur even in the absence of such a driving force if the 'phase space' in which a trait is evolving is constrained and the trait originally arises near one of the constraints (a so-called 'passive' trend) [38]. For example, the trend of increasing biological complexity could be the result of the earliest single-celled organisms arising near a 'left-wall' of minimum complexity, i.e. it was almost impossible for them to have been any less complex [34]. Initially any changes in complexity must be in the direction of increased complexity. Subsequently, increases and decreases are possible, yet over time the maximum degree of complexity will increase. Similar mechanisms could explain the trend towards increasing political complexity (Figure 18.3).

Biologists have employed PCMs to investigate trends in biological evolution [39]. Here we use a PCM to directly estimate the number of changes between forms of political organization to assess whether increases in complexity have actually been more common than decreases. As a first step we inferred the form of political organization in the ancestral Austronesian society under the best-fitting model of evolution from the previous analysis, the UNILINEAR model. The results suggest that the ancestral Austronesian society was politically acephalous (proportional support for different forms of organization: Acephalous = 0.76, Simple Chiefdom = 0.22, Complex Chiefdom = 0.01, State = 0.00) (Figure 18.1), which confirms that the *maximum* degree of hierarchical political organization in Austronesian societies has indeed increased over time. We then used a PCM to infer the number of increases and decreases between levels of complexity under the UNILINEAR model of trait evolution. Figure 18.1 shows the distributions of the estimated numbers of changes from these analyses. We can see that increases in complexity have occurred more frequently than decreases (Table 18.1) (although in the comparison between changes A → sC and sC → A, the mean difference was less than one). As the more complex forms of political organization evolved later, the significant differences in the first three comparisons could be owing to the fact that more time has been spent in the form of lower complexity, therefore allowing for more opportunities for increases to occur. The final two comparisons are situations where there were equal opportunities for increases or decreases and in these comparisons increases are again significantly

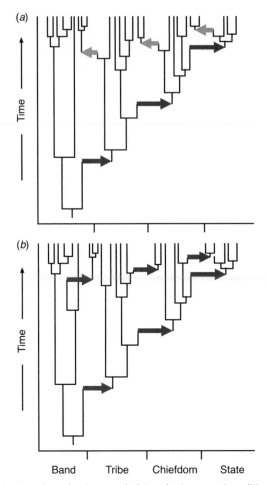

Figure 18.3 Alternative trend mechanisms underlying the increase in political complexity over time. (*b*) In a driven trend, change is biased with increases in complexity more likely than decreases (this represents an extreme example in which only increases have occurred). (*a*) In a passive trend, increases and decreases are equally likely. An increase in the maximum degree of complexity over time occurs because the ancestral lineage arose near a 'left wall' of minimum complexity, meaning evolution in the direction of decreasing complexity was initially limited. Phylogenetic comparative methods can be used to test between these scenarios.

greater than decreases. These results suggest that increases in political complexity in Austronesian-speaking societies have generally been more common than decreases.

18.2.3 Coevolution of social and political traits

Another aspect of social evolution that has been the subject of considerable debate is the idea that different aspects of social organization are correlated with one another, i.e. classificatory schemes such as Band, Tribe, Chiefdom and State are based on regular hypothesized differences between these categories in such things as subsistence practices, degree of social differentiation, inherited inequalities and permanent offices of leader-ship [1, 7, 9]. An associated idea is that change from one category to another involves the relatively rapid restructuring of these different aspects of social organization, i.e. socio-political evolutionary change is *punctuational* [2]. However, it has been argued that different aspects of social organization do not coevolve this closely and that societies exhibit too much variation to fit easily into categories such Band, Tribe, Chiefdom and State [19].

There has been a lack of quantitative comparative analyses attempting to address this question. We examined whether political organization coevolves with hereditary social stratification (i.e. some individuals or groups of individuals within a society are afforded higher social status and have greater influence owing to who their ancestors were). In traditional social evolutionary theories, Chiefdoms and States are thought to be socially stratified along these lines, while such hereditary ranking is thought to be absent in socie-ties organized politically only at the level of the local community (i.e. Bands and Tribes) [6, 7, 9]. Table 18.2 shows the co-occurrence of these two aspects of sociopolitical organiza-tion in our sample, which suggests that Acephalous societies generally lack hereditary forms of social stratification, while it is generally present in Chiefdoms and States. However, as societies are hierarchically related they may have several features in com-mon, not because they are functionally linked, but because they have all been inherited from a common ancestral society (e.g. most of the Polynesian societies in the sample are organized as chiefdoms and have hereditary social stratification (see electronic supple-mentary material, figure S2), which potentially could be owing to either process). Therefore, societies cannot be treated as independent data points in a cross-cultural analysis. Phylogenetic comparative analyses can overcome these problems by identifying whether the traits under investigation are coevolving while controlling for the historical relatedness between societies [5].

To formally test whether political organization has coevolved with the wider presence of hereditary social stratification, we use a PCM to compare two alternative models of trait evolution: (i) a *dependent* model where the rate of change of one trait is different depend-ing on the state of the other, and (ii) an *independent* model where the rate of trait change does not vary according to the state of the other (see electronic supplementary material, figure S1). For our sample of Austronesian-speaking societies, the dependent model of evolution fits the data much better than the independent model (Figure 18.4 and electronic supplementary material). These results support the hypothesis that political

Table 18.2 Contingency table showing the occurrence of different forms of political organization and the presence or absence of hereditary social stratification in our sample

political organization		
hereditary social stratification	Acephalous	Chiefdoms/States
absence	31	3
presence	12	37

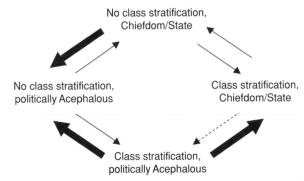

Figure 18.4 Flow diagram showing the estimated rates of change between different combinations of the binary variables of Class Stratification and Jurisdictional Hierarchy under the dependent model of evolution. This dependent model has a much better fit to the data (AIC: 176.2) than the independent model of evolution (AIC: 215.6) (see electronic supplementary material). Relative thickness of arrows represents relative estimated rate parameters, with the dotted line representing an estimated rate of zero.

organization, as represented by the number of hierarchical jurisdictional levels, has indeed coevolved with the wider presence of hereditary social stratification in Austronesian societies.

Figure 18.4 shows the estimated rates of change between the different combinations of these variables, and thus shows the most likely pathways of evolution of these traits. It appears that Acephalous societies lacking hereditary class distinctions can develop either hereditary class distinctions or a chiefdom form of political organization first. However, the rate of change from Acephalous society to Chiefdom is greater in the presence of hereditary class distinctions, while the particular form of political organization does affect the rate at which hereditary class distinctions evolve. Interestingly, the rates of change away from the intermediate states (i.e. Bands or Tribes exhibiting hereditary class distinctions and vice versa) are generally higher than those going towards these intermediate states. This suggests that these intermediate forms of organization are unstable, which is consistent with the idea that different features of social organization may alter relatively rapidly once other elements have changed.

18.3 **Discussion**

In this chapter we have demonstrated how PCMs can be used to test hypotheses about the macro-evolutionary patterns and processes of socio-political evolution. Despite suggestions that Darwinian and Spencerian evolutionary approaches are incompatible, we actually found support for three defining features of Spencerian evolutionary theories. First, political organization has evolved through a regular sequence in the direction of increasing levels of hierarchal complexity. Secondly, the overall direction of political evolution has been from less hierarchically complex to more hierarchically complex, and the number of increases in complexity appears to have been greater than the number of decreases. Finally, hierarchical political organization appears to have coevolved with hereditary forms of social stratification with politically Acephalous societies lacking hereditary distinctions, while they are generally present in societies organized politically as Chiefdoms and States. Interestingly, the intermediate combinations of these traits were relatively less stable, which is consistent with a punctuational process of socio-political change. These studies illustrate the benefits a Darwinian evolutionary framework can have in addressing important questions relating to these aspects of social and cultural change, while avoiding many of the problems associated with the traditional Spencerian studies.

Despite the logical possibility that political evolution could involve larger jumps in hierarchical complexity, our results indicate that in fact only sequential increases have occurred. This may reflect constraints imposed by a number of micro-evolutionary forces, such as a social psychology, that evolved in the context of life in small-scale groups requiring the evolution of cultural 'work-arounds' [40], the difficulty in reorganizing existing institutions that rely on the coordination of large numbers of individuals, or the requirement for certain pre-existing institutions or cultural practices [33]. More complex forms of political organization appear to result from the welding together of smaller pre-existing units [6], a process which requires the cultural evolution of institutions that allow these large-scale groups to be stable. For example, it has been argued that a stable form of state organization uniting previously independent Chiefdoms in Hawaii was made possible only by the presence of administrative institutions such as local land managers (*konohiki*) under the control of district chiefs [2]. Just as biologists seek to understand what constrains biological evolution to take small steps in 'design space' rather than large, saltational jumps [41], future work could examine what factors have been most important in preventing larger increases in political organization.

The results suggest that while decreases in political complexity have occurred, increases have been more common. This is consistent with the idea that increases in complexity over time have been the result of a driven trend mechanism [38]. This may be owing to selection having favoured more complex forms of political organization because they improve the coordination, cooperation and division of labour between individuals, thus providing an advantage in direct or indirect competition between groups [6, 33, 42]. It should be stressed that these potential advantages to more complex forms of political organization may not always be realized and may be contingent on the presence of other factors. For example, environmental instability in the Pleistocene appears to have created a 'right wall' of maximum complexity that could not be breached until the climatic amelioration of the Holocene allowed the evolution of agriculture [3]. Furthermore, the rate of political evolution has not been even across the world, a fact that has had important consequences for the present day [6, 33, 42]. Future work should aim to empirically investigate rates of political evolution and which factors have been most important in determining these rates.

We also found support for the idea that different aspects of socio-political organization evolve together. Furthermore, the estimated rates of change were consistent with a punctuational process of socio-political evolution. So, as forms of socio-political organization follow a pattern of sequential increases in complexity, the change from one form to another may involve the relatively rapid change of several different aspects of social structure. This highlights the fact that a Darwinian view of evolution does not require an adherence to the idea that evolutionary change is always a continuous, gradual process. Indeed, investigating the rate at which evolution proceeds, and how it can vary over time or across different traits, is important for both biological and cultural phenomena [27, 28]. The coevolutionary techniques we have outlined will be applied to test the extent to which other social and cultural features (such as those described in §18.2.3) evolve in a correlated fashion. This will allow us to build up a network of the dependencies between these traits in a manner similar to the way in which PCMs have been used to investigate networks of functional linkages between genes [43]. Additionally, many different factors have been proposed to be important in leading to more complex forms of political organization including such things as intensification of subsistence practices, warfare and trade [1, 9]. With their ability to make inferences about the order in which traits change, these methods raise the possibility of being able to provide more rigorous tests of such causal hypotheses. For example, Holden and Mace [29] show that in Bantu-speaking societies of sub-Saharan Africa, the adoption of cattle-herding led to the loss of matrilineal forms of inheritance.

It is important to point out that the idea that sociopolitical organization can be classified as falling into a limited number of forms does not imply that societies belonging to these categories will be *exactly* the same. Instead, it is proposed that there is a 'limited array of basic designs underlying the apparently wide range of variability' [2]. For example, in Hawaiian society, both secular and religious power were concentrated in the paramount *Ali'i ai moku* chiefs, while in Tonga, a dual paramountship was in operation with the *Tu'i Tonga* as a spiritual figurehead and the *Hau* chief wielding political authority [44]. Yet both societies can be classified as Complex Chiefdoms in terms of the number of hierarchical decision-making levels. Furthermore, the question of whether or not several features of social and political organization coevolve does not mean that any functional associations between traits must follow the previously proposed schemes such as Band, Tribe, Chiefdom and State. Other forms of patterned variation not captured by these schemes may be observable. For example, Blanton and colleagues [45] argue that the Mesoamerican archaeological sites they investigate are best described as representing either 'network' polities, characterized by self-aggrandizing rulers, or 'corporate' polities, in which leaders had minimized personal identities and visibility. We feel the extent to which societies can be usefully classified based on different features is an empirical question that is best answered using the kind of quantitative analyses we have advocated in this chapter.

We have argued that the focus of Spencerian and Darwinian evolutionary approaches has often been very different, with Spencerians tending to focus on broad-scale macro-evolutionary phenomena. An important goal of research in Evolutionary Biology is to understand the relationship between micro-evolution and macro-evolution [46]. A Darwinian view of cultural evolution is also well suited to addressing such questions with respect to cultural and social evolution [33]. Recent empirical research has begun to explore how cultural transmission between individuals relates to patterns of cultural diversity at the population level [16]. Similarly, attention needs to be paid to how particular forms of social and political organization emerge and are maintained from the perspective of the interactions between individuals and the transmission of institutions, customs, practices and rules of behaviour within and between generations. Mathematical models and computer simulations of such micro-evolutionary processes promise to shed light on the evolution of socio-political organization (e.g. [17]) and provide an important complement to the phylogenetic techniques we have employed here.

The use of PCMs avoids some of the problems attributed to the Spencerian approach. For example, Shennan [14] argues that often archaeological investigations within this framework have done little more than propose that the remains of a society found at an archaeological site are indicative of a particular stage of evolution, without understanding the processes by which societies and culture change. Spencerian evolutionary theory has also been criticized for taking a progressive, archaic, ladder-like view of evolution [22]. The use of PCMs makes the fact explicit that the societies under investigation are contemporaries and enables us to make inferences about the sequence in which the *traits* of these societies, such as their form of political organization, have evolved. Furthermore, they allow us not only to infer the pattern of trait changes over time, but also what processes have occurred to give rise to the diversity of forms of organization we witness in the ethnographic record.

Our goal in this chapter has been to highlight the huge potential that the use of PCMs within a Darwinian evolutionary framework hold for addressing questions relating to the pattern and process of socio-political evolution. Although Darwinian and Spencerian evolutionists have often had fundamental disagreements about the concept of 'evolution', and despite suggestions that the two approaches are incompatible, we have demonstrated how some of these differences can be resolved. In biology, the concept of evolution provides a unifying principle around which a large body of information can be organized and synthesized [47]. Given the great success of Darwinism in helping us understand the natural world, it is hoped that the theory of evolution as 'descent with modification' can be the same kind of organizing principle for anthropology that it is in biology [15]. The use of PCMs to investigate socio-political evolution is a key step forward in this endeavour, allowing us to go beyond the purely verbal arguments which have hitherto dominated the debates on this topic, and to provide quantitative tests of opposing hypotheses.

Acknowledgements

T.E.C. was supported by an ESRC/NERC Interdisciplinary Research Studentship and a Japan Society for the Promotion of Science Postdoctoral Fellowship. R.M. was supported by a European Research Council grant. We thank Russell Gray and Simon Greenhill for providing the Austronesian phylogenetic trees, and who, along with Robert Foley, Michael Dunn and Fiona Jordan, provided many valuable comments at various stages during this research. We also thank Andrew Whiten and two anonymous reviewers for their comments on the manuscript.

Note

[1] In addition to the references listed below an extended bibliography is available as electronic supplementary material.

References

1 Carneiro, R. L. 2003 *Evolutionism in cultural anthropology*. Boulder, CO: Westview Press.

2 Spencer, C. S. 1990 On the tempo and mode of state formation: neoevolutionism reconsidered. *J. Anth. Arch.* **9**, 1–30.

3 Richerson, P. J. & Boyd, R. 2005 *Not by genes alone*. Chicago, IL: University of Chicago Press.

4 Laland, K. N. & Brown, G. R. 2002 *Sense and nonsense*. Oxford, UK: Oxford University Press.

5 Mace, R. & Holden, C. J. 2005 A phylogenetic approach to cultural evolution. *Trends Ecol. Evol.* **20**, 116–121.

6 Diamond, J. 1997 *Guns, germs and steel*. London, UK: Vintage.

7 Service, E. R. 1962 *Primitive social organization*. New York, NY: Random House.

8 Earle, T. 1994 Political domination and social evolution. In *Companion encyclopedia of anthropology* (ed. T. Ingold), pp. 940–961. London, UK: Routledge.

9 Flannery, K. V. 1972 The cultural evolution of civilizations. *Ann. Rev. Ecol. Evol. Syst.* **3**, 399–426.

10 Marcus, J. 2008 The archaeological evidence for social evolution. *Ann. Rev. Anth.* **37**, 251–266.

11 Graber, R. B. 2007 Bye-Bye BABY! A cultural evolutionist's response to evolutionary culture theorists' complaints. *Social Evol. Hist.* **6**, 3–28.

12 Dunnell, R. C. 1980 Evolutionary theory and archaeology. *Adv. Archaeol. Method Theory* **3**, 35–99.

13 Boyd, R. & Richerson, P. J. 1985 *Culture and the evolutionary process*. Chicago, IL: Chicago University Press.

14 Shennan, S. 2002 *Genes, memes, and human history*. London, UK: Thames & Hudson.

15 Mesoudi, A., Whiten, A. & Laland, K. N. 2006 Towards a unified science of cultural evolution. *Behav. Brain Sci.* **29**, 329–383.

16 Shennan, S. 2011 Descent with modification and the archaeological record. *Phil. Trans. R. Soc. B* **366**, 1070–1079.

17 Henrich, J. & Boyd, R. 2008 Division of labor, economic specialization, and the evolution of social stratification. *Curr. Anth.* **49**, 715–724.

18 Mesoudi, A. & O'Brien, M. J. 2008 The cultural transmission of Great Basin projectile-point technology. I. an experimental simulation. *Am. Antiquity* **73**, 3–28.

19 Feinman, G. M. 2008 Variability in states: comparative frameworks. *Social Evol. Hist.* **7**, 54–66.

20 Campbell, R. B. 2009 Toward a networks and boundaries approach to early complex polities: the Late Shang case. *Curr. Anth.* **50**, 821–848.

21 Bondarenko, D. M., Grinin, L. E. & Korotayev, A. V. 2002 Alternative pathways of social evolution. *Social Evol. Hist.* **1**, 54–79.

22 Yoffee, N. 1993 Too many chiefs? (or, safe texts for the '90s). In *Archaeological theory: who sets the agenda?* (eds N. Yoffee & A. Sherratt), pp. 60–78. Cambridge, UK: Cambridge University Press.

23 Tainter, J. A. 2006 Archaeology of overshoot and collapse. *Ann. Rev. Anth.* **35**, 59–74.

24 Eriksen, T. H. & Nielsen, F. S. 2001 *A history of anthropology*. London, UK: Pluto Press.

25 Henrich, J., Boyd, R. & Richerson, P. J. 2008 Five misunderstandings about cultural evolution. *Hum. Nat.* **19**, 119–137.

26 Jordan, F. M., Gray, R. D., Greenhill, S. J. & Mace, R. 2009 Matrilocal residence is ancestral in Austronesian societies. *Proc. R. Soc. B* **276**, 1957–1964.

27 Calude, A. S. & Pagel, M. 2011 How do we use language? Shared patterns in the frequency of word use across 17 world languages. *Phil. Trans. R. Soc. B* **366**, 1101–1107.

28 Gray, R. D., Atkinson, Q. D. & Greenhill, S. J. 2011 Language evolution and human history: what a difference a date makes. *Phil. Trans. R. Soc. B* **366**, 1090–1100.

29 Holden, C. J. & Mace, R. 2003 Spread of cattle led to the loss of matrilineal descent in Africa: a coevolutionary analysis. *Proc. R. Soc. Lond. B* **270**, 2425–2433.

30 Pagel, M. 1999 Inferring the historical patterns of biological evolution. *Nature* **401**, 877–884.

31 Dalerum, F. 2007 Phylogenetic reconstruction of carnivore social organizations. *J Zool* **273**, 90–97.

32 Currie, T. E., Greenhill, S. J., Gray, R. D., Hasegawa, T. & Mace, R. 2010 Rise and fall of political complexity in island South-East Asia and the Pacific. *Nature* **467**, 801–804.

33 Richerson, P. J. & Boyd, R. 2001 Institutional evolution in the Holocene: the rise of complex societies. In *The origin of human social institutions* (ed. W. G. Runciman), pp. 197–234. Oxford, UK: Oxford University Press.

34 Gould, S. J. 1997 *Life's grandeur: the spread of excellence from Plato to Darwin*. London, UK: Vintage.

35 McShea, D. W. 1998 Possible largest-scale trends in organismal evolution: eight 'live hypotheses'. *Ann. Rev. Ecol. Syst.* **29**, 293–318.

36 Lee, S. H. & Wolpoff, M. H. 2003 The pattern of evolution in Pleistocene human brain size. *Paleobiology* **29**, 186–196.

37 Kingsolver, J. G. & Pfennig, D. W. 2004 Individual-level selection as a cause of Cope's rule of phyletic size increase. *Evolution* **58**, 1608–1612.

38 McShea, D. W. 1994 Mechanisms of large-scale evolutionary trends. *Evolution* **48**, 1747–1763.

39 Marcot, J. D. & McShea, D. W. 2007 Increasing hierarchical complexity throughout the history of life: phylogenetic tests of trend mechanisms. *Paleobiology* **33**, 182–200.

40 Richerson, P. J. & Boyd, R. 1999 Complex societies: the evolutionary origins of a crude superorganism. *Hum. Nat.* **10**, 253–289.

41 Dennett, D. C. 1996 *Darwin's dangerous idea: evolution and the meanings of life*. New York, NY: Simon & Schuster.

42 Currie, T. E. & Mace, R. 2009 Political complexity predicts the spread of ethnolinguistic groups. *Proc. Natl Acad. Sci. USA* **106**, 7339–7344.

43 Barker, D. & Pagel, M. 2005 Predicting functional gene links from phylogenetic-statistical analyses of whole genomes. *PLoS Comput. Biol.* **1**, e3.

44 Kirch, P. V. 1984 *The evolution of the Polynesian chiefdoms*. Cambridge, UK: Cambridge University Press.

45 Blanton, R. E., Feinman, G. M., Kowalewski, S. A. & Peregrine, P. N. 1996 A dual-processual theory for the evolution of Mesoamerican civilization. *Curr. Anth.* **37**, 1–14.

46 Penny, D. & Phillips, M. J. 2004 The rise of birds and mammals: are microevolutionary processes sufficient for macroevolution. *Trends Ecol. Evol.* **19**, 516–522.

47 Dobzhansky, T. 1973 Nothing in biology makes sense except in light of evolution. *Am. Biol. Teacher* **35**, 125–129.

Chapter 19

How Copying Affects the Amount, Evenness and Persistence of Cultural Knowledge: Insights from the Social Learning Strategies Tournament*

Luke Rendell, Robert Boyd, Magnus Enquist,
Marcus W. Feldman, Laurel Fogarty
and Kevin N. Laland

Darwinian processes should favour those individuals that deploy the most effective strategies for acquiring information about their environment. We organized a computer-based tournament to investigate which learning strategies would perform well in a changing environment. The most successful strategies relied almost exclusively on social learning (here, learning a behaviour performed by another individual) rather than asocial learning, even when environments were changing rapidly; moreover, successful strategies focused learning effort on periods of environmental change. Here, we use data from tournament simulations to examine how these strategies might affect cultural evolution, as reflected in the amount of culture (i.e. number of cultural traits) in the population, the distribution of cultural traits across individuals, and their persistence through time. We found that high levels of social learning are associated with a larger amount of more persistent knowledge, but a smaller amount of less persistent expressed behaviour, as well as more uneven distributions of behaviour, as individuals concentrated on exploiting a smaller subset of behaviour patterns. Increased rates of environmental change generated increases in the amount and evenness of behaviour. These observations suggest that copying confers on cultural populations an adaptive plasticity, allowing them to respond to changing environments rapidly by drawing on a wider knowledge base.

Keywords: social learning; cultural evolution; simulation modelling

* Electronic supplementary material is available at http://dx.doi.org/10.1098/rstb.2010.0376 or via http://rstb.royalsocietypublishing.org.

19.1 **Introduction**

Understanding the evolution of human culture is one of the greatest challenges facing science. The gulf between the complexity of human culture and cognition and that observed in other animals is so vast that to many it has seemed unbridgeable. Nonetheless, evolutionary links are there to be found. Most behavioural biologists now acknowledge, for example, the existence of diverse behavioural traditions observed in other apes and monkeys [1–3], the surprisingly complex cognition of corvids [1], and the impressive collective decision-making and rich social behaviour of insect societies [2, 3]. Yet, the fact remains that however much we talk up these phenomena, there is a chasm between our achievements and theirs. If one accepts, as we do, the argument that chimpanzees, and for that matter monkeys, whales, birds and fishes, have some semblance of culture, then one must acknowledge that the 'culture' of nonhuman animals is very different from our own.

Such reasoning leads to two kinds of question. First, in what ways do the processes that underlie human culture differ from those observed in other animals, such that they can create such distinct patterns of behavioural, social and technological complexity. Second, how did those processes that underlie human culture evolve out of the kind of rudimentary capabilities observed in other animals? In simple terms, we can ask 'what is the gap?' and 'how can we bridge it?' The traditional routes to addressing these questions are well represented in the other contributions to this issue [4–7]. Here we take a different approach, drawing on and extending the insights into the evolution of culture that emerged from the social learning strategies tournament [8]. In this chapter, we will first review the setup and results of this tournament, and then use the same model framework to investigate how the strategies that were successful in the tournament affect cultural evolution.

Our tournament was a competition designed to understand the most effective means to learn in a complex, changeable world. Similar tournaments have proved an effective means for investigating the evolution of cooperation [9]. The background to the tournament was the observation that while social learning is central to the capacity for human culture, and while human culture is widely thought to be responsible for our success as a species [10], it remains something of a mystery as to why individuals profit by copying others and how best to do this (note that throughout this chapter, we use the term 'copying' as synonymous with social learning in the broad sense—any form of socially contingent learning by which individuals come to do what others already do [11]). At first sight, social learning appears advantageous because it allows individuals to avoid the costs of trial-and-error learning. However, theoretical work shows that this advantage can be offset if social learning leads individuals to acquire inappropriate or outdated information in non-uniform and changing environments [10, 12–15]. Current theory suggests that to avoid these errors individuals should be selective in when and how they use social learning [10, 16], and that natural selection should favour the best 'social learning strategies'—psychological mechanisms that specify when individuals copy and from whom they learn [17]. Formal theoretical analyses [10, 15, 18–21] and experimental studies [22–24] have explored a small number of strategies. However, for a more authoritative understanding the relative merits of a large number of alternative social learning strategies must be assessed. To address this, we organized a computer tournament, in which strategies competed in a complex and changing simulation environment, with a €10 000 prize awarded to the winner [8]. In this article, we extend our earlier analyses of the tournament results to consider how the strategies that did well affect the *amount, evenness* and *persistence* of cultural traits.

Among the striking differences between human and animal culture is the sheer amount of culture that humans possess. Here, the *amount* of culture refers to the number of cultural traits that a population knows about, or actually expresses in behaviour, which we call the amount of knowledge and behaviour, respectively. We explore the relationship between these quantities and the learning strategies deployed in a population, expressed as the amount and type (social or asocial) of learning used.

We also consider how evolutionarily successful strategies affect the *evenness* of culture, which we define as the flatness or uniformity of the distributions of knowledge and expressed behaviour across a population. Logic suggests that copying should increase the behavioural evenness exhibited by a population, since copying generates homogeneity in exhibited behaviour, but it is less clear whether and how copying will affect the evenness of acquired knowledge. Once again, we use the output from the tournament to shed light on this issue.

Finally, we examine how these strategies affect the *persistence* of cultural traits, which we define here as the average length of time individual traits persist, given that they became known or expressed by at least one individual, either in the knowledge or the expressed behaviour of at least one individual in a population. Human culture is uniquely cumulative, with each generation building upon the cultural knowledge of the previous generations [25]. Cumulative culture requires cultural traits to persist for long enough to allow refinements or elaborations of acquired knowledge [26]. The cultures of other animals are frequently characterized by 'lightning traditions', which rapidly sweep through a group of animals, and then are replaced as quickly, with little sign of any accumulation of knowledge [27]. Conversely, humans today possess knowledge first acquired many thousands of years ago. It is plausible that the preservation of acquired knowledge over long periods of time creates the opportunity for refinement, elaboration and diversification [26], and that this again explains some of the uniqueness of human culture. We use the data generated by the tournament to explore how the longevity of cultural knowledge is affected by the proportion of learning that is copying. We consider how the level of copying affects the average persistence of both exploited behaviour and behavioural knowledge in the population's repertoire.

One of the challenges facing a developing theory of cultural evolution is to link the small-scale, social-learning decisions of individuals to the creation and subsequent evolution of the collections of knowledge, tradition, language and behaviour that characterize populations at the level analysed in other contributions to this collection [28, 29] (here, Chapters 16 and 18). As we describe below, the tournament is effective both because it proposes specific means by which copying may be implemented strategically to enhance copying efficiency, and because it illustrates the population-level consequences of such strategies. In the sections below we first summarize the methods and findings of the social-learning strategies tournament [8]. Second, we present analyses of tournament simulations designed to shed light on how copying affects the longevity, evenness and amount of cultural knowledge in the virtual 'cultures' constructed by the strategies that did well in our tournament. Finally, we will attempt to collate these insights to shed light on both the field of cultural evolution and, more generally, understanding of the evolution of culture.

19.2 **The tournament**

19.2.1 **Methods**

To investigate why copying is so widespread in the animal kingdom, and in humans in particular, we organized a computer simulation tournament [8]. Entrants were challenged to specify a strategy to enable agents to survive and prosper in a simulated environment.

In this simulated environment 100 agents could learn about 100 different behavioural acts, each with a distinct payoff, drawn from an exponential distribution. This learning problem belongs to a class termed 'restless multi-armed bandits' commonly used in a variety of fields to study learning [30, 31]. The environment varied, as payoffs changed with a fixed probability, p_c, per simulation iteration.

The goal for entrants to the tournament was to design a simple piece of software (submitted either in code or pseudo code) that specified the circumstances under which individuals with their strategy should learn asocially (play INNOVATE), learn socially (play OBSERVE) or perform an act (play EXPLOIT). INNOVATE returned accurate information about the payoff of a randomly selected behaviour previously unknown to the agent. OBSERVE returned noisy information about the behaviour and payoff currently being demonstrated in the population by $n_{observe}$ other agents, selected at random from those playing EXPLOIT (i.e. at least one individual in the population needed to be performing a behaviour pattern for it to be observable by others). Playing OBSERVE could return no behaviour if none was demonstrated or if a behaviour that was already in the agent's repertoire was observed. Finally, playing EXPLOIT performed an act from the individual's repertoire, chosen by the agent (more specifically, the strategy controlling that agent), and the agent received the associated payoff—this was the only way in which an agent could actually acquire payoffs.

OBSERVE moves were error prone in two ways. There was a small probability of acquiring a behaviour different from that being observed, $p_{copyActWrong}$, in which case an individual added a random act from the 99 unperformed acts to its repertoire. This act was still associated with the payoff received by the observed individual. Independently, the payoff associated with each act observed was subject to a normally distributed random error with mean 0 and standard deviation $\sigma_{payoffError}$.

Entrants were given some information about the simulation environment, and strategies had access to agents' own personal histories. They were free to estimate parameters like $n_{observe}$, p_c, and the errors associated with each move using this information. Each agent also possessed a behavioural repertoire, empty at birth. The agent could only acquire knowledge, with which it could then acquire payoffs through playing EXPLOIT, by adding to its repertoire using either of the two learning moves OBSERVE or INNOVATE.

The evolutionary dynamics of the tournament simulation were modelled as a death–birth process with each individual having a per-iteration probability of dying, fixed at 1/50, giving each agent an expected lifespan of 50 rounds. After each death, individuals were selected to reproduce in proportion to their mean lifetime payoff (p, the sum of the payoffs gained by playing EXPLOIT divided by the number of iterations the individual had been alive) and their offspring replaced dying individuals. The probability of individual z reproducing was $p_z/\Sigma p$, where Σp was the summed mean lifetime payoff of the population in that iteration. Offspring generally inherited their parent's strategy, but could mutate and so carry a different strategy. This mutation rate (set at a probability of 1/50 per birth) allowed new strategies to invade the population.

The tournament was run in two stages, a pairwise round-robin stage and a melee that included the top 10 strategies from the first stage. Each pairwise contest consisted of 10 simulations in which agents performing strategy A were introduced (using the mutation process described above) into a population containing only strategy B and 10 simulations in which strategy B was introduced into a population containing only strategy A. In each simulation, the dominant strategy was introduced and run for 100 rounds without mutation so that agents could establish their behavioural repertoires. Mutation was then introduced, providing the second strategy with the opportunity to invade, and simulations were run for a further 10 000 rounds. The mean frequency of a strategy over the last 2500 simulation rounds was its score for that simulation. These scores were then averaged over the 20 simulations, and this average recorded as the contest score for that strategy in that contest. These simulations were run with the parameter set ($p_c = 0.01$, $p_{copyActWrong} = 0.05$, $\sigma_{payoffError} = 1$, $n_{observe} = 1$). A further set of simulations was run across a range of conditions using the 24 highest ranked strategies and the top 10 strategies were picked from among these. This top 10 set proceeded to the melee round.

In the melee simulation there were two sets of conditions, one systematic and one random. For the systematic condition set, we selected a number of values for each of the four parameters, p_c, $n_{observe}$, $p_{copyActWrong}$ and $\sigma_{copyPayoffError}$. Fifty simulations were run with each of the 280 possible combinations of these parameter values giving 14 000 simulations. To check that the results of this process were not unduly affected by the specific parameter values we chose, we also ran random conditions, where parameter values were chosen at random from statistical distributions. For biological plausibility these distributions were weighted towards lower values of p_c, $n_{observe}$ and $p_{copyActWrong}$. We selected 1000 unique sets of parameter values and ran a single simulation with each set of values. Systematic and random analyses gave identical returns on the ranked performance of the 10 strategies, computed across all simulations and based on their frequency in the last quarter of each simulation.

19.2.2 **Results**

The most striking outcome of the tournament was the success of strategies that relied heavily on copying when learning, in spite of the absence of a fixed additional cost to asocial learning. Copying paid under a surprisingly broad range of conditions, even when it was highly error prone, even when only a single individual was copied, and even when copying revealed no information about the payoff to the copied behaviour. The effectiveness of social learning was observed in spite of the absence of an inherent cost to asocial learning, and in the presence of costs to social learning. We also found that the presence of the copy error, $p_{copyActWrong}$, was an important source of new information for strategies relying almost exclusively on social learning. The results showed that when the value of $p_{copyActWrong}$ was set to 0, the positive effect of reliance on social learning on mean individual fitness reversed, becoming strongly negative ($r = -0.30$, $p < 0.001$). Thus, when there is no copy error, high levels of social learning are associated with reduced average individual fitness in the population.

Our analyses suggested that copying pays because other individuals filter behaviour, making adaptive information available for others by only performing the highest-payoff behaviour in their repertoires. This means that even random copying is typically far more efficient than trial-and-error learning, because copiers select from a subset of the most effective actions. This helps us to understand why copying is widespread in animals [32].

However, to be successful in the tournament, strategies had to do far better than copy at random. Successful strategies restricted learning and maximized exploiting, timing bouts of copying for when payoffs drop, such that they acquired new knowledge that enhanced their performance after a change in the environment. The winning strategy, *discountmachine* (entered by Dan Cownden and Tim Lillicrap), evaluated current information based on its age, and judged how valuable it would be in the future, a form of mental time travel that greatly increased its learning efficiency. Copying only increased the mean individual fitness of individuals in the population when conducted in the efficient manner exhibited by the best performing strategies. This may help explain why human culture, but not that of animals, has led to demographic success, an observation that previous analytical theory has found difficult to explain [13]. Conceivably, only humans have the psychological attributes to be able to copy with this kind of efficiency.

19.3 **The dynamics of cultural knowledge and behaviour: factors affecting amount, evenness and persistence**

19.3.1 **Methods**

The initial tournament analysis [8] focused primarily at the individual level, asking how and why individuals using certain strategies performed well. However, the tournament framework also allowed us to explore factors such as how copying affects the amount of cultural knowledge at the population level. Each simulation contains 100 individuals, and each of those individuals has, at any one time, a set of behaviour patterns in its repertoire (almost always a subset of the 100 possible behaviour patterns defined in the multi-armed bandit). These combined repertoires thus constitute the combined knowledge of that population. The population can also be characterized by the set of behaviour patterns it is performing, provided at least one individual is playing EXPLOIT at a given time. This distinction between things individuals know about and things individuals actually do, between knowledge and behaviour, is not often captured in theoretical studies of cultural evolution, and cultural evolution theory has been criticized precisely for this reason [33]. It is, however, a core feature of the tournament model that we can distinguish between behaviour and knowledge. Here, we investigate these two aspects of culture independently, running simulations that kept track of three simple measures that together characterized the knowledge and behaviour present in these virtual cultures.

The first quantity we tracked was simply the number of different behaviour patterns present, which we expressed as a proportion of the 100 possible behaviour patterns defined by the multi-armed bandit. We measured both the proportion (out of 100) of possible behaviour patterns that were known—i.e. that were present in the repertoire of at least one individual—and the proportion that were actually performed in an EXPLOIT move by at least one individual. We call these proportions the *amount* of knowledge and behaviour, respectively; they measure the number of behaviour patterns known about, or performed, by a population at a given time.

Second, to describe what we term *evenness* in the context of this chapter, we measured the flatness of the frequency distribution of behaviour patterns across the population using Pielou's evenness index [34]. This is a measure used in quantifying species evenness in ecological communities based on the Shannon–Wiener diversity index, and is given by

$$J = \frac{-\sum_{i=1}^{S} p_i \ln p_i}{\ln(S)}, \tag{3.1}$$

where S is the number of species present in a sample, and p_i is the relative frequency of species i in the sample. In our case, we are using it as a measure of the distribution of behaviour patterns, so S is the number of possible behaviour patterns (100) and p_i is the number of individuals in the population at that iteration with that behaviour. The value of J can range from 0 to 1, the latter representing maximum evenness. For example, consider a sample of 100 individuals, in an environment where five behaviour patterns were possible. Maximum evenness would be if 20 individuals each performed one behaviour ($p = [0.2\ 0.2\ 0.2\ 0.2\ 0.2]$, $J = 1$), while minimum evenness would be if 100 individuals performed one behaviour and none performed the others ($p = [1\ 0\ 0\ 0\ 0]$, $J = 0$). An uneven distribution of behaviour with most individuals choosing the same behaviour could come about through conformism, the strategy of preferentially copying the most commonly seen behaviour, the importance of which in human culture is an area of active debate [35, 36]. However, we were interested to use our tournament model to explore the extent to which apparently conformist outcomes, such as an uneven distribution of behaviour, could arise in the absence of explicitly conformist strategies being deployed by individual agents [37].

Finally, we measured the rate of cultural turnover by calculating what we term the *persistence* of knowledge and expressed behaviour. Persistence was the average number of continuous iterations that behaviour patterns were known (as before, present in the repertoire of at least one individual) or for which they were performed (as before, being chosen in an EXPLOIT move by at least one individual), given that they had become known or expressed by at least one individual (such that persistences of zero did not occur).

We concentrated our analysis on the top ten strategies (Figure 19.1) as, being highly effective, we reasoned, these are the strategies most likely to occur at high frequency in nature and so it is their behaviour that is of greatest relevance here. We gathered data on amount, evenness and persistence by running two batches of tournament simulations. The first recreated the *random melee* section of the tournament, where the top ten strategies competed simultaneously across varied simulation parameters, to investigate how variation in learning strategies affects cultural dynamics. Varying simulation parameters reflect different assumptions about the environmental conditions. The cultural measures we analysed could change in response to this variation through both the way strategies themselves changed their behaviour in response to varying parameter values, and also the way in which the parameter values themselves altered the simulation dynamics by changing the error rates and relative cost associated with social learning. We were interested in the consequences of these strategic shifts on cultural dynamics at the population level.

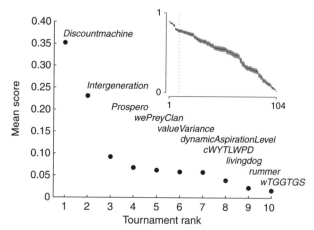

Figure 19.1 Performance of entered strategies. Plot shows ranked overall strategy scores in the final stage of the tournament (*cWYTLWPD* = *copyWhenYoungThenLearnWhen-PayoffsDrop* and *wTGGTGS* = *whenTheGoingGetsToughGetScrounging*). Scores are averaged over all final stage simulations. Inset plot shows mean scores for all 104 entered strategies in the pairwise round; error bars show standard deviation. The dotted black line on the inset indicates the 10 highest scoring strategies. From *Science*, **328** (5975), L. Rendell, R. Boyd, D. Cownden, M. Enquist, K. Eriksson, M. W. Feldman, L. Fogarty, S. Ghirlanda, T. Lillicrap, and K. N. Laland, Why Copy Others? Insights from the Social Learning Strategies Tournament, pp. 208–213. Reprinted with permission from AAAS.

The second set of simulations took each strategy in turn and ran simulations with only that strategy present, using the same parameter values as the *pairwise* tournament phase. We then repeated this exercise twice, in each case making a major alteration to the model assumptions. First, we set the probability of copying the wrong behaviour when playing OBSERVE, $p_{copyActWrong}$ = 0, removing the assumption that copying errors could introduce new behaviour into a population. Secondly, we set the standard deviation of a normally distributed error applied to payoffs returned by OBSERVE, $\sigma_{copyPayoffError}$, = 100, making information about the payoffs of behaviour acquired by social learning too inaccurate to be useful. We then compared the characteristics of the virtual cultures constructed by the single strategies under these varied assumptions.

19.3.2 Results

This was not a standard simulation study in which one changes a parameter to analyse how this parameter causally affects some measure in the results, rather it was a correlation study, where both dependent and independent variables were outcomes of variation in other variables. Several noteworthy results emerged. We first characterized the learning approach of the mixed strategy populations simply as the average proportion of learning in each round that was social (i.e. the number of individuals playing OBSERVE divided by the number of individuals playing either learning move—OBSERVE plus INNOVATE), and then examined how this single feature affected the population level measures described above (Figure 19.2). In general, we found that there was a step change in the relationships we examined, that, for the parameter sets explored, occurred after the proportion of OBSERVE exceeded around 0.7.

High levels of social learning were associated with increased amounts of knowledge until the proportion of OBSERVE exceeded approximately 0.7, after which we observed a ceiling effect with populations generally knowing all possible behaviour patterns (Figure 19.2a). This is a counterintuitive result because, compared to reliance on asocial learning, a reliance on social learning must reduce the amount of new information entering a population [38]. We interpret this apparent paradox as being due to two factors. It results in part from the assumption that copy error could introduce new behaviour into a population, hence more social learning leading to more copying errors leading to more knowledge, an interpretation which is supported by the results of our switching off copying errors, presented below. Secondly, more copying also means that behaviour patterns are more likely to be retained within the population, since multiple copies of any given variant are more likely to be generated. This can increase the amount of cultural knowledge in the population, because any knowledge that is built up over time is much less likely to be lost (Figure 19.2e) thereby compensating for the reduced introduction of variants that would have occurred through innovation. However, for increases in copying to be associated with increases in the amount of culture there has to be a source of new variants present, either stemming from innovation (even at low levels) or copy-error.

Conversely, high levels of social learning were associated with reduced numbers of expressed behaviour patterns, especially when the proportion of OBSERVE exceeded approximately 0.7 (Figure 19.2b). Accompanied by the concurrent reduction in the

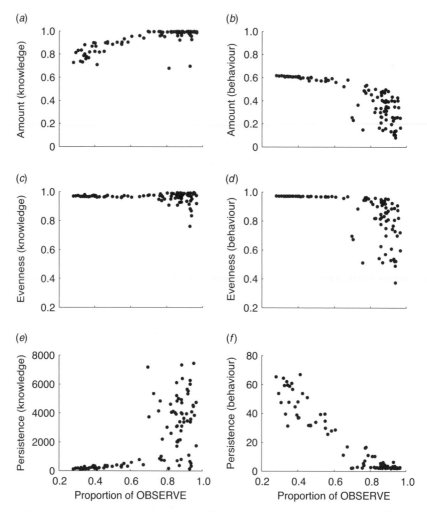

Figure 19.2 How effective learning strategies affect culture at the population level. Plots show quantitative measures of the (a,b) amount, (c,d) evenness, and (e,f) longevity of knowledge (a,c,e), and behaviour (b,d,f), plotted against the proportion of learning that was social, in mixed-strategy populations running under the *random melee* tournament conditions. Each point represents the average value across all iterations for a single 10 000 iteration simulation run. Note the order of magnitude difference in y-axis scales between (e) and (f).

evenness of behaviour apparent in Figure 19.2d, this observation suggests that in populations containing effective strategies and with high levels of social learning, individuals concentrate on performing relatively few behaviour patterns even though they have knowledge of many. Those few behaviour patterns performed are drawn from those with the best payoffs available at that time as many individuals choose to adopt them.

As these patterns in the amount of culture were counterintuitive, we were curious as to whether they could be explained either by simply the amount of learning that strategies did (quantified as the proportion of moves that were either OBSERVE or INNOVATE), or directly from the variation in simulation parameter values. We first fitted simple GLMs with identity link and normal error [39] to the data on the amount of knowledge, using as predictors the average proportion of learning in each simulation, which we term $p(\text{learn})$, and the values of the four simulation parameters (p_c, $n_{observe}$, $\sigma_{copyPayoffError}$ and $p_{copyActWrong}$). We used these predictors, including all first-order interactions, in a model selection analysis, testing all possible combinations to see which gave the best fit, as determined by the lowest AIC value. Once the best model had been identified, we then compared its AIC with that of an identical model but with the average proportion of learning that was social (which we term $p(\text{OBSERVE})$) as an additional predictor. The best model without $p(\text{OBSERVE})$ contained all predictors and interactions save $\sigma_{copyPayoffError} * p_{copyActWrong}$ and $\sigma_{copyPayoffError} * p(\text{learn})$, with an AIC of -7013.5. The same model with $p(\text{OBSERVE})$ added as a predictor had an AIC of -7093.4, some 79.9 units smaller, comfortably exceeding 3, the rule of thumb generally used to indicate a better fitting model [40]. This analysis shows that while other factors certainly had an effect, the proportion of learning that is social still independently explains a significant amount of variation in the amount of knowledge.

High levels of social learning did not affect the evenness of knowledge (Figure 19.2c), but drastically reduced the evenness of behaviour (Figure 19.2d). Once the proportion of OBSERVE exceeded approximately 0.7 we saw populations where most individuals performed just one or two behaviour patterns.

High levels of social learning (especially greater than approx. 0.7) were sometimes associated with very large increases in the persistence, or longevity, of knowledge in these populations (Figure 19.2e). Given that the average lifespan of individuals in these populations is 50 iterations, it is clear that increased levels of social learning can, in this model, lead to knowledge that far outlives its original innovators, lasting for tens and sometimes hundreds of generations. Conversely, in populations with high levels of social learning, persistence of behaviour was reduced, because effective strategies were quick to stop exploiting behaviour that did not return payoffs as high as expected, leading to a low average persistence (as the most effective strategies were the ones that did most social learning, populations with high levels of social learning are probably dominated by those strategies).

We found that only the evenness and amount of behaviour (not knowledge) were affected by varying the simulation parameters (Figure 19.3), while persistence was not affected at all. We found that increased rates of environmental variation were associated with both greater evenness and more expressed behaviour patterns (Figure 19.3a,c), even though the evenness and amount of knowledge were not affected. It is not inevitable that an increased amount of expressed behaviour is linked to increased evenness—it would be perfectly possible, for example, for a population to contain one very popular behaviour and a lot of relatively unpopular ones—but in these simulations they do appear to be linked, a result of individuals diverging in their estimates of what is currently the best behaviour to be deploying. Surprisingly, the extent to which social learning was error-prone appeared to have no effect on knowledge and behaviour at the population level (Figure 19.3b,d), even when it reached extreme levels such as 0.5.

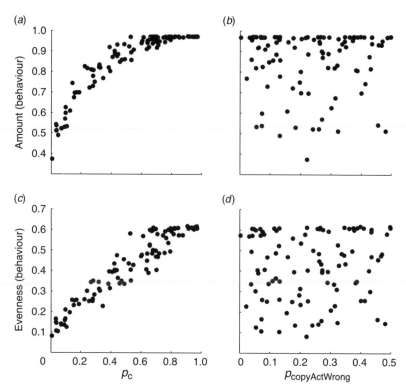

Figure 19.3 How the rates of environmental change and copying error affect the amount and evenness of expressed behaviour when effective strategies are present. Plots (*a,b*) show the proportion of the 100 possible behaviour patterns being used (i.e. by playing EXPLOIT) in mixed-strategy populations running under the *random melee* tournament conditions, as a function of (*a*) the rate of environmental change, and (*b*) the standard deviation of error in the estimated payoff of a behaviour learned socially (i.e. by OBSERVE). Plots (*c,d*) show the evenness of the distribution of behaviour patterns being used, in the same populations, as a function of (*c*) the rate of environmental change, and (*d*) the standard deviation of error in the estimated payoff of a behaviour learned socially. Each point represents the average value across all iterations for a single 10 000 iteration simulation run.

We also examined how two important assumptions in our tournament structure may have affected our results. These assumptions were first, that social learning carries a probability of learning the wrong behaviour (copy error) and thereby introduces new knowledge into a population, and second, that social learners are capable of learning the payoff associated with a given behaviour (payoff information). It is easy to envisage situations where these might not apply—for example, in the first case where strict error-correcting mechanisms are deployed to maintain fidelity (reproduction of classical music, or ballet steps), and in the second case, when the behaviour is one with delayed or opaque payoffs (e.g. planting seeds). We ran simulations containing single strategies explicitly, considering the effect of no copy error and no payoff information (Figure 19.4).

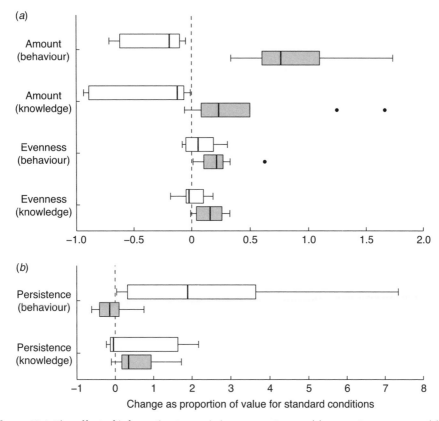

Figure 19.4 The effect of information transmission parameters on (a) amount, evenness and (b) persistence of knowledge and behaviour (note differing x-axis scales between panels). Boxplots show the change from the standard conditions used in the tournament when (white bars) the probability of copying the wrong behaviour when playing OBSERVE, $p_{copyActWrong}$ = 0 or when (grey bars) the social learning of payoffs is so error-prone as to be uninformative (the standard deviation of a normally distributed error applied to payoffs returned by OBSERVE, $\sigma_{copyPayoffError}$ = 100). Values are taken from averages over ten 10 000 iteration simulations in each of which only one of the 10 best tournament entries was present.

We found that these factors had strong effects on the amount of behaviour and knowledge. Both were reduced in the absence of copying errors but increased in the absence of useful payoff information (Figure 19.4). They had either no effect (in the absence of copy error) or relatively little effect (in the absence of payoff information) on the evenness of either behaviour or knowledge, except that a lack of payoff information slightly increased the evenness of both knowledge and behaviour. Switching off copy error profoundly affected the persistence of behaviour, increasing it up to seven-fold for some strategies, but did not affect the persistence of knowledge. A lack of payoff information appeared to have little general effect on persistence, although in some strategies it appeared to increase the persistence of knowledge. These effects are generally intuitive. The switching off of copying errors reduces the supply of new information into a population when that population learns mostly by social learning, which is thought to be an important weakness of social learning in general [10, 38], resulting in reduced amounts of knowledge and behaviour. Individuals in these populations were forced to rely heavily on that reduced set of behaviour patterns they did know about, resulting in an increased persistence of behaviour in a population. Finally, increased evenness of behaviour in the absence of payoff information probably reflects a reduced ability by the strategies in question to identify the currently optimal behaviour.

19.4 Discussion: what does the tournament imply for cultural evolution?

Analysis of the social learning strategies tournament [8] revealed that social learning is a more effective means of knowledge gain than asocial learning under most biologically plausible conditions, even when it is highly error prone. Copying pays because the copied individual is usually rational in performing his or her most effective (i.e. highest-payoff) behaviour, such that only the subset of high-performance behaviour patterns are exploited, thereby inadvertently filtering behaviour for the copier. This is probably why copying is widespread in nature, since even random copying is more effective than trial-and-error learning, and effective copying can be performed in the absence of cognitively challenging learning rules. Social learning thus can have benefits that may have been previously underappreciated [41]. However, this does not detract from the utility of strategic copying. The most successful strategies were highly selective about when they copied, which they achieved by engaging in bouts of copying only when payoffs dropped significantly, and evaluating information based on its age. It was only when copying was conducted in this efficient manner that it increased mean fitness within the population. This may explain why a reliance on social learning has led to demographic success in humans but not in other animals; conceivably, only we copy with sufficient efficiency and fidelity to give the demographic success observed in human history [10].

The analyses of population-level cultural characteristic produced a number of interesting insights. Noting that humans possess a great deal more cultural knowledge than other animals, we suggested that this might go hand-in-hand with our greater reliance on social learning compared to other animals. Our results were consistent with this hypothesis in establishing a positive relationship between the proportion of learning that was OBSERVE and the amount of cultural knowledge in the population (Figure 19.2a). While, in principle, this relationship need not be a causal one, the aforementioned analyses, plus further simulations presented in the electronic supplementary material, lead us to the view that it probably is. Under some circumstances increased reliance on copying can increase the amount of culture present in the population because the transmission of knowledge between individuals allows it to outlive any single individual, thereby reducing the rate at which a population loses knowledge. However, it is also the case that the relationship between reliance on social learning and amount of knowledge is partly, but not solely, a product of selection between alternative strategies, perhaps favouring strategies associated with large repertoire sizes. Learning strategies can also be characterized by the amount of learning they do, and our statistical analyses showed that this also affected the amount of culture present in a positive way, which is an intuitive result. The amount of learning was, however, a less powerful predictor of our data than the amount of social learning, which is perhaps less intuitive. High levels of copying were associated with complete knowledge saturation, such that all theoretically possible behaviour was represented in the repertoire of at least one individual in the population. This knowledge was retained in spite of the fact that enhanced copying led to a much smaller average proportion of behaviour actually being expressed at any point in time (Figure 19.2b). In the electronic supplementary material we present the results of simulations that raise the number of possible behaviour patterns to 10 000, conducted to gain a deeper understanding of the analyses presented here. The objective of allowing such a large number of behaviour patterns was to prevent any ceiling effects associated with knowledge saturation. The simulations also utilized a single strategy to remove the possibility of selection among strategies. Even under such conditions, we find that an increased reliance on social learning can be associated with increases in the amount of cultural knowledge, by virtue of it allowing behaviour to persist for longer than it otherwise would.

This relationship is not monotonic, however, as we find a peak in the amount of culture at some probability of social learning less than unity. In the extreme, when there is no copy error and only social learning, the amount of knowledge collapses to virtually zero.

We think these results are best understood in conjunction with the striking effect of copying on the retention of knowledge within a population (Figure 19.2e). A heavy reliance on social learning led to an average duration of knowledge within populations that was several orders of magnitude longer than for populations reliant on asocial learning. We observed a threshold level of copying, above which cultural knowledge could be retained for many hundreds of generations (given an average lifespan of 50 iterations). We suggest that it is this retention of knowledge that allows knowledge repertoires to approach saturation when populations rely heavily on social learning, because even with very low levels of innovation, if knowledge persists then it will, over time, accumulate. The caveat here is that there must be a source of new variation present, either through copying errors or occasional innovation. Once again, there is a marked contrast with the strong negative effect of copying on the persistence of behaviour (Figure 19.2f). High levels of copying lead to rapid turnover in the behaviour patterns exploited, without a concurrent loss of knowledge from the population's repertoire. These observations have parallels in human populations, where we simultaneously witness fads and fashions that change rapidly, representing high turnover in behaviour, and the retention of cultural knowledge over millennia. By illustrating how copying enhances the persistence of knowledge, our analyses explain why these observations should not be viewed as conflicting.

These observations help to resolve the conundrum that, while logic dictates that copying promotes behavioural homogeneity, humans have accumulated large amounts of cultural knowledge. As expected, individuals converge, through copying, on high-payoff behaviour, such that increasing levels of copying reduce the proportion of behaviour exploited to the high-performance end of the spectrum. However, in a changing environment, with individuals born naive, inevitably there is some low-level exploitation of poor-performing behaviour too. It would seem that copying may sometimes promote the maintenance of cultural knowledge in a population, by preventing such knowledge from being lost when individuals die. This illustrates, once again, the striking adaptive advantages of social learning: individuals rapidly converge on, and reap the benefits of, exploiting high-payoff behaviour, yet at the same time high-copying populations retain high levels of cultural knowledge, conferring the plasticity to switch behaviour when environments change.

As expected, we also found that copying typically reduced the evenness of exploited behaviour, because it leads to a small number of high-performance behaviour patterns being disproportionately performed (Figure 19.2d). Indeed, even in the absence of an explicit 'conformist learning' rule being deployed by individual agents, we witnessed some semblance of conformity emerging at the population level, reflected in lower evenness of the distribution of behaviour (Figure 19.2d) a finding consistent with other analyses [42]. This did not, however, greatly affect the size of the cultural knowledge base (Figure 19.2a), since, as we have described, it allowed more knowledge to be retained over a greater period. Our tournament simulations focused on a single focal population, and we envisage that, were multiple populations to be involved, the large cultural knowledge base promoted by copying would lead to extensive cultural diversity between populations.

We also considered how some other parameters in our analyses affected the amount, persistence and evenness of culture. One of the cleanest and most intuitive relationships was between the rate of environmental change and amount of culture, where greater rates of turnover in the environment led to a greater range of behaviour patterns being performed (Figure 19.3a). High rates of change also resulted in more even distributions of behaviour, as no single high-performance behaviour was persistently optimal in the changing world (Figure 19.3c). Unlike much previous theory, which has suggested that a reliance on social learning can sometimes hinder the adaptive tracking of temporally changing environments [13, 14, 43], a heavy reliance on social learning did not compromise the ability of agents in our tournament to adjust to changing environments. This probably reflects the greater biological realism of the tournament over analytical models, since only in the former do individuals possess a repertoire of behaviour. Possessing knowledge of multiple behaviour patterns allows individuals to switch rapidly to an alternative high-performing action when changes in the environment reduce the payoff to the current behaviour. This flexibility dramatically reduces the costs of copying.

Perhaps surprisingly, copy error had little effect on the amount of expressed behaviour (Figure 19.3b,d), except at the extreme where there was no copy error at all (Figure 19.4). Error-free copying reduced the amount of both cultural knowledge and behaviour, since new behaviour could no longer be introduced by this route. While it is no surprise that without copy error behaviour patterns persisted for longer (Figure 19.4), it is less intuitive that this would lead to individual actions being exploited for longer (on average, twice as long). This reflects the fact that a great deal of copying (53% of all OBSERVE moves in the first tournament phase) failed to introduce new behaviour into individuals' repertoire, as individuals observed behaviour patterns that they already knew about. In the tournament, copy error increases the chances that individuals will acquire new behaviour when they play OBSERVE. These findings reinforce our view that copy error may be an important source of adaptive variation within natural populations [44].

One of the more surprising findings from the tournament was that copying paid even when copiers had no information about the payoff associated with the copied behaviour [8]. Like many others [30], we had assumed that one advantage to copying would be that it allowed individuals to home in on high-performance behaviour; and indeed, this assumption may yet be correct. However, copying offers advantages over trial-and-error learning even if observers receive no payoff information, because even blind copiers benefit from the aforementioned filtering of behaviour by the copied agents [10]. This insight could help explain the extreme reliance of children on imitation, leading them faithfully to copy even superfluous actions in a demonstrated task [45]. When children copy adults, they are typically taking advantage of decades of information filtering by the adult, making it on average simply more efficient to take their word for it. We also find that, in the absence of payoff information, greater amounts of cultural knowledge are retained and exploited (Figure 19.4), since the potential to be selective in the acquisition and performance of behaviour is reduced by a lack of payoff information. This also leads to greater evenness in behaviour across the population.

The tournament has proved an effective means of exploring a number of questions and paradoxes concerning cultural evolution. By illustrating the striking utility of copying across such a broad range of conditions, and drawing attention to the adaptive filtering performed by individual agents, it helps to explain why social learning is widespread in nature. By isolating the factors that lead strategies to be successful, it allows us to make a series of predictions as to the patterns of strategic copying likely to be observed in nature (e.g. copying should increase when payoffs drop, but rapidly drop off once effective behaviour is found). A focus on the winning strategy leads us to the insight that mental time travel, combined with the ability to estimate rates of environmental change, may be a vital feature of human copying, since it allows individuals to assess the probable utility of current information in the future. Our analyses also help explain how a highly culturally dependent species like humans might accumulate large amounts of cultural knowledge, when copying leads to behavioural homogeneity. Provided copying errors or innovation introduce new behavioural variants, copying can simultaneously increase the knowledge base of a population, and reduce the range of exploited behaviour to a core of high-performance variants. Similar reasoning accounts for the observation that copying can lead to knowledge being retained over long periods of time, yet trigger rapid turnover in behaviour. Low-level performance of sub-optimal behaviour is sufficient to retain large amounts of cultural knowledge in copying populations, over long periods. Indeed, a high level of copying is associated with the retention of cultural knowledge being increased by several orders of magnitude.

These observations suggest that copying confers an adaptive plasticity on cultural populations, allowing them to respond to changing environments rapidly by drawing on a deep knowledge base. In biological evolution the rate of change is positively related to genetic diversity [46], and formal analyses suggest a similar relationship between the rate of cultural evolution and the amount of cultural variation [10, 18]. Accordingly, we might envisage that populations heavily reliant on culture would rapidly diverge behaviourally, exploiting the rich levels of variation retained in their knowledge base. Our tournament suggests that the ecological and demographic success of our species, our capacity for rapid change in behaviour, our cultural diversity, our expansive knowledge base, and the sheer volume of cultural knowledge we exhibit, may all be direct products of the heavy, but smart, reliance of our species on social learning.

Acknowledgements

We are very grateful to Kimmo Eriksson whose discussion and comments greatly improved our manuscript. The authors would like to acknowledge the use of the UK National Grid Service (www.grid-support.ac.uk) in carrying out this work. We thank all those who entered the tournament for contributing to its success. We are also very grateful to Robert Axelrod for providing advice and support with regard to the tournament design. This research was supported by the CULTAPTATION project (European Commission contract FP6–2004-NESTPATH-043 434).

References

1 Emery, N. J. & Clayton, N. S. 2004 The mentality of crows: convergent evolution of intelligence in corvids and apes. *Science* **306**, 1903–1907.

2 Sumpter, D. J. T. 2006 The principles of collective animal behaviour. *Phil. Trans. R. Soc. B* **361**, 5–22.

3 Conradt, L. & List, C. 2009 Group decisions in humans and animals: a survey. *Phil. Trans. R. Soc. B* **364**, 719–742.

4 Whiten, A. 2011 The scope of culture in chimpanzees, humans and ancestral apes. *Phil. Trans. R. Soc. B* **366**, 997–1007.

5 Perry, S. 2011 Social traditions and social learning in capuchin monkeys (*Cebus*). *Phil. Trans. R. Soc. B* **366**, 988–996.

6 Henrich, J. & Broesch, J. 2011 On the nature of cultural transmission networks: evidence from Fijian villages for adaptive learning biases. *Phil. Trans. R. Soc. B* **366**, 1139–1148.

7 van Schaik, C. P. & Burkart, J. M. 2011 Social learning and evolution: the cultural intelligence hypothesis. *Phil. Trans. R. Soc. B* **366**, 1008–1016.

8 Rendell, L. *et al.* 2010 Why copy others? Insights from the social learning strategies tournament. *Science* **328**, 208–213.

9 Axelrod, R. 1980 Effective choice in the prisoner's dilemma. *J. Conflict Resolution* **24**, 3–25.

10 Boyd, R. & Richerson, P. J. 1985 *Culture and the evolutionary process.* Chicago, IL: Chicago University Press.

11 Whiten, A., Horner, V., Litchfield, C. A. & Marshall-Pescini, S. 2004 How do apes ape? *Learn. Behav.* **32**, 36–52.

12 Enquist, M. & Ghirlanda, S. 2007 Evolution of social learning does not explain the origin of human cumulative culture. *J. Theor. Biol.* **246**, 129–135.

13 Rogers, A. 1988 Does biology constrain culture? *Am. Anthropol.* **90**, 813–819.

14 Feldman, M. W., Aoki, K. & Kumm, J. 1996 Individual versus social learning: evolutionary analysis in a fluctuating environment. *Anthropol. Sci.* **104**, 209–231.

15 Enquist, M., Eriksson, K. & Ghirlanda, S. 2007 Critical social learning: a solution to Rogers' paradox of non-adaptive culture. *Am. Anthropol.* **109**, 727–734.

16 Giraldeau, L.-A., Valone, T. J. & Templeton, J. J. 2002 Potential disadvantages of using socially acquired information. *Phil. Trans. R. Soc. Lond. B* **357**, 1559–1566.

17 Laland, K. N. 2004 Social learning strategies. *Learn. Behav.* **32**, 4–14.

18 Cavalli-Sforza, L. L. & Feldman, M. W. 1981 *Cultural transmission and evolution: a quantitative approach*. Princeton, NJ: Princeton University Press.

19 Henrich, J. & McElreath, R. 2003 The evolution of cultural evolution. *Evol. Anthropol.* **12**, 123–135.

20 Borenstein, E., Feldman, M. W. & Aoki, K. 2008 Evolution of learning in fluctuating environments: when selection favors both social and exploratory individual learning. *Evolution* **62**, 586–602.

21 Wakano, J. Y., Aoki, K. & Feldman, M. W. 2004 Evolution of social learning: a mathematical analysis. *Theor. Popul. Biol.* **66**, 249–258.

22 Galef Jr, B. G. 2009 Strategies for social learning: testing predictions from formal theory. *Adv. Study Behav.* **39**, 117–151.

23 Pike, T. W. & Laland, K. N. 2010 Conformist learning in nine-spined sticklebacks' foraging decisions. *Biol. Lett.* **6**, 466–468.

24 Pike, T. W., Kendal, J. R., Rendell, L. E. & Laland, K. N. 2010 Learning by proportional observation in a species of fish. *Behav. Ecol.* **21**, 570–575.

25 Tomasello, M. 1994 The question of chimpanzee culture. In *Chimpanzee cultures* (eds R. W. Wrangham, W. C. McGrew, F. B. M. de Waal & P. G. Heltne), pp. 301–317. Cambridge, MA: Harvard University Press.

26 Enquist, M., Strimling, P., Eriksson, K., Laland, K. & Sjostrand, J. 2010 One cultural parent makes no culture. *Anim. Behav.* **79**, 1353–1362.

27 Laland, K. N., Richerson, P. J. & Boyd, R. 1993 Animal social learning: towards a new theoretical approach. In *Perspectives in ethology*, vol. 10, *Behavior and evolution* (eds P. P. G. Bateson, P. H. Klopfer & N. S. Thompson), pp. 249–277. New York, NY: Plenum Press.

28 Currie, T. E. & Mace, R. 2011 Mode and tempo in the evolution of socio-political organization: reconciling 'Darwinian' and 'Spencerian' evolutionary approaches in anthropology. *Phil. Trans. R. Soc. B* **366**, 1108– 1117.

29 Gray, R. D., Atkinson, Q. D. & Greenhill, S. J. 2011 Language evolution and human history: what a difference a date makes. *Phil. Trans. R. Soc. B* **366**, 1090–1100.

30 Schlag, K. H. 1998 Why imitate, and if so, how? *J. Econ. Theory* **78**, 130–156.

31 Gross, R., Houston, A. I., Collins, E. J., McNamara, J. M., Dechaume-Moncharmont, F. X. & Franks, N. R. 2008 Simple learning rules to cope with changing environments. *J. R. Soc. Interface* **5**, 1193–1202.

32 Leadbeater, E. & Chittka, L. 2007 Social learning in insects—from miniature brains to consensus building. *Curr. Biol.* **17**, R703–R713.

33 Cronk, L. 1995 Commentary on Laland KN, Kumm J & Feldman MW Gene-culture coevolutionary theory: a test case. *Curr. Anthropol.* **36**, 147–148.

34 Smith, B. & Wilson, J. B. 1996 A consumer's guide to evenness indices. *Oikos* **76**, 70–82.

35 Eriksson, K., Enquist, M. & Ghirlanda, S. 2007 Critical points in current theory of conformist social learning. *J. Evol. Psychol.* **5**, 67–87.

36 Henrich, J. & Boyd, R. 1998 The evolution of conformist transmission and the emergence of between group differences. *Evol. Hum. Behav.* **19**, 215–241.

37 Franz, M. & Matthews, L. J. 2010 Social enhancement can create adaptive, arbitrary and maladaptive cultural traditions. *Proc. R. Soc. B.* **277**.

38 Rendell, L., Fogarty, L. & Laland, K. N. 2010 Roger's paradox recast and resolved: population structure and the evolution of social learning strategies. *Evolution* **64**, 534–548.

39 Faraway, J. H. 2006 *Extending the linear model with r: generalized linear, mixed effects and nonparametric regression models*. Boca Raton, FL: Chapman & Hall/CRC.

40 Burnham, K. P. & Anderson, D. R. 2002 *Model selection and multimodel inference: a practical information-theoretic approach*, 2nd edn. New York, NY: Springer.

41 Rieucau, G. & Giraldeau, L.-A. 2011 Exploring the costs and benefits of social information use: an appraisal of current experimental evidence. *Phil. Trans. R. Soc. B* **366**, 949–957.

42 Matthews, L. J., Paukner, A. & Suomi, S. J. 2010 Can traditions emerge from the interaction of stimulus enhancement and reinforcement learning? An experimental model. *Am. Anthropol.* **112**, 257–269.

43 Boyd, R. & Richerson, P. J. 1988 An evolutionary model of social learning: the effects of spatial and temporal variation. In *Social learning: psychological and biological perspectives* (eds T. Zentall Jr & B. G. Galef Jr), pp. 29–48. Hillsdale, NJ: Lawrence Erlbaum.

44 Henrich, J. & Boyd, R. 2002 On modeling cognition and culture: why cultural evolution does not require replication of representations. *J. Cogn. Cult.* **2**, 87–112.

45 Lyons, D. E., Damrosch, D. H., Lin, J. K., Macris, D. M. & Keil, F. C. 2011 The scope and limits of over-imitation in the transmission of artefact culture. *Proc. R. Soc. B.* **366**, 1158–1167.

46 Fisher, R. A. 1930 *The genetical theory of natural selection*. Oxford, UK: Clarendon Press.

Chapter 20

What Drives the Evolution of Hunter–Gatherer Subsistence Technology? A Reanalysis of the Risk Hypothesis with Data from the Pacific Northwest

Mark Collard, Briggs Buchanan, Jesse Morin and Andre Costopoulos

Recent studies have suggested that the decisions that hunter–gatherers make about the diversity and complexity of their subsistence toolkits are strongly affected by risk of resource failure. However, the risk proxies and samples employed in these studies are potentially problematic. With this in mind, we retested the risk hypothesis with data from hunter–gatherer populations who lived in the northwest coast and plateau regions of the Pacific Northwest during the early contact period. We focused on these populations partly because the northwest coast and plateau differ in ways that can be expected to lead to differences in risk, and partly because of the availability of data for a wide range of risk-relevant variables. Our analyses suggest that the plateau was a more risky environment than the northwest coast. However, the predicted differences in the number and complexity of the populations' subsistence tools were not observed. The discrepancy between our results and those of previous tests of the risk hypothesis is not due to methodological differences. Rather, it seems to reflect an important but hitherto unappreciated feature of the relationship between risk and toolkit structure, namely that the impact of risk is dependent on the scale of the risk differences among populations.

Keywords: toolkit variation; risk; subsistence; hunter–gatherers; northwest coast; plateau

20.1 **Introduction**

Identifying the factors that influence the number and intricacy of the tools that hunter–gatherers use to obtain food is an important task for researchers interested in the evolution of culture. The reason for this is twofold. First, artefacts linked to the acquisition and processing of food dominate our main source of information about the evolution of hominin culture, the archaeological record. Recent discoveries suggest that hominins have been producing material culture for 3.4 Myr [1, 2]. More or less all of the artefacts that have been recovered from the first 3.3 Myr of this time period appear to have been employed in subsistence activities. Artefacts that were used for purposes other than subsistence increased in frequency around 100 000 years ago [3, 4], but subsistence-related artefacts continued to make up a substantial portion of the archaeological record well into the Holocene. One implication of the dominance of the archaeological record by subsistence-related artefacts is that to understand the evolution of hominin culture, we have to understand the evolution of hominin subsistence technology. Second, hominin history is dominated by hunting and gathering. Current evidence indicates that the hominin clade originated about 7 Myr ago [5]. The earliest evidence for farming dates to around 11 500 years ago [6, 7]. Thus, for 99 per cent of the time that hominins have existed as a distinct lineage, they have relied on wild resources. The obvious corollary of this is that to understand the evolution of hominin subsistence technology, we have to understand the evolution of hunter–gatherer subsistence technology.

   In this chapter, we report a study in which we used data from early contact-era hunter–gatherer populations living in the Pacific Northwest to reassess the most widely supported of the hypotheses that have been put forward to account for the variation in the structure of the toolkits that hunter–gatherers use to obtain food. This hypothesis holds that the differences among hunter–gatherer populations in the number and intricacy of the tools they use to obtain food reflect differences in the level of risk of resource failure experienced by the populations. We begin by outlining a method that anthropologists have developed to quantify toolkit structure. We then describe the main hypotheses that have been put forward to account for the variation in the structure of hunter–gatherer toolkits. Next, we review the results of recent tests of these hypotheses, and explain why a reassessment of the risk hypothesis is warranted. Subsequently, we describe our study. Lastly, we discuss the results of our study in relation to the results of previous work on the causes of variation in the structure of hunter–gatherer toolkits.

20.2 **A method of quantifying toolkit structure**

Oswalt [8, 9] laid the foundations for systematic research on the factors that influence hunter–gatherer toolkit structure by developing a cross-culturally applicable typology of tools and several measures of toolkit structure. Oswalt limited his studies to tools that are employed directly in the acquisition of food, which he termed 'subsistants'. Oswalt recognized three types of subsistants: instruments, weapons and facilities. Instruments are 'hand-manipulated subsistants that customarily are used to impinge on masses incapable of significant motion and relatively harmless to people' [9, p. 64]. A digging stick is perhaps the most obvious example of an instrument. A weapon is 'a form that is handled when in use and is designed to kill or maim species capable of significant motion' [9, p. 79]. Weapons include boomerangs, crossbows and toggle-headed harpoons. A facility is 'a form that controls the movement of a species or protects it to man's advantage' [9, p. 105]. A deadfall trap is an example of a facility. Oswalt also drew a distinction between simple and complex tools. A simple tool 'retains the same physical appearance before, during, and after it is brought into play' [8, p. 27], while a complex one 'always has more than one component and its parts change in their physical relationship to one another during use' [8, p. 28]. The weapons mentioned earlier illustrate this distinction. Boomerangs are simple weapons, whereas crossbows and toggle-headed harpoons are complex weapons.

Oswalt [9] devised three measures of toolkit structure. The first is the total number of subsistants (STS), which is an indicator of the size or what Torrence [10–12] and Shott [13] called the 'diversity' of a toolkit. The second is the total number of 'technounits' (TTS). Put simply, technounits are the different kinds of parts in a tool. More formally, a technounit is an 'integrated, physically distinct, and unique structural configuration that contributes to the form of a finished artefact' [9, p. 38]. The total number of technounits included in a toolkit is a measure of its 'complexity' [9, 10–12]. Oswalt's third measure of toolkit structure is the average number of technounits per subsistant (AVE). Again, this is a measure of toolkit complexity [9, 10–13].

Recently, some additional toolkit structure variables have been proposed. Henrich [14] introduced the sum of the technounit counts for the most complex instrument, weapon, untended facility and tended facility in a given toolkit (MXT). Read [15] has proposed three new toolkit structure variables. One of these is the number of complex subsistants, where—following Oswalt [9]—a complex subsistant is one whose parts change their physical relationship to one another during use (NCT). Read's other two variables are the number of technounits in complex subsistants (CSTS) and the number of complex subsistant types (CTTS).

20.3 Factors hypothesized to influence toolkit structure

Numerous factors have been hypothesized to drive hunter–gatherer toolkit structure [9, 10–21], but attention has been focused primarily on the nature of the resources exploited for food, risk of resource failure, residential mobility and population size. A primary role for the first of these in shaping hunter–gatherers' decisions regarding the structure of their toolkits was initially proposed by Oswalt [9]. Based on an analysis of the toolkits and diets of 20 hunter–gatherer populations, Oswalt argued that there is a relationship between a population's degree of reliance on mobile resources and the complexity of its toolkit. He suggested that the exploitation of resources that are mobile is more difficult and therefore demands more complex tools than the exploitation of immobile resources. Thus, populations that rely on animals can be expected to have more complex toolkits than populations whose diets are plant dominated. Oswalt also argued that, because aquatic animals are more mobile than terrestrial animals, populations that depend on aquatic animals are likely to have more complex toolkits than populations that hunt mainly terrestrial animals.

The latter point has also been made by Osborn [18]. Osborn argued that when considering hunter–gatherer toolkit structure, it is important to recognize that the organizational demands of terrestrial hunting differ from those of aquatic hunting and fishing. He then reported the results of an analysis in which the diversity and complexity of 21 populations' toolkits were correlated, first, with the percentage contribution to their diets made by terrestrial animals, and then with the percentage contribution to their diets made by marine animals. Osborn found that, generally, the procurement of marine animals explained more of the variability in toolkit diversity and complexity than terrestrial animal procurement (marine r^2 range = 0.12–0.54; terrestrial r^2 range = 0.02–0.44). The only toolkit complexity measure that correlated more strongly with terrestrial animal procurement than with the procurement of marine animals was the diversity of simple instruments (terrestrial r^2 = 0.28; marine r^2 = 0.12).

The notion that risk of resource failure is the chief influence on hunter–gatherer toolkit structure has its roots in Torrence [10]. In this paper, Torrence focused on time stress. She hypothesized that as time stress increased, hunter–gatherers could be expected to produce more specialized tools and therefore more diverse and complex toolkits. Torrence tested the time stress hypothesis by measuring the statistical association between toolkit structure and latitude in Oswalt's [9] sample of 20 hunter–gatherer populations. She employed latitude as a proxy for time stress on the grounds that, all other things being equal, the length of the growing season for plants decreases with increasing latitude. The significance of this, according to Torrence, is that as latitude increases, the number of edible plants available for hunter–gatherers decreases, and therefore they have to depend more heavily on animal resources, which as noted above are more taxing as far as search and pursuit time are concerned. Torrence's analyses strongly supported the time stress hypothesis. She found that toolkit diversity and complexity were positively and significantly correlated with latitude.

Subsequently, Torrence [11, 12] abandoned the time stress hypothesis in favour of one based on risk, which she defined as the effects of stochastic variation in the outcome associated with some behaviour. She explained that she had come to believe that the necessity for increasing speed of capture and for budgeting limited time are merely the proximate causes of the variation in toolkit structure, and that the ultimate causes of the variation are the timing and severity of risk. Torrence went on to argue that the use of more specialized and therefore more elaborate tools reduces the risk of resource failure. Thus, populations that experience high resource failure risk will produce toolkits that are diverse and complex, whereas those that experience lower resource failure risk will settle for more simple toolkits. In support of her revised hypothesis, Torrence highlighted the correlation that she had previously identified between toolkit structure and latitude, as well as the correlation that Oswalt had found between toolkit structure and degree of reliance on mobile resources. She argued that the former correlation supports the risk hypothesis because distance from the equator is a proxy for overall resource abundance, which in turn is a proxy for the scale of risk. The correlation between toolkit structure and degree of reliance on mobile resources supports the risk buffering hypothesis, Torrence argued, because a prey's mobility affects the probability of a hunter–gatherer capturing it: the higher the mobility, the larger the risk of failure.

The hypothesis that residential mobility influences hunter–gatherer toolkit structure was proposed by Shott [13]. Such a relationship exists, he argued, because carrying costs constrain the number of the tools a population can employ regularly. Thus, according to Shott, populations that move frequently and/or long distances every year will have less diverse toolkits than those that move less frequently and/or shorter distances. The corollary of this is that the tools employed by highly mobile populations will be less specialized than those used by less mobile populations, since they will be applied to a broader range of tasks. Shott carried out two sets of analyses to test the mobility hypothesis. The first set of analyses focused on residential mobility. These analyses employed data for 14 historically documented hunter–gatherer populations. Shott carried out parametric and non-parametric analyses in which the number of subsistants and average number of technounits per subsistant were correlated with several measures of mobility, including number of residential moves per year, distance travelled annually during residential moves in kilometres, average length of each residential move in kilometres and total area occupied in square kilometres. In the second set of analyses, which were based on samples that were smaller than those used in the first set of analyses, Shott examined the relationships between the technological variables and two measures of logistic mobility, the number of days spent in the main winter camp and intensity of land use. In addition to examining the correlations between the technological variables and measures of mobility, Shott carried out analyses that evaluated the strength of the statistical association between the technological variables and effective temperature and net primary productivity on the grounds that Kelly [22] argued that these variables play a role in structuring hunter–gatherer mobility strategies.

The results of Shott's first set of analyses were mixed. Toolkit diversity and mobility frequency were found to be significantly and negatively correlated, suggesting that, as predicted, populations that move frequently employ a smaller number of subsistants than groups that are more sedentary. However, the rest of the residential mobility-focused analyses did not support the mobility hypothesis. Toolkit diversity was not significantly correlated with total distance covered per year; toolkit complexity was not significantly correlated with either frequency of residential moves per year or the average distance covered during those moves, and neither toolkit diversity nor toolkit complexity was significantly correlated with territory size. The results of the second set of analyses were also mixed. Shott found that there was a significant positive correlation between toolkit diversity and number of days at the winter camp, which supports the mobility hypothesis. But toolkit diversity was not significantly correlated with intensity of land use, and toolkit complexity was not significantly correlated with either number of days at the winter camp or intensity of land use. Lastly, Shott found that the relationships between the technological variables and the two environmental parameters, effective temperature and net primary productivity, were not significant.

The hypothesis that hunter–gatherer toolkit structure is affected by population size was independently proposed by Collard *et al.* [21] and Henrich [23]. Collard *et al.* suggested that the diversity and complexity of hunter–gatherer toolkits might be influenced by population size in the light of cultural evolutionary modelling work carried out by Shennan [24]. Shennan employed two models, both of which were adapted from a population genetics model developed by Peck *et al.* [25]. In Peck *et al.*'s model, mutations can be either beneficial or deleterious; there is a correlation between an allele's fitness prior to mutation and its post-mutation fitness, and many mutations produce only very small changes in fitness. In his models, Shennan treated cultural innovations as equivalent to Peck *et al.*'s mutations. To create his first model, Shennan altered Peck *et al.*'s model so that transmission was only possible from one parent to one offspring. To produce his second model, Shennan modified Peck *et al.*'s model to allow transmission between individuals belonging to different generations where the older individual is not the biological parent of the younger individual. In simulation trials, Shennan found that there was a marked increase in the mean fitness of the population as effective population size increased, and that this occurred regardless of whether transmission was purely between relatives or involved unrelated individuals too. Shennan concluded from these results that larger populations have a major advantage over smaller ones when it comes to cultural innovation due to the decreasing role of sampling effects as populations get larger. When effective population size is large, there is a far greater probability of fitness-enhancing innovations being maintained and deleterious ones being deleted than when the effective population size is small. Collard *et al.* argued that a corollary of Shennan's findings is that, because each technounit represents an innovation, small populations can be expected to have less complex toolkits than large ones. Thus, there should be a significant positive correlation between population size, on the one hand, and measures of toolkit diversity and complexity, on the other hand.

Henrich [23] also drew on a cultural evolutionary model to argue that hunter–gatherer toolkits should be affected by population size. However, his model differs from Shennan's [24] in a number of respects. Henrich's model assumes that when copying a behaviour, especially a complex one, individuals will try to imitate the most skilful person in their population. Most people will not do as well as the best practitioner, but occasionally an individual will strike it lucky and, in a failed attempt to imitate, produce a behaviour that gives a better result than the previous best. This then becomes the new goal for the rest of the population. As a result, so long as the new behaviour is not more difficult to copy than the previous best, the skill level of the whole population will be improved. If the new behaviour is more difficult to copy than the previous best, the population's skill level will probably not improve. Thus, the likelihood of cumulative cultural evolution is partly dependent on the difficulty of copying a new behaviour. It is also partly dependent on population size, since in large populations even improbable events—in this case arriving at a behaviour that gives a better result than the previous best—occur now and again, and the larger the population is, the more likely this is. Depending then on the difficulty of copying a new behaviour, a larger or smaller population size will be required for cumulative cultural evolution to take place. It follows that, for a level of copying difficulty, if the size of the interacting population changes for some external reason, then this will affect the rate of cumulative cultural evolution. If population size increases, then the probability of cumulative improvement increases. On the other hand, if population size drops, then it is likely that the number of adaptive cultural behaviours will decline, because the probability of someone improving on the existing situation, or even equalling the current best, is small. Thus, in the next generation, the best individual to copy is likely to be slightly worse than in the generation before, and this process will be repeated through the generations, until some equilibrium is reached. Henrich argued that his model explains the apparent loss of cultural adaptations in Tasmania after it became separated from the Australian mainland with rising sea levels at the end of the last Ice Age, since this isolation meant that the Tasmanians were no longer part of a larger interacting continental population.

20.4 **Rationale for current study**

Three recent studies have compared the relative merits of the nature of the food resources, risk of resource failure and residential mobility as explanations for variation in hunter–gatherer toolkit structure, and reached different conclusions [14, 15, 21]. Collard *et al.* [21] tested the competing hypotheses by subjecting Oswalt's [9] toolkit structure data and a series of proxies for the putative explanatory factors to stepwise multiple regression. They found that the only significant predictors of STS, TTS and AVE were the two proxies for risk of resource failure they employed, effective temperature (ET) and net above ground productivity (NAGP). As part of a reply to Read [26], Henrich [14] used Collard *et al.*'s [21] dataset to investigate the impact of ET, NAGP, number of residential moves per year, the percentage contribution of terrestrial animals to the diet and the percentage contribution of aquatic animals to the diet on MXT. He found that ET was the only variable that explained a significant proportion of the variation in MXT. Read [15] argued that Collard *et al.*'s [21] results are problematic because they are dependent on the authors' choice of regression technique. He then reported a study in which he reassessed the relative merits of the three putative explanations for hunter–gatherer toolkit structure using several types of multiple regression. Read used Oswalt's [9] toolkit structure data and the same proxy data as Collard *et al.*'s [21], but also used additional toolkit variables and another proxy for risk of resource failure. The additional toolkit variables he employed are NCT, CSTS and CTTS. The additional risk proxy Read used is the length of the growing season (GS). Read found that in the majority of his analyses, the measures of toolkit structure were most strongly influenced by GS but were also affected—to a lesser extent—by the number of residential moves per year. He went on to create a model in which toolkit structure is driven by the interaction between GS and number of residential moves per year.

Currently, then, it appears that risk of resource failure is the most important of the factors that have been hypothesized to affect hunter–gatherer toolkit diversity and complexity. However, the studies that support this conclusion suffer from potentially important shortcomings. One concerns the proxies for risk of resource failure used by Collard *et al.*

[21] and Read [15]. To reiterate, Collard *et al.*'s risk proxies were ET and NAGP, while Read's were ET, NAGP and GS. While these variables are undoubtedly closer to the factors that directly affect hunter–gatherer technological decision-making than the other proxy for risk that has been used, latitude, they all relate to primary biomass (i.e. plants and other organisms that obtain their energy directly from the solar radiation), and there is a reason to think that the availability of primary biomass is less important to hunter–gatherers than the availability of secondary biomass in the form of animals [27]. As such, there is a reason to retest the risk hypothesis with data pertaining to the availability of secondary biomass. Another shortcoming is that none of the studies included what Torrence [11, 12] contends is the key risk variable—species diversity. Lastly, there is a reason to be concerned about the sample used by Collard *et al.* [21], Henrich [14] and Read [15]. By any standard, 20 populations is a small sample. A modest sample need not be problematic if it is representative, but the sample in question is not representative. It is biased towards high-latitude environments and also coastal environments [21]. Accordingly, it is not clear whether we can be confident about the conclusions drawn in any of the studies.

The study we report here was designed to address the first of these shortcomings. In the study, we tested the risk hypothesis with data from hunter–gatherer populations living in the Pacific Northwest in the early contact period. We focused on these populations not only because the climates and ecologies of the two main regions in which they lived—the northwest coast and the plateau—differ in ways that can be expected to lead to differences in the risk of resource failure, but also because data pertaining to the availability of secondary biomass are available. As such, they allow a more precise test of the risk hypothesis to be carried out.

20.5 **Predictions tested in current study**

The study focused on 16 hunter–gatherer populations. Eight of these populations lived on the northwest coast, and eight on the plateau. The northwest coast populations are, from north to south, the Tlingit, Kwa'Kwa'Ka'Wk (Kwakiutl), Nuu-Chan-Nulth (Nootka), Coast Salish, Makah, Upper Stalo, Twana and Quinalt. The plateau populations are—again from north to south—the Shuswap, Lillooet, Thompson, Okanogan, Coeur D'Alene, Sanpoil/Nespelem, Flathead and Klamath. The approximate spatial distribution of the populations is shown in Figure 20.1.

The northwest coast extends from Yakutat Bay in Alaska to Cape Mendicino in California. It is bounded by the Pacific Ocean on the west and by the Chugach, Coast and Cascade mountain ranges on the east. Much of the northern and central northwest coast is indented by deep fjords and contains many islands, while the southern portion consists of a relatively straight exposed coastline without islands. Many large rivers including the Stikine, Nass, Skeena, Fraser and Columbia flow westward across the region. The climate of the northwest coast is temperate. Summer temperatures rarely exceed 18°C, and winter temperatures rarely drop below 0°C. Annual rainfall is relatively high, with many locations receiving more than 2000 mm of rain per year. Dense coniferous forests cover

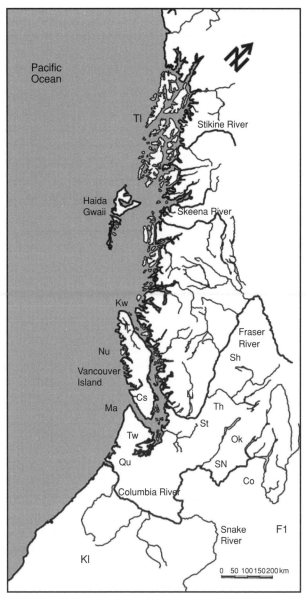

Figure 20.1 Map showing the approximate locations of the 16 hunter–gatherer populations included in the study. The abbreviations for the populations are as follows: Tl, Tlingit; Kw, Kwa'Kwa'Ka'Wk; Nu, Nuu-Chan-Nulth; Cs, Coast Salish; Ma, Makah; St, Upper Stalo; Tw, Twana; Qu, Quinalt; and the abbreviations for the groups in the plateau region are as follow: Sh, Shuswap; Li, Lillooet; Th, Thompson; Ok, Okanogan; Co, Coeur D'Alene; SN, Sanpoil/Nespelem, Fl, Flathead; Kl, Klamath.

nearly the entire region. Upwelling cool, nutrient-rich waters support a highly productive local marine food chain. Halibut, sealions and grey whales are among the species resident in the waters of the northwest coast. In addition, massive runs of salmon and several other fish species usually occur once a year. By comparison, the terrestrial fauna of the northwest coast is much less abundant.

The plateau is bounded by the Coast Mountains in the west, the Rocky Mountains in the east, the Subarctic in the north and the Great Basin in the south [28]. The region consists of steep mountains, rolling hills, river valleys and several large lake systems. Almost the entire region is drained by the Columbia and Fraser River systems. The climate of the plateau is more extreme than that of the northwest coast. Summers tend to be very hot and winters very cold. In addition, there is much less precipitation than on the northwest coast. The ecology of the plateau is diverse, and is influenced by altitude and precipitation. Typically, lower elevation areas are dominated by shrub and bunchgrass steppe, while higher elevations are dominated by xeric montane forests (ponderosa and lodgepole pine) intermingled with some mesic montane forests (western hemlock and western red cedar) [29]. Not surprisingly, the plateau has far fewer aquatic animal species than the northwest coast. Less obviously, its terrestrial fauna is more diverse than that of the northwest coast.

The differences between the climates and ecologies of the northwest coast and plateau are such that it seems likely that the hunter–gatherers who occupied the latter faced greater risk of resource failure than the hunter–gatherers who occupied the former. Thus, if the risk hypothesis is correct, the toolkits of the plateau populations should have been more diverse and complex than those of the northwest coast populations.

20.6 **Comparison of risk on the northwest coast and the plateau**

We began by testing the hypothesis that risk of resource failure was higher for the populations that lived on the plateau than for the populations that lived on the northwest coast. We collected data for environmental variables relevant to testing the risk hypothesis for each of the 16 populations. These variables included ET, NAGP, GS, mean temperature of the coldest month (MCM), mean temperature of the warmest month (MWM), mean annual rainfall (RMEAN), mean rainfall for the wettest month (RHIGH), mean rainfall for the driest month (RLOW) and species richness (RICH). Data for ET, NAGP, GS, MCM, MWM, RMEAN, RHIGH and RLOW were obtained from Binford [20]. Data for RICH were taken from Jorgensen [30].

Once we had collected the environmental data, we subjected them to principal components analysis (PCA). We pursued this course of action because risk of resource failure is likely influenced by multiple environmental variables, and is therefore unlikely to be adequately represented by a single such variable. We reasoned that, because principal components reflect covariation among two or more variables, principal components derived from multiple environmental variables might approximate risk of resource failure more closely than any of the individual variables. We employed the Kaiser criterion for principal component extraction, and therefore only extracted principal components with eigenvalues that exceeded unity. A total of two principal components were extracted in the PCA. The first principal component (PC1) accounted for approximately 64.5 per cent of the variation in the dataset, and the second (PC2) for a further 25.2 per cent. The scores for these principal components were incorporated into the dataset alongside the values for the environmental variables.

Subsequently, we used the t-test to evaluate the significance of the differences between the northwest coast and plateau populations in the environmental variables. Prior to carrying out the t-tests, we tested all the variables for kurtosis and skewness. None of the variables was found to exhibit significant kurtosis, and only one variable was significantly skewed. This variable, RLOW, was $\log_e$ transformed to avoid violating the assumptions of the t-test. In the t-tests, we used the Bonferroni correction to adjust the significance level to account for the fact that we were carrying out multiple unplanned tests. The Bonferroni correction modifies the critical value by dividing it by the number of tests conducted [31]. We carried out a total of 11 tests. Thus, the significance level was 0.005.

Most of the environmental variables not only differed between the northwest coast and plateau in the expected direction, but also did so significantly. RMEAN, RHIGH, RLOW, MCM, GS, RICH and PC1 were all significantly lower for the plateau than for the

Table 20.1 Results of t-tests in which northwest coast and plateau hunter–gatherer populations' values for nine risk variables and four toolkit structure variables were compared. MCM, Mean temperature of coldest month; MWM, mean temperature of warmest month; ET, effective temperature; RMEAN, mean annual rainfall; RHIGH, mean rainfall for wettest month; LRLOW, natural log of mean rainfall for driest month; GS, growing season; NAGP, net above ground productivity; PC1, first principal component obtained in PCA of environmental variables; PC2, second principal component obtained in PCA of environmental variables. The Bonferroni-corrected significance level for this analysis was 0.005

variable	northwest coast mean	plateau mean	predicted direction?	p
MCM	3	−5	Y	0.000[a]
MWM	16	19	Y	0.002[a]
ET	12	12	N	0.727
RMEAN	1652	458	Y	0.001[a]
RHIGH	263	68	Y	0.001[a]
LRLOW	4	2	Y	0.001[a]
GS	7	6	Y	0.375
NAGP	740	324	Y	0.000[a]
RICH	50	28	Y	0.000[a]
PC1	0.86	−0.86	Y	0.000[a]
PC2	0.21	−0.21	Y	0.412

[a]Statistically significant difference.

northwest coast, while MWM was significantly higher for the plateau than for the northwest coast (Table 20.1). The remaining three environmental variables—GS, ET and PC2—were not significantly different between the two subsamples. However, GS and PC2 differed between the northwest coast and plateau in the expected direction. Thus, overall, the environmental variables supported the idea that the plateau is a more risky environment for hunter–gatherers than the northwest coast.

20.7 Comparison of toolkit structure on the northwest coast and plateau

Using Oswalt's [8, 9] methodology, we recorded the subsistants and technounits of six of the northwest coast populations (the Kwa'Kwa'Ka'Wk, Nuu-Chan-Nulth, Coast Salish, Makah, Upper Stalo and Quinalt) and seven of the plateau populations (Shuswap, Lillooet, Thompson, Okanogan, Coeur D'Alene, Sanpoil/Nespelem and Flathead). We obtained subsistant and technounit data for the remaining three populations (the Twana, Tlingit and Klamath) from Oswalt [9].

From the subsistant and technounit data, we calculated Oswalt's [9] three statistics for describing toolkit structure, total number of subsistants (STS), total number of technounits (TTS) and average number of technounits per tool (AVE). We also computed the statistic proposed by Henrich [14], the sum of the technounit counts for the most complex instrument, weapon, untended facility and tended facility in a given toolkit (MXT). We did not calculate Read's [15] toolkit structure statistics—the number of complex subsistants, the number of technounits in complex subsistants and the number of complex subsistant types—because we are not convinced by Read's rationale for using them and because trials showed that they are redundant with one or more of the other toolkit structure statistics. In addition, trials also showed that Read's number of complex subsistant types statistic is excessively prone to subjectivity.

Subsequently, we used the t-test to evaluate the significance of the differences between the northwest coast and plateau populations in the toolkit structure variables. As in the previous analysis, the variables were tested for kurtosis and skewness prior to the t-tests

Table 20.2 Results of t-tests in which northwest coast and plateau hunter–gatherer populations' values for four toolkit structure variables were compared. STS, Total number of subsistants; TTS, total number of technounits; AVE, average number of technounits per subsistant; MXT, sum of technounit counts for the most complex instrument, weapon, untended facility and tended facility in a toolkit. The Bonferroni-corrected significance level for this analysis was 0.013

variable	northwest coast mean	plateau mean	predicted direction?	p
STS	39	39	N	0.984
TTS	212	178	N	0.350
AVE	5	5	N	0.038
MXT	37	31	N	0.097

being carried out, and the Bonferroni correction was used to adjust the significance level to account for the fact that we were carrying out multiple unplanned tests. None of the variables was found to exhibit significant kurtosis, and none was significantly skewed. Applying the Bonferroni correction reduced the significance level to 0.013.

None of the toolkit variables was found to differ significantly between the northwest coast and the plateau populations (Table 20.2). Moreover, none of the toolkit variables differed between the northwest coast and the plateau populations in the expected direction. The mean values for the northwest coast populations were all higher than the mean values for the plateau populations. Thus, the comparison of the toolkit variables did not support the predictions of the risk hypothesis.

20.8 **Discussion**

The climate and ecological variables we examined strongly suggest that the plateau is a more risky environment than the northwest coast. According to the risk hypothesis, this should mean that plateau hunter–gatherer populations created more diverse and complex toolkits than hunter–gatherer populations on the northwest coast. However, the results of our comparison of the toolkits of hunter–gatherers from the plateau and northwest coast were not consistent with this prediction. The plateau populations in our sample did not create more diverse and complex toolkits than the northwest coast populations. As such, the results of our study do not support the risk hypothesis.

There are several possible explanations for the discrepancy between the results of our analyses and the results of the analyses reported by Collard *et al.* [21], Henrich [14] and Read [15], which, as we explained earlier, supported the risk hypothesis. One is that our research protocol was inadvertently biased against identifying the impact of risk of resource failure on toolkit structure. It is possible that classifying the environments of the two groups as 'lower risk' and 'higher risk' and then comparing the groups' values for the toolkit structure variables with the *t*-test is too crude. To evaluate this possibility, we ran a series of correlation analyses in which each toolkit structure variable was correlated with each risk variable. As in the *t*-tests, the *p*-value was divided by the number of tests to account for the fact that we were carrying out multiple unplanned tests ($p = 0.001$). These analyses did not support the risk hypothesis either. None of the risk variables was significantly correlated with the toolkit structure variables (Table 20.3). Thus, it does not seem to be the case that the discrepancy between the results of our analyses and the results of the analyses reported by Collard *et al.* [21], Henrich [14] and Read [15] can be explained by our research protocol.

Another possible explanation for the discrepancy between the results of our analyses and the results of the analyses reported by Collard *et al.* [21], Henrich [14] and Read [15] concerns the risk variables we used. It could be that, contrary to what we have been assuming, our risk variables do not reflect risk of resource failure as well as the risk variables employed by Collard *et al.* [21], Henrich [14] and Read [15]. However, this explanation is also unsatisfactory. The reason for this is that our set of risk variables included all the risk variables employed by Collard *et al.* [21], Henrich [14] and Read [15]. To reiterate, Collard

Table 20.3 Results of correlation analyses in which toolkit structure variables were correlated with risk variables. The upper value in each cell is the Pearson correlation coefficient; the lower is the p-value. After the Bonferroni correction, the significance level for the analyses was 0.001

	MCM	MWM	ET	RMEAN	RHIGH	LRLOW	GS	NAGP	RICH
STS	−0.030	0.015	0.073	−0.216	−0.209	−0.408	−0.250	−0.032	−0.011
	0.913	0.956	0.789	0.421	0.438	0.117	0.351	0.907	0.969
TTS	0.201	−0.510	0.161	−0.033	−0.019	−0.152	−0.009	0.178	0.243
	0.456	0.850	0.551	0.903	0.943	0.575	0.973	0.508	0.365
AVE	0.509	−0.106	0.289	0.348	0.370	−0.331	0.477	0.464	0.569
	0.440	0.696	0.278	0.186	0.159	0.211	0.062	0.070	0.021
MXT	0.384	−0.180	0.138	0.298	0.301	0.204	0.056	0.367	0.474
	0.142	0.506	0.609	0.261	0.257	0.448	0.836	0.162	0.064

et al. used effective temperature and net above ground productivity as proxies for risk, Henrich employed effective temperature and Read used effective temperature, net above ground productivity and growing season. It might be objected that our first set of *t*-tests did not find a significant difference between the effective temperature values for the two groups of populations, and that this is consistent with the risk hypothesis. However, it is clear from the regression analyses reported in the previous paragraph that this result is misleading, and that effective temperature does not, in fact, impact the toolkits of the Pacific Northwest populations in the manner predicted by the risk hypothesis. As such, the discrepancy between the results of our analyses and the results of the analyses reported by Collard *et al.*, Henrich and Read is not a consequence of our choice of risk proxies.

A third possibility is that our results differed from those of Collard *et al.* [21], Henrich [14] and Read [15] because the risk hypothesis holds at the global scale, but not necessarily at the regional level. It is feasible that risk of resource failure is the dominant influence on toolkit structure variation when differences in risk of resource failure are large—as seems likely to be the case between, say, Africa and the Arctic—but is less influential when differences in risk of resource failure are small. In such situations, other factors may be equally, if not more, important. The results of a recent study by Kline & Boyd [32] are consistent with this idea. Kline & Boyd used data from Polynesian fisher–farmer populations to test the hypothesis that population size influences cultural evolution. They found that population size has a significant impact on both number of subsistants and average number of technounits per subsistant, which is consistent with the predictions of the population size hypothesis. Significantly for present purposes, Kline & Boyd selected the populations in their sample to minimize risk differences, and when they evaluated the relative importance of risk and population size, they found—as expected—that population size was more important than risk. This is consistent with the hypothesis that risk is the dominant influence on toolkit structure variation when risk differences are large, but becomes less important than other factors as risk differences among populations decrease.

To evaluate the possibility that our results differ from those of Collard *et al.* [21], Henrich [14] and Read [15] because the importance of risk versus other factors is dependent on the magnitude of the differences in risk among populations, we carried out a further analysis. First, we combined our TTS and ET data with Collard *et al.*'s [21]. Next, we generated 20 ten-population subsamples by random sampling with replacement, log transformed the values for ET (LET) and calculated the variance of LET for each subsample. Subsequently, we computed the Pearson correlation coefficient for the correlation between the number of technounits and LET for each subsample. Lastly, we correlated the variances for LET with the Pearson correlation coefficients. We reasoned that if the hypothesis is correct, there should be a significant negative correlation between variance of LET and the strength of the relationship between TTS and LET. The reason the relationship should be negative is that toolkit diversity and complexity are predicted to increase as ET decreases, since low-ET locations are expected to be more risky than high-ET locations. The analysis supported the hypothesis. As predicted, there was a significant negative correlation between the variances for LET and the Pearson correlation coefficients ($r = 20.450$, $p = 0.046$). As such, it seems reasonable to conclude that our results differ from those of Collard *et al.* [21], Henrich [14] and Read [15] not because there is a problem with our analyses, but rather because the importance of risk versus other factors is dependent on the magnitude of the differences in risk among populations.

With regard to future research, there are two obvious challenges. One is to further evaluate the idea that the influence of risk is dependent on the scale of risk differences among populations. This will require additional regional comparisons and/or studies that compare populations from parts of the world that are geographically separate but have similar levels of risk. In addition, there is a need to confirm that the results of the global-scale analyses are reliable and do not simply reflect population history [33]. The other challenge is to determine what influenced hunter–gatherer toolkit structure in the Pacific Northwest during the early contact period. If risk of resource failure was not the main influence, what was? Based on the findings of Henrich [14] and Kline & Boyd [32], population size is an obvious possibility to investigate. The study reported by Rendell *et al.* [34] suggests that degree of reliance on copying may also be worth considering.

20.9 **Conclusions**

A number of recent studies have supported the hypothesis that the diversity and complexity of hunter–gatherer toolkits are driven by risk of resource failure such that populations living in more risky environments create and use more diverse and complex toolkits than populations living in less risky environments [14, 15, 21]. In the study reported here, we carried out a further test of the risk hypothesis using data from hunter–gatherer populations who occupied the Pacific Northwest in the late nineteenth and early twentieth centuries. Our analyses indicated that the two main regions of the Pacific Northwest—the northwest coast and the plateau—differ significantly in variables that can be expected to affect risk of resource failure. Specifically, they indicated that the plateau is a more risky environment than the northwest coast. According to the risk hypothesis, this should mean that plateau hunter–gatherer populations created more diverse and complex toolkits than hunter–gatherer populations on the northwest coast. However, the results of our comparison of the toolkits of hunter–gatherers from the two regions were not consistent with this prediction. The plateau populations did not create more diverse and complex toolkits than the northwest coast populations. As such, the results of our study did not support the risk hypothesis. The discrepancy between our results and those of previous tests of the risk hypothesis is not due to methodological differences. Rather, it seems to reflect an important but hitherto unappreciated feature of the relationship between risk of resource failure and toolkit structure, namely that the impact of risk is dependent on the scale of the risk differences among populations. It appears that when risk differences are large, risk is the most important influence on toolkit structure variation. However, when risk differences among populations are small, other factors are as, if not more, influential as determinants of toolkit structure variation.

Acknowledgements

M.C. is supported by the Social Sciences and Humanities Research Council, the Canada Research Chairs Program, the Canada Foundation for Innovation, the British Columbia Knowledge Development Fund and Simon Fraser University. B.B.'s work on this project was supported by the Social Sciences and Humanities Research Council and the University of Missouri.

References

1 McPherron, S. P., Alemseged, Z., Marean, C. W., Wynn, J. G., Reed, D., Geraads, D., Bobe, R. & Béarat, H. A. 2010 Evidence for stone-tool-assisted consumption of animal tissues before 3.39 million years ago at Dikika, Ethiopia. *Nature* **466**, 857–860.

2 de la Torre, I. 2011 The origins of stone tool technology in Africa: a historical perspective. *Phil. Trans. R. Soc. B* **366**, 1028–1037.

3 d'Errico, F. & Stringer, C. B. 2011 Evolution, revolution or saltation scenario for the emergence of modern cultures? *Phil. Trans. R. Soc. B* **366**, 1060–1069.

4 Foley, R. A. & Mirazón Lahr, M. 2011 The evolution of the diversity of cultures. *Phil. Trans. R. Soc. B* **366**, 1080–1089.

5 Lebatard, A. *et al.* 2008 Cosmogenic nuclide dating of *Sahelanthropus tchadensis* and *Australopithecus bahrelghazali*: Mio-Pliocene hominids from Chad. *Proc. Natl Acad. Sci. USA* **105**, 3226–3231.

6 Bellwood, P. 2005 *First farmers: the origins of agricultural societies*. Malden, MA: Blackwell.

7 Gray, R. D., Atkinson, Q. D. & Greenhill, S. J. 2011 Language evolution and human history: what a difference a date makes. *Phil. Trans. R. Soc. B* **366**, 1090–1100.

8 Oswalt, W. H. 1973 *Habitat and technology: the evolution of hunting*. New York, NY: Holt, Rinehart, and Winston.

9 Oswalt, W. H. 1976 *An anthropological analysis of food-getting technology*. New York, NY: Wiley.

10 Torrence, R. 1983 Time budgeting and hunter–gatherer technology. In *Hunter–gatherer economy in prehistory* (ed. G. Bailey), pp. 11–22. Cambridge, UK: Cambridge University Press.

11 Torrence, R. 1989 Re-tooling: towards a behavioral theory of stone tools. In *Time, energy and stone tools* (ed. R. Torrence), pp. 57–66. Cambridge, UK: Cambridge University Press.

12 Torrence, R. 2000 Hunter–gatherer technology: macro-and microscale approaches. In *Hunter–gatherers: an interdisciplinary perspective* (eds C. Panter-Brick, R. H. Layton & P. Rowley-Conwy), pp. 99–143. Cambridge, UK: Cambridge University Press.

13 Shott, M. 1986 Technological organization and settlement mobility: an ethnographic examination. *J. Anthropol. Res.* **42**, 15–51.

14 Henrich, J. 2006 Understanding cultural evolutionary models: a reply to Read's critique. *Am. Antiquity* **71**, 771–782.

15 Read, D. 2008 An interaction model for resource implement complexity based on risk and number of annual moves. *Am. Antiquity* **73**, 599–625.

16 Bousman, C. B. 1993 Hunter–gatherer adaptations, economic risk, and tool design. *Lithic Technol.* **18**, 19–35.

17 Vierra, B. J. 1995 *Subsistence and stone tool technology: an Old World perspective*. Tempe, AZ: Arizona State University Press.

18 Osborn, A. J. 1999 From global models to regional patterns: possible determinants of Folsom hunting weapon design diversity and complexity. In *Folsom lithic technology, explorations in structure and variation* (ed. D. S. Amick), pp. 188–213. Ann Arbor, MI: International Monographs in Prehistory.

19 Kuhn, S. L. & Stiner, M. C. 2000 The antiquity of hunter–gatherers. In *Hunter–gatherers: an interdisciplinary perspective* (eds C. Panter-Brick, R. H. Layton & P. Rowley-Conwy), pp. 99–143. Cambridge, UK: Cambridge University Press.

20 Binford, L. R. 2001 *Constructing frames of reference: an analytical method for theory building using ethnographic and environmental data sets*. Berkeley, CA: University of California Press.

21 Collard, M., Kemery, M. D. & Banks, S. 2005 Causes of toolkit variation among hunter–gatherers: a test of four competing hypotheses. *Can. J. Archaeol.* **29**, 1–19.

22 Kelly, R. L. 1983 Hunter–gatherer mobility strategies. *J. Anthropol. Res.* **39**, 277–306.

23 Henrich, J. 2004 Demography and cultural evolution: why adaptive cultural processes produced maladaptive losses in Tasmania. *Am. Antiquity* **69**, 197–218.

24 Shennan, S. J. 2001 Demography and cultural innovation: a model and some implications for the emergence of modern human culture. *Camb. Archaeol. J.* **11**, 5–16.

25 Peck, J. R., Barreau, G. & Heath, S. C. 1997 Imperfect genes, Fisherian mutation and the evolution of sex. *Genetics* **145**, 1171–1199.

26 Read, D. 2006 Tasmanian knowledge and skill: maladaptive imitation or adequate technology. *Am. Antiquity* **73**, 599–625.

27 Kelly, R. L. 1995 *The foraging spectrum: diversity in hunter–gatherer lifeways*. Washington, DC: Smithsonian Institution Press.

28 Walker, D. 1998 Introduction. In *Handbook of North American Indians*, vol. 12, *Plateau* (ed. D. Walker), pp. 1–7. Washington, DC: Smithsonian Institution Press.

29 Chatters, J. 1998 Environment. In *Handbook of North American Indians*, vol. 12, *Plateau* (ed. D. Walker), pp. 29–48. Washington, DC: Smithsonian Institution Press.

30 Jorgensen, J. G. 1980 *Western Indians*. San Francisco, CA: W. H. Freeman.

31 Beal, K. G. & Khamis, H. J. 1991 A problem in statistical analysis: simultaneous inference. *Condor* **93**, 1023–1025.

32 Kline, M. A. & Boyd, R. 2010 Population size predicts technological complexity in Oceania. *Proc. R. Soc. B* **277**, 2559–2564.

33 Mace, R. & Pagel, M. 1994 The comparative method in anthropology. *Curr. Anthropol.* **35**, 549–564.

34 Rendell, L., Boyd, R., Enquist, M., Feldman, M. W., Fogarty, L. & Laland, K. N. 2011 How copying affects the amount, evenness and persistence of cultural knowledge: insights from the social learning strategies tournament. *Phil. Trans. R. Soc. B* **366**, 1118–1128.

Chapter 21

On the Nature of Cultural Transmission Networks: Evidence from Fijian Villages for Adaptive Learning Biases*

Joseph Henrich and James Broesch

Unlike other animals, humans are heavily dependent on cumulative bodies of culturally learned information. Selective processes operating on this socially learned information can produce complex, functionally integrated, behavioural repertoires—cultural adaptations. To understand such non-genetic adaptations, evolutionary theorists propose that (i) natural selection has favoured the emergence of psychological biases for learning from those individuals most likely to possess adaptive information, and (ii) when these psychological learning biases operate in populations, over generations, they can produce cultural adaptations. Many laboratory experiments now provide evidence for these psychological biases. Here, we bridge from the laboratory to the field by examining if and how these biases emerge in a small-scale society. Data from three cultural domains—fishing, growing yams and using medicinal plants—show that Fijian villagers (ages 10 and up) are biased to learn from others perceived as more successful/knowledgeable, both within and across domains (prestige effects). We also find biases for sex and age, as well as proximity effects. These selective and centralized oblique transmission networks set up the conditions for adaptive cultural evolution.

Keywords: cultural transmission; networks; prestige-biased transmission; dual inheritance theory; Fiji; cultural adaptations

21.1 Evidence from Fijian villages for adaptive learning biases

Long before agriculture and the emergence of complex societies, humans with the same basic genetic endowments expanded across the globe into a dizzying range of environments, from the arid deserts of Australia to the frozen tundra of Alaska. Survival in this range of environments, many of which are ill-suited for a tropical primate like us, depends

---

* Electronic supplementary material is available at http://dx.doi.org/10.1098/rstb.2010.0323 or via http://rstb.royalsocietypublishing.org.

on large bodies of culturally transmitted practices, beliefs, values and know-how. Examples include the (i) complicated manufacturing processes for arrow poisons, bows, traps, blowguns and kayaks; (ii) complex practices to detoxify critical food sources, such as acorns, cycads and cassava [1, 2] or to release essential nutrients from plants [3]; (iii) taboo repertoires that protect mothers and their offspring from dangerous marine toxins [4]; and (iv) recipes and taste preferences for anti-microbial spices that reduce pathogen threats posed by meat in warm climates [5, 6]. Such cultural products appear functionally well-designed to address local environmental challenges, usually in subtle ways not recognized or explicitly understood by the people reliant on them. Such anthropological observations mean that understanding the nature and success of our species requires explaining the emergence of such *cultural adaptations* [7].

To approach this issue, we draw on work applying evolutionary thinking to understanding culture and cultural change. This enterprise can be partitioned into three interrelated lines of research. The first involves applying evolutionary reasoning, often aided by the construction of formal models, to generate hypotheses about how natural selection might have shaped human psychology to most effectively extract adaptive ideas, practices, beliefs and values from the behaviour of others (e.g. [8, 9]). Building on this foundation, the second line takes these hypothesized, and empirically grounded, elements of human psychology and considers how they create and influence population-level processes of cultural evolution, including the emergence of cultural adaptations. That is, this line of research, which is itself disciplined by formal cultural evolutionary models [10], considers how aspects of our psychology, operating through interaction in social groups, can give rise to everything from sophisticated technologies (like arrow poisons) and adaptive taboos to large-scale cooperation, social norms [11], ethnicity [12] and social stratification [13]. Using culture–gene coevolutionary models, the third line explores how the emergence of such cultural products, including both sophisticated tools and social institutions, feeds back to influence the genetic evolutionary processes that shape our brains and bodies [14–16].

Here, we aim to contribute to understanding the evolution of cultural adaptations by empirically exploring the psychological biases in observational learning, and the consequent transmission networks that they produce. The application of evolutionary theory to understanding to whom learners should pay attention for cultural transmission and how they should integrate information from different models has generated a wide range of hypotheses about human cognition, many of which have found empirical support, especially from recent laboratory experiments (see below). Hypotheses about *model selection biases* propose that learners should preferentially attend to those individuals in their social world ('models') deemed most likely to possess adaptive information that can be acquired by learners [17]. To locate these *preferred models*, learners should give weight to a variety of cues that indicate which individuals are most likely to be worthy of imitation (i.e. possess adaptive information). Sets of proposed cues include (i) skill (competence), knowledge, success and prestige, (ii) health, (iii) age and (iv) self-similarity (e.g. based on sex, ethnicity, personality and physical attributes). These cues allow learners to identify not only those individuals in their social environment who are likely to possess adaptive information, which could be acquired via cultural learning, but also select those most likely to have information suitable to the learner in future roles, or as stepping stones in the acquisition of increasingly complex skills or repertoires. A variety of models (examples cited above) formalize these assumptions about human learning and examine how they generate cumulative cultural products over generations.

This line of theorizing also proposes that learners should weigh the potential gains of learning from their preferred models against the costs of accessing those models [17]. If access costs are too high, learners should adjust their selected models to those with lower access costs. In particular, this consideration emphasizes that some potential models have evolutionary incentives to transmit adaptive information to the learner, such as parents, siblings and other close relatives. Much cultural transmission benefits from the consent or cooperation of the model. Novice learners in particular, who have little to gain from community experts over their own family early in their development, should learn first from their most accessible models, later shifting over to their preferred models (see electronic supplementary material). In its simplest form, this proposal suggests a two-stage learning model in which individuals first acquire information from their parents (or other household members), and then later update this information based on transmission from their preferred models [18]. Recent empirical work in Fiji broadly supports this two-stage model in the domain of food taboos [4].

This theoretical framework in general, and these predictions about model selection biases in particular, organize a large body of findings from laboratory experiments across the social sciences. Work in psychology and economics supports the above predictions by showing that people use cues of success, competence and prestige in learning from others by modifying their preferences, beliefs, practices, opinions and food choices—among other things. Participants do this spontaneously, unconsciously and whether or not they are paid for their performance (reviewed in [19]). There is also evidence that success in one domain crosses over to influence other domains [17]. Recent experimental work has tested these models in sophisticated ways, sometimes measuring the relative importance of success biases over other learning mechanisms (e.g. individual experience). Success-bias consistently emerges as an important component of complex learning strategies [20, 21], though access costs are important, as expected [22].

Developmental psychology has recently focused on selective imitation in young children, providing evidence consistent with the above predictions. Young children (typically 3- and 4-year-olds) spontaneously track the competence of potential models in labelling objects and knowing the function of artefacts, and then preferentially imitate more competent models, even after a one-week delay (reviewed in [23]). Although children show a capacity to identify skill differences indirectly using cues about age, confidence and experience [24, 25], they selectively weigh competence over age by taking the word of a previously accurate child over an inaccurate adult [26, 27].

These studies contribute substantially to exploring and testing the psychological foundations of cultural learning predicted by our evolutionary approach. However, they are limited in being laboratory studies. It remains to be established how important these psychological biases are in real life, and whether they could generate adaptive cultural evolution in fitness-relevant domains. We begin to bridge this gap between the laboratory and field by assessing whether these same predictions bear out in the cultural transmission networks of a small-scale society.

Here we sharpen some of the model selection hypotheses mentioned above with the goal of testing them using data from three Fijian villages. In presenting these predictions, we sketch the supporting evolutionary logic (see further discussion in the electronic supplementary material):

Perceived success or knowledge: since perceived success or knowledge in a particular domain is a potential indicator of the adaptive value of cultural variants possessed by an individual, a learner's perceptions of others' success or knowledge in a domain should be an important predictor of their model choice. We examined this using five measures of perceived success and knowledge.

Cross-domain success (prestige): because more direct cues of success and skill may be noisy, unreliable or unavailable, learners should also weight perceived success or prestige in other locally valued domains. For example, individuals perceived as great fishermen may also be selected as models for learning about yams. Such cross-domain weightings may be adaptive for a number of reasons. Individuals who are most effective at acquiring skills from one domain may also be effective at acquiring adaptive information in other domains; or, successful individuals may possess general traits or practices, which can be acquired, that promote success in multiple domains (e.g. thrift and temperance). We use perceived success from two highly valued domains to predict model selection in other domains.

Age: it is a potentially valuable cue to possessing fitness-enhancing information for three reasons [17]. First, older individuals have had more years to acquire know-how through both social learning and experience. Second, merely by getting to be old, individuals have passed through a selective filter—not everyone gets to be old. Therefore, learners should preferentially target more senior community members, *ceteris paribus*. However, this effect may be nonlinear as very old individuals may experience cognitive losses. Finally, children may focus on somewhat older models as a way of scaffolding themselves up to increasingly complex skills.

Sex: if there are divisions in the skills or specializations of community members based on individual-level factors (e.g. sex), learners should target their attention using cues related to these factors in two ways. First, since learners want to acquire know-how that is suitable to them in their social roles (or future roles), attending to those who are similar to oneself on these factors customizes information acquisition. That is, for sex, we should expect that women should preferentially choose other women as models, *ceteris paribus*. Second, when sexual divisions of skill sets exist, learners can use sex as an indirect cue of their chances of knowing much about a particular domain (e.g. if a boy wants to know about nursing an infant, he should probably not ask a man).

Access: learners must balance the costs of accessing high-quality models against the quality of information available for transmission [17]. Thus, we expect learners to differentially copy from others that live in their same households and villages, as well as preferentially learn from those to whom they are most closely related. Since we are primarily testing adolescents and adults, we expect households and relatives to be less important as many of our participants will have learned nearly all they can from their co-householders and close relatives.

Network centrality: if there is a distribution in the perceived quality of potential models (e.g. variation in perceived success or suitability), the overall patterns of model selections for different kinds of cultural information should reflect this at the network or community level. The more important these cues are, and the more agreement among community members on these cues, the more centralized the transmission networks should be. If most people suggest their parents, other family members or vary idiosyncratically in their model selection, these networks should not be particularly centralized.

21.2 Ethnographic sketch and methods

The data presented here were collected as part of an in-depth, ongoing study of life on Yasawa Island, which lies in the northwestern corner of the Fijian archipelago. Our project mixes ethnographic observation with extensive interviewing and a range of experiments. Economically, Yasawans rely primarily on horticulture, fishing and littoral gathering. Fishing is the most important source of protein, and spear-fishing is the most productive form of fishing for those with sufficient skill. People also fish with lines and nets. Yams and cassava provide the caloric staples, although yams are preferred, traditional and necessary for ceremony life. Men compete informally to grow the largest yams. Political units are composed of interrelated clans called Yavusa, which are governed by a council of elders and a hereditary chief. Social life is organized by a complex web of kinship relations and obligations. At the time of the study there were no cars, TVs, markets or public utilities in these villages. These data come from the villages of Teci, Dalomo and Bukama, with populations ranging from 100 to 250 people in each. Teci and Dalomo, which lie about 10 min apart, jointly form one Yavusa. Bukama is about 2.5 h away (on foot) and forms its own Yavusa.

These data were collected between 2003 and 2008 by trained Fijian interviewers who did not have kinship or other ties with the communities. Interviews about preferred models and perceived success networks were conducted in private settings with only the researchers present. The methods deployed to gather each of our measures are discussed in turn (details in the electronic supplementary material):

Cultural transmission networks: These interviews were conducted in 2008 with everyone in the three villages over the age of 6. Participants' responses were used to construct the cultural transmission networks that serve as our three outcome variables for the regressions below. These naturally bounded networks are created by asking individuals to whom they would go for advice if they had a question in a given domain. We asked 'who would you go to for advice if you had a question about' (i) 'fish or fishing' (hereafter Fishing); (ii) 'planting or growing yams' (Yams); or (iii) 'using a plant as a medicine'

(Medicinal Plants). When people stopped listing names they were prompted with 'Is there anyone else?' This continued until the participant communicated that he had finished. People readily listed between zero and five individuals, self-limiting to five or fewer. We emphasize here that these are not direct measures of actual cultural transmission events. Instead, we assume these data approximate who individuals would look to, or rely on, in acquiring information in these domains. Below, we discuss the limitations of using such data as a proxy for the actual pathways of cultural transmission, and consider how this approach complements and converges with other lines of work on cultural transmission.

Perceived success and knowledge measures: In 2006, the team conducted an interview with all villagers over the age of 10 that was designed to measure perceptions of who in the community were considered to be the most successful, skilled or knowledgeable across a variety of domains. After participants' initial responses, they were queried as to whether there was anyone else besides those listed who should be added. This continued until participants communicated that no one needed to be added. All questions followed a similar format, asking participants to name those in their Yavusa first. We used participant responses from these questions: who (i) knows the most about fishing, (ii) are the best line fishers, (iii) are the best spear fishers, (iv) are the best yam growers, (v) knows the most about growing yams, and (vi) knows the most about medicinal plants, to construct perceived success/knowledge measures. These data are unavailable for Bukama.

Note that these success and knowledge interviews were conducted *2 years prior* to the network interview above, which served as our dependent variables. If these instruments were deployed at the same time (despite asking different questions), or within a relatively short delay, it is possible that participants might be responding similarly to both sets of questions because they were linking their two responses in some way. However, given the long delay between interviews, it seems unlikely that participants would recall their responses to the success/knowledge interviews when responding to the cultural transmission network questions.

An important question is how well people's subjective perceptions correspond to actual measurements of success or production. Our aggregate ranking of the best fisherman correlates 0.84 with our actual measures of fishing efficiency, based on weights for over 1700 fish collected over 6 years (see electronic supplementary material). These findings are consistent with work on hunting among foragers, which also indicates that locals' subjective evaluations are very accurate [28]. We lack data to evaluate success in growing yams and using medicinal plants.

Demographic measures: Using a demographic database that has been updated yearly since 2003, we drew information on age, gender and years of formal schooling for all respondents.

Kinship measures: Using a kinship diagram going back approximately three generations from those living in 2003, we calculated a coefficient of relatedness (r) matrix for Teci and Dalomo.

Time allocation measures of association: From 2003 to 2008 our team collected time allocation for a few months each year. Every day during each sampling month, several individuals were randomly selected to be sampled at a random time. At the appointed time, researchers located the individual and recorded what he or she was doing, and who they were with. We used these observations to generate a matrix where a cell in row i, column j, would contain the proportion of times that individual j was present when individual i was sampled. This control variable allows us to show that our findings do not represent merely common association patterns.

Using these measures, we estimated a series of regression models to assess the relative importance of each of our predictor variables for selecting the cultural models (based on our outcome variable). To statistically examine the relationship between our predictor and outcome variables, given the non-independence of network data, we constructed exponential random graph (ERG) models [29]. Our ERG models assume every tie (a selection of one person as a cultural model by another person) between every possible pair of individuals to be a random variable that can take a value of 1 if the tie is present or 0 if it is not. Assuming this, it is possible to construct all of the possible network configurations that have the same number of nodes as the observed network. If the process that generates the connections between individuals in the observed network was completely random, one would expect there to be identical probabilities for every tie existing between every dyad in the network. However, if this process is non-random, for example if individuals are more likely to go to people who are of the same sex for their cultural information, then the probability of ties between same-sex individuals will be higher than ties between individuals of the opposite sex. If one specifies how a set of variables relates to the probability of a tie existing between two individuals, it is possible to compare the observed network with the distribution of possible networks and estimate coefficients that maximize the probability of generating networks that are similar to the observed network. The electronic supplementary material expands on ERG models.

We explore two categories of effects with this approach: (i) *main effects*, which capture the relationship between individual-level attributes (e.g. age, sex and education) with the number of times that an individual is selected as a model by others, and (ii) *dyad effects*, which measure the effects of similarities and differences between dyads, or some character of their joint relationship. If, for example, two individuals match on sex this may influence the likelihood of a connection (directed tie) between them. Alternatively, the coefficient of relatedness matrix (r) can be used to estimate how kinship influences the likelihood of a cultural transmission tie. Because we have all the variables discussed above for both Teci and Dalomo but only a subset of them for all three villages, we present our findings in reference to the *Teci-Dalomo sample* ($n \sim 65$ individuals with 4160 directed ties), and the *full sample* (approx. 200 individuals with 39 800 directed ties).

While small, these communities provide a particularly suitable environment for our methodological approach. The small size and remote nature of these communities mean that we have bounded networks, and little concern that people might obtain information in these domains from books, newspapers, the Internet or formal education. We explain below that these cultural transmission networks naturally bounded themselves, with very few people seeking models beyond their Yavusa, and no one in the Teci–Dalomo sample doing so. This avoids otherwise prickly analytical challenges.

21.3 **Results**

Before presenting the regression models, we discuss what the network visualizations tell us. Figure 21.1 shows the networks for all three villages in our three domains. Visual inspection suggests that all three networks are centralized. Network centralizations range from 16 per cent for the full yams network to 41 per cent for the Teci–Dalomo medicinal plants network (see electronic supplementary material). A network in which everyone is selected equally frequently has a centralization of 0 per cent while a network in which everyone picks the same person has a centralization of 100 per cent. This degree of centralization is consistent with the prediction that people substantially share notions about who is a good cultural model (network centrality), but that individuals' model selections are influenced by multiple factors.

Figure 21.1 also reveals that people see their primary sources of cultural information to be members of their own Yavusa. Yasawans in villages of Teci and Dalomo, which together form a Yavusa, are inclined to select those in their own village, but do also look to the other village within their Yavusa. They do not look to Bukama (the next closest village). Those in Bukama limit their choice almost entirely to their own Yavusa, with just a handful of people from Bukama choosing models in distant communities (not shown). The fact that Bukama forms bounded networks independent of Teci–Dalomo in Figure 21.1 is not owing to our explicit instructions: Yasawans spontaneously limited themselves in this fashion, though substantial rates of inter-village marriage mean that individuals flow readily among all these communities.

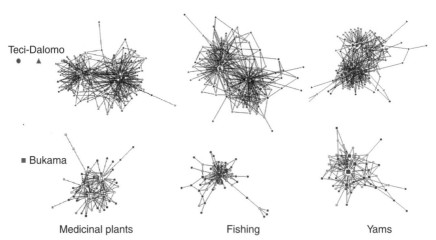

Figure 21.1 (Also see Colour Plate 8) Inferred cultural transmission networks for our three domains. The top row shows the networks for the villages of Teci and Dalomo while the bottom row shows Bukama. Each column represents one of the three domains. Nodes represent individuals. The lines and arrows point towards the selected model. Node sizes are proportional to the number of individuals who selected that person as a model. Node shapes and colours mark individuals' villages and sexes. Blue, males; red, females. *Note: this caption refers to the version of the figure in the Colour Plate Section.*

To present our findings, we focus on our Teci–Dalomo sample (4160 dyads) and use our set of theoretically relevant variables to create baseline models. These baseline models, one for each domain, use the following variables to predict a person's chances of being selected as a model: (i) perceived success or knowledge within the target domain, (ii) age and age difference, (iii) sex and same sex (1 for same-sex dyads and 0 otherwise), (iv) proximity (same village and same household) and genetic relatedness (r), and (v) education. We also discuss models that add cross-domain success measures as predictors to this baseline and models that add our time-allocation measures of association to the baseline. Finally, using the full sample (39 800 dyads), we consider how dropping our measures of success, knowledge and relatedness affect the other coefficients on the predictor variables. This allows us to assess the robustness of our coefficient estimates using a larger sample.

Figure 21.2*a, b* presents our regression coefficients as odds ratios. All the variables represented come from our baseline regressions, *unless* they are cross-domain success and knowledge variables—in which case they come from a model that includes the baseline predictors plus our cross-domains success and knowledge measures. For example, if you are looking at the odds ratio for predicting who people seek out for information about yams (in red, see Colour Plate 8), the bars for best spear fisher come from a model that has the cross-domain predictors added to the baseline model. However, the odds ratio shown for most yam knowledge and sex are from the baseline model. Mixing coefficients drawn from different models greatly simplifies the presentation, and is justified because none of our baseline estimates of our coefficients change significantly when we add our cross-domain predictors. Unless otherwise stated below, all of our findings are robust across several alternative specifications and in the full sample regressions (see electronic supplementary material).

Within-domain success and knowledge: As expected, individuals' perceptions (measured 2 years earlier) were by far the most powerful predictors of being selected as a model. For the domain of Fishing, believing someone to be among the best spear or line fishers increases their chances of selection by 9.9 and 2.2 times, respectively (95% CI are on Figure 21.2). For yams, believing someone to be among the best yam growers or the most knowledgeable about yams increases their chances of selection by 7.3 and 2.2 times, respectively. For the domain of Medicinal Plants, believing someone to be among the most knowledgeable about such plants increases their chances of selection by 25 times.

It is interesting to note that in the two domains in which we did use measures of both knowledge and success—Fishing and Yams—we find that success is far more important than knowledge. The coefficient for our measures of perceived fishing knowledge is small, and cannot be distinguished from unity. For our measure of yam knowledge, the coefficient is significant, but the coefficient on yam success is more than three times larger. Coupled with our finding on the immense importance of medicinal plant knowledge on model choice, we suspect that when certain cultural domains provide clear direct (observational) evidence of success (e.g. catching big fish and growing big yams), people weight this more heavily in selecting their models. Healing people with plants is a fuzzier business.

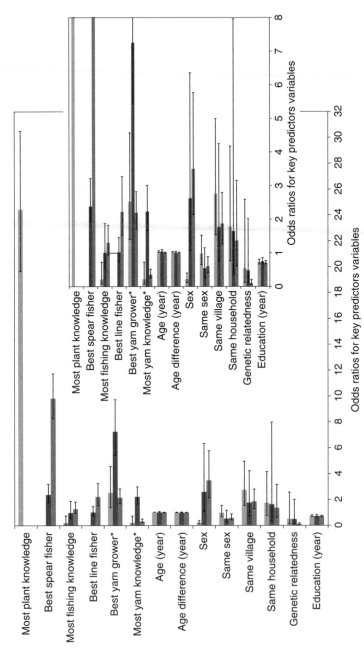

Figure 21.2 (Also see Colour Plate 9) Effect sizes and confidence intervals for our primary predictor variables in odds ratios. The inset plot is the same as the larger plot except that the axis is rescaled so the smaller odds ratios can be seen. The bars give the odds ratios for our estimated coefficients. Odds ratios greater than 1 indicate positive effects while those less than 1 indicate negative effects. The error bars are 95% CI estimated by resampling. The bar colours mark the different cultural domains. Green, Medicinal Plants odds ratio; red, Yams odds ratio; blue, Fishing odds ratio. *Note: this caption refers to the version of the figure in the Colour Plate Section.*

Cross-domain success (prestige): To explore this, we used our measures of success and knowledge in one *valued* domain to predict selection as a model in another domain. To select our valued domains, we used data collected in 2005–2006 in which a sample of participants listed those arenas of village life that had to be mastered to be considered a respected member of the community. Fishing and yam growing were near the top, though medicinal plant usage was not (see electronic supplementary material). For learning about fishing, being perceived as a successful yam grower makes one 2.2 times more likely to be selected as a model. This effect size is roughly equal to that found for the effect of success in line-fishing on selection as a model for Fishing, but much less than within-domain success of spear-fishing. For Yams, success in spear-fishing increases one's likelihood of selection by 2.4 times, which is not distinguishable from the impact of our measures of possessing the most yam knowledge. For Medicinal Plants, our measures of yam success increase one's chance of selection as a model by 2.5 times (see electronic supplementary material).

Age: We examined both a main effect for age (are older people selected more frequently?) and a dyadic effect using age difference (do learners seek out people older than themselves?). Age was a significant predictor for the Yam and Medicinal Plant models for the Teci–Dalomo sample, and for Fishing and Medicinal Plant models in the full sample (interestingly, the coefficient on age for the yam model in the full sample is larger than that for the other two domains, but it is not estimated with sufficient accuracy). For medicinal plants and yams in the Teci–Dalomo sample, an individual who is 20 years older than another receives between two and two-and-a-half times more selections as a cultural model. In analyses not shown, we also examined the coefficient on age^2 and found no evidence for an elderly decline in the age cue. By contrast, age difference was never a significant predictor in any of our models, including in the full sample.

We would expect age, as an indirect cue of possessing adaptive know-how, to be most important when information about success is less available or less accurate. If success in spear fishing is most evident to learners, then the pattern observed in the Teci–Dalomo sample (with success controlled for) makes sense. And, it also makes sense that when our success measures are dropped, age emerges as an important predictor of whom to seek out for fishing information. However, why the significance of the age effect disappears for yams in the full sample remains puzzling.

Sex: We analysed sex for a main effect, asking if either males or females are preferentially selected as models, and as a dyadic effect (same sex), asking if males tend to pick males and females tend to pick females. Consistent with ethnography, analyses of sex indicate that both Fishing and Yams are predominantly male domains (everyone is biased to pick males), while Medicinal Plants represent a predominantly female domain (everyone is biased to pick females). Being male, independent of other variables including perceived success, makes one between 2.5 and 3.5 times more likely to be selected as a cultural model for fishing and yam growing. However, in the full sample analysis for yams, with our success and knowledge measures dropped, sex is not significant, though its coefficient remains large.

Same sex: For both yams and fishing, learners were roughly twice as likely to select those of the *opposite* gender when compared with one's own. For medicinal plants, we found no effect in the Teci–Dalomo sample but did find the same opposite-sex effect in the full sample. We discuss and interpret this unanticipated finding below.

Proximity and relatedness (access costs): Broadly, being from the same village increases an individual's likelihood of being selected as a model between 1.8 and 2.76 times across all three domains. However, while the coefficient on same village for yams is significant in the full sample analysis and across all our other specifications, it is not significant in our baseline model (see the electronic supplementary material).

Clear results do not emerge from our analyses of our same household variable or from genetic relatedness variable. In our baseline models for yams and medicinal plants neither coefficient is significant. For Fishing, the coefficient on genetic relatedness actually predicts that greater relatedness makes an individual less likely to be selected as a cultural model. However, in additional analyses in the electronic supplementary material, we show that this result depends on having both same household and genetic relatedness in the model at the same time. If same household is dropped, the coefficient for genetic relatedness is non-significant. In the full sample analyses, which lack our success/knowledge variables and our genetic relatedness measures, same household is a significant predictor for medicinal plants and fishing, but not for yams.

Education: More years of formal education reduce selection as a model in all three of these traditional domains, across all specifications and in the full sample. In the baseline model for Fishing, if two individuals varied only in their level of education, the one who completed 10 years of schooling would be 30 times less likely to be sought after for advice than an individual who had had no formal schooling. Effects in the other two domains are of similar magnitude.

Time allocation: The electronic supplementary material provides models that include our measures of time allocation as dyadic predictor variables. Theoretically, it is not clear that such time-allocation measures should be controlled for, as time allocation could be seen as the consequence of selecting preferred models (along with many other variables) rather than as a predictor. However, as a robustness check, we included a model specification in which our time-allocation measures were included as predictors. The above described results all hold when this variable is included. Time allocation itself is significantly associated with selecting cultural models for learning about yams and medicinal plants, but not for fishing. For yams and medicinal plants, the proportion of times that two individuals were observed together during random point samples is related such that a 10 per cent increase in the proportion of times individual *j* was observed with individual *i* would result in *i* being 1.2 (yams) and 1.5 (medicinal plants) times more likely to go to *j* for advice.

21.4 Discussion

These results add to and complement prior work on establishing the pathways and mechanisms of cultural transmission in small-scale societies (reviewed in [30]). This prior work suggests important roles for both vertical and oblique transmission, but provides only hints about the nature of that oblique transmission (see electronic supplementary material), including whether it is capable of producing cultural adaptations. The above findings fill an important gap regarding the nature of this oblique transmission, addressing the question of whether people select their oblique models in an adaptive and predictable manner capable of generating cumulative cultural evolution.

Methodologically, our efforts provide an additional tool for addressing the puzzles of cultural transmission. Much prior work—though not all—has typically asked about cultural learning retrospectively, or relied on general ethnographic descriptions. Research on social network methods suggests that retrospective approaches tend to underestimate the so-called 'weak ties' [31], which may be precisely the kind of pathways in which we are interested. Our work, while still interview-based, asks people whom they would go to for cultural information now, given what they currently know. This approach avoids two potential shortcomings of prior methods in which memory biases (recalling past learning) and cultural beliefs about socialization (which biases recall and frame discourse) could influence the results. Of course, as we discuss below, our approach has its own limitations.

This retrospective method may help explain the long emphasis on vertical (parent–offspring) transmission that emerged from this work [4, 30]. Consider, for example, what this approach would elicit if our two-stage model of cultural transmission were correct. Young learners would first acquire cultural information from their family, and principally from their parents. Then, perhaps starting in adolescence, learners would update their cultural information by attending to a set of preferred models, selected using the above described cues. Even though in this system the process of updating from selected models is the essential mechanism for generating cultural adaptations, recall-based interviews and casual ethnographic observation will mostly elicit stage 1 (vertical or family-based transmission) for two reasons. First, if the system is at or near the adaptive equilibrium, many learners would not update from their preferred models because their parents would have already transmitted to them the same information possessed by nearly everyone else in the community. Thus, stage 2 would not often occur when the system is at equilibrium [4]. Second, assuming learners do update from their preferred models, they would still have learned much of what they know from their parents. The updating process only refines previously acquired knowledge. If you ask an individual where they learned to make a bow, and they learned it first (80%) from their dad and then updated (20%) from the best hunter, they might be inclined to name their father (say, 80% of the time, or more).

To look for any evidence that younger (mostly adolescent) learners were more likely to choose genetic kin (e.g. parents) as models, we performed an additional set of ERG models where we split the sample into two subsets, one for ages 10–20 and another for ages 20 and older. If younger participants were more likely to choose genetic kin as models, we would expect differences in the significance, magnitude or direction of the coefficients for our genetic relatedness variable. We observed no such differences in any of our three domains. Further, there were no significant relationships between the age of the learner and the models that they nominated in any of the domains. It seems that neither the 10–20 age cohort, nor the group adults over 20 were inclined to seek out parents or other close relatives.

As our approach asks people whom they would seek out now, given their current knowledge, we are targeting more precisely the updating (second stage) component of the two-stage process. We think that this view of our method best explains why perceptions of within-domain success and knowledge are so potent, along with indirect assessments of the likelihood of possessing adaptive information (not already possessed by the learner), including cross-domain perceptions of success, age and sex. Both the within- and cross-domain effects, as well as age, are consistent with prior theoretical predictions. The effects for age, independent of perceived success and knowledge measures, are consistent with evolutionary arguments about why elders receive prestige-based deference across many societies [17]. Below we propose an explanation for why the effect of age disappeared for the Fishing domain. The effects of sex indicate a distinct sexual division of cultural information, with two of our domains being male (fishing and yams) and one being female (Medicinal Plants).

We think this view of our cultural transmission networks helps make sense of some of our more puzzling findings. First, our variable same sex had coefficients that went in the opposite direction to that predicted in two domains, and had no significant impact in the third. Viewing this post hoc and in light of the strong sexual division of information, we now suspect that individuals may have figured that opposite-sex people were more likely to possess useful information *not already possessed by the learner*, once success and knowledge-related measures are controlled for. That is, given one does not know something and one has learned most of what one knows from same-sex individuals, it is more likely that someone of the opposite sex knows it, *controlling* for success and knowledge. People may be more sophisticated cultural learners than our method anticipates.

Also puzzling was that neither same household nor genetic relatedness revealed the expected effects robustly. However, taking into account the 'right now' nature of our measures, this is less surprising. By adulthood, or even adolescence, individuals may have already sapped their household models and close relatives of much cultural information. The predictive effects observed for same village are consistent with this view, in that individuals have probably not yet fully tapped everyone in their village by adulthood. Beyond the village, a lack of sufficient information about potential cultural models, or simply higher access costs, might deter individuals from tapping those outside their village and Yavusa. It is also possible that both same household and genetic related-ness have their influence through our success or knowledge measures.

For the final puzzle, we found no effect for age difference. While age is an indirect cue of possessing adaptive information, age difference should be most important for younger children who need to scaffold themselves up to complex skills. Given that we focused on adolescents and adults (but not children), it is not surprising that we obtained a null result for this variable. Taken together, these patterns suggest that our measures tap the second stage—locate preferred models—in the two-stage transmission model.

Our results also reveal several patterns that were not anticipated by the existing theoretical work, and deserve further study. To begin, in domains where we have measures of both perceived knowledge and success, there are stronger effects for perceived success. In fact, cross-domain success is about as important as within-domain knowledge. This may be owing to the relative perceived accuracy of assessments of these in different domains. Assessing success in some domains can be accomplished by attending to distinct outcomes (e.g. who brings home the largest fish catch). Ethnographic observations suggest that not only are these outcomes most salient to observers, but they are also readily spread among community members. Information about spear-fishing success, in particular, comes in on a daily or weekly basis, while yam growing success arrives yearly. Information about line-fishing success also circulates, especially when big fish are caught, but line fishing does not produce many large fish, or the substantial hauls, of spear-fishing. Meanwhile, successes with medicinal plants are relatively noisy and sporadic (medicines of all kinds frequently fail) such that asking about success directly is unproductive. Another possibility is that knowledge may be seen as less connected to what the learner themself wants to achieve. Modelling work has begun to address such cultural dynamics [32].

A second related pattern that emerged, which we did not predict *a priori* (but should have), involves understanding why the effects of age disappear in the fishing domain. The relative accuracy of individuals' perceived assessments of success may illuminate this phenomenon. Effects from indirect cues like age should be strongest when other clear indicators of success are not available to learners. The clearer the direct indicators of success in a particular domain, the less important indirect cues like age should be.

This same effect may also explain why our time-allocation measures are not predictive for Fishing, but are for the other two domains. Accurately assessing model quality in Fishing may be easier than for Yams and Medicinal Plants, which may require the close contact captured by our time-allocation measures. As noted, our ethnography strongly suggests that people's assessments of success in fishing are likely to be substantially more accurate than in the other two domains. Although more work is needed to quantify the differences between our cultural domains, these findings suggest that future research should attend to the details of how learners acquire information about their models.

A third pattern, which has been suggested elsewhere, is that education is negatively associated with selection as a model in all three of our domains. This is interesting as some readers might view formal education as a general proxy for intelligence, skills or knowledge. However, for the domains under investigation, being in school means not spending time fishing, planting yams or dealing with medicinal plants. While formal education does promote skills that are valued in the developed world, the hours spent in school may result in fewer opportunities for learning other life skills that are not taught in schools [33].

This opens the largely unaddressed question of how cross-domain success (prestige) effects operate. Theorists have suggested that success or prestige achieved in one domain (e.g. Nobel prizes) should carry over to and influence learning in other domains, especially domains perceived as similar to the source domain. Our findings are broadly consistent with this view, as success in fishing predicts being selected as a cultural model for learning about yams, *independently* of success in yam growing, but it does not predict being sought for information about medicinal plants. Success in growing yams predicts being sought for information about both fishing and medicinal plants. Greater education, which does ethnographically carry a general air of prestige, negatively predicts being sought for advice in all three domains. We speculate (wildly) that growing yams and fishing are perceived as similar because they are both male domains, that growing yams and using medicinal plants are perceived as similar because both involve culturally valued plants, and that education is perceived negatively for learning about these domains because it runs opposite to pursuing a traditional Fijian livelihood.

The major limitation in this approach—as in other field studies—involves the connection between our interview-based measures of whom people would seek out for cultural transmission and from whom they actually learn. The methods employed here may not fully capture the dynamics of cultural learning events. For example, learners may observe multiple preferred models and then copy the most commonly observed strategy (conformist transmission). Our method would potentially capture the models that a learner might assess, but it would not capture the learning algorithms used to integrate the information obtained from different models.

An alternative approach we are currently pursuing in Fiji involves studying the correlations in actual cultural traits among individuals and trying to analytically back out the transmission pathways. This avenue avoids having to rely on participant reports of transmission, but it can only be done in cultural domains with at least moderate degrees of inter-individual variation. Empirically, however, we have found many cultural domains, including some of the most important, which show very little inter-individual variation [4]. Under many conditions, this is what we would expect when the two-stage model has reached equilibrium in an important domain. Thus, even this approach has limitations. Ongoing fieldwork in our Fijian communities aims to illuminate more precisely the connection between our networks and the actual distributional patterns of various cultural traits.

Given that all approaches to assessing the pathways of cultural transmission in humans have important—but different—limitations, we believe our findings here are best interpreted in light of converging research lines from psychology, where laboratory-experimental evidence reveals similar patterns of transmission to those inferred from our village networks, and from phylogenetic analyses of actual cultural traits, which reveal patterns of oblique transmission consistent with our findings [34]. It is only through converging lines of evidence using different methodological approaches in diverse populations that we can address this key evolutionary question.

21.5 Conclusion

Understanding the success of our species involves delineating the processes responsible for assembling the adaptive information about tracking, tool manufacture, plant use, environmental dangers and shelter construction that have allowed a tropical primate to inhabit such a diversity of environments. Theorists have proposed three kinds of mechanisms capable of generating these cultural adaptations: (i) individual learning (plus vertical cultural transmission), (ii) selective cultural learning biases, and (iii) natural selection acting on cultural variation [7]. Our findings, combined with prior field studies and recent experimental work, point towards the importance of selective cultural learning biases. This does not mean that neither individual learning nor natural selection are unimportant in particular circumstances. However, it does suggest that if our learning biases are as strong as they appear, cultural evolution driven by such biases can overcome individual learning effects in creating cultural products, and natural selection will often have little impact on cultural variation, as the rates of adaptive cultural evolution created by such biases will often be very fast compared with natural selection. Efforts to model cultural evolution and culture–gene interactions should consider the effects of selective learning biases, as well as vertical cultural transmission, and individual learning.

References

1 Whiting, M. G. 1963 Toxicity of cycads. *Econ. Bot.* **17**, 271–302.

2 Beck, W. 1992 Aboriginal preparation of cycas seeds in Australia. *Econ. Bot.* **46**, 133–147.

3 Katz, S. H., Hediger, M. L. & Valleroy, L. A. 1974 Traditional maize processing techniques in the New World: traditional alkali processing enhances the nutritional quality of maize. *Science* **184**, 765–773.

4 Henrich, J. & Henrich, N. 2010 The evolution of cultural adaptations: Fijian food taboos protect against marine toxins. *Proc. R. Soc. B* **277**, 3715–3724.

5 Billing, J. & Sherman, P. W. 1998 Antimicrobial functions of spices: why some like it hot. *Q. Rev. Biol.* **73**, 3–49.

6 Sherman, P. W. & Hash, G. A. 2001 Why vegetable recipes are not very spicy. *Evol. Hum. Behav.* **22**, 147–163.

7 Richerson, P. J. & Boyd, R. 2005 *Not by genes alone: how culture transformed human evolution.* Chicago, IL: University of Chicago Press.

8 Boyd, R. & Richerson, P. J. 1985 *Culture and the evolutionary process.* Chicago, IL: University of Chicago Press.

9 Rendell, L., Boyd, R., Enquist, M., Feldman, M. W., Fogarty, L. & Laland, K. N. 2011 How copying affects the amount, evenness and persistence of cultural knowledge: insights from the social learning strategies tournament. *Phil. Trans. R. Soc. B* **366**, 1118–1128.

10 Cavalli-Sforza, L. L. & Feldman, M. 1981 *Cultural transmission and evolution.* Princeton, NJ: Princeton University Press.

11 Henrich, J. & Boyd, R. 2001 Why people punish defectors: weak conformist transmission can stabilize costly enforcement of norms in cooperative dilemmas. *J. Theor. Biol.* **208**, 79–89.

12 McElreath, R., Boyd, R. & Richerson, P. J. 2003 Shared norms and the evolution of ethnic markers. *Curr. Anthropol.* **44**, 122–129.

13 Henrich, J. & Boyd, R. 2008 Division of labor, economic specialization, and the evolution of social stratification. *Curr. Anthropol.* **49**, 715–724.

14 Laland, K. N., Odling-Smee, J. & Myles, S. 2010 How culture shaped the human genome: bringing genetics and the human sciences together. *Nat. Rev. Genet.* **11**, 137–148.

15 Durham, W. H. 1991 *Coevolution: genes, culture, and human diversity.* Stanford, CA: Stanford University Press.

16 Boyd, R. & Richerson, P. J. 1983 The cultural transmission of acquired variation: effects on genetic fitness. *J. Theor. Biol.* **100**, 567–596.

17 Henrich, J. & Gil-White, F. 2001 The evolution of prestige: freely conferred deference as a mechanism for enhancing the benefits of cultural transmission. *Evol. Hum. Behav.* **22**, 165–196.

18 Henrich, J. 2004 Demography and cultural evolution: why adaptive cultural processes produced maladaptive losses in Tasmania. *Am. Antiquity* **69**, 197–214.

19 Mesoudi, A. 2009 How cultural evolutionary theory can inform social psychology and vice versa. *Psychol. Rev.* **116**, 929–952.

20 Efferson, C., Lalive, R., Richerson, P. J., McElreath, R. & Lubell, M. 2008 Conformists and mavericks: the empirics of frequency-dependent cultural transmission. *Evol. Hum. Behav.* **29**, 56–64.

21 McElreath, R., Bell, A. V., Efferson, C., Lubell, M., Richerson, P. J. & Waring, T. 2008 Beyond existence and aiming outside the laboratory: estimating frequency-dependent and pay-off-biased social learning strategies. *Phil. Trans. R. Soc. B* **363**, 3515–3528.

22 Mesoudi, A. 2008 An experimental simulation of the 'copy-successful-individuals' cultural learning strategy: adaptive landscapes, producer-scrounger dynamics, and informational access costs. *Evol. Hum. Behav.* **29**, 350–363.

23 Harris, P. L. & Corriveau, K. H. 2011 Young children's selective trust in informants. *Phil. Trans. R. Soc. B* **366**, 1179–1187.

24 Birch, S. A. J., Akmal, N. & Frampton, K. L. 2010 Two-year-olds are vigilant of others' non-verbal cues to credibility. *Dev. Sci.* **13**, 363–369.

25 Jaswal, V. K. & Malone, L. S. 2007 Turning believers into skeptics: 3-year-olds' sensitivity to cues to speaker credibility. *J. Cogn. Dev.* **8**, 263–283.

26 Jaswal, V. K. & Neely, L. A. 2006 Adults don't always know best: preschoolers use past reliability over age when learning new words. *Psychol. Sci.* **17**, 757–758.

27 VanderBorght, M. & Jaswal, V. K. 2009 Who knows best? Preschoolers sometimes prefer child informants over adult informants. *Infant Child Dev.* **18**, 61–71.

28 Hill, K. & Kintigh, K. 2009 Can anthropologists distinguish good and poor hunters? Implications for hunting hypotheses, sharing conventions, and cultural transmission. *Curr. Anthropol.* **50**, 369–377.

29 Hunter, D., Handcock, M., Butts, C., Goodreau, S. & Morris, M. 2008 ERGM: a package to fit, simulate and diagnose exponential-family models for networks. *J. Stat. Softw.* **24**, 1–29.

30 Hewlett, B. S., Fouts, H. N., Boyette, A. H. & Hewlett, B. L. 2011 Social learning among Congo Basin hunter–gatherers. *Phil. Trans. R. Soc. B* **366**, 1168–1178.

31 Marsden, P. 2005 Recent developments in network measurement. In *Models and methods in social network analysis* (eds P. J. Carrington, J. Scott & S. Wasserman), pp. 8–30. New York, NY: Cambridge University Press.

32 Tanaka, M. M., Kendal, J. R. & Laland, K. N. 2009 From traditional medicine to witchcraft: why medical treatments are not always efficacious. *PLoS ONE* **4**, e5192.

33 Reyes-Garcia, V., Kightley, E., Ruiz-Mallen, I., Fuentes-Pelaez, N., Demps, K., Huanca, T. & Martinez-Rodriguez, M. R. 2010 Schooling and local environmental knowledge: do they complement or substitute each other? *Int. J. Educ. Dev.* **30**, 305–313.

34 Tehrani, J. J. & Collard, M. 2009 On the relationship between interindividual cultural transmission and population-level cultural diversity: a case study of weaving in Iranian tribal populations. *Evol. Hum. Behav.* **30**, 286–300.

Chapter 22

Natural Pedagogy as Evolutionary Adaptation

Gergely Csibra and György Gergely

We propose that the cognitive mechanisms that enable the transmission of cultural knowledge *by communication* between individuals constitute a system of 'natural pedagogy' in humans, and represent an evolutionary adaptation along the hominin lineage. We discuss three kinds of arguments that support this hypothesis. First, natural pedagogy is likely to be human-specific: while social learning and communication are both widespread in non-human animals, we know of no example of social learning *by* communication in any other species apart from humans. Second, natural pedagogy is universal: despite the huge variability in child-rearing practices, all human cultures rely on communication to transmit to novices a variety of different types of cultural knowledge, including information about artefact kinds, conventional behaviours, arbitrary referential symbols, cognitively opaque skills and know-how embedded in means-end actions. Third, the data available on early hominin technological culture are more compatible with the assumption that natural pedagogy was an independently selected adaptive cognitive system than considering it as a by-product of some other human-specific adaptation, such as language. By providing a qualitatively new type of social learning mechanism, natural pedagogy is not only the product but also one of the sources of the rich cultural heritage of our species.

Keywords: social learning; communication; evolution; cultural transmission; natural pedagogy

22.1 **Introduction**

Imagine that you are in a foreign country and observe a man as he turns a bottle upside down, twists its cap three times to the left and then another time to the right, turns it upside again, then opens it and drinks its content. What should you learn from this observation? The action sequence does not make much sense as it is not clear why he has performed it. Part of your problem is that the action sequence appears *teleologically opaque* to you. You may attempt to resolve this by assuming that the (familiar) outcome (i.e. drinking the bottle's content) is the agent's goal that explains his behaviour as a means action. You would still be puzzled, however, about what part of the behaviour was necessary to achieve this end result as the action sequence would remain *causally opaque* to you. Was turning the bottle upside down causally relevant for its opening or just the twisting? You may try to rely on your background knowledge about bottles to answer this question. At this point, you would still not know whether it is worth memorizing this action sequence or not. It may be useful to do so, but only if this manner of manipulation should be applied not just to this particular bottle, which you may never encounter again, but to all bottles of this kind. In other words, you need to infer whether it is reasonable for you to *generalize* your observation outside the episodic bounds of the particular situation. In this regard, it would also help to know whether what you observed was just an idiosyncratic fact about that particular individual, or that the way the action was performed is common practice among other members of the cultural community as well. Is it *shared knowledge* in this culture that this kind of bottle is to be opened this way (whether because of its construction or because this is a convention)?

Teleological and causal opacity, and the uncertainty about genericity and sharedness of knowledge are common problems, with which any observational learner is confronted. These problems are not entirely insurmountable. For example, trial-and-error learning can help to clarify the causally relevant aspects of the action and its generalizability to other bottles, and statistical observational learning may help to figure out the extent of the genericity and the shared nature of the acquired knowledge. These learning processes take time and require significant cognitive resources.

There is, however, a special type of social learning that allows for the acquisition of reliable (shared and generalizable) cultural knowledge without the extended acquisition process that trial-and-error learning and statistical observational learning necessitate. If the man with the bottle does not merely perform his peculiar action sequence, but performs it manifestly *for you* by clearly indicating that this is a demonstration presented to you as its addressee, you will learn significantly more from the same action than you would from simply observing it performed. The demonstration can highlight the important action elements and direct your attention to them as causally relevant, and can also mark the desired outcome as the goal of the action presented. In addition, the explicitly communicative nature of the demonstration can license the conclusion that the knowledge gained from it is likely to be generic to the object kind (i.e. the type of bottle) involved in the action and that this knowledge is shared by the cultural community. As a result, you would most probably conclude that the person is not just opening a bottle, but he demonstrates to you how to open that *kind* of bottle and that this is common practice and shared knowledge among locals.

The theory of natural pedagogy [1] states that the latter scenario illustrates a fundamentally new type of social learning system in humans. Human communication makes it possible to efficiently convey knowledge with opaque content to others in a single act of demonstration not only because the recipient is prepared to recognize such actions *as* communicative demonstrations, but also because the addressee has the default expectation that the content of the demonstration represents shared cultural knowledge and is generalizable along some relevant dimension to other objects, other occasions or other individuals. The most obvious beneficiaries of such a cultural transmission system are children, who have to acquire the technological, social, conventional and institutional knowledge and skills that are necessary for survival in their culture.

During recent years, we have documented that human infants and children possess specialized cognitive mechanisms that allow them to be at the receptive side of such cultural transmission. By being sensitive to *ostensive signals* (such as direct eye contact, infant-directed speech or contingent reactivity), infants are prepared to identify and interpret others' actions as communicative acts that are specifically addressed to them [2, 3]. They also display interpretive biases that suggest that they expect to learn generic and shared knowledge from such communicative acts. For example, infants expect that ostensive signals will be followed by referential signals [4], pay preferential attention to generalizable kind-relevant features of objects that are referentially identified by demonstrative communicative acts addressed to them [5, 6], learn causally opaque means actions from communicative demonstrations [7] and assume that communicated valence information about objects (i.e. whether they are evaluated positively or negatively) is shared by others [8]. These and other findings suggest that pre-verbal human infants are prepared to receive culturally relevant knowledge from benevolent adults who are, in turn, spontaneously inclined to provide it.

This chapter advances the hypothesis that the cognitive systems that make natural pedagogy possible reflect an evolutionary adaptation in the hominin lineage. This account can be contrasted with other explanations, according to which this type of social learning is not human-specific, or is the result of cultural rather than cognitive (hence biological) evolution and therefore not universal across human cultures, or is a by-product of some other basic adaptation. We think that empirical and theoretical arguments can be advanced against these proposals.

22.2 Is natural pedagogy human-specific?

One way to characterize natural pedagogy is that it is a particular kind of social learning in which knowledge or skill transfer between individuals is accomplished by communication. Both social learning and communication are widespread in non-human animals. It is thus a plausible assumption that these two phenomena will overlap in some species, producing instances of communication that transfers knowledge from one party to another. However, so far we have not been able to find convincing examples for this kind of communication in non-human species.

To convey generalizable knowledge, communication must be 'referential' in order to anchor the manifested content to the kind of referents to which it can be generalized beyond the 'here and now'. Whether animal communication can be referential in the same way as human language is a matter of debate [9]. Nevertheless, there are several examples of animal signals that are functionally referential: their 'meaning' is restricted to a specific stimulus class in the environment, and they are interpreted appropriately by receivers even when the corresponding stimulus is not present [10]. Well-known examples of these signals are alarm calls that functionally refer to predator classes [11], food calls [12] or recruitment signals [13], and even the bee dance that refers to specific locations of food sources and quantities of food retrievable from those locations. Note, however, that, unlike referential noun phrases of human languages, these signals cannot identify just a specific stimulus class (like 'aerial predator') as their referent: they can make reference only to an inseparable configuration of a referent with a fixed predicate content (such as 'aerial predator approach'). In addition, their referential scope is also severely restricted to episodic facts in the 'here and now' and cannot express content that is generalizable to other situations, other locations or other individuals. (Monkey alarm calls cannot communicate that 'aerial predators usually come during daytime'.) In this sense, referential communication in non-human animals tends to be inherently *episodic* in nature, transferring only pre-specified types of information about particulars, but not generalizable knowledge.

By emphasizing the episodic nature of animal communication, we do not mean to imply that such communication cannot be involved in learning. A pied babbler that gets fledglings' attention to a food source by purr calls communicates an episodic fact, but the resulting behaviour of the youngsters (approaching the indicated location) provides them with an opportunity to learn about properties of likely food sources [14, 15]. One can even assume that one of the functions of emitting the call is to facilitate such learning by luring the targeted youngsters to the food source (although local benefits, such as allowing fledglings to find food, could also explain such a behaviour). Note, however, that the generalizable knowledge gained in this situation does not come from the content of the communication, but is produced by individual learning, which is, in turn, triggered by the responses to the food call. If one accepts that such communicative behaviours serve the purpose of training of youngsters, these would also be qualified as acts of teaching. However, they are not examples of natural pedagogy in the specific sense we propose for this term.

A similar argument can be made about other examples of animal teaching as well. The most studied kind of teaching in non-human animals is 'opportunity teaching' in meerkats and other carnivores [16–18]. Adult meerkats supply the pups with intact, disabled or dead scorpions according to the perceived age and skills of the young, which provides them with optimal conditions for learning prey handling. These behaviours do not just satisfy generally accepted criteria for teaching [19], but also demonstrate the teachers' behavioural adjustment of the curriculum to the pupils' knowledge, which strongly suggests a pedagogical function. However, no communication is involved in this kind of teaching, which resembles more the type of environmentally supported learning called 'scaffolding' in developmental psychology [20]. A further significant difference between natural pedagogy and the type of animal teaching through coordinated scaffolding is that the latter is restricted to facilitate learning about a fixed, domain-specific content.

Another recent finding reported teaching by communication in tandem-running ants [21]. In this species, knowledgeable individuals (leaders) guide naive ants (followers), by running in tandem, towards a food source. In fact, the leader in the tandem not only directs the follower to a location but also adjusts its behaviour to its pupil: it slows down or stops to allow the follower to 'memorize' the route, and if the teaching is interrupted, it waits for the pupil to return [22]. Thus, this behaviour is based on bidirectional signals, and transfers valuable information to the pupil, who will find the food faster with guidance than without it. However, whether or not this behaviour is qualified as teaching [23], it is clear that it transfers episodic information about temporary food sources that are not generalizable. The sophisticated bidirectional communication that allows such information to be passed on from the leader ant to the follower ant serves the coordination problem of getting from location A to location B together rather than transferring knowledge between individuals. And again, the type of information acquisition that this teaching system is designed to facilitate seems highly domain-specific: there is no evidence that the bidirectional communicative signals could be recruited in the service of transferring any other kind of functional information (even if it is only episodic: say, leaders directing followers away from danger).

We suggest, therefore, that at present none of the documented cases of animal teaching [24] seem to qualify as communicating generalizable knowledge, i.e. as an example of natural pedagogy. This does not necessarily mean that it would be impossible to find such an adaptation in non-human animals. Some types of behaviour come very close to actions that would be classified as demonstrations for novices. For example, mother hens seem to attract chicks to palatable food by increased pecking, especially when they perceive that the chicks are feeding on unpalatable food [25]. If it could be shown that the hen's behaviour is directed to demonstrating that a particular *type* of food is palatable rather than to directing the chicks to the location of a particular supply of palatable food, and that the chicks learn from these demonstrations better than they do from pure observation of the hen, this would be an example of natural pedagogy. Another, more recent, study found that mother dolphins slow down and modify their hunting behaviour when their infant observes them from a close distance [26]. If this effect is not produced by the divided attention demanded from the mother by the situation, and the mother dolphin's behaviour modification is prey-specific and does facilitate the calf's acquisition of hunting, the modified behaviour will qualify as pedagogical communication under our account.

We do not find it inconceivable that these or other examples of animal teaching will be shown to be analogous to human natural pedagogy described in the previous section. If this is proved, it will show that natural pedagogy is not human-specific. Nevertheless, this would not disconfirm our hypothesis that the cognitive systems that enable pedagogical knowledge transmission in humans represent a hominin adaptation, because analogous adaptations can emerge independently in distinct lineages. Crucially, no convincing example of teaching has been found in non-human apes or other primates [24]. Thus, if natural pedagogy is an evolutionary adaptation, it must have emerged in the hominin lineage.

Why is it then that, despite the fact that neither social learning nor communication is human-specific, and knowledge transmission to kin seems to be adaptive [27], one cannot find good examples of overlap between these phenomena in non-human species? We suggest that at least two factors explain the lack or scarcity of pedagogical knowledge transmission in non-human animals. The first one is that it is not needed. Non-human animals' behavioural repertoire, even when it incorporates local traditions, does not include opaque elements that characterize many human instrumental actions and social conventions. In the absence of long chains of instrumental actions involving various artefacts and/or time delay or spatial separation between interventions and effects, the adaptive nature of to-be-acquired actions is usually evident from observation of their outcomes and does not require active social guidance to be recognized. In other words, behavioural skills of non-human animal species, even when they involve population-specific cultural traditions, tend to be teleologically and causally 'transparent' to the observer. In contrast, the inter-generational transfer and cultural stabilization of cognitively opaque knowledge exemplified by human technological skills and cultural traditions would pose a learnability problem for the purely observational learning mechanisms of non-human species [28]. In human cultures, almost any action, even when it seems arbitrary, unnecessary, or even counterproductive, could, for some reason, be relevant and important to be learnt [7, 29–31]. A benevolent teacher who highlights through selective marking and manifest foregrounding (i.e. explicitly emphasizing [32]) the relevant aspects of these actions, or the kind-relevant properties of the objects involved, could thus not just facilitate, but in fact make such learning possible [33].

The second factor that explains the apparent uniqueness of human pedagogy is that it does not come for free. Even if a species has excellent social learning abilities and a well-developed communicative system that incorporates referential signals, it does not guarantee that the members of the species will be able to transfer generic knowledge to each other. Communicating knowledge about categories of objects, actions or situations requires either signals that refer to kinds of objects, actions and situations without fixed predicates, and/or mutual assumptions between communicators with respect to the possibility and scope of potential generalization of the information conveyed. The evolution of such specialized, hence costly, cognitive systems may not be expected in the absence of a significant body of adaptive but, from an evolutionary point of view, arbitrary knowledge that characterizes human cultures.

22.3 Is natural pedagogy universal?

The second implication of the hypothesis that natural pedagogy is a hominin evolutionary adaptation is that it must be universal across human cultures. The cognitive mechanisms that enable people to transmit and receive generic knowledge by communication must be present in virtually all members of the species and must be used whenever it is in the interests of the individuals of a community to preserve their cultural traditions and pass on the to-be-acquired knowledge or skills that are opaque. This prediction does not entail that pedagogy emerges in the same form or is practised in the same amount in every society. Cultural and environmental factors, for example, the extent of cognitive opacity of local traditions and artefact use, should also influence what kind of knowledge is communicated to novices and how much pedagogy is required for children to become full members of their community. Nevertheless, if there were a human culture where no generic knowledge was communicated to others in any form, it would seriously undermine the hypothesis according to which natural pedagogy is a hominin evolutionary adaptation.

It is a widespread belief among anthropologists and cultural psychologists that teaching, of which natural pedagogy is a subspecies, is not practised at all in many non-Western societies [34]. In an unpublished but frequently cited manuscript, Fiske [35] asserts, 'children learn most of their cultures on their own initiative, without pedagogy'. This is probably correct and applies also to Western societies. Children's learning is supported by domain-specific mechanisms in many cognitive domains [36], and social learning is also available to them in non-interactive, observational forms [37]. The question to be answered in order to evaluate the claim about universality of natural pedagogy is whether there is a society in which novices are left with these options without having opportunities to learn from experts by communication. Note that we use the terms 'novices' and 'experts' here because they describe their functional role in pedagogical knowledge transmission. Although these roles map naturally to children and adults, respectively, adults also learn new skills from others by communication, and children may play the role of teachers of younger children, especially in traditional societies [38].

In an influential paper on 'cultural panthropology', Whiten et al. [39] argued that chimpanzee 'cultures' share many characteristics of human cultures—except teaching practices. This does not, however, imply a sharp difference between the species because 'the role of teaching in the human case must also be questioned. In observational studies of everyday interactions between children and caretakers, relatively little sign of overt teaching was found, particularly in a traditional African society [40]. Anthropologists appear to have come to similar conclusions. In particular, to the extent that hunter–gatherer societies provide our best models for the kind of childhood experiences likely in the greater part of ancestral, pre-agricultural human life, a repeated message of ethnographers is that little overt teaching occurs among foraging peoples [39, pp. 96, 41, 42].

We think that the examples cited in this short section are not convincing concerning the absence of teaching in traditional societies. In their observational studies, Whiten & Milner [40] did not find any evidence of teaching of young children in rural Nigeria, but their specific definition of 'teaching' required that adults should help the infant by actively intervening in the execution of difficult actions. By contrast, they found clear examples of 'demonstration', in which the adult showed to the child how to perform certain actions, and frequent incidents of providing information about object properties specifically for the child. Both of these types of child-directed actions exemplify communication of generic knowledge and satisfy the criteria of natural pedagogy. Thus, parents of these Nigerian infants did practise natural pedagogy. Note that when Whiten applied the same coding scheme to the analysis of the parenting behaviour of a gorilla, he found no examples of teaching but also no cases of demonstration either [43].

The second work cited for showing the lack of teaching by Whiten et al. [39] is a description of children's life among the !Kung [41]. !Kung adults have a laissez faire attitude towards children, intervening seldom in what they do. However, even in this society, adults interrupt and change children's behaviour about 1.5 to 2 times an hour [41]. It is not clear how many of these interruptions are pedagogical in nature, but even if only a small fraction of them (e.g. a single occasion a day) allows the child to learn directly from the adult, it would expose !Kung children to more teaching than a young chimpanzee ever receives. In addition, other characteristics of the same society suggest that the concept of teaching is not alien to them. In the same volume, Blurton Jones & Konner [44] reported 'an enlightening argument between some younger men who hunt very little and some older and more active men. The inactive young men accused the older men of having neglected to teach them hunting. The older men countered that this was something that one just did. 'You teach yourself'—a very common phrase among the !Kung—would be applicable here' (pp. 338–339). While this report provides evidence of the absence of teaching of hunting among the !Kung, it also demonstrates that (i) the !Kung have a concept and a word for *teaching*, and (ii) the norm that adults are expected to conform to is teaching since they had to justify why they had *not* taught a certain skill. Thus, while the !Kung illustrate how different a traditional society could be from Western cultures in terms of child-rearing practices, they hardly demonstrate the complete absence of natural pedagogy.

Whiten *et al.* [39] also cite the work by Hewlett & Cavalli-Sforza [42] among the Aka in West Africa. They found that the dominant mode of cultural transmission among the Aka is *vertical* (parent-to-child and one-to-one) as opposed to *oblique* (teacher-to-pupil and one-to-many). People reported that they had learnt most (80%) of their skills from their parents, often by teaching. This indicates that there is hardly any *institutionalized* teaching in this society. However, most skills were reported to have been acquired from the parents by *demonstration* and *instruction*, indicating pedagogical practices.

David Lancy is one of the anthropologists who argue strongly against the universality of pedagogy [45], and his monograph on the development of Kpelle children in Liberia [46] is often cited as an illustration of a society without teaching practices. Indeed, he insists that Kpelle 'parents influence children by example and by setting limits on their behaviour, but not through direct *teaching*' (p. 78). The evidence presented in the book, however, does not seem to support this conclusion. The section that concludes with the sentence above cites direct quotes from Lancy's informants that seem to contradict the above conclusion. They say, for example, that 'If I am cutting brush, I give him [his son] the machete for him to know how to cut brush. If work becomes hard, I'll show him how to make it easier' (p. 76). 'Showing how to make it easier' is a prototypical pedagogical activity of demonstrating a means action and functional artefact use. Furthermore, Lancy also cites one of his informants as explicitly saying that 'We will teach our children our work' (p. 76). And the book provides many more examples of pedagogical activities. To mention only a few, knowledgeable adults teach their children about medicines (p. 68) and board games (p. 116), give advice about making traps (p. 146), guide children's hands when learning how to weave a bag (pp. 151–152) and demonstrate how to make a hammock (p. 154).

Other societies that have been suggested to us by anthropologists as examples of pedagogy-free cultures do not seem to show a complete lack of teaching either. Ultimately, whether there is such a society is an empirical question, and ongoing studies in several traditional societies will testify how much of the predictions of the theory of natural pedagogy can be confirmed outside Western cultures (see [47] and http://www.philosophy.dept.shef.ac.uk/culture&mind/). Nevertheless, the sharp contrast between some anthropologists' insistence of the non-existence of teaching and the empirical data demands an explanation. We think that at least three factors contribute to this apparent contradiction. The first one is a certain type of methodological commitment to participatory data collection, as opposed to relying on verbal interviews, for understanding how other cultures work [35]. People in many non-Western societies are reluctant or even unable to explain or justify their customs or beliefs, and do not readily give instructions to an outsider when he or she attempts to acquire their skills. Thus, an anthropologist had better try to integrate into the society he or she studies and acquire their culture by participation in its life rather than expecting the locals to enlighten them by revealing crucial information about their culture. We are not in a position to decide whether this methodological commitment represents the right way to study other cultures. But we think that it contributes to some anthropologists' conviction that teaching is almost non-existent in certain cultures.

A related factor behind this controversy is that anthropologists may apply a different concept of pedagogy from ours. While animal behaviourists' definition of teaching is much wider than our notion of natural pedagogy, anthropologists' examples for the lack of teaching suggest a much narrower concept. What they find lacking in traditional societies is the habit of systematic teaching, explanations that accompany demonstrations, verbal instructions and enforcing behavioural norms [48]. While these behaviours exemplify some characteristics of child rearing in Western societies [45], none of them is necessary for confirming that a society practises natural pedagogy. Occasional non-verbal but communicative (i.e. addressed and tailored to a novice) demonstrations of means actions, artefact functions or object properties that potentially result in knowledge acquisition in the addressee would count as acts of teaching, not just under our description of natural pedagogy but also under animal behaviourists' functional definition [19].

This brings us to the third factor that explains why some anthropologists insist that natural pedagogy cannot be universal. Apparently, the baseline norm they apply for significant frequency of occurrence of teaching differs from ours. This is evident from phrases like 'children learn *much* of their cultures … without pedagogy' [35], 'adults … *seldom* "teach" ' (Maretzki & Maretzki 1966, cited in [35]), '*relatively little* sign of overt teaching was found' [39], or 'in most small-scale human societies there is *very little* active teaching' [34] (italics added). None of these claims asserts the actual absence of teaching practices in non-Western cultures, but they quantify it as much less than some unspecified norm. We suspect that the comparison baseline that these authors apply here is the frequency of teaching in Western societies. However, when the question is the universality of a human behaviour, the proper baseline is not the frequency of a behaviour in an admittedly 'WEIRD' culture [49] but that of non-human animals. As communicative teaching does not seem to exist among non-human animals, even 'rare' pedagogical activities that can be identified in some non-Western cultures confirm, rather than disprove, our hypothesis that natural pedagogy is a hominin adaptation.

Undoubtedly, there are enormous cultural differences in how societies organize child rearing and how they ensure that children acquire the knowledge and skills they need [45, 48]. Many societies do not institutionalize this learning process in the form of schools and may not even exert any coercion on children's learning. Whether or not there is a culture where no natural pedagogy is exercised at all is an empirical question, and so far we have not managed to identify one. Nevertheless, the fact that children in some traditional cultures that do not emphasize the importance of teaching display similar learning biases to Western children (when novel actions are demonstrated to them in a communicative context) suggests that the cognitive mechanisms of natural pedagogy are universal in humans [31].

22.4 **The evolution of natural pedagogy**

Even if natural pedagogy is human-specific and universal across cultures, it does not have to be an evolutionary adaptation. Whether or not it is an adaptation is primarily a historical question of when and how it emerged during human evolution, and secondarily a question of plausibility of the hypothesis that the cognitive systems supporting natural pedagogy were selected for achieving this very function. Although the archaeological record can speak to the first question [50], it is unlikely that sufficient data will ever exist to uncover hominin cognitive evolution in such detail.

The second question contrasts our hypothesis with claims according to which natural pedagogy could be a fortunate by-product of a more basic adaptation. There are several candidates for this role. The most obvious one is the ability for linguistic communication. As all human languages share certain essential features, like their predicate-argument structure and their combinatorial properties, which are ideal for expressing arbitrary contents, natural pedagogy may just be a specific domain where this extraordinary faculty, supposedly evolved to fulfil some other function, has found one of its uses. Indeed, it has been suggested that the primary function of linguistic abilities is to enable combinatorial composition of human thought [51]. As soon as such abilities are in place, and a natural language exists in which such thoughts could be expressed, generic sentences and other linguistic utterances that communicate knowledge that is valid beyond the 'here and now' make it possible to practise natural pedagogy between members of a linguistic community. However, we find it unlikely that natural pedagogy was a by-product of the evolution of language. Non-verbal communication, for example, demonstrations of artefact use, can express generic content, and, given the presence of ostensive signals, will be interpreted as such by addressees. In fact, even pre-verbal infants display biases to do so, as we have demonstrated in many studies [5–7]. Thus, we think that some form of non-verbal natural pedagogy is likely to have evolved before language, and can operate without direct linguistic support.

If language is not necessary, then perhaps the general ability for human communication is the key for the emergence of natural pedagogy. Ostensive communication might have evolved to support the manipulation of the mental states of others [52]. In this scenario, specifically human communicative abilities arose from our extended social cognitive skills, and in particular the metarepresentational capacities that allow sophisticated mental state attributions to be made to others, which, in turn, might have been the result of the increase in group size [53] or other factors. Alternatively, human ostensive communication may simply be a consequence of our heightened motivation to collaborate and cooperate with others [54]. Communication, whether it is verbal or non-verbal, allows mutual adjustment of actions towards common goals, sharing information that is necessary to build common plans and to confirm and verify commitments to collaborative efforts. The evolutionary pressure that produced the emergence of specific forms of human communication thus must lie in some environmental circumstances that made extended cooperation among humans inevitable at some point during hominin evolution.

While we acknowledge that human communication serves both competition and collaboration, we do not see how the communicative system that they necessitate would also satisfy the requirements of natural pedagogy. The crucial point here is that both Machiavellian and cooperative functions demand information transfer that is episodic in nature. Except in special circumstances, it is rarely in the interest of competitors to implant (true or false) beliefs about generic object kinds, action types or situations into the other's mind. This is why the question of trust and epistemic vigilance (protection against misleading information, see [55, 56]) arises mainly with communicative contents that can be potentially deceptive [57]. Typically, these contents refer to particulars rather than kinds, and are restricted in validity in space and time. Similarly, most collaborative actions require information to be shared about the here and now, or about a particular episode in the past or future. Such communication calls for the establishment of an episodic, rather than a semantic, common ground [54]. Thus, neither the manipulative nor the collaborative function of communication explains why human communicators, including preverbal infants, display perceptual and cognitive biases to find generalizable content in the messages directed to them.

We propose that another evolutionary factor had a shaping influence on the cognitive systems that underlie human communication. This factor is the technological challenge that growing up and living in societies that employed more and more sophisticated artefacts and longer and longer means-end sequences posed to humans, and especially to children (see also [58]). Human artefacts and instrumental actions tend to be *opaque* both in terms of their adaptive function (teleological opacity) and in terms of their modus operandi (causal opacity). Much of this information can be acquired by trial-and-error or by passive observation, but not all human actions can efficiently be learnt this way [33]. Even Lancy [46], who denied the importance of teaching among the Kpelle, observed that there are always skills that are 'so complex [they] cannot be acquired through observation, imitation, trial, and error' (p. 163). This is when communicative demonstration, or even just directing the pupil's attention to the relevant aspects of the situation, can make a difference in learning [58]. Crucially, such demonstration or verbal information subserves the acquisition of generic knowledge that is not tied to the particular situation or to the actual artefact used in the demonstration, but is generalizable to other locations, other times and other objects of the same kind.

We believe that what we know about human evolution supports our hypothesis at least as strongly as the alternative proposals with respect to the environment in which specifically human communication emerged. Our hominin ancestors made stone tools at least 2.5 [59], if not 3.4 Myr ago [60], and used them to produce tools of perishable materials (wood, hide) about 2 Myr ago. The production of these tools was so difficult that acquiring the skills to make them was likely to require extended learning periods, cultural transmission and active participation of the experts [61–63]. One cannot find these tools in the archaeological record, but other data also support an early emergence of human technological skills. In particular, our hominin ancestors made fire and cooked their food at least a million, possibly even 2 Myr ago [64]. In fact, Wrangham argues that changing the diet from raw to cooked food (both meat and plants) fundamentally changed the hominin physiology of digestion and contributed to human evolution by freeing up our ancestors' time. Making and maintaining fire is a complex skill, which may even vary from location to location because of differing ecologies. Food preparation by various modes of cooking is full of completely opaque elements that are maintained by local traditions and passed on through generations. The acquisition of these skills, and the social conventions attached to them, can surely be facilitated by demonstrations of cooking techniques, and by providing information about food kinds, ingredients, methods of preparation, etc. Thus, the technological diversity that might have made natural pedagogy useful was present in early hominin cultures.

When discussing its evolutionary origin, beyond its benefits, we should also consider the costs of natural pedagogy, especially that its costs and benefits may be asymmetrically distributed across teachers and pupils. If pedagogical activity can increase the (cultural) fitness of the recipient, we would expect that adults use this investment only if it benefits their offspring. However, neither ostensive communication nor cultural practices of pedagogy are restricted to kin-to-kin interactions. Although the emotional bonding between parents and their children remains special in human societies, children seem to be promiscuous in accepting adults as potential source of knowledge. Infants smile to any adult who communicates to them, more probably follow a strangers' gaze than that of the mother [65] and preferentially target them when they need more information about the situation [66]. This openness of children coupled with adults' willingness to teach non-kin children is explained by the fact that we are a *cooperative breeding* species [67]. In fact, we are the only apes who share the care of children within a group and have been doing so for at least a million years or so. This arrangement has made it possible that human (or even *Homo erectus*) children enjoy a much longer childhood than any other mammalian species [68], which seems to be necessary for a protracted and metabolically costly development of the brain [69]. We propose that the coevolution of the uniquely long childhood period and the cooperative breeding practices in early hominins is supplemented by the emergence of a communication system that provided 'food for thought' for the not only metabolically but also informationally hungry developing brain of children. In other words, the cognitive mechanisms of natural pedagogy, this asymmetric but cooperative social learning system, might have evolved together with the technological, neurobiological and social factors that made such an adaptation necessary and possible [70].

22.5 **Conclusions**

We have collected arguments to support the hypothesis that communicative knowledge transmission (as opposed to non-communicative social learning and communicative information sharing) is a hominin adaptation. Natural pedagogy is uniquely human because no such behaviour or cognitive mechanism is found in other species, though there are examples for other types of teaching. Natural pedagogy is also universal because, despite the huge differences across cultures, so far no society has been found that would not share knowledge by verbal or non-verbal communication. These claims can be falsified by finding a species that teaches by communication or a human society that does not do so.

Unlike other theorists, we do not think that there is a single cognitive or psychological factor (like language or motivation to cooperate) that makes humans unique. We do not think this, not because we do not believe that humans are unique in some sense, but because there are many differences between the cognitive makeup of humans and other species, just like between any two species that are separated by at least 6 Myr of evolution. It is also true that the cognitive mechanisms that underlie natural pedagogy grew out of cognitive mechanisms that were, and are, present in our ape ancestors and cousins. For example, the ostensive signals that humans employ to indicate their communicative intent evolved from signals that had already carried natural meaning for our ancestors [2]. We also agree that the special type of teaching that we call natural pedagogy could only have evolved because individual social learning mechanisms that extracted knowledge from the observation of conspecifics' actions [71] were probably well developed in early hominin societies (cf. [25]).

Our proposal is that the adaptation for natural pedagogy was made necessary by the cognitively opaque knowledge and skills required by technological inventions during early human evolution. This technology, including its materialization as artefacts and its know-how as expertise, was inherently cultural in nature. However, communicative knowledge transfer, with its assumptions about genericity and culturally shared information, must have opened up new domains of cultural contents to be preserved or stabilized by communicative means. Conventions, rituals and novel symbol systems could also be transmitted to the next generation by natural pedagogy, and the operation of modern social institutions is unimaginable without communicative knowledge transfer. In this sense, natural pedagogy is not just the product but also one of the sources of the rich cultural heritage of our species.

Acknowledgements

We thank Emma Flynn, Robert Hinde, John. S. Watson and Andrew Whiten for their helpful comments on an earlier version of this chapter. This work was supported by an Advanced Investigator Grant by the European Research Council (no. 249519, OSTREFCOM).

References

1 Csibra, G. & Gergely, G. 2009 Natural pedagogy. *Trends Cogn. Sci.* **13**, 148–153.
2 Csibra, G. 2010 Recognizing communicative intentions in infancy. *Mind Lang.* **25**, 141–168.

3 Sperber, D. & Wilson, D. 1995 *Relevance: communication and cognition*, 2nd edn. Oxford, UK: Blackwell.

4 Senju, A. & Csibra, G. 2008 Gaze following in human infants depends on communicative signals. *Curr. Biol.* **18**, 668–671.

5 Futó, J., Téglás, E., Csibra, G. & Gergely, G. 2010 Communicative function demonstration induces kind-based artifact representation in preverbal infants. *Cognition* **117**, 1–8.

6 Yoon, J. M. D., Johnson, M. H. & Csibra, G. 2008 Communication-induced memory biases in preverbal infants. *Proc. Natl Acad. Sci. USA* **105**, 13 690–13 695.

7 Gergely, G., Bekkering, H. & Király, I. 2002 Developmental psychology: rational imitation in preverbal infants. *Nature* **415**, 755.

8 Gergely, G., Egyed, K. & Király, I. 2007 On pedagogy. *Dev. Sci.* **10**, 139–146.

9 Seyfarth, R. M. & Cheney, D. K. 2003 Signalers and receivers in animal communication. *Annu. Rev. Psychol.* **54**, 145–173.

10 Marler, P., Evans, C. S. & Hauser, M. D. 1992 Animal signals: motivational, referential, or both? In *Nonverbal vocal communication: comparative and developmental approaches* (eds H. Papousek, U. Jurgens & M. Papousek), pp. 66–86. Cambridge, UK: Cambridge University Press.

11 Cheney, D. K. & Seyfarth, R. M. 1990 *How monkeys see the world*. Chicago, IL: University of Chicago Press.

12 Slocombe, K. E. & Zuberbuhler, K. 2005 Functionally referential communication in a chimpanzee. *Curr. Biol.* **15**, 1779–1784.

13 Slocombe, K. E. & Zuberbühler, K. 2007 Chimpanzees modify recruitment screams as a function of audience composition. *Proc. Natl Acad. Sci. USA* **104**, 17 228– 17 233.

14 Radford, A. N. & Ridley, A. R. 2006 Recruitment calling: a novel form of extended parental care in an altricial species. *Curr. Biol.* **16**, 1700–1704.

15 Rapaport, L. G. 2006 Parenting behaviour: babbling bird teachers? *Curr. Biol.* **16**, R675–R677.

16 Thornton, A. & McAuliffe, K. 2006 Teaching in wild meerkats. *Science* **313**, 227–229.

17 Thornton, A. 2008 Variation in contributions to teaching by meerkats. *Proc. R. Soc. B* **275**, 1745–1751.

18 Thornton, A. & Clutton-Brock, T. 2011 Social learning and the development of individual and group behaviour in mammal societies. *Phil. Trans. R. Soc. B* **366**, 978–987.

19 Caro, T. M. & Hauser, M. D. 1992 Is there teaching in nonhuman animals? *Q. Rev. Biol.* **67**, 151–174.

20 Wood, D., Bruner, J. S. & Ross, G. 1976 The role of tutoring in problem solving. *J. Child Psychol. Psychiatr.* **17**, 89–100.

21 Franks, N. R. & Richardson, T. 2006 Teaching in tandem-running ants. *Nature* **439**, 153.

22 Richardson, T. O., Sleeman, P. A., McNamara, J. M., Houston, A. I. & Franks, N. R. 2007 Teaching with evaluation in ants. *Curr. Biol.* **17**, 1520–1526.

23 Leadbeater, E., Raine, N. E. & Chittka, L. 2006 Social learning: ants and the meaning of teaching. *Curr. Biol.* **16**, R323–R325.

24 Hoppit, W. J. E. *et al.* 2008 Lessons from animal teaching. *Trends Ecol. Evol.* **23**, 486–493.

25 Nicol, C. J. & Pope, S. J. 1996 The maternal feeding display of domestic hens is sensitive to perceived chick error. *Anim. Behav.* **52**, 767–774.

26 Bender, C. E., Herzing, D. L. & Bjorklund, D. F. 2009 Evidence of teaching in Atlantic spotted dolphins (*Stenella frontalis*) by mother dolphins foraging in the presence of their calves. *Anim. Cogn.* **12**, 43–53.

27 Thornton, A. & Raihani, N. J. 2008 The evolution of teaching. *Anim. Behav.* **75**, 1823–1836.

28 Gergely, G. & Csibra, G. 2006 Sylvia's recipe: the role of imitation and pedagogy in the transmission of cultural knowledge. In *Roots of human sociality: culture, cognition and interaction* (eds N. J. Enfield & S. C. Levinson), pp. 229–255. Oxford, UK: Berg.

29 Lyons, D. E., Young, A. G. & Keil, F. C. 2007 The hidden structure of overimitation. *Proc. Natl Acad. Sci. USA* **104**, 19 751–19756.

30 Lyons, D. E., Damrosch, D. H., Lin, J. K., Macris, D. M. & Keil, F. C. 2011 The scope and limits of overimitation in the transmission of artefact culture. *Phil. Trans. R. Soc. B* **366**, 1158–1167.

31 Nielsen, M. & Tomaselli, K. 2010 Overimitation in Kalahari bushman children and the origins of human cultural cognition. *Psychol. Sci.* **21**, 729–736.

32 Gergely, G. 2007 Learning 'about' versus learning 'from' other minds: human pedagogy and its implications. In *The innate mind: foundations and the future* (eds P. Carruthers, S. Lawrence & S. Stich), pp. 170–189. Oxford, UK: Oxford University Press.

33 Csibra, G. & Gergely, G. 2006 Social learning and social cognition: the case for pedagogy. In *Processes of change in brain and cognitive development. Attention and performance XXI* (eds Y. Munakata & M. H. Johnson), pp. 249–274. Oxford, UK: Oxford University Press.

34 Henrich, J. 2004 Cultural group selection, coevolutionary processes and large-scale cooperation. *J. Econ. Behav. Organ.* **53**, 3–35.

35 Fiske, A. P. 1997 Learning a culture the way informants do: observing, imitating and participating. See http://www.bec.ucla.edu/papers/learning_culture.htm.

36 Atran, S. & Sperber, D. 1991 Learning without teaching: its place in culture. In *Culture, schooling, and psychological development* (ed. L. T. Landsmann), pp. 39–55. Norwood, NJ: Ablex.

37 Odden, H. & Rochat, P. 2004 Observational learning and enculturation. *Edu. Child Psychol.* **21**, 39–50.

38 Maynard, A. E. 2002 Cultural teaching: the development of teaching skills in Maya sibling interactions. *Child Dev.* **73**, 969–982.

39 Whiten, A., Horner, V. & Marshall-Pescini, S. 2003 Cultural panthropology. *Evol. Anthropol.* **12**, 92–105.

40 Whiten, A. & Milner, P. 1984 The educational experiences of Nigerian infants. In *Nigerian children: developmental perspectives* (ed. H. V. Curran), pp. 34–73. Boston, MA: Routledge.

41 Draper, P. 1976 Social and economic constraints on child life among the !Kung. In *Kalahari hunter–gatherers: studies of the !Kung San and their neighbours* (eds R. B. Lee & I. DeVore), pp. 199–217. Cambridge, MA: Harvard University Press.

42 Hewlett, B. & Cavalli-Sforza, L. L. 1986 Cultural transmission among Aka pygmies. *Am. Anthropol.* **88**, 922–934.

43 Whiten, A. 1999 Parental encouragement in gorilla in comparative perspective: implications for social cognition. In *The mentality of gorillas and orangutans* (eds S. T. Parker & H. L. Miles & R. W. Mitchell), pp. 342–366. Cambridge, UK: Cambridge University Press.

44 Blurton Jones, N. G. & Konner, M. 1976 !Kung knowledge of animal behavior. In *Kalahari hunter–gatherers: studies of the !Kung San and their neighbours* (eds R. B. Lee & I. DeVore), pp. 325–348. Cambridge, MA: Harvard University Press.

45 Lancy, D. F., Gaskins, S. & Bock, J. (eds) 2009 *The anthropology of learning in childhood*. Lanham, MD: Altamira Press.

46 Lancy, D. F. 1996 *Playing on the mother-ground: cultural routines for children's development*. New York, NY: Guilford Press.

47 Hewlett, B. S., Fouts, H. N., Boyette, A. H. & Hewlett, B. L. 2011 Social learning among Congo Basin hunter–gatherers. *Phil. Trans. R. Soc. B* **366**, 1168–1178.

48 Paradise, R. & Rogoff, B. 2009 Side by side: learning by observing and pitching in. *Ethos* **37**, 102–138.

49 Henrich, J., Heine, S. J. & Norenzayan, A. 2010 The weirdest people in the world. *Behav. Brain Sci.* **33**, 61–83.

50 Tehrani, J. J. & Riede, F. 2008 Towards an archeology of pedagogy: learning, teaching and the generation of material cultural traditions. *World Archeol.* **40**, 316–331.

51 Chomsky, N. 1980 *Rules and representations*. Oxford, UK: Blackwell.

52 Sperber, D. 2001 An evolutionary perspective on testimony and argumentation. *Phil. Top.* **29**, 401–413.

53 Dunbar, R. 1998 *Grooming, gossip, and the evolution of language.* Cambridge, MA: Harvard University Press.

54 Tomasello, M. 2008 *Origins of human communication.* Cambridge, MA: MIT Press.

55 Mascaro, O. & Sperber, D. 2009 The moral, epistemic and mindreading components of children's vigilance towards deception. *Cognition* **112**, 367–380.

56 Sperber, D., Clément, F., Heintz, C., Mascaro, O., Mercier, H., Origgi, G. & Wilson, D. 2010 Epistemic vigilance. *Mind Lang.* **25**, 359–393.

57 Sterelny, K. 2008 *The fate of the third chimpanzee.* Jean Nicod Lectures. See http://www. institutnicod.org/Session_1.pdf.

58 Sterelny, K. 2007 Social intelligence, human intelligence and niche construction. *Phil. Trans. R. Soc. B* **362**, 719–730.

59 Schick, K. D. & Toth, N. 1993 *Making silent stones speak: human evolution and the dawn of technology.* New York, NY: Simon and Schuster.

60 McPherron, S. P., Alemseged, Z., Marean, C. W., Wynn, J. G., Reed, D., Geraads, D., Bobe, R. & Béarat, H. A. 2010 Evidence for stone-tool-assisted consumption of animal tissues before 3.39 million years ago at Dikika, Ethiopia. *Nature* **466**, 857–860.

61 Nonaka, T., Blir, B. & Rein, R. 2010 How do stone knappers predict and control the outcome of flaking? Implications for understanding early stone tool technology. *J. Hum. Evol.* **59**, 155–167.

62 Stout, D. 2011 Stone toolmaking and the evolution of human culture and cognition. *Phil. Trans. R. Soc. B* **366**, 1050–1059.

63 Goren-Inbar, N. 2011 Culture and cognition in the Acheulian industry: a case study from Gesher Benot Yaáqov. *Phil. Trans. R. Soc. B* **366**, 1038–1049.

64 Wrangham, R. 2009 *Catching fire: how cooking made us human.* New York, NY: Basic Books.

65 Gredebäck, G., Fikke, L. & Melinder, A. 2010 The development of joint visual attention: a longitudinal study of gaze following during interactions with mothers and strangers. *Dev. Sci.* **13**, 839–848.

66 Stenberg, G. 2009 Selectivity in infants social referencing. *Infancy* **14**, 457–473.

67 Hrdy, S. B. 2009 *Mothers and others: the evolutionary origins of mutual understanding.* Cambridge, MA: Harvard University Press.

68 Gibbons, A. 2008 The birth of childhood. *Science* **322**, 1040–1043.

69 Skoyles, J. R. 2008 Human metabolic adaptations and prolonged expensive neurodevelopment: a review. *Nat. Pre.* See http://precedings.nature.com/documents/1856/version/2.

70 Burkart, J. M., Hrdy, S. B. & van Schaik, C. P. 2009 Cooperative breeding and human cognitive evolution. *Evol. Anthropol.* **18**, 175–186.

71 Csibra, G. & Gergely, G. 2007 'Obsessed with goals': functions and mechanisms of teleological interpretation of actions in humans. *Acta Psychol.* **124**, 60–78.

Chapter 23

The Scope and Limits of Overimitation in the Transmission of Artefact Culture*

Derek E. Lyons, Diana H. Damrosch, Jennifer K. Lin, Deanna M. Macris and Frank C. Keil

Children are generally masterful imitators, both rational and flexible in their reproduction of others' actions. After observing an adult operating an unfamiliar object, however, young children will frequently *overimitate*, reproducing not only the actions that were causally necessary but also those that were clearly superfluous. Why does overimitation occur? We argue that when children observe an adult intentionally acting on a novel object, they may automatically encode all of the adult's actions as causally meaningful. This process of *automatic causal encoding* (ACE) would generally guide children to accurate beliefs about even highly opaque objects. In situations where some of an adult's intentional actions were unnecessary, however, it would also lead to persistent overimitation. Here, we undertake a thorough examination of the ACE hypothesis, reviewing prior evidence and offering three new experiments to further test the theory. We show that children will persist in overimitating even when doing so is costly (underscoring the involuntary nature of the effect), but also that the effect is constrained by intentionality in a manner consistent with its posited learning function. Overimitation may illuminate not only the structure of children's causal understanding, but also the social learning processes that support our species' artefact-centric culture.

Keywords: imitation; overimitation; causal learning; cognitive development; artefacts

23.1 Introduction

Though we understand much about how imitation shapes the human mind, there are some aspects of imitative learning that remain mysterious. Imagine a preschool-aged

* Electronic supplementary material is available at http://dx.doi.org/10.1098/rstb.2010.0335 or via http://rstb.royalsocietypublishing.org.

child watching an adult open a simple novel object to retrieve a toy. Imagine that the adult approaches this task in a way that is clearly inefficient, for example, adjusting superfluous rods and levers on the outside of the object before opening it. How would we expect the child to later open the same object him or herself?

We know that even infants are capable of rationally selective imitation [1, 2], i.e. of copying only those components of an action sequence that are appropriate given their goals and physical context. Thus, we might expect our hypothetical preschooler to 'edit' the observed actions, copying only the necessary parts of the adult's behaviour. Yet this is not always what occurs. Horner & Whiten [3] presented both children and chimpanzees with a display very much like the one described above. Both groups watched an adult opening a simple 'puzzle fruit' using a short sequence of necessary and visibly unnecessary actions, and were subsequently allowed to try and open the fruit for themselves. While chimpanzees ignored the adult's irrelevant actions, children did not; in fact, the children tended to reproduce everything that the adult had done—even the actions that were plainly superfluous.

We term this curious phenomenon *overimitation* [4]. It is not a new occurrence; many instances of overimitation-like behaviour can be found in the social learning literature of the past two decades (e.g. [5–10]). Until recently, however, the effect attracted little comment. It was generally assumed that the surface oddity of overimitation (i.e. children seeming to be outsmarted by chimpanzees) could be easily resolved by appeal to some plausible configuration of social motivations.

23.2 **Prior theories of overimitation**

Theorists have long argued that imitation plays a critical dual role during development, serving as an early socialization strategy as well as a learning mechanism ([11, 12]; see also [8, 13, 14]). Thus, one common reading of overimitation has been that it simply reflects the social end of the imitative continuum. On this view, overimitation is ascribed to children's desire to 'be like' an adult model [8], and their willingness to privilege this social concern above instrumental efficiency. In essence, the argument is that children overimitate because they *want* to.

In a related vein, the procedural details of some prior studies may have led children to overimitate because they believed that they were *supposed* to. For example, in Horner & Whiten's experiments [3], participants watched the adult repeat the same sequence of relevant and irrelevant actions three times in succession before acting on the object themselves (see also [15, 16]). Though this procedure was arguably necessary in Horner & Whiten's comparative context (i.e. to ensure that the chimpanzee participants were attending), children may have reasonably interpreted the repeated displays as a non-verbal mandate to 'do it like so …'.

A third theory of overimitation, what Whiten and colleagues have termed the 'copy-all, refine/correct-later' view [17, p. 2425], argues that 'we are such a thorough-going cultural species that it pays children, as a kind of default strategy, to copy willy-nilly much of the behaviour they see enacted before them. Children have the longest childhoods of any primate ... so there is plenty of opportunity to weed out wrongly assimilated aspects of the actions observed' ([18, p. 280]; see also [10, 15]). This perspective sees overimitation as a kind of cultural Pascal's wager: even if an adult's actions appear irrelevant, children reproduce them because they have little to lose (and, in our artefact-centric culture, potentially much to gain) by assuming that the actions may serve some non-obvious purpose. This is a logically appealing possibility, and one that would help to explain why older children may actually be *more* prone to overimitation than younger ones ([15, 19]; see also [20] for extension to adults). That is, the copy-all/correct-later view predicts the increase of overimitation over development, as we would expect older children to be more sophisticated about withholding judgement on seemingly irrelevant actions.

23.3 An alternative view of overimitation: automatic causal encoding

The above explanations all share an important commonality. The unifying assumption is that children overimitate not because they are actually confused about the causal importance of the actions they have observed, but rather because they are *choosing* (for social or pragmatic reasons) to copy actions that appear to be unnecessary. Several years ago we began to consider an alternative theory of overimitation, one that challenges this core assumption [4]. Our motivation stemmed in part from considering the unique causal learning challenges that children face during development.

Children must contend with an environment that is dense with tools and artefacts, many of which are difficult or impossible to understand through direct inspection alone. This problem of *causal opacity* is obvious for modern devices like computers and cell phones, but it actually extends to far simpler (and far more evolutionarily salient) kinds of artefacts. Indeed, Gergely & Csibra [21–23] have argued that once cognitive innovations like inverse teleology (the ability to stably conceptualize tools in terms of the goals they enable)[1] and recursive teleology (the ability to conceptualize objects as tools for making other tools) arise, understanding the structure and usage of even 'simple' artefacts quickly becomes a daunting inferential problem. Because these teleological modes allow tool-mediated actions to occur separately from the goals they ultimately serve, it is often impossible to predict *a priori* which *features* of a tool or which *aspects* of its usage are the causally important ones to attend to (see [24] for more discussion of this issue). Since learners can no longer rely solely on physical and environmental cues to understand the artefacts around them, some form of social support becomes necessary.

We wondered whether overimitation might reflect a unique human social learning mechanism that would help children to overcome this problem of causal opacity. We hypothesized that when young children view an adult acting intentionally on a novel object, they may automatically (and in some cases mistakenly) encode all of the adult's purposeful actions as causally necessary. In other words, children 'may implicitly treat the adult's actions as highly reliable indicators of the object's "inner workings" or causal structure, revising their causal beliefs about it accordingly' [4, p. 19751]. Such an *automatic causal encoding* (ACE) process would normally be very helpful, allowing children to extract accurate causal beliefs about complex artefacts by observing adults' intentional actions. However, in the unusual event of an adult *intentionally* performing *unnecessary* actions, this mechanism would cause children to incorrectly encode the irrelevant actions as causally important. This mistaken encoding, and the distortions in object-specific causal beliefs that it would cause, might explain why children are vulnerable to overimitating unnecessary actions that other apes more readily ignore.

To review: whereas prior theories of overimitation have assumed that children copy irrelevant actions because they *want* to (for social reasons), or because they think they are *supposed* to (owing to task demands), our hypothesis stakes out different ground. We believe that children may overimitate because, in an important sense, they *have* to: the normally adaptive ACE process blinds them to the irrelevance of the adult's unnecessary actions. Among prior theories, our view is most similar to Whiten *et al.*'s copy-all/correct-later hypothesis, as both perspectives see overimitation as an adaptive human social learning strategy. The ACE hypothesis differs, however, in its assertion that overimitation is an entirely automatic response to a specific class of stimuli (i.e. intentional action enacted on a novel object) rather than a deliberate strategy arising from experience.

In the remainder of this chapter, we synthesize data from a variety of sources, including several new experiments, to construct a detailed appraisal of the ACE hypothesis. We begin by briefly reviewing the studies that initially supported the ACE theory, and then progress to new evidence that more fully illustrates the scope and limits of the effect.

23.4 The story so far: initial tests of the automatic causal encoding hypothesis

The ACE hypothesis makes an unambiguous prediction: if children truly overimitate because they have mis-encoded adults' purposeful actions as causally meaningful, then they should be unable to avoid doing so—even in situations where copying superfluous actions would be inappropriate. We first tested this prediction in a series of experiments in which 3-to 5-year-olds were trained to identify irrelevant actions as 'silly' and unnecessary [4]. Children watched as an experimenter used sequences of relevant and irrelevant actions to remove toys from familiar, transparent household containers such as plastic food jars, clear zipper pouches, etc. The children then received effusive praise for successfully pointing out the actions that the experimenter had not needed to perform. This training made clear to children both that: (i) the experimenter was an 'unreliable' model, frequently performing actions with no bearing on his goal, and (ii) that performing irrelevant actions was not desirable.

Immediately following this training, children watched the same experimenter retrieving toys from inside simple (but now *novel*) 'puzzle objects'. As during the training phase, the adult's retrieval method was always markedly inefficient, incorporating obviously irrelevant actions (e.g. pulling out an extraneous wooden dowel on top of the object) alongside necessary ones (e.g. opening the door to a compartment containing the toy). Also as in training, each of the puzzle objects was constructed predominantly from transparent materials (e.g. Plexiglas) such that the causal significance of each of the adult's actions was plainly visible. The question of interest was whether children would overimitate on the puzzle objects, despite having just been trained to ignore irrelevant actions in a nearly identical context. We predicted that the novel puzzle objects would trigger ACE and overimitation, even among those children who had shown no difficulty filtering out irrelevant actions enacted on familiar objects.[2]

Despite their extensive contrary preparation, children did indeed show a near universal tendency to overimitate on the puzzle objects. This finding was not simply a reflection of the puzzle objects being overly complex, as participants in an age-matched baseline group seldom operated the irrelevant mechanisms when opening these objects independently. Moreover, children's tendency to overimitate was independent of the ease with which they completed the training phase; participants who easily identified the irrelevant actions on the familiar training objects were just as likely to overimitate on the novel puzzle objects as children who found the training more challenging. Consistent with the ACE theory, we found that a single observation of an adult performing purposeful but unnecessary actions on a novel object was enough to lock even 'causally precocious' children into overimitation.[3]

Subsequent experiments confirmed and expanded these findings, demonstrating that overimitation was not diminished by increasingly blatant countervailing information. For example, in a 'covert' follow-up immediately after the above experiment, participants were led to believe that the study was over. As the experimenter cleaned up, he asked the child for help in verifying that an assistant had correctly replaced all of the toys in the puzzle objects (the experimenter claimed that another participant was due to arrive at any moment and that he was thus pressed for time). Despite the time-sensitive nature of this task, children continued to overimitate at levels indistinguishable from the first study when opening the puzzle objects. A third experiment found that even directly *telling* children not to overimitate failed to curtail the effect.

Together these findings weigh against prior social views of overimitation, in which the effect was seen as arising from the child's desire to interact with the experimenter or to accommodate perceived task demands. The persistence of overimitation—even when situational demands strongly discourage it—is instead more consistent with the ACE hypothesis, and its contention that ACE can sometimes render children unable to avoid copying irrelevant actions.

However, while these initial studies provide a solid foothold for the ACE theory, limitations remain. Our puzzle objects were deliberately designed to be appealing to children, with colours, textures, knobs and handles used to highlight each object's mechanistic affordances. Given that these kinds of properties encourage children to manipulate and explore objects [27], might children have persisted in overimitation simply because they were curious?[4] Alternatively, returning to the copy-now/correct-later view of Whiten and colleagues [17], might the demands we used to oppose overimitation simply have been insufficient to dislodge a deliberate, productive strategy of high-fidelity copying? Having hypothesized that overimitation is essentially unavoidable, we need to be thorough in our evaluation of these voluntary alternatives.

23.5 **Using competition to test the scope of overimitation**

Though our prior experiments were designed to discourage overimitation, it is important to note that there was no actual cost to indulging in it. Thus, one way of testing the ACE hypothesis more rigorously would be to attach a salient price to the reproduction of irrelevant actions. For example, what if overimitation placed children at a disadvantage in a competition, making them less likely to win or gain an enticing prize?

Competition is an important dimension of childhood from an early age. By the time children reach preschool, informal competitions such as being the first to the toy box have become ubiquitous features of their daily routine [29]. Preschoolers spontaneously describe photos of potentially competitive situations (e.g. a girl and a boy running side-by-side) in terms of winning and losing, are able to give detailed accounts of which peers usually win in competitive contexts [29], and attach greater value to success in competitive settings [30]. Additionally, whereas older children and adults show a long-term negative relationship between competition and intrinsic motivation [31, 32], competition seems to actually enhance preschoolers' interest in and motivation to master novel tasks [33–35].

Given that competition is such a highly motivating context for preschoolers' learning, it seems an ideal tool for further exploring the ACE hypothesis. In experiment 1, we thus presented children with a situation in which overimitation posed a distinct competitive disadvantage. We hypothesized that even in this highly motivating context, automatic causal encoding of the adult's purposeful actions would render children unable to avoid overimitation. Contrastingly, if children in our original studies were overimitating simply out of curiosity or as part of a habitual learning strategy, then we would expect that the more acute incentive of competition would block the effect.

23.6 **Experiment 1: does associating a competitive cost with overimitation eliminate the effect?**

23.6.1 **Procedure**

As in our prior work, we began with a training phase designed to oppose overimitation.[5] Children aged 4 and 5 years ($n = 64$) watched an experimenter removing toy dinosaurs from eight familiar household containers using sequences of relevant and irrelevant actions. For the first four training items, children were asked to verbally identify the experimenter's 'silly' unnecessary actions; on the final four training items, children were invited to try retrieving the dinosaur faster than the experimenter. Children who responded by correctly identifying or skipping the irrelevant steps received enthusiastic reinforcement, while those who missed or copied the unnecessary actions were verbally corrected and guided towards the correct solution (see the electronic supplementary material for full details). This action-based training procedure allowed children to practise inhibiting copying, and also helped to establish an explicit causal relationship between skipping unnecessary steps and reaching a desired goal state more quickly.

23.6.1.1 Non-competitive phase

Immediately after training, children were introduced to the 'monkey box', a novel puzzle object consisting of two symmetrical halves separated by an opaque divider (Figure 23.1; electronic supplementary material, Figures S3 and S4). Each of the identical halves was very similar to the puzzle box used in prior studies [3, 4] and incorporated analogous relevant and irrelevant mechanisms. Children watched the experimenter retrieve a toy turtle from the monkey box using a combination of irrelevant and necessary actions partially depicted in Figure 23.1. After reassembling the object outside of the child's view, the experimenter explained that he was going to briefly step outside; he told participants: 'if you want to, you can get the turtle out while I'm gone. You can get it out however you want'. The experimenter then left the room, a step we took to minimize any perceived social pressure to copy his actions. Children were free to retrieve the turtle in whatever manner they chose.

23.6.1.2 Competitive phase

After the child retrieved the turtle, the experimenter returned to the room. Moving an opaque divider aside, the experimenter revealed a 'cabana' (electronic supplementary material, Figure S1) out of which emerged a seemingly autonomous orang-utan puppet named Felix. Felix was operated by a second experimenter hidden inside the structure, who used a concealed puppetry rig to move Felix's limbs and torso; a live closed-circuit video feed allowed this experimenter to observe the child, enabling a high degree of contingent interactivity in Felix's movements and vocalizations. Once the child was comfortable, the experimenter pointed out the monkey box's symmetrical ends and explained their design: 'that's so you and Felix can have a *race*! You can both try to get the turtle out *at the same time!*' The experimenter explained that he would use a vertical tube on top of the box (electronic supplementary material, Figure S5) to drop a single turtle into the centre of the object, and that whoever opened their side of the box fastest would retrieve the turtle and win. A verbal manipulation check was used to ensure that children

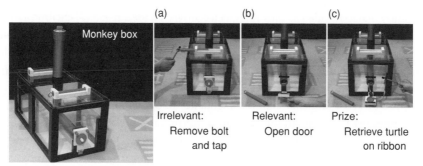

Figure 23.1 The experimenter retrieved the toy turtle from the monkey box by (a) removing the irrelevant red bolt and tapping the wand in the empty upper compartment, (b) opening the door to the prize compartment, and (c) using the wand to pull out a ribbon to which the turtle was attached. See electronic supplementary material, methods and Figure S4 for full details.

understood these key points. See electronic supplementary material, video S1 for a complete example of this introduction procedure.

Following this set-up, the experimenter began a series of 'races' between the child and Felix. At the start of each race, the child watched the experimenter deposit a single turtle into the tube at the centre of the box; a cardboard barrier was then fitted over the box's middle so that the child could no longer see Felix. Moving to the door of the room, the experimenter counted aloud: '1 … 2 … 3 … Go!' On the 'go' signal the experimenter left the room, and the child (as well, purportedly, as Felix) was allowed to start opening the box. Electronic supplementary material, Video S2 provides an example of this procedure.

Unbeknownst to the child, the outcome of each race was yoked to overimitation; all children 'lost' to Felix on race 1, and the outcome of race $n + 1$ was then determined by whether the child overimitated on race n (see electronic supplementary material for more details on this design). In losing races, children opened the monkey box only to find that it was empty; when the central divider was subsequently removed children saw that Felix had won and was holding the turtle. The question of interest was whether, over the course of up to three consecutive races, children would adapt to Felix's apparent expertise by beginning to omit irrelevant actions, thus enabling them to open the box more quickly.

23.6.2 Results and discussion

An initial analysis confirmed that children did understand the competitive nature of the racing task. We found that all children—regardless of whether they overimitated—opened the monkey box significantly more quickly on the first competitive trial than on the non-competitive trial that preceded it (mean improvement: from 18.6 to 5.6 s); significant improvements continued to be evident across races 2 and 3 as well. While some fraction of these changes can no doubt be attributed to a practice effect, the steep slope of the initial improvement—averaging 302 per cent faster on the first competitive trial—argues that children understood the competition and were adapting their behaviour accordingly. The fact that this large speed improvement was evident even among overimitators is important, as it shows that the continued reproduction of irrelevant actions was not caused by a failure to grasp the competitive nature of the task. Indeed, as electronic supplementary material, video S3 illustrates, Felix proved an ideal means of eliciting a full and animated competitive response from children without any of the sting that might have accompanied losing to a confederate child. As intended, overimitation imposed a large competitive cost, with overimitators needing an average of four times as long to open the monkey box as non-overimitators (7.7 versus 1.9 s, $t_{51} = 5.3$, $p < 0.001$).

How did this cost influence children's tendency to overimitate? As Figure 23.2 shows, the beginning of the competition did reduce overimitation relative to the non-competitive phase of the experiment (McNemar test, $n = 60$, $p < 0.001$). Thus, we cannot rule out the possibility that at least some of the children in our initial experiments may have been overimitating out of curiosity or habit. However, though overimitation decreased on the first race, the *majority* of participants were unsuccessful at avoiding it—even when the pressure of repeatedly losing to Felix began to mount on the second and third trials. Most importantly, the rate of overimitation across all three of these contests was a significant

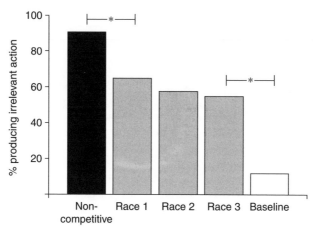

Figure 23.2 Children continue to overimitate even when doing so places them at a disadvantage in a time-critical race. Though the competitive cost of overimitation did dissuade some participants, most children continued to overimitate across all three races. Even after the final race, irrelevant action production remained 4.6 times more frequent than in the baseline condition.

4.6–5.4 times greater than the rate of irrelevant action production observed among age-matched baseline participants ($n = 28$) who opened the monkey box independently (race 1: $X^2(1, n = 85) = 19.8$, $p < 0.001$, odds ratio $= 13.6$; race 2: $X^2(1, n = 84) = 14.8$, $p < 0.001$, odds ratio $= 10.0$; race 3: $X^2(1, n = 83) = 13.4$, $p < 0.001$, odds ratio $= 9.0$). Although fully 88 per cent of baseline participants ignored the irrelevant mechanism when opening the monkey box independently, children in the experimental group tended to fixate on overimitation despite (i) their increasing first-hand experience with the monkey box itself, and (ii) repeatedly discovering that Felix had apparently opened the box more quickly.

Overimitation's persistence during competition is consistent with the ACE hypothesis, but there is another possible explanation for these results. Perhaps children believed that the experimenter's irrelevant actions were intended to be *part of the race*, i.e. that performing these actions was mandated by the rules of the contest. We find this possibility unlikely (it runs strongly counter to the contrary training phase that began the experiment), but it does bear consideration. To resolve this alternative we undertook a second competitive experiment, covertly presented to participants immediately following experiment 1.

23.7 **Experiment 2: overimitation and 'real-world' competition**

23.7.1 **Procedure**

After the final race in experiment 1, Felix retired to his cabana and participants were told that the game was over. The experimenter brought in a new puzzle object (Figure 23.3; electronic supplementary material, Figures S7 and S8), which he identified as a box of prizes. Indicating that he was going to retrieve a prize for the child, the experimenter proceeded to open the box using a series of relevant and irrelevant steps; a bell attached

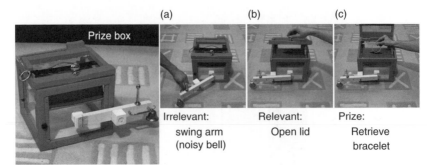

Figure 23.3 The experimenter retrieved the toy bracelet from the prize box by (a) swinging the irrelevant yellow arm from right to left (causing the bell to jingle loudly), (b) opening the lid to the prize compartment, and (c) removing the bracelet. See electronic supplementary material, methods and Figure S8 for full details.

to the irrelevant mechanism caused the box to jingle noisily when the experimenter performed the unnecessary action.

The experimenter removed a prize from the box and handed it to the child. As the child examined their reward, Felix unexpectedly re-emerged from his cabana. The experimenter interpreted as Felix gestured and vocalized: 'I think Felix wants to see your prize. Would you mind showing it to him?' Unfortunately, once the participant agreed, Felix took the prize and disappeared back into the cabana in a flurry of excited chattering. After feigning shock, the experimenter remarked that Felix must have taken the prize because of being awakened by the loud jingling bell (attached to the irrelevant mechanism).

With the original prize now gone, the experimenter presented the child with a new plan. The experimenter proposed that he would leave the room, thus fooling Felix into thinking that everyone had gone home. The child would then have an opportunity to stealthily open the prize box and retrieve another reward—this time without alerting Felix. After explaining this idea the experimenter left, leaving the child to determine how best to proceed (electronic supplementary material, Video S4 provides an example of this procedure). Would this real-world competitive scenario push children to ignore the noisy irrelevant mechanism?

23.7.2 Results and discussion

Children approached this task with great seriousness, often pausing to consider their strategy and moving with stealthy slowness (electronic supplementary material, Video S5). Yet despite this caution, children were remarkably blind to the strategy of simply ignoring the noisy irrelevant mechanism. As Figure 23.4 shows, children continued to overimitate at a rate indistinguishable from that observed in a non-competitive comparison condition. This finding was all the more striking given that none of the participants in a baseline control group ever operated the prize box's irrelevant mechanism. These results thus confirm and extend those of experiment 1, demonstrating that children will persist in overimitating even when doing so imposes a direct competitive cost. Indeed,

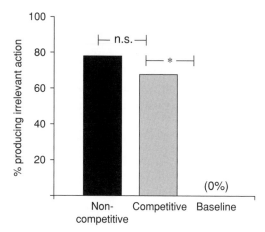

Figure 23.4 Experiment 2 participants continued to overimitate even when doing so directly imperilled their prospects for obtaining a desirable prize. The rate of overimitation observed during the competitive phase of the study was indistinguishable from that observed in the non-competitive phase.

consistent with the ACE hypothesis, children continued to reproduce observed irrelevant actions as though there was no other choice.

These competitive studies expand the scope of overimitation beyond our initial work, demonstrating that children will continue to overimitate even when doing so imposes motivationally salient costs. This degree of persistence is consistent with the proposed automaticity of the ACE process, and argues that ACE may be a better explanation for overimitation than more voluntary alternatives.

23.8 **The limits of overimitation**

Interestingly, we have now reached the point where the very robustness of overimitation begins to pose a challenge for our theory. That is, overimitation surprises us precisely because children's causal intuitions usually seem much more accurate. By the time they reach 3–5 years of age, children routinely operate (and watch others operate) devices that are much more complex than our puzzle objects without being diverted by causally irrelevant steps. At the same time though, our central claim is that children often base their understanding of new objects on a profoundly uncritical encoding of others' actions. How can both of these things be true? If children's causal understanding is as malleable to observed actions as we have suggested, then why is it not riddled with errors and inconsistencies by the end of early childhood? If ACE does occur, it must be subject to constraints that normally confine it to contexts where it will clarify children's causal understanding rather than undermining it.

23.8.1 **Prior investigation of constraints: core knowledge**

Our previous work began to examine the issue of constraints by focusing on 'core knowledge': the set of foundational rules that infants use to structure their earliest interpretation of physical events [36]. One particularly elemental aspect of core knowledge is the contact principle, which specifies that mechanical interactions cannot occur at a distance. Infants as young as three months of age display surprise when this principle appears to be violated, such as when two balls react as though they have collided without actually touching [37]. Because the contact principle is so deeply rooted in our causal knowledge, we predicted that children would not causally encode (and thus, would not overimitate) actions that appeared to violate it.

In a test of this prediction [4], two groups of 3- to 5-year-old children watched an adult open a puzzle object comprising two distinct halves, performing relevant actions on one half of the object and irrelevant actions on the other. The only difference between the groups pertained to the presence or absence of a small connector tube between the halves of the object. Participants in the *connected* condition saw the experimenter performing his actions with the tube in place (hence the relevant and irrelevant actions occurred on a single continuous object), while in the *disconnected* condition the tube was removed. Despite identical experimenter actions in both cases, only children in the connected condition overimitated; children in the disconnected condition ignored the experimenter's unnecessary actions. The ACE process was blocked when the irrelevant action implied a violation of the contact principle.

This initial result was an important 'existence proof' for our theory, demonstrating that overimitation is indeed subject to at least some constraints consistent with its posited learning function. However, if ACE is to be a net benefit to children's causal understanding, more constraints are needed. An especially useful kind of constraint—one that has been implicit in our theory from the outset—involves intentionality.

23.9 Experiment 3: does intentionality constrain overimitation?

In introducing our hypothesis, we framed the ACE process as one that helps to extract causal information from *purposeful* (intentional) adult actions. Indeed, the theory depends on this assumption, as intentionality is a prime indicator that an adult's actions are likely to reflect a target object's causal structure. Conversely, the functional value of ACE breaks down when an observed adult's actions are unintentional and therefore unlikely to convey meaningful information. If our theory is correct, it follows that ACE and overimitation should shut off with a circuit-breaker-like crispness when an adult's irrelevant actions no longer appear to be intentional.

23.9.1 Procedure

To test this prediction, a new group of 3- to 5-year-olds ($n = 27$) underwent training as in experiment 1, and then observed the experimenter opening one of the previously described puzzle objects using relevant and irrelevant actions.

In the case of the monkey box, the experimenter's actions began with waving a wooden paddle left, right and left again over the box's irrelevant red bolt, which now had a vertical 'wing' component attached perpendicularly to its left end (electronic supplementary material, Figure S11). When the experimenter waved the paddle back to the left for the final time, he did so along a lower trajectory that caused the face of the paddle to strike the bolt's wing and knock the bolt out of its bracket. Upon completing this irrelevant sequence, the experimenter opened the relevant door mechanism using one of the same techniques used in experiment 1 (electronic supplementary material, Figure S11 illustrates the complete action sequence).

The experimenter's actions on the prize box followed a similar structure. He began by waving a red wooden wand left, right and left again over the end of the irrelevant arm. When waving the wand back to the left for the final time the experimenter lowered it slightly, thus hitting the vertical metal rod on the arm's end and causing it to swing from right to left. After these unnecessary steps, the experimenter finished opening the object using the same relevant actions as in experiment 2 (electronic supplementary material, Figure S12).

All children saw the experimenter performing these same actions, but different participants saw them embedded in different contexts. For each puzzle object, half of the children saw the adult's irrelevant actions presented as *intentional*, while half saw the same irrelevant actions presented as *unintentional*. The intentional case was exactly analogous to prior experiments, with the experimenter performing all of the irrelevant actions—including the back-and-forth waving of the paddle or wand—in a purposeful, intent manner (electronic supplementary material, Video S6). In the unintentional case, however, a new procedural wrinkle was used to suggest that the experimenter's irrelevant actions were actually accidental in nature. Specifically, just as the experimenter was about to begin his action sequence, he received a call on his cellular phone, purportedly from his mother.

The experimenter answered the phone, listened for a moment, and said: 'oh, really? You can't find it?' He then looked up thoughtfully (away from the object) and continued: 'let's see ... Did you try looking on the side of the yard over by the dog house?' While saying this, the experimenter began his action sequence by waving the wand/paddle to the left, an action that now appeared to represent gesturing towards a point in imagined space. 'No, it's not there?' he continued. 'Well, did you look on the other side of the yard, over by the tree?' The experimenter now waved the paddle back to the right, again appearing to gesture at an imagined landmark. 'It's not there either?' he said. 'Well, you know, I really feel like I saw it over by the dog house'. During this last phrase, the experimenter waved the wand/paddle back towards the left for the final time, striking and actuating the irrelevant mechanism in the process. Critically though, the operation of this mechanism now appeared to be *accidental*: an unintended by-product of gesturing during his conversation (electronic supplementary material, Video S7).

After striking the irrelevant mechanism, the experimenter ended his phone conversation and (without comment) proceeded to complete the relevant portion of the action sequence. The experimenter then left the room, and children were evaluated for overimitation in the same manner as in prior studies.

23.9.2 **Results and discussion**

Children showed a strong propensity for overimitation when the adult's irrelevant actions appeared to be intentional, copying the unnecessary actions 69 per cent of the time on both objects. However, when the very same irrelevant actions were contextualized as being unintentional, overimitation rates declined significantly (Figure 23.5; monkey box: $X^2(1, n = 27) = 11.1, p = 0.001$, odds ratio $= 29.3$; prize box: $X^2(1, n = 25) = 9.6, p = 0.002$, odds ratio $= 24.8$). In fact, children in the unintentional condition were no more likely to operate the irrelevant mechanisms than participants in the baseline group who opened the objects independently. The same pattern held in between-subjects analyses as well, where we found that individual participants were significantly less likely to overimitate on the unintentional object than they were to do so on the intentional object (McNemar test, $n = 25, p < 0.001$).

Importantly, data from a separate age-matched control experiment (see electronic supplementary material for full details) argue that the absence of overimitation in the unintentional condition was not simply a byproduct of reduced attention. Children in this control experiment saw exactly the same display as those in the unintentional group, but afterwards they were *asked to copy* what the experimenter had done rather than simply being given the opportunity to open the puzzle box. In this circumstance, we found that 81 and 78 per cent of children were able to reproduce the experimenter's unintentional irrelevant actions on the monkey box and prize box, respectively. Thus, we can infer that in the unintentional condition children's memories of the adult's actions were, in principle, detailed enough for overimitation to have matched the level observed in the intentional case. The steep decline of overimitation thus supports our theory's proposal that ACE is constrained by intentionality.

Although future work will likely reveal more boundary conditions on overimitation, these experiments demonstrate that the effect is not indiscriminate. Instead,

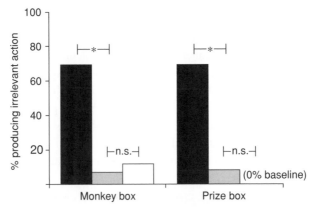

Figure 23.5 Overimitation is firmly constrained by intentionality. Children will ignore irrelevant actions that appear unintentional, even though the same actions presented in an intentional context trigger high levels of overimitation. Black bars, intentional; grey bars, unintentional; white bar, baseline.

overimitation is bounded in a manner consistent with the learning function we have ascribed to it.

23.10 **Conclusions and future directions**

As adults we often use social information to guide our causal learning, looking to the ways that others manipulate novel artefacts in order to infer causally important operations. Here, we have argued that children engage in a very similar process, but that they do so in a way that is often surprisingly automatic. When children observe an adult performing intentional actions on a novel object, they have a strong tendency to encode those actions as causally meaningful—even when there is clear visible evidence to the contrary. This ACE process gives children a powerful boost in understanding our species' artefact-rich cultural environment, but it can also lead to vivid errors. In particular: in the rare case of an adult intentionally performing *unnecessary* actions, children are extremely susceptible to encoding those actions as causally meaningful. We argue that the resulting distortions in children's causal beliefs are the true cause of overimitation.

Because overimitation is rooted in a highly automatic learning process, it is an effect that is remarkably difficult to extinguish. In our previous work, we showed that opposing task demands and even direct contrary instruction were insufficient to block overimitation. Here, we have expanded the scope of these findings, demonstrating that children will continue to overimitate even when doing so imposes a direct and motivationally significant cost.

At the same time though, overimitation is not indiscriminate; the effect is subject to boundary conditions that are coherent in light of its posited learning function. In particular, our studies are the first to show that intentionality imposes a significant boundary on overimitation, just as the ACE hypothesis predicts. Combined with our prior demonstration of core knowledge constraints [4], these results begin to suggest the first contours of what is certain to be a rich and interesting landscape of overimitation boundary conditions.

Looking to the future, one of the interesting under-explored dimensions of overimitation is its potential human universality. The ACE hypothesis predicts that all humans, regardless of their cultural background or exposure to sophisticated modern devices like computers and remote controls, should exhibit overimitation. Because the effect is posited to arise from the evolutionarily ancient advances of inverse and recursive teleology [21–24], one should not need to grow up in a highly technological culture to show the effect. In fact, Nielsen & Tomaselli [16] have recently contributed the first evidence that this prediction may be accurate, demonstrating that Kalahari Bushman children are just as likely to overimitate as the urban American children we have studied. While firm conclusions on the issue will require additional data and replication, these findings present an intriguing first piece of evidence that overimitation may indeed be a universal feature of human learning in the way that the ACE hypothesis predicts.

In the laboratory, overimitation often looks like an error—an unfortunate suggestibility that leads children into mistakes other primates do not make. However, we believe that in more naturalistic settings, overimitation actually represents a profound learning advantage, one that helps to support and propagate our species' artefact-centric culture. The ACE process, operating in tandem with the kinds of powerful constraints we have begun to describe here, affords us a uniquely human perspective for understanding one another's contributions to the designed world.

Acknowledgements

We wish to thank the children and preschools whose participation made this work possible; Deena Skolnick Weisberg for her generous assistance; Andrew Whiten for his invitation and helpful commentary; and Paul Bloom, Uta Frith, Paul Harris, Robert Hinde, Marcia Johnson, Laurie Santos, Brian Scholl, Michael Weisberg and an anonymous reviewer for their insightful feedback on this work. D.E.L. was supported by a National Science Foundation Graduate Research Fellowship. F.C.K. was supported by Yale University and National Institutes of Health Grant R37 HD023922.

Endnotes

[1] Gergely & Csibra [22] contrast this with the 'simple teleology' of chimpanzees, who appear to see objects as tools only transiently, and only when prompted by the immediate presence of a desirable goal state.

[2] Recall that our hypothesis frames ACE as a learning mechanism triggered by observing intentional action on an unfamiliar object. The familiar nature of the training items was thus an important aspect of our design, as otherwise children would have been expected to overimitate during both phases of the experiment.

[3] It is interesting to compare these results to tasks in which preschoolers are asked to evaluate their trust of adults. Children will report less trust for adults who have proven unreliable in prior situations [25, 26]—not unlike the experimenter's unreliable modelling during the training phase of our study—yet overimitation is not diminished by similar circumstances. In this respect, the ACE process seems to bind children more strongly than conversational inferences.

[4] Although it is true that children in our baseline control conditions were not sufficiently curious about the irrelevant mechanisms to explore them, the experimental conditions introduced further elements of stimulus enhancement (i.e. the adult actually acting on the irrelevant mechanisms). Given that similar kinds of action-based 'highlighting' have been shown to influence preschoolers' behaviour [28], the curiosity alternative needs to be taken seriously.

[5] More detailed procedures, results and discussion for each of the experiments reported in this chapter can be found in the electronic supplementary material.

References

1 Gergely, G., Bekkering, H. & Király, I. 2002 Rational imitation in preverbal infants. *Nature* **415**, 755.

2 Schwier, C., Van Maanen, C., Carpenter, M. & Tomasello, M. 2006 Rational imitation in 12-month-old infants. *Infancy* **10**, 303–311.

3 Horner, V. & Whiten, A. 2005 Causal knowledge and imitation/emulation switching in chimpanzees (*Pan troglodytes*) and children (*Homo sapiens*). *Anim. Cogn.* **8**, 164–181.

4 Lyons, D. E., Young, A. G. & Keil, F. C. 2007 The hidden structure of overimitation. *Proc. Natl Acad. Sci. USA* **104**, 19751–19756.

5 Call, J., Carpenter, M. & Tomasello, M. 2005 Copying results and copying actions in the process of social learning: chimpanzees (*Pan troglodytes*) and human children (*Homo sapiens*). *Anim. Cogn.* **8**, 151–163.

6 Carpenter, M., Call, J. & Tomasello, M. 2002 Understanding 'prior intentions' enables two-year-olds to imitatively learn a complex task. *Child Dev.* **73**, 1431–1441.

7 Nagell, K., Olguin, K. & Tomasello, M. 1993 Processes of social learning in the tool use of chimpanzees (*Pan troglodytes*) and human children (*Homo sapiens*). *J. Comp. Psychol.* **107**, 174–186.

8 Nielsen, M. 2006 Copying actions and copying outcomes: social learning through the second year. *Dev. Psychol.* **42**, 555–565.

9 Want, S. C. & Harris, P. L. 2002 How do children ape? Applying concepts from the study of non-human primates to the developmental study of 'imitation' in children. *Dev. Sci.* **5**, 1–41.

10 Whiten, A., Custance, D. M., Gomez, J.-C., Teixidor, P. & Bard, K. A. 1996 Imitative learning of artificial fruit processing in children (*Homo sapiens*) and chimpanzees (*Pan troglodytes*). *J. Comp. Psychol.* **110**, 3–14.

11 Uzgiris, I. C. 1981 Two functions of imitation during infancy. *Int. J. Behav. Dev.* **4**, 1–12.

12 Meltzoff, A. N. 2007 'Like me': a foundation for social cognition. *Dev. Sci.* **10**, 1–126.

13 Nielsen, M., Simcock, G. & Jenkins, L. 2008 The effect of social engagement in 24-month-olds' imitation from live and televised models. *Dev. Sci.* **11**, 5–722.

14 Tomasello, M., Carpenter, M., Call, J., Behne, T. & Moll, H. 2005 Understanding and sharing intentions: the origins of cultural cognition. *Behav. Brain Sci.* **28**, 675–735.

15 McGuigan, N., Whiten, A., Flynn, E. & Horner, V. 2007 Imitation of causally-opaque versus causally-transparent tool use by 3- and 5-year-old children. *Cogn. Dev.* **22**, 353–364.

16 Nielsen, M. & Tomaselli, K. 2010 Overimitation in Kalahari Bushman children and the origins of human cultural cognition. *Psychol. Sci.* **21**, 730–736.

17 Whiten, A., McGuigan, N., Marshall-Pescini, S. & Hopper, L. M. 2009 Emulation, imitation, overimitation, and the scope of culture for child and chimpanzee. *Phil. Trans. R. Soc. B* **364**, 2417–2428.

18 Whiten, A., Horner, V. & Marshall-Pescini, S. 2005 Selective imitation in child and chimpanzee: a window on the construal of others' actions. In *Perspectives on imitation: from neuroscience to social science* (eds S. Hurley & N. Chater), pp. 263–283. Cambridge, MA: MIT Press.

19 McGuigan, N. & Whiten, A. 2009 Emulation and 'over-emulation' in the social learning of causally opaque versus causally transparent tool use by 23- and 30-month olds. *J. Exp. Child Psychol.* **104**, 367–381.

20 McGuigan, N., Makinson, J. & Whiten, A. 2011 From over-imitation to super-copying: adults imitate causally irrelevant aspects of tool use with higher fidelity than young children. *Br. J. Psychol.* **102**, 1–18.

21 Gergely, G. & Csibra, G. 2005 The social construction of the cultural mind: imitative learning as a mechanism of human pedagogy. *Interact. Stud.* **6**, 463–481.

22 Gergely, G. & Csibra, G. 2006 Sylvia's recipe: the role of imitation and pedagogy in the transmission of cultural knowledge. In *Roots of human sociality: culture, cognition, and human interaction* (eds N. J. Enfield & S. C. Levenson), pp. 229–255. Oxford, UK: Berg.

23 Csibra, G. & Gergely, G. 2006 Social learning and social cognition: the case for pedagogy. In *Processes of change in brain and cognitive development. Attention and performance*, vol. 21 (eds Y. Munakata & M. H. Johnson), pp. 249–274. Oxford, UK: Oxford University Press.

24 Lyons, D. E. 2008 The rational continuum of human imitation. In *Mirror neuron systems* (ed. J. A. Pineda), pp. 77–103. New York, NY: Humana Press.

25 Harris, P. 2007 Trust. *Dev. Sci.* **10**, 1–135.

26 Harris, P. L. & Corriveau, K. H. 2011 Young children's selective trust in informants. *Phil. Trans. R. Soc. B* **366**, 1179–1187.

27 Henderson, B. & Moore, S. G. 1980 Children's responses to objects differing in novelty in relation to level of curiosity and adult behavior. *Child Dev.* **51**, 2–457.

28 Henderson, B. B. 1984 Social support and exploration. *Child Dev.* **55**, 4–1246.

29 Sheridan, S. & Williams, P. 2006 Constructive competition in preschool. *J. Early Child. Res.* **4**, 3–291.

30 Higgins, E. T. & Eccles-Parsons, J. E. 1983 Social cognition and the social life of the child: stages as subcultures. In *Social cognition and social development: a sociocultural perspective* (eds E. T. Higgins, D. N. Ruble & W. W. Hartup), pp. 15–62. New York, NY: Cambridge University Press.

31 Deci, E. L., Betley, G., Kahle, J., Abrams, L. & Porac, J. 1981 When trying to win: competition and intrinsic motivation. *Pers. Soc. Psychol. Bull.* **7**, 79–83.

32 Heyman, G. D. & Dweck, C. S. 1992 Achievement goals and intrinsic motivation: their relation and their role in adaptive motivation. *Motiv. Emot.* **16**, 3–231.

33 Butler, R. 1989 Interest in the task and interest in peers' work in competitive and noncompetitive situations: a developmental study. *Child Dev.* **60**, 3–562.

34 Butler, R. 1989 Mastery versus ability appraisal: a developmental study of children's observations of peers' work. *Child Dev.* **60**, 6–1350.

35 Butler, R. 1990 The effects of mastery and competitive conditions on self-assesment at different ages. *Child Dev.* **61**, 1–201.

36 Spelke, E. S., Breinlinger, K., Macomber, J. & Jacobson, K. 1992 Origins of knowledge. *Psychol. Rev.* **99**, 605–632.

37 Spelke, E. 1994 Initial knowledge: six suggestions. *Cognition* **50**, 431–445.

Chapter 24

Social Learning Among Congo Basin Hunter–Gatherers[*]

Barry S. Hewlett, Hillary N. Fouts, Adam H. Boyette and Bonnie L. Hewlett

This chapter explores childhood social learning among Aka and Bofi hunter–gatherers in Central Africa. Existing literature suggests that hunter–gatherer social learning is primarily vertical (parent-to-child) and that teaching is rare. We use behavioural observations, open-ended and semi-structured interviews, and informal and anecdotal observations to examine the modes (e.g. vertical versus horizontal/oblique) and processes (e.g. teaching versus observation and imitation) of cultural transmission. Cultural and demographic contexts of social learning associated with the modes and processes of cultural transmission are described. Hunter–gatherer social learning occurred early, was relatively rapid, primarily vertical under age 5 and oblique and horizontal between the ages of 6 and 12. Pedagogy and other forms of teaching existed as early as 12 months of age, but were relatively infrequent by comparison to other processes of social learning such as observation and imitation.

Keywords: hunter–gatherers; social learning; cultural transmission; Africa

24.1 Introduction

Anthropologists have long been interested in social learning [1, 2], and several excellent monographs exist on social learning in small-scale cultures [3–5]. However, the majority of research in social anthropology and developmental psychology has been conducted with horticultural or intensive farming cultures, where craft specialization and various forms of hierarchy, such as gender or age inequality, exist. Characterizations of social learning in 'traditional' cultures are largely limited to these contexts. According to Harris [6], common features of learning in traditional societies are that physical punishment is commonly used to help children learn, infants are taught little because

---

[*] Electronic supplementary material is available at http://dx.doi.org/10.1098/rstb.2010.0373 or via http://rstb.royalsocietypublishing.org.

parents consider infants to be incapable of learning, older siblings and children have the right to dominate younger children to show them how to do tasks, and parents are not the friends or playmates of their children. These may be common features of social learning in farming communities but not necessarily in hunter–gatherer communities.

Studies of hunter–gatherer social learning are essential to a comprehensive understanding of how culture evolves, because this way of life characterized 99 per cent of human history and constituted the environment(s) of evolutionary adaptation. While contemporary hunter–gatherers are not Stone Age relics of the past, they can provide insights into a way of life that was characterized by mobility, small population size (25–35 individuals), minimal gender and age hierarchy, and lack of both storage and strong political leaders. Given the potential importance of hunter–gatherers for understanding social learning in humans, it is ironic that more books and other publications exist on chimpanzee social learning than that on hunter–gatherer social learning.

Here we assemble what we currently know about social learning among the most intensively studied hunter–gatherer juveniles—the Aka and Bofi 'Pygmy' children of the Central African Republic and Republic of Congo. We have conducted several years of qualitative and quantitative research with these children, each of us covering a different age range. Not all of our research directly addressed social learning, but our systematic observational and interview data from infancy through adolescence enable us to begin to quantitatively address social learning questions and hypotheses.

This section of the chapter introduces two prominent social learning questions, while §24.2 summarizes the methods we used to answer the questions. Section 24.3 examines modes of thought, patterns of daily life and demographic features of Congo Basin hunter–gatherers and farmers. These two modes of production and thought are too often grouped together and characterized as traditional, small-scale, tribal or non-Western societies. Instead, we highlight the distinctive features of hunter–gatherers by comparing them with their farming neighbours. The two groups live in the same natural environment, the tropical forest, and interact on a regular basis. The relatively distinct hunter–gatherer modes of thought, patterns of daily life and demography are essential for contextualizing our results. Section 24.4 presents data to address social learning questions, and §24.5 summarizes and discusses what we currently know about hunter–gatherer social learning.

The chapter distinguishes modes of cultural transmission from processes of social learning. Modes of transmission refer to individuals from whom children learn and include vertical, horizontal, oblique, conformist and prestige-bias. Processes of social learning include teaching, emulation, imitation and collaborative learning. The different modes of transmission may involve different processes of social learning: for example, vertical transmission may take place by emulation or teaching. We do not examine all modes of transmission and processes of social learning. Two questions are examined: (i) do hunter–gatherers learn primarily from parents (vertical) or others (horizontal or oblique)? (ii) does teaching exist in hunter–gatherers? We define teaching as modification of one's behaviour to facilitate learning of information, knowledge or skills in another.

Our studies do not distinguish imitation from emulation as defined in other papers in this collection [7] (here, Chapter 7) because the differences were difficult to capture in our naturalistic behavioural observations. Consequently, from this point forward, 'imitation' can be emulation or imitation as defined in other chapters in this volume, unless otherwise noted.

24.1.1 Modes of transmission: from whom do children learn?

Harris's [8] critical review of the child development literature addresses one of the issues in this chapter—from whom do children learn? Her review concluded that peers, friends and other adults contributed substantially more to social learning than did parents. Her conclusion was also supported by her literature review of learning in 'traditional' cultures [6], unsurprisingly, because most socialization studies in small-scale cultures were conducted in farming cultures where older siblings and children have key roles in child rearing [9, 10].

The importance of parents versus other children and adults is also a contentious issue in evolutionary studies of cultural transmission. Early social anthropologists interested in learning and education used the term 'cultural transmission' [11] to refer to this issue, but the term took on a different meaning when Cavalli Sforza & Feldman [12] published *Cultural Transmission and Evolution*. They used the term to refer to an innovative evolutionary approach to culture that used analogies from population genetics and epidemiology to mathematically model several modes of cultural transmission. Mendel revolutionized genetics by identifying mechanisms of genetic transmission, and Cavalli Sforza and Feldman aimed to revolutionize cultural anthropology by identifying specific mechanisms of cultural transmission. Paralleling Mendel's early studies in genetic transmission, Cavalli Sforza and Feldman's models focused on who transmitted culture. Vertical or parent-to-child transmission was modelled after genetic transmission so that a cultural belief or practice transmitted vertically was predicted to be highly conserved and contributed to intracultural diversity (i.e. each parent transmitting a cultural variant). Horizontal (friends and peers) and oblique (other adults) transmission were based on disease transmission models in epidemiology and were hypothesized to contribute to the rapid spread of a belief or practice if contact with friends, neighbours or other adults was frequent.

Early tests of Cavalli Sforza and Feldman's models suggested that vertical transmission was particularly important. Stanford University undergraduate students were reported to acquire their religious and political beliefs vertically 50–70% of the time [13]. Aka hunter–gatherer adults, adolescents and children were asked how they learned a list of 50 skills and indicated that about 80 per cent of their knowledge about subsistence, childcare, sharing and other skills was transmitted from their parents, generally from the same sex parent [14]. Other interview-based studies with active [15, 16] or former [17] hunter–gatherers also identified parents as primary transmitters of knowledge or skills. Hewlett's ethnographic survey of cultural transmission among 40 hunting–gathering cultures from the Standard Cross-Cultural Sample was consistent with these field studies; parents were primary transmitters of culture to boys in 70 per cent and to girls in 80 per cent of the cultures. Other categories of individuals, such as uncles, aunts or peers, trained boys and girls in the remaining 20–30% of cultures. Vertical transmission is also reported to be a primary mode of transmission in farming communities with craft specialization [18, 19].

Boyd & Richerson [20, 21] expanded this field, mathematically modelling two relatively new non-vertical transmission mechanisms, conformist transmission (copy the beliefs or practices of the majority) and prestige bias (copy the successful). The emerging fields of human behavioural ecology and life-history theory influenced their cultural transmission theories, and unlike their predecessors, they evaluated the efficiency and tradeoffs of different transmission mechanisms. Henrich & McElreath [22] refined these models and continued to emphasize the importance of non-vertical transmission mechanisms, and simulations by McElreath & Strimling [23] showed that vertical transmission was only adaptive in relatively stable environments. Harris's [6, 8] review of the developmental psychology literature, social anthropologists' descriptions of the importance of sibling care in farming cultures [10] and MacDonald's [24] review of the hunter–gatherer ethnographic literature on how children learn hunting skills supported Boyd, Richerson, Henrich & McElreath's emphasis on the importance of horizontal and other non-vertical forms of cultural transmission.

24.1.2 Processes of social learning: does teaching exist in hunter–gatherers?

Social anthropologists suggest that teaching is absent or rare in small-scale cultures, whereas developmental psychologists tend to assume that it is part of human nature. The first section of a recent review of children's social learning by social anthropologists Lancy & Grove [25] is titled 'The absence of teaching'. Like many social anthropologists, they indicate that teaching seldom occurs in small-scale cultures and emphasize the importance of observational [26] and informal learning [27]. MacDonald's [24] hunter–gatherer study also concluded that 'teaching is unimportant'.

Mead [28] characterized many small-scale cultures as 'learning cultures' because children in these cultures acquired culture easily and quickly without teaching. Social anthropologists past [29] and present [26] used the term 'osmosis' to refer how easy it was for children in small-scale cultures to acquire a wide variety of knowledge and skills without teaching; it was automatic, without effort and nobody failed. Among hunter–gatherer researchers, Lewis [30] concluded that explicit teaching did not exist among hunter–gatherers because it was inconsistent with an egalitarian ethos; 'pedagogic action' (education) took place through practices, changes in physical maturity such as menstruation, and the natural curiosity and motivation of individuals.

The conclusion of Lancy & Grove and other social anthropologists that teaching does not exist in small-scale cultures may be exaggerated. Mead's classic work [24] concluded 'Manus teach very young children things which they consider most important such as physical skill, prudery and respect for property. They [parents, others] teach them these things firmly, unrelentingly, often severely.' Kruger & Tomasello [31] provide several examples of teaching in small-scale cultures, but the vast majority of examples come from horticultural societies, such as the Manus, or intensive farmers where craft specialization is common.

The view that teaching is rare in small-scale cultures contrasts dramatically with the recent proposition by cognitive psychologists that teaching or pedagogy is an innate and relatively unique feature of human cognition [32–34]. Pedagogy is defined by them as when one individual (teacher) provides explicit signals of generalizable (to other situations or individuals) knowledge to another individual (learner) who can read and interpret the content of the signals. They hypothesize that pedagogy evolved to solve the recurring problem of faithfully transmitting opaque knowledge (e.g. tool functions) to the learner. Learners evolved to pay attention to particular cues such as eye and body movements, and teachers evolved the skills to convey important information to learners such as pointing, looking or making sounds. It is hypothesized that other learning processes such as observation, imitation and emulation were not sufficient for learning tasks and behaviours that were opaque to the learner. They concede that others have pointed out the importance of teaching in human evolution [31, 35], but suggest that their hypothesis is distinct from previous ones because it does not require the coevolution of cognitive abilities to read the intentions of others or language. However, Csibra and Gergely point out that effective learning is more likely to take place if the learner trusts (reads the intentions of) the teacher.

This is a provocative new hypothesis, but the data used to support it come entirely from infant and child development studies of parent–infant eye contact, gaze and infant-directed speech in urban-industrial cultures, where these types of parent–infant interactions and formal, institutionalized teaching are common. Studies of parent–infant interactions in small scale, particularly hunter–gatherer groups, are needed. It is also important to point out that pedagogy is one type of teaching. Positive reinforcement and other simple modifications of one's behaviour to facilitate learning of information, knowledge or skill in another are not necessarily pedagogy as defined by Gergely and Csibra.

24.1.3 Connections between modes and processes of transmission

Theoretical and conceptual connections exist between the modes and processes of cultural transmission. Gergely & Csibra [32], Shennan & Steele [18] and Tehrani & Collard [19] assume that teaching is an important component of vertical transmission. Teaching entails costs to the teacher because he or she has to spend time and energy to accommodate the learner, and other processes of social learning (imitation and emulation) are not as efficient as teaching. Gergely & Csibra [32] and Shennan & Steele [18] hypothesize that teaching is more efficient than other processes of learning and that parents (vertical transmission) are more likely to invest in training of their children than are others; the potential roles of older brothers, sisters or cousins (horizontal transmission) are not mentioned. Shennan and Steele also hypothesize that learning should be early rather than late so as to free up parent's time to have another child and that learners should demand more than teachers are willing to give (based on parent–offspring conflict theory).

Researchers who emphasize horizontal transmission tend to downplay the role of teaching. Other processes, such as observation and interactions with older children, copying what the majority are doing or acquiring traits of successful adults, are more likely to be emphasized by researchers who model horizontal transmission.

Given this overview, if teaching is part of human nature it should be common at a relatively young age in hunter–gatherers. If teaching is a product of cultural structures, such as increasing inequality associated with farming cultures [30], specialization or institutional developments, it should be absent or rare in hunter–gatherers.

24.2 **Methods**

Our data come primarily from Aka and Bofi hunter–gatherers and Ngandu and Bofi farmers in the southern forests of the Central African Republic. About 20 000 Aka and 3000 Bofi hunter–gatherers occupy the area; the number of Ngandu and Bofi farmers is substantially greater, but we do not have reliable estimates. The Aka have economic, ritual and kinship relationships with several different farming groups, including the Ngandu. The Bofi hunter–gatherers are neighbours of the Aka and were Aka until about 70 years ago when they started to affiliate with Bofi farmers and speak the Bofi language. From this point on, whenever we use the term 'hunter–gatherers' or 'foragers', we are referring to the Aka or Bofi foragers, unless otherwise noted, and when we say 'farmers' we are referring to the Ngandu or Bofi farmers, unless otherwise noted. We do not want to diminish the dramatic diversity that exists among Congo Basin hunter–gatherer and farmer groups but want to simplify the chapter to reduce potential confusion between groups.

Focal follows of individuals from infancy through adolescence provide key data used to answer the two social learning questions. Each child was followed for 6–12 h over several randomly selected days. Anywhere from 20 to 30 behaviours were coded every 30 s. The data have been collected over the past 15 years. The coded behaviours for infancy and early childhood were similar, whereas the coded behaviours for children 4–18 years of age were similar in some domains (e.g. who is proximal to focal child) but different in others (e.g. codes for teaching and imitation). Electronic supplementary material provides greater detail on the samples from each age group and the procedures and behavioural codes used in each study. Qualitative methods such as participant observation, open-ended and semi-structured interviews and structured questionnaires were also used to understand cultural perceptions of social learning, which individuals said they learned from and how they learned particular skills and knowledge. Each of the authors has spent at least two field seasons with Congo Basin foragers.

24.3 **Cultural and demographic contexts of Congo basin hunter–gatherer social learning**

This section describes foundational schema (cultural values and ways of thinking and feeling that pervade several domains of life), features of daily life and demographic contexts essential to understanding forager social learning. Comparisons with neighbouring farmer groups are used to help identify distinctive features of hunter–gatherer social learning.

24.3.1 Foundational schema

Three foundational schemas pervade hunter–gatherer life: egalitarianism, autonomy and sharing. An egalitarian way of thinking means others are respected for what they are and it is not appropriate to draw attention to oneself or judge others to be better or worse than others. Men and women, young and old, are viewed as relatively equal and have similar access to resources. Respect for an individual's autonomy is also a core cultural value. One does not coerce others, including children. Men and women, young and old, are generally free to do what they want. If an infant wants to play with a machete, she is allowed to do so. A giving or sharing way of thinking also pervades hunter–gatherer life; hunter–gatherers share 50–80% of what is acquired by hunting and gathering, Aka share with everyone in camp, every day.

The farmers cultivate manioc, corn, plantains and peanuts. They exchange some of their crops for meat and other forest products of hunter–gatherers. Women plant, maintain and harvest the fields and provide the majority of the dietary calories, whereas men fish, hunt and trade. Foundational schemas among the farmers include: gender and age hierarchy, communalism and material/economic dimensions to social relations. Women are expected to defer to the requests of men and the young should be respectful of elders, be they older siblings or parents. Communalism refers to the cultural value placed on putting the needs of the group, generally clan members or the extended family, over the needs of an individual. The third foundational schema refers to the thoughts and feelings that interpersonal relations have economic or material components. Material and economic dimensions of relationships are embedded within the social and emotional aspects of relationships.

Foundational schemas are learned early in life because sanctions exist for them. If a forager child does not share, others gesture, comment or tease the child. Young children often hear stories about how people who do not share properly face sanctions (e.g. illness, death, death of a child). Among farmers, sanctions tend to be harsh. Corporal punishment is not an uncommon response for young farmer children who do not listen to or respect their parents or older siblings [36].

24.3.2 Habitus and demographic contexts of hunter–gatherer social learning

This section describes relatively distinct features of forager *habitus* [37]—daily, lived experiences—and demography that are important for understanding social learning. The habitus is shaped by the foundational schema and is also the means by which children learn the foundational schema and other cultural knowledge. Forager habitus and demography are again contrasted with those of neighbouring farmers to highlight forager patterns.

24.3.2.1 Physical and emotional intimacy

Physical and emotional proximity is particularly important to hunter–gatherers [38]. Forager camps are generally very dense, often occupying a space the size of a large dining and living room in the USA or the space of one or two farmer houses. When hunter–gatherers sit down in the camp, they are usually touching somebody. At night, foragers sleep very close together and usually sleep with someone; our study of co-sleeping found that forager children and adolescents never slept alone, whereas farmer children over 7 years old slept alone 30–40% of the time. In terms of holding during infancy and early childhood, forager three to four month old infants were held 91 per cent of the day while farmer infants were held 54 per cent of the day [39]. Forager 2-, 3- and 4-year-olds were held 44, 27 and 8 per cent of daylight hours, whereas farmer children of the same age were held 18, 2 and 0 per cent of the day [40].

The importance of emotional proximity to others is illustrated in two studies. In a study of conflicts between toddlers and older juveniles among hunter–gatherers and farmers, Fouts & Lamb [41] found that hunter–gatherer toddlers were substantially more likely to have conflicts over staying close to juveniles (38% of conflicts among forager toddlers versus 2% of conflicts among farmer toddlers), whereas farmer toddlers were more likely to have conflicts with juveniles over competition for objects (48% of farmer toddler conflicts versus 14% of forager toddler conflicts) or over the juvenile hitting the toddler, which never occurred among the hunter–gatherer toddlers. This study illustrates early acquisition and manifestation of cultural values—emotional proximity to others among the hunter–gatherers and the economic-material dimensions of social relations among the farmers.

In another study, hunter–gatherer and farmer adolescents were asked about their experiences and feelings about the death and loss of friends and relatives [42]. Forager expressions of grief emphasized their love and emotional connections to the person, whereas farmer expressions of grief focused on materials objects the lost relative gave or provided.

24.3.2.2 Self-motivated and directed learning

Hunter–gatherer children are granted autonomy during the day, whereas farmer children are subject to the control of parents and older children. For instance, Hewlett found that forager three to four month old infants took the breast on their own to nurse during 58 per cent of feeding bouts by comparison to only 2 per cent of feeding bouts among farmers. Farmer mothers directed infant nursing while it was infant-directed among foragers. At weaning, hunter–gatherer mothers said that the child decided when he or she wanted to wean, whereas farmer mothers said they decided. The hunter–gatherer mothers said that if they initiated the weaning it would cause the child to get sick, whereas the farmers said nursing too long causes the child to become lazy [43]. In the co-sleeping study, forager parents indicated that their children slept wherever they wanted, whereas the farmer parents said that they told their children where to sleep. Recent studies in social anthropology on informal learning emphasize self-motivation [27], but hunter–gatherer children probably initiate learning and discovery more often than children in other modes of production. Forager children's high motivation to learn occurs early and often. Infants climb into their parents' laps to watch them cook, play an instrument or make a net. Children want to learn more than what parents and others want to give, but forager parents seldom refuse the intrusions of a child, because of their egalitarian and autonomy ethos.

24.3.2.3 Trust of others

The development of trust of others is important to some degree in all cultures, but the socialization for trust of several others is particularly pronounced in hunter–gatherers, which relates to their extensive sharing and giving. Hunter–gatherer infants and young children were breastfed on demand, averaging about 4 bouts per hour, whereas farmers averaged about 2 bouts per hour. Young forager infants were often breastfed by other women, generally aunts and grandmothers (sometimes even fathers offered their breast), whereas among farmers, breastfeeding by other women was thought to cause infant sickness and was not practised except under unusual circumstances. Forager caregivers were significantly more likely than farmer caregivers to respond to infant crying, and farmer infants cried significantly longer and more frequently than did forager infants [39, 44]. Hunter–gatherer infants and young children were held twice as often as neighbouring farmers, and this additional holding came from many different individuals—fathers, grandmothers, siblings and others. In early infancy, mothers provided the most care, but all others together provided more holding than did mothers [38]. Likewise, hunter–gatherer toddlers received most plates of food from mother, but all other categories of providers together (grandmothers, aunts, etc.) provided more plates of food to children than did mothers [45].

24.3.2.4 Mixed adult–child groups

Konner [46] indicates that after weaning, hunter–gatherer children move from a relationship with mother to relationships with children in mixed aged playgroups. Our data question his representation of hunter–gatherers and indicate that parents and other adults are frequently around children and even adolescents. Time with parents and other adults, generally grandparents, gradually declines with age, but by comparison to farmers, foragers spend considerably less time in child-only groups. Table 24.1 summarizes Fouts's data on who is proximal (i.e. within arm's reach) to hunter–gatherer and farmer young children; hunter–gatherer children were much more likely to be proximal to more categories of people and parents and other adults than were farmers. By age 4–5, hunter–gatherers are still proximal to parents and adults 33 per cent of the time, whereas farmer children are proximal to them only 6 per cent of the day. Farmer children at this age spent 59 per cent of their day in child-only groups, whereas hunter–gatherer children spent only 18 per cent of their day in proximity to child-only groups. Boyette found that 4-to 12-year-old forager children spent more time in mixed aged groups, but they were still within visual range of an adult 77 per cent of the day, and parents and other adults were among their nearest neighbours (defined as those equally close to the child) 33.1 per cent of the day.

Table 24.1 Percentage of observation intervals hunter–gatherer and farmer children were within arm's reach of adults and children

	age					
proximity	2-years-old		3-years-old		4-years-old	
	hunter–gatherers	farmers	hunter–gatherers	farmers	hunter–gatherers	farmers
adults only	63.5	34.5	47.5	23.4	33.1	5.6
children only	7.0	28.3	18.7	29.2	18.5	59.2
adults and children	21.6	13.5	23.0	9.5	28.9	2.7

Another behavioural study found that forager children in late childhood spent 40 per cent of their day in mixed adult–child proximity groups (defined as three closest individuals to child) and 30 per cent of their day in child-only proximity groups while in a camp setting [47]. Outside of the camp, these children spent 70 per cent of their time with an adult social or work group and 30 per cent of their time with a child-only social or work group. This is consistent with Boyette's recent finding that children were more likely to spend time with adults in the forest and less likely to spend time with younger children in camp, as they got older. Neuwelt-Truntzer [47] found that this pattern continued into adolescence.

At night, the co-sleeping study found that forager children and adolescents were three times more likely than farmer children of similar age to sleep with parents or other adults.

24.3.2.5 Play

Play is an important learning context. Several researchers have reported that hunter–gatherer children spend most of the day playing and are not expected to contribute much to subsistence or maintenance [46, 48]. By comparison, children in farming communities are more likely to be given responsibilities for childcare and other tasks [49]. Boyette found that forager 4- to 12-year-old children spent a considerable amount of time playing (31.4% of day) and laying around (idle, 37.9% of day). Unfortunately, comparative data on farmers are not available. Forager play is relatively equally divided between solitary play, social play and work play (children imitating/emulating adult tasks). Kamei's [50] study of types of play among 7- to 15-year-old Baka hunter–gatherers, Cameroonian neighbours of the Aka, identifies 85 different types of games, the majority (61%) dealing with hunting–gathering, camp life (cooking and childcare) and singing–dancing. All of this play takes place in child-only groups, and most of the play involves learning about making a living as a hunter–gatherer.

It is essential to understand the cultural and demographic contexts of forager social learning. Foragers value autonomy and egalitarianism, so parents, older children or other adults are not likely to think and feel that they know what is best or better for a child and are generally unlikely to initiate, direct or intervene in a child's social learning. This is consistent with our finding that forager social learning is self-motivated and directed, but it also suggests that teaching and explicit instruction should be rare or absent. Sharing and giving are also forager core values, so what an individual knows is open and available to everyone; if a child wants to learn something, others are obliged to share the knowledge or skill. If forager children regularly asked questions, teaching could be common, but forager children seldom ask questions about how to do things. The mixed adult–child demographic data on where children are at different ages suggest that parents are proximal and very available for social learning, especially before age 5, but that after age 5 children are more likely to be around children and other adults. Vertical transmission is likely at younger ages and horizontal and oblique transmissions more likely in middle and late childhood. Forager children also play much with other children, creating opportunities for horizontal transmission. Since learning is self-motivated and directed and takes place in intimate and trusting contexts, hunter–gatherer children are generally very confident and self-assured learners. Finally, intimacy and socialization for trust with many individuals suggest that social learning may be rapid in foragers, as developmental psychologists [32] showed that trust facilitates social learning.

24.4 Modes and processes of social learning

24.4.1 Modes of transmission: from whom do hunter–gatherer children learn?

24.4.1.1 The case for vertical transmission

Vertical transmission should be important in hunter–gatherers given our great ape phylogenetic heritage of mother-to-offspring transmission [51] and parents' potential inclusive fitness benefits from taking the time to transmit knowledge or skills [18]. Theoretically, one can make the case, but this is also what hunter–gatherers say when asked how they learned a wide range of skills and knowledge [14, 17, 52]. In a recent study, Hattori [16] found that Baka hunter–gatherer women said that they learned about the uses of 90 plants from their mothers 80 per cent of time, fathers 15 per cent of time and others 5 per cent of time; Baka men said that they learned about the plants from their mothers 10 per cent of the time, fathers 65 per cent of the time, siblings 11 per cent of the time and others 13 per cent of the time. An interview-based qualitative study of forager adolescents [53] is replete with expressions of vertical transmission. One adolescent boy explained 'father showed me how to care for younger brothers and sisters and to have a good character. He showed me how to hunt and find honey. (My mother) showed me how to guard the baby and how to wash and comfort the babies'. Often the same sex parent was identified as the person transmitting knowledge, such as when a forager adolescent male stated 'I love my father because he shows me everything', but this is not always the case in hunter–gatherers where gender flexibility is pervasive; an adolescent female stated 'father showed me how to care for the *moanna* (baby) and to give her food and to wash her'.

In a more quantitative study, Boyette asked 39 5- to 18-year-old forager children to list anyone who taught them to share food. On average, 60 per cent of the Aka children said that their mothers taught them to share food, 27 per cent listed their fathers, 20 per cent other kin and 3 per cent mentioned a non-family member (children could list more than one individual). Learning to share was often attributed to the same sex parent. Girls mentioned mothers 84 per cent of the time and boys mentioned fathers 65 per cent of the time.

The habitus and demographic contexts of social learning also contribute to patterns of vertical transmission. In terms of intimacy, hunter–gatherer infants were held most of the day and parents provided over 80 per cent of the holding [37]. Fathers and others provided more holding than mothers while in the camp setting in early infancy, but outside of camp and by late infancy, mothers and fathers provided most of the holding. Fouts found that in early childhood, hunter–gatherer children were within an arm's reach of a parent 40–50% of the day. Mothers and fathers continued to do most of the holding until age 4.

At night, hunter–gatherer infants and children up to the age of 12 slept with their parents. In late childhood and adolescence, hunter–gatherer children spent less time with parents, but they continued to regularly interact with, eat and sleep with them.

24.4.1.2 The case for horizontal and oblique transmission

While our phylogenetic history suggests that vertical transmission should be important, humans are distinct from great apes in that cooperative breeding is part of human nature. Allomaternal care is pronounced in hunter–gatherers [39], and it would be surprising to find that individuals other than parents did not influence cultural transmission.

Hattori's [16] study with Baka foragers examined the degree of agreement between informants in how plants were used. Plants used for food or material culture showed 80–95% agreement between informants, but plants used for medicine showed only 25–30% agreement and considerable intracultural variability. The intracultural diversity of medicinal plant use is consistent with the theoretical expectations of vertical transmission, but the uniformity found in food and material culture suggests that other modes of transmission, possibly conformist bias, influence social learning. Hattori suggests that plants used for food and material culture are public and open to observation, whereas medicinal plant use is relatively private.

Forager parents are more accessible to their young children than parents are among farmers, but other adults and juveniles play significant roles in forager children's daily lives and probably stimulate horizontal and oblique transmission. In infancy, parents are most likely to hold the baby but many others are nearby and interact with the child. If a parent sits down with their infant, they place the infant in their lap facing away from them and towards other camp members. Other adults and children were more likely than mothers or fathers to engage infants in any type of play, but especially in face-to-face play during early infancy [38].

In early childhood, parents, especially mothers, were proximal and provided most of the holding, but other caregivers interacted with toddlers just as often as did parents. Table 24.2 shows that hunter–gatherer parents were more interactive with their 2-year-old than were others, but by 3 and 4 years of age, children were interacting with others just as frequently as parents.

Table 24.2 Frequency (percentage of intervals observed) hunter–gatherer parents and others provided caregiving (e.g. clean and wash), showed affection or vocalized to the child during daylight hours

	2-year-olds	3-year-olds	4-year-olds
parents	6.7	3.1	4.3
others	2.8	3.9	3.7

By middle and late childhood, adults are often nearby, but children spend most of the day in multi-aged child groups. Boyette found that forager children at this age spent most of their day with other children and that children frequently observed and imitated/emulated other children's behaviour. All the types of play he described occurred with other children. The potential for oblique transmission also increases at this time as the chances of children living in step-parent households increase; 42.4 per cent of 11- to 15-year-olds do not live with both biological parents [38].

Hunter–gatherer parents are important contributors to cultural transmission, especially by comparison to farmer parents. Foragers say that parents as a category provide more cultural transmission than any other similar category, such as siblings, cousins, aunt/uncles, grandparents or friends. Behavioural observations also indicate that children spend substantial parts of the day near parents up until age 5. However, other adults and juveniles also spend considerable time with children, especially after age 5. The roles of 'others' in hunter–gatherers (i.e. all friends, cousins, etc.) are poorly understood and probably underestimated, and more systematic studies are needed to evaluate the nature and impact of their contributions to social learning.

24.4.2 Processes of social learning: does teaching exist in hunter–gatherers?

Evolutionary approaches to culture identify several processes of social learning [51], but we focus here on teaching because anthropological literature [25] says that it is rare or does not exist in hunter–gatherers, whereas other recent literature [32–34] indicates that it is part of human nature. We define teaching as modification of one's behaviour to facilitate learning of information, knowledge or skill in another. Pedagogy as defined by Gergely and Csibra is one type of teaching. Qualitative and quantitative data suggest that pedagogy and other forms of teaching exist in hunter–gatherers.

Parents make small axes, digging sticks, baskets and spears for infants and young children. These are small-sized artefacts that reflect the size of the infant or child and are not toys. Mothers place these implements in their baskets and while resting on a net hunt or other subsistence activity, they will be given to infants. The infants chop, dig, etc., and the parents watch, laugh, make sounds and sometimes physically take the infants' hands to show them how to use the implement. Hewlett made 1 h naturalistic video recordings of 10- to 12-month olds, and preliminary analysis indicates that parents in at least three of the videos exhibited pedagogy; parents moved the arm of the infant to show her how to dig or use a knife, or pointed to objects or actions that helped the infant obtain oblique information about a tool or a particular task (e.g. build a house). Parents in half of the videos gave their infants a knife or machete to play with during the 1 h video. All co-authors have observed parents place fabric slings on toddlers, sometimes placing a bottle or corncob in it to represent an infant. Young children are also frequently asked to deliver food to other houses and parents use eye contact and gestures to indicate where to take the food.

In Hewlett's [36] study of women's lives, she asked women to teach her how to 'be an Aka woman'. In order to show her how to make a basket, a woman sat next to her, touching her and never left her side. The woman started the basket, ripped it apart, then asked her to try it on her own. As Hewlett tried to weave, some people laughed and commented; after a short time, a 12-year-old girl came over, sat next to her in the same way and demonstrated again how to do it and then handed it back for her to try. Hewlett was not weaving correctly so the girl took her hand and helped her weave the twine. The mother and 12-year-old spent three weeks, hours at a time, sitting right next to Hewlett until she completed the small children's basket. Both the mother and young girl clearly had pedagogic skills, knew how to scaffold (i.e. build on the knowledge Hewlett was acquiring over time) and promoted learning in a novice.

As part of the same study, Hewlett asked Aka women what were the important lessons they learnt from their mother. Several women indicated that learning edible versus inedible food items was the most important thing they had been taught. Women described how when they were very young their mothers laid out several types of mushrooms or wild yams in front of them and explained how to identify edible versus inedible varieties.

Boyette is conducting the only systematic observational study of hunter–gatherer social learning. In a preliminary study, he observed 35 children aged 4–18 years and coded instances (every 30 s) of the focal child observing others, imitating others (child performs behaviour just observed), receiving instruction from others (child gives verbal or gestural signal intended to change focal child's behaviour) and giving instruction to others (child gives verbal or gestural signal intended to change the behaviour of another child). The last two codes were measures of teaching. Consistent with existing anthropological studies, he found that observation was common, taking place 72 min per day, but that children received instruction 14 min per day, gave instruction 5 min per day and imitated others 3 min per day. Somewhat surprisingly, imitation was rare, but this is due, in part, to how it was defined (child tries to replicate behaviour just observed). This definition did not distinguish emulation from imitation because focal techniques were not detailed enough to evaluate the unique qualities of each type of social learning. As expected, amount of time in observation, receiving instruction and imitation declined with age, whereas giving instruction increased with age. Giving instruction was particularly common during child-only productive activities and when children were in play, imitating productive activities. This study is important because it demonstrates that some forms of teaching (not limited to pedagogy as defined by Gergely and Csibra) exist on a daily basis and that horizontal transmission is prevalent at these ages as forager children are learning from other children in a variety of ways (observation, imitation and teaching).

Examples of teaching among other hunter–gatherer groups come primarily from research with the !Kung. Konner [54] described how !Kung taught their infants to sit and walk, while Draper [55] found that 4- to 14-year-old girls received 1.5 'adult interruptions' per hour (a measure of adults 'shaping a child's behaviour') and boys received about 2 per hour. Wiessner [56] described how parents removed beads from infants' necklaces and had them give the beads to appropriate kin relations so they could learn about sharing networks. Konner [51] also indicated that !Kung learn to share early: '!Kung value sharing very highly, and from the time their infants are six months of age mothers and other adults frequently say 'Na' meaning 'Give' when a bit of food is in the infant's hand and on the way to its mouth. The criterion is that they should inhibit the very strong impulse to eat and reliably turn the morsel over to the adult making the demand'.

An example of the early parent–infant social learning hypothesized by Gergely and Csibra comes from Guemple's [57] descriptions of teaching kinship categories to infants among the Inuit foragers. While on the mother's back, a young infant is asked to identify which individual in the room belongs to a kinship category, for instance, *nuak* or paternal aunt. Other individuals in the room look at the person with that kin term and when the infant looks at the correct relative the mother looks approvingly at him or her and others in the room cheer. At 12 months of age, infants are asked to point to particular kin and by 14–18 months a child can identify everyone in the camp by an appropriate kin term.

24.5 Summary and discussion

Existing studies of social learning in small-scale cultures come primarily from farming communities. This chapter uses quantitative and qualitative data on Congo Basin hunter–gatherer children and literature on a few other forager groups to examine what we know about social learning in hunter–gatherers. Data are limited, but we propose the following generalizations.

Social learning occurs early and is relatively rapid. Twelve-month-olds know core cultural values, kinship terms and have had experience with a broad range of subsistence activities. Children know most subsistence, childcare, sharing and essential skills and knowledge to make a living by age 10, if not earlier.

Vertical transmission is pronounced up to age 4–5. Foragers are frequently around parents in early childhood and this is whom forager adults and children say taught them a wide range of cultural knowledge and skills. Vertical transmission probably occurs after this age because parents continue to be around their children and forager camps are small, living density is high, physical and emotional proximity is valued and co-sleeping with parents continues until early adolescence.

Horizontal and oblique transmission are dominant modes of cultural transmission between the ages of 5 and 12. Children in middle and late childhood spend most of their day in multi-aged child groups playing or resting (idle, including visiting). Non-parental adults are also usually within sight and accessible to children. Adolescents spend considerable time in child-only groups, but they begin to spend more time with adults, especially when outside of the camp setting during subsistence activity. Children at this age spend most of their time observing and imitating other children and adults.

Pedagogy and other forms of teaching exist in hunter–gatherers. Systematic observational studies suggest that older children and other adults modify their behaviour to help younger children learn, but that this teaching is relatively rare by comparison to observation and imitation. Informal observations and limited video data indicate that pedagogy exists in infancy. Parents used eye contact, pointed and moved infant's arms to help them learn how to use tools, perform tasks such as house building, and learn foundational schema such as how to share. Foragers said parents and others explicitly taught them particular cultural knowledge and had no problem teaching field researchers how to do a variety of tasks. Data are limited and substantially more are needed to evaluate the types and developmental aspects of teaching and other processes of social learning in hunter–gatherers.

Learning to trust others is central to forager life and is transmitted early via a variety of modes and processes. It facilitates pedagogy and other forms of teaching, probably contributes to early and rapid learning, and is central to maintaining extensive sharing common to hunter–gatherer cultures.

Social learning is usually a self-motivated and guided discovery process. Parental interruptions and sanctions are relatively rare due to limited parental authority, especially by comparison to farmers. Respect for autonomy and an egalitarian ethos promote self-discovery and an intrinsic motivation to learn. Children often want to learn more than what others are willing to provide.

Play permeates hunter–gatherer child daily life, but its role in social learning is poorly understood. Lack of parental direction provides more time for play and horizontal transmission.

Our data have several theoretical implications. The data support Shennan and Steele's [18] hypothesis that hunter–gatherer social learning should be early, rapid, primarily vertical and take place via teaching. Hunter–gatherer infants are given small artefacts, parents sometimes use direct instruction to show infants and young children how to use the tools and parents hold or are within arm's reach of infants and young children most of the day. But the hypothesis underestimates the significance of horizontal and oblique transmission and the roles of observation and imitation. Our data indicate that 5- to 18-year-olds teach each other and children are likely to observe and imitate older children. The children who receive or provide instruction are usually siblings and/ or cousins so horizontal transmission may enhance their inclusive fitness, but unlike the parents, and a factor that may motivate older children to invest in younger children, is that the younger children will be their future sharing and subsistence partners.

Qualitative and quantitative data also support the Gergely and Csibra [32–34] hypothesis that pedagogy is a human universal. As they suggest, it occurs early in life and is primarily vertical, at least in infancy. Data indicate that various forms of teaching, broadly defined, occur daily, but that other processes of social learning, such as observation and imitation, are more prevalent. The Gergely and Csibra hypothesis also underestimates the importance of teaching by other children and adults. Other children and adults modify their behaviour to enhance the learning of children. Better methods (e.g. videotapes and field experiments) are needed to evaluate pedagogy with older children. Trust may enhance social learning, and this is an essential factor for understanding the effectiveness of hunter–gatherer social learning.

Social anthropologists and others may have overlooked pedagogy and other forms of teaching because of preconceived notions of formal teaching; it is often thought to be explicitly linguistic and involve easily observable self-conscious efforts of teachers. Pedagogy may not be verbal or very explicit. Researchers are unlikely to catch it with scan sampling techniques or participant observation. Pedagogy was captured with videotapes, and other forms of teaching (modifying behaviour to help others learn) were captured with focal follows.

Social anthropologists [25], developmental psychologists [6, 8] and several cultural evolution theorists [20, 21] emphasize the importance of horizontal transmission, and it occurs regularly among hunter–gatherers, especially after age 5, but it is more likely to be a characteristic feature in farming cultures. Farmer children are weaned relatively early, usually by 18 months, mothers and others stop holding children years before this happens among foragers, farmer infants are often placed in the care of older siblings, and as Table 24.1 indicates, they spend a majority of the day in child-only groups because both mothers and fathers leave the village to work and socialize. These data are consistent with existing studies of farmers. Horizontal transmission has specific features, and it may contribute to more rapid culture change and greater cross-cultural diversity than is observed among hunter–gatherers.

Social learning always takes place in a biology–culture interface. Social anthropologists tend to ignore biology, and evolutionary biologists tend to neglect the role of culture. Hopefully, this chapter provides implicit examples of biology–culture interactions. Pedagogy, reading the intentions of others, attachment, cooperative breeding and paying attention to successful individuals all influence social learning and appear to be part of human nature and biology. Cultural niche construction, such as the differences between forager and farmer modes of production, and cultural ideologies, such as the differences between forager and farmer foundational schema, also influence social learning and can amplify or diminish the expression of the biological propensities. Formal educational institutions clearly amplify the role of pedagogy, and Lewis [30] is probably correct that explicit teaching is less likely to occur in hunter–gatherers than in farmers because of their egalitarian ethos and respect for autonomy. In contrast, farmers expect men to tell women what to do and parents and older children will tell younger children what to do and how to do it. Better data are needed to test these hypothesized differences between foragers and farmers.

Finally, this chapter has several limitations. We focused on social learning in childhood and used data on tropical forest hunter–gatherers with extensive relationships with farmers.

Social learning continues into adulthood, and we have few data on foragers in other natural and social environments. The most pronounced limitation is the lack of systematic data on hunter–gatherer social learning. We assembled what we knew at this point in time and often relied upon indirect methods to evaluate social learning (e.g. who is around and interacting with the child), but there is so much we do not know—who do children watch, how often do children initiate learning, how are vertical and horizontal transmission similar and different, what are the roles of conformist and prestige bias and how early do pedagogy and other forms of teaching occur? We know very little about social learning in hunter–gatherer adolescence. Systematic research on hunter–gatherer social learning is urgently needed. This way of life will not be part of the human landscape for much longer.

References

1 Mead, M. 1930 *Growing up in New Guinea*. NY: New American Library.

2 Fortes, M. 1970 [1938] Social and psychological aspects of education in Taleland. In *From child to adult* (ed. J. Middleton), pp. 14–74. Garden City, NY: Natural History Press.

3 Greenfield, P. 2005 *Weaving generations together: evolving creativity in the Maya of Chiapas*. Santa Fe, NM: School of American Research.

4 Rogoff, B. 1990 *Apprenticeship in thinking: cognitive development in social contexts*. New York, NY: Oxford University Press.

5 Lancy, D. F. 1996 *Playing on the mother ground: cultural routines of children's development*. New York, NY: Guilford.

6 Harris, J. R. 1998 *The nurture assumption: why children turn out the way they do*. New York, NY: Free Press.

7 Whiten, A. 2011 The scope of culture in chimpanzees, humans and ancestral apes. *Phil. Trans. R. Soc. B* **366**, 997–1007.

8 Harris, J. R. 1995 Where is the child's environment: a group socialization theory of development. *Psychol. Rev.* **102**, 458–489.

9 Weisner, T. S. & Gallimore, R. 1977 My brother's keeper: child and sibling caretaking. *Curr. Anthropol.* **18**, 169–180.

10 Levine, R. A., Levine, S., Dixon, S., Richman, A., Leiderman, P. H., Keefer, C. H. & Brazelton, T. B. 1994 *Child care and culture: lessons from Africa*. Cambridge, UK: Cambridge University Press.

11 Spindler, G. 1973 Cultural transmission. In *Culture in process* (eds A. R. Beals, G. D. Spindler & L. Spindler), 2nd edn. New York, NY: Holt, Rinehart and Winston.

12 Cavalli Sforza, L. L. & Feldman, M. 1981 *Cultural transmission and evolution: a quantitative approach*. Princeton, NJ: Princeton University Press.

13 Cavalli Sforza, L. L., Feldman, M. W., Chen, K. H. & Dornbusch, S. M. 1982 Theory and observation in cultural transmission. *Science* **218**, 19–27.

14 Hewlett, B. S. & Cavalli Sforza, L. L. 1986 Cultural transmission among Aka pygmies. *Am. Anthropol.* **88**, 922–934.

15 Aunger, R. 2000 The life history of culture learning in a face-to-face society. *Ethos* **28**, 1–38.

16 Hattori, S. In press. 'My medicine (ma a le)': variability of medicinal plant knowledge among adult Baka hunter–gatherers of Southeast Cameroon. *Afr Study Monogr*.

17 Ohmagari, K. & Berkes, F. 1997 Transmission of indigenous knowledge and bush skills among the western James Bay Cree women of subarctic Canada. *Hum. Ecol.* **25**, 197–222.

18 Shennan, S. J. & Steele, J. 1999 Cultural learning in hominids: a behavioural ecological approach. In *Mammalian social learning: comparative and ecological perspectives* (eds H. O. Box & K. R. Gibson), pp. 367–388. Cambridge, UK: Cambridge University Press.

19 Tehrani, J. & Collard, M. 2009 An integrated analysis of inter-individual and inter-group cultural transmission in Iranian tribal populations. *Evol. Hum. Behav.* **30**, 286–300.

20 Boyd, R. & Richerson, P. J. 1985 *Culture and the evolutionary process*. Chicago, IL: University of Chicago Press.

21 Richerson, P. J. & Boyd, R. 2005 *Not by genes alone: how culture transformed human evolution*. Chicago, IL: University of Chicago Press.

22 Henrich, J. & McElreath, R. 2003 The evolution of cultural evolution. *Evol. Anthropol.* **12**, 123–135.

23 McElreath, R. & Strimling, P. 2008 When natural selection favors learning from parents. *Curr. Anthropol.* **49**, 307–316.

24 MacDonald, K. 2007 Cross-cultural comparison of learning in human hunting. *Hum. Nat.* **18**, 386–402.

25 Lancy, D. F. & Grove, M. A. 2010 The role of adults in children's learning. In *The anthropology of learning in childhood* (eds D. F. Lancy, J. Bock & S. Gaskins), pp. 145–180. Lanham, MD: AltaMira Press.

26 Gaskins, S. & Paradise, R. 2010 Learning through observation in daily life. In *The anthropology of learning in childhood* (eds D. F. Lancy, J. Bock & S. Gaskins), pp. 85–118. Lanham, MD: AltaMira Press.

27 Paradise, R. & Rogoff, B. 2009 Side by side: learning by observing and pitching in. *Ethos* **37**, 102–138.

28 Mead, M. 1964 *Continuities and discontinuities in cultural evolution*. New Haven, CT: Yale University Press.

29 Spindler, G. 1974 The transmission of culture. In *Education and cultural process* (ed. G. D. Spindler), 237–310. New York, NY: Holt, Rinehart and Winston.

30 Lewis, J. 2007 Ekila: blood, bodies, and egalitarian societies. *J. R. Anthropol. Inst. (N.S.)* **14**, 297–335.

31 Kruger, A. C. & Tomasello, M. 1996 Cultural learning and learning culture. In *Handbook of education and human development: new models of learning, teaching, and schooling* (eds D. Olson & N. Torrance), pp. 369–387. Oxford, UK: Blackwell.

32 Gergely, G. & Csibra, G. 2006 Sylvia's recipe: the role of imitation and pedagogy in the transmission of human culture. In *Roots of human sociality: culture, cognition, and human interaction* (eds N. J. Enfield & S. C. Levinson), pp. 229–255. Oxford, UK: Berg.

33 Csibra, G. & Gergely, G. 2006 Social learning and social cognition: the case for pedagogy. In *Processes of change in brain and cognitive development. Attention and performance* (eds Y. Munakata & M. H. Johnson), pp. 249–274. Oxford, UK: Oxford University Press.

34 Csibra, C. & Gergely, G. 2011 Natural pedagogy as evolutionary adaptation. *Phil. Trans. R. Soc. B* **366**, 1149–1157.

35 Caro, R. M. & Hauser, M. D. 1992 Is there teaching in nonhuman animals? *Quart. Rev. Biol.* **67**, 151–174.

36 Hewlett, B. L. In press. *Women of the forest and village: ethnographic narratives from the Congo Basin*. Oxford, UK: Oxford University Press.

37 Bourdieu, P. 1977 *Outline of a theory of practice*. Cambridge, UK: Cambridge University Press.

38 Hewlett, B. S. 1991 *Intimate fathers: the nature and contexts of Aka Pygmy father–infant relations*. Ann Arbor, MI: University of Michigan Press.

39 Hewlett, B. S., Lamb, M. E., Leyendecker, B. & Scholmerich, A. 2000 Internal working models, trust, and sharing among foragers. *Curr. Anthropol.* **41**, 287–297.

40 Fouts, H. N., Hewlett, B. S. & Lamb, M. E. 2005 Parent–offspring weaning conflicts among Bofi farmers and foragers of Central Africa. *Curr. Anthropol.* **46**, 29–50.

41 Fouts, H. N. & Lamb, M. E. 2009 Cultural and developmental in toddlers' interactions with other children in two small-scale societies in Central Africa. *J. Eur. Dev. Sci.* **3**, 259–277.

42 Hewlett, B. L. 2005 Vulnerable lives: death, loss and grief among Aka and Ngandu adolescents of the Central African Republic. In *Hunter–gatherer childhoods: evolutionary, developmental and cultural perspectives* (eds B. S. Hewlett & M. E. Lamb), pp. 322–342. New Brunswick, NJ: Aldine Transaction.

43 Fouts, H. N., Hewlett, B. S. & Lamb, M. E. 2001 Weaning and the nature of early childhood interactions among Bofi foragers in Central Africa. *Hum. Nat.* **12**, 27–46.

44 Hewlett, B. S., Lamb, M. E., Shannon, D., Leyendecker, B. & Scholmerich, A. 1998 Culture and early infancy among Central African foragers and farmers. *Dev. Psychol.* **34**, 653–661.

45 Fouts, H.N. & Brookshire, R. 2009 Who feeds children? A child's-eye-view of caregiver feeding patterns among the Aka foragers in Congo. *Soc. Sci. Med.* **69**, 285–292.

46 Konner, M. 2005 Hunter–gatherer infancy and childhood: the !Kung and others. In *Hunter–gatherer childhoods: evolutionary, developmental and cultural perspectives* (eds B. S. Hewlett & M. E. Lamb), pp. 19–64. New Brunswick, NJ: Aldine Transaction.

47 Neuwelt-Truntzer, S. 1981 Ecological influences on the physical, behavioral and cognitive development of Pygmy children. Ph.D. dissertation, University of Chicago, Chicago, IL.

48 Gosso, Y., Otta, E., Morais, M., Riberiro, F. J. L. & Bussab, V. S. R. 2005 Play in hunter–gatherer societies. In *The nature of play: great apes and humans* (eds A. D. Pellegrini & P. K. Smith), pp. 213–253. New York, NY: Guilford.

49 Barry, H., Child, I. L. & Bacon, M. 1959 Relation of child training to subsistence economy. *Am. Anthropol.* **61**, 51–63.

50 Kamei, N. 2005 Play among Baka children in Cameroon. In *Hunter–gatherer childhoods: evolutionary, developmental and cultural perspectives* (eds B. S. Hewlett & M. E. Lamb), pp. 343–362. New Brunswick, NJ: Aldine Transaction.

51 Konner, M. 2010 *The evolution of childhood: relationships, emotion, mind.* Cambridge, MA: Harvard University Press.

52 Aunger, R. 1994 Are food avoidances maladaptive in the Ituri Forest of Zaire? *J. Anthropol. Res.* **50**, 277–310.

53 Hewlett, B. L. 2001 Adolescent culture: an exploration of the socio-emotional development of the Aka adolescents of the Central African Republic. *Orient. Anthropol. (India)* **1**, 84–96.

54 Konner, M. 1976 Maternal care, infant behavior and development among the !Kung. In *Kalahari hunter–gatherers: studies of the !Kung San and their neighbors* (eds R. B. Lee & I. DeVore), pp. 218–245. Cambridge, MA: Harvard University Press.

55 Draper, P. 1976 Social and economic constraints on child life among the !Kung. In *Kalahari hunter–gatherers: studies of the !Kung San and their neighbors* (eds R. B. Lee & I. DeVore), pp. 199–217. Cambridge, MA: Harvard University Press.

56 Wiessner, P. 1982 Risk, reciprocity, and social influences on !Kung San economics. In *Politics and history in band societies* (eds E. Leacock & R. Lee), pp. 61–84. Cambridge, UK: Cambridge University Press.

57 Guemple, L. 1988 Teaching social relations to Inuit children. In *Hunters and gatherers 2: property, power, and ideology* (eds T. Ingold, D. Riches & J. Woodburn), pp. 131–149. Oxford, UK: Berg.

Chapter 25

Young Children's Selective Trust in Informants

Paul L. Harris and Kathleen H. Corriveau

Young children readily act on information from adults, setting aside their own prior convictions and even continuing to trust informants who make claims that are manifestly false. Such credulity is consistent with a long-standing philosophical and scientific conception of young children as prone to indiscriminate trust. Against this conception, we argue that children trust some informants more than others. In particular, they use two major heuristics. First, they keep track of the history of potential informants. Faced with conflicting claims, they endorse claims made by someone who has provided reliable care or reliable information in the past. Second, they monitor the cultural standing of potential informants. Faced with conflicting claims, children endorse claims made by someone who belongs to a consensus and whose behaviour abides by, rather than deviates from, the norms of their group. The first heuristic is likely to promote receptivity to information offered by familiar caregivers, whereas the second heuristic is likely to promote a broader receptivity to informants from the same culture.

Keywords: credulity; trust; epistemic reliability; consensus

25.1 **Introduction**

Young children are trusting disciples. They are ready to learn from adult caregivers [1, 2]. When presented with a demonstration or claim that conflicts with their own knowledge, they are willing to set aside that knowledge. For example, in solving practical problems, they are prone to reject their own accurate and efficient causal understanding so as to more closely imitate the actions of a model [3–5]. Similarly, in classifying objects and in drawing inferences about the objects' properties, they are prepared to abandon their own initial classification if they hear a different classification proposed by an adult [6]. When informed (via pointing or words) about simple matters of fact—for example, the location of an object—they act on that information even in the face of repeated evidence of its falsity [7, 8]. Young children also endorse and extrapolate from demonstrations and claims that they have no way to check for themselves. Introduced to a new practice, for example, they treat it as a generalized prescriptive norm, not just as a local behavioural regularity [9]. Told about un-observable processes and entities in domains such as religion and science, they incorporate them into their explanations and predictions [10].

Taken together, these empirical findings imply that human children are receptive pupils who trust adult models or informants. They rarely express doubt even when the information supplied runs counter to their own understanding or judgement. This emphasis on early credulity has a distinguished history in philosophy. Reid [11], a leading member of the Scottish Enlightenment, argued that an original principle implanted in us: 'is a disposition to confide in the veracity of others and to believe what they tell us ... It is unlimited in children'. Twentieth-century philosophers were in agreement with this argument. Russell [12] wrote: 'Doubt, suspense of judgement and disbelief all seem later and more complex than a wholly unreflecting assent'. Similarly, Wittgenstein [13] claimed that: 'A child learns there are reliable and unreliable informants much later than it learns the facts which are told it'. The same emphasis on early credulity and the absence of doubt can be found among contemporary psychologists and biologists. Gilbert [14], for example, proposed that: 'Children are especially credulous, especially gullible, especially prone toward acceptance and belief', and Dawkins [15] called attention to the alleged biological advantages of such credulity: 'Theoretically, children might learn from personal experience not to go too near a cliff edge, not to eat untried berries, not to swim in crocodile-infested waters. But, to say the least, there will be a selective advantage to child brains that possess the rule of thumb: believe, without question, whatever your grown-ups tell you'.

We argue, nevertheless, that any implication of early, indiscriminate credulity is implausible, both biologically and psychologically. The body of findings just reviewed concerns information that is provided to a child by a single informant. In such cases, children may indeed set aside what they know to be the case or take on trust claims that they cannot verify. However, evolutionary approaches to cultural transmission [16, 17] have led to the plausible conclusion that a variety of selection principles are likely to bias children to learn from particular models or informants. In this chapter, we present a large set of recent experimental findings showing that children do, in fact, select whom to approach for information and whom to believe. One set of findings shows that young children trust informants to varying degrees depending on their history of interaction with those informants. A second set of findings shows that they assess unfamiliar informants for their cultural typicality, preferring those who conform to local norms. In short, we argue that even if children are surprisingly indiscriminate in choosing *what* to believe, they are nonetheless quite selective in choosing *whom* to believe.

25.2 **Attachment**

The history of research on attachment has long suggested that any assumption of indiscriminate trust in early childhood is likely to be misplaced. Human infants are equipped with a non-verbal repertoire (eye contact, crying and facial expressions) that they use to engage potential caregivers. Following an initial period when they indiscriminately 'court' all potential caregivers, infants become increasingly selective in whom they trust to supply reassurance and a secure base [18–20]. Such selectivity is more or less universal among children who grow up under normal rearing conditions. Only after prolonged and severe neglect—of the kind observed in Romanian orphanages during the Ceausescu regime—do children display persistent signs of indiscriminate trust (so-called disinhibited attachment) towards unfamiliar as well as familiar adults [21].

Granted this near-universal selectivity in the socio-emotional sphere, young children are likely to display the same type of selectivity in choosing which informant to trust. More specifically, a straightforward prediction from attachment theory is that young children will be more receptive to information offered by a familiar caregiver than to that offered by a stranger. With the help of two preschool caregivers, one working in preschool A, the other in preschool B, we obtained support for this prediction [22].

Children from each preschool watched a film in which the two caregivers proposed conflicting names or functions for novel objects. Children could indicate which caregiver they wanted to ask about the novel objects. In addition, once the two caregivers had proposed conflicting names or functions, children were invited to endorse one or the other. The experimenter said, for example: 'C. in the pink shirt said it's a snegg and S. in the black shirt said it's a hoon. What do you think it's called—a snegg or a hoon?' Children attending preschool A placed more trust—as indexed by their choice of whom to ask and endorse—in the information provided by caregiver A than in that provided by unfamiliar caregiver B, whereas children attending preschool B placed more trust in familiar caregiver B than in unfamiliar caregiver A. Figure 25.1 confirms children's preference for the familiar caregiver at 3, 4 and 5 years (the data have been averaged across each preschool).

Attachment theory implies that familiarity is not in itself sufficient to evoke trust. A history of responsive caregiving is needed. By implication, children might not invariably prefer information from a familiar informant. Their receptivity should be undermined if the familiar person is consistently unavailable or unresponsive. We tested this prediction in a longitudinal study [23]. Based on the standard strange situation procedure, children were identified at 15 months as having a secure, avoidant or ambivalent relationship with their mother. We returned approximately 4 years later when children had just turned 5 years of age to assess their trust in their mother as an informant. Children were shown pictures of animal hybrids. Figure 25.2 illustrates an example. The mothers categorized these hybrids in one way—for example, as a horse—whereas an unfamiliar adult whom the child had

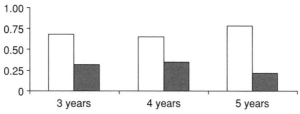

Figure 25.1 Proportion of choices directed at familiar (white bar) and unfamiliar (grey bar) caregiver by 3-, 4-and 5-year-olds (averaged across preschools A and B). Modified from Corriveau, K. H. & Harris, P. L. 2009 Choosing your informant: weighing familiarity and recent accuracy. *Dev. Sci.* **12**, 426–437.

Figure 25.2 Example of an animal hybrid—a cow-horse. Reprinted from *Child Development* **80**, Kathleen H. Corriveau, *et al.* Young children's trust in their mother's claims: Longitudinal links with attachment security in infancy, pp. 750–761, copyright (2009) with permission from John Wiley and Sons.

just met categorized them differently—for example, as a cow. Children were invited to say which person they wanted to ask for information about the hybrids—and when they offered conflicting information, which person they agreed with.

Figure 25.3 shows how often children with each type of attachment trusted the information supplied by their mother as compared to that supplied by the stranger. If children invariably preferred information from a familiar caregiver, such as their mother, we should observe that preference in all three attachment groups. However, if children are guided by their prior attachment, we would expect any preference for the mother's claims to be evident in secure and ambivalent children but to be attenuated or even absent among avoidant children. That is, in fact, the pattern that emerged. Children with an avoidant attachment to their mother treated her no differently from a stranger, whereas the other two groups trusted the claims made by their mother over those made by the stranger.

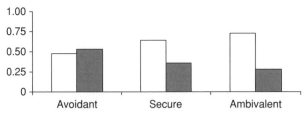

Figure 25.3 Proportion of choices directed at the mother (white bar) versus a stranger (grey bar) by attachment classification. Reprinted from *Child Development* **80**, Kathleen H. Corriveau, *et al.* Young children's trust in their mother's claims: Longitudinal links with attachment security in infancy, pp. 750–761, copyright (2009) with permission from John Wiley and Sons.

A plausible way to conceptualize the findings presented so far is to propose a theoretical marriage. Children are trusting disciples—in line with the findings on cultural learning reviewed earlier. However, their trust is selective in just the way that attachment theory would predict. More specifically, children are especially receptive to information provided by a familiar caregiver rather than to that provided by a stranger, so long as they do not have an avoidant relationship with that caregiver. Based on this analysis, young children select among potential informants on socio-emotional grounds. A person who has provided responsive and reassuring caregiving is regarded as trustworthy in the epistemic as well as the emotional domain.

25.3 Monitoring for accuracy

However, recent findings show that such an arranged marriage between attachment theory and cultural learning will not work. In the first place, there is evidence that children monitor potential informants for their epistemic history and not just for their caregiving history. Even more problematically, children increasingly weigh an informant's epistemic history more heavily than his or her caregiving history when selecting whose information to trust. We document these two claims below, starting with evidence for children's attention to an informant's epistemic history.

In an initial study, 3- and 4-year-old children were introduced to two unfamiliar adults [24]. In an induction phase, children were given an opportunity to assess the comparative reliability of these two potential informants by watching them name a series of four familiar objects. One informant named all the four objects in the series correctly. Presented with a ball, for example, she said: 'That's a ball'. The other informant, by contrast, named all the four objects incorrectly. Presented with a ball, for example, she said: 'That's a cup'. Because children knew the names of these objects, they were in a position to conclude that one informant was an accurate source of information, whereas the other was not. In a subsequent test phase, we checked whether children had, in fact, drawn this conclusion and also whether they used it to guide their subsequent trust in the claims made by the two informants. We found that children in both age groups appropriately judged one informant to be more accurate than the other. Moreover, their willingness to make that judgement predicted their trust. When unfamiliar objects were presented— whose names were not known to the children—they preferred to ask for information from the accurate as opposed to the inaccurate informant. Moreover, when the two informants supplied conflicting names for any given unfamiliar object, children were likely to endorse the name supplied by the hitherto accurate informant.

Subsequent research has clarified and consolidated several aspects of this basic result [25]. First, on the basis of the initial findings, children's sensitivity to informant accuracy might operate in only a circumscribed domain, namely the domain of object names. However, when tested in a similar procedure, namely an induction phase with two informants followed by a test phase, children also selected between accurate and inaccurate informants when the test domain concerned factual information about objects rather than objects' names [26]. Second, children's selective trust might not reflect a spontaneous tendency to engage in accuracy monitoring but a response to leading questions on the part of the experimenter about the accuracy of the two informants. Based on this argument, selective trust should evaporate if children are not prompted by questions about the relative accuracy of the informants. However, in two follow-up studies, conducted in different laboratories, removal or postponement of such questions did not undermine the basic pattern. Children continued to trust the accurate informant rather than the inaccurate informant [27, 28]. Third, the induction phase involved a somewhat unnatural contrast in informant accuracy. One informant named objects correctly and the other named them incorrectly in each of the four trials. In subsequent research, this contrast between the informants has been attenuated. For example, children watched one informant who was predominantly correct (75% of the trials) and another who was predominantly incorrect (75% of the trials) during induction. Even though both informants had been sometimes right and sometimes wrong, children still went on to invest greater trust in the more accurate of the two [29]. Indeed, 4-year-olds monitor apparent differences in accuracy even when no obvious errors are involved. Having watched one informant name objects accurately and another informant make either non-committal remarks about them (e.g. 'Let me look at that') or express ignorance, children subsequently invested more trust in the accurate as opposed to the non-committal [30] or ignorant informant [31]. Fourth, accuracy monitoring can reverse a pre-existing pattern of trust. Although preschoolers typically trust an adult informant over a peer, this preference is reversed if the peer proves more accurate [32]. Finally, selective trust in particular informants is not transient. When a second test phase was administered, either 3–4 days or indeed an entire week after the induction and initial test phases, 3- and 4-year-olds still invested more trust in the previously accurate informant [28].

Summing up, these studies offer persuasive evidence that young children monitor informants for their epistemic reliability. More precisely, children rapidly and spontaneously assess the comparative accuracy of two unfamiliar informants and use that assessment over a protracted period to guide their judgments about which informant to ask for information and whose claims to endorse. We may now turn to the second obstacle to any straightforward marriage between attachment theory and theories of early cultural learning. Do children weigh an informant's accuracy more heavily than his or her history of caregiving?

25.4 **Weighing accuracy against familiarity**

In all the experiments just reviewed, the two adults who differed in their apparent accuracy were initially unfamiliar to the children. They formed an impression of the comparative reliability of the adults during the induction phase that lasted only a few minutes. Arguably, in the absence of an established caregiving relationship, children use this brief exposure to the epistemic reliability of the two informants as a proxy for longer term indices of their trustworthiness. More specifically, it could be argued that children ordinarily accumulate sustained evidence for the trustworthiness of a familiar informant in the context of the child–caregiver relationship. Faced with two unfamiliar informants, their monitoring of accuracy might be a back-up strategy, one used only in the absence of a prior relationship. Based on this hypothesis, children's sensitivity to informant's accuracy would be a supplement to, or substitute for, the trust that is ordinarily grounded in a long-standing attachment. In that case, we would not expect recent evidence of inaccuracy to undermine the cumulative trust that is established on the basis of a long history of caregiving.

However, an alternative hypothesis is that children's sensitivity to accuracy is distinct from their sensitivity to the pattern of caregiving they have received. Their monitoring of epistemic reliability is not just a substitute for the safeguards ordinarily provided by a prior history of caregiving. Instead, accuracy monitoring is a distinct mode of appraisal, one that is critically important for a species that relies so heavily on cultural learning, especially learning that is transmitted obliquely to the child by less familiar informants rather than vertically by long-standing caregivers. If this view is correct, we would expect that even when an informant is a familiar caregiver, children will continue to check on his or her accuracy. In fact, faced with a choice of whom to trust, they might prefer to learn from an evidently accurate but hitherto unfamiliar informant than from someone who has cared for them over a long period but has proven inaccurate in the recent past.

To assess these competing possibilities, we extended the testing session that was conducted in preschools A and B as described earlier [22]. Recall that 3-, 4-, and 5-year-olds first watched as two preschool caregivers proposed conflicting names and functions for unfamiliar objects. During this pre-test, all the three age groups displayed a preference for the caregiver with whom they were familiar. In the subsequent induction phase, half the children in each age group saw their familiar caregiver name familiar objects accurately, whereas the unfamiliar caregiver named them inaccurately. The remaining children saw the reverse arrangement: the familiar caregiver named familiar objects inaccurately, whereas the unfamiliar caregiver named them accurately. In the succeeding post-test, the two caregivers again supplied conflicting information about novel objects just as they had in the pre-test. The key experimental question was how far children would continue to display trust in the familiar caregiver rather than in the unfamiliar caregiver—as they had done in the pre-test phase (Figure 25.1). Figure 25.4 shows the proportion of post-test

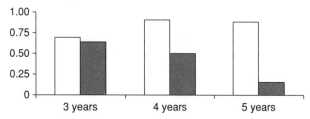

Figure 25.4 Proportion of choices directed at the familiar caregiver in the post-test depending on whether children had observed her being accurate (white bar) or inaccurate (grey bar) in naming well-known objects during the preceding induction phase. Modified from Corriveau, K. H. & Harris, P. L. 2009 Choosing your informant: weighing familiarity and recent accuracy. *Dev. Sci.* **12**, 426–437.

trials in which children in each age group displayed trust in the familiar caregiver following the induction phase.

Inspection of Figure 25.4 shows that 3-year-olds were unaffected by the induction phase: whether they had witnessed the familiar caregiver being accurate or inaccurate in the induction phase, they continued to favour the information that she provided in the test phase. Thus, their familiarity with one of the two caregivers trumped any evidence of inaccuracy that children may have registered during the induction phase. By contrast, the two older groups were affected by the induction phase. If the more familiar caregiver had proven to be accurate, they displayed a marked preference for the information that she supplied. By contrast, if she had proven to be inaccurate, they abandoned the preference for her that they had shown in the initial test. Indeed, 5-year-olds now switched their preference to the less familiar caregiver, granted that she had proven to be the more accurate during the induction phase.

Why did the induction phase not lead to a shift in the pattern of selective trust among 3-year-olds? It is worth noting that two initially plausible explanations are inadequate. Arguably, 3-year-olds are unable to notice and remember an informant's errors. Hence, any selection that they make among informants can only be based on familiarity rather than on accuracy. However, the solid body of evidence described earlier shows that this explanation cannot be correct. When faced with two unfamiliar informants, 3-year-olds do keep track of their relative accuracy and distribute their trust accordingly [24, 28, 30]. Apparently, it is only when they are confronted with a familiar informant who makes mistakes that they 'forgive' those errors and continue to invest more trust in her.

A second possible explanation is that granted their history of interaction with a familiar caregiver, 3-year-olds set aside or overlook any recent evidence of inaccuracy because it counts for little when set alongside a cumulative history of reliable information from the same caregiver. However, there is also a clear objection to the second explanation. If anything, 4- and 5-year-olds are likely to have had a longer or more intense interaction with their preschool caregiver than 3-year-olds. Therefore, if children were weighing recent inaccuracy against a cumulative prior history of accuracy, we would expect the exact opposite of the pattern of results illustrated in Figure 25.4. We would expect 3-year olds to be more troubled by recent inaccuracy than 4- and 5-year-olds, given that 4- and 5-year-olds are likely to have accumulated a longer history of accuracy on the part of a familiar caregiver.

Granted these two points, the most plausible explanation is that there is a major shift in the weight that children attach to two indices of trustworthiness: a prior history of caregiving and epistemic reliability. Three-year olds are sensitive to both but they favour prior caregiving even in the face of evidence for epistemic unreliability. By contrast, 4-year-olds and particularly 5-year-olds favour epistemic reliability even when this means rejecting information from a familiar caregiver.

A key implication of these results is that although attachment theory can help to explain selective trust, it cannot explain the overall developmental pattern. Children attend to an informant's epistemic record, and in the case of older children, this focus is pre-emptive.

When the epistemic record proves unsatisfactory, they mistrust the information supplied, even if the person is familiar to them. More broadly, these results imply that in the course of early development, children's selective trust is increasingly guided by epistemic factors rather than by socio-emotional factors. In acquiring new information, they trust accurate informants rather than familiar caregivers.

In terms of the broader pattern of cultural learning, these experimental findings confirm the expectation that there is likely to be an initial disposition towards vertical trust—a preference for seeking and accepting information from those familiar adults and older children who provide care. However, in the course of development, trust in what others demonstrate and claim is likely to be increasingly oblique or horizontal—extended to those outside the circle of caregiving, especially when they have a demonstrable record of accuracy in a given domain.

25.5 **Group membership**

In learning from other people, it is plausible that children seek true information rather than false information. The fact that they monitor informants for the accuracy of their claims is likely to increase the probability that they learn from truthful informants. However, certain cultural practices are not true or false in any straightforward, factual sense. Nevertheless, they are likely to be favoured by members of a given culture. How do children maximize the likelihood that what they learn is representative of the cultural group to which they belong? One strategy that young children might adopt is to trust informants who are culturally prototypical—who act or talk in ways that reflect the surrounding culture. If this hypothesis is correct, we can expect children to favour learning from cultural conformists rather than from cultural misfits. Several recent findings indicate that children display exactly this strategy. For example, they endorse claims made by informants who respect rather than deviate from the morphological rules of their language. They endorse demonstrations of tool use by models who speak with a native as opposed to a foreign accent. They endorse claims made by informants who elicit bystander approval rather than disapproval. Finally, they endorse claims made by members of a consensus rather than those made by lone dissenters. We briefly describe these findings and then consider their implications.

In many of the experiments described so far, the two informants differed in terms of accuracy. One correctly identified a series of objects, whereas the other misidentified the same objects. We have found that such errors of fact are not needed to trigger selective trust. Four-year olds listened to two informants who varied in terms of their morphological production [33]. In the induction phase, one speaker produced minor morphological errors (e.g. she said 'a shoes' or 'some shoe'), whereas the other speaker produced these morphological forms correctly (e.g. she said 'a shoe' or 'some shoes'). In the subsequent test phase, these two speakers made conflicting claims about the names of unfamiliar objects as well as the past tense forms of unfamiliar verbs. Children preferred to seek and endorse information from the good morphologist in both the semantic domain (i.e. learning new names) and the morphological domain (i.e. learning new past tense forms).

Children are also sensitive to other markers that an informant belongs to the same linguistic community as themselves. Having briefly listened to two speakers similar in age, appearance and gender but differing in accent, infants and young children prefer to interact with the person who has a native rather than a foreign accent [34]. We tested if children also use accent in deciding which speaker to trust for new information [35]. One group of 3-, 4- and 5-year-olds watched and listened as two speakers narrated a short passage from the story of 'Curious George'. One spoke English with a native (North-American) accent. The other spoke English with a foreign (Spanish) accent. A second group of children of the same age watched and listened as the two speakers narrated a short passage from 'Jabberwocky'—the nonsense poem by Lewis Carroll. Although syntactically well-formed, the sentences in this passage were not meaningful so that any differences in trust following this induction could not be attributed to differential comprehension of the two speakers. Following both types of induction, children were given an opportunity to seek and endorse information about the use of four unfamiliar artefacts from the two speakers. They offered conflicting demonstrations of how to use any given artefact. For example, one speaker looked through a plastic sprinkler attachment as if it were a telescope, whereas the other speaker held it to her mouth and blew in it.

Children preferred to seek and endorse information from the native-accented speaker. This preference was equally strong in all three age groups and equally strong following the meaningful, 'Curious George' induction and the meaningless, 'Jaberwocky' induction. Note that the induction phase and the test phase of this experiment differed in both modality and domain. The induction phase involved audible differences in accent. The test phase involved visible differences in tool use. Nevertheless, children used the audible cues of group membership to guide their learning about tool use.

In both of the studies just described—the study of morphology and accent—children could appraise the two speakers in terms of their conformity to practices that they—the children themselves—subscribed to and knew about. Because the children were native speakers of English, they were sensitive to departures from standard practice. Yet, there are often occasions when children encounter informants who profess beliefs or engage in practices that are quite unfamiliar to them—practices that children cannot gauge for cultural representativeness. In these circumstances, how can young children optimize the likelihood that a potential informant is providing information that is culturally typical rather than marginal or deviant? One strategy that children might adopt is to behave like sociologists— to look for signs of consensus or dissent among a group of potential informants.

In more concrete terms, suppose that children encounter two informants who make conflicting claims that are novel and therefore impossible for children to adjudicate themselves. However, the claims made by one informant elicit approval from bystanders, whereas the claims made by the other elicit disapproval. Do children use such bystanders' reactions to moderate their trust in the novel claims made by each informant? To examine this possibility, we had 4-year-olds watch as two speakers produced conflicting names for a series of unfamiliar objects [36]. For example, faced with the sprinkler attachment, one speaker might call it a 'feppin' and the other might call it a 'merval'. The two bystanders reacted differently to the two speakers. Having listened to one, they nodded and smiled. Having listened to the other, they shook their head and frowned. Subsequently, children were asked for their judgement. They were reminded that one speaker had called it a feppin and the other had called it a merval—what did they think? Children overwhelmingly endorsed the speaker who had attracted bystanders' approval rather than disapproval.

In the next stage of the experiment, we tested if children would continue to regard the speaker who had received bystanders' approval as more trustworthy even in the absence of any feedback from the bystanders. To assess this possibility, the two bystanders left the room, and testing continued as before with the two informants making conflicting claims about unfamiliar objects. Children continued to display selective trust in the two speakers—they were more likely to endorse the names supplied by the speaker who had received bystanders' approval even though, at this point in the experiment, the bystanders were no longer present and could supply no cues. By implication, the cultural typicality of the two speakers—the extent to which their claims had met with approval versus disapproval—led children to regard one of them as a more trustworthy informant.

However, an alternative interpretation of these results is that children did not conclude that the two informants differed in terms of cultural typicality but in terms of likeability. After all, in expressing their approval, the bystanders had smiled at one informant, and in expressing their disapproval, they had frowned at the other. Arguably, children preferred to endorse the speaker whom they inferred to be more likeable, as indexed by the bystanders' reactions.

In a follow-up study, we again had two informants as well as an additional pair of adults who sided with one informant and not with the other ([37]; study 1). However, we altered the way in which this endorsement was expressed. Several unfamiliar objects were set out on a table and the experimenter asked the adults to say which of them was, for example, 'a slod'. Three of the adults pointed to the same object, whereas the fourth—the lone dissenter—pointed to a different object. This pattern was repeated for four trials with the same person always in the role of a lone dissenter. After watching the adults' responses, children were invited to express their view. As in the previous study, children strongly favoured the majority view, effectively endorsed by three of the adults, as opposed to the minority view endorsed by only a single adult.

The next stage of the experiment resembled what had happened in the previously described bystanders' study. Two of the three adults who had formed a consensus left, leaving only one member of the consensus behind, together with the so-called lone dissenter. These two adults now supplied conflicting names for unfamiliar objects, and children were invited to seek and endorse information from either of them. As expected, children displayed greater trust in the informant who had been part of the consensus as opposed to the lone dissenter. Note that in this study, no signs of liking or disliking had been expressed towards either informant. In the initial induction phase, the four adults had simply pointed wordlessly and with a neutral facial expression. Therefore, if the member of the consensus elicited more trust in the second stage of the study, it was because children had noted that her behaviour was more typical.

Two additional studies have lent further support to the hypothesis that children are actively looking for cultural conformists—people who represent the norms of their group. First, we repeated the study just described but with three adults, two who formed a consensus and one who was the lone dissenter ([37]; study 2). As before, in the induction phase, children were more likely to endorse information provided by the informants who were in agreement. In addition, when one of the two left, children were more likely to trust the remaining member of the pair than the lone dissenter. By implication, children's sensitivity to a consensus is acute. Two persons in agreement override a single other.

Finally, we tested whether the composition of the consensus was important to children. We found that in both Boston and Taipei, it did make a difference [38, 39]. When children were faced with a consensus composed of women from their own race (i.e. women with a European-American appearance in Boston and an East Asian appearance in Taipei), we replicated previous findings. In the induction phase, children trusted the consensus over the lone dissenter. Subsequently, in the test phase, they trusted a single member of the consensus over the lone dissenter. However, when we altered the cultural identity of the consensus—substituting three East Asian women in Boston and three European-American women in Taipei, the preference for the consensus over the lone dissenter was attenuated in the induction phase, and there was no preference for the consensus member over the lone dissenter in the test phase. By implication, when children meet informants who come from a different group, they are less attentive to any consensus that they form. This makes sense if children look to members of a consensus for guidance about the norms that prevail in their own group.

25.6 **Conclusions**

We started this chapter with a brief review of evidence showing that young children are credulous. They are guided by other people's claims and demonstrations even when they run counter to what children would say and do if left to their own devices. In some cases, children's acceptance of guidance from others can even lead them to adopt a less efficient rather than a more efficient strategy. Granted children's hyper-receptivity, it is tempting to endorse the long-standing assumption, voiced in both philosophical and biological analyses, that children are indiscriminate in their cultural learning.

The evidence in this chapter shows that such a conclusion would be mistaken. No matter how non-selective children are in *what* they learn from others, they are selective in *whom* they learn from. We have identified two broad classes of heuristics—one class helps children to select among informants with whom they have had previous interactions, and the second class helps children to differentiate among relatively unfamiliar informants whom they have just met.

Within the first class, children display two biases. First, they display a preference for the information supplied by a familiar caregiver versus a stranger (provided that they have not developed an avoidant relationship with that caregiver). Second, children prefer information supplied by someone who has proven to be a reliable source of information in the past. Taken together, these two biases are likely to converge on a proclivity for vertical cultural learning—a bias to endorse and imitate the claims and demonstrations of adults who have a record of providing reliable care, accurate information, or both.

Consider, for example, the ethnographic data reported by Hewlett *et al.* [40]. In early childhood, hunter–gatherer children are within the reach of their mother or father for 40–50% of each day, and it is their parents who provide them with miniaturized cultural artefacts (baskets, axes, digging sticks and spears). Insofar as children prefer to learn from people who have provided reliable care and accurate information, we may expect them to trust information provided by their parents. Consistent with this expectation, Baka hunter–gatherers reported that almost all of their knowledge about the use of plants came from their parents, not from other people [41].

Note, however, that the bias towards attachment figures and the bias towards those who have proven accurate will not always converge on the same informant. Children may notice that in some epistemic domains, an attachment figure is less accurate than someone with whom they have no history of attachment. Our findings suggest that in such cases, children will increasingly opt for the more accurate informant. Indeed, observation of cultural transmission networks in small-scale societies by Henrich & Broesch [42] lends support to the proposal that vertical transmission is increasingly supplemented by the oblique or horizontal transmission of information and expertise.

The second class of biases enables children to differentiate among informants with whom they have had no protracted interaction. As noted, this class leads children to prefer informants who appear to be culturally typical, either in the sense that the informants signal that they belong to the same group as the children (because of the way that they speak or look) or in the sense that other potential informants assent to, rather than dissent from, the information offered by the informant. These biases are likely to promote oblique and horizontal cultural learning that is relatively conservative. When children encounter someone who is not a familiar caregiver, they will be more inclined to accept guidance from that person if he or she appears to belong to, and receives endorsement from, the children's cultural group. Stated differently, children's receptivity to both oblique and horizontal learning does not extend to all-comers. They are less likely to trust information that is provided by members of another cultural group or by deviants from within their own group.

In future research, it will be important to test how children weigh both what they learn and from whom they learn. By way of illustration, consider recent findings illustrating children's deference to a model in the domain of tool use. Young children overimitate inefficient and irrelevant actions that are included in the demonstration of a tool or apparatus—despite various prompts not to do so [3–5]. Such deference is striking but, arguably, it may be displayed only in conditions which, from a cultural learning perspective, are impoverished. In overimitation experiments, children are typically offered a single demonstration by a single informant, whereas in everyday life, they are likely to have access to multiple demonstrations by multiple informants.

How might children respond when they have access to multiple informants? Two different possibilities warrant investigation. One possibility is that—particularly in 'opaque' domains such as tool use where the possibilities for exhaustive and autonomous analysis are limited—children defer more or less automatically to any apparently effective demonstration that they encounter. Based on this hypothesis, the selectivity among informants that has been described in this chapter would not be in evidence. An alternative possibility, however, is that children might deploy either of the two classes of heuristics so as to be more selective about what they imitate. For example, faced with conflicting demonstrations by informants with a different attachment status or a different history of accuracy, children might copy in a selective fashion rather than in an indiscriminate fashion, copying and indeed overimitating one model rather than the other. Similarly, having observed ingroup and outgroup members model different tool-based procedures, children might engage in more sedulous imitation of ingroup members.

Finally, it is important to remember that developmental psychology has long demonstrated children's capacity for autonomous observation and interpretation. There are occasions when children use that cognitive capacity—including the distinctively human capacity for asking questions—to query the cultural information that they receive, even from familiar sources [10, 43, 44]. Indeed, children are especially likely to direct their sustained—and sometimes sceptical questions—at trusted caregivers [45].

References

1 Gergely, G. & Csibra, G. 2006 Sylvia's recipe: the role of imitation and pedagogy in the transmission of cultural knowledge. In *Roots of human sociality: culture, cognition and interaction* (eds N. J. Enfield & S. C. Levinson), pp. 229–255. Oxford, UK: Berg.

2 Csibra, C. & Gergely, G. 2011 Natural pedagogy as evolutionary adaptation. *Phil. Trans. R. Soc. B* **366**, 1149–1157.

3 Horner, V. & Whiten, A. 2005 Causal knowledge and imitation/emulation switching in chimpanzees (*Pan roglodytes*) and children (*Homo sapiens*). *Anim. Cogn.* **8**, 164–181.

4 Lyons, D. E., Young, A. G. & Keil, F. C. 2007 The hidden structure of overimitation. *Proc. Natl Acad. Sci. USA* **104**, 19751–19756.

5 Lyons, D. E., Damrosch, D. H., Lin, J. K., Macris, D. M. & Keil, F. C. 2011 The scope and limits of overimitation in the transmission of artefact culture. *Phil. Trans. R. Soc. B* **366**, 1158–1167.

6 Jaswal, V. K. 2004 Don't believe everything you hear: preschoolers' sensitivity to speaker intent in category induction. *Child Dev.* **75**, 1871–1885.

7 Couillard, N. L. & Woodward, A. L. 1999 Children's comprehension of deceptive points. *Br. J. Dev. Psychol.* **17**, 515–521.

8 Jaswal, V. K., Croft, A. C., Setia, A. R. & Cole, C. A. 2010 Young children have a specific, highly robust bias to trust testimony. *Psychol. Sci.* **21**, 1541–1547.

9 Rakoczy, H., Warneken, F. & Tomasello, M. 2008 The sources of normativity: young children's awareness of the normative structure of games. *Dev. Psychol.* **44**, 875–881.

10 Harris, P. L. & Koenig, M. 2006 Trust in testimony: how children learn about science and religion. *Child Dev.* **77**, 505–524.

11 Reid, T. 1764/2000 *An inquiry into the human mind on the principles of common sense* (ed. D. R. Brookes). Edinburgh, UK: Edinburgh University Press.

12 Russell, B. 1921 *The analysis of mind*. New York, NY: McMillan.

13 Wittgenstein, L. 1969 *On certainty*. Oxford, UK: Blackwell.

14 Gilbert, D. T. 1991 How mental systems believe. *Am. Psychol.* **46**, 107–119.

15 Dawkins, R. 2006 *The God delusion*. London, UK: Bantam Press.

16 Cavalli-Sforza, L. L. & Feldman, M. W. 1981 *Cultural transmission and evolution: a quantitative approach*. Princeton, NJ: Princeton University Press.

17 Richerson, P. J. & Boyd, R. 2005 *Not by genes alone: how culture transformed human evolution*. Chicago, IL: University of Chicago Press.

18 Ainsworth, M. D. S., Blehar, M. C., Waters, E. & Wall, S. 1978 *Patterns of attachment: a psychological study of the strange situation*. Hillsdale, NJ: Erlbaum.

19 Bowlby, J. 1969 *Attachment and loss*, vol. 1 *Attachment*. London, UK: Hogarth Press.

20 Hrdy, S. B. 2000 *Mother nature*. New York, NY: Ballantine Books.

21 Rutter, M., Sonuga-Barke, E. J., Beckett, C., Castle, J., Kreppner, J., Kumsta, R., Schlotz, W., Stevens, S. & Bell, C. A. 2010 Deprivation-specific patterns: effects of institutional deprivation. *Monogr. Soc. Res. Child Dev.* **75** (serial no. 295).

22 Corriveau, K. H. & Harris, P. L. 2009 Choosing your informant: weighing familiarity and recent accuracy. *Dev. Sci.* **12**, 426–437.

23 Corriveau, K. H. *et al.* 2009 Young children's trust in their mother's claims: longitudinal links with attachment security in infancy. *Child Dev.* **80**, 750–761.

24 Koenig, M., Clément, F. & Harris, P. L. 2004 Trust in testimony: children's use of true and false statements. *Psychol. Sci.* **10**, 694–698.

25 Harris, P. L. 2007 Trust. *Dev. Sci.* **10**, 135–138.

26 Clément, F., Koenig, M. & Harris, P. L. 2004 The ontogenesis of trust in testimony. *Mind Lang.* **19**, 360–379.

27 Birch, S., Vauthier, S. & Bloom, P. 2008 Three- and four-year-olds spontaneously use others' past performance to guide their learning. *Cognition* **107**, 1018–1034.

28 Corriveau, K. H. & Harris, P. L. 2009 Preschoolers continue to trust a more accurate informant 1 week after exposure to accuracy information. *Dev. Sci.* **12**, 188–193.

29 Pasquini, E. S., Corriveau, K., Koenig, M. & Harris, P. L. 2007 Preschoolers monitor the relative accuracy of informants. *Dev. Psychol.* **43**, 1216–1226.

30 Corriveau, K. H., Meints, M. & Harris, P. L. 2009 Early tracking of informant accuracy and inaccuracy. *Br. J. Dev. Psychol.* **27**, 331–342.

31 Koenig, M. & Harris, P. L. 2005 Preschoolers mistrust ignorant and inaccurate speakers. *Child Dev.* **76**, 1261–1277.

32 Jaswal, V. K. & Neely, L. A. 2006 Adults don't always know best: preschoolers use past reliability over age when learning new words. *Psychol. Sci.* **17**, 757–758.

33 Corriveau, K. H., Pickard, K. & Harris, P. L. 2011 Preschoolers trust particular informants when learning new names and new morphological forms. *Br. J. Dev. Psychol.* **29**, 46–63.

34 Kinzler, K., Dupoux, E. & Spelke, E. S. 2007 The native language of social cognition. *Proc. Natl Acad. Sci. USA* **104**, 12577–12580.

35 Kinzler, K. D., Corriveau, K. H. & Harris, P. L. 2011 Children's selective trust in native-accented speakers. *Dev. Sci.* **14**, 106–111.

36 Fusaro, M. & Harris, P. L. 2008 Children assess informant reliability using bystanders' non-verbal cues. *Dev. Sci.* **11**, 781–787.

37 Corriveau, K. H., Fusaro, M. & Harris, P. L. 2009 Going with the flow: preschoolers prefer non-dissenters as informants. *Psychol. Sci.* **20**, 372–377.

38 Chen, E. E. 2010 Children's use of social group membership versus consensus cues when learning from others. Paper presented at the Harvard–Yale Social Cognitive Development Workshop, Harvard University, 15 May.

39 Chen, E. E., Corriveau, K. H. & Harris, P. L. In press. Children are sociologists. *An. Psicologia.* **27**, 625–530.

40 Hewlett, B. S., Fouts, H. N., Boyette, A. H. & Hewlett, B. L. 2011 Social learning among Congo Basin hunter–gatherers. *Phil. Trans. R. Soc. B* **366**, 1168–1178.

41 Hattori, S. 2010 'My Medicine (Ma a le)': variability of medicinal plant knowledge among adult Baka hunter–gatherers of southeast Cameroon. Paper presented at annual meeting of Society for Cross Cultural Research, Albuquerque, NM.

42 Henrich, J. & Broesch, J. 2011 On the nature of cultural transmission networks: evidence from Fijian villages for adaptive learning biases. *Phil. Trans. R. Soc. B* **366**, 1139–1148.

43 Chouinard, M. 2007 Children's questions: a mechanism for cognitive development. *Monogr. Soc. Res. Child Dev.* **72** (Serial no. 286).

44 Frazier, B. N., Gelman, S. A. & Wellman, H. M. 2009 Preschoolers' search for explanatory information within adult-child conversation. *Child Dev.* **80**, 1592–1611.

45 Tizard, B. & Hughes, M. 1984 *Young children learning*. London, UK: Fontana.

Index